COMPANY LAW

SECOND EDITION

BEN PETTET

PEARSON
Longman

Harlow, England • London • New York • Boston • San Francisco • Toronto
Sydney • Tokyo • Singapore • Hong Kong • Seoul • Taipei • New Delhi
Cape Town • Madrid • Mexico City • Amsterdam • Munich • Paris • Milan

Second edition published 2005

ISBN-13: 978-0-582-89418-1
ISBN-10: 0-582-89418-2

British Library Cataloguing-in-Publication Data
A catalogue record for this book is available from the British Library

Library of Congress Cataloging-in-Publication Data
Pettet, B. G.
    Company law / Ben Pettet.—2nd ed.
    p. cm.—(Longman law series)
    Includes index.
    ISBN 0-582-89418-2
    1. Corporation law—Great Britain. I. Title. II. Series.
    KD2079.P48 2005
    346.41'066—dc22
                                             2005043015

10 9 8 7 6 5 4 3
10 09 08 07 06

Typeset in 10/12pt Plantin by 3
Printed in Great Britain by Henry Ling Ltd., at the Dorset Press, Dorchester, Dorset.

The publisher's policy is to use paper manufactured from sustainable forests.

CONTENTS

Supporting resources
Visit **www.pearsoned.co.uk/pettet** to find valuable online resources

Companion Website for students
• Regular updates to keep you up to date in the field of Company Law

For more information please contact your local Pearson Education sales representative or visit **www.pearsoned.co.uk/pettet**

PREFACE TO THE FIRST EDITION

In writing this book I have three aims. The first is to move the subject of company law closer to what is usually called securities regulation (or capital markets law). I have become ever more convinced in recent years that one cannot understand company law from a practical or theoretical angle without a clear perception of the principles and aims of securities regulation. As an academic and practical subject, company law needs to include securities regulation, and I have tried to demonstrate that in this work.

My second purpose is to provide a lively and thought-provoking analysis of the main legal rules of company law. Readers will find that I have departed somewhat from the list of topics often contained in company law texts, and so some areas have a much lower profile in this book than they have received elsewhere. It has also been necessary to vary the depth of coverage in order for the book to remain short enough for it to claim to be a student textbook. On the other hand, I have given special attention to areas which I have seen students struggle with over the years, and in some chapters I have picked on the facts of seminal cases, or constructed examples, which have then been used to illustrate at length the ideas which I have wished to convey. As far as I am able, and where relevant, I have tried to present the rules in the social and practical context in which they operate, both as a means of making the subject of more interest and to enhance understanding.

My third aim is to give an account of, and assessment of, the important theoretical or jurisprudential issues which are current in this field, with a view to enabling the reader to develop views on the appropriate direction of future reforms. In this regard, it is an exciting time to be considering company law reform, because the DTI's Company Law Review is currently questioning the rationale of many areas, and because a substantially new system of securities regulation is coming into being as a result of the passing of the Financial Services and Markets Act 2000. Also, national and international scholarship on fundamental theoretical issues has continued unabated into the new Millennium, spurred both by scholarly interest and by the competitive pressures between different systems of company law created by the global market for capital.

This book is arranged in six Parts: Foundation and Theory, The Constitution of the Company, Corporate Governance, Corporate Finance Law, Securities Regulation, Insolvency and Liquidation. An explanation of the contents of these Parts and the reasons for organising the book in this way are set out in Chapter 1. It has of course been necessary to draw a line under the inclusion of material, and I have endeavoured to present the law and developments as they stand at 1 August 2000. With respect to the Financial Services and Markets Act 2000, the account assumes that the Act is in force, which is very likely to be the case by the time this book is published. As regards my very occasional references to the secondary legislation in that area, I have written on the basis of the draft orders and made this clear in the footnotes, since the finalised versions are unlikely to be available before about autumn 2001. This book has its own companion website and the reader will find on it material which supports the book: http://www.booksites.net/pettet.

I wish to thank Professor Roger Rideout and the other editors, for first encouraging me to write a text on company law, so many years ago, and Pearson Education Ltd for their patience in waiting for it; also Pat Bond, of Pearson Education, who has been a pleasure to work with and a source of helpful advice. Credit is also due to Pearson Education's efficient production team, in particular Anita Atkinson, Kathryn Swift and Sarah Phillipson. I owe much to a generation of students for their enthusiastic criticism and probing of some of my ideas, and of course the debt of any author to past and present scholars and lawyers in the field is immense. In this regard I wish to record special thanks to Guido Ferrarini, Jim Fishman, David Sugarman, Jim Wickenden, and others, who have read and commented on some of the material in draft form. Needless to say, the responsibility for the views expressed here and for errors and omissions remains mine, and mine alone.

This book is dedicated to my wife, Corry, and to my children, Emily, Roland and Florence, in grateful recognition of their loving support and encouragement in the years I was writing, particularly during that lost summer of 2000.

Ben Pettet
Faculty of Laws
University College London
September 2000

PREFACE TO THE SECOND EDITION

It is almost four years to the day since I sent the text of the first edition of this book to my publishers. In the fields covered in this work much has changed, and the text reflects that. But perhaps the most significant change of all is the increasing influence of the European Union in the development of company law, and capital markets law. In company law we now have the EC Commission's Action Plan for Company Law, a huge programme replacing the rather sedate progress of pre-existing company law harmonisation. In the capital markets field we have, in the five years which have elapsed since the Financial Services Action Plan was published, seen a stream of complex legislation which will take many years to implement and which presents a tough challenge to the UK's Financial Services Authority. We have also seen the reform of the EC legislative process itself with the introduction of the Lamfalussy procedures, and the formation of the Committee of European Securities Regulators (CESR), events of enormous importance in the context of the development of Pan-European securities regulation. Set against the backdrop of enlargement of the EU to 25 Member States, these events have changed forever the processes of law reform in this field.

Much of the new material in this edition is therefore concerned with the major legislation which has now emerged, such as the Directive on Takeover Bids, the Directive on Insider Dealing and Market Manipulation (Market Abuse), the Directive on Markets in Financial Instruments, and the new Prospectus Directive. In the UK we have seen significant legislative initiatives from our Department of Trade and Industry, such as the Enterprise Act 2002, and the Companies (Audit, Investigations and Community Enterprise) Act 2004. As ever there have been interesting developments in case law. At the time of writing, the DTI are preparing a major Companies Bill which will be published in draft form for consultation before it enters the legislative process.

Readers should be aware that where the text refers to human persons generally, using the masculine gender, this is of course intended to equally make reference to persons of female gender and vice versa.

I wish to record my gratitude to my editor Michelle Gallagher for her helpful advice and for her patience in waiting for this new edition, also to the rest of the efficient production team at Pearson.

Ben Pettet
Faculty of Laws
University College London
September 2004

ACKNOWLEDGEMENTS

We are grateful to the following for permission to reproduce copyright material:

Financial Services Authority for extracts from *Combined Code on Corporate Governance* by the Financial Reporting Council 23rd July 2003, *FSA Handbook of Rules and Guidance, Principles for Business* August 2004 and *UK Implementation of the EU Market Abuse Directive (Directive 2003/6/EC)* June 2004; and HMSO for an extract from *Law Commission Report No 246*.

In some instances we have been unable to trace the owners of copyright material and we would appreciate any information that would enable us to do so.

TABLE OF CASES

xix

TABLE OF STATUTES

TABLE OF STATUTORY INSTRUMENTS

NORTHERN IRELAND

TABLE OF EUROPEAN LEGISLATION

PART I

FOUNDATION AND THEORY

1

THE NATURE OF COMPANY LAW

1.1 PRELIMINARY

At the heart of the UK capitalist system, the free market economy, lies company law. Its web of rules establishes the parameters within which the process of bringing together and organising the factors of production can take place. Company law does this by setting up or regulating two environments, the company, which is the organisational structure within which the production takes place, and the capital market through which the money is raised to finance the production process.

In the capital market people will supply the company with its capital by taking up securities when the company issues them. These will usually be either share capital or debt. The securities will give the holders claims against the company. In the case of shares, it will usually give rights to assets remaining in a future liquidation after the holders of debt securities and other creditors have been paid; they are residual rights. The shareholders will also usually have the right to elect the managers of the company, the board of directors. These managers, will buy in the factors of production, consisting of assets and labour. The company will then exchange the goods and/or services which it produces in return for money or other assets. If over a period of time the company receives more back from its activities than it has received from those who have supplied capital, then wealth will have been created for the shareholders. This wealth will usually find its way back to the shareholders either by way of small periodic payments called dividends and/or by a rise in the share price on the market reflecting the fact that the company's assets have increased. Alternatively, though rarely, it may be distributed to the shareholders in a liquidation. More usually, a liquidation marks the end of the company's useful life as a business organisation and will be an insolvent liquidation where the assets are insufficient to pay the creditors all that they are owed.

This analysis relates to what in this book will be described as the 'dispersed-ownership' company, which is a company where its shares are widely held by the public, and where the management have a relatively small or insignificant shareholding, leading to some degree of what is often called separation of ownership and control. Such companies exhibit very different characteristics and face very different problems from companies which in this book will be described as 'small closely-held' companies, where the managers own all or most of the shares and where there is no substantial separation of ownership and control.[1]

---

[1] These definitions, the significance of them and their relationship to legal terms of art such as 'public' company and 'private' company, are explored in more detail below.

1.2 RATIONALE, ABSTRACT AND AGENDA

The first Part of this book, 'Foundation and Theory', introduces some of the main doctrines of company law, and explores past and current theoretical and practical challenges and the way attempts are being made to resolve them. Company law draws various technical distinctions between different types of companies and there are various types of business vehicle in existence, but the focus of the subject can initially be narrowed down to a consideration of public and private companies limited by shares and created by registration.[2] Companies are treated by the law as having legal personality, as being separate from the shareholders, which means, for instance, that the company and not the shareholders, is the owner of its property. In most situations there is a related doctrine of limited liability, under which the maximum amount which the shareholders stand to lose is the amount which they have invested or agreed to invest. Thus, if the company goes into insolvent liquidation, the shareholders will not be required to make good the shortfall. The doctrine of limited liability has many effects but in particular it plays an important role in enabling companies to raise capital from the public because it enables individuals to invest small amounts in the shares of a company without risking personal insolvency if the company goes into insolvent liquidation.[3] Jurisprudential writings on company law have produced a rich body of legal theory which both seeks to describe the impact produced by the operation of the rules of company law and to prescribe what those rules should be. Of particular current interest is the impact of economic analysis of law and the continuing challenges of stakeholder company law.[4] The Company Law Review, under the auspices of the Department of Trade and Industry, has undertaken a comprehensive investigation into the purposes and effectiveness of company law. In the course of this, many of the issues in the theory of company law have been considered. In due course it is likely that many thoughtful reforms will reach the statute book.[5]

'The Constitution of the Company' is the subject of Part II of this book, dealing with the ways in which provisions in the constitution of the company affect the contractual rights of various persons dealing with it, and broadly, the way in which functions are divided between the shareholders and directors. The statutory parts of the constitution of a company permit shareholders to entrench rights subject to alteration by prescribed statutory procedures designed to produce a system of checks and balances. Additionally, by means of contractual arrangements called shareholder agreements it is sometimes possible to entrench rights and make detailed provision for an almost unlimited variety of contingencies.[6] The constitution normally vests the power to manage the business of the company in the board of directors, although subject to interference by the shareholders in certain circumstances. Historically, under what is termed the *ultra vires* doctrine, the powers of the company have been limited by the constitution with the result that acts beyond

---

[2] These matters are dealt with in this chapter.
[3] See Chapter 2 below.
[4] See Chapter 3 below.
[5] See Chapter 4 below.
[6] See Chapter 5 below.

those powers have been regarded as ineffective; this has been curtailed by statute but still continues to give rise to analytical difficulties if the powers of the directors to bind the company are similarly limited.[7] The related question of how a company enters into contractual relations with other legal persons is largely determined by the law of agency. In company law the area has been made unnecessarily obscure by the development of a doctrine known as the 'indoor management rule' and by the effect of limitations on the powers of directors and other agents contained in the constitution.[8]

'Corporate Governance' is dealt with in Part III. The term corporate governance denotes the system by which the company is controlled and governed, but in dispersed-ownership companies it carries the additional connotation that the managers will need to be controlled, otherwise they will be likely to pursue their own interests. So, broadly, it involves an analysis of the ways in which the law seeks to align the interests of the managers with those of the shareholders. The relationship between the board of directors and the shareholders is largely delineated by the provisions in the legislation regulating the calling of meetings and passing of resolutions which are supplemented by provisions contained in the constitution of the company. In dispersed-ownership companies, the realities of the situation make it difficult for the meeting structure to be an effective control mechanism.[9] As a primary alignment mechanism, the law casts common law duties of care and skill on directors and fiduciary duties of good faith. However, these duties are owed to the company, rather than the shareholders as individuals, which, by reason of case law makes litigation for breach of them difficult.[10] Other constraints on directors' powers come about by provisions which enable the shareholders to dismiss the directors, and by statutory provisions which seek to enforce fair dealing by directors and so restrict the extent to which directors are able to benefit from transactions with the company. Also relevant here are rules which require disclosure of financial and other information.[11] Insufficiencies in corporate governance mechanisms have resulted in the appearance of codes of corporate governance, supplementing the legal requirements and relying on elements of self-regulation for compliance.[12] Litigation by shareholders is a last resort and historically the common law has discouraged it, in particular by developing doctrines which restrict the standing of shareholders to bring proceedings.[13] The recent development of litigation based on standing given by legislation to redress conduct which is 'unfairly prejudicial' has resulted in very significant developments in the remedies available to shareholders. However, the increased possibility of litigating matters has, not surprisingly, been of little interest to shareholders in dispersed-ownership companies who have little economic incentive to fight issues of principle through the courts and who will normally 'exit' by sale on the market.[14]

---

[7] See Chapter 6 below.
[8] See Chapter 7 below.
[9] See Chapter 8 below.
[10] See Chapter 9 below.
[11] See Chapter 10 below.
[12] See Chapter 11 below.
[13] See Chapter 12 below.
[14] See Chapter 13 below.

'Corporate Finance Law' is the subject of Part IV. This is concerned with basic doctrines of corporate finance and the techniques by which companies raise capital as well as the rules which apply to restrict the situations in which the capital raised can be returned to the shareholders. Techniques of corporate finance range from the entrepreneur using his savings to subscribe for shares in his newly formed business, through to venture capital, and on to an initial public offering and flotation on the Stock Exchange. These and other techniques are made possible by the ability of the company to issue shares and to borrow in various ways.[15] Company law has developed a doctrine of nominal value of shares under which the share is given a fixed value at the time of its issue and it retains that nominal value even though the actual market value may later have changed. From this concept rules have been developed which govern the payment for shares when issued. Subsequently, the company comes under restrictions, known as the doctrine of maintenance of capital regulating how and when it can return capital to the shareholders and related matters.[16] A particular problem developed early in the last century in which a company's assets were used to enable a syndicate to purchase the shares in it. This led to legislation to prohibit what became known as financial assistance for the acquisition of shares. The legislation and related case law have raised problems ever since.[17]

'Securities Regulation' is covered in Part V of this book and its inclusion in a text on company law is probably the most controversial topic considered here. Securities regulation, or as it is sometimes called, 'Capital Markets Law', is often thought to be a discrete field, separate and distinct from company law. Culturally it seems different, the state has a high profile through the presence of a powerful regulatory authority as opposed to the often permissive nature of company law rules and low profile presence of the state. It seems more part of public law, and alien to the mainly private law feel of company law with its emphasis on entrepreneurs and common law concepts of property and contract. And yet, investor protection has been a major theme of company law texts for many years and company law books almost invariably give some coverage to some of the central areas of securities regulation, such as takeovers, insider dealing and public offerings of shares but it is usually approached from the perspective of the managers and others trying to get a result, by carrying out the takeover or, for instance, getting through the regulatory hurdles involved in a public offering. Part of the reason for this approach perhaps lies in the fact that the UK has only had a comprehensive system of securities regulation since 1986 and the challenge, as to whether securities regulation should be seen as an indispensable part of the overall picture of what we call company law, is a relatively new one. But there is an important theoretical reason as to why securities regulation/capital markets law is part of company law.[18] A traditional analysis of the human participants in a company involves seeing it as comprised of the directors and the shareholders. They are both 'in' the company, in the sense of being

---

[15] See Chapter 14 below.
[16] See Chapter 15 below.
[17] See Chapter 16 below.
[18] These arguments are taken up again at p. 313 *et seq.* below and amplified by practical and other perspectives.

indispensable to its functioning in the manner prescribed by the companies legislation, even if those functions are carried out by the same people. Historically, the legislation contemplates the running of the company through meetings in which people will be present in the room, either in shareholder meetings, voting to elect or remove directors, or in board meetings as directors. It perhaps draws on the concepts of government from the Ancient World in which all the involved parties can and will turn up at a meeting, albeit a large one. Lastly, the shareholders are 'in' the company in the sense that they are committed to it emotionally and financially, and if it is not running properly they will often want to litigate, as the exponential growth in often bitterly contested shareholder litigation in recent decades testifies. Thus, securities regulation, with its emphasis on what happens on capital markets, seems to be outside company law. The shareholders are clearly, 'in' the company. But this picture of being bound up with the company in all these ways and so 'in' the company is only true of the small closely-held company. In dispersed-ownership companies it is a mistaken analysis to regard the shareholders as being 'in' the company in any of the above senses. Typically in dispersed-ownership companies shareholders will not vote; there is little point since their relatively small overall stake (perhaps 1%) will give them very little influence over any outcome. If they do vote, it will usually be by filling in a proxy form; they will not be 'in' the meeting listening to arguments and explanation. Nor will they be sufficiently committed to the company's fortunes, either financially or emotionally to want to litigate disputes. If they do not like what seems to be happening in the company they will 'exit' by selling their shares on a liquid market, and re-invest in something else. So if the shareholders in dispersed-ownership companies are not 'in' the company, then where are they? They are in the market. But we obviously have to study their position. It cannot be left out – as not really part of 'company law'; the rights and concerns and position of shareholders of dispersed-ownership companies are part of company law. And so, if we are to get a proper perspective of these matters, and the way the law protects their position, it is necessary to study that part of company law which is called 'securities regulation' or 'capital markets law'.[19]

Policy and theory in securities regulation differs from traditional company law theory in a number of respects. The most striking feature is perhaps the cultural differences which arise from the high profile role of the state, making its pervasive presence felt through the agency of the regulator. The main goal of securities regulation is investor protection and much of the policy and theoretical writing is concerned with the different techniques employed by the regulator to achieve an adequate level of protection on the one hand, but on the other, to ensure that the financial services industry or parts of it, are not made uncompetitive by overheavy regulation.[20] The legislation sets up a comprehensive system under which people offering financial services are usually required to seek authorisation from the regulator, the Financial Services Authority. Authorisation will bring with it responsibilities to comply with detailed rules regulating how their business is to be carried

---

[19] The terms are used interchangeably in this book, although with the preference towards the longstanding American expression, securities regulation.
[20] See Chapter 17 below.

out.[21] When shares are offered to the public there is a high risk of fraud if the offer documents are not carefully regulated. Thus, one of the oldest forms of securities regulation is the requirement for adequate disclosure of information about the issuer and the securities in a prospectus.[22] Insider dealing broadly involves the use of inside information by a party to a transaction on a stock exchange which the other party does not have and which enables him to make a profit or avoid a loss. Although the matter is not entirely free from controversy, it has long been felt by regulatory authorities that insider dealing damages investor confidence in markets and for this reason, and others, it falls to be regulated along with other forms of market abuse.[23] Hostile takeovers can easily produce unfairness for shareholders of the target company and for this reason takeovers are subjected to timetable require-ments and many other rules designed to ensure that the shareholders are treated equally. Takeover regulation is currently the main remaining example of UK secu-rities regulation which retains major elements of self-regulation.[24]

'Insolvency and Liquidation' is the final Part. It contains a brief account of the processes which are available to deal with corporate insolvency and winding up gen-erally. The legislation contains complex procedures for the winding up of solvent and insolvent companies and eventual dissolution of the corporate entity.[25] A remarkable feature of company law has been its development of a facility for expul-sion of directors from its world, the corporate world. In the last two decades there have probably been more reported cases on disqualification of directors than any other single aspect of company law. Whether the law has got the balance right between protecting the public from abuses of limited liability and not creating unnecessary deterrents to enterprise is open to question.[26]

1.3 SCOPE OF THIS WORK

It is clear that this book marks out a conceptually broader field than usual for core company law. On the other hand, it is possible to exaggerate the practical effect of this. Most company law texts will usually give some attention to most of the main areas of securities regulation, insider dealing, public offerings of shares and takeovers. This book differs, since in doing this it places the emphasis on the regulatory aspect of these areas, and sets them in the context of the policy and theory of securities regulation. More generally, in order for the book to remain short enough to claim to be a text for use by students, it has been necessary to vary the depth of coverage.[27] It is felt that this is preferable to an artificial restric-tion of a subject area which for good theoretical and practical reasons needs to be seen as a unified whole. Even so, the book leaves out altogether a whole range of

---

[21] See Chapter 18 below.

[22] See Chapter 19 below. The subject of public offerings of shares is also covered from the corporate finance perspective in Chapter 14 below.

[23] See Chapter 20 below.

[24] See Chapter 21 below.

[25] See Chapter 22 below.

[26] See Chapter 23 below.

[27] It has also resulted in a lower profile being given to certain areas which commonly receive a whole chapter in company law texts.

subjects which undoubtedly affect the way companies are structured and how they go about their business; among these are revenue law, competition law, environmental law, health and safety law, labour law, and consumer law. It is not felt that these areas can be covered in sufficient depth to be meaningful, and they are best left to specialist texts. Although this work is primarily for the student market, it is hoped that some practitioners will also find the book of use and interest.

1.4 THE GENESIS OF COMPANY LAW

English company law is mainly concerned with the creation and operation of registered companies, that is, companies with separate legal personality created by the process of registering them with the Registrar of Companies under the Companies Act 1985. This facility of creating companies simply by registration has been available in England since the Joint Stock Companies Act 1844.

Prior to that time companies were created by Royal Charter (a special authorisation from the Crown) or by a special Act of Parliament. These forms of company became common in the 16th century and were called 'joint stock' companies because the members of it contributed merchandise or money, and the company traded with the outside world as an entity distinct from the members. At first these companies were colonial companies, formed mainly to open up trade with new colonies, but by the late 17th century most of the new companies were created for domestic enterprises. At this time, there was also considerable growth in the numbers of large partnerships which were using various legal devices to make them as much like the chartered and statutory companies as possible. In the early 18th century there were many speculative flotations of various types of company and a stock market collapse. This reached a climax in 1720 when the share price of the South Sea Company collapsed; this event was known as the South Sea 'Bubble' because once it burst, there was nothing (no assets) there. Legislation was then passed which was designed to prevent the large partnerships from acting as though they were companies. Known as the Bubble Act, it was not repealed until 1825, by which time it had been realised that it was economically desirable to permit the easy creation of companies. It also soon became necessary to clarify the status of the many partnerships which had now begun to flourish. In England, legislation in 1844 permitted incorporation by registration for the first time and limited liability was made available in 1855. These provisions were then re-enacted in the Joint Stock Companies Act 1856. In 1862 this and other subsequent legislation was consolidated in the Companies Act 1862. Thereafter, the growth of company law followed a pattern which continues to the present day. In the years following a consolidating Act more reforms are conceived, either as a result of an inquiry into company law by an expert outside committee appointed by the government department responsible for companies, the Department of Trade and Industry (DTI) or, as is more common these days, as a result of policy decided by the DTI itself. The proposed reforms then become legislation and after many years of this process, another consolidating Act is passed and for a few years thereafter all the statutory material on company law is available in one consolidated Act. The latest consolidation is the 1985 consolidation.[28]

The facility of creating companies by registration was widely used in the second half of the 19th century not only by those wishing to operate a large company with an offer of shares to the public, but also by many who ran small businesses either as single traders or in partnership who now wanted the advantages of limited liability and the corporate form. Partnership law ceased to be the focus of concern by the legislature and, following the Partnership Act 1890 and the Limited Partnership Act 1907 (both of which are currently in force), there was little interest by the legislature in the subject[29] until the closing years of the 20th century, when it became clear that a new business vehicle combining aspects of partnership law with company law might be desirable. In due course the Limited Liability Partnerships Act 2000 was passed.[30]

1.5 THE PRESENT COMPANIES LEGISLATION

The last great consolidation in the UK was in 1985. The present primary legislation relating to companies is as follows: the main Act containing most of the basic companies legislation is the Companies Act 1985. There is also the Companies Consolidation (Consequential Provisions) Act 1985.[31] The following year saw a consolidation of insolvency law into the Insolvency Act 1986,[32] which now includes the law on all company liquidations (not just insolvent ones as the Act's name might suggest), and this led to a repeal of those parts of the Companies Act 1985 which had dealt with company liquidations. Also in 1986 was the Company Directors Disqualification Act into which was consolidated the various scattered provisions relating to the disqualification of directors. Companies were further affected by the Financial Services Act 1986 which amended, repealed and replaced various parts of the Companies Act 1985. Then three years later the Companies Act 1989 was passed, some of which stands on its own and other parts of which amend earlier legislation. Subsequently, the Financial Services and Markets Act 2000 completely restructured the securities regulation aspects of company law and so replaced the Financial Services Act 1986. Thus there is no effective consolidation at the present day. The legislation on company law is spread out between various statutes, not to mention the mass of statutory instruments which the main Acts have spawned. Nevertheless, in a broad sense, the basic Act is the Companies Act 1985.[33] References in this book will be to sections in this Act, unless the con-

---

[28] See below.

[29] Although the courts continued to develop some aspects of partnership law.

[30] See further p. 20 below.

[31] At the time of the consolidation the provisions on insider dealing were contained in the Company Securities (Insider Dealing) Act 1985; the current provisions are now in the Criminal Justice Act 1993. Additionally, the Business Names Act 1985 will have some relevance to a company if it trades under a name other than the name with which it is registered. There is also now the Companies and Business Names (Chambers of Commerce) Act 1999, which is relatively insignificant.

[32] Amended subsequently by the Insolvency Act 2000 and the Enterprise Act 2002.

[33] And it has just been amended again, by the Companies (Audit, Investigations and Community Enterprise) Act 2004.

text makes it clear that some other statute is intended. It will be seen that in addition to copious statute law, case law features in many areas of company law, either as interpretation or application of statutory provisions, or as a result of remedies given in the statutes, or, some areas, entirely independently of statute. Unless otherwise stated or clear from the context, the law described in this book is the English law.[34]

1.6 EUROPEAN COMMUNITY LEGISLATION

A The harmonisation programme[35]

As part of the process of creating the common market with free movement of goods, persons, services and capital, the European Community has felt it necessary to attempt to co-ordinate the laws affecting companies in the various Member States. There is to be approximation of laws, not in the sense of making them exactly the same, but similar in their main characteristics, making the safeguards for members and others 'equivalent throughout the Community'.[36] The company law[37] harmonisation policy is based on the EC Treaty, art. 44 (2) (g). The usual pattern has been for the European Commission to make proposals for Directives[38] which, after various subsequent stages, are finally adopted by the Council of Ministers and the European Parliament. Unlike a Regulation, which automatically becomes law in the Member States, a Directive is usually a set of principles[39] which the individual Member States are required to enact into their own law, making whatever adaptations are necessary to key it in with their domestic law. The Directives are to be binding only as to the result to be achieved. In some limited circumstances they do have direct effect on the domestic law of the Member States. It has been made clear that a national court which hears a case falling within the scope of an EC Directive is required to interpret its national law in the light of the wording and purpose of that Directive.[40]

B The Company Law Programme: UK Implementation

The UK entered the European Community by the European Communities Act 1972. Section 9 of the 1972 Act was an attempt to translate into UK law the

---

[34] I.e. England and Wales. As regards Scotland, much of the legislation will automatically be applicable there, subject sometimes to minor exceptions, although there are major differences in some areas such as insolvency. As regards Northern Ireland, nearly all of the English legislation becomes applicable there by virtue of enactment by Order in Council; thus the Northern Ireland equivalent of the Companies Act 1985 is the Companies (Northern Ireland) Order 1986 (SI 1986 No. 1032, NI6). Some of the English legislation is applicable directly in Northern Ireland (e.g. some parts of the Companies Act 1989).

[35] For a detailed account of this, see V. Edwards *EC Company Law* (Oxford: OUP, 1999). See also the EU website http://europa.eu.int and the DTI website http://www.dti.gov.uk.

[36] See EC Treaty, art. 44 (2) (g) (art. 54 (3) (g), pre-Amsterdam).

[37] Capital markets harmonisation is dealt with at p. 330 below.

[38] Occasionally a Regulation has been used.

[39] In practice these have often been very detailed.

[40] See Case C-106/89 *Marleasing SA* v *La Comercial SA* [1993] BCC 421, ECJ.

relevant provisions of the First Company Law Directive.[41] The main changes necessary in the UK related to doctrines under which persons dealing with companies could find themselves unable to enforce the contracts they had entered into, by virtue of being given 'constructive notice' of constitutional limitations on the power of the company or its officers and agents, to enter into the contracts. Section 9 was not well drafted to achieve the stated aims of the Directive and further measures were brought in by the Companies Act 1989.[42] Other provisions of the First Directive related to publicity and to the doctrine of nullity.[43]

The Second Directive[44] set out minimum requirements relating to the raising and maintenance of capital and the formation of companies. These were implemented by the Companies Act 1980[45] and although it was not necessary to make very radical changes to the existing UK rules on capital, the Directive did require more legal distinctions to be drawn between public and private companies than had formerly been the case. In particular, since 1980, the end name 'Limited' or 'Ltd' has been applicable only to a private limited company, while public company names must end with the words 'public limited company' or 'plc'.

The Third Directive[46] was implemented by the Companies (Mergers and Divisions) Regulations 1987.[47] Because takeovers in the UK are usually carried out by share exchange, the Third Directive, which relates to mergers by transfers of assets, is not of very great significance.

The Fourth Directive[48] related to the annual accounts of companies, prescribing in detail how those should be presented. It was implemented by the Companies Act 1981 (now contained in the Companies Act 1985).[49]

The Sixth Directive[50] is concerned with demergers of public companies, termed 'scissions' or 'divisions'. It was implemented, along with the Third Directive by the Companies (Mergers and Divisions) Regulations 1987.[51]

The Seventh Directive[52] is supplementary to the Fourth Directive and makes provision for the regime governing group accounts. It was implemented by the Companies Act 1989.

The Eighth Directive[53] relates to the qualifications and independence of auditors. It was implemented by the Companies Act 1989. The substantive law in this area already required high standards and not much change was required to comply with the Directive, although a new supervisory structure was created.

---

[41] Which had been adopted by the European Council on 9 March 1968; Directive 68/151/EEC.
[42] See p. 123 below.
[43] Nullity was a doctrine unknown to UK law.
[44] 79/91/EEC.
[45] And are now contained in the Companies Act 1985.
[46] 78/855/EEC.
[47] SI 1987 No. 1991.
[48] 78/660/EEC.
[49] The Fourth Directive, and its counterpart the Seventh Directive, have both been amended by many subsequent Directives. There is now also Regulation (EC)1606/2002 on the application of International Accounting Standards; this is dealt with at p. 186 below.
[50] 82/891/EEC.
[51] SI 1987 No. 1991.
[52] 83/349/EEC.
[53] 84/253/EEC.

The Eleventh Directive on the disclosure requirements of branches of certain types of company[54] was implemented by the Oversea Companies and Credit and Financial Institutions (Branch Disclosure) Regulations 1992.[55]

The Twelfth Directive[56] on single member private limited companies was implemented by the Companies (Single Member Private Limited Companies) Regulations 1992.[57]

The Directive on Takeover Bids[58] (formerly called the Thirteenth Directive on Takeover Bids) was adopted in 21 April 2004[59] after a 15-year struggle. It will have many long-term implications for Europe's capital markets and corporate governance.

The European Company Statute (the '*Societas Europaea*' or '*SE*') was enacted by EC Regulation in 2001.[60] It allows companies with operations in more than one Member State to operate voluntarily as European companies, that is European corporate entities, governed by a single law applicable in all Member States.[61] In order to enable Member States to take account of differences between national systems, the politically sensitive area of the involvement of employees has been dealt with by a Directive.[62]

C The EC Commission's Company Law Action Plan

On 21 May 2003 the European Commission published a communication: *Modernising Company Law and Enhancing Corporate Governance in the European Union – A Plan to Move Forward*[63]containing an 'Action Plan' for the development of company law in Europe for many years to come. The plan envisages 15 new Directives, and several EC Regulations and Commission Communications with a view to enhancing corporate governance and modernising company law.

The detailed plans involve increases in corporate governance disclosure, electronic access to information, recommendations about board conduct in conflict of interest situations, strict rules on the collective responsibility of directors for financial statements,[64] the introduction of a version of the UK's successful wrongful trading law, new ideas and rules on groups[65] of companies and many other

---

[54] Directive 89/666/EEC.

[55] SI 1992 No. 3179. This also implemented the 'Bank Branches' Directive 89/117/EEC.

[56] 89/667/EEC.

[57] SI 1992 No. 1699.

[58] 2004/25/EC.

[59] For a detailed analysis of this see Chapter 21 below.

[60] Regulation (EC) 2157/2001.

[61] However, in many circumstances, some of the applicable corporate laws will be those operating in the Member State in which it has its registered office, in respect of public limited liability companies.

[62] Directive 2001/86/EC, implemented in the UK by the European Public Limited-Liability Company Regulations 2004 (SI 2004 No. 2326), which also have relevance for certain aspects of the EC Regulation.

[63] COM (2003) 284 final. This Action Plan was a response to an earlier report of a group of eminent company law experts chaired by Professor Jaap Winter: *Report of the High Level Group of Company Law Experts on a Modern Regulatory Framework for Company Law in Europe* (Brussels: CEC 2002).

[64] In this the Commission is therefore not planning to take Europe down the American road adopted in their Sarbanes-Oxley Act of 2002 whereby the Chief Executive Officer (CEO) and the Chief Finance Officer (CFO) are fixed with an enhanced responsibility for the financial statements of their company.

[65] They are not planning to reintroduce the proposal for a Ninth Directive which in some circumstances

matters.[66] As part of the plan the Commission is pressing ahead with new proposals for two previously planned Directives relating to corporate mobility and re-structuring.[67] It is clear that the earlier rather cautious company law harmonisation programme has been replaced with a new energetic concept of forging a modern and competitive company law for Europe's companies.

1.7 COMPANY LAW, CORPORATE LAW OR CORPORATIONS LAW?

It has become quite common in England in recent years to see the American term 'corporation' used instead of 'company'. Some universities have chairs of 'corporate' law.[68] Courses on company law in American universities are usually called 'Corporations Law' and their legislation, state 'corporations' statutes. Over the years the word 'company' has been used in the UK instead of 'corporation' probably mainly for historical reasons. The early joint stock companies used 'company' rather than 'corporation' and the word became part of the title of the statute which was the foundation of modern company law, the Joint Stock Companies Act 1844. Since 1862 the statutes have been entitled 'Companies Act' and their provisions invariably refer to 'company' and 'companies'. Nearly all the textbooks speak of 'company law' and university courses are usually similarly titled. However, the Companies Act makes it clear that a company is a corporation, and, for example, s. 13 (3) of the Companies Act 1985 provides that the effect of registration under the Act is that from the date of 'incorporation' the members of the company 'shall be a body corporate'.

The problem with using the word 'corporations' instead of companies in English law is that, even at the present day, 'corporations' is a wider concept than 'companies'. There are two main types of corporations – corporations 'sole' and corporations 'aggregate'. A corporation sole is basically an office or public appointment that is deemed to be independent of the human being who happens to fill the office from time to time. Originally most corporations sole were of an ecclesiastical nature so that archbishops, bishops, canons, vicars and so on, were, and still are, corporations sole. But there are also many lay corporations sole, such as the Sovereign, government ministers (for example the Secretary of State for Defence)

---

would have resulted in the group or the dominant undertaking in the group having liability for the debts of subsidiaries, although it may be that some detailed new ideas will emerge along these lines; if so, they would prove controversial in the UK. See generally K. Hopt 'Common Principles of Corporate Governance in Europe?' in B. Markesinis (ed.) *The Clifford Chance Millennium Lectures: The Coming Together of the Common Law and the Civil Law* (Oxford: Hart Publishing, 2000) p. 126.

[66] In the light of the proposed reforms of corporate governance and the board in the Action Plan, it is clear that there is no longer any intention to revive the earlier proposal for a Fifth Directive which foundered on the rock of trying to impose some form of structured worker participation in corporate decision-making. For the history of the various versions of the proposals see: A. Boyle 'Draft Fifth Directive: Implications for Directors' Duties, Board Structure and Employee Participation' (1992) 13 Co. Law. 6; J. Du Plessis and J. Dine 'The Fate of the Draft Fifth Directive on Company Law: Accommodation Instead of Harmonisation' [1997] JBL 23.

[67] Proposal for a Tenth Company Law Directive on Cross-border Mergers, and the proposal for a Fourteenth Company Law Directive on the transfer of seat from one Member State to another.

[68] The 'corporate' title perhaps deriving from the use of the term by City law firms which endow the chairs.

and non-ministerial offices such as the Treasury Solicitor. A corporation sole will have the normal incidents of corporateness such as perpetual succession, so that when the individual occupying the office dies, the corporation sole, unchanged, is still there and can be filled by someone else, either immediately or at some later point in time. It is clear from all this that a company is not a corporation sole, hence, perhaps, the historical English law reluctance to use 'corporation' as a synonym for 'company', for while all companies are corporations, not all corporations are companies. Thus a company is a corporation aggregate, a corporation made up from a totality of individuals.[69]

1.8 FOCUS – THE MAIN BUSINESS VEHICLE

A Company limited by shares

The main business vehicle through which most economic activity is carried on in the UK is the company limited by shares and created by registration under the Companies Act 1985. It is a corporate body, having legal personality separate from its members, and the liability of the members to contribute to its assets in an insolvent liquidation is limited to the amount unpaid on any shares held by them.[70] Within the legislation, there are two technically separate forms of it, the public company, and the private company. It will be seen below that there are many other types of company[71] and organisation, but these will not generally be covered in this book other than in this chapter below, for comparative purposes and perspective.[72]

B Public or private

The registered company limited by shares can be formed either as a private company or as a public company. Most in fact begin life as private companies and then convert to public companies when they have grown large enough for the managers and shareholders to feel that they can benefit from being able to raise large sums of capital by an offering of their shares to the public. They will also usually want to be a quoted company, that is, for their shares to be quoted on the London Stock Exchange (either as a listed company on the Main Market, or unlisted but quoted on the Alternative Investment Market (AIM))[73] which, of course, has the advantage that investors can feel confident of being able to sell their holdings if they wish, thus making them a more attractive and liquid investment. It is important to realise that being a public company does not automatically mean that prices on its shares are quoted in that way. Many public companies are unquoted.[74] Also, it

---

[69] It is not proposed to explore here all the incidents of corporateness. These are dealt with at pp. 23–24 below and for the related theories of incorporation, see p. 48 below.

[70] See Companies Act 1985, s. 1 (2) (a).

[71] There are sometimes various methods available of converting one type to another; see Companies Act 1985, ss. 43–55.

[72] Thus, to avoid confusion, unless the context shows otherwise, the company which is being referred to will be the company limited by shares, created by registration and either public, or private.

[73] See further p. 258 below.

[74] The majority in fact; only about 2,600 public companies are quoted on the London Stock Exchange

should be realised that in economic terms some public companies are quite small, smaller perhaps, than some of the larger private companies. The mere fact that its legal type is 'public' does not of itself guarantee economic size.

In recent years, partly (though not entirely) due to the influence of the EC Harmonisation Directives, there has been an increase in the differences between the legal rules affecting public and private companies, though much of company law still continues to apply to both types. The main technical legal differences between public and private companies are as follows:

(1) The name endings are different; the public company name must end with 'public limited company' which can be abbreviated to 'plc' and a private limited company must end its name with the word 'limited' which can be abbreviated to 'Ltd'.[75]

(2) A public company may offer its shares to the public; a private company may not do this.[76]

(3) A public company must have a minimum issued share capital of a minimum of £50,000 paid up to at least one quarter of the nominal value[77] and the whole of any premium on it.[78]

(4) A public company must have at least two members, but a private company need have only one member.[79]

(5) A public company must have at least two directors, but a private company need have only one.[80]

(6) A public company must ensure that its company secretary is properly qualified whereas a private company has no statutory obligation to do this.[81]

(7) Public companies are often required by the statutes to go through more onerous procedures than private companies.[82]

C Small closely-held and dispersed-ownership companies

As a means of classifying companies in a meaningful way, the technical legal 'public and private' distinction has its limitations. In company law theory, the really important distinction to be made is between those companies which are wholly or

---

(1,900 on the Main Market and 790 on AIM; see generally p. 259 below), whereas on 31 March 2004 there were 11,700 public companies on the Great Britain register. It is also worth noting that there are many more private companies than public, although their significance for the economy in terms of economic size is arguably less. On 31 March 2004 there were 1,831,100 private companies on the register; see *Companies in 2003–2004* (London: DTI, 2004) p. 34.

[75] See Companies Act 1985, ss. 25–26. Welsh equivalents are permitted; *ibid.*

[76] Companies Act 1985, s. 81.

[77] For these concepts, see p. 263 below.

[78] Companies Act 1985, ss. 11, 101, 117–118.

[79] *Ibid.* s. 1 (1), (3A).

[80] *Ibid.* s. 282.

[81] *Ibid.* s. 286. Directors' common law or fiduciary duties might import such a requirement in certain circumstances.

[82] Private companies, furthermore, may take advantage of what is called the 'elective regime' under which they may pass an elective resolution agreed to by all the members entitled to vote (Companies Act 1985, s. 379A) disapplying certain procedural requirements of the legislation; see *ibid.* ss. 80A, 252, 366A, 369 (4), 378 (3), 386.

substantially owner managed and controlled, and those where there is a major separation of ownership and control. The reasons for this have already been explained,[83] but, in a nutshell, the point is that those two types of companies raise very different problems of corporate governance.[84] In the former type, the owners will be in charge and if things go wrong, that is largely their own problem; they have lost their own money and wasted their own time. In the latter type of company, the shareholders are confronted with the difficulty of trying to ensure that the managers are motivated to act in the interests of the shareholders.

There is a need to identify an expression which conveys accurately these two paradigms. The terms public and private are only partially useful because many public companies are not companies which have dispersed ownership of shares. Fewer than 3,000 of the 12,000 public companies on the register are quoted on the Stock Exchange.[85] The remaining 9,000 or so are in many cases owner managed and controlled. Various expressions are commonly used by company lawyers to refer to companies which are managed and controlled by their owners: small private companies, close companies, companies with concentrated ownership of shares, quasi-partnership companies, small and closely-held companies, SMEs,[86] owner-managed companies, micro companies. Similarly, there are those which are used to describe the companies which have dispersed ownership of shares: large public companies, quoted companies, companies with fragmented ownership of shares, Berle and Means companies,[87] 'public and listed and other very large companies with real economic power'. These expressions all have varying degrees of accuracy and some have potential for confusion; some are cumbersome. As stated earlier, the expressions which will be adopted in this book are: 'small closely-held' companies[88] and 'dispersed-ownership' companies.[89] These expressions are pithy, and more or less accurate for the situations in which they will be used.

D The Company Law Review and law reform

One of the key areas identified by the Company Law Review[90] as needing reform was 'small companies'.[91] Subsequently, the Review developed a major 'think small first' strategy,[92] which involves simplifying the law for all private companies and

---

[83] See pp. 5–8 above.

[84] Corporate governance is the system by which the company is managed and controlled; see further Part III below.

[85] See n. 74 above.

[86] Small and medium-sized enterprises; the expression comes from the EC Directive which created exemptions from certain reporting requirements.

[87] See pp. 50–53 below.

[88] These will in fact usually be companies which are private, small in the sense of few shareholders, and of relatively minor economic significance.

[89] These will usually be public, quoted (either on the Main Market or on AIM), with very many shareholders, and of relatively large economic significance.

[90] See generally Chapter 4 below.

[91] DTI Consultation Document (February 1999) *The Strategic Framework* paras 2.31, 5.2.33. The subject of the appropriateness of the private company form had been under academic scrutiny for some years; see e.g. J. Freedman 'Small Businesses and the Corporate Form: Burden or Privilege?' (1994) 57 MLR 555; A. Hicks 'Corporate Form: Questioning the Unsung Hero' [1997] JBL 306.

[92] DTI Consultation Document (March 2000) *Developing the Framework* paras 6.5 *et seq.*

especially for small private companies.[93] Many of the complex procedural requirements which currently apply to companies, public and private would no longer
apply to private companies. The idea was therefore that future companies legislation
would set out the law relating to private companies first and then build in extra
requirements relating to public companies and public companies which are listed on
the Stock Exchange. In the Company Law Review Final Report some of these ideas
were reiterated, along with various technical recommendations concerning registration of companies and provision of information.[94]

1.9 OTHER BUSINESS VEHICLES[95]

A Other types of companies

The other types of companies which can be formed by registration under the
Companies Act 1985 are the company limited by guarantee[96] and the unlimited
company.[97] The first of these is not commonly used for trading, since it cannot be
formed with any share capital and is not appropriate for raising any capital
from the members. Its use is therefore mainly confined to clubs, societies and
charitable institutions such as schools. The unlimited company has corporate personality but, as the name suggests, the members' liability for debts is not limited.
Not surprisingly, the unlimited company is not a very common vehicle through
which to do business, although in earlier times it may have provided a useful
alternative to large partnerships which were prohibited by s. 716 until the removal
of limits in 2002.[98]

Sometimes companies which are formed under the Companies Act also attract
detailed statutory regulation by other legislation if the company is carrying on a
specialised type of business. Thus, for instance, registered companies which are
banks will need to comply with the Banking Act 1987 and insurance companies
with the Insurance Companies Act 1982. Sometimes, as with investment
companies and shipping companies, there are special provisions within the
Companies Act itself.

Companies formed by Act of Parliament (other than the Companies Act) are
usually referred to as 'statutory companies'. There are various (General) Public
Acts[99] under which corporate bodies may be formed for special purposes.
Additionally, they can individually be formed by Private Act, as were most of the

---

[93] *Ibid.* paras 6.22 *et seq.*
[94] See *Modern Company Law for a Competitive Economy Final Report* (London: DTI, 2001), paras.
2.1–2.37, 4.1–4.62. See also the subsequent government White Paper *Modernising Company Law* July
2002, Cmnd. 5553.
[95] This book will not have any further focus on these except to the extent that they become relevant from
time to time in Chapter 18.
[96] Companies Act 1985, s. 1 (2) (b), (4).
[97] *Ibid.* s. 1 (2) (c).
[98] See n. 117 below.
[99] Such as the Industrial and Provident Societies Acts 1965–1978, the Credit Unions Act 1979 and the
Building Societies Act 1986.

early canal companies, or by (Special) Public Act, as where a nationalised industry is set up. Common form provisions set out in the Companies Clauses Consolidation Act 1845 will apply unless the creating Act specifically excludes them and creates its own.

Chartered companies are those formed by a charter from the Crown, either under the Royal Prerogative or specific statutory powers. In the Companies Act, these are referred to as companies 'formed ... in pursuance ... of letters patent'.[100] At the present day companies are usually only created by charter if they have a broadly charitable or public service character, although a few of the old chartered trading companies still remain.

Generally speaking, statutory companies and chartered companies are regulated by the law contained in their statute or creating charter, but subject to that will be governed by general principles of company law built up by case law over the last century or so. They will be covered in this book only in so far as they are relevant to the registered company limited by shares.

The European Economic Interest Grouping (EEIG) is a relatively new type of what can probably be called a company, which can be formed in the UK under the European Economic Interest Grouping Regulations 1989.[101] It is a non-profit-making joint venture organisation which, although not giving limited liability to its members, does have corporate personality.

The European Company ('*Societas Europaea*' or '*SE*') is a concept that has been worked on for a long time. It can be used as a corporate vehicle in various cross-border situations.[102] The concept has recently been taken further, into the non-profit area by permitting the creation of an entity called the European Cooperative Society ('*Societas Cooperativa Europaea*' or '*SCE*').[103]

Lastly, it should be mentioned that there is in existence a new legal entity in the form of the Community Interest Company (CIC) which has been specially created for use by not-for-profit organisations pursuing community benefit.[104]

The open-ended investment company (OEIC) is a new type of company which can be formed to operate collective investment schemes. The role and structure of these is considered below.[105]

In some situations companies will fall to be regulated by the Companies Act even though they are not formed under it. Since the UK is an open economy, many foreign companies do business here and will find that they are subjected to various requirements in the Companies Act under the 'oversea companies' regime and/or under the 'branch' regime.[106]

---

[100] Companies Act 1985, s. 680(1)(b).
[101] SI 1989 No. 638; and Regulation (EEC) 2131/85.
[102] For more detail and legislative background see p. 13 above.
[103] Regulation (EC) 1435/2003, OJ 2003, L 207/1.
[104] These are a new legal creature contained in the Companies (Audit, Investigations and Community Enterprise) Act 2004; further details are available on the DTI website: http://www.dti.gov.uk/cld.
[105] At pp. 350–355.
[106] See Companies Act 1985, ss. 690A–703R. Section 718 of the Companies Act 1985 and the Companies (Unregistered Companies) Regulations 1985 (SI 1985 No. 680) will also sometimes have the effect of subjecting companies to the Companies Act regimes.

B Other organisations and bodies

There are various other types of organisations within English law. Some of these are unincorporated associations and thus not corporate bodies, while others have a status which while closely resembling corporate bodies fall some way short of that. Examples of unincorporated associations are:[107] clubs and societies, where the members are bound to each other contractually by the club rules and the club property is vested in trustees; syndicates, where unlike partnerships, the members put a limit on their liability when they make contracts with third parties. There are also various organisations whose legal status is difficult to classify in any very satisfactory way.[108] Unit trusts, for instance, resemble unincorporated associations, but it was held in *Smith v Anderson*[109] that they are not unincorporated associations but that the investors in a unit trust are in legal terms merely beneficiaries under a trust and do not 'associate' with one another. Trade unions have many of the attributes of corporations but it is expressly provided that they are not corporate bodies.[110] The separate legal personality concept is probably the main basis of distinction between unincorporated associations and corporations. However, it should be noticed that occasionally the courts have been prepared to hold that in some situations unincorporated associations have legal personality separate and distinct from their members but not so as to make them corporate bodies.[111] These rather hybrid associations are sometimes referred to as quasi-corporations or near-corporations.

C Partnerships

There are currently three types of partnership available as business vehicles in English law: the partnership,[112] the limited partnership and the new, limited liability partnership (LLP). It has been estimated that there are around 600,000 general partnerships.[113]

The partnership is governed by the Partnership Act 1890,[114] the common law, in so far as it is not inconsistent with the Act, and the terms of any partnership agreement, again, in so far as they do not conflict with the Act. Partnership is defined as 'the relation which subsists between persons carrying on business in common with a view of profit'.[115] No formalities are necessary for the creation of a partner-

---

[107] The case of partnerships is dealt with below.

[108] The new limited liability partnership (LLP) is probably a new example of this; see below.

[109] (1880) 15 Ch D 247.

[110] Trade Union and Labour Relations (Consolidation) Act 1992, s. 10.

[111] See e.g. *Willis v British Commonwealth Association of Universities* [1965] 1 QB 140, where an unincorporated association, the Universities Central Council on Admissions (UCCA), was regarded by Lord Denning MR as a body with a distinct legal personality, although it did not (apparently) amount to a body corporate.

[112] Often referred to as the 'general' partnership. Reforms are being worked on; see DTI Consultation Document of April 2004, *Reform of Partnership Law: The Economic Impact.*

[113] Within the UK. This is a DTI estimate; there are no precise statistics available because there is no registration requirement for the formation of an ordinary business partnership. Additionally, there are estimated to be around 400,000 sole traders, so that the combined figure for unincorporated business enterprises in the UK (600,000 partnerships and 400,000 sole traders) is around the million mark. As regards limited partnerships, on 31 March 2004 there was a Great Britain total of 11,287 limited partnerships registered under the Limited Partnerships Act 1907.

[114] Which codified and amended aspects of the pre-existing common law.

[115] Partnership Act 1890, s. 1.

ship,[116] it will exist if the definition is satisfied.[117] The partners will have unlimited liability for the debts of the firm, arising in various circumstances.[118] Broadly speaking, and usually in the absence of contrary provision, partners will share profits equally,[119] be entitled to take part in the management of the firm,[120] and be able to bind the firm within the scope of the partnership business.[121]

Limited partnerships are under the same regime as general or ordinary partnerships except that they are also subject to the Limited Partnerships Act 1907.[122] The limited partnership provides a vehicle by which one or more partners can have limited liability so long as certain conditions are fulfilled. However, the partnership must also consist of one or more persons who have no limitation of liability. Most limited partnerships are used in tax avoidance schemes or venture capital structures rather than as trading partnerships.

Limited liability partnerships (LLPs) were originally conceived as a new business vehicle for professionals designed to ameliorate the problems being faced, in particular, by audit firms who were finding that litigation for negligence was placing partners in danger of liability well above the limits covered by their professional indemnity insurance policy. The government also feared that accountancy firms would be tempted to relocate to Jersey, where more attractive forms of partnership had been developed. Under that spur, the UK developed one of its first new business forms[123] since the Limited Partnerships Act 1907. The Limited Liability Partnerships Act 2000 introduces a new type of business association, an interesting hybrid entity which possesses some characteristics which derive from company law and some from partnership law. Although originally conceived as a business vehicle for professionals, in its current form it is available to any two or more persons carrying on a lawful business with a view to profit.[124] The Act provides that there shall be a new entity called a limited liability partnership.[125] It provides that the LLP is a body corporate[126] to be created by registration with the Registrar of Companies.[127] There are to be no problems with the *ultra vires* doctrine since it will have unlimited capacity.[128] It must have a minimum of two members.[129]

---

[116] Although the law may impose other formalities as to how they go about business; see e.g. the Business Names Act 1985.

[117] See also Partnership Act 1890, ss. 2, 45. Until recently the Companies Act 1985 required incorporation if the maximum number of partners was more than 20 (although subject to exceptions). This requirement was removed by the Regulatory Reform (Removal of 20 Member Limit in Partnerships etc) Order 2002 (SI 2002, No. 3203).

[118] See Partnership Act 1890, ss. 9, 10, 12.

[119] *Ibid.* s. 24.

[120] *Ibid.* s. 24 (5).

[121] Subject to *ibid.* ss. 5, 8.

[122] And various statutory instruments.

[123] The other was the introduction of open-ended investment companies (OEICs) in 1996. See p. 351 below.

[124] Limited Liability Partnerships Act 2000, s. 2 (1) (a). Academics had criticised the earlier restrictive concept, see J. Freedman and V. Finch 'Limited Liability Partnerships: Have Accountants Sewn up the "Deep Pockets" Debate?' [1997] JBL 387.

[125] Limited Liability Partnerships Act 2000, s. 1 (1).

[126] *Ibid.* s. 1 (2).

[127] *Ibid.* s. 3.

[128] *Ibid.* s. 1 (3).

[129] *Ibid.* s. 2 (1) (a).

Membership of the LLP comes about by subscribing the incorporation document or by agreement with the existing members.[130] The constitution of the LLP is derived from the agreement between the members, or between the limited liability partnership and its members.[131] Pre-incorporation agreements between the members may carry over into the LLP to some extent.[132] It is provided that every member of an LLP is the agent of it.[133] On the matter of limited liability, the legislation provides that the members of an LLP have 'such liability to contribute to its assets in the event of its being wound up as is provided for by virtue of this Act'.[134]

With their new entity the DTI seem to have met a commercial need that was actually there; the LLP is being used.[135] It takes the advantage of limited liability from company law and combines it with what some will regard as advantageous aspects of partnerships, namely partnership taxation. On the important question of disclosure, it much resembles a company in that it must file annual reports and accounts,[136] so in respect of disclosure it looks as though there is going to be little advantage over an ordinary private company.

---

[130] *Ibid.* s. 4 (1), (2).

[131] *Ibid.* s. 5.

[132] *Ibid.* s. 5 (2).

[133] *Ibid.* s. 6 (1). Although in some circumstances a member without actual authority to act will not be able to bind the partnership to a third party: s. 6 (2).

[134] *Ibid.* s. 1 (4). The Limited Liability Partnerships Regulations 2001 (SI 2001 No. 1090), reg. 5, apply the provisions of the Insolvency Act 1986 so as to bring about limited liability (i.e. s. 74 thereof).

[135] At 31 March 2004 there were 7,396 on the register (Great Britain); source *Companies in 2003–2004* (London: DTI, 2004) p. 50.

[136] See reg. 3 of the LLP Regulations.

2

CORPORATE ENTITY, LIMITED LIABILITY AND INCORPORATION

2.1 CORPORATE ENTITY

A The '*Salomon*' doctrine

Incorporation by registration was introduced in 1844 and the doctrine of limited liability followed in 1855.[1] Subsequently, in 1897, in *Salomon* v *Salomon & Co*[2] the House of Lords explored the effects of these enactments and cemented into English law the twin concepts of corporate entity and limited liability. Incorporation gives the company legal personality, separate from its members, with the result that a company may own property, sue and be sued in its own corporate name. It will not die when its members die. In many areas of company law, the legal rules are shaped by and to some extent flow from the concept of separate personality. Thus, the share capital, once subscribed must be maintained by the company, it no longer belongs to the members and cannot be returned to them except subject to stringent safeguards.[3] The rule that for a wrong done to the company, the proper claimant is the company itself is similarly largely the result of this principle.[4] The separate personality concept is often spoken of as though it also necessarily involves the idea that the liability of the company's members is limited but of course this is not always so; it is perfectly possible to form an unlimited company under s. 1 (2) (c) of the Companies Act 1985. It has no limited liability, but under the corporate entity doctrine it will have separate legal personality. In practice, most companies are limited companies and so corporate personality and limited liability[5] tend to go hand in hand.

The corporate entity principle was firmly settled at the end of the 19th century in the *Salomon* case.[6] It concerned a common business manoeuvre whereby Aron Salomon, the owner of a boot and leather business, sold it to a company he formed, in return for fully paid-up shares in it, allotted to him and members of his family.

---

[1] Joint Stock Companies Act 1844; Limited Liability Act 1855. For a more detailed account of these events and related matters, see B. Pettet 'Limited Liability – A Principle for the 21st Century?' (1995) 48 *Current Legal Problems* (Part 2) 125 at pp. 128–132.
[2] [1897] AC 22.
[3] See further p. 280 below.
[4] This is part of the rule in *Foss* v *Harbottle*; see further p. 213 below.
[5] Limited liability is discussed at p. 31 below.
[6] [1897] AC 22.

Salomon also received an acknowledgement of the company's indebtedness to him, in the form of secured debentures. These were later mortgaged to an outsider. Soon after formation, the company went into liquidation at the behest of unpaid trade creditors. The debentures, being secured by a charge on the company's assets ranked in priority to the trade creditors and so the mortgage to the outsider was paid off. About £1,000 remained and Aron Salomon, now as unencumbered owner of the debentures, claimed this in priority to the trade creditors. He succeeded and also defeated their claim that he should be made to indemnify the company in respect of its debts. The House of Lords affirmed the principle that the company was a separate legal person from the controlling shareholder, and that it was not to be regarded as his agent.[7] It was also made clear that he was not liable to indemnify the creditors, thus giving effect to the limited liability doctrine.

The corporate entity principle, often now referred to as the '*Salomon*' principle, is applied systematically in most cases and these have gradually built up a picture of its ramifications.[8] It was held that it was possible to regard a shareholder who was employed as a pilot by the company as a 'worker' (within the meaning of a statute) even though he controlled the company and was its chief executive.[9] Another case quite logically confirmed that the shareholder was not the owner of the property of the company.[10]

B Piercing the corporate veil

At times, the *Salomon* principle produces what appear to be unjust and purely technical results and in such circumstances judges[11] come under a moral and/or intellectual pressure to sidestep the *Salomon* principle and produce a result which seems more 'just'. For instance, a number of cases have revolved around versions of this problem: Company A has a subsidiary, Company B. Company A owns land on which stands a factory. Its subsidiary Company B operates the factory business. A

---

[7] This was necessary to the result reached, for if the company had been Salomon's agent, he would have been liable to the creditors, as principal, on the contracts he had made; on agency generally, see further Chapter 7.

[8] It continues to stimulate academic interest, particularly on the question of piercing the corporate veil, as the undiminishing flow of scholarship testifies; see e.g. R. Grantham and C. Rickett (eds) *Corporate Personality in the 20th Century* (Oxford: Hart Publishing, 1998); H. Rajak 'The Legal Personality of Associations' in F. Patfield (ed.) *Perspectives on Company Law: 1* (London: Kluwer, 1995) p. 63; L. Sealy 'Perception and Policy in Company Law Reform' in D. Feldman and F. Meisel (eds) *Corporate and Commercial Law: Modern Developments* (London: LLP, 1996) 11. And on 'piercing the veil' (see below): S. Ottolenghi 'From Peeping Behind the Veil, To Ignoring it Completely' (1990) 53 MLR 338; J. Gray 'How Regulation Finds its Way through the Corporate Veil' in B. Rider (ed.) *The Corporate Dimension* (Bristol: Jordans, 1998) p. 255; C. Mitchell 'Lifting the Corporate Veil in the English Courts: an Empirical Study' [1999] CFILR 15.

[9] *Lee v Lee's Air Farming* [1961] AC 12, PC.

[10] *Macaura v Northern Assurance Co.* [1925] AC 619, where the beneficial owner of all the shares in a company did not realise that he was not owner of the company's property and so when he insured that property by policies in his own name and the property was later damaged by fire, he failed to recover. Similarly, it has been held that it is possible for the sole shareholders and directors to steal from their company: *R v Philippou* (1989) 5 BCC 665.

[11] In some circumstances the corporate entity principle will be set aside by statute, as is common in taxation legislation. In company law, apart from the rules on group accounts (see below), the main examples of this are ss. 24 and 349 (4) of the Companies Act 1985.

local government authority makes a compulsory purchase of the land. The statute under which it does this provides for compensation for the landowner in respect of disturbance to a business carried on by him on the land. In our problem, applying the *Salomon* doctrine strictly, Company A cannot claim, since it has no business which is disturbed, nor can Company B since although it does have a business which has been disturbed, it has no land. Obviously in reality the two companies function as a single unit, but in law they are separate. There are a number of reported cases on this kind of problem[12] which reveal differing approaches. In one case, *Smith, Stone & Knight v Birmingham Corporation*[13] the judge managed to decide that Company B was the agent of Company A and so compensation was payable. The problem with this reasoning is that *Salomon* makes it clear that a company is not, without more, the agent of its shareholder. Of course, if there happens to be a genuine agency relationship between them, perhaps created by express contract, there is no conflict with *Salomon*, but in *Smith, Stone & Knight* it seems that the judge was merely inferring an agency, on very little evidence, in order to get round the *Salomon* principle. A more robust approach was tried by Lord Denning MR[14] in *DHN Ltd v Tower Hamlets*,[15] where he suggested that the corporate 'veil' could be lifted, that the companies were in reality a group, and should be treated as one, and so compensation was payable.[16] In *Woolfson v Strathclyde DC*,[17] in an analogous situation, the House of Lords[18] held that the corporate veil could only be lifted in this way in circumstances where the company is a 'facade', and they criticised Lord Denning's approach. Accordingly, compensation was not payable.

There are many other reported examples of the courts having to grapple with applications of the *Salomon* doctrine in difficult cases. In several cases, the judges have openly stated that if justice requires it then the precedent of *Salomon* can be by-passed. Thus in *Re A Company*[19] the Court of Appeal seemed to be taking the view that *Salomon* was of *prima facie* application only: 'In our view, the cases ... show that the court will use its powers to pierce the corporate veil if it is necessary to achieve justice ...'[20] and in *Creasey v Breachwood Motors Ltd*[21] it was held that the court had power to lift the veil 'to achieve justice where its exercise is necessary for that purpose'.[22] However, the judicial movement in support of piercing the corporate veil to 'achieve justice' has been firmly suppressed in several influential Court of Appeal cases concerned with how the *Salomon* doctrine should be applied to the way in which group structures are organised. In *Adams v Cape Industries plc*[23] the idea that a court was free to disregard *Salomon* merely because it considered that

---

[12] Although not *exactly* on those facts.
[13] [1939] 4 All ER 116.
[14] Although the remainder of the Court of Appeal adopted a more orthodox analysis.
[15] [1976] 1 WLR 852.
[16] This was followed by the Northern Ireland Court of Appeal in *Munton Bros v Sect of State* [1983] NI 369.
[17] (1978) 38 P & CR 521.
[18] Hearing an appeal from the Court of Session in Scotland.
[19] (1985) 1 BCC 99,421.
[20] *Ibid.* at p. 99,425.
[21] [1992] BCC 638.
[22] *Ibid.* at p. 647, per Judge Southwood QC.
[23] [1990] BCC 786.

justice so required was firmly rejected and the court gave strong support to the idea[24] that there is really only one well-recognised exception to the rule prohibiting the piercing of the corporate veil and that is that: '[I]t is appropriate to pierce the corporate veil only where special circumstances exist indicating that it is a mere facade concealing the true facts.'[25] A number of subsequent cases have generally followed the *Adams* v *Cape* approach,[26] and *Creasey* v *Breachwood Motors*, which did not, was recently flatly overruled by the Court of Appeal in *Ord* v *Belhaven Pubs Ltd*.[27] In *Ord* v *Belhaven Pubs Ltd*, the claimants had taken a 20-year lease of a pub from the defendant company in 1989 and were later claiming damages for misrepresentation. The claimants became worried that restructuring of assets between 1992 and 1995 within the group of companies which the defendant was a part of, had left the defendant company without sufficient assets to pay their claim if it was eventually successful. The claimants applied to substitute the defendant's holding company and/or another company in its group for the defendant. Although the claim was successful at first instance, the Court of Appeal reversed this and delivered a resounding affirmation of the *Salomon* doctrine and gave us a useful example of an application of the 'mere facade' test:

> The defendant company was in financial difficulties. None of the things that were done in 1992 and 1995 in any way exacerbated those difficulties; in fact, they relieved those difficulties, they did not adversely affect the balance sheet of the defendant company in any way that prejudiced the plaintiffs ...
>
> All the transactions that took place were overt transactions. They were conducted in accordance with the liberties that are conferred upon corporate entities by the Companies Act and they do not conceal anything from anybody. The companies were operating at material times as trading companies and they were not being interposed as shams or for some ulterior motive ...
>
> In the course of its judgment [in *Adams* v *Cape*] the Court of Appeal considered both what is described as the single economic unit argument of groups of [companies] and ... piercing the corporate veil. They discussed the authorities and clearly recognised that the concepts were extremely limited indeed ... The approach of the judge in the present case was simply to look at the economic unit, to disregard the distinction between the legal entities that were involved and then to say: since the company cannot pay, the shareholders who are the people financially interested should be made to pay instead. That of course is radically at odds with the whole concept of corporate personality and limited liability and the decision of the House of Lords in *Salomon* ... On the question of lifting the corporate veil, they expressed themselves similarly ... but it is clear that they were of the view that there must be some impropriety before the corporate veil can be pierced. It is not necessary to examine the extent of the limitation of the principle because, in the present case, no impropriety is alleged. [The Court of Appeal] quoted what was said by Lord Keith in *Woolfson* ... [that] it is appropriate to pierce the corporate veil only where special circumstances exist, indicating that it is a mere facade concealing the true facts ... The plaintiffs in the present case cannot bring themselves within any such principle. There is no facade

---

[24] Which had been developing in *Woolfson* v *Strathclyde DC* (1979) 38 P & CR 521.
[25] [1990] BCC 786 at p. 822.
[26] E.g. *Re Polly Peck plc* [1996] BCC 486; *Re H Ltd* [1996] 2 All ER 391; *Yukong Lines Ltd of Korea* v *Rendsberg Investments Corp* [1998] BCC 870.
[27] [1998] BCC 607.

that was adopted at any stage; there was [no] concealment of the true facts ... it was just the ordinary trading of a group of companies under circumstances where, as was said in [*Adams* v *Cape*] the company is in law entitled to organise the group's affairs in the manner that it does, and to expect that the court should apply the principles of [*Salomon*] in the ordinary way ...[28]

It seems therefore that almost exactly 100 years after *Salomon* was decided, the courts may have settled down to the idea that it has to be followed,[29] unless the situation can be brought within the 'facade' test. It is likely that in future cases judges will find themselves focusing on what it is to mean.

There is already a little guidance. In *Adams* v *Cape* it was felt that the motive of the person using the company would sometimes be highly material and the Court of Appeal clearly felt that *Jones* v *Lipman*[30] was a good example of a case which would satisfy the facade test and that the judge there was right to pierce the corporate veil. The first defendant there, Lipman, had agreed to sell some land to the claimants, but after entering into the contract he changed his mind. So he sold it to a company of which he owned nearly all the shares. The judge made an order for specific performance against Lipman and the company. The Court of Appeal approved[31] of the judge's description of the company as 'the creature of the first defendant, a device and a sham, a mask which he holds before his face in an attempt to avoid recognition by the eye of equity'. In *Trustor AB* v *Smallbone and others (No. 3)*[32] the managing director of Trustor had transferred money to Introcom, a company which he controlled, and one of the issues which arose was whether the corporate veil of Introcom could be pierced so as to treat receipt by Introcom as receipt by him. Morritt V-C held that the court would be 'entitled to pierce the corporate veil and recognise the receipt by a company as that of the individual(s) in control of it if the company was used as 'a device or façade to conceal the true facts thereby avoiding or concealing any liability of those individual(s)'[33] and that on the facts this was satisfied.

As regards what is not a facade, we can have regard to the parts of the above-quoted passage from *Ord* v *Belhaven*, which emphasises that what happened there:

> ... did not adversely affect the balance sheet of the defendant company in any way that prejudiced the plaintiffs ... All the transactions that took place were overt transactions ... The companies were operating at material times as trading companies and they were not being interposed as shams or for some ulterior motive ... it was just the ordinary trading of a group of companies under circumstances where ... the company is in law entitled to organise the group's affairs in the manner that it does ...[34]

---

[28] *Ibid.* at p. 615, per Hobhouse LJ; (Brooke and Balcombe LJJ agreeing).
[29] The House of Lords' decision in *Williams* v *Natural Life Health Foods* [1998] BCC 428 is further support for the idea that departure from *Salomon* is going to be very difficult to bring about; see further p. 29 below.
[30] [1962] 1 WLR 832.
[31] *Ibid.* at p. 825.
[32] [2002] BCC 795.
[33] *Ibid.* at p. 801.
[34] *Ibid.*

No doubt as the years go by, future cases will gradually result in the courts developing a detailed jurisprudence of the façade concept.

C Corporate liability for torts and crimes

1 The problem of the corporate mind

The doctrine of separate legal personality of companies runs into problems as soon as it meets those parts of the general law which apply to natural persons and which involve assessing the mental state of the person for the purpose of imposing liability. In these circumstances, the courts have recourse to the expedient[35] of treating the state of mind of the senior officers of the company as being the state of mind of the company.[36] The idea was put nicely by Denning LJ in *Bolton Engineering* v *Graham*,[37] where a landlord company opposed the grant of a new tenancy on the ground that it intended to occupy the land for its own business. There had been no formal board meeting or other collective decision which could be said to show the company's intention, but it was argued that in a managerial capacity, the directors simply had that intention. The Court of Appeal held that the intention of the company could be derived from the intention of its officers and agents. Denning LJ said in his graphic prose which was to become so familiar in subsequent years:

> A company may in many ways be likened to a human body. It has a brain and a nerve centre which controls what it does. It also has hands which hold the tools and act in accordance with directions from the centre. Some of the people in the company are mere servants or agents who are nothing more than the hands to do the work and cannot be said to represent the mind or will. Others are directors and managers who represent the directing mind and will of the company and control what it does. The state of mind of these managers is the state of mind of the company and is treated by the law as such.[38]

It has become clear that in special circumstances, persons lower down the managerial hierarchy might be regarded as the 'directing mind and will' or the persons whose state of mind should be attributed to the company. In *Meridian* v *Securities Commission*[39] the Privy Council held that a company's chief investment officer and a senior portfolio manager were the persons whose knowledge was to count as the knowledge or state of mind of the company for the purposes of the application of a New Zealand Securities Act. They were not board members, but unless they were held to be the directing mind and will in the context of a duty to notify an acquisition of shares, then the purposes of the Act would be defeated.

---

[35] In a jurisprudential sense it tends to suggest that the fictional entity theory (see the discussion at p. 48 below) is not a sufficient explanation of the phenomenon of corporate personality and that, to some extent, the company soon has to be regarded in law as the people in it, thus lending support to the real entity theory of incorporation.

[36] See e.g. *Lennard's Carrying Company Ltd* v *Asiatic Petroleum Co. Ltd* [1915] AC 705.

[37] [1957] 1 QB 159.

[38] *Ibid.* at p. 172. On this kind of basis the knowledge of a director can sometimes be imputed to a company so as to make it liable for knowing receipt of trust property; see *Trustor AB* v *Smallbone and others* [2002] BCC 795. Other aspects of this case are discussed at p. 27 above.

[39] [1995] BCC 942.

The problem of the corporate mind has often become relevant in relation to the company's tortious and criminal liability.

2 Corporate liability for torts

A company acts through its servants or agents and in the context of tortious liability, it is well established that it is vicariously liable for torts committed by its servants or agents acting in the course of their employment, just as any other principal or employer would be vicariously liable. Companies are sued on this basis all the time.[40]

The employee who actually commits the act will also be liable as the primary tortfeasor. So if an employee of a bus company drives a bus negligently and injures someone, in addition to creating vicarious liability for his employer company, he will himself be liable as the individual primary tortfeasor. This aspect of tortious liability has recently been giving rise to problems. Suppose the controlling shareholder and managing director of a company sets in motion all the events which produce a tort committed against a third party. It would seem under the above principles that he would be personally liable. Apart from the obvious situation of his driving the bus, where causation is not in doubt, in many cases his liability will depend on his having done enough to set the events in motion to be able to regard him as the primary tortfeasor. In the past, the test adopted has sometimes been whether he has acted in such a way as to 'make the tort his own'.[41] Of course, in a situation where he is the major shareholder and managing director, the practical effect of holding him liable as primary tortfeasor will be, in effect, to strip him of the protection generally assumed to be afforded to incorporators by the *Salomon* doctrine.

In *Williams v Natural Life Health Foods*[42] the House of Lords had to grapple with these issues in a situation where the claimant was seeking damages under the *Hedley Byrne* principle for negligent misrepresentation. The company had become insolvent, and so the claimant was seeking to make the major shareholder and managing director liable. The question arose of whether there was the necessary special relationship for the purposes of his liability for negligent misstatement. The House of Lords took the view that the manager would not be liable unless it could be shown that there was an assumption of responsibility by him, sufficient to create the

---

[40] The argument that a company could not be liable for an *ultra vires* tort has never been generally accepted by the courts (see e.g. *Campbell* v *Paddington Corporation* [1911] 1 KB 869) and has probably been finally laid to rest by the Companies Act 1985, s. 35 (1). On *ultra vires* generally see further p. 114 below. An interesting use of tort principles to try (in effect) to circumvent the separate entity doctrine of *Salomon*, occurred in *Lubbe* v *Cape (No. 2)* [2000] 4 All ER 268, HL, where, in circumstances where injury had been negligently caused by a subsidiary company, it was argued against the holding company that it had exercised de facto control over the subsidiary and therefore owed a duty of care to those injured, in relation to its control of and advice to its subsidiary. The proceedings were eventually settled without this issue having been the subject of judicial decision, so it is not clear whether the interesting argument would have succeeded.

[41] *Fairline Shipping Corp* v *Adamson* [1975] QB 180; *Trevor Ivory Ltd* v *Anderson* [1992] 2 NZLR 517, Cooke P; *Evans* v *Spritebrand* [1985] BCLC 105; *Mancetter Developments Ltd* v *Garmanson Ltd* [1986] 1 All ER 449, (1986) 2 BCC 98,924; *Attorney General of Tuvalu* v *Philatelic Ltd* [1990] BCC 30; *Noel* v *Poland* [2001] 2 BCLC 645.

[42] [1998] BCC 428.

necessary special relationship, and here there was no such assumption, particularly since he had chosen to conduct his business through the medium of a limited liability company.[43] Different issues arose in the subsequent case of *Standard Chartered Bank v Pakistan National Shipping Corporation (No. 2)*,[44] where the managing director had made a fraudulent misrepresentation. He was held liable in the tort of deceit for which it was not necessary to establish a duty of care. All the elements of the tort were proved against him. It was irrelevant that he made the representation on behalf of the company or that it was relied on as such.

That this is an area where there are 'deep waters' needing careful negotiation is shown by the fact that the Court of Appeal in the *Standard Chartered* case unanimously managed to reach a conclusion which was subsequently unanimously reversed by the House of Lords.

3 Corporate liability for crimes

Until 1944, companies had no general common law liability for crimes,[45] although the principle of vicarious liability had been used to make companies liable for certain 'strict liability' offences, where *mens rea* was not a required element of the offence. In *DPP v Kent and Sussex Contractors Ltd*[46] it was decided that the state of mind of the officers of the company could be imputed to it for the purpose of establishing 'intent' to deceive. Companies can therefore now have direct criminal liability imposed on them[47] by the use of this technique of 'identifying' senior individuals whose state of mind can be regarded as that of the company for the purposes of establishing *mens rea*.

Corporate liability for manslaughter has recently shown up some of the limitations of this approach. It was established in *R v P & O European Ferries (Dover) Ltd*[48] that a company could be indicted for manslaughter but that it was necessary to be able to identify one individual who had the necessary degree of *mens rea* for manslaughter, and so the prosecution against the company failed.[49] Subsequently, the Law Commission has made recommendations for the introduction of a new offence of corporate killing where the conduct of the company falls below what could reasonably be expected, and death will be regarded as having been caused by the conduct of the company if it is caused by a failure in the way the company's activities are managed and organised.[50]

---

[43] The further argument that the managing director and the company could be joint tortfeasors was disposed of on the policy grounds that it would 'expose directors and officers to a plethora of new tort claims' ([1998] BCLC 428 at p. 435).

[44] [2002] BCLC 846, HL.

[45] Subject to certain exceptions.

[46] [1944] KB 146.

[47] Obviously there is a wide range of crimes that it is impossible for the company to commit.

[48] (1990) 93 Cr App R 72.

[49] A successful prosecution for corporate manslaughter was subsequently brought against a company where the managing director himself had been convicted of manslaughter; see *R v OLL Ltd* (1994) unreported but noted by G. Slapper in 144 NLJ 1735.

[50] Law Com. Report No. 237 *Legislating the Criminal Code: Involuntary Manslaughter* (1996). The area was subject to further consultation; see Home Office Consultation Paper (23 May 2000) *Reforming the Law on Involuntary Manslaughter: The Government's Proposals*, but it seems that no legislation is currently contemplated.

2.2 LIMITED LIABILITY

A The meaning of limited liability

Eleven years after the passing of the Joint Stock Companies Act 1844 which for the first time permitted the creation of companies by registration, limited liability became generally[51] available in the Limited Liability Act 1855. By 1855 it was felt by the legislature that limited liability was a necessary addition to the facility of incorporation by registration.[52]

Outside of company law, limited liability is not a term with any very precise meaning and is commonly used to describe the situation where a person has done an act which under the generally prevailing rules of the legal system would incur a liability to pay money but is excused, wholly or partly, from incurring that liability. Within company law, the notion of limited liability is very technical and often misunderstood. Sometimes wrongly referred to as 'corporate' limited liability,[53] it is the principle or principles as a result of which the members of an insolvent company do not have to contribute their own money to the assets in the liquidation to meet the debts of the company.[54] Under the Insolvency Act 1986 the members have a liability to contribute to the assets of the company in the event of its assets in the liquidation being insufficient to meet the claims of the creditors.[55] It is this liability which is limited.[56]

B The continuing debate about the desirability of limited liability

When limited liability was introduced in 1855, the preceding public debate had been about whether it was morally justified and efficient. However, owing to the relatively undeveloped nature of tort law at that time, no consideration was given to how limited liability would impact on someone who was a tort creditor as opposed to a contract creditor.

---

[51] Prior to this, limited liability could be secured on an ad hoc basis by the creation of a company by statute or by the grant of a charter of incorporation. However, obtaining legislative incorporation was difficult and charters granted sparingly.

[52] About half a century of public debate and argument had preceded it.

[53] The liability of the company for its various debts is unlimited; in an insolvent liquidation, where the debts over-top the assets available, all of the assets will be used up in satisfying the claims of creditors and not all creditors will be paid in full. There is no point at which, prior to exhaustion of its assets, the company is relieved of its liability; it is emptied.

[54] It is often said that their liability for the company's debts is limited, but this is wrong; they are not liable at all for the company's debts.

[55] Insolvency Act 1986, s. 74.

[56] Limited to the amount 'unpaid' on the shares (Insolvency Act 1986, s. 74 (2) (d)), called a 'company limited by shares', or limited to the amount which the members have undertaken to contribute to the assets of the company in the event of its being wound up (s. 74 (3)), called a 'company limited by guarantee'. There is also the possibility of forming a company which does not have any limit on the liability of its members, called 'an unlimited company'. In each case, the names given to the company by the Companies Act 1985 in s. 1 (2) are misleading; the *company* is not limited by shares nor by guarantee, and all these companies are unlimited in the sense just described. The names only make any sense if they are taken to refer to the financial backup that is ultimately available in a liquidation, so that 'company limited by shares' really means 'company where shareholder backup is limited to the amount unpaid on their shares'.

As regards contract creditors, the essence of the argument in favour of permitting limited liability is along the lines that manufacturing, trade and economic activities generally are good for us because they create the goods and services which we like having around us and which enrich our lives. Thus, a business form which is conducive to economic activity is preferable to one which is not and limited liability is needed because it encourages the channelling of resources into productive businesses. The encouragement is given by enabling the investor who has capital to invest it in the company without having to worry much about the liabilities being incurred by the company. The main argument against this is that limited liability encourages recklessness in business ventures and innocent creditors have to bear the loss.

It is clear that the arguments in favour of limited liability for contract debts have won the day. Limited liability for contract debt is here to stay and there is no great movement for its abolition. On the contrary, it is usually regarded as one of the main pillars of company law and our economic system and in addition to the usual intuitive arguments of lawyers and politicians the copious literature dealing with economic analysis[57] of limited liability is generally in favour of it. The economists lay stress on the idea that the creditor chooses to give credit and when he enters into the agreement he can compensate himself for the risk he runs that his debt will not be paid. Thus a bank will charge a higher interest rate if the loan is unsecured or is otherwise deemed risky, or it can bargain around the limitation of liability by requiring a personal guarantee from the incorporators, or a trade creditor can raise the price of his goods to compensate for the fact that during the course of the year he knows he will probably encounter some bad debts. Thus the limited liability doctrine does not empower the company to cause harm to the contract creditor; he is a voluntary creditor and is in a position to look after himself.

It is highly arguable that it is different with a tort creditor because tort creditors are involuntary creditors. Suppose, for instance, the company's factory emits poisons which afflict the surrounding population. They have not been in a position to bargain with the company. As a result the company may not have bothered to ascertain whether appropriate care had been taken by it, for it knew that any loss arising from failure to take care would be borne by the local people and not by the shareholders. The risk has been shifted away from the company and may well have enabled it to take decisions which are inefficient for society as a whole. Such effects are described by economists as 'third party effects' or 'externalities'. These issues have been the subject of considerable academic debate which has not closed. My own views to the effect that an insurance solution is desirable have been expressed elsewhere and the reader wishing to pursue the debate is referred there.[58]

---

[57] On economic analysis of company law generally, see p. 66 below.
[58] B. Pettet 'Limited Liability – A Principle for the 21st Century?' (1995) 48 *Current Legal Problems* (Part 2) 125 at pp. 152–159.

C Fraudulent trading and wrongful trading

Within the field of company law there have been two major attempts to curb situations in which it is arguable that limited liability[59] is being abused. These are fraudulent trading and wrongful trading.

The fraudulent trading provisions were first introduced in 1929.[60] Under the present form of the provisions the court has power to declare that persons who have carried on a company with intent to defraud creditors are liable to make contributions to the company's assets. There is also the possibility of criminal liability which can attract up to seven years' imprisonment.[61] The provisions have not been much used; the main problem being that because criminal liability was in issue the courts developed a test for intent which was in practice difficult to satisfy. In *Re Patrick & Lyon Ltd*[62] it was held that what was necessary was 'actual dishonesty, involving, according to current notions of fair trading among commercial men, real moral blame'. However, despite their shortcomings the provisions are by no means a dead letter and are still used in cases where the necessary intent can be established. For example, in *Re Todd Ltd*[63] the director was liable for debts of the company amounting to £70,401. Moreover, in clear cases of fraud the criminal offence of fraudulent trading is frequently used.

Wrongful trading liability was conceived as an attempt to discourage and penalise abuses of limited liability which stemmed from negligent rather than fraudulent conduct.[64] If the requisite conditions set out in s. 214 of the Insolvency Act 1986 are satisfied, the court may declare that the director is liable to make such contribution to the company's assets as the court thinks proper. Liability will arise where the company has gone into insolvent liquidation and at some time before commencement of the winding up, the director: '... knew or ought to have concluded that there was no reasonable prospect that the company would avoid going into insolvent liquidation ...'[65] The provision is not designed to remove limited liability

---

[59] Technically it is arguable that they merely impose penalties on managers and do not seek to remove limited liability from shareholders. However, the reality is that most of the situations in which they are used concern small private companies where the managers are the major shareholders, and thus the effect is to create a kind of removal of limited liability.

[60] Amended since, the provisions are now contained in s. 213 of the Insolvency Act 1986 and s. 458 of the Companies Act 1985. Section 213 provides: '(1) If in the course of the winding up of a company it appears that any business of the company has been carried on with intent to defraud creditors of the company or creditors of any other person, or for any fraudulent purpose, the following has effect. (2) The court, on the application of the liquidator may declare that any persons who were knowingly parties to the carrying on of the business in the manner above-mentioned are to be liable to make such contributions (if any) to the company's assets as the court thinks proper.' Criminal liability is added by s. 458 of the 1985 Act, which applies whether or not the company has been, or is in the course of being wound up. Since 1986 the court has had the additional power to defer debts owed by the company to persons who have carried on fraudulent trading: Insolvency Act 1986, s. 215 (4).

[61] See Companies Act 1985, Sch. 24.

[62] [1933] Ch 786 at p. 790.

[63] [1990] BCLC 454.

[64] Sir Kenneth Cork *Report of the Review Committee on Insolvency Law and Practice* (the Cork Report) (London: HMSO, Cmnd. 8558, 1982) Chap. 44 had recommended the creation of civil liability without need for proof of dishonesty. This led to the introduction in 1985 of liability for what has generally become known as 'wrongful trading'; the provisions are now in the Insolvency Act 1986, s. 214.

[65] Insolvency Act 1986, s. 214 (2) (b).

altogether the instant that a company becomes insolvent. It is perfectly possible for some companies to trade out of a position of insolvency and so avoid going into insolvent liquidation. Many directors of insolvent companies doubtless carry on with this hope in mind. What the statute is saying is that there may however come a 'moment of truth' when the reasonable[66] director should realise that the company cannot recover. If he carries on[67] trading thereafter he does so with the risk that in the subsequent insolvent liquidation the court will order him to make a contribution and the case law shows that he is likely to have to shoulder any worsening in the company's position after the moment of truth.[68]

The first reported case on the new provisions was a strong one in the sense that it involved no deliberate course of wrongdoing but had severe consequences for the directors involved. This was *Re Produce Marketing Consortium Ltd (No. 2)*[69] in 1989, where the company was operating a fruit importing business. From a relatively healthy position of solvency in 1980 it gradually drifted into a position of insolvency with losses amounting to £317,694 in 1987. The business was mainly run by the two directors who worked full-time in the company and at no time did they stand to get much out of it; their remuneration for the last three years being around £20,000 per annum.[70] For various reasons it was held that they should have put the company into creditors' voluntary liquidation earlier than they did and were jointly ordered to pay the liquidator £75,000.[71] Subsequent cases have shown that the directors will not always lose. In *Re Sherborne Ltd*[72] the company was formed with a paid-up capital of £36,000. The first year trading loss was of £78,904 and then the directors injected more of their own funds into it so that the capital was increased to £68,000. The final deficiency was £109,237. The directors were not regarded as having acted unreasonably in all the circumstances and escaped liability. Judge Jack QC counselled against '. . . [T]he danger of assuming that what has in fact happened was always bound to happen and was apparent'.[73]

Later cases have contained extremely important developments for groups of companies. In *Re Hydrodam Ltd*[74] the question arose as to whether a holding company could be liable for wrongful trading in respect of its subsidiary company.[75]

---

[66] *Ibid.* s. 214 (4).

[67] The Insolvency Act 1986 also gives a defence if the director can show that, after he should have realised that there was no reasonable prospect that the company would avoid going into insolvent liquidation, he took every step that he ought with a view to minimising the potential loss to the company's creditors: s. 214 (3). In practice this will often mean that he must speedily take steps to put the company into creditors' voluntary liquidation.

[68] See *Re Produce Marketing Consortium Ltd (No. 2)* (1989) 5 BCC 569 at p. 597, *per* Knox J. 'Prima facie the appropriate amount that a director is declared to be liable to contribute is the amount by which the company's assets can be discerned to have been depleted by the director's conduct which caused the discretion under s. 214 (1) to arise.'

[69] (1989) 5 BCC 569.

[70] *Ibid.* at p. 589.

[71] For a recent example of liability and where the defences failed, see *Re Brian D Pierson (Contractors) Ltd* [1999] BCC 26.

[72] [1995] BCC 40.

[73] *Ibid.* at p. 54.

[74] [1994] 2 BCLC 180. See further generally the analysis by G. Morse 'Shadow and de facto Directors in the Context of Proceedings for Disqualification on the Grounds of Unfitness and Wrongful Trading' in B. Rider (ed.) *The Corporate Dimension* (Bristol: Jordans, 1998) p. 115.

[75] Actually a sub-sub-subsidiary on the facts of the case.

The legislation is clear in principle that in appropriate circumstances this could happen, since by virtue of s. 214 (7), director is defined so as to include 'shadow director'. The Insolvency Act definition of shadow director is 'a person in accordance with whose directions or instructions the directors of the company are accustomed to act'.[76] Thus the question arises as to what level of interference by the holding company, or by its individual directors, could make it (and/or those individual directors)[77] liable as shadow directors. In *Hydrodam* a decision had been taken to dispose of a company's business and the question for consideration was whether the holding company (or its directors) had been sufficiently implicated so as to make them into shadow directors. Millett J said:

> It is a commonplace that the disposal of a subsidiary or a subsidiary's business by its directors would require the sanction or approval of the parent, acting in this instance as the shareholder. Provided that the decision is made by the directors of the subsidiary, exercising their own independent discretion and judgment whether or not to dispose of the assets in question, and that the parent company only approves or authorises the decision, then in my judgment there is nothing which exposes the parent to liability for the decision or which constitutes it a shadow director of the subsidiary.[78]

A later case gave further guidance on the problem: in *Re PFTZM Ltd*[79] the holding company had lent money to the subsidiary and the holding company directors were in the habit of attending weekly management meetings. On the point whether the holding company might be liable as shadow director, Judge Paul Baker said:

> [The definition of shadow director] is directed to the case where nominees are put up but in fact behind them strings are being pulled by some other persons who do not put themselves forward as appointed directors. In this case, the involvement of the [holding company directors] here was thrust upon them by the insolvency of the [subsidiary] company. They were not accustomed to give directions. The actions they took, as I see it, were simply directed to trying to rescue what they could out of the company using their undoubted rights as secured creditors. It was submitted to me that it was a prima facie case of shadow directors, but I am bound to say that this is far from obvious ... The central point, as I see it, is that they were not acting as directors of the company; they were acting in defence of their own interests. This is not a case where the directors of the company ... were accustomed to act in accordance with the directions of others ie the [holding company directors] here. It is a case where the creditor made terms for the continuation of credit in the light of threatened default. The directors of the company were quite free to take the offer or leave it.[80]

Although these two cases turn on their own facts, it is perhaps clear from the tenor of the judgments that a considerable level of involvement by holding company

---

[76] Insolvency Act 1986, s. 251.

[77] Liability of the individual directors is very unlikely because in most situations they will be acting on behalf of the holding company rather than on their own behalf, and the pressure on the subsidiary to abide by their suggestions will come about as a result of the fact that the holding company holds a controlling interest in the subsidiary rather than by virtue of any special charisma of the individual holding company directors.

[78] [1994] 2 BCLC 180 at p. 185.

[79] [1995] BCC 280.

[80] *Ibid.* at pp. 291–292.

directors in the affairs of the subsidiary is likely to be required before a holding company will be held to be a shadow director.[81] Nevertheless, in structuring and operating the control relationships between companies in a group, incorporators need to have regard to the shadow director problem if they are to preserve the limited liability doctrine within the group.

Other interesting effects may arise from s. 214 of the Insolvency Act 1986. English company law has no doctrine of adequacy of capital[82] under which the company, when first incorporated, must have capital sufficient to enable it to be likely to meet its business obligations, otherwise the law will not accord to it the advantages of incorporation, in particular limited liability. However, in *Re Purpoint Ltd* [83] Vinelott J expressed the view that arguably the company being dealt with in the case was, at the outset, so undercapitalised in relation to its business undertakings that it might have been insolvent from the moment of commencement of business.[84] If so, the implication was that wrongful trading liability would have been present throughout the life of the company and, presumably, would have covered the whole of the shortfall between assets and debts. It remains to be seen whether a doctrine of adequacy of capital will grow from these ideas.

There are different views about the extent to which s. 214 has been a success. It is clear that, in many cases, liquidators will not want to risk incurring the costs of bringing the proceedings against the directors, since the prospect of a successful outcome is uncertain[85] and all that happens is that the assets which might otherwise have been available for the creditors in the liquidation are wasted on legal proceedings. Thus, wrongful trading proceedings are a rarity compared, say, to proceedings for the disqualification of directors.[86]

On the other hand, the infrequency of proceedings is probably not an accurate pointer to the effectiveness of the provisions. In many situations the wrongful trading provisions are probably operating on the minds of directors, who will have been warned by their accountants about the dangers they face once the company becomes insolvent and it will have been put to them that they should consider

---

[81] Although concerned with disqualification proceedings against individuals, some of the more general statements made by the Court of Appeal in *Secretary of State for Trade and Industry* v *Deverell* [2000] BCC 1057 may have some bearing on the liability of holding companies as shadow directors. In particular, the court cautioned against the use of epithets or graphic descriptions such as 'puppet' in place of the actual words of the statute; *per* Morritt LJ at p. 1,068. It was also stressed that the directions or instructions given by the shadow director do not have to extend over all or most of the corporate activities of the company; *ibid*.

[82] Public companies must have a nominal capital at or above the authorised minimum of £50,000 but this is a different concept; see p. 16 above.

[83] [1991] BCC 121.

[84] 'I have felt some doubt whether a reasonably prudent director would have allowed the company to commence trading at all. It had no capital base. Its only assets were purchased by bank borrowing or acquired by hire purchase ...' [1991] BCC 121 at p. 127. Ultimately, he took the view that this was not the position on the facts: 'However, I do not think it would be right to conclude that ... [the director] ought to have known that the company was doomed to end in an insolvent winding up from the moment it started to trade': *ibid*.

[85] Also, in many cases, even if the case against the directors is clear, they may not have any money since they will have given personal guarantees to banks and others and will often be facing personal insolvency.

[86] See at p. 417 below.

putting the company into creditors' voluntary liquidation.[87] But, as suggested above,[88] directors of small businesses which are sinking will already be facing personal insolvency and in such cases the threat of wrongful trading liability will hardly make matters seem any worse. In any event, the legislation represents an important theoretical limitation on the doctrine of limited liability. However, if limited liability (for contract debts) is seen as a morally desirable and efficient doctrine, then the question does of course arise as to whether the wrongful trading provisions are misconceived. Intuitively, the answer which can be given is that in most situations they remove the protection of limited liability at more or less the time when the contract creditors (in particular the trade creditors) cease to be able to influence the extent to which the company is now shifting its losses onto them, for they will usually lack the detailed information about the week to week trading position of the company such as might enable them to protect themselves by refusing further credit. They are, so to speak, 'sitting ducks',[89] and legal provisions designed to discourage and compensate for this must therefore be appropriate.[90]

2.3 GROUPS OF COMPANIES

Behind the apparent simplicity of the *Salomon* doctrine, with its shareholders separate from the company and its emphasis on business carried on by small private companies, lies the more complex reality that most large businesses are carried on through the medium of groups of companies. A listed public company will often have hundreds of private company subsidiaries. The reasons for this are many and various. Often there are taxation advantages. In other situations, the holding company is deliberately running a risky business through a subsidiary in order to avoid liability for its activities. Sometimes companies are arranged in a pyramid structure which can have the effect of enabling those who own a majority of shares of the holding company to control a large amount of capital.[91]

English company law is remarkably unreactive to the phenomenon of corporate groups[92] and almost invariably proceeds to apply the *Salomon* entity concept separately to each company in the group. Thus, limited liability for corporate debts is the

---

[87] On which, see at p. 408 below.

[88] See p. 32.

[89] Put in the language of economic analysis, one might say that the wrongful trading provisions remove the protection of limited liability at more or less the precise moment when the business starts to make a negative social input and survives only by externalising its losses onto the creditors.

[90] The same justifications would broadly apply to liability for fraudulent trading.

[91] For a further explanation of pyramiding, see p. 51, n. 29 below. For an interesting analysis of group structures and policy implications, see T. Hadden 'Regulation of Corporate Groups: An International Perspective' in J. McCahery, S. Picciotto and C. Scott (eds) *Corporate Control and Accountability: Changing Structures and the Dynamics of Regulation* (Oxford: Clarendon Press, 1993) p. 343 and D. Milman 'Groups of Companies: The Path Towards Discrete Regulation' in Milman (ed.) *Regulating Enterprise: Law and Business Organisations in the UK* (Oxford: Hart Publishing, 1999) p. 219. Where the group operates on a transnational basis the economic power that it exercises will often raise issues for the development of economic policy in the states in which it operates: see generally T. Muchlinski *Multinational Enterprises and the Law* (Oxford: Blackwell, 1995). Some restriction is placed on the arrangement of group structures by the Companies Act 1985, s. 23, which provides that a company may not hold shares in its holding company.

[92] The policy issues in developing a group law are probably too complex for meaningful case law development, and the legislature has been largely silent.

automatic right of the holding company. It was put clearly by Templeman LJ in *Re Southard Ltd*:[93]

> English company law possesses some curious features, which may generate curious results. A parent company may spawn a number of subsidiary companies, all controlled directly or indirectly by the shareholders of the parent company. If one of the subsidiary companies, to change the metaphor, turns out to be the runt of the litter and declines into insolvency to the dismay of its creditors, the parent company and the other subsidiary companies may prosper to the joy of the shareholders without any liability for the debts of the insolvent subsidiary.[94]

Similarly, the holding company has a right to deliberately set about creating structures which minimise its own liability. In *Adams* v *Cape Industries plc*[95] this right was expressly recognised by Slade LJ in this way:

> ... [W]e do not accept as a matter of law that the court is entitled to lift the corporate veil as against a defendant company which is a member of a corporate group merely because the corporate structure has been used to ensure that the legal liability (if any) in respect of future activities of the group ... will fall on another member of the group rather than the defendant company. Whether or not this is desirable, the right to use a corporate structure in this manner is inherent in our corporate law. [Counsel] urged on us that the purpose of the operation was in substance that [Cape Industries plc] would have the practical benefit of the group's asbestos trade in the US, without the risks of tortious liability. This may be so. However, in our judgment [Cape Industries plc] was entitled to organise the group's affairs in that manner and ... to expect that the court would apply the principle of *Salomon* v *Salomon* in the ordinary way.[96]

Other areas of company law proceed in a similar way, and thus directors of a company owe their duties to the individual company which they happen to be directors of, rather than to the group as a whole.[97] Occasionally, company law does bend to the group reality. The main example of this is in relation to the rules on financial reporting; group accounts are required showing the position for the group as a whole in a consolidated balance sheet and profit and loss account.[98] Not all countries have been content to follow the English approach. West Germany, for example, has had special rules governing groups of companies since 1965, the 'Konzernrecht', in which the parent company will be liable to make good the losses of the subsidiary in certain circumstances.[99] It is possible that the UK may eventually find that it has to change its position if the draft Ninth Directive is ever adopted, although this seems highly unlikely at present.[100]

The Companies Act 1985 contains definitions of the various terms used to

---

[93] [1979] 3 All ER 556.
[94] *Ibid.* at p. 565.
[95] [1990] BCC 786.
[96] *Ibid.* at p. 826.
[97] *Pergamon Press* v *Maxwell* [1970] 1 WLR 1167; *Charterbridge Corp* v *Lloyds Bank* [1970] Ch 62; *Lonhro* v *Shell Petroleum* [1981] 2 All ER 456.
[98] See further p. 186 below.
[99] For an account of recent developments, see J. Peter 'Parent Liability in German and British Law: Too Far Apart for EU Legislation' [1999] *European Business Law Review* 440.
[100] See p. 13 above.

describe companies in groups. These are technical and somewhat at odds with the way in which the terms are used in common parlance. The main general distinction in the Act is between 'holding company' and 'subsidiary'. This is confusing, since people will generally talk about 'parent' and subsidiary whereas the term 'parent company' is very technical[101] and confined to the areas of legislation which deal with the duty to prepare group accounts and matters incidental thereto.[102]

The general definition is contained in s. 736 (1):

A company is a 'subsidiary' of another company, its 'holding company', if that other company –
(a) holds a majority of the voting rights in it, or
(b) is a member of it and has the right to appoint or remove a majority of its board of directors, or
(c) is a member of it and controls alone, pursuant to an agreement with other shareholders or members, a majority of the voting rights in it, or if it is a subsidiary of a company which is itself a subsidiary of that other company.

Various expressions in s. 736 are supplemented and explained by lengthy provisions in s. 736A.[103] No doubt people will continue to use the expressions 'holding company' and 'parent company' as if they were completely interchangeable and most of the time this will probably not give rise to misunderstandings.

2.4 INCORPORATION

A Formal requirements

Forming a company by registration is relatively simple[104] and costs very little. All that is necessary is for certain documents to be delivered to the Registrar of Companies along with the registration fee. Often the layperson will choose to purchase from his solicitors, or accountant or other commercial supplier, a company which has already been formed (an 'off-the-shelf' company) and then change its name and constitution to suit himself. However, the ease of formation can create the wrong impression, for as will gradually become clear throughout this book, and not least in the last chapter,[105] the use of the legal facilities provided by the corporate form brings with it many obligations, liabilities and pitfalls.

There are five documents which may need to be delivered to the Registrar of Companies prior to registration, depending on the type of company being formed and the circumstances. These are: the memorandum of association, the articles of association, the statement of first directors and secretary and intended situation of

---

[101] In essence, as one would expect, it is similar to the definition of holding company, but it is wider since it is being used in legislation designed to curb off-balance sheet financing; see Companies Act 1985, ss. 258–260 and Sch. 10A.

[102] Namely, Pt VII of the 1985 Act.

[103] The expression 'wholly-owned subsidiary' is defined in the Companies Act 1985, s. 736 (2) as follows: 'A company is a "wholly-owned subsidiary" of another company if it has no members except that other and that other's wholly-owned subsidiaries or persons acting on behalf of that other or its wholly-owned subsidiaries.'

[104] Compared, say, to trying to get incorporation by Royal Charter or private Act of Parliament.

[105] On disqualification of directors.

registered office, the statutory declaration of compliance, and the application for commencement of business.

The memorandum of association, usually along with articles of association, forms the statutory constitution of the company.[106] A memorandum of association is essential for a company, whereas it is not necessary for a company limited by shares to have articles of association, though most do.[107] By s. 2 of the Companies Act 1985 the memorandum must state: (a) the name of the company; (b) whether the registered office is to be situated in England and Wales,[108] or in Scotland;[109] and (c) the objects of the company. The memorandum of a company limited by shares must also state that the liability of its members is limited,[110] and also, state the amount of share capital with which the company proposes to be registered and the division of the share capital into shares of a fixed amount. It must be signed by each subscriber in the presence of at least one witness[111] and must be in one of the forms specified by the Companies (Tables A to F) Regulations 1985.[112] If the company is to be a public company, the memorandum must also state that fact, immediately after the statement of its name.[113] Also it is clear from Tables A to F that the memorandum must also contain what is usually referred to as an 'association clause', which declares that 'we the subscribers to this memorandum of association wish to be formed into a company pursuant to this memorandum: and we agree to take the number of shares shown opposite our respective names'. Finally, it is quite common for other additional clauses to be put in the memorandum which are not required to be there by statute. To some extent this can have the effect of entrenching them in a constitutional sense, although this is subject to ss. 17, 125 and 425 of the Companies Act 1985.[114]

The memorandum raises other matters which need consideration. The objects clause and the capital clause are dealt with in Chapters 5 and 14 respectively below. Here it is necessary to examine the provisions relating to company names. Sections 25–34 of the Companies Act 1985 contain some of the rules about company names. The public company name must[115] end with 'public limited company' which can be abbreviated to 'plc' and a private limited company must end its name with the word 'limited' which can be abbreviated to 'Ltd'.[116] Subject to this, and to various statutory prohibitions, a company can have any name. It is clear that a company will not be registered with a name which is the same as a name already appearing in the Registrar's index of company names, so a search of the register is

---

[106] See further Chapters 5 and 6 below.
[107] They are necessary for unlimited companies or companies limited by guarantee; see Companies Act 1985, s. 7 (1).
[108] As regards Wales, the 1985 Act provides, *inter alia*, that as an alternative to 'England and Wales' the memorandum may contain a statement that the company's registered office is to be situated in Wales.
[109] Similar provisions pertain in Northern Ireland.
[110] There are further provisions about companies limited by guarantee.
[111] Companies Act 1985, s. 2 (6).
[112] SI 1985 No. 805.
[113] Table F, para. 2.
[114] See further p. 87 below.
[115] Companies Act 1985, s. 25.
[116] Welsh equivalents are permitted; see *ibid.* ss. 25–27.

one of the steps to take in the formation of a company.[117] There are certain rules of construction for helping to determine when the names are the same[118] and there are guidance notes issued by the DTI.[119] There are various other prohibitions[120] such as, use of a name which would, in the opinion of the Secretary of State (in effect, the DTI), constitute a criminal offence, or be offensive; nor is it possible[121] to use names which would be likely to give the impression that the company is connected with the government.[122] It is relatively easy for a company to change its name. All that is needed is a special resolution[123] and compliance with the above provisions.[124] The Companies Act 1985 also contains provisions pertaining to the use of the name by the company. Identification of the company is provided for by requirements for its name to be painted or affixed (and kept so) outside every office or place in which its business is carried on, in a conspicuous position and in easily legible letters. Its name (and various other details) must be mentioned in legible characters in all business letters of the company and in other documents through which it deals with the public.[125] This last point is of particular interest to directors and other officers who[126] become personally liable[127] on, for instance, any cheque or order for goods in which the company's name is not mentioned as required.[128] Lastly, it should be made clear that if a company trades under a name other than its registered name, then it must comply with the Business Names Act 1985.

The articles of association set out the internal rules as to the running of the company and cover such matters as appointment and removal of directors, quorum and frequency of meetings. Table A[129] is a common form table of the sort of provisions that most companies would probably require. Table A will automatically apply to a company limited by shares unless, and to the extent that, it is excluded.[130] In practice, most new companies adopt Table A but make a few modifications which suit their particular circumstances. It is important to be aware that

---

[117] *Ibid.* s. 26.

[118] *Ibid.* s. 26 (3).

[119] DTI Guidance Notes on Company Names, May 1984. Using a name or similar name is unwise, in any event, since it could make the company liable at common law for the tort of passing off (see e.g. *Erven Warnink BV* v *Townend (J) & Sons (Hull) Ltd (No. 1)* [1979] AC 731, HL), or it may infringe a registered trade mark; see Trade Marks Act 1994.

[120] In Companies Act 1985, s. 26.

[121] Except with the consent of the Secretary of State.

[122] The Secretary of State also has power in some circumstances to require a company to change its name if its name is too like a name on the register of names (or which should have been on the register) or if the name gives so misleading an indication of the nature of its activities as to be likely to cause harm to the public: Companies Act 1985, ss. 28, 32. Certain companies are, by s. 30, exempt from having to use the word 'limited' as part of their name; the main requirement being that the objects of the companies will be the promotion of commerce, art, science, charity etc. Further limitations have recently been added by the Companies and Business Names (Chambers of Commerce) Act 1999.

[123] Broadly, three-quarters of members present and voting, or voting by proxy; see p. 152 below.

[124] Companies Act 1985, s. 28 (1).

[125] *Ibid.* ss. 348–351.

[126] By s. 349 (4).

[127] In addition to the company.

[128] See e.g. *Blum* v *OCP Repartition SA* [1988] BCLC 170, CA. The most common error is to miss off the end word 'Limited' or 'Ltd'.

[129] As set out in the Companies (Tables A to F) Regulations 1985 (SI 1985 No. 805).

[130] Companies Act 1985, s. 8 (2).

Table A gets amended from time to time and that the Table A which forms a company's articles will be that which is in force at the date of incorporation. A later change in Table A will not automatically amend the articles of the company and these will have to be changed if the company wants the 'up-to-date' Table A.[131] The constitutional significance of the articles of association is dealt with in Chapter 5 below, and various other aspects are considered throughout the text.[132]

The statement of first directors and secretary, and intended situation of registered office, are details which are required to be delivered to the Registrar of Companies in the prescribed form.[133]

The Statutory Declaration of Compliance basically involves filling in the prescribed form.[134] The main purpose of this seems to be to ensure that those who are forming the company are 'solemnly and sincerely aware of their obligations to prepare the documents properly and comply with all the legal requirements of the Act'.[135] In view of the package of obligations which descends on the incorporators, this enforced 'solemnity' is perhaps no bad thing.

Commencement of business[136] is not permitted in the case of a public company unless the Registrar has issued it with a certificate under s. 117 of the 1985 Act. He can only issue the certificate if, on an application made to him in the prescribed form,[137] he is satisfied that the nominal value of the company's allotted share capital is not less than the 'authorised minimum'.[138] The 'authorised minimum' is a minimum capital requirement of £50,000[139] for public companies set by the Second Directive.[140]

B Certificate of incorporation

Once the documents have been delivered to the Registrar of Companies and he is satisfied that the legal formalities have been complied with, then he registers the documents and issues a certificate of incorporation.[141] From the 'date of incorporation mentioned in the certificate, the subscribers of the memorandum, together with such other persons as may from time to time become members of the company, shall be a body corporate by the name contained in the memorandum . . .'.[142] The presence of the word 'shall' in ss. 12 (2) and 13 (1) of the Companies Act 1985 makes it clear that, provided that the Act has been complied with, the

---

[131] For this reason, there are companies in existence whose articles adopt Table A, either expressly (or automatically by not excluding it) and the Table A in question is an earlier version than the 1985 one.

[132] See index.

[133] Currently form 10; see Companies Act 1985, s. 10.

[134] Form 12.

[135] Companies Act 1985, s. 12.

[136] Or exercise of any borrowing powers.

[137] Form 117.

[138] And a statutory declaration in accordance with s. 117 (3) is also delivered to him.

[139] It can be increased by statutory instrument.

[140] As with all public company share capital, the authorised minimum must be paid up to at least one quarter of the nominal value, and the whole of any premium; Companies Act 1985, s. 101. On this see p. 265 below.

[141] Companies Act 1985, s. 12.

[142] *Ibid.* s. 13 (3).

Registrar has no discretion as to whether to register the company and if he refuses, proceedings can be brought by the promoters to compel him to register.[143]

The certificate of incorporation is 'conclusive evidence' that the requirements of the Act 'in respect of registration and of matters precedent and incidental to it have been complied with, and that the association is a company authorised to be registered and is duly registered . . .'. The effect of this is generally thought to be to preclude the existence of any doctrine of nullity in UK law (under which a company might be regarded as defectively incorporated with consequent complications for persons who might have acquired rights against it). It was against this problem that arts 11 and 12 were included in the First Directive[144] under which persons who have dealt with the defective company would be protected if it was later annulled in court proceedings. No steps have been taken to implement these provisions of the Directive in the UK.[145]

If a company is incorporated for what turns out to be an unlawful object then it can be wound up.[146] It has been suggested that the Attorney General can initiate proceedings to get the certificate of incorporation cancelled or revoked.[147] If this were to become a frequent occurrence it might raise problems which fall within the ambit of arts 11 and 12 of the First Directive, and then a court might be faced with the argument that even though it had not been implemented in a UK statute, the parties could nevertheless perhaps rely on it under the doctrine of direct effect.

C Publicity and the continuing role of the Registrar

On receipt of the incorporation documents, the Registrar of Companies will open a file on the company which is then open to inspection.[148] Thereafter, more information will appear on the file from time to time in pursuance of the Companies Act provisions relating to annual returns and accounts.[149] Also, 'Official Notification' is necessary under which the Registrar must publish in the *Gazette* notice or the issue or receipt by him of various documents, one of which is the issue of any certificate of incorporation.[150]

---

[143] *R v Registrar of Companies, ex parte Bowen* [1914] 3 KB 1161.

[144] 68/151/EEC.

[145] Although there is one situation where, by statute, s. 13 (7) of the 1985 Act is overridden, for s. 10 (3) of the Trade Union and Labour Relations (Consolidation) Act 1992 contains provisions making void any attempted incorporation of a trade union.

[146] Under Insolvency Act 1986, s. 122 (1) (g); see also *Princess of Reuss v Bos* (1871) LR 5 HL 176.

[147] *R v Registrar of Companies, ex parte Central Bank of India* [1986] QB 1114 at pp. 1169 (Lawton LJ) and 1177 (Slade LJ).

[148] Companies Act 1985, s. 709.

[149] See p. 185 below.

[150] Companies Act 1985, s. 711 (1). Failure to comply with official notification by the Registrar (which is unlikely) might have adverse consequences under s. 42, for it provides that a company is not entitled to rely against other persons on the happening of certain events (such as the alteration of the memorandum or articles) if the event had not been officially notified at the material time (and certain other conditions are satisfied). The issue of the certificate of incorporation is not one of the matters referred to in s. 42 which, in this respect, can therefore not produce difficulties.

D Promoters and pre-incorporation contracts

Those who set up a company will, in addition to all the legal duties that descend on them after incorporation, usually find that they owe a fiduciary duty to the company covering matters relating to the setting up of it. These are known as promoters' duties. The term 'promoter' has accordingly acquired a fairly specific meaning, expressed in the language of Lord Cockburn CJ as '[O]ne who undertakes to form a company with reference to a given project and to set it going, and who takes the necessary steps to accomplish that purpose'.[151] On the other hand, people who act merely in a professional capacity such as solicitors and accountants will not be promoters unless they step outside their professional sphere of activity and become involved in the business side of formation.[152]

Cases on the duties of promoters have been very rare over the last 100 years for two reasons. First, most companies start life as small private companies where the promoters immediately become the shareholders and first directors, and not surprisingly they are not in a hurry to raise legal complaints against the promoters. No one else is involved for many years until the company starts to expand and seeks more shareholders, by which time the possible wrongdoing of the company's founders many years earlier is of little interest to the new shareholders in a thriving and expanding business. Secondly, if a public offering of shares is to have any chance of being fully subscribed for by the public it will need to be underwritten by an investment bank and such institutions will usually find it in their commercial interests to ensure that problems about promoters breaching their legal duties do not arise, and if they do arise, are probably quickly and quietly settled.

The ideas are established by the (mainly) 19th-century cases. Promoters are regarded as standing in a fiduciary relationship[153] to the company. It is entirely in their hands, they create it and shape it, and because of this they owe it fiduciary duties. Most of the cases involve the promoters selling some item of their own property to the newly formed company which only later finds out that it was their property, or that the property was worth a good deal less than the price the company paid, or that, whatever the value of the property, the promoters had sold it to the company at a higher price than they had paid. The case law is confused at times and overlapping, but the following two principles seem to be supportable. First, promoters must disclose to the company any interest which they have in the property they are selling to the company, and furthermore the disclosure must be made to a board of directors (or group of shareholders) who are truly independent so that they can decide on the company's behalf, whether the terms of the contract are prudent or not. It the directors are not independent, the disclosure is obviously useless.[154] Failure to make disclosure in this way will entitle the company to rescind the contract once an independent board does discover the true facts, provided both

---

[151] *Twycross v Grant* (1877) 2 CPD 469 at p. 541.
[152] *Re Great Wheal Polgooth Ltd* (1883) 53 LJ Ch 42.
[153] On this concept in relation to directors, see p. 164 *et seq.* below.
[154] See *Erlanger v New Sombrero Phosphate Co.* (1878) 3 App Cas 1218 at pp. 1236, 1239, *per* Lord Cairns LC referring to the need for 'the intelligent judgment of an independent executive'.

that it is reasonably possible to put the contracting parties back into the position they were in before the contract was entered into and that there has not been sufficient delay to amount to acquiescence. Thus, in *Erlanger v New Sombrero Phosphate Co.*[155] the promoters had sold an island to the company in breach of these principles and ended up getting it back and having to return the money and shares they had received for it. Secondly, promoters who make a profit by selling to the company for a higher price than they themselves paid will be liable to hand that over (ie account to the company) if, at the time when they purchased it, they had already become promoters to the extent that it is possible to regard them as trustees who at the time should have been trying to make a profit for the trust (ie the company) rather than themselves.[156]

Pre-incorporation contracts are another feature of incorporation procedure which have occasionally given rise to legal difficulties.[157] If a promoter makes a contract purportedly on behalf of the company but prior to its incorporation, it is well established that, as regards the company, the contract is a nullity, since the company was not in existence at the time when the contract was entered into.[158] However, the promoter who enters into such a void contract may find himself personally liable on it, for s. 36C (1) of the Companies Act 1985 provides:

A contract which purports to be made by or on behalf of a company at a time when the company has not been formed has effect, subject to any agreement to the contrary, as one made with the person purporting to act for the company or as agent for it, and he is personally liable on the contract accordingly.

The words 'subject to any agreement to the contrary' have been held to mean 'unless otherwise agreed' and it has been held that it is not sufficient in this regard, merely for the promoter to sign 'as agent for' the company.[159] In *Braymist Ltd v Wise Finance Co Ltd*[160] a firm of solicitors entered into a contract as agents on behalf of a company which was not yet formed, in which the company agreed to sell some land to some developers. Later the developers changed their minds and the solicitors sought to enforce the contract against them under s. 36C. The Court of Appeal held that the words of the section did not merely create an option enabling the developers to sue the agent if they so wished, but specified that the contract had 'effect', and thus the contract was enforceable by the agent.

---

[155] (1878) 3 App Cas 1218.

[156] *Re Cape Breton Co.* (1885) 29 Ch D 795 at pp. 801–805 *passim, per* Cotton LJ; *Erlanger v New Sombrero Phosphate Co.* (1873) 3 App Cas 1218 at pp. 1234–1235, *per* Lord Cairns LC.

[157] A related problem concerns the question of how promoters go about getting compensated for expenses incurred or remunerated for work done in promoting the company. In most cases this raises no practical difficulty and the method adopted is to put a power into the company's articles enabling the first directors of the newly formed company to pay promoters' expenses and remuneration.

[158] Nor is it possible for the company once formed to ratify a pre-incorporation contract or to purport to adopt it merely by ratification; it is necessary to enter into a new contract: *Natal Land Co. v Pauline Syndicate* [1904] AC 120.

[159] *Phonogram v Lane* [1982] QB 938 at p. 944, *per* Lord Denning MR.

[160] [2002] BCC 514.

E Right of establishment

As part of the process of creating the common market with free movement of goods, persons, services and capital, the EC Treaty[161] gives a right of establishment to natural persons to carry out business in any Member State.[162] Similarly, a right of establishment is given to companies by the provision that companies shall be treated in the same way as natural persons, provided that they have been formed in accordance with the law of a Member State and that they have their registered office, or central administration or principal place of business within the European Community.[163] The principle was recently tested in the *Centros* case and the European Court of Justice gave a ruling firmly upholding the doctrine.[164]

2.5 COMPANY LAW REVIEW AND LAW REFORM

The Final Report of the Company Law Review[165] contains proposals which would affect incorporation procedure, in particular by requiring only one document of constitution rather than memorandum or articles.[166]

---

[161] The Treaty of Rome.

[162] EC Treaty, art. 43 (art. 52, pre-Amsterdam).

[163] By EC Treaty, art. 48 (art. 58, pre-Amsterdam).

[164] Case C-212/97 *Centros Ltd* v *Erhvervsog Selskabsstyrelsen* [1999] BCC 983. For analysis of the interesting issues raised by the case, see E. Micheler 'The Impact of the Centros Case on Europe's Company Laws' (2000) 21 Co Law 179. The doctrine has been emphatically confirmed in several subsequent ECJ cases.

[165] See generally Chapter 4 below.

[166] See *Modern Company Law for a Competitive Economy Final Report* paras. 9.1–9.11. See also the subsequent government White Paper *Modernising Company Law* (July 2002, Cmnd. 5553) and *Company Law. Flexibility and Accessibility: A Consultative Document* (London: DTI, 2004).

3

LEGAL THEORY AND COMPANY LAW

3.1 THE ROLE OF THEORY IN COMPANY LAW

Company law 'theory', is a body of writing which has grown up over the years which is primarily concerned not with the exposition of the legal rules themselves. Instead, theoretical writing about company law normally has two components: a descriptive aspect and a normative aspect. The descriptive aspect involves examining the operation of legal rules and the structures produced by them in an objective and contextual way; it will often involve the writer in spotting an underlying rationale or illogicality contained in the rules. The normative aspect involves the writer in making normative propositions. This will usually be either that the structures or individual legal rules ought to change, in other words that they are not morally justified, or, that they ought to remain as they are, in other words, that they are morally justified. Recent and contemporary writings use the expression moral 'legitimacy' instead of moral 'justification'. In practice the distinction between descriptive writing and normative writing is rarely clear cut, not least because the way in which a descriptive writer sees and interprets a situation is value laden and subjective, in the sense that he or she is not always aware that their selection of material will influence people's conclusions about the moral legitimacy of the structure being described.

It is the normative aspect which lends dynamism and force to legal theory, because, essentially, we are looking at arguments about the way we should be living; arguments which are of fundamental social and political importance. In the context of company law, legal theory will be trying to tell us what sort of company law we have, and what sort of company law we should have.

This chapter analyses the main issues which have emerged in the last century or so. The focus is primarily on the Anglo-American writing although occasional reference is made to theory emanating from continental Europe. Theoretical issues relating to securities regulation are dealt with in a separate chapter, largely because the subject has developed independently of mainstream company law.[1] The areas covered here overlap, and are interwoven in countless ways. Nevertheless, for the sake of convenience they are grouped under headings as follows: the nature and origins of the corporation, managerialism, corporate governance, stakeholder company law (including social responsibility and industrial democracy), and economic analysis of corporate law.

---

[1] Chapter 17 below.

3.2 THE NATURE AND ORIGINS OF THE CORPORATION

A The theories

The industrial revolution in Europe and America coupled with increased legal facilities for incorporation in some of the world's major legal systems[2] fuelled a juristic interest in the phenomenon of the corporation. The nature of the corporation, particularly its corporate personality, became the focus of thought. It is possible to identify two main and distinct theories: the fiction theory and the real entity theory.[3]

The fiction theory[4] asserts that the legal person has no substantial reality, no mind, no will; it exists only in law. The corporation is 'an artificial being, invisible, intangible, and existing only in contemplation of law'.[5] It is a theory which asserts that the corporate body is merely a creature of the intellect.[6] It seems that it can be traced to the canon law of the Roman church of the 13th century and earlier.[7] The real entity theory is of later origin and is generally regarded as the work of 19th-century German realists, particularly Gierke.[8] Gierke saw corporate personality not merely as a juristic conception, but as a social fact with an actual living nature. It is a living organism, for when individuals associate together, a new personality arises which has a distinctive sphere of existence and will of its own. The function of the law is to recognise and declare the existence of the personality.[9]

The arguments about the nature of the corporation became linked and at times confused with a separate issue, namely the origins of the corporation. Two main theories were developed to explain the origins of the corporation: the concession theory and the contract theory. The essence of the concession theory is that the corporation's legal power is derived from the state. The idea seems to have emerged as a state response to the problem of how to check the power of groups arising within it; the answer being that a corporation could only achieve recognition and acceptability through a validation process emanating from the state, whether a grant by Royal Charter or registration under some state-created system.[10]

The contract theory essentially ran counter to the thrust of the concession theory, and sought to show that companies were associations formed by the agreement of

---

[2] E.g. Joint Stock Companies Act 1844 in the UK, various state incorporation statutes in the USA dating from early in the century such as 1811 in New York.

[3] The latter is sometimes referred to as the 'natural entity' theory or 'organic' theory.

[4] It is sometimes suggested that there is separate theory which sees the company merely as an aggregate of individuals; but this is really the corollary of the fiction theory, for if the company is a legal fiction, that will leave the people involved with it as merely an aggregate of individuals.

[5] *Trustees of Dartmouth College* v *Woodward* (17 US) 4 Wheat 518 at p. 636, *per* Marshall CJ.

[6] See J. Dewey 'The Historic Background of Corporate Legal Personality' 35 Yale LJ 655 (1926) at p. 669.

[7] Dewey, n. 6 above, at pp. 667–668. It is possible that the fiction theory was in the minds of the Roman jurists as Savigny has claimed; see F. Hallis *Corporate Personality: A Study in Jurisprudence* (London: OUP, 1930) p. 6, n. 3.

[8] *Das Deutsche Genossenschaftsrecht* (1887), translated in O. Gierke *Political Theories of the Middle Age* (F.W. Maitland (ed.), 1900).

[9] See generally the summaries in Hallis, n. 7 above, at p. 150 and E. Freund *The Legal Nature of Corporations* (Chicago, IL: University of Chicago Press, 1897) at p. 13.

[10] See generally Dewey, n. 6 above, at p. 668. It seems that the choice of the word 'concession' was influenced by Roman law; *ibid.*

the shareholders.[11] The corporate structure was in substance the outcome of a series of contracts between the shareholders and the managers and so was really hardly any different from a partnership. It followed that there was no reason why individuals should need to obtain permission from the legislature in order to form a company. This, while being a theory about the origins of the company, also has implications for the nature of the company. The idea of the company as a contract, or as a nexus of contracts, has undergone a renaissance with the development in the 1970s of the economic theory about the nature of the firm.[12]

B Rationale and application of the theories

The above ideas have been presented as analytically separate and distinct, but in many of the writings they were linked together in various ways. The way they were linked seems to have varied depending on the social or political agenda possessed by those advancing the theories. The fiction theory about the nature of the corporation was often run alongside the concession theory[13] and so the proposition became that a company was a fictional entity created by the exercise of state power. In this form the proposition reflected 19th-century political theory based on liberal individualism: state consent was needed for the formation of a group and even then the 'groupness' was fictional, the company was merely an aggregate of individuals. The proposition in this form also provided a justification for state regulation of companies, for in giving the concession, the state had done something gratuitous or special, in return for which it could expect that its right to regulate companies had been acknowledged. By contrast, the real entity theory of Gierke and others clearly had logical links with the contract theory of creation of the corporation, which stressed the underlying reality of the contractual organisation and denied that the state had a major role in creating it, or therefore, in regulating it. Historically, the realist theory, with its emphasis on the reality of groups can be seen[14] as part of the challenge to individualist political theory and its associated fiction theory of incorporation posed by the emergence by the late 19th century of powerful groups such as corporations.

The question of whether these theories have had or still have any useful role has attracted a lively debate which has simmered on into modern times. In his article in 1926[15] Dewey mounted a powerful legal realist diatribe against the usefulness of theorising about the nature of the corporation, arguing that the theories have been used variously to serve opposing ends[16] and that the discussion was needlessly encumbered with traditional doctrines and old issues.[17] By the early 1930s jurisprudence in company law was pursuing different paths and theorising about

---

[11] M. Horwitz in '*Santa Clara* Revisited: The Development of Corporate Theory' 88 W Va L Rev 173 (1985) at p. 203 attributes the theory to a work by V. Morawetz *A Treatise on the Law of Private Corporations* 2nd edn (Boston, MA: Little, Brown, 1886).

[12] See further p. 66 below.

[13] Dewey, n. 6 above, at p. 670.

[14] For this view, see Horwitz, n. 11 above, at pp. 180–181.

[15] See n. 6 above.

[16] Dewey, n. 6 above, at p. 671.

[17] *Ibid.* at p. 675.

the nature and origins of the corporation dried up.[18] The area has been revisited more recently. Professor Horwitz, taking a stance against the Critical Legal Studies position that legal conceptions have little or no influence in determining outcomes, argued[19] that in specific historical settings legal theory can influence the direction of legal understanding and in particular sought to show that the rise of the natural (i.e. real) entity theory was a significant factor in legitimating the concept of the large business enterprise. In a subsequent critique of this approach Millon argued that at the same time that theory is influencing legal doctrine, it in turn is being influenced by legal doctrine.[20] It is clear that to some extent the relevance of theory as providing justification for state intervention has been overtaken by events. The state has largely won the battle, in the UK certainly, and elsewhere. The corporation is the plaything of the state and has been subjected to an elaborate apparatus of regulation, both from Westminster and Brussels, and in the UK the new superpowerful Financial Services Authority has been created to watch over investment business. Almost as a faint echo of *laissez-faire*, the individual interest, the principle of freedom from state intervention is now represented by human rights legislation which puts down markers as to the limits of state intervention.[21] But state intervention itself is not in doubt. Having said this, though, it is clear from the 'stakeholder' debate[22] that the extent of state intervention is very much a live issue; and it will be for legislators of the future to decide the extent to which company law must facilitate the representation of interests in corporate governance, beyond merely the shareholders. Here lies the current interest in what the corporation actually is. There has been renewed interest in these early writings as modern juristic activity strives to find a sound philosophical basis for the new 'stakeholder' ideas. In particular, some of the ideas about the company's 'social conscience' can be seen as developments of the real entity theory.[23]

3.3 MANAGERIALISM

The publication in 1932 of *The Modern Corporation and Private Property* by Adolf Berle and Gardiner Means[24] changed the focus of theoretical scholarship in corporate law for many decades and the central thrust of their thesis continues to be an axiom in modern times.[25] They adopted[26] the broad notion that control of a company resides in the hands of the individual or group who have the power to

---

[18] See below.
[19] See Horwitz, n. 11 above.
[20] D. Millon 'Theories of the Corporation' Duke LJ 201 (1990). He also takes issue with Horwitz's stance on the meaning of legal concepts.
[21] See further p. 426 below.
[22] See p. 58 below.
[23] See further p. 58 below.
[24] New York: Harcourt, rev. edn 1968. First published in 1932.
[25] See e.g. E. Herman *Corporate Control, Corporate Power* (New York: CUP, 1981) p. 14, who expressed the view that control of large corporations generally by top management is an 'established truth'. See also the discussion of convergence at p. 55 below.
[26] A. Berle and G. Means *The Modern Corporation and Private Property* (New York: Harcourt, rev. edn 1968) p. 66.

select the board of directors[27] and proceeded[28] to identify five types of control: control through almost complete ownership (where the corporation might well be described as private); majority control (which will usually give the power to select the board); control through legal device without majority ownership (for example by 'pyramiding');[29] minority control (less than 50.1% will often give working control in the absence of organised opposition from the remainder); and management control. It is in 'management control' that the kernel of their thesis resided. They defined management control as where ownership is so widely distributed that no individual or small group has an interest large enough to dominate the affairs of the company and so the existing management will be in a position to become a self-perpetuating body.[30] They then sought to discover the extent to which each type of control existed among the largest US non-banking[31] companies. In spite of the necessity of a certain amount of guesswork, the clarity of the results was startling.[32] They found that 44% of companies by number and 58% by wealth[33] were subject to management control and that 21% by number and 22% by wealth were controlled by legal device involving only a small proportion of the ownership. They concluded that the fact that 65% of the companies and 80% of their combined wealth should be controlled by management or legal device showed clearly the extent to which ownership and control of companies had become separate.[34] One of the main effects of this separation of ownership and control was, they argued, that management might pursue their own goals of personal profit, prestige or power.[35]

Although later studies have criticised their empirical methods and definitions and lack of sophistication,[36] the essence of the Berle and Means' thesis remains a central fact of company law theory: dispersed ownership, combined with shareholder passivity, leads to a separation of ownership and control, with control substantially residing in the managers. This management control premise is what is meant by the term 'managerialism'.[37]

There is an important caveat, necessary to an understanding of the significance of managerialism in its worldwide setting, namely that it needs to be emphasised

[27] The directors of course usually having control over the day-to-day activities of a company.

[28] Berle and Means, n. 26 above, at pp. 66–84.

[29] Pyramiding involves owning the majority of the shares of one corporation which in turn holds the majority of another, and so on. The effect is to create a situation where the majority at the top of the pyramid control a huge business concern even though the overall wealth they have invested is but a small percentage of the total: Berle and Means, n. 26 above, at p. 69.

[30] The background being that when they receive the proxy forms for the election of the board, most of the individual shareholders (having insignificant stakes in the company) will either not bother to vote, or will sign the proxy form giving their vote to the proxy committee, which itself will have been nominated by the management; it will then re-appoint the management: Berle and Means, n. 26 above, at pp. 80–81.

[31] I.e. non-financial: Berle and Means, n. 26 above, at p. 18, n. 2.

[32] Although not altogether surprising, for the phenomenon had not gone unnoticed, even if the evidence for it tended to be anecdotal; see Herman, n. 25 above, at pp. 6–8.

[33] I.e. 58% of the total wealth of the largest 200 companies.

[34] Berle and Means, n. 26 above, at p. 110.

[35] *Ibid.* at pp. 112–116.

[36] See e.g. the list in Herman, n. 25 above, at pp. 11–14.

[37] See Herman, n. 25 above, at p. 9.

that it is a thesis about the effects of dispersed ownership on corporate control. It is a thesis about patterns of ownership then, and largely still, pertaining in the US. It has similar relevance in the UK which has dispersed ownership patterns. It has very little application to most of the other countries of the developed world, for these have concentrated ownership patterns. These different ownership patterns and the different systems of corporate governance which exist under them has, in the last decade, become the fascinating focus of what might be termed 'convergence' scholarship.[38]

The research by Herman published in 1981[39] was essentially a reexamination and re-assessment of the phenomenon of managerialism in the light of developments in the half-century or so since Berle and Means. Herman was careful to stress that managerial discretion and power are realities and not seriously open to question.[40] However, he criticised Berle and Means on the basis that they had failed to explore the limits and constraints on managerial power and, in essence, he argued that their position on control was unsophisticated, that they took the view that either there was control, or there was not. Herman put forward a theory of constrained managerial control. He argued that 'strategic position' in the sense of occupancy of high office in the company was the source of control[41] (although ownership should be seen as an important basis for obtaining strategic position).[42] By 'control', Herman meant the power to make the key decisions of a company and he contrasted this with 'constraint', which he said was a form of control, but was merely a power to limit certain choices or involved power over only a narrow range of corporate activities.[43] Thus, whilst he found a huge decline in the exercise by financial institutions of direct control[44] he maintained that they still exercised powerful constraints over management.[45]

Interestingly, whilst Herman found the impact of the managerialist phenomenon on corporate performance difficult to assess (in view of all the other occurrences which might have had an influence),[46] he ultimately reached a conclusion at odds with the fears expressed by Berle and Means that management would eschew the profit maximisation objective required by the stockholders in favour of goals of their own. Herman's view was that companies with management control seemed as committed to profitable growth as companies dominated by shareholder owners and that this was partly due to an internalisation of profit maximisation criteria in corporate culture and internal operating rules.[47] Herman's empirical data and thoughtful reasoning made an important contribution to our understanding of the phenomenon of managerialism.

The fact of managerialism is linked to other major issues in the theory of company law. The separation of ownership and control has been seen as raising an

---

[38] This is discussed at p. 55 below.
[39] E. Herman *Corporate Control, Corporate Power* (New York: CUP, 1981).
[40] *Ibid.* p. 14.
[41] *Ibid.* p. 26.
[42] *Ibid.* p. 27.
[43] *Ibid.* p. 19.
[44] *Ibid.* p. 157.
[45] *Ibid.* p. 153.
[46] *Ibid.* pp. 106–107.
[47] *Ibid.* p. 113.

inquiry into the legitimacy of corporate power. It is clear that large public corporations have colossal economic strength. The power that these kinds of companies can wield over the lives of ordinary people is very significant. In democratic countries we expect power, political or otherwise, to be subject to controls and constraints. Uncontrolled power is seen as lacking moral legitimacy and thus the separation of ownership and control raises important questions as to whether there are sufficient controls on managerial power.[48] Two major issues in company law theory bear on this question. The first is what has come to be called the corporate governance debate, the second being the social responsibility debate. The corporate governance debate[49] is principally concerned with whether there are, as a matter of fact, sufficient controls, legal or otherwise, on boards of directors, to ensure that their powers are exercised for the benefit of stockholders. The social responsibility debate has origins which are broader than the legitimacy question but to some extent it can be seen as a response to the legitimacy deficiency in terms of trying to change, to broaden out the goals of corporate life,[50] to give managerial power legitimacy by making the exercise of it statesmanlike, and of direct benefit to a wider range of people than merely the shareholders and creditors. The second issue has often been referred to as the social responsibility debate or social enterprise theory but recent developments have given us another name: stakeholder company law. These two issues will now be considered.

3.4 CORPORATE GOVERNANCE

A Alignment

The term 'corporate governance' is essentially a reference to a system. What system is there to ensure that the providers of capital get any return on their investment? To a large extent, the company is, after all, a collection of assets which fall under the control of the managers. The assets have arisen from capital contributions from the shareholders and retained profits arising from the trading activities of the company. Of course, the assets may also have arisen from inputs made by creditors, whose interests are clearly also part of the corporate governance picture.[51] And so

---

[48] See e.g. M. Stokes 'Company Law and Legal Theory' in W. Twining (ed.) *Legal Theory and Common Law* (Oxford: Blackwell, 1986) p. 155.

[49] Some writers use the term 'corporate governance' to include what is here characterised as the second branch. See e.g. IPPR Report *Promoting Prosperity: A Business Agenda for Britain* (London: Vintage, 1997) p. 103. The IPPR Report argues that corporate governance is the system whereby managers are ultimately held accountable to all stakeholders for their stewardship. In view of the fact that the UK committees on corporate governance said very little about the wider 'stakeholder' constituency, it is probably in the interests of clarity if the term corporate governance continues to exclude the 'stakeholder' debate. There are very different institutions and interest groups involved in each field. This will not affect the outcome of that debate because there is no great advantage anyway in calling it 'corporate governance' but it will avoid confusion. Eventually, if the wider constituencies become part of our company 'law' (whether as codes or otherwise) then the fields will probably merge and the IPPR Report description of the term corporate governance will be appropriate; at the moment, it is not.

[50] An approach described by Stokes as the corporatist countervision; see n. 48 above, at p. 178.

[51] In some circumstances, there is even legal recognition that the company must be run in the interests of the creditors; see *Winkworth* v *Baron* [1987] 1 All ER 114; *West Mercia Safety Wear* v *Dodd* [1988]

corporate governance is about alignment; that is, it is about what system of legal or other mechanisms exist to ensure that the interests of the managers of the company are aligned with those of the shareholders:[52] to ensure that the managers do not pursue their own interests which might embrace anything, from, on the one hand, doing as little as possible in return for their remuneration, to, on the other, walking away with the money.

Corporate governance systems contain both internal and external mechanisms. The internal elements will involve the extent to which the law puts in the hands of shareholders the ability to control or influence the board of directors, through voting in meetings, or perhaps by the use of litigation to enforce the legal duties owed by directors. The external mechanisms are to be found in the regulatory environment in which the company operates, for instance, the existence of facilities for the detection and prosecution of corporate fraud, or the existence of rigorous corporate insolvency procedures. In recent years, great interest has been shown in the idea that the stock markets play an important part in providing mechanisms of corporate governance. This comes about through the idea that the price of a company's share can influence the managers. If confidence in their abilities is low, then this will be reflected in a relatively low price for the company's stock, resulting in criticism in the financial press, or in company meetings. Additionally, if management have been given share options, then a fall or rise in the company's share price will have a direct bearing on the personal wealth of the directors. In countries where companies are susceptible to being taken over by hostile takeover bid, then the existence of this 'market for corporate control' is thought to provide a powerful mechanism for disciplining management. The idea being that, if management are underperforming, then the share price will be lower than those of other companies in that sector of industry. This will make the company vulnerable to a hostile bid which if successful will usually result in the dismissal of the directors.[53]

B The Cadbury Report and self-regulation

The last two decades of the 20th century saw an upsurge in public and political interest in corporate governance in the UK.[54] Corporate scandals and frauds were not an invention of the 1980s but that decade saw a series of very high profile scan-

---

BCLC 250. The doctrine was put thus by Leslie Kosmin QC in *Colin Gwyer & Associates Ltd* v *London Wharf (Limehouse) Ltd* [2003] BCC 885 at p. 906: 'Where a company is insolvent or of doubtful solvency or on the verge of insolvency and it is the creditors' money which is at risk the directors, when carrying out their duty to the company, must consider the interest of the creditors as paramount and take those into account when exercising their discretion.'

[52] The point has already been made (n. 49 above) that the discussion of corporate governance will proceed here on the orthodox basis that the only stakeholders are the shareholders; the issues relating to widening this constituency are considered below under the heading 'Stakeholder company law'.

[53] The effectiveness or otherwise of these mechanisms is the subject of much current research and argument: see e.g. J. Franks and C. Mayer 'Hostile Takeovers and the Correction of Managerial Failure' (1996) 40 J Finan Econ 163, arguing that there was little evidence of poor performance prior to bids and hostile takeovers do not therefore perform a disciplining function. Also under scrutiny is the issue of whether good corporate governance can be linked with strong performance, see J. Millstein and P. MacAvoy 'The Active Board of Directors and the Large Publicly Traded Corporation' 98 Col LR 1283 (1998).

[54] And elsewhere; the corporate governance movement is worldwide.

dals involving very large companies. These pointed up failures in the way companies were being run, and exposed failures in the response of the regulatory system.[55] It became common to sue the auditors of a company which had collapsed in circumstances where it was at least arguable that the auditors should have spotted the problems earlier. Accountancy firms are not usually limited liability companies[56] and so, under partnership law, the partners of these firms were personally liable for the debts of the partnership. Additionally, the size of the claims often exceeded the amounts covered by professional indemnity insurance policies. Accountancy firms took a variety of steps to improve their position. The most significant in terms of the overall development of company law, was their role, along with the Financial Reporting Council and the London Stock Exchange, in setting up in May 1991 the Committee on the Financial Aspects of Corporate Governance, to be chaired by Sir Adrian Cadbury. This led to the famous 'Cadbury' Report with its controversial emphasis on the role of self-regulation in corporate governance. These issues are taken up below.[57]

C Global convergence in corporate governance

1 Two patterns of share ownership and two systems of corporate governance

During the 1990s in the US there emerged an important sequel to the Berle and Means' thesis of separation of ownership and control, dispersed ownership, and shareholder passivity; a focus of scholarship which remains very alive. It had become very clear that the world seemed to have divided itself broadly into two patterns of share ownership: countries like the US and UK which have dispersed ownership of shares, with small stakes in the company being held widely by many shareholders, and most other countries where there is concentrated ownership of shares.[58] The differences in ownership patterns produce different background systems of corporate governance. In countries with dispersed ownership of shares, individual shareholders will often have little incentive to monitor management because their small stakes in the company give them very little power to do so. On the other hand, this is counterbalanced by the presence of highly developed and liquid equity markets that enable the minority shareholder to exit from the company and, furthermore, the presence of large numbers of small shareholders also makes the company vulnerable to takeover offers, the possibility of which has the effect of disciplining management.[59] In countries with concentrated ownership of shares, the corporate governance systems are different. In these countries large blocks of shares are held by families or by banks or by other companies under cross-holding arrangements; and these are sometimes described as 'networked' systems because of the link-ups between the shareholders. The result is that the

---

[55] See further p. 389 *et seq.* below.
[56] Incorporation of audit firms was not permitted until the passing of the Companies Act 1989.
[57] See further p. 194 below for discussion of these issues and subsequent developments.
[58] See generally the reference in n. 60 below.
[59] See further p. 389 below.

shareholders are often in a position to exercise quite direct controls over management. Conversely, such systems are usually characterised by relatively undeveloped stock markets and little possibility of effective takeover bids; hence their stock markets provide little in the way of controls on management via takeover bids. The current academic debate largely centres around the question of what causes these two patterns of ownership and resultant systems of corporate governance and whether they will 'converge', in the sense that one or other will become the sole pattern and the other will change.[60]

2 Causes of dispersed share ownership

There are three discernible trends of thought about the causes of dispersed share ownership which can conveniently be labelled as: the efficiency approach, the politics and path dependency approach, and legal protection of minority approach. The first of these derives from traditional economic theory that corporate law and corporate structures will come to assume the form which is most efficient in the sense of producing the greatest profit for the shareholders.[61] Under this approach, the large public firm with dispersed ownership evolved as an efficient response to the needs of industry for large scale organisations which could only be created by the aggregation of share capital from very many shareholders.

This view has been challenged, principally in the work of Professor Mark Roe,[62] who argued that politics played a major part in the evolution of the large public corporation. He observed that in other countries the large companies have concentrated institutional ownership and maintained that as well as the usual efficiency considerations, the reason for the development and retention of fragmented ownership in the US was that politicians (and the electorate) did not want the Wall Street institutions to have the power to control large corporations. This therefore led to legal constraints which prohibited or raised the costs of banks and other institutions holding large blocks of shares.[63] Roe's conclusion was that politics confined the terrain on which the large public corporation evolved, with the result that the corporation with fragmented ownership evolved and survived rather than some other organisation (e.g. with concentrated ownership).[64] In his later work, Roe developed a theory of 'path dependency', which seeks to explain observed persistent differences in the world's corporate ownership structures: dispersed, on the one hand, concentrated on the other.[65] Under the idea of 'path dependence' current circum-

---

[60] A similar debate has been going on in the EU about the harmonisation of capital markets and corporate governance systems; see generally K.J. Hopt, H. Kanda, M.J. Roe and E. Wymeersch (eds) *Comparative Corporate Governance – The State of the Art and Emerging Research* (Oxford: Clarendon Press, 1998).

[61] See generally F. Easterbrook and D. Fischel *The Economic Structure of Corporate Law* (Cambridge, MA: HUP, 1991) pp. 1–39 and 212–218. According to Easterbrook and Fischel, corporate law works and should work like a standard form contract, containing the terms investors would have negotiated if the costs of negotiating were sufficiently low.

[62] M. Roe 'A Political Theory of American Corporate Finance' 91 Col LR 10 (1991).

[63] E.g. the prohibition on bank ownership of equity in the US Glass–Steagall Act 1933 (now partially repealed).

[64] Roe, n. 62 above, at p. 65.

[65] M. Roe 'Chaos and Evolution in Law and Economics' 109 Harv LR 641 (1996).

stances are ascribed partly to the circumstances which existed in earlier times.[66] Thus it is argued[67] that initial ownership structures have an effect on subsequent ownership structures[68] and further that initial ownership structures can have an influence on legal rules[69] which in turn will influence the way subsequent structures are chosen.

The third approach to the problem of explaining different patterns of corporate ownership emphasises the role of law. Professor Coffee has argued[70] that dispersed share ownership may be the result of giving strong legal protection to minority shareholders. This means that they are content with being minority shareholders in corporations and do not feel that they have to network themselves into the controlling group in order to avoid being expropriated or otherwise badly treated. Their strong legal position protects them, with the result that corporate ownership remains dispersed into small fractional holdings.

3 Prospects for convergence

The fascinating question arising out of the existence of the two patterns of corporate ownership is 'what will happen in the future'? Faced with global competition between companies in markets for products, it is interesting to speculate as to the effects of competition between the dispersed and concentrated systems of corporate governance. If one system is inherently better than the other, it is arguable that companies in the weaker system will ultimately be forced either to join the stronger system by obtaining a stock exchange listing there, or seek to change their weaker system.

The three trends of thought discussed above all have interesting angles on the convergence question. The efficiency approach tends towards the idea that the two rival systems of corporate governance have, through globalisation, been put into competition with one another and the most efficient will ultimately win.[71] For instance, it is sometimes argued that the US/UK system of corporate governance is more efficient than European systems[72] because the former have a developed and liquid market for corporate control which enables companies to make share for share takeover offers and grow in size. The politics and path dependency approach stresses that politics and path dependency factors will constrain convergence and so, broadly, the two systems will continue to exist alongside each other. As regards the legal protection of minority approach Coffee stresses the need for regulators to

---

[66] Roe gives the example of the winding road which was originally constructed to avoid dangerous areas. Once the dangers have disappeared there is no need for the road to wind and bend; a straight road could be put through. And yet, it may not be economically efficient to build a completely new straight road, and so the old remains; see Roe, n. 65 above, at p. 643.

[67] See L. Bebchuk and M. Roe 'A Theory of Path Dependence in Corporate Ownership and Governance' 52 Stan LR 127 (1999).

[68] Described as 'structure-driven path dependence'.

[69] Called 'rule-driven path dependence'.

[70] J. Coffee 'The Future as History: The Prospects for Global Convergence in Corporate Governance and its Implications' 93 Nw ULR 654 (1999).

[71] See the analysis in Coffee, n. 70 above, at pp. 645–646.

[72] For a trenchant European view of this see: K. Hopt 'Corporate Governance in Germany' in K. Hopt and E. Wymeersch (eds) *Capital Markets and Company Law* (Oxford: OUP, 2003) p. 289.

address the policy question of whether the Anglo-American approach should be adopted[73] and argues that some degree of convergence can and will be brought about on a voluntary basis by companies electing to join the US corporate governance system by obtaining a listing in the US. This will then enable them to use the capital raising and takeover mechanisms of the US markets to grow to global scale.

4 Conclusions

It seems clear that each of the approaches discussed above brings a valuable insight to the complex problem of trying to identify the forces which are responsible for shaping corporate structure. It is also becoming clear that convergence is coming about in a practical sense in two ways.[74] First, there have been examples of European companies seeking listings in the US; the most significant of these in recent years being that of the German company Daimler getting a listing on the New York Stock Exchange in 1993 and subsequently being able to make a successful share for share takeover offer for the US company Chrysler.[75] Secondly, it seems that back in continental Europe, things are changing, and the market for corporate control is beginning to look more open. The new Directive on Takeover Bids will almost certainly contribute to this process.[76]

3.5 STAKEHOLDER COMPANY LAW

A Social responsibility

As well as the Berle and Means' thesis on the separation of ownership and control,[77] the early 1930s also saw the famous Berle and Dodd debate on the question 'For whom are corporate managers trustees?'[78] Dodd argued that the existence of the corporation as an entity separate from the individuals who compose it meant that it could be conceived as a person imbued with a sense of social responsibility.[79] Berle himself, although originally in favour of a narrow interpretation of the company's responsibilities, later explored the idea that the company had a 'conscience' which could lead it to assume wider responsibilities to society than merely profit maximisation within the law. Berle saw conscience as something which must be built into

---

[73] Coffee, n. 70 above, at pp. 649–650.

[74] For a more detailed analysis of these and related issues, see K. Hopt 'Common Principles of Corporate Governance in Europe' in B. Markesinis (ed.) *The Clifford Chance Millennium Lectures: The Coming Together of the Common Law and the Civil Law* (Oxford: Hart Publishing, 2000) p. 105. See also K. Hopt 'Modern Company and Capital Markets Problems: Improving European Corporate Governance after Enron' (2003) 3 JCLS 2001.

[75] For other examples, see Coffee, n. 70 above, at n. 129.

[76] See further p. 400 below.

[77] In addition to their managerialist thesis, Berle and Means developed ideas on social responsibility; see n. 26 above, especially at pp. 219–243, 293–313.

[78] A. Berle 'Corporate Powers as Powers in Trust' 44 Harv LR 1049 (1931) and M. Dodd 'For Whom are Corporate Managers Trustees?' 45 Harv LR 1145 (1932). For a detailed analysis of the debate and the later literature, see: S. Sheikh *Corporate Social Responsibilities: Law and Practice* (London: Cavendish, 1996) pp. 153–157.

[79] Dodd, n. 78 above, at p. 1161.

institutions so that it could be invoked as a right by the individuals and interests subject to the corporate power.[80] The conscience was the existence of a set of ideas, widely held by the community, and often by the organisation itself and the people who direct it, that certain uses of power were contrary to the established interest and value system of the community.[81] Some aspects of the conscience idea are more than just saying that a company owes a duty to society to behave responsibly. There is also an element of realist jurisprudence, strongly evocative of the real entity theory.[82] The corporation is seen not as a mere fiction of law, but existing in a real sense; the real sense of social reality.[83]

The development of social responsibility within the UK was comprehensively stunted by legal doctrine, which not only enshrined profit maximisation as a major corporate goal, but made it clear that it was the only permissible goal. It was the decision in *Hutton* v *West Cork Railway Company*[84] which held up the development of corporate social responsibility in the UK. The company was in the process of being wound up when a general meeting endorsed a proposal of the directors to compensate corporate officers for the loss of their employment, not because of any legal claim for salary that they then had but as a gratuity.[85] It was held that the payments would be *ultra vires* the company. *Hutton* enshrined the profit driven mechanism of our capitalist system – it is unlawful to give the workers anything unless it is good for the shareholders; meaning, unless it increases efficiency and therefore increases profits. *Hutton* cemented the shareholders' legal rights to the efficient use of resources at the disposal of the board of directors. Because of this use of the *ultra vires* doctrine to block corporate giving, future developments in the arena of corporate social responsibility tended to concentrate on finding ways of circumventing the doctrine so as to at least make it lawful for companies to make gratuitous distributions for philanthropic reasons if they wanted to. The *ultra vires* doctrine has been eroded by statute and common law doctrine.[86] From the beginning of the 1980s Great Britain has seen a significant increase in corporate giving to the wider community.[87] The Annual Reports of many large companies reveal the high profile

---

[80] A. Berle *The Twentieth Century Capitalist Revolution* (London: Macmillan, 1955) pp. 89–90.

[81] A. Berle *Power Without Property* (New York: Harcourt Brace, 1959) p. 90.

[82] See p. 48 above.

[83] Such themes have been developed by German social systems theorists. Teubner has referred to academic views about the nature of the legal person that stress its 'dynamic social reality'. See G. Teubner 'Enterprise Corporatism: New Industrial Policy and the Essence of the Legal Person' 36 *American Journal of Comparative Law* 130–155 (1988).

[84] (1883) 23 Ch D 654.

[85] Also to apply about £1,500 in remuneration for the past services of the directors, who had never received any remuneration.

[86] See pp. 114–130 below. *Hutton* was overturned in the Companies Act 1980 so that in circumstances of cessation of business a company can make provision for employees, even though it is not in the best interests of the company; see now Companies Act 1985, s. 719 (2).

[87] Sheikh, n. 78 above, at p. 45 and n. 22, cites statistics showing a substantial rise during the 1980s. Since then that picture has continued and statistics during the 1990s from *The Major Companies Guide 1997–1998* (London: Directory of Social Change, 1998) p. 9 show increases in corporate giving, funded by increases in profits (although the percentage of pre-tax profit being given has fallen). Thus Top *400* Corporate Donors:
1990–91: Charity Donations 133m (% ptp 0.25%) and Community Contributions 225m (0.42%)
1995–96: Charity Donations 182m (% ptp 0.21%) and Community Contributions 252m (0.29%).

which they accord to their philanthropic activities. Many companies give contributions to political parties; historically, mainly the Conservative Party.[88]

B Industrial democracy

Industrial democracy, participation of the workforce in corporate decision making, has in recent years formed a major part of the social responsibility debate in the UK. By the late 1970s it had acquired a high public profile, when the majority report of the Bullock Committee recommended having worker representation on company boards.[89] In 1980 Parliament enacted that boards of directors must have regard to the interests of their employees as well as their members.[90] In broadening the constituency in this way company law had taken a great leap, even though the technicalities ensured that it would be virtually impossible for employees to get any legal remedies.[91] During the 1980s, numerous academics emphasised the challenges posed for company law by industrial democracy.[92] In his influential article 'The Legal Development of Corporate Responsibility: For Whom Will Corporate Managers be Trustees?',[93] Lord Wedderburn argued that no solution for managerial authority would be found without some renegotiation of the legitimacy on which corporate government rests and that that could not be accomplished without the acceptance of the workers as an integral constituent, albeit a conflictual constituent, in the business corporation.[94]

In the 1990s the movement towards industrial democracy made some progress. In the face of opposition from the UK, little satisfactory progress was made with the draft EC Fifth Directive, the earliest draft of which would have required larger companies to have a two-tier board structure, consisting of a top-tier supervisory

[88] Corporate donations to political parties are now subject to controls contained in the Companies Act 1985, ss. 347A–K, which were inserted by the Political Parties, Elections and Referendums Act 2000. These prohibit donations and political expenditure by companies unless the donation or expenditure has been authorised by an approval resolution. There are special rules for subsidiaries. Certain procedures are specified and there are various exemptions.

[89] *Report of the Committee of Inquiry on Industrial Democracy* (London: HMSO, Cmnd. 6706, 1977).

[90] Companies Act 1980, s. 46; now Companies Act 1985, s. 309. See further p. 176 below.

[91] See B. Pettet 'Duties in Respect of Employees under the Companies Act 1980' (1981) 34 *Current Legal Problems* 199, at pp. 200–204. Conservative government policy remained one of promoting employee involvement voluntarily; an example of this being the statement about employee involvement required in the Directors' Report by what is now Companies Act 1985, Sch. 7, Pt V.

[92] Wedderburn 'The Legal Development of Corporate Responsibility: For Whom Will Corporate Managers be Trustees?' in K. Hopt and G. Teubner (eds) *Corporate Governance and Directors' Liability: Legal, Economic and Sociological Analyses of Corporate Social Responsibility* (Berlin: de Gruyter, 1985); Wedderburn 'The Social Responsibility of Companies' (1985) 15 *Melbourne University Law Review* 1; Wedderburn 'Trust, Corporation and the Worker' (1985) 23 *Osgoode Hall Law Journal* 203; G. Teubner 'Corporate Fiduciary Duties and their Beneficiaries: A Functional Approach to the Legal Institutionalisation of Corporate Responsibility' in K. Hopt and G. Teubner (eds) *Corporate Governance and Directors' Liability: Legal, Economic and Sociological Analyses of Corporate Social Responsibility* (Berlin: de Gruyter, 1985); Sealy 'Directors Wider Responsibilities – Problems Conceptual, Practical and Procedural' (1987) 13 Mon LR 164; P. Xuereb 'The Juridification of Industrial Relations through Company Law Reform' (1988) 51 MLR 156; Wedderburn 'Companies and Employees: Common Law or Social Dimension' (1993) LQR 220.

[93] See n. 91 above.

[94] Wedderburn, 'The Legal Development of Corporate Responsibility: For Whom Will Corporate Managers be Trustees?', n. 92 above, at p. 43.

board and an executive, management board and some form of worker represen-tation.[95] Work on the earlier Vredeling Directive[96] and on the European Company Statute had a similar history.[97] However, the 1992 Maastricht Treaty on European Union and its annexed Protocol and Agreement on Social Policy authorised the Member States, to adopt Directives for the information and consultation of employees, and so, despite earlier UK opposition, the European Works Council Directive[98] was adopted in 1994. It covered about 1,500 or so European companies (namely those employing over 1,000 workers with more than 150 in at least two Member States)[99] and required them to establish company wide information and consultation committees for their employees.[100] Subsequently, there has been a fur-ther Directive of more general application, namely the Directive Establishing a General Framework for Informing and Consulting Employees in the European Community.[101] In the long run this legislation might prove to be a catalyst for a major change in corporate culture.

C Stakeholder company law

During the 1990s, the social responsibility debate broadened into philosophical and political arguments about creating a 'stakeholder' society. Although the roots go back further, much of the basic ideology stems from communitarian[102] philosophy which became a quasi-political movement in the US in the early 1990s. The elec-toral success of the Democratic Party in the US may well have inspired an infusion of elements of communitarian ideology into the British Labour Party – which at one stage[103] appeared to endorse the stakeholder concept, although it has since

---

[95] The full story of the subsequent drafts is analysed in detail in J. Du Plessis and J. Dine 'The Fate of the Draft Fifth Directive on Company Law: Accommodation Instead of Harmonisation' [1997] JBL 23.

[96] OJ 1983 C217.

[97] For detail of the proposals, see J. Dine 'The European Company Statute' (1990) 11 Co Law 208; A. Burnside 'The European Company Re-proposed' (1991) 12 Co Law 216.

[98] Council Directive 94/45/EEC on the establishment of a European Works Council or other procedure in Community-scale undertakings or Community-scale groups of undertakings for the purposes of informing and consulting employees, OJ 1994 L254/64.

[99] Council Directive 94/45/EEC, art. 2.

[100] With the coming to power of the Blair 'New Labour' government, policy towards Europe changed, and the UK signed the Protocol, with the result that UK implementation of the Directive became required.

[101] 2002/14/EC.

[102] On communitarianism the main source is A. Etzioni *The Spirit of Community – Rights, Responsibilities and the Communitarian Agenda* (USA: Crown, 1993) (reprinted in the UK by Fontana, 1995). Recent journal sources on corporate responsibility are: A. Sommer 'Whom Should the Corporation Serve? The Berle–Dodd Debate Revisited Sixty Years Later' 16 *Delaware Journal of Corporate Law* 33 (1991); A. Fejfar 'Corporate Voluntarism: Panacea or Plague? A Question of Horizon' 17 *Delaware Journal of Corporate Law* 859 (1992); M. De Bow and D. Lee 'Shareholders, Nonshareholders and Corporate Law: Communitarianism and Resource Allocation' 18 *Delaware Journal of Corporate Law* 393 (1993). There are also distinguished collections in Volume 50 of the *Washington and Lee Law Review* 1373–1723 (1993) and in Volume 43 of the *University of Toronto Law Journal* 297–796 (1993). For earlier material see the extensive bibliography in J.E. Parkinson *Corporate Power and Responsibility: Issues in the Theory of Company Law* (Oxford: Clarendon Press, 1993).

[103] This is widely attributed to Tony Blair's stakeholder speech in Singapore; see *Financial Times*, 9 January 1996. Labour Party thinking in this area was set out in *Vision for Growth: A New Industrial Strategy for Britain* (London: Labour Party, 1996).

backpedalled somewhat – to produce a call for cultural changes in companies.[104] Nevertheless, the genuine public interest in the stakeholder debate in Britain represented a natural desire to search for social consensus, for community. In the UK, the stakeholder philosophy and agenda has been set out in books and articles which appeared spontaneously in a burst of activity in the mid 1990s. Hutton's influential work *The State We're In*[105] argued that the financial system needed to be comprehensively republicanised. Plender's *A Stake in the Future – The Stakeholding Solution*[106] took a milder line than Hutton, setting out the theoretical basis of the doctrine as he saw it.[107]

The word 'stakeholders' originated in the US and it has been argued that it developed as a deliberate play on the American word for 'shareholders', namely 'stockholders'.[108] Arguably it was less subtle than that, and perhaps was adopted because it had a deep historical appeal to the American psyche, carrying the connotation of the hardworking and deserving settler 'staking a claim' by ringfencing a plot of land and thus acquiring it; it denotes a moral claim for participation and for rights not yet recognised by the law.

Plender argued that a stakeholder economy is one which derives competitive strength from a cohesive national culture, in which the exercise of property rights is conditioned by shared values and co-operative behaviour.[109] As a result, not only do people have a greater sense of worth and well-being, but the economy becomes more efficient and grows faster. Some of the efficiency is said by economists to come from lower transaction costs[110] because fewer monitors are needed in the workplace, commercial contracting is simpler and cheaper because of a higher level of trust and shared values between the parties, and less state legislation and costly regulation is needed.[111] Stakeholder theory emphasises the importance of inclusion, the role of intermediate institutions, companies, unions, churches, clubs, campaigning groups.[112]

---

[104] See *Financial Times* 26 June 1996.

[105] London: Vintage, 1996 (first published in 1995 by Jonathan Cape).

[106] London: Brealey Publishing, 1997.

[107] The literature is immense. See also e.g.: *Your Stake at Work: TUC Proposals for a Stakeholding Economy* (London: TUC, 1996); Report of the *Tomorrow's Company* inquiry from the Royal Society of Arts (Royal Society for the Encouragement of Arts, Manufactures and Commerce, 1995); J. Kay and A. Silberstone 'Corporate Governance' *NIESR Review, August 1995* (National Institute of Economic and Social Research Review) p. 84; A. Alcock 'The Case Against the Concept of Stakeholders' (1996) 17 Co Law 177; P. Ireland 'Corporate Governance, Stakeholding, and the Company: Towards a Less Degenerate Capitalism?' (1996) 23 *Journal of Law and Society* 287; P. Ireland 'Company Law and the Myth of Shareholder Ownership' (1999) 62 MLR 32; S. Leader 'Private Property and Corporate Governance Part I: Defining the Interests' and J. Dine 'Private Property and Corporate Governance Part II: Content of Directors' Duties and Remedies' and F. Patfield 'Challenges for Company Law' in F. Patfield (ed.) *Perspectives on Company Law: 1* (London: Kluwer, 1995) pp. 1, 85, 115; J. Dine 'Companies and Regulations: Theories, Justifications and Policing' in D. Milman (ed.) *Regulating Enterprise: Law and Business Organisations in the UK* (Oxford: Hart Publishing, 1999) p. 291.

[108] See P. Ireland 'Corporate Governance, Stakeholding and the Company: Towards a Less Degenerate Capitalism?' (1996) 23 *Journal of Law and Society* 287 at p. 295 and n. 47.

[109] J. Plender *A Stake in the Future – The Stakeholding Solution* (London: Brealey Publishing, 1997) at p. 23.

[110] For this concept, see further pp. 67 *et seq.* below.

[111] See e.g. Plender, n. 106 above, at p. 24 arguing that the historic success of stakeholder economies such as Germany, Switzerland or Japan is partly explained by their lower transaction costs, both inside and outside the firm.

[112] *Ibid.* at p. 256.

The agenda produced by stakeholder theory for the reform of company law is difficult to pin down, but at present it involves participation of employees and other constituencies in corporate decision-making structures, varying the scope of directors' duties, either by including the wider constituencies as the subjects of the duty or redefining the company so as to include them. There are many other suggestions; ranging from rights to training, to requirements for companies to produce a social audit.[113]

Most stakeholder proposals involve a greater or lesser degree of what may broadly be called corporate voluntarism[114] or profit-sacrificing social responsibility;[115] that is, some level of departure from the principle of running the company for the sole benefit of the shareholders. Over the years corporate voluntarism has been subjected to a great deal of theoretical analysis and criticism. The debate revolves around three main criticisms, although these are overlapping and linked and there are many other angles.[116] It is argued, first, that the pursuit of corporate goals other than profit is inefficient and so in the long run we would all be worse off for it. Further it is said that the company and its shares are private accumulations of capital, and any goal other than profit for shareholders is an infringement of private property, a naked redistribution of wealth; sometimes called the shareholders' money argument. Thirdly and alternatively, boards of directors are the wrong people to be making decisions about the distribution of wealth, they are not elected by or accountable to the populace, and it extends their already overlarge powers; it is a state function and they should defer to the state which can make appropriate redistributions through the taxation system. This is sometimes called the deference argument.

Various replies could be mounted. The efficiency argument can be met head on by pointing to the counter efficiencies produced by the reduction of social friction which stakeholder policies would produce. Germany and Japan have forms of worker involvement in larger companies and have clearly been doing better than many countries in recent decades. In his book *Competitive Advantage Through People*[117] Jeffrey Pfeffer, Professor of Organisational Behaviour at Stanford Graduate School of Business, used the example of the five top performing US companies between 1972 and 1992.[118] The factor they had in common was the way in which they managed their workforce. Employment security, high wages and greater employee share ownership can all produce efficiencies and so enhance competitiveness.[119] The shareholders' money argument is arguably diminished by the

---

[113] See: *Your Stake at Work: TUC Proposals for a Stakeholding Economy* (London: TUC, 1996). In fact, in view of the TUC's enthusiasm for their interpretation of stakeholder ideals, it is difficult to see whether the industrial democracy debate survives as a separate issue.

[114] E.g. as in A. Fejfar 'Corporate Voluntarism: Panacea or Plague? A Question of Horizon' 17 *Delaware Journal of Corporate Law* 859 (1992).

[115] J.E. Parkinson *Corporate Power and Responsibility: Issues in the Theory of Company Law* (Oxford: Clarendon Press, 1993) at p. 304.

[116] For a more detailed analysis see Parkinson, n. 115 above, at pp. 304–346.

[117] Boston, MA: Harvard Business School Press, 1994.

[118] J. Pfeffer *Competitive Advantage Through People* (Boston, MA: Harvard Business School Press, 1994) at p. 5. Top performing in terms of the percentage returns on their shares. They were South West Airlines, Tyson Foods, Circuit City and Plenum Publishing.

[119] Pfeffer, n. 118 above, at p. 4.

legitimacy problem created by the immense power that companies in fact exercise over the lives of individuals and in the lack of sufficient controls on that power.[120] The deference argument is challenging but its strength can be diminished by the argument that the general cultural improvement in society resulting from stakeholder policies diminishes the need for strict adherence to democratic theory.[121]

D The Company Law Review and stakeholders

At an early stage the Company Law Review[122] recognised that the stakeholder issue was of great importance; it was picked out as one of the key issues for attention.[123] However, at the time of writing[124] it is looking as though nothing radical will be recommended. The stakeholder issue was, quite properly, linked to the question of identifying the proper scope of company law, meaning, whose interests it should be designed to serve.[125] It was observed that the Review was essentially concerned with law reform and was not concerned with wider ethical issues about the behaviour of participants in companies except to the extent that it was appropriate to reflect them in the law. However, it was made clear the behaviour could be influenced by a wide range of non-legal factors and that the design of the law needed to recognise the importance of these.[126]

The Review identified two broad approaches; 'enlightened shareholder value', and 'pluralist'. The first of these is that the ultimate objective of companies is that which is currently reflected in the law, namely to generate maximum value for shareholders.[127] But that this approach is to be 'enlightened' by the recognition that a wider range of interests can be served as subordinate to the overall aim of achieving shareholder value and indeed will probably need to be so as to avoid short-term concentration on profit levels, and instead have regard to the fostering of co-operative relationships which will bring greater benefits in the longer term.[128] The pluralist approach is that company law should be modified to include other objectives so that a company should be required to serve a range of other interests in their own right and not merely as a means of attaining shareholder value.[129] It was observed that because the enlightened shareholder value approach was not dependent on any change in the ultimate objective of companies, then there would be no need substantially to reform directors' duties.[130]

---

[120] See e.g. *Your Stake at Work*, n. 113 above, at p. 14 with the observation that less than 15% of the votes of pensions funds are cast at AGMs.

[121] E.g. Plender, n. 109 above, at p. 256 arguing that by emphasising the role of intermediate institutions the stakeholding concept consciously downgrades the role of the state.

[122] For an account of the mechanisms of this, see Chapter 4.

[123] DTI Consultation Document (February 1999) *The Strategic Framework*.

[124] July 2004.

[125] DTI Consultation Document (February 1999) *The Strategic Framework* para. 5.1.1.

[126] *Ibid.* para. 5.1.2.

[127] This means shareholder wealth maximisation; *ibid.* para. 5.1.17 and is similar to the concept as used in corporate finance; see p. 254 below.

[128] *Ibid.* para. 5.1.12.

[129] *Ibid.* para. 5.1.13.

[130] *Ibid.* para. 5.1.17.

The Review returned to the issue in a later document.[131] The responses to the consultation showed that there was strong support for retaining the objective of shareholder value, but that it should be framed in an inclusive way[132] and that due recognition was needed of the importance in modern business of developing effective long-term relationships with employees, customers and suppliers, and in the community more widely.[133]

The later Review document also considered the difficulties with implementing the pluralist approach and noted recent trends in continental systems away from 'enterprise law'[134] and towards the primacy of shareholder value.[135] The Final Report contained recommendations along these lines.[136] The likelihood is that the eventual outcome will be a codification of directors' duties framed so as to include an obligation to achieve the success of the company for the benefit of shareholders by taking proper account of all the relevant considerations,[137] but that this will involve a balanced view of the short and long term, the need to sustain ongoing relationships with employees, customers, suppliers and others, the need to maintain the company's business reputation and to consider the impact of its operations on the community and the environment.[138] In the subsequent government White Paper *Modernising Company Law* the draft Bill codifying directors' duties adopted this kind of approach.[139]

The reality is that this is probably the right thing to do for the time being.[140] There does not seem to be any political consensus for the enforcement[141] of the representation of wider interests in companies and nor are the mechanisms through which this might usefully be achieved very obvious. It is true that as regards employee participation, continental systems of law have tried and tested structures[142] but it is also true that many people in those systems are increasingly worried about the ability of their companies to attract international capital unless shareholder value is given legal primacy, and the absence of employee participation in board structure in the UK might be partially offset by the new developments in European Works Councils. In many ways the Review proposals on the stakeholder

---

[131] DTI Consultative Document (March 2000) *Developing the Framework*.

[132] I.e. made clear that it was to be 'enlightened'.

[133] DTI Consultation Document (March 2000) *Developing the Framework* para. 2.11.

[134] I.e. a system under which concepts like the character or integrity of the company can be seen as legally paramount to the wishes or needs of the shareholders.

[135] DTI Consultation Document (March 2000) *Developing the Framework* paras 3.26–3.36.

[136] *Modern Company Law for a Competitive Economy Final Report* (June 2001), paras. 3.4–3.20.

[137] This is to be coupled with enhanced disclosure and consequent public accountability.

[138] DTI Consultation Document (March 2000) *Developing the Framework* summarised at para. 2.19; the Review later sets out a trial draft of the directors' duties reflecting these ideas; *ibid.* at para. 3.40.

[139] July 2002, Cmnd. 5553. See also *Company Law. Flexibility and Accessibility: A Consultative Document* (London: DTI, 2004).

[140] Interestingly, the EC Commission has adopted a definition of Corporate Social Responsibility (CSR) and an approach to CSR which stresses what it regards as its voluntary nature: see the communication *Corporate Social Responsibility: A Business Contribution to Sustainable Development* (COM 2002, 347 final).

[141] The UK government is actively fostering the voluntary approach. We now have a Minister for Corporate Social Responsibility. There is also a CSR Academy, see: http://www.csracademy.org.uk.

[142] E.g. the German system of co-determination (mitbestimmung) under which the executive board (Vorstand) is elected by a supervisory board (Aufsichtsrat) made up of shareholder and worker representatives.

issue are exciting and forward looking, and could be said to represent a partial triumph for the stakeholder doctrine which, if the proposals are enacted, will certainly be seen to have made its mark on the law.

3.6 LAW AND ECONOMICS

A Efficiency as a moral value

Lawyers and the public at large have an inbuilt resistance to the notion that economics can have any relevance to law. Justice is what lawyers like to feel they are about, and however cynical or disillusioned the experienced lawyer can get about the ability of the system to deliver justice, he or she will usually strive to ensure that they are involved in a system which does or should deliver justice. The same is true of the public perception of law. After all, are not the television channels filled with dramas based on people who one way or another are getting justice or just deserts from the legal system, or, if the script writer has really excelled himself, a tale with a difference; injustice? Either way, law is seen as being about justice, and if it is not about justice, then it is not about law.

Anathema then, that economists, with their focus on 'efficiency',[143] could be seen as having anything to say about law or legal systems. Surely it is obvious that efficiency should be irrelevant where matters of justice are concerned? And yet efficiency is not always so. Suppose on a workers' co-operative fish farm it is one day discovered that if the fish in the lakes are fed at sunrise instead of at sunset (as is currently the practice) then the number of fish which can be produced annually is doubled. Suppose also, that no one minds whether they do their feeding duty at sunrise or sunset, that no more food is required, and that no other effects result from changing to the sunrise feeding routine. In these circumstances, a change to sunrise feeding seems a rational course of action. It is clearly more efficient. Doubling the output would make the farm more wealthy and so improve the lot of everyone on it. So it is not difficult to see how arguments about the change in routine could acquire a moral quality. It is not only rational to change to sunrise feeding; it is stupid not to. Perhaps then, even, it is wicked not to; almost deliberatively destructive of ideas of human growth and advancement.

Efficiency will therefore sometimes be seen as an important moral value. We live in a world of scarce resources. We strive to produce goods and services; we need them and we like them. Waste is usually seen as immoral and wasteful ways of doing things will sometimes attract moral condemnation. Nevertheless, efficiency will, in many situations, be trumped by other moral values, and human beings will often regard an inefficient course of action as desirable. Sometimes, then, arguments based on whether the law is efficient, in the sense of producing an optimal use of resources, may not be determinative of the weight of the moral argument on one side or the other. On the other hand, given that efficiency is so fundamental to

---

[143] Economists make technical distinctions between different types of efficiency; see B. Cheffins *Company Law: Theory, Structure and Operation* (Oxford: OUP, 1997) at pp. 14–16.

our values, it is nevertheless useful to know whether a particular legal rule will produce an efficient outcome or not.

Economic analysis of legal rules can sometimes shed light on the values inherent in those rules. It will often show that there is a much closer link between efficiency and legal rules than lawyers, with their lofty notions of 'justice', would like to imagine. Of particular relevance to company law have been the economic theories which try to elucidate the nature of the firm,[144] or which try to explain in economic terms, the operation of concepts or structures produced by company law such as limited liability, or the market for corporate control. The analysis which follows will mainly concentrate on the theories relating to the nature of the firm which will serve to give the reader a picture of the kind of issues which economic analysis of company law raises and from which come many of the basic concepts used in the economic analysis of corporation law.[145] The economic analysis of limited liability has already been discussed[146] and economic aspects of takeovers and the market for corporate control are dealt with below.[147]

B The theory of the firm

1 Transaction cost economics

The 'theory' of the firm is perhaps best seen as a group of closely related writings by economists about various aspects of the firm; about why it exists and about what goes on inside it. Economic scholarship about why the firm exists[148] is generally regarded as having taken a quantum leap forward[149] with the publication in 1937 of an article by Ronald Coase.[150]

Coase sought to explain why production is sometimes co-ordinated by price movements on the market and why it is sometimes co-ordinated by an entrepreneur within the organisation of a firm. Thus, he sought to show why firms exist in an exchange economy in which it is generally assumed that the distribution of

---

[144] 'Firm' in economic theory loosely means business organisation. It is a wider use than the English lawyer's term of art for partnership.

[145] For a work which deals with the whole picture of company law from the economic angle, see: F. Easterbrook and D. Fischel *The Economic Structure of Corporate Law* (Cambridge, MA: Harvard University Press, 1991) arguing that corporation law is a sort of common form contract which should and in fact does supply the rules that investors would contract for if it were easy to contract sufficiently fully. For an interesting recent example of the counterview that company law is public regulation arising from a choice among policies, see: D. Sugarman 'Is Company Law Founded on Contract or Public Regulation? The Law Commission's Paper on Company Directors' (1999) 20 Co Law 162; D. Sugarman 'Reconceptualising Company Law: Reflections on the Law Commission's Consultation Paper on Shareholder Remedies: Part 1' (1997) 18 Co Law 226, and Part 2, *ibid.* 274.

[146] See pp. 34–35.

[147] At p. 410. For the 'Efficient Capital Markets Hypothesis' and other economic aspects of the theory of securities regulation, see p. 324 below.

[148] This term embraces both companies and partnerships in this context.

[149] Prior to that, the neoclassical approach was the dominant analysis; and it continues to survive. Neoclassical theory views the firm as a set of feasible production plans presided over by a manager who buys and sells assets with a view to maximising the welfare of the owners; see O. Hart 'An Economist's Perspective on the Theory of the Firm' in P. Buckley and J. Michie (eds) *Firms, Organizations and Contracts: A Reader in Industrial Organisation* (Oxford: OUP, 1996) pp. 199, 200.

[150] R. Coase 'The Nature of the Firm' *Economica*, New Series, IV, 386 (1937).

resources is organised by the price mechanism,[151] in other words, why organisations exist if production is regulated by price movements and could be carried on without any organisation at all.[152] Coase observed that the main reason why it is profitable to establish a firm would seem to be that there is a cost of using the price mechanism.[153] He went on to consider the various costs (i.e. disadvantages) such as the costs of negotiating and concluding contracts for each exchange transaction on the market.[154] In particular he argued that a firm would be likely to emerge in cases where a short-term market contract would be unsatisfactory; such as where it was for the supply of a service and where the details of what the supplier is expected to do are left to be decided on later by the purchaser.[155] Thus he argued that by forming an organisation and allowing an entrepreneur to direct the resources, certain marketing costs are saved[156] and so a firm, therefore, consists of the system of relationships which comes into existence when the direction of resources is dependent on an entrepreneur.[157] Then, as it were, approaching the problem from the other end, he considered why there are any market transactions at all if by organising one can eliminate certain costs and in fact reduce the cost of production, and raised the question of why production is not carried on by one big firm.[158] The answer being, that a firm will expand until the costs of organising an extra transaction within the firm become equal to the costs of carrying out the same transaction by means of an exchange on the open market.[159]

The emphasis given to the costs of transacting on the market as compared with the costs of organising within a firm has resulted in this kind of analysis being referred to as 'transaction cost' economics. Many later writers have developed aspects of Coase's theory; in particular, Oliver Williamson, a major exponent of the transaction cost approach, has argued that the modern corporation is mainly to be understood as the product of a series of organisational innovations that had the purpose and effect of economising on transaction costs,[160] and so transactions will be organised by markets unless market exchange gives rise to substantial transaction costs.[161] Furthermore, for Williamson, the reduction in transaction costs achieved by the use of the firm in some situations provides a moral justification for allowing firms to exist, on the basis that since transaction cost economising is socially valued, then it follows that the modern corporation serves affirmative economic purposes.[162] This is a crucial insight, for it encapsulates one of the main tenets of the economic analysis of corporation law, that one of the reasons for the existence of corporation law is the reduction of transaction costs.

---

[151] *Ibid.* at p. 393.
[152] *Ibid.* at p. 388.
[153] *Ibid.* at p. 391.
[154] Usually referred to by later economists as the costs of 'writing contracts'.
[155] Coase, n. 150 above, at pp. 391–392 *passim*.
[156] *Ibid.* at p. 392.
[157] *Ibid.* at p. 393.
[158] *Ibid.* at p. 394.
[159] Or the costs of organising in another firm; *ibid.* at p. 395.
[160] O. Williamson 'The Modern Corporation: Origins, Evolution, Attributes' (1981) 19 *Journal of Economic Literature* 1537.
[161] Williamson, n. 160 above, at p. 1547.
[162] *Ibid.* at p. 1538.

2 Shirking, agency costs and nexus of contracts

Other economic theorists have concentrated more on what goes on inside a firm (rather than how and why it comes into existence) and provided some important perspectives. Alchian and Demsetz[163] maintained in 1972 that their view of the firm was not necessarily inconsistent with Coase's observation that the higher the cost of transacting across the markets the greater will be the comparative advantage of organising resources within the firm.[164] However, in order to move the theory forward, they argued that it was necessary to know what is meant by a firm and to explain the circumstances under which the cost of managing resources is low relative to the cost of allocating resources through market transaction.[165] Their approach stresses that a firm should not be characterised by the existence of authoritarian power and argued that a firm has no power of fiat, or authority or disciplinary action any different from ordinary market contracting between any two people[166] and therefore that the employee 'orders' the owner of the team to pay him money in the same sense that the employer directs the team member to perform certain acts.[167] They thus placed their focus on contract, as the mechanism which brings about exchange, and locate the firm in circumstances which they describe as the team use of inputs and a centralised position of some party in the contractual arrangements of all other inputs.[168] They described the need for the firm to monitor carefully who is doing what and to reward those who deserve it, referring to this process as 'metering'.[169] In relation to this they identify the problem of what they term 'shirking' and argue that there is a higher incentive for people to shirk when they are part of a team (because it is more difficult to monitor than if they work singly).[170] They therefore move to the position that because it involves team production, one of the firm's chief difficulties is the monitoring of shirking.[171] In identifying how the firm structure seeks to provide the monitor[172] they raise what at first sight looks like a red herring but in fact provides a powerful insight into the firm's organisational structure. They raise the question of who will monitor the monitor[173] and in considering this they see the point that the firm structure has a particular answer to this, to be found in the concept of the residual claimant (i.e. the equity shareholder(s)) because if you give someone the title to the net earnings of the team then they have an incentive not to shirk as

---

[163] See A. Alchian and H. Demsetz 'Production, Information Costs, and Economic Organisation' 62 *American Economic Review* 777 (1972).

[164] *Ibid.* at p. 783.

[165] *Ibid.* at pp. 783–784.

[166] *Ibid.* at p. 777.

[167] *Ibid.* at p. 783.

[168] *Ibid.* at p. 778.

[169] Metering is seen as important because if the economic organisation meters poorly, with rewards and productivity only loosly correlated, then productivity will be smaller: *ibid.* at p. 779.

[170] *Ibid.* at p. 779.

[171] The shirking-information problem.

[172] Alchian and Demsetz use the term monitor to connote activities such as measuring output performance, apportioning rewards, and giving assignments or instructions in what to do and how to do it (in addition to its normal disciplinary connotation): Alchian and Demsetz, n. 163 above, at p. 782.

[173] *Ibid.* at p. 782.

a monitor.[174] Ultimately, they summarise the bundle of rights possessed by the equity shareholder,[175] and conclude that the coming together of them has arisen because it resolves the shirking-information problem of team production better than the non-centralised contractual arrangement.[176]

The Alchian–Demsetz analysis is an important elucidation of the problem of aligning the interests of the various participants in corporations towards an efficient outcome. In this respect, their analysis is closely related to Jensen and Meckling's influential work on agency costs to which it is now necessary to turn.

Jensen and Meckling bring a wide range of perspectives to the theory of the firm.[177] Perhaps the most influential aspects are those which derive from their analysis of the firm as a 'nexus'[178] of contracts, and their analysis of the role of agency costs.[179] They define the firm as simply one form of legal fiction[180] which serves as a nexus for contracting relationships. It is also characterised by the existence of divisible residual claims on the assets and cash flows of the organisation which can generally be sold without permission of the other contracting individuals.[181] One of the claims which they make for this approach is that it serves to make it clear that it is seriously misleading to personalise the firm by reference to its social responsibility. The firm is not an individual, it is a legal fiction which serves as a focus for a complex process in which the conflicting objectives of individuals are brought into equilibrium within a framework of contractual relations.[182]

In their paper, Jensen and Meckling focus on an analysis of agency costs generated by the contractual arrangements between the owners and the top management of the corporation. They define an agency relationship as a contract under which one or more persons (the principal(s)) engage another person (the agent) to perform some service on their behalf which involves delegating some decision-making authority to the agent.[183] They argue that agency costs come about because if both

---

[174] *Ibid.* at p. 782.
[175] To be a residual claimant; to observe input behaviour; to be the central party common to all contracts with inputs; to alter the membership of the team; to sell these rights.
[176] *Ibid.* at p. 783.
[177] See M. Jensen and W. Meckling 'Theory of the Firm: Managerial Behaviour, Agency Costs and Ownership Structure' 3 *Journal of Financial Economics* 305 (1976).
[178] 'Nexus' has the dictionary meaning of 'bond, link or connection'.
[179] The term 'agency costs' is used here to denote the costs of organising resources within firms, as opposed to the term 'transaction costs' which is generally used to denote the costs of organising across markets. This perhaps is in keeping with the approach originally used by the writers and may help to avoid confusion; see e.g. H. Demsetz 'Theory of the Firm Revisited' in O. Williamson and S. Winter (eds) *The Nature of the Firm: Origins, Evolution, and Development* (New York, Oxford: OUP, 1993) at pp. 161–162 referring to the terminology problem arising if the term transaction costs is used to cover both. (Demsetz also preferred the term 'management costs' instead of 'agency costs'.) However, quite often agency costs are equated with and are regarded as a species of transaction cost; see e.g. S. Deakin and A. Hughes 'Economics and Company Law Reform: A Fruitful Partnership' (1999) 20 Co Law 212.
[180] Legal fiction is earlier defined as the artificial construct under the law which allows certain organisations to be treated as individuals: Jensen and Meckling, n. 177 above, at n. 12.
[181] *Ibid.* at p. 311.
[182] *Ibid.* It is interesting to compare this claim, which makes little allowance for realist theory, with writings about social responsibility; see p. 58 above.
[183] Jensen and Meckling, n. 177 above, at p. 308.

parties to the relationship are utility maximisers there is good reason to believe the agent will not always act in the best interests of the principal[184] and trying to align the interests of the agent and the principal gives rise to costs.

These 'agency costs' are defined as the sum of (1) the monitoring expenditures by the principal,[185] (2) the bonding expenditures by the agent,[186] and (3) the residual loss.[187] The core of Jensen and Meckling's paper consists of formal mathematical economic analysis of the effect of outside equity on agency costs by comparing the behaviour of a manager when he owns 100% of the residual claims on a firm to his behaviour when he sells off a portion of those claims to outsiders. Their general concluding observations are that agency costs are as real as any other costs and the level of agency costs depends among other things on statutory and common law and human ingenuity in devising contracts and that whatever its shortcomings, the corporation has thus far survived the market test against potential alternative forms of organisation.[188]

3 Property rights theory

Subsequently, a 'Property Rights' approach has been developed, initially in an article by Sanford Grossman and Oliver Hart.[189] This seeks to take further Coase's observation that transactions will be organised in the firm[190] when the cost of doing this is lower than the cost of using the market[191] by exploring the content of the idea that there are benefits of organising the transaction within the firm.

The background to the property rights approach, and the platform from which it moves forward, lies in the development of transaction cost theory subsequent to Coase, largely by Williamson.[192] It is useful to start[193] with the observation that contracts are 'incomplete' in the sense that the parties will not provide for every single contingency in their contracts.[194] The result of this is that as their business relationship progresses the parties will seek to 'renegotiate' the contract. This renegotiation process will involve costs; for example, because the parties will haggle over the new terms. The costs may be so high that it becomes worth the while of

---

[184] *Ibid.*
[185] 'Monitoring' here includes any rules designed to control the behaviour of the agent; see Jensen and Meckling, n. 177 above, at n. 9.
[186] 'Bonding' refers to situations where it will pay the agent to enter into arrangements which guarantee that he will act in the principal's interests.
[187] Jensen and Meckling, n. 177 above. 'Residual loss' means that even given optimal monitoring and bonding activities between principal and agent, there will still be some divergence between the agent's decisions and those decisions which would maximise the welfare of the principal.
[188] Jensen and Meckling, n. 177 above, at p. 357.
[189] S. Grossman and O. Hart 'The Costs and Benefits of Ownership: A Theory of Vertical and Lateral Integration' 94 J Pol Econ 691 (1986); O. Hart *Firms, Contracts and Financial Structure* (Oxford: Clarendon Press, 1995).
[190] I.e. there will be integration.
[191] Grossman and Hart, n. 189 above, at p. 692.
[192] See generally O. Williamson *The Economic Institutions of Capitalism* (New York: Free Press, 1985).
[193] This summary is largely derived from Chapters 1 and 2 *passim* of O. Hart *Firms, Contracts and Financial Structure* (Oxford: Clarendon Press, 1995).
[194] The incompleteness comes about largely as a result of difficulties in seeing all the contingencies and of 'writing' them into the contract.

the parties to go their separate ways and find other partners. However, they will be deterred from doing this, and will be willing to put up with quite a lot of renegotiation costs if they have already put a lot of work or money (i.e. investment) into preparations for the business relationship – this is referred to as an 'ex ante relationship-specific investment'. This puts us into a position to comprehend one other renegotiation cost which may arise. Prior to the parties' entering into a contract setting up a relationship-specific investment, they will tend to look ahead, and may well anticipate that the incomplete contract governing it will sooner or later need to be renegotiated and that they could then well find that the trading gains which they hope to make from it will be eaten up by the other party being difficult[195] in those renegotiations. This fear might well be so significant that it causes them never to enter into the contract for the relationship-specific investment in the first place, even though that would have been their best option in efficiency and trading terms. Instead, they decide to opt for a less relationship-specific investment which will sacrifice some of the efficiency benefits[196] which the more specific investment would have brought, but avoids the risks arising from the incomplete contract and potential hold-up behaviour. Thus we have been examining the transaction costs which are potentially present in transactions between separate firms (i.e. firms which are non-integrated). It is part of transaction cost theory (stemming from Coase) that in some circumstances these costs will be less within an integrated firm.[197] Hart argues that transaction cost theory does not tell us why, but that property rights theory does.[198]

Hart starts his explanation[199] by focusing on the effect of an acquisition by firm A, of firm B, and argues that what A actually gets out of it is that it becomes owner of firm B's assets. He uses the phrase 'nonhuman assets' to take in the point that the firm does not own the people employed by it.[200] He then observes that because contracts are incomplete, they will not specify all aspects of the use of the asset, there will be gaps, and so the question will arise of which party has the right to decide about the gaps. Hart takes the view that the owner of the asset has the residual control right.[201] The core of the theory is that in view of the incompleteness of contracts, this residual control will affect bargaining power during the renegotiation of incomplete contracts. Hart summarises that the benefit of integration is that the acquiring firm's incentive to make relationship-specific

---

[195] This 'being difficult' is often referred to as 'hold-up' behaviour.
[196] The loss of the efficiency benefits is thus the cost.
[197] I.e. if the transaction is being carried out within a firm (the integrated situation) rather than across a market (i.e. between two non-integrated firms).
[198] See O. Hart *Firms, Contracts, and Financial Structure* (Oxford: Clarendon Press, 1995) at p. 28. He later makes it clear that the theory applies most directly to owner-managed firms, but that the main insights of the property rights approach continue to be relevant to the large company cases; see *ibid.* pp. 61–62 and Chaps 6–8.
[199] Hart, n. 198 above, pp. 30–32 *passim*.
[200] Although obviously it will be the owner of any rights (choses in action) which it has against those people by virtue, e.g. of their employment contracts.
[201] Hart argues (citing Oliver Wendell Holmes Jr) that this view of ownership seems consistent with the standard view of ownership adopted by lawyers and seems to accord with common sense: Hart, n. 198 above, at p. 30.

investments increases since, given that it has more residual control rights, it will receive a greater fraction of the *ex post* surplus[202] created by such investments. On the other hand, the cost of integration is that the acquired firm's incentive to make relationship-specific investments decreases since, given that it has fewer residual control rights, it will receive a smaller fraction of the incremental *ex post* surplus created by its own investments.[203]

This proposition is then formalised in mathematical models.[204] The essence of the theory is that changes in ownership[205] can affect the severity of the hold-up problem that arises owing to the incompleteness of contracts for relationship-specific investments.[206] It remains to be seen whether the difficult insights of this theory will become as influential as those provided by the earlier transaction cost and agency cost analyses.

4 Assessment

How should we assess the relevance of these economic writings on the nature of the firm for the study of company law? First, it needs to be said that, famous though they are, there is a danger in presenting the above[207] theories as if they represented some settled orthodoxy within the discipline of economics. This is not the case. Work on the theory of the firm has evolved over many years and continues to do so both in terms of criticism of the existing theories and in the evolution of new theory. Even self-criticism is not lacking. For instance, Demsetz, later felt able to observe that the Alchian and Demsetz analysis of abating the cost of shirking helped to explain the firm's inner organisation but provided no rationale for the firm's existence.[208] Others have mounted sharp critiques of the theories; thus, in 1993, Winter, when considering the explanations offered by economics of the role of the business firm in a market economy, wrote of a state of incoherence, of significantly conflicting answers, of an interesting babble.[209] In recent years, many new theories, ideas and approaches

---

202 '*Ex post* surplus' broadly means the trading gains accruing to the parties after the contract has been entered into.
203 Hart, n. 198 above, at p. 33.
204 *Ibid.* at pp. 33 *et seq.* The theory seems to be assuming that the acquired firm retains considerable rights of autonomy as regards how it continues to undertake business.
205 Meaning, changes in the boundaries of firms (i.e. the integration of non-integrated firms).
206 This is paraphrased from Hart, n. 198 above, at p. 87. Hart uses the hold-up example, but points out (*ibid.*) that although the hold-up problem is a useful vehicle for developing the property rights approach, it is not an essential part of the approach. That is, even in the absence of a hold-up problem, asset ownership would still generally matter and what is required for a theory of asset ownership is that there is some inefficiency in the economic relationship, which the allocation of residual control rights can influence.
207 Or others.
208 S. Winter 'The Theory of the Firm Revisited' in O. Williamson and S. Winter (eds) *The Nature of the Firm: Origins, Evolution, and Development* (New York, Oxford: OUP, 1993) pp. 159, 168.
209 'On Coase, Competence, and the Corporation' in O. Williamson and S. Winter (eds) *The Nature of the Firm: Origins, Evolution, and Development* (New York, Oxford: OUP, 1993) p. 179. Also somewhat sceptical is C. Goodhart 'Economics and the Law: Too Much One-Way Traffic?' (1997) 60 MLR 1.

have emerged.[210] Hart makes reference to the vast literature on aspects of agency theory.[211]

How relevant are these theories to an understanding of company law? The question is difficult to answer with any precision. Roberta Romano, in 1993, expressed the enthusiastic view that corporate law has undergone a revolution and that legal scholarship has been transformed by the use of the new analytical apparatus of the economics of organisation.[212] There is obviously much truth in this in the sense, at least, that legal academics have continued to develop a respectful interest in the economic analysis of law. And certainly, some of the economic concepts have become common parlance among legal teachers and students. 'Reduction of agency costs' is a phrase which would be used freely in any discussion of laws dealing with the alignment of management with shareholder interests and people would share the connotations which it carried in respect of the function and policy of the law. But most lawyers are not economists, and whilst, with effort, they can get on top of the broad thrust of an economist's explanation of his theory, most will stop well short of being able to comprehend the formal mathematical proofs which are so important to many economists.

Perhaps a better approach is to ask how relevant economic theory would be to the reform of company law. Is this not the litmus test? If economic analysis could identify absurdities in the policies currently enforced by the law and then point the way to the socially optimal policy, it would be the indispensable tool of the law reformer and politician. Interest in economic analysis from law reform agencies has not been absent in recent years.[213] But the reliance on economic analysis seems tentative and very much at the experimental stage and it seems that, in the UK at any rate, most law reform in corporate law proceeds on the basis that the arguments are still lost and won by intuitive moral reasoning, the lawyers' and politicians' traditional chosen field of battle.

---

[210] See generally the collection in M. Casson (ed.) *The Theory of the Firm* (Cheltenham: Elgar, 1996) and the survey in P. Milgrom and J. Roberts 'Economic Theories of the Firm: Past, Present and Future' in P. Buckley and J. Michie (eds) *Firms, Organizations and Contracts: A Reader in Industrial Organization* (New York: OUP, 1996). For a fascinating analysis of corporate law which seeks to identify the common structure of corporate law across national boundaries, see R. Kraakman et al, *The Anatomy of Corporate Law: A Comparative and Functional Approach* (Oxford: OUP, 2004). Recent writings include: S. Deakin and A. Hughes 'Economic Efficiency and the Proceduralisation of Company Law' [1999] CFILR 169; M. Whincop 'Painting the Corporate Cathedral: The Protection of Entitlements in Corporate Law' (1999) 19 OJLS 19; S. Copp 'Company Law Reform and Economic Analysis: Establishing Boundaries' (2001) 1 JCLS 1; A. Macneil 'Company Law Rules: An Assessment from the Perspective of Incomplete Contract Theory' (2001) 1 JCLS 401; B. Maughan and M. McGuinness 'Towards an Economic Theory of the Corporation' (2001) 1 JCLS 141; J. Armour and M. Whincop 'The Proprietary Foundations of Corporate Law' (version 12 September 2004) available at http://www.hertig.ethz.ch/LE_2004–05_files/Papers/Armour_Corporations_2004.pdf.

[211] Hart, n. 198 above, p. 19.

[212] R. Romano *Foundations of Corporate Law* (New York: OUP, 1993) preface.

[213] The Law Commission's efforts to involve economic analysis in the reform of directors' duties quickly stimulated a sharp and lively debate: see Law Com. Consultation Paper No. 153, Scottish Law Commission Consultation Paper No. 105 *Company Directors: Regulating Conflicts of Interests and Formulating a Statement of Duties* (1998). See e.g.: C. Maughan and S. Copp 'The Law Commission and Economic Methodology: Values, Efficiency and Directors' Duties' (1999) 20 Co Law 109; S. Deakin and A. Hughes 'Economics and Company Law Reform: A Fruitful Partnership?' (1999) 20 Co Law 212; C. Maughan and S. Copp 'Company Law Reform and Economic Methodology Revisited' (2000) 21 Co Law 14.

Much of the problem with economic analysis of corporate law really stems from the fact that it does not tell us much more than our vague orthodox processes based on moral reasoning. Reference has been made to economic analysis of the concept of limited liability and yet it is clear that on careful examination, the ideas and analyses which the economists of the late 20th century expounded were already present in the committee reports and parliamentary debates of the mid-19th century.[214] This is largely because corporate law is founded on the intuitive concepts of efficiency embraced by the *laissez-faire* economic systems of the 19th century.[215] Neither the mid-19th century reformers nor the late-20th century economists were able to demonstrate a conclusive scientific case for having limited liability; the arguments run either way and the balance of them falls broadly in favour of limited liability.[216] The 19th-century reformers stumbled towards having limited liability and the 20th-century economic justifications chart a similarly erratic path.

Part of the difficulty lies with the complexity of the problems which confront any reformers. Many of the economists' articles recognise the need to try to produce formal models of the theories.[217] But formal models tend to be a simplification of the real world. If it tries to embrace all the considerations needed, the model loses its force. As Hanson and Hart have pointed out, the most common and potent criticisms of law and economics are either that its models are indefensibly unrealistic or that the analysis is insufficiently scientific.[218] However, we should not lose sight of two important facts. First, that an economic analysis of a problem will often throw up useful perspectives which can then be assessed using the normal intuitive processes which lawyers and law reformers usually use. Although the economic perspective will be geared towards showing whether the outcome is efficient or not, this will often be of interest to the reformer, since in the absence of some other moral value which is felt should govern the situation and therefore trumps efficiency, the reformer will probably be morally right to opt for a law which produces an efficient outcome. Secondly, that in some situations the economist will have empirical research behind his analysis which will tend to show how the existing law or an existing problem is actually affecting matters and so it is possible that there are occasions when the input of law and economics will tend towards being conclusive of a policy discussion which may have been going on for years on an intuitive basis.

3.7 FUTURE ISSUES

It is interesting to speculate as to the path of future scholarship in the legal theory of company law. First, it is clear that what might be called 'technical' improvements will continue to be made as a result of law reform agencies and scholars identifying areas of law which are not working in the way that people feel they should. Many

---

[214] This is demonstrated in detail in B. Pettet 'Limited Liability – A Principle for the 21st Century' (1995) 48 *Current Legal Problems* (Part 2) 125 at pp. 143–150.

[215] See in particular, Posner's comments; cited in Pettet, n. 214 above, at p. 143.

[216] See Pettet, n. 214 above, pp. 141–157.

[217] *Ibid.* at p. 156, nn. 142, 153.

[218] J. Hanson and M. Hart 'Law and Economics' in D. Patterson (ed.) *A Companion to Philosophy of Law and Legal Theory* (Oxford: Blackwell, 1996) p. 329.

of the thoughtful recommendations of the Company Law Review which is discussed in the next chapter are of this quality. Certain procedural requirements will be removed, others will be introduced; and unless there is some overriding moral reason, all changes will be made in order to enable the corporate law system to function more efficiently, or to put it in economic terms, to reduce transaction costs.

Secondly, globalisation will continue to provide a fertile area for research and interest not only by scholars but also by companies themselves who will increasingly be forced to consider whether it is worth their while getting a listing on a stock market other than that operated by their own country. The clash between the two rival systems of corporate governance, dispersed ownership and concentrated ownership, is only just beginning.

Finally, the stakeholder debate will not go away. It will survive at two levels. First, if stakeholder policies do in fact produce more efficient firms, and more efficient economies, then, in the course of time, this will become painfully apparent to countries which have not developed such systems and it will be difficult for them to compete successfully in international markets. Secondly, even if the pursuit of stakeholder policies is in fact, either not proven to be more efficient or is even seen to damage corporate performance at the margin, it may well nevertheless come to be seen as one of those areas of corporate law where our usual striving to produce an efficient system needs to be trumped by the moral imperative of adopting corporate structures which ensure a humanisation of corporate power.

4

CURRENT REFORM MECHANISMS

4.1 MODERN COMPANY LAW

There could not be a more exciting time to be writing about company law. Early in the new century and the new millennium we find ourselves in the midst of a rolling programme of reform of company law. In March 1998 the DTI published a Consultation Paper entitled *Modern Company Law – for a competitive economy*,[1] the effect of which was to launch a complex review mechanism spanning several years. These mechanisms and the progress to date are explored below and set in the context of 150 years of company law reform by the Department of Trade and Industry and its predecessors.

4.2 THE AGENCIES OF COMPANY LAW REFORM

A Department of Trade and Industry

The basic structure of UK company law, the 1844 Act and its successors, which created the facility of incorporation by registration, was the product of parliamentary reform mechanisms, of committees, and of political and commercial pressure groups. It was not the product of the judge-made common law. Although judges have had an influence on the incremental development of the law, their influence has been relatively slight; company law has developed with periodic but distinct leaps forward, usually preceded by the enunciation of clear and distinct policy.

From the earliest pre-1844 days the Department of Trade and Industry or its predecessor, the Board of Trade, has had a dominant role in the process of company law reform. It was the trenchant energy of William Ewart Gladstone as President of the Board of Trade, which saw through the passage of the 1844 Act which gave birth to the UK company law system. Thereafter, although the DTI would periodically produce its own agenda derived from difficulties which had been brought to its attention or which it had come across, company law reform was often the product of recommendations of committees set up to inquire into particular problems or simply to rove through known problem areas.

If a major reform has been in contemplation, then the input of time and care is apparent from a reading of the committee reports, which remain fascinating sources

---

[1] To avoid confusion with an earlier less ambitious review launched in 1992, it will be referred to in this book as the 'Company Law Review'.

of company law history. For instance, there were four inquiries in which the matter of limited liability was canvassed:[2] Bellenden Ker's Report (on limited partnerships) in 1837,[3] the Select Committee on Investments for the Savings of the Middle and Working Classes 1850,[4] the Select Committee on the Law of Partnership 1851,[5] and the Royal Mercantile Law Commission 1854.[6] Eventually, Parliament took the plunge and enacted the controversial Limited Liability Act 1855, which added the facility of limited liability to the 1844 Act's facility of incorporation by registration.

In the 20th century, the usual pattern was that a committee would be set up periodically under the chairmanship of a member of the judiciary distinguished in company law. The Loreburn Committee of 1906 led to the introduction of the distinction between public and private companies. Other reforms, of a wide-ranging nature, were instituted as a result of the Wrenbury Committee (1918). The Greene Committee (1926) left its mark on company law by[7] the introduction of the first legislation against financial assistance for the purchase of shares. The Cohen Committee (1945) was responsible for the introduction of legislation against directors' loans, and for the 1948 consolidation. The last such committee was chaired by Lord Jenkins. Its report in 1962 was full of recommendations. Many of these never reached the statute book but one that did changed UK company law forever, for it was the Jenkins Committee which recommended the introduction of the unfair prejudice remedy. Although these committees were given wide terms of reference, they generally remained focused on specific problems which had become apparent to practitioners generally or to the DTI. They were not committees which embarked on a wholesale reassessment of fundamental principles.

The Jenkins Committee was the last of its type. For some years thereafter, the DTI adopted the policy of securing the appointment of committees to look into specific areas of malfunction such as the Cork Report[8] which led to reforms in the Insolvency Act 1985. Another technique was to secure the appointment of a distinguished academic to look into a matter and report. In this way the appointment of Professor Jim Gower produced the Gower Report[9] and ultimately led to the Financial Services Act 1986 which set up the first comprehensive system for the regulation of financial services in the UK. Other academics were asked to take on the task of inquiring into particularly knotty academic problems, such as *ultra vires*[10] and company charges.[11]

In November 1992 the DTI announced that it was launching a 'Company Law Review'.[12] This turned out to be a series of consultation documents on various

---

[2] Although no significant weight of opinion in favour of the principle emerged.

[3] BPP Vol. XLIV.

[4] BPP Vol. XIX.

[5] BPP Vol. XVII.

[6] BPP Vol. XXVII.

[7] Among other things.

[8] Sir Kenneth Cork *Report of the Review Committee on Insolvency Law and Practice* (London, Cmnd. 8558, 1982); also the White Paper *A Revised Framework for Insolvency Law* (Cmnd. 9175, 1984).

[9] See further p. 339.

[10] Professor D. Prentice produced a report on the *ultra vires* doctrine in 1986.

[11] Professor A. Diamond produced a report into company charges in 1989.

[12] This is not to be confused with the later Company Law Review launched in March 1998. They are very different creatures.

problem areas. Although it covered a broad range of topics it was clear that this 'Review' was not intended to be a thorough re-examination of basic principles. By the beginning of 1995 the DTI had produced detailed consultation papers and proposals covering, such topics as: financial assistance for the purchase of shares; shareholders' written resolutions; simplifying accounts; simplifying disclosure of interests in shares; a new company voluntary arrangements procedure; partnership companies; simpler summary financial statements; late payment of commercial debts; draft uncertificated securities regulations for CREST; registration of charges; and model articles of association for partnership companies. Many of these led to legislation[13] and others will in time. Some proposals have been undergoing further refinement.[14] It seems that the 1992 Company Law Review ended around 1994–95. Thereafter, the DTI simply continued its work of reform by producing consultation documents[15] and they no longer bore the legend 'Company Law Review', but merely, 'Company Law Reform'.

The post-1995 consultation documents on 'Company Law Reform' covered a similarly diverse range of matters: Disclosure of Directors' Emoluments Draft Regulations;[16] Shareholder Communications at the Annual General Meeting;[17] Private Shareholders: Corporate Governance Rights;[18] Disclosure of Directors' and Company Secretaries' Particulars;[19] Share Buybacks;[20] Investment Companies Share Repurchases using Capital Profits;[21] Political Donations by Companies;[22] Directors' Remuneration.[23] A good number of the issues dealt with in these consultation papers are unresolved and some have found their way onto the agendas of the 1998 Company Law Review described below.

Additionally, there have been two big projects on shareholder remedies and limited liability partnerships. The first of these had largely been a Law Commission venture[24] but the DTI later produced its own consultation document.[25] For the second of them the DTI produced three consultation documents, and this work has recently found fruition in the passing of the Limited Liability Partnerships Act 2000.[26]

As has been seen above, the DTI has also been responsible for the sometimes awesome task of implementing the EC Directives on company law and financial

---

[13] E.g. the consultation letter of August 1993 on the problems with the new written resolution procedure in the Companies Act 1989 led to the Deregulation (Resolutions of Private Companies) Order 1996 (SI 1996 No. 1471).

[14] E.g. the well-known difficulties with the area of financial assistance for the purchase of shares were examined in Consultation Document (October 1993) *Proposals for the Reform of Sections 151–158 of the Companies Act 1985*, but there was subsequent output on this in September 1994, November 1996, and April 1997. The matter has since been taken up in the 1998 Company Law Review (see below).

[15] And prepared to conduct a Review of far greater magnitude.

[16] January 1996.

[17] April 1996.

[18] November 1996.

[19] February 1997.

[20] May 1998.

[21] March 1999.

[22] March 1999.

[23] July 1999.

[24] See Law Com. Consultation Paper No. 142 and the Law Com. Report No. 246 on *Shareholder Remedies*.

[25] *Shareholder Remedies* (November 1998).

[26] See further p. 21 above.

services, although since 1992 the Treasury has had responsibility for such matters relating to financial services.

B The Law Commission

Since 1994 the Law Commission[27] has been making a significant input into company law reform. It has investigated various matters which have been referred to it by the DTI and has produced consultation papers, reports and draft legislation. Its investigations have ranged across company law, covering such matters as alternatives to small private companies, the offence of corporate killing, review of partnership law, codification and review of directors' duties, execution of documents and shareholder litigation. In addition, the Law Commissioners have given unstinting leadership to the academic and practitioner communities with the intention of widening the constituency of input into the inquiry and reform process. The work of the Law Commission will have done much to assist the task of the 1998 Review in some areas.

C City and institutional input

In recent years it has become apparent[28] that the City, its institutions and professions are willing to participate in the reform process. The example of the work of the Cadbury, Greenbury and Hampel committees on corporate governance, in conjunction with the Stock Exchange, spanning nearly a decade, has shown the innovative possibilities of self-regulation.

Also looking at company law reform has been the Law Society's Standing Committee on Company Law. Comprised of leading practitioners and academics, this group have taken a keen interest in reform. In 1991 they produced a memorandum document called 'The Reform of Company Law' which critically considered the adequacy of the present structures of company law and recommended the establishment of an independent standing Company Law Commission which would harness the experience of civil servants, practitioners and academics. It would publish draft legislation well in advance of enactment so that it could be scrutinised publicly. The Law Society's Standing Committee has also been performing the useful function of responding to the output of DTI and Law Commission consultation material.[29]

The Institute of Chartered Accountants of England and Wales (ICAEW) has also made considered responses on matters which would affect the interests of those engaged in the financial reporting industry. They have been particularly active in recent years in trying get something done about what is widely seen as the over-exposure of accountants to litigation in respect of their audit functions. Other accountancy bodies have from time to time also joined the debate.

---

[27] On some projects, such as the investigation into shareholder remedies, the Scottish Law Commission also is involved.

[28] See p. 194 below.

[29] The Financial Law Steering Group has made similar inputs.

D Academics

Down the years the academics have also contributed, not only through the traditional forms of academic output, of writing articles and books, but also through undertaking investigations into problem areas, through sitting on reform committees, editing journals and collections, or generally getting involved in the reform process.[30]

E European Commission

The input made to company law by the EC Harmonisation Programme has already been described, as have the major new initiatives set out in the Commission's Action Plan for Company Law.[31] As will be seen later, there has been a similar, but more radical, programme in the field of capital markets law, designed to create a single market in financial services within the EU.[32]

4.3 THE 1998 REVIEW

A Structure

The Consultation Paper *Modern Company Law – for a competitive economy* set out the mechanisms and the timetable for the running of the Company Law Review. It seemed that the Review was to be substantially a DTI project. The structure of the mechanisms for bringing about the Review preserve the historical primacy of the role of the DTI in company law reform. Overseeing the management of the project was the Steering Group, and this was chaired by the Director of the Company Law and Investigations Directorate of the DTI. There was also a Consultative Committee chaired by the DTI's Director General, Competition and Markets. The Project Director was Jonathan Rickford.

The Steering Group was a small committee made up of senior lawyers, representatives of large and small businesses, the chairpersons of the various Working Groups, a Scottish representative and the Project Director. The role of the Steering Group was to ensure that the outcome was clear in concept, well-expressed, internally coherent and workable. The Consultative Committee included representatives from key groups such as the accountancy bodies, the Law Society, the CBI, the TUC, other government departments. Wider interests were also represented including those of small business and shareholders. In addition to the Steering Group and the Consultative Committee, there were Working Groups which did much of the work of analysis of policy and problems and producing draft proposals under the overview of the Steering Committee. At the outset of the Review it was intended that the Final Report would be published in conjunction with a White Paper by March 2001.

---

[30] See e.g. the story of Professor Gower's role in creating the UK's first comprehensive system of securities regulation at p. 318 below.

[31] At p. 13 above.

[32] See further p. 334 below.

B Guiding principles

It was clear from the objectives and terms of reference set out in the Consultation Paper[33] that the primary guiding principle is intended to be the competitiveness of British companies. The objectives and terms of reference overlapped to some extent but several clear themes emerged. The Review was to help achieve a company law which was competitive in the sense of helping to provide a framework within which British businesses can grow and compete effectively in an economic sense. But the DTI also had in mind what is sometimes referred to as the 'Delaware effect', under which a legal system which has a desirable framework of company law will attract businesses to it with all the benefits to the economy which that brings in terms of employment and investment.

Another theme was the need for company law to embrace a basic *laissez-faire* approach to the regulation of the business-world giving maximum choice and freedom of action to the managers of the business and yet square this with the need to secure the interests of others who have contact with or are in some way involved with the business. This is expressed to include not only those who provide the working capital of the business, shareholders and creditors, but also the employees and possibly others. Essentially here, the Review was to be required to investigate whether company law strikes the right balance between these interests, and the language used was sufficiently wide arguably to require a consideration of the desirability of concepts of stakeholder company law. The promotion of proper standards of corporate governance was another area for investigation and in particular here, the pros and cons of the use of self-regulation needed to be considered.

Accessibility of the law was another main focus. Over the years, company law has acquired a reputation as a field of law known only to lawyers, and even then yielding up its secrets only after painstaking analysis. The Review was required to consider how the drafting of company law can be modernised, so as to ensure that it can be understood by the people in the business world who are going to have to use it.

C Swift progress

The Company Law Review speedily produced a series of high quality and very clearly written consultation documents.[34] The first of these, *The Strategic Framework*,[35] described the way in which the Review had started its work and the future arrangements for the process. The document discussed the objectives of the Review:[36] the predominant objective was law for a competitive economy, and modern law, in the sense of being well fitted to meet current and foreseeable future

---

[33] See generally, *Modern Company Law – for a competitive economy* (London: Department of Trade and Industry, 1998), paras 5.1–5.2.

[34] The Review has also produced a number of other useful background documents, such as: C. Jordan *International Survey of Company Law* and Centre for Law and Business, Faculty of Law, University of Manchester *Company Law in Europe: Recent Developments*. These and others are accessible on the Review website: http://www.dti.gov.uk. Also available on the website are summaries of the responses to the consultation procedures.

[35] DTI Consultation Document (February 1999).

[36] DTI Consultation Document *The Strategic Framework* pp. 8 *et seq.*

needs; with an optimal balance between freedom for management and risk of abuse; the reforms should be coherent and comprehensive; and take account of key trends such as globalisation, Europeanisation, other regulators, information technologies, changing patterns of share ownership and the increasing importance of human resources; small private companies were particularly important in job creation and needed an optimal legal climate. With the objectives in mind, the Review sought to develop Guiding Principles: facilitation of transactions, with a presumption against prescription; accessibility, ease of use and identification of the law; observance of regulatory boundaries.

Eight key issues were then identified as priorities for early work.[37] Seen as of paramount importance were 'the scope of company law' (i.e. the stakeholder issue) and the 'problems of the small, or closely-held company'. Also key issues were the questions of the boundaries of regulatory and self-regulatory bodies, and, international aspects of law. Finally, also chosen as 'key' were company formation, company powers, capital maintenance, and, electronic communications and information.

The later consultation documents obviously reflected the choice of these key issues and contained ideas and sought views on specific matters. The second consultation document *Company General Meetings and Shareholder Communication*[38] raised the question of whether the law should abandon the requirement for public companies to hold an annual general meeting and considered the use of electronic communication. The third consultation document *Company Formation and Capital Maintenance*[39] contained radical proposals for the restructuring of the constitution of the company, and relaxations of the capital maintenance doctrine. *Reforming the Law Concerning Oversea Companies*[40] reviewed the legal treatment of companies which are incorporated overseas and which operate in the UK without incorporating there. The fifth consultation document *Developing the Framework*[41] dealt with corporate governance and the policies for the legislative treatment of small private companies. This document was also described as the second 'strategic' document since it contained plans for how the remainder of the work of the Review should proceed. Subsequently there has been a further document *Capital Maintenance: Other Issues*[42] focusing on a small number of residual technical issues. Then a consultation document called *Registration of Company Charges*[43] and lastly, drawing together many of the previous issues, came *Completing the Structure*[44] which prepared the way for the final report.

D The Final Report and subsequent developments

The Review Steering Group presented the Final Report (*Modern Company Law for a Competitive Economy Final Report*) to the Secretary of State in June 2001.[45] The

[37] *Ibid.* p. 19.
[38] DTI Consultation Document (October 1999).
[39] DTI Consultation Document (October 1999).
[40] DTI Consultation Document (October 1999).
[41] DTI Consultation Document (March 2000).
[42] DTI Consultation Document (June 2000).
[43] DTI Consultation Document (October 2000).
[44] DTI Consultation Document (November 2000).
[45] The Final Report is available on the web at http://www.dti.gov.uk/cld.

Report is in three parts, Part 1 consisting of an overview of the objectives and core proposals. Part II goes into the recommendations in more detail and Part III contains examples of how parts of the legislation might be drafted. As would be expected, it is a final gathering together of the ideas which were the subject of extensive discussion and consultation during the Review years. The Report identifies three core policies which are at the heart of the Review: (1) the 'think small first' stategy for small and private companies, (2) an open, inclusive and flexible regime for company governance, (3) an appropriate institutional structure for law reform, enforcement and related matters.

Further references are made to some of the detail of the Final Report's recommendations in chapters throughout this book.

Subsequently, in July 2002 the government produced a White Paper *Modernising Company Law*[46] setting out some of its proposals. It did not accept all the recommendations of the Review. However a 'mini' Bill, the Companies (Audit, Investigations and Community Enterprise) Bill, was introduced in the House of Lords on 3 December 2003 and passed into legislation the following year. The Act seeks to strengthen several regimes: the regulation of auditors; the enforcement of accounting and reporting requirements; and company investigations. It also makes provision for the setting up of Community Interest Companies (CICs). Its provisions are dealt with at appropriate places in this book.[47]

In the meantime, work continues on implementing some of the main ideas in the Company Law Review. The DTI intend to produce a draft Bill for consultation before it is introduced to Parliament. There is no current indication of timescales. At the time of writing the latest indication of the shape of future legislation is the document *Company Law. Flexibility and Accessibility: A Consultative Document* (May 2004, DTI).

E Treatment in this book

This chapter has largely confined itself to illustrating the mechanisms at work in the reform process and it has not considered in detail any of the substantive ideas being raised by the Company Law Review. This is because it is felt that it will be of more use to the reader if the main Review ideas are considered alongside the discussion of those areas of the law to which they primarily relate.[48]

---

[46] Cmnd. 5553; also on the DTI website.

[47] Also dealt with in appropriate places are the relevant provisions of the Enterprise Act 2002, the provisions of which mainly relate to insolvency law.

[48] For coverage of the Company Law Review elsewhere in the text, see pp. 4, 17, 46, 64–66, 111, 130, 142, 159, 178, 193, 210–211, 228–230, 249, 275, 292–293, 308–309.

PART II

THE CONSTITUTION OF THE COMPANY

5

ENTRENCHMENT OF RIGHTS

5.1 ENTRENCHMENT OF EXPECTATION VERSUS FLEXIBILITY

When the promoters of a company set it up they usually have in mind that the company will grow and that they will all make a great deal of money out of it. The other major concern will be how much money each one of them will make and how much influence and power each will have over the company's operations. The legal rules relating to shares go some way towards settling these issues. The organisation of the constitution of the company largely completes that picture. This chapter is concerned with the way company law attempts to resolve the tension which arises between, on the one hand, the desire of the promoters to secure for themselves firmly entrenched rights and, on the other hand, their realisation that if the company is to grow and respond to business situations, it will be necessary for those entrenched rights to give way sometimes to change. We will see that the law provides some quite sophisticated methods of resolving these issues. This chapter therefore looks first at the way in which the constitutions of companies are organised and then looks at the range of processes by which the various rights enshrined in the constitution can be altered. Chapter 6 describes the way in which the constitution sets up the major functioning parts of the company and considers the difficult question of limitations on corporate power contained in the constitution. Chapter 7 investigates how the constitution impacts on mechanisms whereby the company enters into contractual relations with third parties.

5.2 MEMORANDUM OF ASSOCIATION

As has been seen, the constitution of most companies consists of two formal documents: the memorandum of association and the articles of association.[1] Some companies also have what is in effect a third constitutional document called a shareholder agreement.

In a sense, compared to the articles, the memorandum of association can be seen as the 'senior' constitutional document. This will become particularly apparent later in this chapter when we see that rights which are enshrined in the

---

[1] A memorandum of association is essential, whereas it is not strictly necessary for a company limited by shares to have articles of association, although most do. Articles are necessary for unlimited companies or companies limited by guarantee; see Companies Act 1985, s. 7 (1).

memorandum can be a lot more difficult to alter than if they had been contained in the articles.[2]

The Companies Act 1985 prescribes what the memorandum of association shall consist of, but subject to that, other matters can be added. The 1985 Act establishes[3] that the memorandum must state: (a) the name of the company; (b) whether the registered office is to be situated in England and Wales, or in Scotland (similar provisions pertain in Northern Ireland);[4] and (c) the objects of the company. The memorandum of a company limited by shares must also state that the liability of its members is limited[5] and also state the amount of share capital with which the company proposes to be registered and the division of the share capital into shares of a fixed amount. The Companies (Tables A to F) Regulations 1985[6] specify various formats, and the memorandum must comply with one of these.[7] It is apparent from those formats that the memorandum must also contain what is usually referred to as an 'association clause', which declares that 'we the subscribers to this memorandum of association wish to be formed into a company pursuant to this memorandum: and we agree to take the number of shares shown opposite our respective names'.[8] Most of these matters are technical and not of great significance although the objects clause has had a considerable impact on the development of the law and will be considered in detail in the next chapter.[9] The memorandum of association binds the members of the company under the same principles as apply to the articles of association, namely by the operation of s. 14 of the 1985 Act. Since all the case law on this convoluted topic relates to the articles of association, discussion of it appears below.

5.3 ARTICLES OF ASSOCIATION

The articles of association set out the internal rules as to the operation of the company and, for example, cover matters relating to meetings, such as quorum, length of notice, voting, and matters relating to directors such as appointment and retirement, remuneration, proceedings. The Companies (Tables A to F)

---

[2] The seniority idea also sometimes has significance when it comes to construing the constitution as a totality. In *Re Duncan Gilmour* [1952] 2 All ER 871, there was a discrepancy between the rights given by the memorandum and those given by the articles. The articles gave more extensive rights to preference shareholders and they were arguing that they were entitled to these. It was held that the memorandum was the primary document and that if it was clear on its face, then doubts could not be raised as to its meaning by reference to the articles. If, however, the memorandum was on its face ambiguous, and posing difficulties of construction, reference to the articles is possible to help resolve the doubt. In the circumstances the memorandum was unambiguous and so the preference shareholders were disappointed.

[3] By s. 2.

[4] As regards Wales, the 1985 Act provides, *inter alia*, that as an alternative to 'England and Wales' the memorandum may contain a statement that the company's registered office is to be situated in Wales.

[5] There are further provisions about companies limited by guarantee.

[6] SI 1985 No. 805.

[7] Or be as near to that form as circumstances permit; see generally Companies Act 1985, s. 3.

[8] By the Companies Act 1985, s. 2 (6) the memorandum must be signed by each subscriber in the presence of at least one witness. If the company is to be a public company, the memorandum must state that fact, immediately after the statement of its name; see Table F, para. 2.

[9] The capital clause is revisited on p. 263 below and as regards company names, see p. 41 above.

Regulations 1985[10] contain a common form list (Table A) of the sort of provisions that most companies would probably require. In practice most companies adopt Table A but make modifications which are necessary in their particular case. It is important to realise that the effect of s. 8 (2) of the Companies Act 1985 is that, as regards companies limited by shares, Table A will automatically apply unless, and to the extent that it is excluded.[11]

One would have thought that the law would provide that the members would be able to enforce the articles. Otherwise there would not be much point in the first place of going through the process of meeting with professional advisers and getting them (and the memorandum) drafted up and then registered with the Registrar of Companies as public documents. There would not, it might be thought, be much point in calling them articles of *association*, if they were not meant to govern the way in which the members thereafter *associate*. Unfortunately, for those of this mind, UK case law has prepared a disappointment. The mechanism adopted by the draftsman of the legislation was simple enough. He must have instinctively turned to the idea which was in use for pre-1844 deed of settlement companies which, being essentially partnerships by nature, linked their members to one another by the use of contractual obligations. The result, which has passed down through successive Companies Acts, is what is now s. 14 (1) of the 1985 Act, which provides:

> Subject to the provisions of this Act, the memorandum and articles, when registered, bind the company and its members to the same extent as if they respectively had been signed and sealed by each member, and contained covenants on the part of each member to observe all the provisions of the memorandum and of the articles.

The courts have admitted a certain level of enforceability. They have also developed doctrines which restrict enforceability. The former are considered next.

First, and not surprisingly, given the background analogy with partnerships inherent in s. 14, it has been held that the members can enforce the articles against each other. This is apparent from the somewhat difficult case of *Rayfield v Hands*.[12] Here, article 11 of the articles of association provided that a member who wished to transfer his shares should inform the directors of that intention and the said directors 'will take the said shares equally between them at a fair value'. This was probably meant to be a kind of pre-emption clause designed to give the directors and shareholders a method of preventing transfer to an outsider who they would not want to work with. But the wording, far from giving them merely a right of pre-emption, actually cast an obligation upon them to buy the shares. Rayfield had spotted this and argued that they should take his shares. Vaisey J, whilst lamenting that the articles were 'very inarticulately drawn by a person who was not legally expert', nevertheless upheld his claim. So the case is an example of the powerful

---

[10] SI 1985 No. 805.

[11] From time to time the legislature amends Table A. The Table A which forms a company's articles will be that in force at the date of incorporation: Companies Act 1985, s. 8 (2). A later change in Table A will not automatically change the articles of the company (s. 8 (3)) and so if the company wants the up-to-date Table A it will have to change its articles. For this reason, there are companies in existence whose articles adopt Table A, either expressly or automatically (by not excluding it) and the Table A in question is an earlier version than the 1985 one.

[12] [1958] 2 All ER 194.

contractual effect that the articles can have between the members. There is a difficult aspect of the decision which will be looked at below when considering the limitations on enforceability.

Secondly, it has been established that a member may enforce the articles against the company.[13] In *Wood* v *Odessa Waterworks Co.*[14] the articles empowered the directors to declare a dividend 'to be paid' to the shareholder. Wood was a shareholder who objected to the directors' plan to pay a dividend in debentures rather than cash. He successfully obtained an injunction to prevent payment by the issue of debentures since the court accepted his argument that 'to be paid' *prima facie* meant paid in 'cash'. Wood was able to enforce the articles against the company here, even though the shareholders in general meeting had resolved, by ordinary resolution, to carry out the directors' idea. The case is a very important example of the principle of majority rule,[15] which normally ascribes a binding effect to a decision of the majority of shareholders in general meeting, giving way to the principle that a shareholder can enforce the constitution.

Thirdly, as the converse of the second situation, it has been held that a company can enforce the articles against the members. This is clear from the seminal case, *Borland's Trustee* v *Steel Brothers & Co Ltd.*[16]

However, these three situations are subject to two doctrines which in some circumstances will deprive the member of the chance of enforcing the article. One doctrine is connected with the 'rule' in *Foss* v *Harbottle*[17] which in some situations will maintain that matters of internal management, or internal disputes between the shareholders, cannot be litigated. In at least one case[18] the courts have used this principle to prevent a member from being able to insist that the management or conduct of the company be conducted in accordance with the memorandum or articles. This whole topic is explored later in this book.[19] The other doctrine, which will be examined in detail here, is that of insider and outsider rights.

Broadly, the idea is that, under s. 14, a member may only enforce those rights which affect him in his capacity as a member (an insider) and that he may not enforce rights which affect him in some other capacity, such as a director (an outsider). It may seem strange to refer to a director as an outsider in this context, since in a very obvious sense he or she is intimately connected with the company, but what is meant is that the director is, *in that capacity*, a stranger to the membership contract and all its mutual obligations. The doctrine was first set out in authorita-

---

[13] In this context, there is a problem at the outset arising from the wording of s. 14, namely that there is no mention of the company signing and sealing the memorandum and articles, and so under what principle does it become bound, at all? The problem was considered by Astbury J in *Hickman* v *Kent or Romney Marsh Sheepbreeders Association* [1915] 1 Ch 881 and his solution, which seems sensible, was 'the section cannot mean that the company is not to be bound when it says that it is to be bound ... Much of the difficulty is removed if ... the company is treated in law as a party to its own memorandum and articles': *ibid.* at p. 897.

[14] (1889) 42 Ch D 676.

[15] See further, at p. 214 below.

[16] [1901] 1 Ch 279.

[17] (1843) 2 Hare 461.

[18] *McDougall* v *Gardiner (No. 2)* (1875) 1 Ch D 13, CA.

[19] At p. 227.

tive form in 1915 by Astbury J in *Hickman* v *Kent or Romney Marsh Sheepbreeders Association*.[20] He reviewed the case law and concluded that:

> ... No right merely purporting to be given by an article to a person, whether a member or not, in a capacity other than that of a member, as, for instance, as solicitor, promoter, director, can be enforced against the company.[21]

The effects of the doctrine are quite dramatic, so that, for instance, if the articles provide for a salary for a director, he will not be able to rely on s. 14 to sue for it.[22]

The doctrine was taken up by the Court of Appeal in 1938 in *Beattie* v *E. Beattie Ltd*,[23] where the issues were subtle but the result was a clear enunciation and application of the doctrine. In *Beattie* the issue arose as to whether part of an action could be stayed pursuant to an arbitration clause contained in the articles. The action was being brought by a shareholder against one of the directors, Ernest Beattie (who was also a shareholder), and the part of the action which formed the subject matter of these proceedings was brought in respect of alleged improper payments of remuneration by him. Ernest Beattie applied to have this part of the action stayed on the basis of an arbitration clause contained in clause 133 of the articles which provided that disputes arising between the company and any member or members (concerning various matters) should be referred to arbitration. In order to bring himself within the Arbitration Act then governing the situation it was necessary for Ernest Beattie to be able to point to a written agreement (i.e. contract) for submission to arbitration. There was nothing except the articles, and so it became necessary for Ernest Beattie to establish that clause 133 of the articles constituted a contract to submit to arbitration. This threw the spotlight onto the contractual effect of what is now s. 14.[24] Sir Wilfred Greene MR delivered the judgment of the court[25] holding that:

> ... Ernest Beattie is, and was at all material times, a director of the company and it is against him, in his capacity as director that these claims are made. It is as a director in charge of the company's funds that he is responsible for their proper application, in accordance with the regulations which govern the company ... [T]he contractual force given to the articles of association by the section is limited to such provisions of the articles as apply to the relationship of the members in their capacity as members ... the real matter which is here being litigated is a dispute between the company and the appellant in his capacity as a director ... and by seeking to have it referred [to arbitration] he is not, in my

---

[20] [1915] 1 Ch 881. An earlier example is said to be *Eley* v *Positive Life Co.* (1876) 1 Ex D 88 but this is the explanation offered in *Hickman* although it is difficult to discern the principle in the case itself.

[21] [1915] 1 Ch 881 at p. 900.

[22] This is the effect of *Eley*, n. 20 above, as explained in *Hickman*. The director may however be able to rely on the doctrine of implied contract under which the courts will infer the existence of a contract from the course of dealing between the parties and obtain the detailed terms by reference to the articles; see *Swabey* v *Port Darwin Gold Mining Co.* (1889) 1 Meg 385; *Re New British Iron Co, ex parte Beckwith* [1898] 1 Ch 324. In practice, a written employment contract is used to avoid these problems.

[23] [1938] 1 Ch 708.

[24] Actually then, s. 20 of the Companies Act 1929. There was also another issue in the case, namely whether clause 133 of the articles, on its true construction, actually applied to the present dispute. It had been held at first instance that it did not apply, but the Court of Appeal did not 'find it necessary to resolve' that matter: [1938] 1 Ch 708 at p. 719.

[25] Scott and Clauson LJJ concurring.

judgment, seeking to enforce a right which is common to himself and all other members . . . He is not seeking to enforce a right to call on the company to arbitrate a dispute which is only accidentally a dispute with himself. He is seeking, as a disputant, to have the dispute to which he is a party referred. That is sufficient to differentiate it from the right which is common to all the other members of the company under this article.[26]

It is clear from this passage that a major part of the underlying rationale of the insider/outsider doctrine is the notion that insider rights are those which are common between the shareholders. This idea seemed to have helped Vaisey J reach his decision in *Rayfield* v *Hands*[27] for a possible objection to his conclusion was that the action was being brought against the directors (i.e. outsiders). On the other hand, the right to have their shares purchased was common to all the members and he laid stress on the idea that the articles were 'a contract between a member and member-directors in relation to their holdings of the companies shares'.[28]

Not surprisingly, this area of law has been the subject of steady academic scrutiny spanning many decades. The literature has variously questioned the wisdom of the doctrine, puzzled to find a rationale, and struggled with cases that seem out of line. Writing in 1957,[29] Lord Wedderburn developed the idea that a member would sometimes be able to enforce indirectly an outsider right as long as he made it clear that he was suing in his capacity as a member. Using this concept, he sought to explain the House of Lords' decision in *Salmon* v *Quinn & Axtens*,[30] where one of two managing directors was entitled to an injunction to enforce a veto over certain board action which had been given to him in the articles. In 1972,[31] Goldberg endeavoured to enunciate a new explanation of what was really going on in the cases. He argued that the true position was that a member would be able to enforce any clause in the articles provided that the clause was ascribing a function to a particular organ of the company. Thus he explained the *Salmon* case on the basis that the organ prescribed by the articles for the particular board action was: board + two managing directors. Salmon's action was designed to ensure that that organ was indeed the one which carried out that function, and so succeeded. One of the difficulties with this thesis is that the cases do not purport to be decided on this basis. Drury, writing in 1986,[32] argued that this area had to be looked at in the light of the fact that the articles were a long-term contract and therefore it was inappropriate that a party could point to particular clauses and demand that they be enforced. The difficulty with this is that, as will be seen below, the legislation contains detailed provisions under which the articles and class rights can be altered, with the obvious purpose of providing long-term flexibility, but with built in safeguards of

---

[26] [1938] 1 Ch 708 at pp. 718–722 *passim.*
[27] [1958] 2 All ER 194, see p. 95 above.
[28] [1958] 2 All ER 194 at p. 199. Subsequently, the doctrine has received tacit support in the House of Lords in *Soden* v *British and Commonwealth Holdings plc* [1997] BCC 952.
[29] 'Shareholders' Rights and the Rule in *Foss* v *Harbottle*' [1957] CLJ 194 at p. 212 and [1958] CLJ 93.
[30] [1909] AC 442. It is noteworthy that the decision pre-dated the high level of articulation given to the doctrine in *Hickman.*
[31] 'The Enforcement of Outsider-Rights under s. 20 (1) of the Companies Act 1948' (1972) 35 MLR 362.
[32] 'The Relative Nature of a Shareholder's Right to Enforce the Company Contract' [1986] CLJ 219.

checks and balances so as to give a measure of protection to settled expectations and bargains.

Gregory's article,[33] written in 1981, adopted a somewhat different approach, but one which has much to commend it. His view was that, contrary to what Astbury J claimed, the analysis in *Hickman* was wrong and that prior to *Hickman* the courts were in the habit of enforcing the articles without limitation. One of the great strengths of this approach is that it gives effect to the wording of the statute. The gloss put upon it by the *Hickman* case is not justified by any established principle of statutory interpretation and the result is hardly edifying.

In fact, it is possible to construct two quite fundamental objections to the *Hickman* doctrine, both deriving from very significant but relatively recent developments in other areas of company law.

First, the developments in the case law on unfair prejudice[34] have taken the opposite direction to *Hickman* to such an extent as to make it highly arguable that it no longer represents the law, even if it ever really did. Under the unfair prejudice case law the courts will often give effect to equitable expectations which go *beyond* the express terms of the articles. These expectations will often include matters which under the *Hickman* approach would probably be regarded as outsider rights. Early case law in this field had a similar attitude, so that in *Re Lundie Bros*[35] the removal of a director in a small partnership style company (quasi-partnership company) was held not to amount to 'oppression' under the then prevailing legislation because it affected the petitioner in his capacity as a director and not (as the statute required) as a member. Under the unfair prejudice legislation which replaced the oppression remedy in 1980,[36] the principle that the prejudice had to affect the member in his capacity as a member was reiterated,[37] but tempered by the idea that in appropriate circumstances his membership rights might well include expectations of management, directorship and accompanying financial rewards. These kinds of matters would have been regarded as 'outsider' or non-membership rights in the *Lundie Bros* era. They are no longer so regarded. What matters now is not any rigid classification based on narrow notions of what the membership contract involves, but what the justice of the situation demands. It is therefore perhaps arguable that the current position with the s. 14 contract is that all the terms of the articles are *prima facie* enforceable.[38]

Secondly, there has been a substantial growth in the use by small companies of complex written shareholder agreements.[39] These will require registration with the Registrar of Companies if they can be regarded as amounting to a document of the constitution.[40] Shareholder agreements are enforceable by dint of the common law,

---

[33] 'The Section 20 Contract' (1981) 44 MLR 526.
[34] See generally p. 232 below.
[35] [1965] 1 WLR 1051; a case on the old s. 210 of the Companies Act 1948.
[36] Now s. 459 of the Companies Act 1985.
[37] *Re a Company 00477/86* (1986) 2 BCC 99,171.
[38] In some circumstances it will no doubt be unfairly prejudicial to rely on the article, or a particular article.
[39] See further p. 94 below.
[40] This is probably a reasonable shorthand expression of the effect of Companies Act 1985, s. 380 (4) (c).

of contract, and are not dependent on s. 14. For this reason, they are often used by practitioners to secure the enforcement of rights which would otherwise be in danger of being unenforceable under the *Hickman* doctrine. To some extent, the development of shareholder agreements illustrates the absurdity of the law in s. 14. Promoters who wish to define the terms on which they are going to associate must be careful not to put certain matters into the articles of *association*, for these will possibly not in fact regulate how they are required to associate. Instead, they must put the terms into a document which is enforceable by the law of contract, even though the section in the Companies Act which it has become necessary to avoid says, in effect, that the articles are to be enforceable contractually!

The Law Commission in its report *Shareholder Remedies*,[41] after consultation, took the view that this area was not in need of reform because it was not a problem in practice.[42] It may well be that practitioners nearly always avoid difficulty, they have after all studied company law at some stage in their education. Nevertheless, the *Hickman* doctrine is an anachronism, vague, confusing and unjustifiable. Although the matter was looked at by the Company Law Review, the subsequent White Paper *Modernising Company Law* contained no commitment to deal with the problem.[43]

5.4 SHAREHOLDER AGREEMENTS

It is common these days, in small private companies, for the memorandum and articles to be supplemented by a shareholder agreement.[44] Theoretically, since they operate under normal contract law, it is not necessary for them to be put in writing and there are situations where an oral shareholder agreement will be enforceable. Sometimes the courts have even been prepared to imply the existence of a shareholder agreement arising from the course of dealing between the parties.[45] However, it is obviously preferable for the agreement to be in writing[46] and the complexity of modern ones normally makes this essential.

At the outset, it is clear that shareholder agreements have some significant disadvantages which will need to be overcome if the agreement is to be effective. The most obvious point is that if they are going to be used to try to create what is in effect a third part of the constitution of the company, then they are really only suitable for small companies, since the agreement of all the members will be necessary if the mechanism is to be effective.[47] Furthermore, the transfer of a share by a member will pose a challenge for the draftsman of a shareholder agreement. The transferee of a share will not be bound by the shareholder agreement. He will how-

---

[41] Law Com. Report No. 246. See further p. 228 below.

[42] *Ibid.* para. 7.11.

[43] London: DTI, 2002.

[44] For a detailed treatment of the subject, see G. Stedman and J. Jones *Shareholder Agreements* 3rd edn (London: Sweet & Maxwell, 1998).

[45] See e.g. *Pennell* v *Venida* (unreported) noted by S. Burridge (1981) 40 MLR 40.

[46] There will normally be sufficient mutuality of obligations for the contractual requirement of consideration to be satisfied, but in exceptional circumstances it may be necessary to circumvent the need for consideration by making the agreement a deed, under seal.

[47] However, agreements between small groups of shareholders in a large company are of course possible, and in the form of voting agreements are quite common.

ever by bound by the terms of the memorandum and articles, since this is the statutory effect of s. 14 of the Companies Act 1985. The statute operates on the situation here so that the transferee automatically steps into the shoes of the transferor as regards rights and obligations arising under the memorandum and articles. Conversely, if the parties to a shareholder agreement want it to have some chance of surviving as a document which binds all the members from time to time it will be necessary to make contractual provisions which bring this about. For instance, it is desirable to include a clause which puts an obligation on an intending transferor of shares to oblige him to put a clause into the sale contract which requires the purchaser to enter into the shareholder agreement.[48]

Why would it ever be desirable to use a shareholder agreement rather than rely on the facilities provided by the memorandum and articles? The common law gives freedom. The parties can construct the agreement to suit themselves. A particular head of agreement may be so important to the parties that they do not want it alterable at a later date by less than 100% agreement. If such a clause is put into the articles it will normally be alterable[49] by a special resolution[50] and this alone may make the articles unacceptable as a constitutional vehicle for carrying out their business plans. Alternatively, the parties may wish that a certain clause or clauses be alterable by a different majority than the 75% of the special resolution, say 90% or 60%; this can easily be done under a shareholder agreement.[51]

If the constitutional mechanisms offered by company law can be by-passed in this way, it becomes pertinent to consider what view company law will take of a shareholder agreement. How much of company law can be ignored by use of the mechanisms of a shareholder agreement?

The first matter is publicity. Legislative policy in this field has been that limited liability comes at a price; the price of publicity. The memorandum and articles have to be registered with the Registrar of Companies and are on public file, open to inspection. But the effect of this registered constitution may in fact be wholly altered by a third document of the constitution, the shareholder agreement, making the policy of disclosure in these circumstances at best incomplete and, at worst, positively misleading. This gap was plugged in 1985,[52] by which time it had been realised that the growth in the use of large scale shareholder agreements was posing a threat to the proper operation of the disclosure mechanism. The statutory provision is contained in s. 380 of the Companies Act 1985 as follows:

(1) A copy of every resolution or agreement to which this section applies shall, within 15 days after it is passed or made, be forwarded to the registrar of companies ...

---

[48] Another similar problem would arise if the company were to issue more shares at a future date. It would be necessary to ensure that the subscribers would be bound by the shareholder agreement. This could perhaps be done by making the company a party to the shareholder agreement and inserting a clause therein which obliged the company to put a clause into the agreement to subscribe which obliged the subscriber to enter into the shareholder agreement.

[49] Under Companies Act 1985, s. 9. See further p. 98 below.

[50] 75% of members voting.

[51] Tampering with the statutory power to alter the articles has not found favour with the courts; see *Allen v Gold Reefs of West Africa* [1900] 1 Ch 656.

[52] By the Companies Consolidation (Consequential Provisions) Act 1985 which amended the Companies Act 1985.

(4) This section applies to – . . .

    (c) resolutions or agreements which have been agreed to by all the members of a company but which, if not so agreed to, would not have been effective for their purpose unless (as the case may be) they had been passed as special resolutions or as extraordinary resolutions.

What this broadly means is that shareholder agreements must be registered if they have substantial constitutional implications of the kind that if the provisions had not been in the shareholder agreement, they would have needed to go into the articles ('passed as special resolutions') in order for them to be effective. Not all shareholder agreements will be registrable, only those falling within the statute. Failure to register a registrable shareholder agreement is punishable with a fine,[53] but it is unlikely that it will invalidate the agreement.

    The second issue to consider is what would be the result of a direct clash between, say, a statutory provision of company law and a contrary provision in the shareholder agreement? Almost obviously, the provision of the shareholder agreement would be void.[54] But this raises the question of the validity of the remainder of the shareholder agreement. These and other issues were explored by the House of Lords in *Russell* v *Northern Bank Development Corp.*[55] The case involved an extensive shareholder agreement, clause 3 of which provided that 'no further share capital should be created without the written consent of each of the parties to the agreement'. The directors were proposing to issue more shares[56] and the claimant sought an injunction to restrain this. He was not deeply opposed to their proposal, but wanted to test the efficacy of clause 3 because he feared that the directors might on a future occasion try to issue more shares in circumstances which might lead to his voting power being reduced. The House of Lords held that, in so far as the clause purported to bind the company, it was void as being contrary to statute. Section 121[57] gives power to a company to increase its share capital. Clause 3 of the shareholder agreement purported to take this power away and accordingly, in so far as it bound the company, which was a party to the shareholder agreement, then it was void. However, the House of Lords upheld the validity of the clause as regards its enforceability between the shareholders on the basis that, as between the shareholders, it could be interpreted as operating as a voting agreement. It being well established in the case law that a voting agreement was valid, this provided a way of upholding the shareholder agreement to a considerable extent. Furthermore, the remainder of the shareholder agreement was not affected by the void aspect of clause 3 which was severed from the agreement. The claimant succeeded in getting a declaration to the above effect, it having been realised that an injunction was an inappropriate remedy in the circumstances, since he had no real objection to the share issue then under consideration.

    The case is significant because it shows a marked lack of judicial hostility to the concept of the complex written shareholder agreement operating as the third con-

---

[53] Companies Act 1985, s. 380 (5).
[54] By analogy with e.g. *Allen* v *Gold Reefs of West Africa* [1900] 1 Ch 656 where a restriction on the statutory power to alter the articles was held void as contrary to statute.
[55] [1992] 3 All ER 161.
[56] It was actually a capitalisation issue.
[57] The case actually concerned the Northern Ireland equivalent.

stitutional document of the company. Where the agreement was unavoidably seen to be in direct conflict with company law then it was 'trumped' by the law and void. Nevertheless, the rigours of company law were upheld only to the extent that this was necessary and overall it could be said that the case gives the 'green light' to shareholder agreements.

The third matter for consideration, which is closely linked to the second, is what would be the result of a clash between a principle of company law established by case law, and a shareholder agreement. There is plenty of scope for this situation to occur and it is clearly something which needs to be borne in mind when drafting a shareholder agreement. One example which might often be relevant is the director's fiduciary duty to exercise an unfettered discretion. If a shareholder agreement binds the board of directors to supporting a particular policy over a long period of time, this might put the directors into an impossible position.[58] Other circumstances might make the enforcement of a shareholder agreement inappropriate. In *Re Blue Arrow*,[59] for example, Vinelott J was unwilling to give effect to an alleged expectation of management, which may have amounted to an informal agreement to that effect,[60] because the policy of the law with regard to publicly quoted companies was that the full extent of the constitution should be publicly available to a would-be investor and that he should not be put in the position of buying shares in a company and then finding that the true constitutional position was subject to understandings of which he could have had no notice.

5.5 CHANGING THE CONSTITUTION AND RECONSTRUCTION

A Introduction

Sooner or later companies find that they are facing different conditions and if they are to survive and prosper, they will need to change. On the other hand, shareholders with settled interests and expectations will want significant protection from change. Company law aims to strike a balance by providing a range of different degrees of entrenchment of rights, and a variety of checks and balances which come into play once an attempt is made to alter those entrenched rights. The analysis here will start by looking at the most simple methods of change and gradually progress to a consideration of the more complex and powerful methods which are needed to deal with high levels of entrenchment of rights or complicated changes.

---

[58] On the other hand, the courts have adopted a very commercially aware approach to this particular duty and if there is a good commercial reason for the directors having fettered their discretion, then this will negate the suggestion that they have broken their fiduciary duty; see *Fulham v Cabra Estates Ltd*, at p. 165 below.

[59] [1987] BCLC 585.

[60] It is not clear whether it did actually amount to a shareholder agreement; but, for the sake of example, it might just as well have done.

B Contract

Much has already been said about the effect of contract in the context of shareholder agreements, but it is worth considering at the outset whether a simple contract will be sufficient to effect the necessary change. In many business situations it will be all that is required. If a shareholder agreement governs the matter and change is required, then perhaps the agreement itself provides a mechanism for effecting the change by compliance with procedures or majority consent. If the shareholder agreement makes no provision, change can be effected by getting the shareholders to agree to a new contract.

Contract has its limitations. The most significant being that the agreement of all the parties is needed for change[61] and in a business context agreement of all parties is often an elusive quality. For this reason, as we will see, one of the salient features of company law in this area is that in its various methods of alteration of constitutional provision it provides mechanisms for binding a minority who disagree.

C Alteration of articles

The position as regards alteration of the articles of association is relatively straightforward. Section 9 (1) of the Companies Act 1985 provides that:

> Subject to the provisions of this Act and to the conditions contained in its memorandum, a company may by special resolution alter its articles.

The use of the special resolution[62] mechanism enables the company to bind a minority who disapprove of the changes. But, on the other hand, the requirement of a special resolution provides a distinctly higher level of protection to the minority than if an ordinary resolution[63] had been required. Thus is the balance struck by the legislature. The courts, however, have decided that more protection for the minority is required and have claimed a jurisdiction to review an alteration. It was established in *Allen* v *Gold Reefs of West Africa*[64] that the power of alteration must be exercised 'bona fide for the benefit of the company as a whole'.[65] The 'company

---

[61] Absent a shareholder agreement authorising something like majority voting.

[62] A special resolution is one which has been passed by a majority of not less than three-fourths (75%) of such members as (being entitled to do so) vote in person or, where proxies are allowed by proxy, at a general meeting of which not less than 21 days' notice, specifying the intention to propose the resolution as a special resolution, has been duly given: Companies Act 1985, s. 378 (2), (1).

[63] An ordinary resolution is one which is passed by a simple majority of 51% of those members who are present and voting at the meeting either in person or by proxy. The ordinary resolution is best thought of as the basic or residual resolution for it can be used in all circumstances unless the legislation or the constitution of the company provides that some other resolution should be used; see p. 152 below.

[64] The case also makes it clear that the s. 9 power to alter the articles is a statutory power and cannot be taken away by any provision in the company's constitution. However, although the company cannot be precluded from altering its articles, it may nevertheless find that the alteration causes it to be in breach of contract with some other party. There are many cases involving directors service contracts; see e.g. *Southern Foundries* v *Shirlaw* [1940] AC 701, HL.

[65] [1900] 1 Ch 656 at p. 671.

as a whole' in this context is not a reference to the fictional entity but is usually regarded as meaning 'the members'.[66]

The application of this deceptively simple test has given rise to divergence of approach. In some cases the approach has been to hold that the term 'bona fide' imports a subjective requirement into the conduct required, so that it is sufficient if the members honestly believe that is is for the benefit of the company as a whole. On this approach, it would not matter if an objective bystander would not have agreed with their view of the situation. Thus the judges have been unwilling to substitute their own views as to what is desirable in place of the views of those actually involved with the company. The policy often appears in cases in other areas of company law. It is felt that it is all to easy to second guess decisions with the benefit of hindsight and in most cases the judges are aware that they would lack the specialist knowledge of that area of commerce which the company was involved in. There are a number of cases which develop this idea but a clear statement of the policy is contained in *Rights and Issues Investment Trust Ltd* v *Stylo Shoes Ltd*.[67] Here, the court was asked to set aside a resolution for the alteration of articles, where the alteration increased the voting rights of one class of shares, called the 'management shares', with the aim of preserving the voting power held by the directors in circumstances where their power would otherwise have been watered down by new share capital that was being issued. The judge, Pennycuick J, upheld the alteration:

> What has happened is that the members of the company . . . have come to the conclusion that it is for the benefit of this company that the present basis of control should continue to subsist, notwithstanding that the management shares will henceforward represent a smaller proportion of the issued capital than heretofore. That, it seems to me, is a decision on a matter of business policy to which they could properly come and it does not seem to me a matter in which the court can interfere.[68]

In spite of this 'subjective' approach, in other cases the courts found themselves drawn into the question of whether the alteration was in fact for the benefit of the members as a whole. Clearly the alteration is sometimes obviously not for the benefit of some of the members and the courts have had to perform a sort of balancing act, weighing the advantage to the majority against the disadvantage to the minority and perhaps reaching the conclusion that sometimes a group of members can be sacrificed to the greater good of the company as a whole. Thus in *Sidebottom* v *Kershaw Leese Ltd*[69] the Court of Appeal allowed an alteration of articles under which any member of the company who competed with it was liable to have his shares compulsorily purchased by the directors. This was so even though some of the members were thus liable to have their shares expropriated under the new article.[70]

---

[66] In *Greenhalgh* v *Arderne Cinemas Ltd* [1950] 2 All ER 1120, Lord Evershed MR took the view that it means 'the corporators as a general body': *ibid.* at p. 1126. In some circumstances it may include the interests of creditors; see p. 53, n. 51 above.

[67] [1965] 1 Ch 250.

[68] *Ibid.* at pp. 255–256.

[69] [1920] 1 Ch 154.

[70] The balance is a difficult one and other decisions, on similar matters went the other way; see *Dafen Tinplate Co. Ltd* v *Llanelly Steel Co. Ltd* [1920] 2 Ch 124; *Brown* v *British Abrasive Wheel Ltd* [1919] 1 Ch 290.

The difference of approach is probably not significant, for the simple reason that if a shareholder or group of shareholders wished to attack an alteration of articles they would almost certainly do it by bringing a petition under s. 459 of the Companies Act 1985, alleging that the alteration was unfairly prejudicial to their interests. In hearing the petition the court would no doubt pay some regard to the reasoning in the earlier case law but it would not be likely to sidestep the issue by saying that it was a matter of subjective honesty for the shareholders. Honesty, if present, might well be a factor to be taken into account, but so also would the issue of whether there was prejudice to the petitioner's interests and, if so, whether it was, in all the circumstances, *unfair* prejudice; this would involve a balancing act of the sort which the courts have become very familiar with in unfair prejudice cases.

D Alteration of the memorandum

The Companies Act 1985 does not provide an overall method for the alteration of the memorandum. Instead, there are different provisions in respect of various parts of the memorandum. In so far as an overall scheme can be discerned, the obligatory clauses of the memorandum each have their own alteration provisions, as do certain other situations which involve altering the memorandum, while clauses which could have been put into the articles but are put into the memorandum instead (i.e. non-obligatory clauses) are governed by s. 17. What is made clear is that there is no general right to alter the memorandum. Section 2 (7) is uncompromising in this respect:

> A company may not alter the conditions contained in its memorandum except in the cases, in the mode and to the extent for which express provision is made by this Act.

If one collects together the alteration provisions for the obligatory clauses, the picture which emerges is one of clauses indiscriminately scattered throughout the 1985 Act. Thus: change of name (s. 28); change of registered office (s. 287 (3));[71] objects clause (s. 4); limited liability clause (ss. 49–52); capital clause (s. 121). Some of these require special resolution, others merely ordinary resolution, although other conditions are sometimes required, such as permission in the articles.

Clauses which are put into the memorandum but are not required to be there, and which could have been put into the articles are, as stated above, alterable only under s. 17. Section 17 (1) provides that these clauses are alterable by special resolution,[72] which is straightforward and logical since it is drawing an obvious analogy with the power to alter articles by special resolution contained in s. 9. This, however, is subject to s. 17 (2). Section 17 (2) (a) is of quite narrow technical effect[73] but s. 17 (2) (b) is of considerable general significance for the structure of this area of law:

---

[71] This is not always going to operate as a change of the clause which is created in compliance with s. 2 (1) (b) for which no alteration method readily appears from the 1985 Act.

[72] In full, s. 17 (1) provides: 'A condition contained in a company's memorandum which could lawfully have been contained in articles of association instead of in the memorandum may be altered by the company by special resolution; but if an application is made to the court for the alteration to be cancelled, the alteration does not have effect except in so far as it is confirmed by the court.'

[73] Section 17 (2) (a) provides: 'this section is subject to s. 16 [which places limits on the extent to which members can find their liabilities increased by alterations subsequent to their becoming members] and also to Part XVII (court order protecting minority)'.

[This section] . . . does not apply where the memorandum itself provides for or prohibits the alteration of all or any of the conditions above referred to, and does not authorise any variation or abrogation of the special rights of any class of members.

Until now it has probably not been immediately obvious to the reader why anyone would want to put a clause into the memorandum when it could just have easily gone into the articles. One reason is now apparent from a reading of s. 17 (2) (b), which makes it clear that it is possible to put provisions into the memorandum and enshrine them by prohibiting variation. Alteration of such provisions is then very difficult and will only be possible by using the scheme of arrangement procedure set up by s. 425 which is subject to very stringent safeguards.[74] It is similarly clear from s. 17 (2) (b) that shareholders' class rights which are put into the memorandum are outside the scope of the alteration power of the section. The alteration of shareholders' class rights is governed by s. 125 and it will be seen below[75] that often the effect of putting class rights into the memorandum is to make them very difficult to alter.

E Variation of class rights

1 Meaning of variation of class rights

The statutory mechanisms for the alteration of the memorandum and articles have been set out above. It is clear that they contain checks and balances designed to produce a workable compromise between the need to protect bargains, and the need to provide a constitution which is flexible. However, there is a further layer of protection for certain types of rights known as shareholders' class rights. If it is sought to alter or vary or remove these class rights, then the legislature has produced a further procedure to be complied with: Companies Act 1985, s. 125. Broadly speaking, this will involve the need for the consent of 75% of those shareholders at a separate class meeting.[76] This will result in the proposals receiving special scrutiny by the shareholders of the class. It will also often have the effect of increasing the commercial bargaining power of the class in the sense that because the procedure will usually enable them to block the proposals if more than 25% of them disapprove, then the directors will have to make sure at the outset that they are being offered a fair deal.[77] Otherwise, the changes proposed will fail to take effect and the whole exercise will have been a waste of time and money.

There is no statutory definition of a class right. It is usually understood as referring to the special rights which are attached to a particular class of shares. For example, a preference share will fairly typically have attached to it the right to a fixed cumulative preference dividend while the company remains a going concern and a prior right to a return of capital on a winding up. These rights are class rights. If they are contained in the articles of association, it is obvious that the level of protection afforded by the alteration procedure under s. 9 might be thought

---

[74] See further p. 106 below.
[75] At p. 106.
[76] For the detail and alternatives, see p. 105 below.
[77] *Re British & Commonwealth Holdings plc* [1992] BCC 58 is an interesting example of this kind of commercial perspective. It is dealt with at p. 107 below.

insufficient, particularly if the preference share capital is a tiny percentage of the overall capitalisation. The rights very much define the commercial nature of the bargain that the shareholder made when he bought or subscribed for those shares. Money is at stake! So they need some special protection from alteration. The protection afforded once s. 125 is triggered is very significant and will often virtually place a veto in the hands of the class. This effect is well illustrated in a recent case which is significant for the further reason that it may have widened the concept of a class right in a way which leaves the boundaries vague.

Cumbrian Newspapers Ltd v *Cumberland & Westmoreland Printing Ltd*[78] concerned a private company (the defendant) which had entered into an agreement with the claimant company under which a number of ordinary shares, amounting to just over 10% of the total share capital, were issued to the claimant. Additionally, and pursuant to the agreement, the articles of the defendant company were altered so as to include various provisions which would enable the claimant to frustrate any attempted takeover of the defendant company. Under these altered articles the claimant was granted (1) pre-emption rights over the ordinary shares, (2) various rights in respect of unissued shares and (3) the right to appoint a director, though this last-mentioned right was subject to the proviso that the claimant retained not less than 10% of the issued ordinary shares. Some years later the board of directors of the defendant wanted to cancel these special rights of the claimant by convening a meeting and getting a special resolution passed altering the articles so as to remove the rights. The claimant sought an injunction to prevent the meeting from being held. It also sought a declaration that its rights under the articles were class rights within s. 125. If they were class rights this would mean that, in the circumstances, they could not be varied or abrogated without the claimant's consent. And the claimant would not be giving consent. The action was successful. It was held that although the claimant's rights were not rights annexed to particular shares in the way that, for instance, preference dividend rights would be clearly annexed to preference shares, they were nevertheless conferred on the claimant in its capacity as a member of the defendant company, though were not attached to any particular share or shares. They were held to be within the wording of s. 125 (1) which provides: 'This section is concerned with the variation of rights attached to any class of shares in a company whose share capital is divided into shares of different classes' on the basis that:

> ... [I]f specific rights are given to certain members in their capacity as members or shareholders, then those members become a class. The shares those members hold for the time being, and without which they would not be members of the class, would represent ... a 'class of shares' for the purposes of section 125 ... [and] ... the share capital of a company is ... divided into shares of different classes, if shareholders qua shareholders, enjoy different rights.[79]

It still remains to be seen whether this bold approach to the wording and scope of s. 125 will be followed by later cases. On the facts of the case, it resulted in the claimant effectively having a veto over the proposal to alter the articles, a result

---

[78] [1987] Ch 1. As regards the parties, the above facts are somewhat simplified.
[79] *Ibid.* at p. 22, *per* Scott J.

which is a graphic example of the dynamic effect that these technical constitutional subtleties can have on the relative rights of the shareholders in a company.

The legislation, whilst it gave no help on the definition of 'class right' does make a small contribution as regards the meaning of the term 'variation'. Section 125 (8) provides:

> In this section and (except where the context otherwise requires) in any provision for the variation of the rights attached to a class of shares contained in a company's memorandum or articles, references to the variation of those rights are to be read as including references to their abrogation.

This is clear enough. However, the judicial contribution here is less helpful. Some years ago, the courts developed the doctrine that an 'indirect' variation of rights would not amount to a variation of rights within the statute. The leading exponent of this heresy is *Greenhalgh v Arderne Cinemas Ltd.*[80] The background to the litigation here was that some years earlier the company had been in financial difficulties and Greenhalgh had put a small fortune into it to put it back on its feet. In return, arrangements were put in hand to give him voting control of the company.[81] Almost immediately the other shareholders set in chain a series of technical manoeuvres aimed at wresting this control from him. Starting in 1941 he waged a 10-year battle against them. It ultimately involved him bringing seven actions, taking five of them to the Court of Appeal. Thus the proceedings in this case occurred about half-way through the struggle. By this stage, there were two types of shares in the company, 2 shilling shares and 10 shilling shares. Greenhalgh held most of the 2 shilling ones. The other faction had enough votes to pass an ordinary (51%) resolution but they probably wanted[82] to be able to pass a special (75%) resolution, so that they would be in a position to alter the articles of association and further whittle away his position.[83]

The prevailing legislation, the Companies Act 1929,[84] contained a power, as it still does, exercisable by ordinary resolution whereby shares of say, £1 nominal value, could be subdivided into multiple shares of a smaller amount. There is a sound technical reason for having such a facility,[85] but it was not relevant here. Here that facility was misused to destroy the constitutional protection which the scheme of the Companies Act was supposed to give to Greenhalgh. The other faction passed an ordinary resolution subdividing each of their 10 shilling shares into five shares, of 2 shillings each. That gave them five times as many votes as they had had a few minutes earlier![86] And so then they were in a position to pass the special resolution and alter the articles. Greenhalgh argued that this amounted to a

---

[80] [1946] 1 All ER 512, CA.

[81] See [1945] 2 All ER 719 at pp. 720–722, Vaisey J.

[82] Presumably; in view of what subsequently happened in *Greenhalgh v Arderne Cinemas Ltd* [1950] 2 All ER 1120.

[83] Lord Greene spoke of his shareholding as 'his safeguard against the passing of special resolutions or extraordinary resolutions which might be contrary to his wishes': [1946] 1 All ER 512 at p. 514. They did eventually pass a special resolution, to satisfactory effect; see *Greenhalgh v Arderne Cinemas Ltd* [1950] 2 All ER 1120.

[84] The provision was s. 50 (combined with art. 37 of the prevailing Table A); now s. 121 (2) (d) of the 1985 Act and art. 32 of Table A of the 1985 Regulations.

[85] See p. 265 below.

[86] 'It was that remaining measure of control which was attacked and sought to be destroyed by the next

variation of his class rights[87] and needed the approval of a class meeting.[88] The Court of Appeal held that his rights had not been varied, they were just the same; the enjoyment of them had been affected, but not the rights themselves. Lord Greene spelled out the results of the reasoning:

> Instead of Greenhalgh finding himself in a position of control, he finds himself in a position where the control has gone, and to that extent the rights of the . . . 2 s[hilling] shareholders are affected, as a matter of business.[89]

But nevertheless, he held: 'As a matter of law . . . they remain as they always were – a right to have one vote per share.'[90]

The decision is surely wrong. Voting rights are only a relative concept; no one votes on their own, if they are the only voter in the constituency. The concept only has human meaning when a person is set against others who vote, and then the votes are added to see who wins. If the votes of one side are quintupled, that must vary the rights of the other side. The court conceded that as a matter of business this *was* true, but as a matter of law it was untrue. The reasoning is technical, legalistic and the factual result both in the instant case and in the 10 year saga generally was profoundly unfair.

Even if the case is binding authority on the technical point that an indirect variation of rights is not a variation of rights which could trigger a class meeting,[91] a person in Greenhalgh's position today would be unlikely to be adversely affected by it. He would bring a petition under s. 459, alleging unfair prejudice. The appearance in 1980 of the unfair prejudice remedy soon spawned a series of cases[92] putting paid to attempts to water down control and voting rights[93] and it is highly unlikely that the subdivision manoeuvre perpetrated on Greenhalgh would survive a petition under s. 459 of the Companies Act 1985.[94]

---

manoeuvre, which was the passing of the resolution now in question under which the issued 10s shares were split, with the consequence that the holders of each of those shares had acquired five times as many votes as they originally had': [1946] 1 All ER 512 at p. 514, *per* Lord Greene MR.

[87] The Court of Appeal assumed, without holding, that the 2 shilling shares were a separate class: [1946] 1 All ER 512 at p. 515. Vaisey J at first instance ([1945] 2 All ER 719) adopted a similar approach although he seemed a little more persuaded, referring to *Re United Provident Assurance Co. Ltd* [1910] 2 Ch 477 which had, surely, settled the point.

[88] As stated earlier, the current provision is s. 125 of the Companies Act 1985; in *Greenhalgh*'s case it was a provision in the articles of association.

[89] [1946] 1 All ER 512 at p. 518.

[90] *Ibid.* at p. 518. As Lord Greene had earlier observed '. . . these things are of a technical nature; . . .': *ibid.* at p. 516.

[91] It cannot be written off lightly; it is a Court of Appeal authority, and the doctrine was given some support in the later Court of Appeal decisions in *White v Bristol Aeroplane Co.* [1953] Ch 65 and *Re John Smith's Tadcaster Brewery* [1953] Ch 308.

[92] *Re Cumana Ltd* [1986] BCLC 430; *Re DR Chemicals Ltd* (1989) 5 BCC 39; *Re Kenyon Swansea Ltd* (1987) 3 BCC 259; *Re a Company 007623/84* (1986) 2 BCC 99,191; *Re a Company 002612/84* (1984) 1 BCC 99,262; *Re a Company 005134/86* [1989] BCLC 383. Also, obviously, s. 89 of the 1985 Act (introduced in 1980) will sometimes be relevant in these kinds of cases; see e.g. the discussion in *Re DR Chemicals* (above) at p. 51.

[93] Even before the appearance of the unfair prejudice remedy, Foster J in *Clemens v Clemens* [1976] 2 All ER 268 was prepared to recognise the element of negative control possessed by a 45% shareholder (in that she could block a special resolution) and an issue of shares to people who would vote with the 55% holder was set aside.

[94] The Court of Appeal decisions in *White v Bristol Aeroplane Co.* [1953] Ch 65 and *Re John Smith's Tadcaster Brewery* [1953] Ch 308 (capitalisation issue of bonus ordinary shares is not a variation of

2 Variation procedure

The procedure for variation is set out in s. 125 of the Companies Act 1985.[95] It is a detailed section which caters for many possibilities. The essence of the kind of procedure being laid down is set out in s. 125 (2):

> Where the rights are attached to a class of shares otherwise than by the company's memorandum, and the company's articles do not contain provision with respect to the variation of rights, those rights may be varied if, but only if –
> (a) the holders of three-quarters in nominal value of the issued shares of that class consent in writing to the variation; or
> (b) an extraordinary resolution passed at a separate general meeting of the holders of that class sanctions the variation;
> and any requirement (howsoever imposed) in relation to the variation of those rights is complied with to the extent that it is not comprised in paragraphs (a) and (b) above.

Other provisions of s. 125 cater for specific situations. Thus, s. 125 (3) sometimes imposes further conditions where the variation of rights is connected with s. 80 or s. 135. Section 125 (4) deals with the situation where variation provisions are contained in the articles.

Of particular interest is s. 125 (5). It has been seen earlier that the memorandum is the senior document of the constitution and that the effect of putting clauses in the memorandum can be to make them more difficult to alter than if they had been contained in the articles. Section 125 (5) shows the extent of the high degree of entrenchment which comes from putting class rights into the memorandum:

> If the rights are attached to a class of shares by the memorandum, and the memorandum and articles do not contain provision with respect to the variation of those rights, those rights may be varied if all the members of the company agree to the variation.

As has been suggested, it will often be difficult to get the consent of every person in a particular group.

If a shareholder objects to the variation that others have consented to, he has the further protection under s. 127, in some situations, of applying to the court to have the variation cancelled. The right to apply is given to the holders of not less in the aggregate than 15% of the issued shares of the class.[96] The test that that court will use in deciding whether to cancel is whether the variation would unfairly prejudice the shareholders of the class.[97]

---

rights of preference shares), although having some similarities with *Greenhalgh*, are also distinguishable in some respects; e.g. they lack the improper motive present in *Greenhalgh*, the long course of unfairly prejudicial conduct, and the liability to watering by bonus issue could be seen as part of the generally understood commercial relationship between preference and ordinary shares. It is not altogether clear that these cases would not be followed at the present day. On the problems in this area generally, see further B. Reynolds 'Shareholders Class Rights: A New Approach' [1996] JBL 554.

[95] See s. 125 (1).

[96] Section 127 (2).

[97] In view of this, it is difficult to see whether the section adds anything to the right of any member to petition under s. 459. It is however possible that the effect of s. 127 is to restrict the ability of a class member to rely on s. 459 since the 15% threshold will be meaningless otherwise.

F Compromises and arrangements under s. 425

1 Rationale

A variety of procedures for altering the constitution of a company have been examined. It will have become apparent that given the balance between entrenchment and flexibility that there are, in the mechanisms looked at above, situations where the entrenchment principle wins. In other words, there are various methods of entrenching rights in such a way that it is either often practically very difficult to alter them, or, not possible at all.

Some examples of this are useful. First, suppose that shareholder class rights are contained in a clause in the memorandum and 98% of all the members of the company are in favour of a proposed alteration. Thus, only a tiny minority are against it. Can the alteration go ahead? An analysis of the available methods draws a blank. The clause is not one of the memorandum's 'obligatory' clauses[98] and it could just as easily have gone into the articles.[99] Therefore, s. 17 is *prima facie* the method for alteration of the clause and, if it applies, will require a special resolution. However, a reading of s. 17 (2) (b) shows that s. 17 does not apply to the variation of class rights. Section 125 deals with the variation of class rights. These class rights are in the memorandum and so s. 125 (5) is applicable; it provides that the rights may be varied 'if all the members of the company agree to the variation'.[100] Since 2% of the company disagree with the variation, s. 125 (5) will not be satisfied and the class rights will remain unaltered.

Secondly, suppose that the memorandum contains a clause[101] containing a condition of some sort, and that the clause itself prohibits variation. As above, the assumption is that it is not one of the 'obligatory' clauses. Again, s. 17 is *prima facie* the method for alteration, but it is clear that it is inapplicable because s. 17 (2) (b) provides that the alteration mechanism in s. 17 'does not apply where the memorandum itself provides for or prohibits the alteration of all or any of the conditions ...'. So, the clause is effectively enshrined in the memorandum and cannot be altered.

To deal with situations like these, the legislature in partnership with the courts has developed a procedure which balances great power to cut through entrenchment with great levels of protection for those whose rights are being varied. Section 425 and its accompanying case law sets up both a process of scrutiny by the members of the class being affected, and a process of scrutiny by an outsider to the transaction, namely the court. As will be seen, s. 425 will not always result in the proposals going ahead, and, as will also be seen, the uses of the procedure range well beyond the examples mentioned above. There are many commercial applications.

The procedure commences[102] with an application to the court to order a meeting (or meetings) of the various classes of members and creditors.[103] If 'three-

---

[98] For the meaning of this, see p. 88 above.
[99] Though with different effect.
[100] The assumption is, for the sake of example, that the memorandum and articles do not contain any provisions for the alteration of class rights.
[101] Not pertaining to class rights.
[102] Various other procedural requirements are contained in the Companies Act 1985, ss. 425–427A.
[103] Companies Act 1985, s. 425 (1).

fourths in value' of the creditors or members present and voting in person or by proxy at the meetings agree to the compromise or arrangement, then, if sanctioned by the court, it will be binding on all of them.[104] It should also be mentioned that the section is not wholly without limit and it has been held that the statutory use of the words 'compromise or arrangement' require that each party should be receiving some benefit under the scheme. If this is not the case, there will be no jurisdiction to sanction the scheme.

> The word 'compromise' implies some element of accommodation on each side. It is not apt to describe total surrender. A claimant who abandons his claim is not compromising it. Similarly, I think that the word 'arrangement' in this section implies some element of give and take. Confiscation is not my idea of an arrangement.[105]

This goes beyond the nominal consideration required in the law of contract, for the loss of the contingent obligation to contribute 5 pence in the liquidation of a company limited by guarantee was held to be *de minimis*.[106]

2 The meetings

The company (i.e. the board)[107] will be proposing the scheme and it will be its responsibility to decide how the meetings are to be structured. A difficulty which the company will sometimes face is that some of the persons it has selected to go into a particular class are thereby put in a position where there will be a conflict of interest. The meetings must only contain 'those persons whose rights are not so dissimilar as to make it impossible for them to consult together with a view to their common interest'.[108] If this point is not dealt with properly, then, when at a later stage the court is asked to sanction the scheme, it will find that it cannot do so. This is well illustrated by *Re United Provident Assurance Company Ltd*,[109] where after the meetings, the company applied to the court for it to approve the scheme. It was held that the holders of fully paid shares formed a different class from the holders of partly paid shares and that there should have been separate meetings of the classes. Swinfen Eady J held: 'In these circumstance, the objection that there have not been proper class meetings is fatal, and I cannot sanction the scheme.'[110]

If the problem is spotted early enough it is possible to get the guidance of the court.[111] An interesting variation on this problem occurred in *Re British & Commonwealth Holdings plc.*[112] A scheme of arrangement was being proposed. The holders of subordinated debt knew that they no longer had any financial interest in

---

[104] *Ibid.* s. 425 (2).
[105] *Re NFU Development Trust Ltd* [1971] 1 WLR 1548 at p. 1555, *per* Brightman J. The case is explored in further detail at p. 108 below.
[106] [1971] 1 WLR 1548 at p. 1554.
[107] Or liquidator or administrator in some circumstances.
[108] *Sovereign Life Assurance* v *Dodd* [1892] 2 QB 573 at p. 583, *per* Bowen LJ.
[109] [1910] 2 Ch 477.
[110] *Ibid.* p. 481.
[111] And it is possible that the tenor of the judgment of Chadwick LJ in *Re Hawk Insurance Ltd* [2001] 2 BCLC 480 will bring about a change of approach so that the court when ordering the meetings actually also directs its mind to the question of whether they are the right meetings.
[112] [1992] BCC 58.

the company because it was clear that even the un-subordinated creditors were not going to be paid in full. Nevertheless, they were threatening to ruin the s. 425 scheme by voting against it in the meetings, and in doing so were trying to use their right to vote as a bargaining chip to get something out of the scheme of arrangement. The court held that they could be left out of the meetings.

3 Review by the court

The court will check that the statutory procedure has been complied with, that the meetings were properly convened and held, and that they were free from conflicts of interest which could vitiate the consent given. In addition to checking these kinds of technical matters, the court has a discretion to take a view as to whether to sanction the scheme or not. The test applied is whether it was an arrangement which 'an intelligent and honest man, considering the interests of the class of which he forms part, might reasonably approve'.[113]

A good example of the court actually refusing to sanction a scheme occurred in *Re NFU Development Trust Ltd.*[114] The company was a company limited by guarantee which had the object of assisting farmers who were involved in fatstock farming and to encourage farming generally. It had about 94,000 farmer members. A scheme of arrangement was proposed for the purpose of reducing administrative expenses. It entailed the farmers losing their membership. Instead, the company would have only seven members some of whom would be nominees of councils of farmers' unions. At the meeting directed by the court 1,439 votes were cast, seven in person and the remainder by proxy. Of those, 1,211 were in favour of the scheme and 228 against, making a majority in favour of the scheme of nearly 85%. At the hearing of the petition to sanction the scheme five persons appeared to oppose the petition.

Brightman J refused to sanction the scheme and produced two alternative reasons for his decision. The first has been discussed above, namely that the lack of give and take in the scheme meant that it did not fall within the statutory words 'compromise or arrangement' and that accordingly there was no jurisdiction to sanction the scheme. His second and alternative reason was that the scheme was unreasonable in that it was not an arrangement which an intelligent and honest man, considering the interests of the class of which he forms part, might reasonably approve:

> Although, therefore, this scheme has been devised in the sincere belief that it could properly be recommended by the board of directors to members for their approval, I do not think that, even if I considered that I had jurisdiction, I would have been justified in sanctioning it.[115]

It is possible that there lurked at the back of the judge's mind a third reason; namely that there had not been fair representation of the members at the meeting. Fewer than 1,500 of the 94,000 had bothered to vote, and it is possible that he took the view that the meeting had not been an adequate safeguard.

---

[113] *Re Dorman Long & Company Ltd* [1934] Ch 635 at p. 657, *per* Maughman J.
[114] [1972] 1 WLR 1548.
[115] *Ibid.* at p. 1555.

The *NFU* case can perhaps be seen as the high point of judicial scrutiny in this field. But cases where the courts have actually gone as far as to turn down a scheme are rare. The schemes are normally carefully prepared by expert practitioners and they are intended to go smoothly through the various gates of the procedure. Most of the shareholders involved will, these days, be institutional investors and quite capable of looking after their own interests or seeking professional advice.

A passage in the judgment of Harman J in *Re MB Ltd*[116] shows these matters being taken into account and their consequential effect on the level of scrutiny which the court brings to bear. The case concerned an international merger which was going through under s. 425:

> Petitions for approval of schemes of arrangement, even when as complicated, international and substantial as this, are usually matters where the court can sanction the scheme without more than a careful check that all the correct steps have been taken. Although the court must be satisfied that 'the proposal is such that an intelligent and honest man ... might reasonably approve ...' yet the underlying commercial purposes need not be investigated by the court since if the persons with whom the scheme is made have been accurately and adequately informed by the explanatory statement and any additional circulars and the requisite majority has approved the scheme, the court will not be concerned with the commercial reasons for approval.

4 Uses of s. 425

To a large extent, the strength of s. 425 lies in its power to bind the dissenting minority. It is often well nigh impossible in a commercial situation to get the agreement of all the parties to a dispute or proposal. The section enables that difficulty to be overcome, subject to the various safeguards.

The applications of s. 425 are many and various. The examples discussed at the beginning of this section showed how the entrenchment provisions of the memorandum and articles can make it difficult or impossible to alter clauses in the constitution of the company. In those kinds of situation, s. 425 is often going to provide a solution.[117] So, for instance, it has been used to alter class rights which are contained in the memorandum.[118] It has been used to reach a compromise between shareholders in dispute about the extent of their class rights as a result of inadequate drafting.[119] The section is quite often used to carry out a takeover; the *MB* case mentioned above was an example of that. It has been held that it is not available for a hostile takeover since the wording of s. 425 (1) envisages that it is the company itself (i.e. its board of directors) that will set the process going and convene the meetings.[120] Some types of takeover find s. 425 particularly appropriate because in some circumstances the powers of s. 427 become available, under which

---

[116] [1989] BCC 684 at p. 686.

[117] But not always; the section is not a panacea. If e.g. the problem stems from the fact that the class which would need to give consent is owned by one person who is implacably opposed to the proposal, then s. 425 will not help. For instance, it would not have helped in *Cumbrian Newspapers Ltd* v *Cumberland & Westmoreland Printing Ltd* [1987] Ch 1 discussed at p. 102 above.

[118] *City Property Trust Ltd, Petitioners* 1951 SLT 371.

[119] *Mercantile Investment and General Trust Co.* v *River Plate Trust Co.* [1894] 1 Ch 578.

[120] See *Re Savoy Hotels Ltd* [1981] 3 All ER 646.

the court can make orders for the transfer of property and liabilities.[121] Section 425 is sometimes used to help a company, in liquidation or otherwise, to reach a compromise with its creditors. A case in 1987 shows it being used another way by liquidators. *Re Exchange Securities Ltd*[122] concerned a large number of commercially interrelated companies which had received money from people to invest in commodities. All the companies were in liquidation and faced terribly complex claims on an intercompany basis. It was going to take years of litigation to sort it out. The liquidator proposed a scheme under s. 425 which involved pooling all the assets and then letting all the outside claimants share in the assets in various percentages to be agreed by them.

G Other methods of reconstruction

The Insolvency Act 1986 contains other methods of reconstruction which will sometimes be of use. These are reconstruction by voluntary liquidation and by company voluntary arrangements (CVA). Only the former of these will be dealt with here. The CVA is considered later in Part VI of this book, Insolvency and Liquidation.

Sections 110–111 of the Insolvency Act 1986 contain a fairly simple reconstruction mechanism not involving any application to the court. The mechanics of it involve a sale in a voluntary liquidation of the business and undertaking of one company to another in return for shares in that other which are then distributed to the shareholders of the company being wound up. Because it involves liquidation,[123] a special resolution is required to operate the mechanism. Dissenters have a right under s. 111 to require the liquidator either to abstain from carrying the resolution into effect or to purchase their shares.

It is a mistake to view this procedure as of equal significance with s. 425 of the Companies Act 1985. It is not. Even at a theoretical level its uses are very limited and in practice it has other limitations. In the past it was sometimes used to get around a potential *ultra vires* problem. If the company found that its objects clause did not permit some new activity that it was planning to do, and that the statutory power to alter the memorandum was not extensive enough to produce a solution, then one solution might be to use the s. 110 procedure[124] to roll the business of the old company into a newly formed company with an appropriate objects clause. These days this will not be necessary since the Companies Act 1989 created a more extensive power to alter the objects.[125] Another use which has become out of date was to use the mechanisms to vary the class rights of shareholder where the articles

---

[121] In some circumstances a conflict has arisen between ss. 428–430F and s. 425. Under the former a 10% minority who have refused to take up a takeover offer can be bought out by the bidder. This, although irksome, may be a lot better for them than simply being part of a losing 25% minority in a s. 425 application. If the minority in a takeover would face a disadvantage as a result of s. 425 being used, then the courts have decided that s. 425 is not available and the s. 428 procedure must be used instead: see *Re Hellenic and General Trust* [1976] 1 WLR 123.

[122] [1987] BCLC 425.

[123] See further p. 408 below.

[124] Or similar provisions in the articles in the days when there was no statutory power.

[125] Companies Act 1985, s. 4, as inserted by the Companies Act 1989, s. 110 (2).

of association contained no clause permitting the variation of class rights. Since 1980[126] there has been a statutory procedure for the variation of class rights and thus if the articles lack it, reliance on a reconstruction by voluntary arrangement would not be necessary. There is a further, more general point here, and that is that the s. 110 procedure is often not much practical use for dealing with a situation where there is likely to be any significant dissent, for the simple reason that the liquidator may find that the scheme cannot be carried out without purchasing the shares of the dissenters. This may well be expensive and possibly will neutralise the commercial advantage of what is being proposed. In many situations it will be easier and cheaper to destroy the opposition by using a s. 425 scheme of arrangement.

5.6 COMPANY LAW REVIEW AND LAW REFORM

In the DTI Consultation Document of October 1999, *Company Formation and Capital Maintenance*, it was proposed that new companies should in future have their constitution in one document, which would be broadly similar to the current articles of association. It was envisaged that this constitution would be capable of alteration by special resolution, but that there would be ways of entrenching certain provisions in the constitution.[127] Additionally, consultation was started on whether the *qua* member doctrine should be retained or modified.

The Final Report[128] adopted the earlier ideas with regard to having only one document of constitution rather than memorandum and articles, and contained further discussion of the problem of personal rights and the *Hickman* (*qua* member) doctrine.[129] The subsequent government White Paper *Modernising Company Law* contained a clear acceptance of the idea of having only one constitutional document.[130]

---

[126] Now Companies Act 1985, s. 125.
[127] DTI Consultation Document (October 1999) *Company Formation and Capital Maintenance*. paras 2.3 *et seq.*
[128] *Modern Company Law for a Competitive Economy Final Report* (London: DTI, 2001).
[129] *Ibid.* paras. 9.1–9.11, 11.1–11.58, 7.34 *et seq.*
[130] July 2002, Cmnd. 5553.

6

ORGANISATION OF FUNCTIONS AND CORPORATE POWERS

6.1 INTRODUCTION

This chapter will explore another important area of law which also largely flows from the constitution, namely the effect which the constitution has on the organisation of the functions of the various major participants within the company. First, the effect which the company's constitution has on the fundamental relationship between the directors and shareholders will be considered. It will then also be seen that the constitution has an effect on the powers of the company and, to some extent the powers of its officers and agents; this will form the major part of the discussion and will focus on the *ultra vires* doctrine in company law.

6.2 THE INSTITUTIONS OF THE COMPANY: THE BOARD AND THE SHAREHOLDERS

English company law is geared to producing companies which have within them two distinct institutions, namely, the board of directors and the shareholders in general meeting. These institutions are often referred to as 'organs' by analogy with the human body, meaning that the organs, the board and the general meeting each have their own internal rules governing how they function, and yet each forms a part of the composite whole, without which, that whole cannot function.

As has been seen, in small closely-held companies this distinction does not have much practical significance in the sense that the shareholders will also be the directors and so the two organs, while they exist in law, in practice are wholly overlapping. However, in larger companies, there will be many shareholders, only a few of whom will be on the board of directors. In such a situation there is a separation of ownership and control, a phenomenon which has major implications for corporate governance and has been the subject of much theoretical writing.[1] Each of the organs is capable of making decisions which can in some circumstances be regarded as decisions of the company. However, most companies adopt art. 70 of Table A,[2] which makes an initial sharing out of the powers of the company between the board of directors and the shareholders in general meeting and which does so in a way

---

[1] See p. 50 above and Part III below.
[2] Or an earlier version of it.

which clearly makes the board of directors the primary decision-making organ of the company.[3] Article 70 reads as follows:

> Subject to the provisions of the Act, the memorandum and the articles *and to any directions given by special resolution*,[4] the business of the company shall be managed by the directors who may exercise all the powers of the company.[5]

Where the board is deadlocked or for some other reason cannot act, or there are no directors for the time being, the case law has established that the powers of the board revert to the shareholders in general meeting.[6] There is no obligation for a company to adopt Table A and it is possible for the articles to adopt some other structure for the exercise of managerial power, such as providing that 'the business of the company shall be managed by a committee consisting of all the shareholders'. In this kind of situation, the shareholders may nevertheless find that the legislation regards them as directors for certain purposes. Section 741 (1) of the Companies Act 1985 provides that 'In this Act "director" includes any person occupying the position of director, by whatever name called' and so the shareholders on their management committee will find that they are afflicted by the statutory obligations which apply to directors.[7]

Article 70 makes it clear that the general meeting can give directions to the directors, by special resolution. This is a considerable improvement on art. 80 of the previous Table A in the 1948 Act[8] which left it very unclear as to how and to what extent the general meeting could interfere with decisions of the board.[9] Thus art. 70 gives a residual power to the general meeting to interfere with board decisions by special resolution. It may seem incongruous that it takes a special (75%) resolution to interfere with a single management decision whereas, as will be seen in Chapter 10, under s. 303 of the 1985 Act only an ordinary resolution (more than 50%) is required for the removal of directors. However, it reveals an unstated policy in the legislation that the normal model of a company under the Companies Act 1985 is one where the management are left free to manage and if the shareholders disagree with them on a matter which they feel is important enough to be worth having a general meeting about then they should remove the management (and will find that easier) rather than give them orders.[10]

---

[3] The special case of litigation is dealt with at p. 226 below where, it will be seen, it is possible that the general meeting and the board share a right to use the company's name in litigation.

[4] Emphasis added.

[5] Article 70 continues: 'No alteration of the memorandum or articles and no such direction shall invalidate any prior act of the directors which would have been valid if that alteration had not been made or that direction had not been given. The powers given by this regulation shall not be limited by any special power given to the directors by the articles and a meeting of directors at which a quorum is present may exercise all powers exercisable by directors.'

[6] See *Barron* v *Potter* [1914] 1 Ch 895; *Foster* v *Foster* [1916] 1 Ch 532.

[7] They are probably also liable to case law duties; these are examined in Chapter 9 below.

[8] And other even earlier versions.

[9] The case law and academic writings on these earlier versions would still be relevant in respect of companies which have not adopted the new art. 70; see generally G. Goldberg 'Article 80 of Table A of the Companies Act 1948' (1970) 33 MLR 177, G. Sullivan 'The Relationship Between the Board of Directors and the General Meeting in Limited Companies' (1977) 93 LQR 569 and *Breckland Group Ltd* v *London & Suffolk Properties Ltd* (1988) 4 BCC 542 which is discussed further at p. 226 below.

[10] In reality the point is not as clear cut as this, since there are often pressures on the shareholders which

6.3 THE *ULTRA VIRES* DOCTRINE

A Introduction

The effects of the company's constitution on the relationship between the directors and the shareholders have been noted. Equally significant, however, is the effect which it has on the *powers* of the company and on the powers of its agents. The first of these matters has given rise to the *ultra vires* doctrine which has bedevilled company law for over a century and in a ghastly way continues to do so despite various efforts of the legislature to ameliorate it. The doctrine and some of its more obvious ramifications were set out reasonably clearly in the House of Lords case of *Ashbury Railway Carriage and Iron Company* v *Riche*.[11] The company had been carrying on business making railway waggons, carriages, signals and other items for use on railways but had not actually been involved in the construction of the railways themselves in the sense of making cuttings, building tunnels and bridges. The directors decided to expand into this activity also and caused the company to purchase a railway concession entitling it to build a railway. The company contracted with Riche for him to build a railway and he set about performance under the contract and received some payment. Later, the shareholders decided that the venture was too risky and the company repudiated its contract with Riche, who then sued for damages. The company claimed the contract was *ultra vires* and therefore void. Thus the principle at stake was of extraordinary significance; could a company point to an aspect of its constitution and use it to escape liability on a contract with a third party? If something had gone wrong within the company, did company law in some way shift the risk of this onto an outside commercial party? If the directors were acting outside the constitution, who would suffer, the shareholders or a commercial creditor?

The objects clause of the memorandum of association included the words 'to carry on the business of mechanical engineers and general contractors'. The House of Lords held that the contract was beyond the powers of the company (*ultra vires*) and void. They did not think that the words 'mechanical engineers' were apt to cover the activity in question and the expression 'general contractors' they felt should be construed *ejusdem generis*[12] with 'mechanical engineers'. Thus, Riche lost his action for damages for breach of contract. The obvious unfairness of this could be partly mitigated on the basis that because the memorandum was a public document, on file in the Companies Registry, Riche had constructive notice of it.[13] Before contracting, he might thus be expected to inspect the memorandum and also understand the full significance which the objects clause would have for the proposed transaction. The risk of not doing this was on him.

The House of Lords made it clear that the policy behind the *ultra vires* doctrine was to protect the shareholders. They had invested money in the company on the

---

would discourage them from using s. 303, such as the company having to pay damages to the dismissed directors for breach of long-term service contracts; see further p. 182 below.

[11] (1875) LR 7 HL 653.

[12] The *ejusdem generis* rule of construction broadly requires that when general words appear at the end of a phrase their meaning is limited by the context in which they appear.

[13] The constructive notice doctrine was enunciated in *Ernest* v *Nicholls* (1857) 6 HLC 407. Its effects have been suppressed by statute in some areas of company law; see pp. 123–130, 138–142, below.

basis that it would be applied for certain purposes set out in the objects clause of the memorandum. If the directors applied it for other purposes the shareholders would not be prejudiced by this, since those acts would be void.[14] Such protection is of course bought at the expense[15] of third parties who dealt with the company. They effectively have a choice of having to expend resources on researching whether the proposed contract is within the powers of the company, or conserving those resources and running the risk that the company may resile from the contract with impunity.

B Reform of the rule – an overview

Despite this policy of protection of shareholders, the doctrine was not popular with incorporators, who often felt that it might unduly restrict the future activities of the company and it became common practice to insert a very long list of objects into the objects clause of the memorandum. The effectiveness of this was damaged by the development of a doctrine known as the 'main objects rule' under which the courts would decide that, as a matter of construction, one object in the list was in fact the main object.[16] This meant that unless the main object was being pursued, the trading would be *ultra vires*.[17] However, by 1918 it had been decided that since the main objects rule was no more than a canon of construction, it would yield to an expressed contrary intention, so that a clause which stated that each object was a separate and independent object and was not ancillary to any other object, would be effective to preclude a court from adopting the main objects rule when construing a memorandum.[18] Between 1918 and 1972 there were several other decisions which helped, by degrees, to diminish the effect of the doctrine.[19] The year 1972 saw the legislature's first attempt to restrict the doctrine and in 1989 a more comprehensive package of reforms was enacted. Before these are examined, it is necessary to introduce some complications, for the above account is a straightforward but somewhat superficial analysis of the rise and fall of the doctrine, and does not take account of the problems underlying some of the basic ideas of the doctrine.

---

[14] There is possibly also a less policy based and more technical reason for the existence of the *ultra vires* doctrine, along the lines that the creation of the company by the Registrar of Companies is an act of delegated legislation and the corporation which is created by the Registrar's issue of the certificate of incorporation only exists in law to the extent of the purposes set out in the objects clause of the memorandum.

[15] It was also held that an *ultra vires* act was non-ratifiable, on the basis that ratification by the principal of an act done by an agent acting beyond his authority is not appropriate if the act was not one which the principal himself could do. On ratification, see further pp. 127, 158, 214, 218, below.

[16] See *Re German Date Coffee Company* (1882) 20 Ch D 169.

[17] This might also have the effect that the company could be wound up for 'failure of substratum' as was the situation in the *German Date* case.

[18] See *Cotman* v *Brougham* [1918] AC 514.

[19] See *Bell Houses* v *City Wall Properties Ltd* [1966] 2 QB 656; *Re New Finance and Mortgage Company Ltd* [1975] 1 All ER 684; *Newstead* v *Frost* [1980] 1 All ER 373 discussed by this author in (1981) 97 LQR 15. Also noteworthy is *Re Horsley & Weight* [1982] Ch 442; this is discussed further at p. 122 below.

C Underlying complications – objects and powers

The difficulties stem from a distinction between objects and powers, which appears in many of the cases, the broad idea being that a company might have, say, an object to run an airline, but would then need powers to perform all the acts necessary to bring this about, such as power to hold land, to buy and sell aircraft etc. Lawyers drafting a memorandum of association would commonly put a list of powers into the objects clause, although the exact status of these could not have been clear, since the legislation merely requires a statement of the objects of the company.[20] Nevertheless, the common law also developed a doctrine of implied powers whereunder a company, in the absence of appropriate express powers in the memorandum, would be deemed to have implied power to carry out any act which was reasonably incidental to its objects.[21] So, for instance, a trading company would have implied power to borrow money for the purposes of its business.[22] This seems reasonably straightforward, but it in fact leads into the quagmire that lies at the heart of the concepts which make up the *ultra vires* doctrine, which is still not wholly resolved at the present day.

Re Introductions Ltd[23] is a good example of one type of approach to the problem of objects and powers. The company had been formed to provide facilities for the 1951 Festival of Britain. It seems to have become dormant at a later stage of its life, but later still, carried on a pig breeding venture. Debentures had been issued to a bank which had lent money to the company. The bank had been sent a copy of the memorandum and, additionally, was aware that the money was to be used for pig breeding. The company was in insolvent liquidation and the liquidator had rejected the bank's claim on the basis that the borrowing was *ultra vires*. The argument was successful. The Court of Appeal held that since the pig breeding was *ultra vires* then the borrowing for pig breeding was *ultra vires*. This was so, even though the objects clause of the memorandum of association contained an express power to borrow money. A power could not stand on its own, it was necessarily ancillary to an object. Thus, express powers need to be 'read down' by reference to the objects.

The case raises some interesting points which are perhaps best illustrated by asking, and attempting to answer, three questions:

(1) Would the result have been different if the bank had not been sent a copy of the memorandum of association, in other words, if it had not had actual notice of the memorandum? The answer here is 'no', for the simple reason that it would anyway have constructive notice under the constructive notice doctrine referred to above.[24]

(2) Would the result have been different if the bank had not had knowledge of the purpose of the loan? There is strong case law authority for the view that the answer here is 'yes'. In *Re Introductions* the Court of Appeal made it clear that

---

[20] Companies Act 1985, s. 2 (1) (c).
[21] *Attorney General* v *Great Eastern Railway* (1880) 5 App Cas 473.
[22] *General Auction Estate* v *Smith* [1891] 3 Ch 432.
[23] [1970] Ch 199.
[24] Again, it is worth mentioning that this aspect of the analysis has been altered by statute, but this was not operative at the time the case was decided. See p. 123 below.

it was significant that the bank had knowledge of the purpose of the loan. Earlier cases had proceeded on a similar basis.[25] The idea is that the exercise of a power to borrow is equivocal; the third party sees[26] the objects in the memorandum (Festival of Britain) and is aware of the existence of the power to borrow. Without more, he is not aware of any impropriety. Only when he knows that the loan is being used for an improper purpose (pigs) should the *ultra vires* nature of the transaction (and hence its impropriety) become clear to him.

(3) If *ultra vires* transactions are void, then why, in the situation discussed in question 2 above, should it be relevant that the third party has knowledge of the purpose? In other words, if the doctrine is that there is no corporate capacity to perform the act, then how does the company suddenly acquire capacity simply by virtue of the fact that the third party has no knowledge of the improper purpose? It is difficult to find an answer to this in the case law. It is probable that in order to protect a third party who is innocent, the courts have allowed an illogicality to creep into the *ultra vires* doctrine.

A later case, *Rolled Steel Products Ltd* v *British Steel Corporation*,[27] provides a very different analysis to the problems posed by the distinction between objects and powers. The analysis has its own difficulties. Here, the claimant company had in its memorandum express power to give guarantees. It gave a guarantee of another company's debt (SSS Ltd) to another company (C Ltd). In return for the guarantee the claimant received a loan from C Ltd to enable it to pay off the claimant company's existing debt to SSS Ltd. The liability under the guarantee was greater than the debt owed by it and so there was a partly gratuitous element in the giving of the guarantee. In other words, to some extent at least, the guarantee was not being given for a proper commercial purpose. Later, the claimant company ran into financial difficulties and to help alleviate its position it brought an action for a declaration that the guarantee was unenforceable. At first instance Vinelott J held that not all the objects in the memorandum were independent objects and the object here to give guarantees was merely a power which was ancillary to the objects of the company. Therefore, if the transaction was for a purpose not authorised by the memorandum it could be *ultra vires* even though it was within the scope of the express powers. Although a third party who did not know of the *ultra vires* purpose would, following *Re Introductions*, nevertheless be able to enforce it, here, the third party, C Ltd, were aware that the guarantee was partly gratuitous and not for the benefit of the claimant company, and so it was unenforceable.

An appeal to the Court of Appeal failed, with the result that the guarantee remained unenforceable. However, the reasons that the court gave, differed substantially from the analysis adopted at first instance. This approach avoids some of the evident illogicality of the *Re Introductions* analysis but, as will be seen, raises puzzles of its own. In essence, the Court of Appeal held that where the objects clause of the memorandum contains an express power to carry out an act, then the

---

[25] *Re David Payne & Co Ltd* [1904] 2 Ch 608 and *Re Jon Beauforte (London) Ltd* [1953] 2 Ch 131.
[26] Or gets constructive notice.
[27] [1986] Ch 246.

company has *vires* (power) to do that act. In other words, express[28] powers are not read down or limited by reference to the objects or purposes of the company.[29] As regards corporate capacity, this approach disposed of the problem in *Rolled Steel*: the company had given a guarantee, it had express power to give guarantees, therefore the guarantee was *intra vires*. However, that was not the end of the analysis. When directors purport to exercise a power, that exercise can sometimes be vitiated. For the purposes of this discussion, there are broadly two ways that this can happen.

First, the exercise may be vitiated because the directors were never given such a power by the constitution of the company. In such a case, their action can be said to be an *excess* of power. This is really an aspect of the law of agency. An agent who exceeds her power and acts outside her actual authority may nevertheless bind her principal if she acts within his apparent authority.[30] However, a third party who is seeking to make the company liable on the basis of apparent authority will not be able to do so where the facts which he has become aware of make it clear to him that the agent has no actual authority, for there is then, no appearance of authority.

The second way in which a power can be vitiated is where it has actually been given to the directors, but is nevertheless exercised for a purpose which is improper. This can be described as an *abuse* of power. The point here is simply is that directors are fiduciaries and are bound to exercise their powers in good faith for the benefit of the company, and for a proper (not collateral) purpose. On this analysis, where directors caused the company to enter into a transaction which did not benefit it in the sense of taking it further down the path described in the objects clause of the memorandum, then this would be an abuse of power. This could occur, for instance, where a power to borrow was exercised for a commercial purpose which was not in the memorandum, such as where it was for a trade not authorised by the memorandum, or was given for improper motives such as to help friends of the directors, or where it was gratuitous and given for solely charitable reasons. A third party, who has become aware of facts which make it clear to him that the action of the directors is an abuse of power, will be in the same position as any other person who deals with a fiduciary, knowing that they are acting in breach of trust.[31]

Traces of both these approaches can be found in *Rolled Steel*. The exercise of the power to give guarantees was variously described as an *excess* of power, and as an *abuse* of power.[32] This is not surprising, as it is obvious that many situations could be analysed in either way, and that both ways broadly amount to the same thing which is being looked at differently through the eyes of the Courts of Common

---

[28] It was suggested that the same approach could be adopted for implied powers (*ibid.*, p. 287). Thus, where the common law would, under the doctrine of implied powers, have implied a power, then such a power would not be read down by reference to the objects. This is probably correct in principle and so the power to borrow, which would be implied for a trading company at common law (*General Auction Estate* v *Smith* [1891] 3 Ch 432), would not be read down by reference to purposes expressed in the objects clause.

[29] As they were in the *Re Introductions* approach (above).

[30] On this agency concept, see further p. 133 below.

[31] They will hold any property received on a constructive trust for the company; see below, for this result in *Rolled Steel*.

[32] [1986] Ch 246 at pp. 281, 286, 297.

Law, and the Courts of Chancery. However, the dominant analysis in *Rolled Steel* seems to have been that based on abuse of power. Thus the giving of the guarantee was an abuse of power and the third party C Ltd was aware of the circumstances which made the giving of the guarantee an abuse of power and therefore held it on constructive trust for the company.[33]

The *Rolled Steel* approach shifts the focus of the analysis away from the problem of the capacity of the company and onto the question of whether the directors have power and whether they have exercised that power in a way which is consistent with their fiduciary obligations, chief of which in the present context is to advance the company down the path[34] laid out in the objects clause of the memorandum and not down some other path of their own choosing. The approach has the merit that it provides a satisfactory answer to question 3 which was discussed above.[35] The explanation is that the situation[36] is not an *ultra vires*[37] problem at all; there is an express power in the memorandum and so the company has capacity and if the directors have abused their power, the third party will not be adversely affected by that unless he is aware of the impropriety.

As well as adopting its new approach, the Court of Appeal in *Rolled Steel* made a valiant effort to 're-explain' the older cases, particularly *Re Introductions*, in such a way as to bring them into line with the new approach. The suggestion that the judicial analysis in *Re Introductions* is the same as the new approach in *Rolled Steel* is unconvincing, with the result that under the doctrine in *Young* v *Bristol Aeroplane Co. Ltd*[38] a later court is free to choose between the two conflicting approaches of the Court of Appeal: on the one hand, the approach in *Re Introductions*[39] and on the other, the analysis in *Rolled Steel*. Subsequent cases have failed to establish any clear preference. The decision of Hoffmann J (as he then was) in *Aveling Barford* v *Perion*[40] arguably has traces of the *Re Introductions* analysis. *Halifax Building Society* v *Meridian Housing Association*,[41] a decision of Arden J (as she then was), contained a clear endorsement and useful example of the *Rolled Steel* approach. Meridian had entered into an agreement to develop a site, consisting of offices and flats. Meridian was now in receivership and the question had arisen of whether it was within Meridian's capacity to develop the site, for office purposes. The objects clause of

---

[33] This presumably neutralised it, on the basis that the guarantee, a chose in action, was held on trust for the person it gave an action against. However, a cloud hangs over this analysis, in view of the approach taken by the House of Lords in *Criterion Properties plc* v *Stratford LLC* [2004] BCC 570, and it is likely that in future cases involving an executory contract between two parties, the analysis will focus on agency concepts rather than fiduciary concepts.

[34] Or at any rate, if no 'path' is evident from the memorandum, to observe the limits on the activities of the company, set out there.

[35] On p. 116.

[36] Envisaged in question 2 and referred to in question 3, pp. 116–117 above.

[37] The term '*ultra vires*' is used in this book to denote the situation where the activity is outside the scope of the objects clause of the memorandum of association (taken together with any implied powers) and hence beyond the capacity of the *company*. It is quite obvious that since the term means (literally) 'beyond the powers', it could also be used to describe the situation where the directors have acted beyond their powers. But to use it in that way is thoroughly confusing in the present context.

[38] [1944] KB 718.

[39] And with it, *Re David Payne & Co Ltd* [1904] 2 Ch 608 (also Court of Appeal).

[40] (1989) 5 BCC 677.

[41] [1994] 2 BCLC 540.

the memorandum of association of Meridian included the following: '2. To carry on the industry business or trade of providing housing or any associated amenities. 3. [Meridian] shall have power to do all things necessary or expedient for the fulfilment of its objects.'

The matter focused on whether the development of the offices *could* ever be performed as reasonably incidental to the pursuit of the objects set out in clause 2. It was held that it clearly could, since it would have been incidental to provide an estate office in connection with residential development. Whether this would have been an improper exercise of power was irrelevant to the question of whether it was within the capacity of Meridian.

It is now necessary to take a closer look at some of the not-so-obvious effects of the *Rolled Steel* approach. The main point really is that the approach has the (probably unintended) effect of abolishing the *ultra vires* doctrine in most situations. It has been common practice for over a century for companies to put a long list of powers into the objects clause, in addition to the long list of objects or purposes; thus, the objects clause will normally contain, for example, power to borrow, power to give guarantees, power to make contracts, power to hold land etc, etc. Even if certain powers are not present, we have already seen that the common law has a doctrine of implied powers[42] and it seems that *Rolled Steel* applies to implied powers as well as express powers. The effect of the existence of these powers is that in virtually any problem which looks like a classic example of *ultra vires* (lack of corporate capacity) the mere existence of the power will be sufficient to give the company capacity.

The point can be reiterated by looking again at *Ashbury Railway Carriage and Iron Company* v *Riche*.[43] There, it was held that the building of the railway was *ultra vires*, because it was not covered by the phrase in the objects clause 'to carry on the business of mechanical engineers and general contractors'. A *Rolled Steel* analysis of the case would go as follows: the memorandum contained express power, to 'make contracts . . .' or although the objects clause of the memorandum contained no express power for the company to 'enter into contracts . . .'; nevertheless since this was a trading company it would clearly need power 'to enter into contracts' and so such a power would be implied.[44] Having been expressly included or implied, it would not be 'read down' by reference to the objects[45] and so, as a matter of corporate capacity, the situation poses no problems; the contract is *intra vires*. Nevertheless, the directors were abusing their powers in that they were causing the company to enter into a contract knowing that it was outside the scope of the purposes expressed in the objects clause. They were therefore in breach of fiduciary duty. Riche, the third party, was aware of the circumstances which showed that they were in breach of duty, namely, he was aware of the nature of the contract and had actual

---

[42] See further at p. 116 above.

[43] (1875) LR 7 HL 653, see p. 114 above.

[44] In accordance with the doctrine of implied powers. An objection might be that a power as general as this would never be implied. But, on the other hand, a general 'power to borrow' would normally be implied for a trading company (see *Anglo Overseas Agencies* v *Green* [1961] 1 QB) and objects clauses frequently contain such wide powers.

[45] As *Re Introductions* would require. See p. 116 above.

or constructive notice of the contents of the memorandum and therefore he held the benefit of the contract on constructive trust[46] for the company.

It is probable that the *Rolled Steel* approach will be followed in later cases.[47] To some extent this is convenient, since it is highly arguable,[48] that the effect of the 1989 legislative reforms is to produce a situation similar to that pertaining at common law under the *Rolled Steel* approach. On the other hand, as will be seen, the drafting of the 1989 legislation does not fully take account of the effects produced by *Rolled Steel*.

D Shareholder intervention

Before looking at the effect of the 1989 statutory reforms on all this, one more aspect of the case law needs to be mentioned. It is clear from a number of cases[49] that a shareholder of a company has a right[50] to seek an injunction to restrain a company and/or its directors from entering into an *ultra vires* act. This has been a well-recognised exception to the principle of *Foss* v *Harbottle*[51] which normally suppresses litigation by shareholders. This aspect of the *ultra vires* doctrine is sometimes referred to as the 'internal' aspect of the doctrine since the action of the directors is restrained before any outside party has become involved and the issue is fought out between the directors and some of the shareholders.

E The current legislation – background matters

The Companies Act 1989 contained a package of provisions which were designed to restrict the *ultra vires* doctrine in various ways. To some extent they were intended to implement the First Company Law Directive, which had required the *ultra vires* doctrine to be removed, as against outsiders dealing with the company. The 1989 provisions replaced an earlier attempt contained in the European Communities Act 1972,[52] which had been felt to be deficient. The 1989 provisions present problems, not least because they are overlaid on what Parliament imagined was the common law of *ultra vires*.

Probably the least difficulty is presented by what is now s. 4 of the Companies Act 1985.[53] This provides that a company may by special resolution alter the

---

[46] Or alternatively, following the approach of the House of Lords in *Criterion* (see fn.33 above), the directors had no actual or apparent authority to bind the company.

[47] It is unlikely that there will be many.

[48] The case is made at p. 127 below.

[49] Examples are *Hutton* v *West Cork Railway Company* (1883) 23 Ch D 654; *Parke* v *Daily News* [1962] Ch 927. To some extent these cases have been overturned by statute: see Companies Act 1985, s. 719.

[50] The extent to which this survives the advent of *Rolled Steel* is discussed at p. 126 below.

[51] See further p. 213 below.

[52] Section 9 (1). This section became s. 35 in the consolidating Companies Act 1985, until its repeal and replacement by new provisions in 1989. It is important to note therefore that between 1972 and 1989 there was a different statutory regime in force which made certain amendments to the common law.

[53] Substituted by Companies Act 1989, s. 110 (2).

objects clause in its memorandum.[54] The previous provision was limited to certain grounds which seriously impinged on the ability of companies to make much use of it. The new section provides much more scope for avoiding *ultra vires*/abuse of power problems, although it is unlikely that small companies who do not have the benefit of a professional company secretary will in fact make much use of it.

Less happy is s. 3A of the Companies Act 1985.[55] It was probably intended to reverse the longstanding corporate practice of putting lengthy lists of powers and purposes into the objects clause. But there is a problem with it. Section 3A provides:

> Where the company's memorandum states that the object of the company is to carry on business as a general commercial company –
> (a) the object of the company is to carry on any trade or business whatsoever, and
> (b) the company has power to do all such things as are incidental or conducive to the carrying on of any trade or business by it.

Paragraph (a) is clearly effective to give the company discretion to engage in a very wide range of commercial activities. However, it is not possible to say that para. (a) gives the company unlimited objects. For instance, could it carry on a *profession*, as an incorporated accountancy firm? Maybe this would be a 'business'. Would para. (a) give the company non-commercial objects, such as to make gratuitous gifts of a charitable or educational or political nature? Probably not; this point is taken up in the next paragraph.

Paragraph (b) raises a problem.[56] Companies often wish to make political or charitable gifts, or make payments which are gratuitous, such as a gift of a pension to a director who is not legally entitled to any pension.[57] The case law shows that arguments that these things are incidental (or conducive or ancillary) to its trade and for its benefit are difficult to maintain (although not impossible).[58] A considerable breakthrough came in 1982 when it was decided by the Court of Appeal in *Re Horsley & Weight*[59] that the objects clause could make it clear that non-commercial purposes (such as charitable or educational purposes) were to be regarded as independent objects of the company sitting alongside its commercial purposes. This had the result that there was no need to show that the pursuit of these non-commercial objects was incidental or conducive to the commercial objects. A company which utilises s. 3A with its para. (b) will find that its power to make non-commercial payments is considerably more limited than if it had drafted its own objects clause, picking up on the points contained in *Re Horsley & Weight*.

One last point remains before turning to an analysis of the main provisions. The Companies Act 1989 contained a provision which purported to abolish the con-

---

[54] Aggrieved parties may apply to the court for the alteration to be cancelled: Companies Act 1985, ss. 4 (2), 5.

[55] Inserted by Companies Act 1989, s. 110 (1).

[56] Although some of that difficulty stems from the limitations of s. 3A (a).

[57] See also pp. 59–60 above. The making of political donations is now subject to procedures contained in the Companies Act 1985, ss. 347A–K.

[58] *Re Lee Behrens & Co Ltd* [1932] 2 Ch 46; *Re W & M Roith* [1967] 1 WLR 432. But, see *Evans v Brunner Mond* [1921] 1 Ch 359 where the gift was held to be of sufficient benefit to the company.

[59] [1982] Ch 442.

structive notice doctrine; not merely in the context of *ultra vires* and related areas, but generally, for all areas of company law.[60] But it was never brought into force. Section 142 of the 1989 Act would have amended the Companies Act 1985 by inserting a s. 711A. This would have provided:

> (1) A person shall not be taken to have notice of any matter merely because of its being disclosed in any document kept by the registrar of companies (and thus available for inspection) or made available by the company for inspection.
>
> (2) This does not affect the question whether a person is affected by notice of any matter by reason of a failure to make such enquiries as ought reasonably to be made.

The drafting of this is unfortunate, because the open-ended provision in subs. (2) seems to cut across the intention of subs. (1), leaving it quite unclear as to when the protection of subs. (1) would be available. Not surprisingly, this has not been brought into force.[61] There are however, other provisions which are designed to abolish constructive notice in the *ultra vires* and related areas. These *are* in force, are fundamental, and are discussed next.

F Core provisions of the legislation

The main provisions affecting the *ultra vires* doctrine are contained in ss. 35, 35A and 35B[62] of the Companies Act 1985.[63] It is by no means clear how they fit together or how they interact with the underlying case law. The relevant[64] provisions are as follows:

> **35.**—(1) The validity of an act done by a company shall not be called into question on the ground of lack of capacity by reason of anything in the company's memorandum.
>
> (2) A member of a company may bring proceedings to restrain the doing of an act which but for subsection (1) would be beyond the company's capacity; but no such proceedings shall lie in respect of an act to be done in fulfilment of a legal obligation arising from a previous act of the company.
>
> (3) It remains the duty of the directors to observe any limitations on their powers flowing from the company's memorandum; and action by the directors which but for subsection (1) would be beyond the company's capacity may only be ratified by the company by special resolution.
>
> A resolution ratifying such action shall not affect any liability incurred by the directors or any other person; relief from any such liability must be agreed to separately by special resolution. . . .
>
> **35A.**—(1) In favour of a person dealing with a company in good faith, the power of the board of directors to bind the company, or authorise others to do so, shall be deemed to be free of any limitation under the company's constitution. . . .
>
> **35B.**—A party to a transaction with a company is not bound to enquire as to whether it is

---

[60] Although it has little significance in most areas.

[61] Its sole function on the statute book has been as a trap for students and textbook writers!

[62] Sections 35A and 35B are discussed further at p. 138 below in the context of agency and the 'Turquand rule'.

[63] They were substituted for the former provision by Companies Act 1989, s. 108.

[64] Relevant for the purpose of gaining a broad understanding of what is going on. No reference is made to ss. 35 (4) and 35A (6) which contain exceptions, where the third parties are directors or their associates (s. 322A), and where the companies are charities.

permitted by the company's memorandum or as to any limitation on the powers of the board of directors to bind the company or authorise others to do so.

In the context of *ultra vires*,[65] it is suggested that the effect of these provisions is as follows.

It seems clear that, taken by itself,[66] s. 35 (1) is intended to abolish the *ultra vires* doctrine; there is reference to 'capacity', i.e. *vires*, and to the 'memorandum', i.e. the objects clause. It is not clear on its face whether s. 35 (1) is also intended to abolish the effect of limitations contained in the memorandum which have an effect on the powers (i.e. capacity) of the *directors* rather than the company. On the face of it, an act done by the directors would still be an act of the company within the meaning of the statute. However, the express reference to the continuing effect of the memorandum on directors' powers in s. 35 (3) probably shows that s. 35 (1) is not meant to be read in this way and that it only refers to corporate capacity. This interpretation is supported by the fact that there are yet further provisions in s. 35A which deal very specifically with the effects on third parties of transactions which are beyond the capacity of directors by reason of the memorandum or (appropriately) the articles.

However, s. 35 (2) makes it clear that the abolition of the *ultra vires* doctrine which is achieved by s. 35 (1) is only partial, and that within the company, it is still operative, so that directors can be restrained from entering into *ultra vires* acts.[67] The way that s. 35 (2) achieves this is curious, seeming to accept that *ultra vires* is abolished by s. 35 (1) but inviting the reader to imagine whether a remedy 'would' have been available 'but for' the abolition. Presumably a would-be litigant has to ask himself the question whether the case law principles under the *ultra vires* doctrine would have entitled him to a remedy. And, presumably, the hearing of his application for the injunction would proceed on the background basis that the proposed act of the company was in fact within the capacity of the company (i.e. *intra vires*) and the live issue between the parties would be what would have been the result had *ultra vires* not been abolished. It is arguable also that the parties would have to proceed on the basis that the development of the case law had been frozen as at the date of the coming into force of s. 35 (1). While all this may be the result of a literal (though uncharitable) reading of the statute, it is likely that a court dealing with this would simply cut through or ignore the theoretical niceties of s. 35 (2) and take a pragmatic view to the effect that the *ultra vires* doctrine exists within the company, and further, that the case law on that matter continues to develop in the normal way.

As briefly mentioned above, s. 35 (3) provides that *it remains* the duty of the directors to observe any limitations on their powers flowing from the company's memorandum. Here, it is pertinent to ask, 'remains? remains after what?'; the answer being: 'after the abolition, by s. 35 (1), of the possibility of an act being called into question on the ground of lack of capacity by reason of the memoran-

---

[65] The effect of ss. 35A and 35B on agency and the *Turquand* rule is discussed at p. 138 below.

[66] But see the next paragraph.

[67] But there is a limit on this; a shareholder will have to catch the directors and intervene before the company has become bound by contract. This is clear from part of s. 35 (2) which reads: 'but no such proceedings shall lie in respect of an act to be done in fulfilment of a legal obligation arising from a previous act of the company.'

dum'. It is clear, therefore, that even after s. 35 (1) has removed the problem of corporate capacity, the directors are still subject to limitations on their powers.

There is an obvious parallel here with the common law analysis under *Rolled
Steel*, which, it will be recalled, in effect removed the problem of corporate capacity
by refusing to read down corporate powers by reference to the objects, but retained
the problem in a different form by treating the objects as limitations on the powers
of the directors (rather than the company), so that an infringement of the limitation
would be seen as either an excess or abuse of power. Thus it can be seen, that,
broadly speaking, the effect of s. 35 is to enact the decision in *Rolled Steel*.

The external effect of *Rolled Steel* (i.e. its effect on a third party) was that if the
third party was aware of the abuse of power (or excess of power) then they would
hold the benefit of the contract on constructive trust for the company. The legislation here is similar in that it contemplates that the third party could be adversely
affected, although it does not spell out under what principles that would happen.[68]
What it does do is to spell out in great detail principles under which the constitution of the company, is removed from the factual matrix to which the underlying
common law is to be applied. This is achieved by ss. 35B and 35A. Section 35B,[69]
in effect, abolishes the doctrine of constructive notice in this area by making it clear
that the third party is 'not bound to enquire' as to whether the transaction is permitted by the memorandum or as to whether there are any limitations on the
powers of the board of directors to bind the company (or authorise others to do so).

Section 35A, which to some extent overlaps with s. 35B, very substantially
restricts the extent to which the constitution of the company can affect a third party.
Section 35A (1) is a deeming provision, which provides that the power of the board
to bind the company[70] shall be deemed to be free of any limitation under the
company's constitution.[71] The deeming effect is expressed to occur only 'in favour
of a person dealing[72] with a company in good faith'[73] and the third party is presumed to have acted in good faith unless the contrary is proved.[74] As well as making
it clear that the burden is not on the third party to prove his good faith, the legislation deals with another problem which could easily arise at common law, namely
that of the unsophisticated third party who has actually been sent the memorandum

---

[68] Broadly leaving the common law principles to govern the situation, although subject to the legislative
amendments of ss. 35A and 35B.

[69] The full text is given above.

[70] '[O]r authorise others to do so.' These words have more significance in the context of agency and the
Turquand rule and are discussed at p. 141 below. Also discussed there is s. 35A (3), which has no relevance in the *ultra vires* context.

[71] It is very important to realise that an infringement of a limitation under the constitution can give rise
to an *excess* of power, or an *abuse* of power as explained at pp. 118–119 above. Or, to put it the other
way round, excess of power or abuse of power situations can both stem from limitations under the
company's constitution and are thus capable of being cured by the deeming provision of s. 35A (1);
provided of course that the conditions in s. 35A are satisfied.

[72] The word 'dealing' has the meaning given in s. 35A (2) (b): 'a person "deals with" a company if he
is a party to any transaction or other act to which the company is a party'. Thus, receiving a gratuitous distribution from the company would fall within the concept of dealing, for while it arguably
does not amount to a 'transaction', such a gift would certainly be an 'other act to which the company
is a party'.

[73] Section 35A (1).

[74] Section 35A (2) (c).

and knows all the facts from which it could reasonably be deduced that the trans-action is *ultra vires* or an abuse or excess of power but who actually has no inkling that there is anything wrong, indeed he has probably not thought about it at all. Although it has never really been finally settled, under the common law there was at least a likelihood that such a person would be held to be aware of the problems and thus adversely affected by the *ultra vires* or improper nature of the transaction; their subjective honesty would be irrelevant if objectively they should have realised what was going on.[75] The solution adopted is in s. 35A (2) (b), which provides:

> a person shall not be regarded as acting in bad faith by reason only of his knowing that an act is beyond the powers of the directors under the company's constitution.

The effect of this is to prevent a court from automatically inferring bad faith (and so depriving the third party of the protection of s. 35A (1)) merely because he has knowl-edge of the factual technicalities which make the act beyond the powers of the direc-tors. It is easy to exaggerate the effect of the provision. It is clearly not intended to make the knowledge that the act is beyond the powers of the directors into an irrele-vance, and it is obvious that anyone who is acting in bad faith will usually have to have such knowledge. Probably all that is really happening here, is that the legislation is emphasising the need to prove subjective bad faith, and so where a third party is genu-inely unaware of the significance of the technicalities he will not be adversely affected by them. With this background in mind, s. 35A (2) (b) makes sense.[76]

It is clear that the deeming effect of s. 35A (1) only operates in favour of a third party. The limitations in the constitution still apply internally so that the directors may be liable for exceeding their powers.[77] Rather oddly, s. 35A (4) appears as a matching provision to s. 35 (2); it provides that s. 35A (1) does not affect any right of a member of the company to bring proceedings to restrain the doing of an act which is beyond the powers of the directors.[78] But would a member have such a right? It is true that he would have a right under the case law[79] to restrain an act which was going to be beyond the capacity of the *company*, i.e. *ultra vires*, as s. 35 (2) indeed contemplates. However, decisions of the courts give no such right to a member to restrain an act which would be beyond the powers of *directors*, for under the case law[80] such an act would usually be held to be a ratifiable breach of duty and so litigation by a member would be prohibited by the rule in *Foss v Harbottle*.[81]

---

[75] Eg, in *Re Jon Beauforte (London) Ltd* [1953] Ch 131 the luckless third party who had supplied coke to the company was expected to have realised from the letter heading that the company was engaged in an *ultra vires* activity. The uncompromising nature of the common law in this field is further revealed by the technical and unrealistic constructive notice doctrine. The imposition of constructive trust liability was similarly rigorous (see *Selangor v Cradock*, at least until the advent of *Royal Brunei Airlines Sdn Bhd v Tan* discussed at p. 307 below).

[76] The approach is in line with the current approach of the common law in *Royal Brunei Airlines Sdn Bhd v Tan*, under which a constructive trust is not to be imposed unless 'dishonesty' can be proved.

[77] Section 35A (5).

[78] With the familiar proviso protecting settled obligations: 'but no such proceedings shall lie in respect of an act to be done in fulfilment of a legal obligation arising from a previous act of the company.'

[79] See p. 121 above.

[80] See at pp. 217–218 below.

[81] Unless the act amounted to a fraud on the minority and hence non-ratifiable. See further at p. 218 below.

It is difficult to be conclusive about the effect of s. 35A (4); but probably its func-tion is to preserve[82] the member's rights in the narrow class of cases falling within the exceptions to the rule in *Foss* v *Harbottle*.[83]

G Ratification

It will be recalled that the traditional *ultra vires* doctrine of *Ashbury Railway Carriage and Iron Company* v *Riche* involved the assumption that the *ultra vires* act was not susceptible of ratification. Section 35 (3) modifies this by providing that action by the directors which, but for s. 35 (1), would be beyond the company's capacity may only be ratified by the company by special resolution. It is difficult to see that the provision makes a great deal of difference, since it is expressed to only apply to mat-ters which s. 35 (1) has acted on and if s. 35 (1) has acted, then the company will be bound anyway whether or not it ratifies. Perhaps it is meant to provide the company with a means of tidying up things internally when faced with the effect of s. 35 (1). A further problem arises from Parliament's failure to consider the effect of *Rolled Steel*, namely that the ratification by special resolution is expressed to apply to action, which but for s. 35 (1) would be beyond the company's capacity. Since the effect of *Rolled Steel* is that action will very rarely be beyond the capacity of the company (there will be an express or implied power which will not be 'read down'), it is unlikely that s. 35 (3) will have made much difference in this respect.

There remains the further difficulty of what happens as regards ratification of the abuse or excess of power. The common law will permit ratification by ordinary res-olution unless the matter amounts to a 'fraud on the minority' when the only method of ratification that will be sufficient is the agreement of all the members of the company.[84] However, it is possible that the effect of the last sentence of s. 35 (3) is to require that the ratification be by special resolution, at least in circum-stances where the matter has been technically *ultra vires* so as to attract the oper-ation of s. 35 (1). Or it may be that the last sentence of s. 35 (3) refers only to the matter of relieving the directors of liability for breach of duty and that the question of whether the company ratifies in the sense of adopting the contract still falls to be dealt with under the common law.

H Pulling it together

So how does this all fit together? A useful way of illustrating this is to turn (again) to the facts of *Re Introductions*[85] and consider how a court would decide the case now. The company, which had originally been formed to provide facilities for the Festival of Britain, was now involved in pig breeding and had borrowed from a bank. The memorandum contained an express power to borrow. The bank had actual notice of the contents of the memorandum, having been sent a copy, and was aware that the money was to be used for pig breeding. The liquidator was arguing that the company

---

[82] Its wording is significantly different from s. 35 (2).
[83] Perhaps the practical solution lies in bringing the claim under s. 459 rather than at common law.
[84] See further p. 158 below.
[85] [1970] Ch 199. The facts of the case are given in more detail at p. 116 above.

did not have to pay the bank because the loan was *ultra vires* and void. In the Court of Appeal this argument succeeded because the express power to borrow was read down by reference to the objects.

At the present day, the argument that the loan was *ultra vires* and void would clearly fail. It would be nullified by s. 35 (1), which provides that the validity of an act done by a company shall not be called into question on the ground of lack of capacity by reason of anything in the memorandum. Additionally, if the judge used the analysis adopted in *Rolled Steel*[86] there would be no problem of corporate capacity anyway, because of the presence in the memorandum of an express power to borrow. Either way, by statute, or by the *Rolled Steel* analysis at common law, the corporate capacity problem is eliminated.[87]

But under s. 35 (3), it would remain the duty of the directors to observe limitations on their powers flowing from the memorandum. This would have been the same at common law under a *Rolled Steel* analysis, so here again, it would seem that the legislation more or less enacts *Rolled Steel*. It is clear that by causing the company to borrow money for pig breeding the directors ignored the limitations on their powers flowing from the memorandum. The question would then arise of whether the third party, the bank, would be adversely affected by this. Under the present law, the answer to this will depend on whether the bank is in 'good faith' because, if it is in good faith, then s. 35A (1) will generate a deemed removal of the limitations on the powers of the board contained in the company's constitution. The removal from the factual matrix of the problem of the constitutional limitations effectively removes the existence of any legal principle under which the transaction could be set aside against the third party bank.

So, is the bank in good faith? Would the liquidator have been able to prove that they were in bad faith? We cannot be sure. Bad faith would be something for the trial judge to find as a proven fact from the evidence before him or her. It is clear from s. 35A (2) (b) that merely showing that the bank knew that the loan was beyond the powers of the directors would not of itself establish bad faith. On the other hand, it might not take all that much more for a judge to reach the conclusion that a commercial organisation like a bank were in bad faith, in the circumstances.[88] So ss. 35 and 35A may have reversed the factual result in *Re Introductions*, or they may not.

Other points can be illustrated if the discussion of *Re Introductions* is continued, but with certain of the facts altered. Suppose, for instance, that a shareholder heard about the plan of the directors to get a loan from the bank and wished to prevent them doing it. Could the shareholder get an injunction on the basis that the threatened act was *ultra vires*? The common law answer to this was probably 'yes', on the basis that a shareholder has a right to restrain the commission of an *ultra vires* act;

---

[86] Rather than the 'reading down' approach actually adopted by the Court of Appeal in *Re Introductions*.

[87] The common law position is only mentioned at this point to show the extent to which the legislation follows the path already laid down by *Rolled Steel*. It is not being suggested that the judge has a choice; the statute prevails.

[88] Again, the Act, to a great extent, mirrors the path of the common law, because there too, the issue would be good faith, or at any rate, lack of dishonesty, for under *Royal Brunei Airlines Sdn Bhd* v *Tan* [1995] 3 All ER 97 (see below) the directors' improper exercise of power would only give rise to a constructive trust if the bank could be shown to have been 'dishonest'.

see *Parke* v *Daily News*.[89] As we have seen, s. 35 (2) puts this on a statutory footing by providing that a member of a company may bring proceedings to restrain the doing of an act which but for s. 35 (1) would be beyond the company's capacity. Effectively it refers back to the common law. But there may be a problem if the *Rolled Steel* method of analysis is adopted, rather than that actually used by the Court of Appeal in *Re Introductions*. For the *Rolled Steel* analysis of the facts of *Re Introductions* would not produce the result that anything *ultra vires* the company was happening. There was an express power to borrow and so the borrowing would have been held to be within the capacity of the company, although an abuse of power by the directors. So, s. 35 (2) would not apply. Section 35A (4) might help, although there is still the problem that at common law, an abuse or excess of power by directors would not give a shareholder a right to an action unless it amounted to a fraud on the minority.[90] Again, s. 35 (2) illustrates the difficulties involved in reforming the law with regard to the *ultra vires* doctrine by leaving the underlying common law intact and bolting on a layer of statute which expressly or impliedly refers back to that common law. It is a tinkering approach, rather than a codification, in an area where the common law was fraught with complexity and uncertainty.

I An alternative approach

In addition to the analysis above, there is another way of looking at the provisions of s. 35 and s. 35A (1) of the Companies Act 1985.[91]

This involves giving a stronger rendering to s. 35 (1) and a weaker rendering to s. 35 (3). Thus, s. 35 (1) is seen as dealing with any capacity problems flowing from the memorandum, whether relating to the capacity of the company, or the capacity of the directors. There is no obvious reason, so the argument runs, why the word 'capacity' in s. 35 (1) should not refer to the capacity of the directors as well as the capacity of the company.[92] This is coupled with a weaker rendering of s. 35 (3) so that it is read as meaning that the limitations in the memorandum on directors' capacity are 'remaining', in the sense that they exist in law only in an internal sense; that they are owed to the company, but that they are not normal fiduciary duties and so a third party who deals with a director, knowing that he is dealing in bad faith and in breach of duty, will not be in danger of being affected by that breach of duty (such as by being made constructive trustee) because of the power of s. 35

---

[89] [1962] Ch 927. NB: the effect of subsequent legislation (s. 719) on the outcome of that case.

[90] See the earlier discussion at p. 127 above and suggested solution.

[91] A number of other perspectives on these sections will become apparent from the analysis of agency law which appears at pp. 138–141 below.

[92] This somewhat flies in the face of s. 35 (2) and (3), which clearly seems to contemplate s. 35 (1) as referring to the company's capacity, since both subss. (2) and (3) contain the phrase 'which but for subsection (1) would be beyond the company's capacity'. Other oddities are produced. If s. 35 (1) applies to directors' capacity (i.e. powers) as well as corporate capacity, then why is s. 35 (2) made expressly only to apply to corporate capacity? 'Perhaps it was not intended to give that right to shareholders in relation to acts which are merely beyond the directors' powers' may be the answer. But this is obviously wrong, in the light of s. 35A (4).

(1) which provides a blanket protection for third parties in its wording the 'validity ... shall not be called into question'.

This interpretation of s. 35 (1) has the effect of leaving ss. 35A and 35B to deal with limitations on authority flowing from parts of the constitution other than the memorandum. This in itself creates a problem for this approach because it sometimes opens a gap in how third parties are treated, with the gap depending entirely on whether the restriction on authority is contained in the memorandum or in the articles. For instance, if the limitation on the capacity of a director is contained in the memorandum, then a third party who deals with him, knowing that the director is acting in breach of his duty will not be adversely affected by that breach. If however, the limitation was contained in the articles, then s. 35 (1) could clearly have no application and so the situation would be governed by s. 35A which would only protect a third party if he was in good faith. This anomaly and the other difficulties mentioned above make this alternative approach to the construction of s. 35 (1) unattractive.

6.4 COMPANY LAW REVIEW AND LAW REFORM

Not surprisingly, the Company Law Review in the DTI Consultation Document of October 1999, *Company Formation and Capital Maintenance*, produced some ideas for consultation, with a view to laying the *ultra vires* doctrine to rest. The main suggestions are[93] that a company should have unlimited capacity, and a provision to that effect would replace s. 35 (1). However, because of the requirements of the Second Directive, public companies will continue to be required to have a statement of objects in their constitution. It seems that there is no intention to change ss. 35A (1)–(3). In the Final Report it was made clear that companies formed under the new legislation contemplated by the Review would have unlimited capacity.[94] The abolition of limitations on corporate capacity is to be welcomed, and will finally confirm the shift of emphasis in analysing the sort of problems which arise in this area onto an inquiry into the scope and propriety of the exercise of directors' powers. Nevertheless, the drafting of legislation here will need careful handling.

---

[93] DTI Consultation Document (October 1999) *Company Formation and Capital Maintenance* paras 2.35 et seq.

[94] *Modern Company Law for a Competitive Economy Final Report* (London: DTI, 2001) para. 9.10. See also the subsequent government White Paper *Modernising Company Law* (July 2002, Cmnd. 5553) and *Company Law. Flexibility and Accessibility: A Consultative Document* (London: DTI, 2004).

7

RELATIONS WITH THIRD PARTIES:
AGENCY AND CONSTITUTIONAL
LIMITATIONS

7.1 CONTRACTUAL RELATIONS WITH THIRD PARTIES

It has been seen that a company is a person in law, separate from its shareholders. One aspect of that corporate entity doctrine which has not yet been looked at in any detail is the question of how the corporate entity enters into contractual relations with other persons in the legal system; either natural persons or corporate persons. It is an area of law which, although potentially very simple, has over nearly 150 years become encrusted with confused judicial and academic doctrine and as a result of the inevitable statutory attempts to sort it out, usually with the economical, but perplexing bolt-on deeming provisions. The underlying principles are in fact straightforward and this account will endeavour to chart a path through by starting with first principles. If the first principles are then kept in mind throughout, most of the difficulties disappear.

The essential point to grasp (and hold in mind) is that, subject to certain statutory exceptions,[1] in English law it is not possible for a person to sue on, or be sued on, a contract, unless that person is a party to it. It is a rule which the contract lawyers call *privity of contract* (and which everybody learns when they first start to study law).[2] There is also a major common law exception, known as the *doctrine of agency*. Much of the confusion in this area in the context of company law comes from the fact that company lawyers thought that they had invented another major exception, called the rule in *Royal British Bank* v *Turquand*,[3] when they had not.

7.2 AGENCY

In daily corporate life, it is this major exception, the doctrine of agency, which provides the vehicle through which most commercial transactions are carried out by the company,[4] for without it, all that is left is the insuperable theoretical problem

---

[1] Mainly now the Contracts (Rights of Third Parties) Act 1999, which will give a person who is not a party to a contract a right to enforce a contractual provision where the contract expressly provides that he or she may or where the provision purports to confer a benefit on him or her. However, this legislation does not generally affect the analysis of agency concepts in this chapter.

[2] See e.g. *Scruttons* v *Midland Silicones* [1962] AC 446.

[3] (1856) 6 El. & Bl. 327; sometimes also called the 'indoor management rule'.

[4] Some, however, are made under the company's common seal. It is possible that where the company makes the contract in writing under its common seal, the effect of s. 36 (a) of the Companies Act 1985 is that the company thereby enters into a direct privity of contract with the third party and that no

that the company, being a fictional entity, cannot do anything on its own account. The basic idea of agency is that if the agent enters into a contract which is within the scope of the authority given to him by the principal, then the contractual rights and obligations which the agent acquires are transmitted[5] to the principal so that the principal can sue and be sued on the contract. Thus in the context of company law, the company, the principal, finds itself able to sue and be sued on contracts which are made by its agents, such as its directors. In fact the position is not as simple as this, first because agency law is more complicated than has been suggested above and secondly because there are difficulties inserted into the company law context by the existence of the constitution of the company and the consequent case law and legislative responses to the agency exception.

The principal will only be bound by the contract if the agent is acting within the scope of his authority although there are two alternative types of authority which the agent can have, and they are both quite distinct ideas, each with a different rationale. The first type is called *actual* authority and the second is called *apparent* authority.[6]

There will be actual authority where the agent is acting entirely within the mandate given to him by his principal. Actual authority comes about as a result of a consensual relationship between the principal and the agent. The principal has asked the agent to act on his behalf, the agent agrees, and then goes and does it. The contractual rights and obligations which the agent acquires are then transmitted to the principal in accordance with the basic principles of agency.[7] Normally actual authority will be created as a result of an express agreement between the principal and the agent. However, it is now clear that actual authority can come about as a result of a course of dealing between those parties as a result of which the court is able to infer that a contractual relationship exists between them. In this book this is described as *implied* actual authority, as opposed to *express* actual authority. The basic notion of implied actual authority was explained by Lord Denning MR in *Hely Hutchinson* v *Brayhead*,[8] where it was held that the chairman of the board had actual authority to act as managing director arising from the fact that the other

---

agency principle is operating. Section 36 appears to be drawing a distinction between a contract being made (a) *by a company* and (b) *on behalf of a company* by any person acting under its authority.

[5] It is not necessary in this work to explore how this comes about. It can be pragmatically accepted as a long-established reality of the common law.

[6] 'Apparent authority' is the expression used in this book because it best describes the basis on which the principal is held liable. It is in use worldwide, and thus for instance is the term used in the American Restatement of Agency. Other expressions are in use denoting the same concept; of particular currency is the term 'ostensible authority' (see e.g. *Armagas* v *Mundogas* [1986] 2 All ER 385, HL). In the past, other expressions have been common, such as 'agency by estoppel', or 'estoppel authority' (useful as it describes the juridical basis of the authority), 'constructive authority' (confusing; easy to muddle with the constructive notice doctrine), 'implied authority' (very confusing; in view of the fact that modern law contains a subdivision of *actual* authority into 'express' and 'implied'). Obviously the principal will also be bound if he chooses to ratify a contract which is outside the scope of the agent's authority.

[7] Where actual authority is present, it is not necessary for the third party to be aware that he is dealing with an agent; see e.g. *Dyster* v *Randall* [1926] Ch 932.

[8] [1968] 1 QB 549. For a recent exploration of these kinds of issues see *SMC Electronics Ltd* v *Akhter Computers Ltd* [2001] 1 BCLC 433, CA.

directors had acquiesced in his acting as chief executive over many months, although he had never been appointed formally as such.

Entirely different is apparent authority. The broad essence of it is that apparent authority will exist where two conditions are satisfied: first, where it *appears* to the third party that the agent has authority to enter into the contract, and secondly, that the appearance has come about through the *fault* of the principal so that it is fair[9] that he is now estopped from denying that appearance. In the context of a principal which is a company, complicating factors enter into the concept, deriving from the fact that a company will be controlled and represented by various officers, and from the fact that the constitution of the company (which may make prescriptions about the authority of its officers) has traditionally been a public document which third parties have constructive notice of.

The most widely accepted judicial formulation of the idea in circumstances where the principal is a company is that of Diplock LJ in *Freeman & Lockyer (a firm)* v *Buckhurst Park Properties (Mangal) Ltd*:[10]

> [T]he ... law ... can be summarised by stating four conditions which must be fulfilled to entitle a contractor to enforce against a company a contract entered into on behalf of the company by an agent who had no actual authority to do so. It must be shown: (1) that a representation that the agent had authority to enter on behalf of the company into a contract of the kind sought to be enforced was made to the contractor; (2) that such representation was made by a person or persons who had 'actual' authority to manage the business of the company either generally or in respect of those matters to which the contract relates; (3) that he (the contractor) was induced by such representation to enter into the contract, that is, that he in fact relied upon it; and (4) that under its memorandum and articles of association the company was not deprived of the capacity either to enter into a contract of the kind sought to be enforced or to delegate authority to enter into a contract of that kind to the agent.

As regards condition (1), it is clear that the representations can take many forms. They can be oral or written, or they may arise, impliedly, from a state of affairs. Sometimes the representation will not be specifically about the authority the agent has, but instead will be a representation about the status possessed by the agent within a particular organisation. A person with a particular status or in a particular position in a company will often have an 'aura' of apparent authority arising from the commercial fact that a person in that position will usually have that authority. The principal has put him there, and will find himself bound by acts which fall within the scope of authority which a person occupying that position would usually have.[11]

Condition (2) is often misunderstood. What Diplock LJ was getting at here is the point that the representation must come from the principal. The agent cannot

---

[9] And it would not be 'fair' if the third party had not in fact relied on the appearance.
[10] [1964] 2 QB 480 at p. 505.
[11] This is sometimes (potentially misleadingly) referred to as *usual* authority. Sometimes the litigation revolves around this issue: see e.g. *Kreditbank Cassel* v *Schenkers* [1927] 1 KB 826 where the matter before the court was whether a branch manager of a company which operated as forwarding agents would normally have authority to endorse a bill of exchange. A similar issue came up in *Armagas* v *Mundogas* (n. 6 above) where it was debated whether an employee in a particular position would normally have authority to commit the company to a three-year charterparty.

create the appearance of authority all by himself, the appearance has to be created by acts of the principal for obviously the principal will only be bound if he has made representations which he can be said to be estopped from denying, or, to put it another way, which it would be unfair to the third party now to let him deny. So, if the representations have come solely from the 'agent', then there is no basis for holding the principal liable.[12] In many cases, the agent will add his own representation, but it is the representation from the principal which is the one which has legal effect. But, of course, in the company law context, that is not straightforward, because the principal, the corporate entity itself, is not able to do anything because it is an inert and fictional entity. So how could it ever be bound by apparent authority? The answer is that the representation must have come from those who are in fact authorised to represent the company, who are, as Diplock LJ says, 'persons who [have] "actual" authority to manage the business of the company ... [etc]'.

Condition (3) is straightforward. The doctrine of apparent authority rests on fairness. If the third party has not relied on the 'appearance' of authority, then there is no basis for invoking an estoppel against the principal.[13]

Condition (4) of Diplock LJ's formulation was a big element at the time the judgment was given, and the matters under consideration in condition (4) played a large part in the formation of the so-called *Turquand* rule. It will be argued below that the *Turquand* rule has no existence. Even if it has, the matters covered by condition (4) will often be removed from the equation by the operation of recent legislative provisions.[14]

7.3 THE *TURQUAND* DOCTRINE

The approach of the Court of Appeal in *Freeman & Lockyer* was firmly rooted in the doctrine of agency. And yet, although English law had a developed doctrine of agency at least since the end of the 18th century,[15] it was one of the first cases[16] to analyse that kind of company law problem without resort to the *Turquand* rule as a kind of *tabula in naufragio*.[17] Indeed, two of the Lord Justices of Appeal[18] did not even mention it. Diplock LJ in particular clearly felt the need to try to explain the older cases and to set out some clear principles in the format that has been discussed above and this is indicative of the confusion that was prevailing in the textbooks at that time. Even at the present day, the *Turquand* rule is often presented as a substantial part of the overall picture of how companies can enter into contractual relations with third parties.

In *Royal British Bank* v *Turquand*[19] the company argued that it was not liable to repay a loan which had been made to it, because the board of directors had no

---

[12] The point recently arose in *Armagas* v *Mundogas SA* [1986] 2 All ER 385, HL.
[13] In contrast to the position with actual authority.
[14] See at p. 138 below.
[15] See e.g. *Wolf* v *Horncastle* (1798) 1 Bos & P 316.
[16] Although it has to be said, that the analysis of Slade J in *Rama Corporation Ltd* v *Proved Tin and General Investments Ltd* [1952] 2 QB 147 was basically an agency approach.
[17] A plank in a shipwreck (of the analysis).
[18] Diplock and Pearson LJJ.
[19] (1856) 6 E & B 327.

power to borrow since they had not obtained the prior authorisation of the general meeting as the company's constitution required. It was held that the company was liable because, although the third party bank was under a duty to inspect the constitution,[20] on finding that the directors could have power to borrow, it could infer that the general meeting had taken place; in other words, it was not adversely affected by mere matters of 'indoor management'.

Various cases then followed this approach[21] so that where there was a problem involving the company's contractual liability to a third party which was complicated by the presence of clauses in the constitution, *Turquand* became a byword for a quick solution.[22]

7.4 THE 'RELATIONSHIP' BETWEEN *TURQUAND* AND AGENCY

Does the rule in *Turquand* exist? Exist, that is, in the sense that it brings to company law a principle, or set of principles, that are not simply already present by virtue of the doctrines of agency. If *Turquand* adds nothing to agency doctrine there is perhaps no point in mentioning it, for having been conceived as a confused analysis of a simple agency problem, its own potential to confuse is substantial. It will indeed be argued here that there is nothing in the *Turquand* rule which cannot be arrived at by a sensible application of the agency concept of apparent authority.[23] And, equally importantly, that there is nothing in the *Turquand* rule by which a non-party can become entitled to sue on a contract or liable to be sued on it.

These ideas can be illustrated by a detailed example[24] containing the kinds of issues which are found in the 150 years of case law on this field. As with the *ultra vires* doctrine, the matter is complicated by statutory intervention, and again (as with *ultra vires*) it helps to get an understanding of whatever principles are subsisting at common law, because the statutory intervention is of the 'bolt-on' variety[25] whereby the common law is left in existence except to the extent that as a result of the statute, certain facts are 'deemed' to be different. Furthermore, the legislation also raises problems of its own. For this reason, the analysis of the example below will initially proceed on the basis that ss. 35A and 35B of the Companies Act 1985 are not in existence. Their effect will then be added to the analysis.

---

[20] The constructive notice doctrine.
[21] E.g. *Mahoney* v *East Holyford Mining Company* (1875) LR 7 HL 869; *Liggett* v *Barclays Bank* [1928] 1 KB 48.
[22] It became known as the *Turquand* rule, or, the 'indoor management rule'.
[23] The general thrust of this argument is not new; see R. Nock 'The Irrelevance of the Rule of Indoor Management' (1966) 30 Conv (NS) at pp. 123 and 163, arguing that although the earlier cases may have treated the rule in *Turquand*'s case as a special principle of company law, the modern cases show that the rule can be explained entirely through agency concepts. Campbell adopted a similar approach but found a role for *Turquand* as a subordinate stage of an analysis based on agency, arguing that *Turquand* operated as a modification of the doctrine of constructive notice in cases where there is apparent authority; see I. Campbell 'The Contracts with Companies' (1959) 75 LQR 469; (1960) 76 LQR 115.
[24] To some extent following the approach of Campbell, n. 23 above.
[25] In other words it is not a codification, but rather leaves the common law basically intact but chooses to suppress or alter some of the results of it.

Assume that the company, Princedrive Ltd (*P*), runs a mini-cab service throughout the county of Devon and has various branches in the major towns. Alice (*A*) is employed by the company as a branch manager. Article 4A of the articles of association of the company provides that 'branch managers shall have no authority to purchase cars on behalf of the company without the prior permission of the shareholders in general meeting'. Although there had been no such permission given, *A*, purportedly on behalf of the company, contracts to buy a car from Tim (*T*). At some time prior to contracting, *T* is given a copy of the memorandum and articles of association. After contracting but before payment, *T* delivers the car, *A* neglects to insure it, writes it off in a crash and disappears. *T* sues *P* for the contract price. Whatever other issues this problem presents, the main hurdle for *T* is clear. He has dealt with *A* but now wishes to sue *P*, who is not a party to the contract.[26] Logically, at the outset, it is necessary to search for a principle of English law which will enable him to do this.

It is clear from the account of agency doctrine given above that agency may well provide the principle which will enable the third party, *T*, to succeed here. We will return to this. But what about *Turquand*? Does the *Turquand* rule set about providing a way for a non-party to be bound by a contract? Can *T* sue *P*, *because* of the *Turquand* rule? *Turquand* says, that a third party dealing with a company is required only to take notice of its external position and need not inquire into matters of indoor management. So how does this help? True, it may be argued that it will become relevant once the analysis of the above example gets under way on an agency basis, but this is to miss the point here. The rule in *Turquand* thus stated will not provide a mechanism for *T* to circumvent the privity of contract rule and sue *P*.[27] This fundamental deficiency means that whatever role can be found for the *Turquand* rule in this analysis, it is necessarily going to be a subordinate role; subordinate to agency, and perhaps only playing a small part in the overall constellation of legal principles which are operating here. It is of course possible to go further and suggest that *Turquand* adds nothing to the concept of agency. Nevertheless, even armed with the simplicity and power of the agency principle, the analysis is not going to be wholly straightforward, for there is a complicating factor: the clause in the articles of association.

The starting point for the analysis here is, as has been seen, the observation that *T* wishes to sue *P*, but *P* is not a party to the contract between *T* and *A*. It is clear from the discussion of agency principle above, that the doctrine of agency provides a way over the barrier created by the doctrine of privity of contract. *T* will be able to sue *P* if *A* was acting within the scope of her actual or apparent authority. The next step must be to inquire whether the agent, *A*, had actual authority, because if

---

[26] He can certainly sue *A*, with whom he has dealt, for *A* is taken to warrant that she has authority to enter into the contract and is therefore liable for breach of warranty of authority. See *Firbanks Executors* v *Humphries* (1886) 18 QBD 54. But *A* has disappeared.

[27] It could be argued that the rule in *Turquand* is really an embryo and incomplete statement of the application in the company context of the doctrine of agency by apparent authority. If so, then much would have to be added to the traditional statement of it. But even then, there is the problem of deciding whether it actually added anything to the widely accepted concept of agency.

she had, then *T* will be able to sue *P.* The shareholders, in the example had not given authority and so it is clear that there is no actual authority.

If there is no actual authority, the next step is to ask: is there any apparent authority? The answer is that there may be. The first point is that *A* is employed as a branch manager, and will have apparent authority to carry out whatever acts are usually carried out by a person in that position. This may involve the court in hearing evidence of what was common practice in that field of commerce.[28] Let us assume, for the sake of argument, that buying a car was a type of contract usually entered into by branch managers in the mini-cab industry.[29] If there were no clause in the articles, then the discussion may be concluded with the observation that *P* will be bound by the contract because, having employed *A* as a branch manager, *P* will be taken to have held out *A*, as having all the authority that a person in that position would usually have. In other words, there will be apparent authority. However, the presence of clause 4A in the articles of association makes the analysis more complex. It was made clear in the facts of the example that *T* had seen a copy of the memorandum and articles prior to contract. Thus the clause in the articles forms part of the overall picture as it appears to him, and it is necessary to consider whether that clause negates the appearance of authority which is otherwise present.

Article 4A states that 'branch managers shall have no authority to purchase cars on behalf of the company without the prior permission of the shareholders in general meeting'. It is possible to argue about the effect of this. The core of the problem is how much can *T* take for granted? Can he assume that the permission has been given? Or does he have to inquire? The law's answer to this is that whether or not permission has been given is a matter of 'indoor management' and so he need not inquire. The case law authority for this proposition is *Turquand*. However, it is equally arguable that the authority for that step in the argument is simply that it is part of the doctrine of apparent authority. The article is equivocal. It does not negate that appearance of authority which is the core of the apparent authority doctrine. So it is possible to reach a conclusion about the effect of the article without recourse to any separate principle of law, such as the rule in *Turquand*. The solution here thus lies with a sensible application of the apparent authority doctrine.[30]

---

[28] As was done in *Kreditbank Cassel GmbH* v *Schenkers* and *Armagas* v *Mundogas*; see n. 11 above.

[29] Notice that *A* is a 'branch manager' and not thereby an officer of the company in the sense of being a director or managing director. Occasionally the courts have had to consider whether certain officers or functionaries within a company will acquire apparent authority simply by virtue of holding that office. Thus, in *Panorama Developments (Guildford) Ltd* v *Fidelis Furnishing Fabrics Ltd* [1971] 2 QB 711 it was held that a company secretary, who in former times was regarded as a mere clerk, now possessed sufficient apparent authority to bind the company in a commercial contract involving the hire of some cars. Since directors act as a board, it is sometimes argued that individual directors acting as such have very little commercial apparent authority. It is perhaps possible that this too may have changed with the passage of time, and certainly in many cases a director will also hold an executive office and will therefore have all the apparent authority which normally attaches to a person in such a position. It is also clear on general principle that someone who occupies the position of a managing director will normally have an apparent authority which will extend to some commercial acts since the board will usually delegate some or all of their powers to him. For interesting discussions of these issues see D. Rice 'The Power of a Director to Bind the Company' [1959] JBL 332; B. Hannigan 'Contracting with Individual Directors' in O. Rider (ed.) *The Corporate Dimension* (Bristol: Jordans, 1998) at p. 273.

[30] This is also true when we consider the rule, part of the *Turquand* jurisprudence, that *Turquand* does

From consideration of the above example it is now possible to see that the rule in *Turquand* was an early example of one tiny facet of the doctrine of apparent authority. *Turquand* adds nothing useful to a careful application of agency doctrine and has no meaningful existence.[31] It has, however, added decades of confusion. It is high time that company lawyers followed the lead given by Diplock LJ in *Freeman & Lockyer* and solved their problems without citing or making reference to *Turquand*.

7.5 SECTIONS 35A AND 35B

What is the effect of legislative intervention on this area of law and, consequently, on the analysis of a problem like 'Princedrive'? The legislative history of ss. 35A and 35B of the Companies Act 1985[32] has already been alluded to and their impact on the *ultra vires* doctrine has been discussed.[33] It is worth recalling the text of s. 35A (1) and s. 35B:[34]

> **35A.**—(1) In favour of a person dealing with a company in good faith, the power of the board of directors to bind the company, or authorise others to do so, shall be deemed to be free of any limitation under the company's constitution. . . .
> **35B.**—A party to a transaction with a company is not bound to enquire as to whether it is permitted by the company's memorandum or as to any limitation on the powers of the board of directors to bind the company or authorise others to do so.

Obviously, in a general sense, the intended effect of these sections is to restrict the extent to which a third party can be adversely affected by limitations on authority contained in the company's constitution. For under the constructive notice doctrine[35] a third party is deemed to have notice of those matters which are on public file, which would include the constitution of the company.[36] To some extent therefore, these sections will have the effect of suspending the operation of that doctrine, where they apply to a particular situation.[37] They may, of course, also have effects which are wider than merely suspending that doctrine, but whether or not this is

---

not apply when the third party is 'put on inquiry'; see e.g. *Liggett* v *Barclays Bank* [1928] 1 KB 48. On this point, Campbell (n. 23 above, at pp. 126–127) gives the example of 'a delegation to the office boy' meaning, that if the third party comes across an implausible situation, he would not be able to rely on the indoor management idea. But then, the point here surely is that there really is no appearance of authority in such a situation.

[31] The decision in *Smith* v *Henniker-Major & Co* [2002] BCC 768, CA, has no bearing on this analysis.
[32] In the account which follows attention will focus on these important provisions. Mention should however be made of s. 285 of the Companies Act 1985 which provides that a director's acts (or those of a manager) 'are valid notwithstanding any defect that may afterwards be discovered in his appointment or qualification'. Over the years, judges have declined to give this provision any great significance and so e.g. in *Morris* v *Kanssen* [1946] AC 459 it was held that it did not extend to the situation where no appointment had been made at all. Thus it probably merely extends to small technical irregularities relating to appointment formalities and share qualification.
[33] See p. 123 above.
[34] It is not proposed to repeat the discussion at pp. 126–127 above as to the effect of s. 35A (2)–(5).
[35] See p. 114 above.
[36] Obviously the memorandum and articles, but also, less obviously, certain shareholder agreements falling within s. 380 (4) (c); see further p. 95 above.
[37] Remember that the general abolition of the constructive notice doctrine was never brought into force; see further p. 123 above.

the case, a third party will be protected, in some situations, from having deemed notice of restrictions in the constitution.[38]

Why is such notice thought to be a matter requiring reversal? The point is that, in some circumstances, the deemed notice will cause the third party to be unable to enforce the contract against the company. A good example of this can be found by altering the facts of 'Princedrive' to produce a second version of it. Suppose that clause 4A of the articles of association stated that 'branch managers shall have no authority to purchase cars on behalf of the company'. *T* is aware of the existence of the clause when he enters into the contract. The contract is one which branch managers in that line of business can normally enter into, but, how can *T* argue that *A* has apparent authority to bind the company when clause 4A makes it clear that she has no such authority? Thus it can be seen, that in some circumstances, restrictions in the constitution will have an adverse affect on a third party's ability to rely on the apparent authority doctrine. This may not produce an unfair looking result in the 'Princedrive' example because *T* knew of the clause in the articles, but it does not look so fair if he is precluded from enforcing the contract by a technical doctrine which deems him to have notice when in fact he had no notice. This is particularly so, if, as is often likely in commercial practice, *T* has not actually inspected the registered documents of the company. The unfairness inherent in the constructive notice doctrine led to the enactment of ss. 35A (1) and 35B.

It is now necessary to look at the question whether s. 35A (1) and/or s. 35B actually have any beneficial effect in the 'Princedrive' example. In order to discuss this, the facts in the second version of the 'Princedrive' example are amended so that *T* has not seen the articles and is unaware of the contents of clause 4A. This third version produces a somewhat sharper focus on the effect of the constructive notice doctrine in some situations. The effect of the constructive notice doctrine is to insert clause 4A into the notional factual matrix being contemplated by the third party, with the result that he is unable to maintain a case against the company based on the apparent authority of *A*, because it is apparent to *T* that *A* could have no authority. So how might s. 35A (1) or s. 35B provide some help for *T* in this situation?

Taking the wording of s. 35A (1) first. Is *T* 'a person dealing with a company'? He is clearly 'a person'. Is he 'dealing with a company'? There is a definition of this in s. 35A (2), to the effect that 'a person "deals with" a company if he is a party to any transaction or other act to which the company is a party'. This looks unhelpful, since the use of the word 'party' might be taken to require that the company has entered into or been involved in some kind of legal relationship with the person, and the whole difficulty here, from the person's point of view is that unless he can show that this or another section applies to eliminate the effect of the constructive notice doctrine, then he will not, on the facts under discussion, be able to establish that the company is a party so that he can sue it. The basic problem here against

---

[38] The unusual facts of *Smith v Henniker-Major & Co* [2002] BCC 768 (CA) show that in circumstances where there is a narrow issue of the legality of procedure within the company (and no third party involved), then it will be difficult to rely on these sections; particularly so for insiders such as directors. However, it has recently been held (as a preliminary issue) that shareholders will be able to rely on the provisions; see *EIS Services v Phipps* [2003] BCC 931.

which s. 35A (1) is being called in aid, is that very issue, to establish that the company is a party. So it appears, that the drafting of s. 35A (1) falls at the first hurdle. The problem can perhaps be overcome if the words 'party . . . to' are interpreted in an imprecise non-legal way so as to mean something like 'in some way involved in'. This might be the only way for s. 35A (1) to ever have any effect, for it will only be called in aid where the problem being faced is that the company is not otherwise a party which the 'person'[39] can sue. To continue the analysis: is *T* 'in good faith'? On the facts of the 'Princedrive' example there is nothing to suggest that *T* is anything other than in good faith and so this poses no problem.[40]

Assuming that *T* can be said to satisfy the above conditions for the applicability of s. 35A (1), what will the section do for him? There are two possibilities envisaged by the section. The first is that '. . . the power of the board of directors to bind the company . . . shall be deemed free of any limitation under the company's constitution'. It is clear that this is of no help to *T* since the part of the constitution which is causing him difficulties (clause 4A of the articles) is not purporting to limit the power of the board to bind the company. The second possibility envisaged by the section is that the power of the board to 'authorise others to' bind the company shall 'be deemed free of any limitation under the company's constitution'. On the face of it, it is certainly arguable that this also has no impact on clause 4A, which states 'branch managers shall have no authority to purchase cars on behalf of the company' because clause 4A is not an attempt to limit the power of the directors to authorise others to bind the company. It is, instead, a limitation in the articles on the power of 'others' to bind the company.

There is, however, another – and better – way of looking at this. If the construction of the words of the statute is approached from the perspective of seeing the board as being the organ responsible for the running of the company (as in art. 70 of Table A), and as being the organ responsible for binding the company to third parties (as is inherent in art. 70), then it can be seen that a different interpretation is possible.[41] Any specific limitation in the constitution on the powers of any person will in fact be a restriction on the board's power to authorise that person to bind the company. This point can be illustrated in the context of the 'Princedrive' example. To be sure, in one sense, clause 4A operates as a restriction on any apparent authority which branch managers might otherwise have, but it is also possible to see the clause as a restriction on the board's power, in the sense that because it provides that branch managers shall have no authority, then it also operates as a limitation on the board's power to authorise branch managers to bind the company, if for instance the board wished to do so. Thus, the statute is aiming to preserve the ability of the board to bind the company and to preserve its discretion to grant authorisation to others in the company, such as agents operating below board level. This, surely, is the better construction of the wording. In the instant example, it produces the result that clause 4A is seen as a limitation on the board's power to

---

[39] I.e. the person in the position of *T* in 'Princedrive'.

[40] The definition of good faith in s. 35A (2) (b) has been discussed at p. 126 above.

[41] The wording of art. 9 (2) of the First Directive (68/151/EEC) is also supportive of this: 'The limits on the powers of the organs of the company, arising under the statutes or from a decision of the competent organs, may never be relied on as against third parties, even if they have been disclosed.'

authorise others (i.e. branch managers) to bind the company. Assuming that *T* were to satisfy the various conditions for the applicability of s. 35A (1), the section would operate by deeming away the limitations on *A*'s authority contained in clause 4A. This would leave *T* able simply to rely on *A*'s apparent authority and thereby enforce the contract against *P*.

Section 35B is open to an analysis on much the same lines. There is a similar problem with the use of the words 'party to a transaction with the company' and similar ambiguities arise as to the meaning of 'authorise others to do so'. Assuming that the difficulties can be resolved, then s. 35B would operate on the 'Princedrive' example slightly differently from s. 35A (1). Its effect is to make it clear that *T* is not bound to inquire as to any limitation on the powers of the board to bind the company or authorise others to do so. Thus the thrust of s. 35B is different. It is not a deeming provision. It operates by providing a focused[42] but indirect abolition of the common law constructive notice doctrine. The constructive notice doctrine effectively coerces *T* to 'inquire', in the sense of reading the registered documents of the company, and establishes that if he does not inquire, he will be deemed to have notice of any matters on public file at the Companies Registry. *T* now has a valid excuse not to inquire – the statute says he need not, and so his failure to do so can therefore no longer provide a rationale for the law to treat him as if he had inquired; in other words, there is no longer a reason to regard him as having 'constructive' notice.[43]

Section 35B would therefore be of use to a person in *T*'s position in the kind of situation envisaged in the third version of 'Princedrive', where the facts were altered so that *T* had no actual notice of the constitution prior to his dealings with *A*. Section 35B would have no impact on the first and second versions of 'Princedrive' because in both of those examples, *T* had knowledge of the terms of clause 4A prior to negotiating the contract. For the sake of the overall perspective, it is worth recalling that s. 35A (1) would have had no impact on the first version of 'Princedrive' because clause 4A in that version did not on its face diminish the apparent authority of *A* and so reliance on the section was not needed. However, s. 35A (1) was potentially of help to *T* in the second version of 'Princedrive' (assuming good faith) because clause 4A clearly destroyed any appearance of authority and without the deeming effect of the section, *T* would not have been able to maintain an action against *P* successfully.

It is obvious that this field is still complicated and that the statutory intervention has a hit and miss quality to it. The statutory technique is to suppress various bits of the common law in certain situations, and the legislation is at times ill-conceived and not well drafted. It is probable that when faced with the need to make a decision on its meaning, the courts will make the best of it and strive to give effect to the obvious intention of the legislation to diminish the circumstances in which the third party is adversely affected by limitations contained in the constitution.

---

[42] Focused in the sense that it is not a general abolition applying to all areas of company law but instead is focused on the problems arising in the areas of *ultra vires* and agency.

[43] It is worth noting that as regards limitations on the powers of the board to bind the company or authorise others to do so, the exemption from inquiry provided by s. 35B is not limited to the constitution although in most situations this will make little difference.

7.6 COMPANY LAW REVIEW AND LAW REFORM

It was seen at the end of the last chapter that the Company Law Review[44] intends to abolish the *ultra vires* doctrine. As regards the problems which have been discussed in this chapter, the recommendations are for the current legislation to be redrafted.[45]

---

[44] See generally Chapter 4.
[45] See DTI Consultation Document (October 1999) *Company Formation and Capital Maintenance* paras 2.37–2.40, and *Modern Company Law for a Competitive Economy Final Report* (London: DTI, 2001) p. 375, Draft Companies Bill, cl. 16.

PART III

CORPORATE GOVERNANCE

8

THE GOVERNANCE PROBLEM AND THE MECHANISMS OF MEETINGS

8.1 ALIGNMENT OF MANAGERIAL AND SHAREHOLDER INTERESTS

As has been seen,[1] corporate governance is about alignment; that is, it is about the system of legal or other mechanisms which ensure that the interests of the managers of the company are aligned with those of the shareholders.[2] The study of corporate governance is therefore concerned with the analysis of the environment in which the directors/managers operate, with a view to considering the totality of the system which is in place to ensure that managers do not pursue their own interests with the company's money, rather than those of the shareholders.

It will be recalled[3] that corporate governance systems contain mechanisms which are internal to the company and mechanisms which are external to the company. The former are the mechanisms which are put into the hands of shareholders which give them some level of ability to control or influence the board of directors. The external mechanisms exist in the regulatory environment in which the company operates and will include the existence of state agencies for the detection of fraud or the existence of insolvency procedures as well as the market mechanisms such as the disciplining effect of the possibility of a hostile takeover. In the following chapters, the emphasis will be on consideration of the internal mechanisms of corporate governance[4] for these form an important part of basic company law and it is interesting to consider those basic elements of the law in the context of their efficacy as governance mechanisms.[5]

The effectiveness of the system will depend very much on what type of company is under observation. In the small closely-held company, the shareholders will also be the directors and so the problem of alignment is often not present, although if there are shareholders who are not also directors, they may well find that they do have to worry about how they can influence what the directors are doing. If, on the

---

[1] The theoretical aspects of corporate governance are discussed in more detail at p. 53 above.

[2] The discussion of corporate governance will proceed here on the orthodox basis that the only stakeholders are the shareholders; the issues relating to widening this constituency have already been considered under the heading 'Stakeholder company law' at p. 58 above.

[3] See p. 54 above.

[4] For a discussion on the external mechanisms, see p. 54 above and for the explanation of the hostile takeover mechanism see further at p. 390 below and see generally p. 257 below (effect of going public).

[5] For a recent analytical perspective on our system see Lady Justice Arden DBE 'UK Corporate Governance after Enron' (2003) 3 JCLS 269.

other hand, the 'dispersed-ownership company' is considered, the problem of who controls the managers, and how will they do it, becomes acute. The shareholders of such companies will have relatively small stakes in it, and therefore little economic incentive to monitor the management or to interfere in what they are doing. Thus the mechanisms of corporate governance will have differing degrees of utility depending on what type of company is under consideration and this needs to be borne in mind in the account which follows.

The approach to the subject in this chapter will be to give an account of the workings of the meeting mechanisms, both in respect of the board of directors and the shareholders in general meetings. In Chapter 9 the general duties which the law imposes on directors will be considered. Chapter 10 will then consider a range of other constraints on the legal and practical position of directors. The input made by the self-regulatory mechanisms developed during the 1990s will be considered in Chapter 11. Chapters 12 and 13 will deal with the ways in which shareholders can bring litigation in respect of failures of corporate governance.

8.2 THE ROLE AND FUNCTIONING OF THE BOARD OF DIRECTORS

A Directors as managers and 'alter ego'

The legislation requires a public company to have at least two directors and a private company to have at least one director.[6] However, the articles of association may require a minimum number greater than these and/or fix a maximum. Table A, which will apply unless excluded,[7] provides that: 'Unless otherwise determined by ordinary resolution, the number of directors ...[8] shall not be subject to any maximum but shall not be less than two.' The current version of Table A dates from 1985 and this is obviously an inappropriate provision for the 'one-man' private company which has been permitted since 1992.[9] Those forming such companies will need to take care to amend the articles appropriately.[10] By s. 741 (1) of the Companies Act 1985 the term 'director' is expressed to include 'any person occupying the position of director, by whatever name called' so if the directors are known by some other title, such as 'the committee of management' they will still be regarded as directors by the legislation. This will involve them in compliance with the many statutory[11] obligations which are cast upon directors and thus it is not possible to avoid the obligations of the Companies Act by simply calling the directors something different.

The normal position in a company is that it will adopt art. 70 of Table A which will ensure that *prima facie*, the directors are the managers of the business of the

---

[6] Companies Act 1985, s. 282.

[7] See *ibid.* s. 8 (2).

[8] '... (other than alternate directors) ...', see p. 147 below.

[9] See the Companies (Single Member Private Limited Companies) Regulations 1992 (SI 1992 No. 1699).

[10] A similar problem arises with the quorum provision in art. 89 of Table A.

[11] And presumably, in appropriate circumstances, with the obligations created by case law.

company.[12] In practice in the larger companies, managerial power will often be devolved to groups or individuals below board level, leaving the board to meet once a month or quarterly.

Because of their managerial role, the directors are sometimes said to be the '*alter ego*' of a company; the word 'alter' meaning here 'the other' (of two). There are various manifestations of this in the case law. One is where the courts are looking for the state of mind of the company. As we have seen,[13] the courts have tended to regard the state of mind of the directors or managing director as the state of mind of the company. Similarly, there are situations where the directors are actually regarded as the company for some purposes. This was illustrated in *Stanfield* v *National Westminster Bank*,[14] where it was held that the proper person to answer interrogatories served on a company was the director or other similar officer:

> Interrogatories administered to a company have of course the special feature that as the company is an artificial person they must be answered not by the litigant, but by some human being who holds a position in relation to the company which enables him to give the answers, such as a director or [here] a liquidator.[15]

The doctrine is not applied rigidly and the courts will not invariably regard the director as a second defendant or second target in every situation.[16]

B Appointment and retirement of directors

The regulation of appointment and retirement of directors is left very much to the articles, although, as will be seen, the legislation does contain a few provisions which are of relevance and which will override the articles in some circumstances. Companies often adopt Table A, which contains detailed provisions in arts 73–80. The broad principle is that the shareholders in general meeting may elect a director by ordinary resolution,[17] although this is made subject to various conditions and procedures in other articles. The directors themselves may appoint a director, although if they do, he must retire at the next following annual general meeting.[18] The directors may appoint one or more of their number to be managing director(s).[19] Provision is also made for the appointment of an *alternate* director who is, in essence, someone who stands in for a director who is temporarily absent; but he is not an agent and is not treated as a director for all purposes.[20] Provision is made for the retirement of directors by rotation. One-third of the directors are to

---

[12] Article 70 of Table A has been discussed at p. 113 above.
[13] At p. 28 above.
[14] [1983] 1 WLR 568.
[15] *Ibid.* at p. 570, *per* Megarry J.
[16] *Attorney General of Tuvalu* v *Philatelic Ltd* [1990] BCC 30. The matter has been discussed at p. 29 above in relation to the director's liability for torts in the light of the House of Lords' decision in *Williams* v *Natural Life* [1998] BCC 428.
[17] Table A, art. 78.
[18] Table A, art. 79.
[19] Table A, art. 84.
[20] Any director may appoint any other director or any other person approved by resolution of the directors to be an alternate director; see Table A, arts 65–69.

retire each year[21] and those that go are those that have been in office longest.[22] They may be reappointed.[23]

The legislation has a few scattered provisions of relevance. When a company is formed, the first directors are appointed by the subscribers to the memorandum.[24] Sections 293–294 of the Companies Act 1985 provide for an upper age limit of 70 in a public company[25] and there is a duty of disclosure of age in some circumstances. However, if certain conditions are satisfied the company in general meeting can appoint or continue with a director of any age.[26] Section 292 provides, in effect, that in a public company the appointment of directors is to be voted on individually. This is to prevent an unpopular or unsuitable candidate being squeezed through the general meeting by putting him into a composite resolution to elect the directors, knowing that the shareholders will probably pass the resolution because they want all the other candidates elected.

The legislative provisions for the removal and disqualification of directors impact very substantially on the extent to which the power of the directors is constrained, and for that reason these matters are dealt with below.[27]

C Proceedings at directors' meetings

The Companies Act 1985 is silent on how the directors are to conduct their meetings. However, arts 88–98 and 100 of Table A lay down details as to the proceedings of directors. Although certain prescriptions are made (for example, as to quorum) they are permissive in style. Article 88 contains the fundamental ideas:

> Subject to the provisions of the articles, the directors may regulate their proceedings as they think fit. A director may, and the secretary[28] at the request of a director shall, call a meeting of the directors. It shall not be necessary to give notice of a meeting to a director who is absent from the United Kingdom. Questions arising at a meeting shall be decided by a majority of votes. In the case of an equality of votes, the chairman shall have a second or casting vote ...[29]

In the absence of express provisions to the contrary in the articles, the case law establishes a few propositions, none of which conflict with the above-mentioned provisions of Table A. Thus, it has been held that notice of meetings must be sent to all those entitled to attend.[30] It has been emphasised that directors

---

[21] Except at the first annual general meeting when all retire.

[22] See generally Table A, arts 73–80 *passim*.

[23] In accordance with art. 80 of Table A.

[24] Companies Act 1985, s. 10 (2) and (3).

[25] Or private company which is a subsidiary of a public company.

[26] Companies Act 1985, s. 293 (5).

[27] At p. 204.

[28] As to company secretary, see p. 190 below.

[29] There is a further provision '... A director who is also an alternate director shall be entitled in the absence of his appointor to a separate vote on behalf of his appointor in addition to his own vote.'

[30] *Young* v *Ladies Club Ltd* [1920] 2 KB 523. It is probable that in the absence of any express provision in the articles, the notice need not state the business or any proposed resolutions; see *La Compagnie de Mayville* v *Whitley* [1896] 1 Ch 788, although there is a dictum to the contrary, in the *Ladies Club* case which suggests that it is necessary to convey to the director what is going to be done.

act collectively, as a board, and that once decisions have been reached by a majority of those present, they bind the others. This rule can sometimes have a significant effect on the opposition to a proposal, for, as was stated by Millett J in *Re Equiticorp plc*:[31] 'Once a proper resolution of the board has been passed ... it becomes the duty of all the directors, including those who took no part in the deliberations of the board and those who voted against the resolution, to implement it ...'

D Remuneration of directors

The law on remuneration of directors has recently been subjected to a thorough examination by the House of Lords in *Guinness* v *Saunders and another*,[32] a civil case which arose out of the Guinness saga. This difficult case is examined in more detail below. We will also return to the subject of remuneration in the next chapter, for it has considerable significance in the self-regulatory context. Before looking at the detail of *Guinness*, it is worth attempting to summarise the main legal propositions.

As with the previous few topics, much depends on what is in the articles. The relatively little legislation on this topic is dealt with below.[33] Directors are fiduciaries[34] and because of this they must not profit from their relationships with the company.[35] Thus, as a *prima facie* rule, it is well established, and reiterated in *Guinness*,[36] that they are not entitled to any remuneration at all. Because of this it is normal for the articles to provide for the award of remuneration. If Table A is adopted, then art. 82 will allow the directors to be awarded 'such remuneration as the company may by ordinary resolution determine'. If there has been no such resolution, the directors will not be entitled to any remuneration. Nor will they be able to argue that they should succeed under a *quantum meruit* for the value of their services. This too, was established in *Guinness*.

The above paragraph refers to the situation where someone is a bare director under the Companies Act and who does not have any full-time contract of employment with the company. However, it is common for directors, especially in the larger companies, to be appointed to paid posts requiring their full-time attention.[37] But here again, their appointments must be properly authorised by the articles or they will not be entitled to any remuneration. They will also have to repay any which they have received. In this context, Table A provides by art. 84:

> Subject to the provisions of the Act, the directors may appoint one or more of their number to the office of managing director or to any other executive office under the company and may enter into an agreement or arrangement with any director for his

[31] (1989) 5 BCC 599 at p. 600.
[32] [1990] BCC 205.
[33] At p. 187.
[34] For this concept see further p. 164 below. Broadly it means that they are like trustees and will owe duties of good faith to the beneficiaries, which in the company law context means the company.
[35] See further pp. 164–178 below.
[36] [1990] BCC 205 at p. 211.
[37] Sometimes the articles themselves appoint the director to executive office at a salary. In the absence of an express contract outside the articles, this can give rise to enforcement problems; see p. 89 above.

employment by the company or the provision by him of any services outside the scope of the ordinary duties of a director. Any such appointment, agreement or arrangement may be made upon such terms as the directors determine and they may remunerate any such director for his services as they think fit.

The difference between this and art. 82 is obvious. Article 82 can only be operated by the shareholders in general meeting, and although the directors may no doubt suggest a level of directors' fees for the meeting to recommend, the matter essentially lies within the control of the meeting. From the directors' point of view, art. 84 is much more useful, for it enables them to appoint themselves to lucrative contracts without the sanction of the shareholders. This has implications for corporate governance which are taken up below.[38] In fact it is not uncommon for an amended version of art. 82 to be adopted which gives greater power to the board to award remuneration. Thus, in *Guinness*, the company's art. 90 gave the power to award remuneration to the board subject to the limitation that remuneration over £100,000 p.a. would need the consent of the general meeting.

These kinds of principles can be seen operating in *Guinness* v *Saunders and another*.[39] The background to these civil proceedings was a takeover battle in which Guinness made a successful bid for the shares of a company called Distillers. Various proceedings were brought against certain officers of Guinness who had been involved with the takeover.[40] Quite early on in the investigation into the matter, it was found that W, an American lawyer who was a director of Guinness, had been paid £5.2m (0.2% of the value of the bid)[41] for acting as a business consultant for advising on the takeover. Guinness immediately brought summary proceedings to recover this sum. Summary proceedings are designed to be used only if there is no arguable defence to the claim and if, during the course of the trial, it becomes clear that there is an issue, then the proceedings will fail and the case will eventually go for trial of the issues. Guinness fought the case to the House of Lords and was in difficulties over its claim that s. 317 of the Companies Act 1985 enabled it to recover.[42] However, the company came up with an alternative argument along the lines that the committee of the board of directors which W claimed had agreed to his remuneration had no power under the articles of association to award special remuneration, only the full board could do this, and it had made no such award. This was successful and W was held to be constructive trustee of the money.[43]

Even if the remuneration is given in accordance with the permissions and procedure set up in the articles, it will not necessarily follow that all remuneration given to directors will be unimpeachable. It is clear from the decision in *Re Halt Garage Ltd*[44] that if the sums paid to the director are so out of proportion to any possible value to the company attributable to him holding office then the court will treat the payments as gratuitous distributions of capital 'dressed up as remuneration'. In such

---

[38] See p. 206.
[39] [1990] BCC 205.
[40] Leading, in one case, to a successful Human Rights challenge; see p. 356, n. 102.
[41] Not actually a huge amount by Wall Street standards.
[42] For discussion of s. 317, see p. 175 below.
[43] W was later acquitted in criminal proceedings arising out of the takeover.
[44] [1982] 3 All ER 1016.

circumstances they will be recoverable. It has also been held in *Re Cumana Ltd*[45] that excessive remuneration can amount to conduct which is unfairly prejudicial.

There are a few legislative provisions in this field. Sections 312–316 regulate payments made to directors in respect of loss of office or retirement in situations where conflicts of interest may arise.[46] Section 318 provides that directors' service contracts are open to inspection. Contracts of employment for more than five years are subjected to further regulation by s. 319; these need to be approved in advance by the general meeting. The inadequacy of this provision as a method of regulating the extent to which directors can entrench themselves with fixed term service contracts has become clear in recent years. The self-regulatory response to the situation is examined below.[47] Lastly, s. 232 and Sch. 6 require extensive disclosure of the level of directors' remuneration in the company accounts. These provisions have altered, largely as a result of pressure arising from the corporate governance debate.

8.3 THE ROLE AND FUNCTIONING OF THE SHAREHOLDERS IN GENERAL MEETING

A The general meeting as the residual authority of the company

It is difficult to state concisely what the role of the shareholders in general meeting is. It is clear that in accordance with art. 70 of Table A the scheme of the legislation is that the business of the company is managed by the board, who 'exercise all the powers of the company'. Thus, the role ascribed to the shareholders is a residual one. In some circumstances the powers of the board will revert to the shareholders,[48] and it is clear from art. 70 that by special resolution the shareholders can give directions to the directors.

There are, however, a number of situations where the shareholders in general meeting are the primary functionaries and are in no sense residual. One is where the Act requires the permission of the shareholders before something can be carried out. An example would be s. 319, referred to above, but there are many, scattered throughout the legislation. Another situation, which is the result of case law rather than statute, is where the question to be decided is whether the company name can be used to commence litigation against, say, one of the directors for breach of duty. In this situation, the traditional response of the case law is to regard the matter as one which is to be decided by a majority of shareholders in general meeting. In fact, as we will see when the matter is examined in Chapter 12, the position is rather muddled and one line of authority suggests that the board may have a role here too.

Reading the above, makes it possible to forget that the shareholders are the *owners* of the company. In this role, although they may be passive most of the time (for a number of reasons)[49] they can hardly be regarded as residual. There will also sometimes come a point when the shareholders decide that it is high time they removed

---

[45] [1986] BCLC 430, CA.
[46] There is also Companies Act 1985, s. 311, which prohibits certain tax-free payments to directors.
[47] At p. 206. See also C. Villiers 'Executive Pay: Beyond Control?' (1995) 15 *Legal Studies* 260.
[48] *Barron v Potter* [1914] 1 Ch 895.
[49] See generally pp. 6–7.

the directors and will use their power under s. 303 of the Companies Act 1985 to do this.[50] As the directors go out of the door for the last time they will understand that the general meeting was not only the residual authority but was in fact the ultimate authority of the company.

B Resolutions at meetings

The two main types of resolution have already been encountered; these are, the ordinary resolution and the special resolution. There is no statutory definition of an ordinary resolution, but it is clear from general usage that an ordinary resolution is one which is passed by a simple majority[51] of those members who are present and voting either in person or by proxy. It can be used in all circumstances unless the legislation or the constitution of the company provide that some other resolution be used. Because of that, it is best thought of as the basic or residual resolution.

A special resolution is one which has been passed by a majority of not less than three-fourths (75%) of such members as, being entitled to do so, vote in person or, where proxies are allowed, by proxy, at a general meeting of which not less than 21 days' notice, specifying the intention to propose the resolution as a special resolution, has been duly given.[52] They must be used where the legislation or constitution of the company so requires. Special resolutions obviously provide a harder task for the meeting and are used by the legislation as a method of achieving a greater safeguard. Thus, for example, an alteration of articles requires a special resolution because it is of a fundamental nature, being an alteration to the constitution of the company.[53]

There is a third type[54] of resolution, the extraordinary resolution. This differs from the special resolution only in terms of the period of notice required, which is 14 days as opposed to 21.[55] There are very few situations where the legislation requires an extraordinary resolution.[56]

C The shareholders' general meetings

The term 'general meeting' is difficult to define, but in essence it means a meeting of the ordinary shareholders together with any other shareholders who are entitled to attend. The general meeting should be distinguished from the shareholders' class meeting. We have already seen[57] that where the company has issued different classes of shares it will sometimes be necessary for the shareholders of a class to

---

[50] As will be seen below, their ability to do this is often circumscribed by other considerations; see further p. 182 below.
[51] I.e. by voting power of more than 50%.
[52] Companies Act 1985, s. 378 (2), (1).
[53] *Ibid.* s. 9.
[54] In some circumstances a written resolution procedure can be used. This is dealt with at p. 158 below.
[55] Companies Act 1985, s. 378 (1), (2).
[56] The main examples being ss. 84 (1) (c) and 165 (2) (a) of the Insolvency Act 1986 (commencement of voluntary winding up on the grounds of insolvency and granting of powers to a liquidator in a members' voluntary winding up).
[57] In Chapter 5.

have their own meeting[58] to consider, for example, proposals for variation of rights or a scheme of arrangement.

The Companies Act 1985 establishes two types of shareholders' general meeting; the annual general meeting (AGM) and the extraordinary general meeting (EGM). An EGM is basically any meeting other than an AGM.[59] The main provision on AGMs is s. 366 of the Companies Act 1985 which makes it clear that in addition to any other meetings which it holds, a company[60] must, every year,[61] hold a general meeting as its AGM.[62] The business of the AGM is whatever is required by the articles as well as any other matters which are being raised. In practice, certain matters are usually dealt with at the AGM such as, the laying of accounts, declaration of dividends, reports of directors and auditors, and election of directors. Minutes must be kept of the proceedings of all general meetings and of meetings of directors (and managers).[63] The minutes must be entered in books kept for that purpose and which are open to inspection by members.[64]

D Convening of meetings and notice

For companies which adopt Table A, art. 37 gives the directors powers to convene[65] general meetings.[66] In the absence of this or any other express provisions in the articles, it is probably reasonably safe to assume that directors may convene meetings (including class meetings) by virtue of their general powers of management of the business of the company. There are also situations where the members, officers and outsiders have rights in relation to the convening of meetings.[67]

As regards notice, s. 370 (1) and (2) requires that notice of meetings must be served on every member of the company, unless the articles otherwise provide. On the other hand, if a member has no voting rights, he will have no right actually to attend the meeting.[68] The length of notice required varies. For an AGM, 21 days' notice in writing is needed whereas for EGMs and other meetings, the period is 14 days. However, if a special resolution is to be passed 21 days is necessary, and the

---

[58] The legal rules discussed here in the Companies Acts concerning meetings and the common law rules will apply to class meetings unless they are expressed to apply or can obviously only apply to general meetings. As regards class meetings connected with variation of rights, s. 125 (6) of the Companies Act 1985 makes express provision for the rules of the statutes to apply, subject to modifications.

[59] Table A, art. 36.

[60] Private companies may elect to dispense with AGMs: Companies Act 1985, s. 366A.

[61] Calendar year.

[62] There is also a requirement that not more than 15 months shall elapse between the date of one AGM and that of the next; Companies Act 1985, s. 366 (3). Section 366 (2) makes special provision for when a company is first formed, and s. 367 (1), (4) governs the situation if the meeting is requisitioned by the Secretary of State.

[63] Companies Act 1985, s. 382. Also to be recorded are any written resolutions passed under s. 381A; see s. 382A.

[64] *Ibid.* s. 383.

[65] Meaning 'call'.

[66] It also provides, in effect, that if insufficient directors are within the UK to call a general meeting, then any director or member may call a general meeting.

[67] See Companies Act 1985, ss. 392A, 367, 371.

[68] *Re Mackenzie Ltd* [1916] 2 Ch 450.

notice must state that a special resolution is going to be proposed.[69] These are minimum prescriptions[70] and the articles may require longer notice.

In some situations a detailed procedure known as 'special notice' is required.[71] As a result of various provisions scattered throughout the legislation, it is required where certain fairly drastic ordinary resolutions are to be passed. An example would be where a director is going to be removed against his will under s. 303.[72]

As regards the contents of notices, the Companies Act 1985 itself is silent, apart from s. 372 (3) which specifies that with a company having a share capital, the notice calling the meeting must contain a statement that a member who is entitled to attend and vote is entitled to appoint a proxy to attend and vote instead of him, and that the proxy need not be a member. So the effect is that the content of the notices and related detailed matters are largely left to the articles. Table A, arts 38–39 and 111–116 make provision in this regard. In particular, art. 38 provides, *inter alia*, that the notice shall specify the time and place of the meeting and the general nature of the business to be transacted and if the meeting is to be an AGM, the notice should say so. As elsewhere in the law relating to meetings, the provisions of the legislation and the articles are sometimes supplemented by the common law of meetings which is created by the case law. In the present context, of content of notices, the effect of the cases is that the substance of any business should be set out in the notice in sufficient detail to enable a member to make a proper decision about whether to attend or not, and special resolutions and extraordinary resolutions must be set out in full with no variations of substance.[73]

E Shareholder independence – meetings and resolutions

The legislation contains ways in which the members can seek to act independently of the board in relation to the convening of meetings and passing of resolutions.

Section 368 (1) and (2) gives the members holding at least one-tenth of the paid-up voting capital the right to require the directors to convene a meeting. The members' 'requisition' must state the object of the meeting.[74] The directors must convene the meeting 'forthwith'.[75] The date fixed for the meeting must[76] be within 28 days of the notice calling the meeting, thus outlawing the old trick of calling (i.e. issuing the notices) the meeting fairly speedily but fixed for a date many months later.[77] If the directors do not duly convene the meeting within the 21 days of the deposit of the duly signed requisition at the company's registered office,

---

[69] Companies Act 1985, ss. 369, 378(2).
[70] *Ibid.* ss. 369 (3), (4) and 378 (3) contain provisions for short notice if the requisite number of members agree to it.
[71] See generally *ibid.* s. 379.
[72] *Ibid.* s. 303 (2).
[73] See *MacConnell* v *Prill Ltd* [1916] 2 Ch 57; *Choppington Collieries Ltd* v *Johnson* [1944] 1 All ER 762; *Re Moorgate Mercantile Ltd* [1980] 1 All ER 40. Companies with a Stock Exchange Listing are under further 'continuing' obligations with respect to notices.
[74] Companies Act 1985, s. 368 (3).
[75] *Ibid.* s. 368 (1).
[76] By virtue of an amendment contained in the Companies Act 1989.
[77] Companies Act 1985, s. 368 (8).

then the requisitionists, or any or them representing more than one half of the total voting rights of all of them, may themselves convene a meeting to be held within three months of the date of the deposit of the requisition, and their reasonable expenses are recoverable from the company.[78]

Resolutions will almost always be proposed and backed by the board of directors. The notice summoning the meeting will have set out the text of the resolution and will usually have been accompanied by a circular explaining the reasons why the directors think that the resolution should be adopted. Sometimes members will feel that simply voting against the board's proposals is too passive a form of opposition. Section 376 provides the means for such members, at their expense, to mount some sort of campaign against the board, by proposing resolutions backed by a carefully argued circular sent out to the members before the meeting happens. This mechanism can be invoked by any number of members representing not less than one-twentieth of the total voting rights of all the members having a right to vote at the meeting in question or alternatively, by not less than 100 members holding shares in the company, paid up to at least £100 per member.[79] Although circulars can be sent round in relation to any general meeting, the right to propose resolutions only relates to resolutions to be moved at the AGM.

F Procedure at meetings

Can you have a meeting at all if there are fewer than two members? According to the decision in *Re London Flats Ltd*,[80] the answer is 'no'. However, both the courts and the legislature have been prepared to recognise a 'meeting of one' in certain circumstances. Section 371 enables the court to order a meeting in some situations, and it empowers the court to direct that 'one member of the company ... be deemed to constitute a meeting'.[81] In *Re RMCA Reinsurance Ltd*[82] the court was prepared to order a meeting of one (to be held in Singapore). Similarly, in *East* v *Bennett*[83] one member who held all the shares of a particular class could constitute a class 'meeting' on his own. Furthermore, since 1992 it has been possible for private companies limited by shares or by guarantee to be formed with only one member.[84] In this situation it is clear that one member can constitute a meeting.[85] Subject to this, however, it is clear that even if there is no quorum requirement, the general rule is that a meeting of one, is no meeting.

---

[78] *Ibid.* s. 368 (4), (6).
[79] *Ibid.* s. 376 (2). Various other conditions and procedures are set out in ss. 376–377. In practice these provisions are seldom used and the limit of 1,000 words is not always helpful in this regard.
[80] [1969] 1 WLR 711.
[81] See *Re Sticky Fingers Restaurant Ltd* [1991] BCC 754.
[82] [1994] BCC 378.
[83] [1911] 1 Ch 163.
[84] Companies (Single Member Private Limited Companies) Regulations 1992 (SI 1992 No. 1699). Prior to 1992, a company which found itself with only one member was subject to the sanction in s. 24 of the Companies Act 1985 which still applies to public companies.
[85] Companies Act 1985, s. 370A makes it clear that a meeting in such circumstances will not be inquorate and it must be implicit from this, that the wider point, as to whether there is a meeting at all, is answered in the affirmative.

A meeting is invalid unless a quorum is present. Unless the articles otherwise provide, two members 'personally present' will constitute a quorum.[86] If Table A applies, art. 40 provides for a quorum of 'two persons entitled to vote upon the business to be transacted' and allows for a person present as a proxy to be counted as part of the quorum.[87] The quorum must be present throughout the meeting which otherwise stands adjourned.[88]

It is normal for a meeting to take place under the direction of a chairman. Indeed, if Table A is applicable, art. 42 will require a chairman to preside over the meeting, and makes provision for this to be the chairman of the board of directors, or in his absence, a director nominated by the board, or failing that, a director elected by the board. If art. 42 does not produce a chairman, then art. 43 requires the members to elect one of their number to be chairman.[89] The chairman's function is to see that the business of the meeting is conducted properly and in accordance with the common law of meetings, the articles and the companies legislation.[90]

Voting at meetings[91] usually takes place on a 'show of hands' of the members present. What this means is that it is done without counting up the votes held by each member. The chairman would then declare the resolution carried or lost by '28 votes to 19' or whatever. Voting by a show of hands is thus a convenient way of getting through the uncontentious business of the meeting. However, if someone present wishes to mount a serious challenge to the resolution then they will demand a poll, either before, or on the declaration of the result by the chairman. A poll is a count of the votes held by each 'hand'.[92] The demand for a poll nullifies the result reached by the show of hands.

The system of proxy voting is a subject which will be returned to below, for it is one of those areas which in its practical workings has been seen to impact adversely on corporate governance.[93] The basic legal position, however, is relatively straightforward and the legislation and Table A contains detailed provisions with regard to proxies.[94] A member of a company who is entitled to attend and vote at a meeting is entitled to appoint another person (who may or may not be a member) as his proxy, to attend and vote instead of him.[95] If the company is listed on the London Stock Exchange the company must send out what are called 'two-way' proxy forms with any notices calling meetings.[96] These forms have on them a clear direction for

---

[86] *Ibid.* s. 370 (4), (1). The special case of the one man private company is dealt with by s. 370A.

[87] Which is not the position under Companies Act 1985, s. 370 (4).

[88] Table A, art. 41.

[89] Companies Act 1985, s. 379 (5) provides that, subject to any contrary provision in the articles, the meeting may be chaired by any member elected by the members present.

[90] See generally *John v Rees* [1970] Ch 345 at p. 382.

[91] See generally, Table A, arts 46–52.

[92] Companies Act 1985, s. 373 (1) (a) preserves and safeguards the common law right of any member to demand a poll, except in relation to the election of chairman or adjournment of the meeting in which cases the right can be restricted by the articles although no further than the extent stated in s. 373 (1) (b). Proxies are also given similar rights to demand a poll: s. 373 (2). Section 374 protects the position of a nominee in some circumstances.

[93] See p. 158 below.

[94] See generally, Companies Act 1985, ss. 372 (1)–(7) and Table A, arts 54–63.

[95] Companies Act 1985, s. 372 (1). In a private company meeting, the proxy may also speak if the member had such a right; *ibid.*

[96] FSA Listing Rules, paras 9.26, 13.28–13.29.

the proxy to vote for or against the resolution which makes it easy for the member to strike out whichever is inapplicable.[97]

8.4 PROBLEMS WITH THE MEETING CONCEPT

It is clear from the above fairly detailed examination of the workings of the board and the general meeting that company law is very dependent on the idea of governance through democratic meetings, and particularly through the shareholders' general meeting. Great power is given to the board by art. 70 of Table A, and yet, the general meeting has a measure of control through its ability to interfere by special resolution, through its ability to remove the directors by ordinary resolution, and through its ability to control the appointment of directors, and in various other lesser ways.

In practice, the extent to which the shareholders' general meeting can operate as an input to the governance of the company is reduced by two factors. The first is that in many situations, in particular where the company is the size of a listed plc, the shareholders would simply think it not worth their while to bother, on the basis that little or no economic advantage could come from their investment of time. The market capitalisation of the average listed plc is so large that any particular shareholder usually owns only a small proportion of the overall voting shares. In that situation, the chance of being able to influence the outcome is negligible. But the problem is more fundamental than this. The shareholder does not see it in his individual economic interest to even try. Investors tend to follow 'portfolio theory',[98] which means that they will try to reduce the risk that a company in which they have invested will collapse, by diversifying, and thus by holding shares in many different companies. Such an investor will not want to spend time worrying about the outcome of some incident or boardroom battle in any one individual company. If the investor senses trouble in the performance of the company, he or she will sell the shares, and invest the proceeds in another company. Currently about 70% of shares are owned by institutions such as pension funds and unit trusts.[99] There is evidence that some of these in recent years have seen it as worth their while to take an interest in the governance of companies which they have invested in.[100] Because of the scale of these funds, they are in a position to buy sizeable stakes in companies and this may have increased their commitment to intervention. It is probable, however, that this is sporadic and it is questionable whether the input to corporate governance is significant. Recent years have seen attempts by the various committees on corporate governance to stir the institutions into more activity in this regard.[101]

The second factor which reduces the effectiveness of the shareholder meeting as an instrument of corporate governance stems from the fact that very few shareholders attend the meetings in person. Instead, if they are minded to take any

---

[97] An ordinary proxy form simply appoints someone as proxy and leaves him or her free to decide how to vote.
[98] See further p. 350 in the context of collective investment schemes.
[99] See p. 208, n. 75 below.
[100] See J. Farrar *Farrar's Company Law* 4th edn (London: Butterworths, 1998) p. 580.
[101] See further p. 197 below.

interest at all, they will appoint a proxy to vote on their behalf. The proxy will usually be one of the directors because if a contentious resolution is coming up at the meeting, the board will have sent out a circular explaining their position and soliciting proxy votes. This means that whatever is said at the meeting will be largely irrelevant because the board will have with them a large pile of proxy votes which will defeat any opposition. If an insurgent shareholder group had mounted an opposition circular it would have arrived after[102] the shareholders had returned their proxy forms, which is a considerable disincentive to voting against[103] the board.[104]

These factors, coupled with the internationalisation of capital markets with the shareholders spread out all over the world, mean that the input which will be made by the shareholders in the governance of companies is seriously limited. Rather like the representative governing bodies of ancient republican Rome, the legal mechanism of UK corporate governance is founded on the idea that all the members of the company can gather together in one place and will actually be enthusiastic enough to do so.[105] And like the Roman bodies, it has found that, in the passage of time, the expansion in size of the human organism to be governed has rendered the governance mechanisms partially obsolete.

8.5 MEETINGS IN SMALL CLOSELY-HELD COMPANIES

In small closely-held companies, special procedures have been developed over the years to enable the shareholders and directors of small closely-held companies to avoid the necessity of holding formal meetings.

First, the common law has developed a doctrine,[106] often referred to as 'shareholder consent', to the effect that if an act may be done by the shareholders formally in a meeting, then such act may be done informally, without a meeting provided that all the shareholders in the company consent. The doctrine can be used in many ways and its existence can produce some unexpected results in litigation.[107] It seems that even long-term acquiescence (coupled with knowledge of the

---

[102] Unless of course the shareholders are able to spot the contentious issue early enough.

[103] In theory the shareholder could change his mind by revoking the appointment of the proxy.

[104] See further M. Pickering 'Shareholder Votes and Company Control' (1965) 81 LQR 248.

[105] In the course of time the use of internet technology might bring about a solution to the problem of global dispersion of shareholders. Already in the UK we have the Electronic Communications Act 2000, which will enable modernisation of the meeting process with regard to matters like appointment of proxies and voting instructions. The first orders have recently been made in that regard: see The Companies Act (Electronic Communication) Order 2000 (SI 2000, No. 3373); and (SI 2002, No. 1986), which effect modifications of the 1985 Act to facilitate the use of electronic communications between companies, their members and others and the Registrar of Companies in a wide variety of circumstances.

[106] See generally *Re Duomatic Ltd* [1969] 1 All ER 161; *Atlas Wright (Europe) Ltd* v *Wright* [1999] BCC 163. It has been held in *Re Torvale Group Ltd* [2000] BCC 626 that the shareholder consent doctrine is not limited to situations where all the shareholders of the company are involved, but is also applicable where statute or the constitution of the company enabled certain acts to be done if a particular group consented.

[107] See e.g. *Multinational Gas Ltd* v *Multinational Services Ltd* [1983] 2 All ER 563 where directors escaped the consequences of breach of duty because all the shareholders knew of their actions and acquiesced in them.

circumstances) can amount to shareholder consent.[108] The consent doctrine has provided a useful vehicle for many years, by which members and directors of small closely-held companies have been enabled legally to circumvent the necessity to hold some of their meetings. In practice the doctrine is often utilised by formulating a proposal in writing and circulating it for successive signature by all the members. Article 53 of Table A enshrines the doctrine in the articles of most companies but is not theoretically necessary.

As part of a package of reforms[109] designed to help small companies operate more efficiently and less burdened with unnecessary procedures by companies legislation, the Companies Act 1989 introduced a statutory procedure whereby written resolutions could be used. Unfortunately, the drafting introduced complications and subsequent amendments were introduced by statutory instrument.[110] The amended provisions, which apply to private companies are contained in ss. 381A–381C of the Companies Act 1985.

8.6 COMPANY LAW REVIEW AND LAW REFORM

The Company Law Review was well aware of the limitations of the meetings concept[111] and addressed a number of issues in its preliminary consultations and recommendations. It was felt that allowing public companies to dispense with the AGM would be premature but the present and future developments in technology might offer alternative forms of communication between directors and shareholders. Accordingly, as well as proposing various technical improvements to the AGM (such as permitting electronic voting), the Review suggested that the DTI should be given a power to enable companies to replace the AGM with a process which they are satisfied sufficiently meets the public policy requirements in this area.[112]

In the Final Report there were many ideas on meetings and the role of shareholders designed to improve corporate governance. These included dispensing with AGMs, standardisation of notice periods, electronic voting, codification of the unanimous consent rule, and proposals designed to ameliorate the hindering of corporate governance by the growth of shareholding by intermediaries.[113]

---

[108] *Re Bailey Hay & Co* [1971] 3 All ER 693.
[109] See also the 'elective regime' in s. 379A.
[110] Deregulation (Resolutions of Private Companies) Order 1996 (SI 1996 No. 1471).
[111] See e.g. DTI Consultation Document (October 1999) *Company General Meetings and Shareholder Communications* paras 14 ff.
[112] See generally DTI Consultation Document (March 2000) *Developing the Framework* paras 4.19–4.64.
[113] See *Modern Company Law for a Competitive Economy Final Report* (London: DTI, 2001) paras. 7.1–7.32. See also the subsequent government White Paper, *Modernising Company Law* (July 2002, Cmnd. 5553) and *Company Law. Flexibility and Accessibility: A Consultative Document* (London: DTI, 2004).

9

DUTIES OF DIRECTORS

9.1 INTRODUCTION

The next stage of the analysis of the legal constraints on the directors of a company[1] is consideration of the case law on directors' duties which has developed slowly over about 150 years, often drawing on even older concepts from the law of trusts. It is traditional to see the duties as falling into two quite distinct categories: common law duties of care and skill and fiduciary duties. This is the result of the idea that the director has two types of function which are treated separately by the law. From one angle the director can be seen as a trustee, whose role it is to protect and preserve the assets for the beneficiary. From the other angle, he is seen as a dynamic entrepreneur whose job it is to take risks with the subscribed capital and multiply the shareholders' investment. This is clearly a wide spectrum of behaviour to regulate and would pose difficulty for any legal system. In the UK there have been attempts to solve the problem by drawing heavily and easily on pre-existing concepts of the law of trusts and, until recent years, largely ignoring the challenges posed by the entrepreneurial function. As a result this area of law has a curious, bifurcated feel, echoing the ancient split between the courts of common law and Chancery.

To add to this strangeness, the enactment of the unfair prejudice remedy in 1980 and the subsequent dynamic case law development of the concept, has added a tinge of irrelevance to the old-established ideas concerning directors' duties. This is particularly true at the procedural level as will be seen below, but it also applies to the substantive law. Very often the directors in a company will find themselves at the receiving end of an unfair prejudice petition brought by a member. Under the case law on unfair prejudice, there are a range of acts which would probably not cause them to break their duties under the established rule on directors' duties but which will be likely to cause them to lose an unfair prejudice petition.[2] For this reason, a director who wishes to stay out of trouble will probably be wise to view the unfair prejudice law as a very broad type of directors' duty.

At a procedural level, the unfair prejudice remedy has an even greater impact on the traditional law on directors' duties. This is because the enforcement mechanisms for breaches of the common law and fiduciary duties lie within the grip of the 'rule in *Foss* v *Harbottle*'.[3] This in itself flows directly from the existence of another

---

[1] For a detailed comparative analysis, see B. Butcher *Directors' Duties: A New Millennium, A New Approach?* (Deventer: Kluwer, 2000).

[2] See further p. 233 below.

[3] (1843) 2 Hare 461. This expression is used here loosely to describe both the restrictions inherent in the *Foss* v *Harbottle* doctrine and the gateways created by the recognised exceptions to it.

rule, namely the rule in *Percival* v *Wright*,[4] which establishes that directors owe their duties to the company of which they are the directors. This means that the shareholders themselves have no cause of action against directors for breach of their duties.[5] Only the company has a cause of action. The ramifications of these rules are explored in Chapter 11. The overall effect, however, is often to make it difficult or impossible for directors to be held accountable. On the other hand, the availability of the unfair prejudice remedy is relatively unrestricted. This, coupled with the wideness and flexibility of the substantive law of unfair prejudice, means that if directors approach their responsibilities solely through the perspective of the traditional common law and fiduciary duties they will be underinformed.

9.2 COMMON LAW DUTIES OF CARE AND SKILL

The common law duties of care and skill represent the courts' attempts to regulate the entrepreneurial side of the director's activities. Until relatively recently, the legal position tended towards regarding holding a directorship as a gentlemanly activity where some gentle coaxing from the courts was sometimes appropriate.[6] Thus, judicial expressions of the duty of care were couched in subjective terms, careful not to require anything approaching the objective concept of reasonable care inherent in the tortious 'neighbour test'. For instance, in *Dorchester Finance Co. Ltd* v *Stebbing*[7] Foster J regarded the law as being that: 'A director is required to take in the performance of his duties such care as an ordinary man might be expected to take on his own behalf.'[8] There was a similar subjective duty of skill: 'A director is required to exhibit in the performance of his duties such degree of skill as may reasonably be required from a person with his knowledge and experience.'[9]

The result of applying a subjective duty of care is apparent from the judicial handling of the subject of attendance at board meetings. On this, in *Re City Equitable Ltd*[10] Romer J said: 'A director is not bound to give continuous attention to the affairs of the company. His duties are of an intermittent nature to be performed at periodic board meetings and committees of the board on which he serves. He is not bound to attend all such meetings, though he ought to go whenever he reasonably can.'[11] The result of the attitude that he ought to go 'whenever he reasonably can' is well illustrated by the risible facts of an earlier case. In *Re Cardiff*

---

[4] [1902] 2 Ch 421.

[5] In some circumstances it has been found that a duty is owed to the shareholders personally. For instance, where the directors have held themselves out as negotiating on behalf of the shareholders, they will owe their duties to them; see *Allen* v *Hyatt* [1914] 30 TLR 444. In a takeover bid, the directors of the offeree company will owe a duty to the shareholders not to mislead them: *Heron International* v *Lord Grade* [1983] BCLC 244. In *Peskin* v *Anderson* [2001] BCC 874, CA, it was held that in order for directors to owe fiduciary duties to shareholders it was necessary to establish a special factual relationship between the directors and the shareholders in the particular case. They do not simply arise from the legal relationship which existed between the company and its directors.

[6] This refers to the non-executive director. Directors with full-time service contracts will normally owe duties of reasonable care in accordance with those contracts.

[7] [1989] BCLC 498.

[8] *Ibid.* at pp. 501–502.

[9] *Ibid.*

[10] [1925] Ch 407.

[11] *Ibid.* at p. 429.

Savings Bank[12] the Marquis of Bute became President and director of the bank when he was six months old. This was in 1848. The bank crashed years later in 1886, having been defrauded, and the liquidator sought to make the Marquis liable for negligence in the performance of his duties. It was established that he had attended a board meeting in 1869 and had signed the minutes on that occasion. Apart from that, he had taken no part in the business of the bank. It was held that he was not liable for breach of duty. The reason offered by the judge was the baffling observation that the 'neglect or omission to attend meetings is not . . . the same thing as neglect or omission of a duty which ought to be performed at those meetings'.[13]

So much for the duty of care. The subjective duty of skill also had its problems. It produced the unfortunate, but logical, result that if a director has no experience and knows nothing, the law will require very little from him. On the other hand, it had a sting in it, for a director who did have a lot of knowledge and experience would find that he was expected to use it. In the *Dorchester Finance* case two of the directors were chartered accountants and this fact was taken into account against them in assessing what could reasonably be expected of them.

Overall, though, the judicial policy of setting the standards low, perhaps justifiable on the basis of not wanting to discourage enterprise, had the effect that directors were more or less immune from suit arising out of their conduct of the entrepreneurial aspect of their functions. There are very few examples of litigation of these matters in the law reports. An additional discouraging factor lay in the special fate[14] which the jurisprudence of the rule in *Foss v Harbottle* accorded to shareholder actions against directors, which effectively limited them to the situations where the company was in liquidation or a new board had been elected on a takeover. It is perhaps possible to trace at least some of the problems of corporate governance which became so apparent in the 1980s to the signal sent by the courts to the business community in these cases.

When the wrongful trading provisions were first introduced in 1985[15] there was considerable interest among company lawyers arising out of s. 214 (4) of the Insolvency Act 1986 which, for the purposes of the new law on wrongful trading, imposed a standard of conduct on directors which was basically objective and yet combined this with the toughest aspects of a subjective duty. By s. 214 (4), the director was required to behave as:

a reasonably diligent person having both—
(a) the general knowledge, skill and experience that may reasonably be expected of a person carrying out the same functions as are carried out[16] by that director in relation to the company, and

---

[12] [1892] 2 Ch 100 (also called the Marquis of Bute's Case).
[13] *Ibid.* at p. 109. A similar kind of case was *Re Denham* (1883) 25 Ch D 752 where a director called Mr Crook attended no meetings in a four-year period and was held not liable in relation to a fraud that had occurred.
[14] Ratifiable. See further below at p. 218 and, in particular, *Pavlides v Jensen* [1956] Ch 656.
[15] Now Insolvency Act 1986, s. 214.
[16] Or are entrusted to him; see Insolvency Act 1986, s. 214 (5).

(b) the general knowledge, skill and experience that that director has.

This combined objective standards in para. (a) with the 'sting' apparent in the *Dorchester Finance* case in the subjective standard in para. (b). The question then was, would the courts uprate the general common law duties of skill and care in line with these new provisions? The answer 'yes' soon came in two cases at first instance, *Norman v Theodore Goddard*[17] and *Re D'Jan Ltd.*[18] It is probable, therefore, that the duties of a director as regards care and skill currently approximate to the level set out in s. 214 (4) of the Insolvency Act 1986. If this is so, it gives added relevance to the practice of many directors who obtain insurance against their potential liability for negligence.

It remains to be seen how the law on directors' common law duties[19] will develop, now that objective standards are required. One area that has almost certainly changed, is the idea, perhaps inherent in the *Cardiff Savings Bank* case that it is possible for someone to be appointed to a board of directors not to act as a full director with normal responsibilities, but just to improve the image of the board or to show that some family connection is being maintained. An American case decided in the New Jersey Court of Appeal in 1978 illustrated the problem. In *Francis v United Jersey Bank*[20] the business of the company had been conducted for many years with the husband and wife, and their sons, as directors. The husband died and the sons carried on running the business. The wife remained a director but had become ill after her husband's death and took no part in the running of the business. The sons perpetrated a fraud which damaged the company, and it was later sought to make the wife liable for breach of her duties as director.[21] The argument that she did not bear the full responsibility of a director was rejected, on the basis that if a person sat on a board it was a representation to the shareholders and creditors that she or he was making an input in the normal way and that it was not possible, when in breach of duty, to 'point to a sign saying "dummy director" '.[22]

Another problem that the courts will need to confront is the argument that in modern companies carrying out very many transactions in dispersed geographical locations, it is often going to be very difficult even for the most diligent director to keep track of what is going on. If the courts are too severe here in their interpretation of what reasonableness requires they will make it difficult for boards to find directors. Indemnity insurance will not solve the problem indefinitely because if claims were too high it would eventually become difficult to obtain. Here then lies a practical problem in corporate governance. How can directors keep track of the business[23] of their companies in a way sufficient to meet their legal liabilities?

---

[17] [1992] BCC 14.

[18] [1993] BCC 646. See also *Re Westlowe Storage & Distribution Ltd (In Liquidition)* [2000] BCC 851.

[19] On the nature of these duties, see: S. Worthington 'The Duty to Monitor: A Modern View of the Director's Duty of Care' in F. Patfield (ed.) *Perspectives in Company Law: 2* (London: Kluwer, 1997) at p. 181; R. Grantham and C. Rickett 'Directors' "Tortious" Liability: Contract, Tort or Property Law' (1999) 62 MLR 139.

[20] 87 NJ 15, 432 A 2d 814 (1981).

[21] By then she had died and the action was actually against her estate.

[22] 432 A 2d 814 (1981).

[23] The problem is particularly acute for non-executive directors, who, by definition, are not required to give all their time or attention to the company. For recent preliminary issue litigation on the extent of the duties owed by NEDs; see *Equitable Life Assurance Society v Bowley* [2003] BCC 829.

9.3 FIDUCIARY DUTIES

A The scope of the duty of good faith

Directors have in their hands the control of the assets of the company and by anal-ogy with the law of trusts, they are regarded as owing fiduciary duties in respect of those assets. We have already seen that the duty is owed to the company rather than the individual shareholders.[24] The courts have described the fiduciary duty as fun-damentally being that of 'good faith'. In *Re Smith & Fawcett*[25] Lord Greene MR said that directors should exercise their powers 'bona fide in what they consider, – not what a court may consider – is in the best interests of the company,[26] and not for any collateral purpose.'[27] Similarly, in *Dorchester Finance* v *Stebbing*[28] Foster J stated: 'A director must exercise any power vested in him as such, honestly, in good faith and in the interests of the company . . .'[29]

It is important to realise that the expression 'good faith' in this context is used by the courts as a kind of shorthand to describe the range of duties which attach to the directors as fiduciaries. They are not 'trustees' in the technical sense of the word because their relationship with the company is not one where they are holding the legal title to the property and the company as a beneficiary holds the equitable title. On the other hand, the relationship is analagous to trustees in the sense that the company's assets are under their close control and they will usually be liable as con-structive trustees if they misapply the assets. They are certainly fiduciaries, how-ever,[30] and in that capacity will owe their duty of good faith. Broadly, good faith in this context means that they must be fair. But 'fair' in this context is a word with wide connotations. For trustees, it means that they must carry out the terms of the trust, that they must deal with the trust property properly, and solely for the ben-efit of the beneficiaries. So too with directors, who having a fiduciary relationship with their company, are also charged by the law to deal with property for the ben-efit of another. Directors obviously have to carry out the business of the company which will involve the assets of the company in business risks,[31] but subject to this, they have a duty to preserve the assets of the company, not to harm the assets and

---

[24] *Percival* v *Wright* at p. 161 above.

[25] [1942] Ch 304.

[26] The 'company' in this context is not usually construed as meaning the company as a detached legal entity and the courts look for some humans by which to gauge it. Thus in *Gaiman* v *Association for Mental Health* [1971] Ch 317 at p. 330 Megarry J said 'I would accept the interests of both present and future members of the company as a whole, as being a helpful expression of a human equivalent.' A similar statement has been noted above in relation to the alteration of articles; see p. 98. It is clear that when faced with the task of assessing the behaviour of the directors or shareholders in the con-text of a duty of good faith towards the company as a whole, the *Salomon* concept of the detached legal entity is temporarily put aside in favour of a pragmatic reckoning based on the social reality of the company, namely the shareholders as a group. In some circumstances the interests of the credi-tors can take the place of those of the shareholders in assessing the nature of the interests of the company; see the discussion at p. 53, n. 51 above.

[27] [1942] Ch 304 at p. 306.

[28] [1989] BCLC 498.

[29] *Ibid.* at pp. 501–502.

[30] *Aberdeen Railway* v *Blaikie* (1854) 1 Macq 461, HL.

[31] For which they may face liability if their conduct has fallen short of the common law duties of care and skill, discussed above.

therefore not to detract from the business of the company. These basic ideas will affect how the directors must go about their conduct of the business of the company. Business decisions taken on behalf of the company must be taken solely for its benefit. They must not be taken with a view to getting some personal benefit or advantage for the directors. The case law contains various illustrations of these ideas being applied in different business contexts. We will look at these now.

The most obvious and fundamental breach of a trustee's duty is for she or he to make off with the trust property.[32] Similarly, directors who take the company's assets will be liable as constructive trustees of any property they take, as will any third parties who take the assets with notice of the breach of duty.[33] If the company is in liquidation the matter is often raised against the directors by what are known as 'misfeasance proceedings', brought under s. 212 of the Insolvency Act 1986.[34] Directors who take the assets of the company may also find themselves liable to criminal proceedings for theft or related offences.[35]

Directors must exercise their powers for the benefit of the company and must not seek any collateral advantage for themselves when doing this. This aspect of the duty of good faith has often arisen in connection with the issue of shares which is a power given to the directors to enable them to raise capital. In some situations they have sought to further their own interests. Thus in *Punt* v *Symons*[36] an issue of shares was set aside because it had been done with a view to creating voting power to enable them to make their own position more secure. In *Howard Smith* v *Ampol Petroleum*[37] an issue of shares was set aside because it had been done to enable a takeover bid to go the way the directors wanted.

Another aspect of the duty of good faith is the idea that directors must exercise an 'unfettered discretion'. What this means is that the company, the beneficiary, is entitled to have a decision on a business matter reached solely on its commercial merits pertaining at the time the decision is taken. A director who has committed himself to vote in a particular way on some issue will be in breach of duty unless that commitment was itself undertaken for genuine commercial reasons. These kinds of issues were recently discussed in *Fulham BC* v *Cabra Estates*,[38] where it was held that, in the circumstances the directors were not in breach of their duty because they had committed themselves to a long-term policy for commercial reasons.

---

[32] Property is a broad notion and can include confidential information in some circumstances; see *Seager* v *Copydex* [1967] 2 All ER 415; *Scherring Chemicals* v *Falkman* [1981] 2 All ER 321. See further p. 167 below on the matter of whether a business opportunity can constitute property.

[33] *Cook* v *Deeks* [1916] 1 AC 554; *Rolled Steel Products Ltd* v *BSC* [1985] 3 All ER 52; *Aveling Barford Ltd* v *Perion* (1989) 5 BCC 677. On bribes, see *Boston Deep Sea Fishing Co.* v *Ansell* (1888) 39 Ch D 399; *Hannibal* v *Frost* (1988) 4 BCC 3.

[34] Although s. 212 is not restricted to the taking of corporate assets.

[35] See e.g. *Attorney General's Reference (No. 2 of 1982)* [1984] 2 All ER 216; *R* v *Rozeik* [1996] BCC 271.

[36] [1903] 2 Ch 506. There are now further statutory controls on the issue of shares; see p. 266 below.

[37] [1974] AC 821.

[38] [1992] BCC 863.

B The no-conflicts rule

1 Rationale of the rule

When adjudicating on an alleged breach of fiduciary duty, by a director, or trustee, the courts are faced with a problem which they have long recognised. The beneficiary is at an almost impossible disadvantage when it comes to proving that there has been a breach of duty. This is particularly true if the beneficiary under a trust is a minor. But the problem is there even if she or he is of full age. And the problem is there in companies. The disadvantage stems from the fact that the directors (or trustee, if a trust) often have in their hands the ability to ensure that the facts appear as they would wish them to appear. This is obviously not always possible. If, for instance, assets have been taken from a trust or from the company's bank account, there may well be independent evidence of this in the hands of the beneficiary or coming into the hands of the court. But where the breach being complained of relates to an exercise of discretion or a decision on a course of action, the problem is almost insurmountable. Suppose the directors of a company have turned down some business offer from a third party with the intention of secretly taking up the offer themselves in their private capacity. They have in their hands the ability to make it appear that their decision was properly reached. They will ensure that there are fictitious minutes of the board meeting showing that the business proposition was discussed carefully, but then rejected, on the perfectly proper grounds that the company did not have enough capital for the project, and also there were worries expressed about the compatibility of the proposed project with the company's existing commitments *etc, etc.* Faced with this, how is a suspicious shareholder to prove that they were in breach of duty and that the board decision was reached, not on a commercial basis as appeared from the minutes, but for reasons of personal advancement?

For hundreds of years, the courts have had a solution to this problem. Any situation which ostensibly gives rise to a conflict between the director's personal interests, and his duty to the company, is treated as a situation from which the director cannot benefit; or can only benefit after protective procedures have been complied with. In a sense, the courts are applying a presumption that the fiduciary duty has been broken, and taking action accordingly. The policy was clearly enunciated in the 18th-century case of *Keech* v *Sandford*.[39] Here, the court was being asked to allow a trustee (who was holding a lease as trust property) to renew the lease for his own benefit, on the genuine basis that the lessor had refused to renew it for the trust. The situation elicited Lord King LC's cynical observation: 'If a trustee, on the refusal to renew, might have a lease to himself, few trust estates would be renewed [for the benefit of the trust].'[40] Translated into the company law situation, the doctrine holds that any situation which is inherently likely to lead to a breach of the duty of good faith should automatically be treated as if the breach had occurred. In such cases therefore, whether the directors are actually in good faith or not, is not in issue.

---

[39] (1726) 25 ER 223.
[40] *Ibid.*

The difficulty which the courts have faced, in this field, is, as in so many others: 'Where to draw the line?' It is easy to say that a director must not put himself into a position where his duty and interest conflict, but how much of a conflict does there have to be before it will trigger the presumption that a breach of fiduciary duty has occurred? We will see that in recent years the courts have become uncomfortable with the severity of the approach normally adopted towards directors who have business interests of their own, and have tried to strike what they see as a fairer balance between the likelihood of damage to the company and the likelihood of damage to the director's own legitimate business interests or career aims.

2 Business opportunities

The question of how to handle directors who take up a business opportunity while they are directors is apparently not easy to answer. There are, however, several ways of looking at the problem.

One view is to see business opportunities coming to the company as the property of the company. In which case, in order to make the directors liable for breach of duty, all that has to be shown is that they have taken up the opportunity themselves.[41] It is arguable that this is what happened in *Cook* v *Deeks*.[42] Here, the defendant directors on behalf of the company negotiated a contract with a third party just as they had done on previous occasions, but when the agreement was formalised, they took the contract in their own names. Although in a sense, the contract had not yet come to the company, the court took the view that the contract 'belonged in equity to the company and ought to have been dealt with as an asset of the company'.[43] There are difficulties with this view. It is not really clear whether it is being held there that a mere business opportunity is a property right, and the case can perhaps be explained on the basis that the contract had actually been negotiated for the company and taken up by it, and that the directors had merely put, what was by then an asset of the company, in their own names. It is perhaps not authority on the wider, and more frequently occurring question which arises where the business opportunity is not in any way taken up on behalf of the company, but is rejected[44] on behalf of the company and then taken up by the directors personally. If the opportunity is property, then it is pertinent to inquire as to the scope of the property right. It is easy to make the assumption that the profits made by the directors are within the scope of the property right, but this is to forget that the directors could have bona fide rejected the opportunity and then not taken it up themselves. A further and perhaps more significant difficulty comes from the fact that it has been held by the House of Lords in *Regal (Hastings) Ltd* v *Gulliver*[45] that the

---

[41] One basis for the idea is that the directors should have decided to take the opportunity for the company (although they could have bona fide rejected it, they can hardly deny this if they did it themselves) and are treated as carrying it out on the company's behalf. The law on promoters reaches a similar position in some situations; see p. 44 above.

[42] [1916] 1 AC 554, PC.

[43] *Ibid.* at p. 564, *per* Lord Buckmaster.

[44] It will not always be clear whether the appropriate organ to do this will be the board, or the general meeting.

[45] [1967] 2 AC 134, [1942] 1 All ER 378

directors can be liable for breach of duty in relation to the opportunity even though it was established that the company itself was not in a position to take up the opportunity. This suggests that perhaps the opportunity was not there seen as an asset of the company[46] and means that there is another principle of liability at work here.

In *Regal Ltd* v *Gulliver*[47] the company owned a cinema and the directors thought it beneficial for the company to acquire two other nearby cinemas. They formed a subsidiary company to hold the leases of these two new cinemas but the lessor required either a personal guarantee from the directors or that the subsidiary should have a paid-up capital of £5,000.[48] The directors were unwilling to give the guarantees and in the circumstances the company was unable to afford to put more than £2,000 into the subsidiary. To enable the deal to go ahead, the directors and some of their business contacts put the money in themselves, taking shares in return. Eventually, the three cinemas were sold as a group, the purchaser agreeing to take all the shares in the two companies, instead of taking the cinemas on their own. The directors and other shareholders made a profit of nearly £3 per share. Thus Regal and its subsidiary passed under different control, that of the purchaser, who then caused Regal to commence an action to recover the profit which the directors had made on their shares. The action against the directors was successful (although the others involved who were not directors were not liable in the circumstances).[49] Citing *Keech* v *Sanford*, the House of Lords held the directors liable to account because by reason and in the course of their fiduciary relationship, they had made a profit. That was sufficient for liability under the 'no-conflict' rule. They had a fiduciary relationship with the company, and had made a profit out of an opportunity which had come to the company. The House of Lords stressed that liability here in no way depended on absence of good faith. It was also apparent that the company itself could not have taken advantage of the chance to buy the shares which the directors and others purchased, since the company was unable to afford more than £2,000.[50] So why was there liability? Is the rule ridiculous?

To understand how the no-conflict rule is working it is necessary to see it from the cynical perspective of Lord King LC in *Keech* v *Sandford*.[51] The directors were held to be in good faith because there was no evidence of bad faith. They may well have made sure that no such evidence existed. Similarly, there is cause for scepticism as to the fact that the company could not find more than £2,000, thus opening the way for the directors nobly to step in and save the deal. Who said it could not find more than £2,000? What steps had the board taken to raise more loan or equity capital for Regal so that it would have the money? Since the *Regal* case,[52] other decisions have followed and enshrined the hard line taken there: *Boardman* v

---

[46] Even if it was an asset, it would presumably have a negligible value if the company was unable to take it up. Nor, in the circumstances would they have been able to assign it for value.

[47] [1967] 2 AC 134, [1942] 1 All ER 378.

[48] As to 'paid-up capital', see p. 264 below.

[49] The action had little moral merit; in effect it was producing a clawback of part of the purchase price.

[50] See also *IDC* v *Cooley* [1972] 1 WLR 443 where it was found that the contract was not likely to be coming to the company.

[51] See the quotation at p. 166 above.

[52] Which was actually decided in 1942 although not fully reported until 1967.

Phipps;[53] *IDC* v *Cooley*;[54] *Carlton* v *Halestrap*;[55] *Attorney General for Hong Kong* v *Reid*.[56]

There is recent evidence of a change of approach. In *Island Export Finance Ltd* v *Umunna*[57] the director won. The company, IEF Ltd, had a contract with the Cameroonian government to supply it with post boxes. Umunna was the managing director. After the contract was ended, he resigned. Later he obtained a new contract in his own capacity.[58] IEF Ltd, perhaps not surprisingly, brought an action for breach of fiduciary obligation. The judge held that the director's fiduciary obligation did not necessarily come to an end when he left the company[59] and that a director was not permitted to divert to himself a maturing business opportunity which the company was actively pursuing. However, he found as a fact that the company was not actively pursuing it at the time Umunna took up the opportunity for himself. Moreover, the knowledge that the market existed was part of Umunna's stock in trade and know-how, and it would be against public policy and in restraint of trade to prevent him using this knowledge. The action failed.

The decision is in line with the no-conflict rule, because even under that rule there will come a point when the business opportunity which is taken up by the director is so remote from what the company does or plans to do, that there is essentially no conflict. It all comes down to what the business of the company is. The *Umunna* case breaks new ground by being quite lenient towards the director in its definition of what the business of the company was. But it is lenient in another way, also related to the definition of the business of the company, because in assessing what that business is, *Umunna* also requires us to have regard to what the business of the director is. If he has a lifetime of general entrepreneurial activity in various markets, it will not be possible for a company which hires him for a few years of that lifetime to argue that all future business in that area becomes the business of the company.

A similar flexible approach can be detected in the subsequent case of *Framlington Group plc* v *Anderson*.[60] Thus, although the no-conflict rule is still law,[61] it is possible that the courts are now sometimes prepared to consider an application of it which seeks to strike a balance that is considerably more in favour

---

[53] [1967] 2 AC 46.

[54] [1972] 1 WLR 443.

[55] (1988) 4 BCC 538.

[56] [1994] 1 AC 324; and see A.J. Boyle '*Attorney-General* v *Reid*: The Company Law Implications' (1995) 16 Co Law 131.

[57] [1986] BCLC 460.

[58] Actually for a company he then owned.

[59] A similar conclusion had been reached in the earlier case of *IDC* v *Cooley* [1972] 1 WLR 443, where Cooley had resigned on the fictitious grounds of ill-health in order to take up a contract which the company he worked for would have been pleased to obtain.

[60] [1995] BCC 611. See also *CMS Dolphin Ltd* v *Simonet* [2002] BCC 600, where the judgment contained a careful analysis of the balance to be struck when a director has resigned his office and thereafter taken up what the company alleges is a corporate opportunity.

[61] And successful litigation against directors in clear cases continues; see for example *Re Bhullar Bros Ltd* [2003] 711, CA, where the directors were held liable for exploiting a commercial opportunity. In *Item Software Ltd* v *Fassihi* [2003] 2 BCLC 1 it was even held that a director would owe a duty to disclose his own misconduct in some circumstances. This was what was described as a 'superadded' duty of disclosure.

of directors than hitherto. Nevertheless, the position has not been reached whereby in other jurisdictions[62] the courts are prepared to go behind the no-conflict rule and to try to make some assessment of whether or not the directors are in good faith. This takes them down the path, forbidden to the English courts by *Regal,* that involves looking at the evidence which the directors may themselves have so carefully manufactured in order for it to give the appearance of their bona fides.

Typical of this approach, which is current in some[63] American states as well as Commonwealth jurisdictions, is the decision of the Minnesota Court of Appeal in *Miller* v *Miller Waste Co.*[64] An action had been brought against the directors on the basis that they had taken the business opportunities of the company by setting up a web of companies around it which were supposedly supporting its business activities, but in reality were siphoning its business away. The court adopted a two-stage test for dealing with the situation. The first stage was the question 'Was the opportunity a *corporate* opportunity?' – the scope of the inquiry here being whether the business opportunity could properly be regarded as one which the company could claim as against any personal claim the directors might have by virtue of their own legitimate business activities. In deciding whether the opportunity was '*corporate*', the court would apply the 'line of business test', which basically meant that it would ask whether it was the sort of thing the company would normally do, or perhaps was currently planning to do. The court would also look at matters such as whether the company realistically had the financial resources to undertake the activity in question. All these matters related to the first stage of the two-stage test. If the court reached the conclusion that the opportunity was non-corporate, then the directors would be free to take it up themselves. If they concluded that it was a corporate opportunity, then the court would proceed to the second stage of the test. This involved answering the question: 'Even if it is a corporate opportunity, would it be fair, in all the circumstances, to allow the directors to take up the opportunity?'[65] Here, the court would hear evidence presented as to why the directors decided that it was not a good idea for the company to take up the opportunity, their good faith, and any other relevant matters. The actual result in the case was that very few of the opportunities were held to be corporate, and those that were, were fairly taken up by the directors.

In the first stage of the test here, there are obviously parallels with the UK approach, in the sense that the question 'was it a corporate opportunity?' is a similar inquiry to whether a conflict exists. If the business opportunity is non-corporate (under the *Miller* test), there will probably be no 'conflict of interest' under the English approach. However, the second stage of the test, the inquiry into the fairness of letting the directors take the opportunity and their good faith, is largely an anathema to the rigid stance taken in *Keech* and *Regal* which embody a resolute

---

[62] For a comparative approach in this area see, J. Lowry and R. Edmunds 'The Corporate Opportunity Doctrine: The Shifting Boundaries of the Duty and its Remedies' (1998) 61 MLR 515.

[63] But not all; versions of the *Regal* approach are to be found in some states.

[64] 301 Minn 207, 222 NW 2d 71.

[65] Or keep the profits if they have already taken it up.

refusal to regard the good faith of the directors as a relevant factor[66] and see the inquiry into it as a trap, in which '. . . few trust estates would be renewed . . .'.[67]

A few final thoughts are pertinent which might help to establish the nature of the relationship between the primary fiduciary duty and the no conflict rule, with special regard to the difficult issues raised by business opportunities. It is interesting to consider the business opportunity situation in the absence of the no-conflict rule. When a company receives a business opportunity, what is the fiduciary duty of the directors in relation to that? It is clear that the *common law* duty of care and skill would require some level of proper assessment of the commercial merits of the situation; we need not discuss that further here. The fiduciary duty requires, as it always will, that the board decision to accept or reject the opportunity is made in a fashion which is wholly consistent, and *exclusively* consistent, with the interests of the company. In particular this will mean that if the opportunity is rejected it is not being rejected so that the directors can then take it up themselves.

Suppose then that the board of directors can be proved to be grossly in breach of this fiduciary duty and that, for instance, documents show that they had rejected the opportunity because 'our formal remuneration is rubbish and it's about time we took the chance to make a bit on the side'. If they then make a profit, on what legal basis does the company litigate this? Presumably it can just go ahead[68] and make the claim for breach of fiduciary duty. The breach alleged is that the directors failed to consider the opportunity in the way their fiduciary duty required, i.e. wholly and exclusively consistent with the interests of the company. On the evidence, the action is going to be successful and the court will then decide what damage the company has suffered as a result of the breach of duty. It is probable that the court will take the profit made by the directors as being the amount recoverable.[69] What is the status of the no-conflict rule here, once the court has clearly established that there is a breach of fiduciary duty? Can it give a second and alternative reason for its decision, that there is a breach of the no-conflict rule because the directors put themselves in a position where their personal interest in taking up an opportunity which lay within the company's line of business conflicted with the company's interest? We have seen that the rationale of the no-conflict rule is to avoid the problem which occurs when the court is faced with trustees (or directors) who are in a position to argue that their conduct was bona fide and the beneficiary is not in a position to contradict that argument (because the trustees/directors are in sole control of the manufacture of evidence in relation to their decision-making process). In such a case, the no conflict rule, when faced with a conflict of interest, presumes the worst because the beneficiary will not be able to prove otherwise, and condemns the trustees out of hand. The rationale of the rule would not extend to the situation where, as here, the court has reached the conclusion on the evidence available that the directors are in breach of fiduciary duty. Thus where there is clear evidence of

---

[66] It was not relevant in *Boardman* v *Phipps* [1966] 3 All ER 721, either, although their good faith obviously helped the court's conclusion that they should receive remuneration 'on a liberal scale'.

[67] See *Keech* v *Sandford* (1726) 25 ER 223, *per* Lord King LC, see p. 166 above and the explanation there.

[68] Assuming there are no problems with the *Foss* v *Harbottle* rule, as discussed in Chapter 12 below.

[69] In *Regal*, the sum recovered was the profit made.

a primary breach of duty, the no-conflict rule is otiose. Thus the rule can be seen to be an adjunct to the main fiduciary duty, ancillary and supportive.[70]

3 Competing directors

It is common for people who hold bare or non-executive directorships[71] to hold directorships in more than one company. Normally this will not, of itself, give rise to a breach of duty to either of the companies. However, if the director holds a directorship in each of two competing companies, there is a danger that he is in a situation where his duty to one will conflict with his duty to the other, and he will possess inside knowledge of both.

The older case law makes light of the problem and suggests that a director is free to direct a competing company. In *London & Mashonaland Ltd* v *New Mashonaland Ltd*[72] Chitty J refused an injunction to restrain the director of one company from becoming a director of a rival company on the basis that a director was not required to give the whole of his time to the company. This does not address the issue of the possible application of the no-conflict rule in this situation and pre-dates the high profile given to that rule in *Regal* and subsequent decisions. This field of company law often draws an analogy with the law of trusts where trustees may not compete with the trust.[73]

Thus from general principle it seems that a director who competes with the company, either in business on his own account, or by being director of a rival company, will run the risk of being found to be in breach of fiduciary duty. Good faith requires loyalty, and would require him to abstain from behaviour which deliberately damages the company.[74] Furthermore, it is an area where the no-conflict rule is likely to become relevant making it unnecessary to prove actual harm. The mere holding of the office of director in each of two competing companies could be sufficient to trigger a remedy in an appropriate case. Where the line would be drawn remains to be seen. How much of an element of competition would there have to be? If the recent approach in *Umunna* is going to be followed, it is likely that the courts would require a very high degree of overlap in what the companies were doing, before they were prepared to invoke the no-conflict principle.[75]

---

[70] In practice a case would usually be argued on both grounds, in case the evidence of primary breach of duty fell short of the mark. In many situations, there will be no evidence at all of the breach of fiduciary duty and the no conflict rule will be all the beneficiary has.

[71] In other words, directorships where the holder does not also have an employment contract requiring full-time attention to some executive role in the company.

[72] [1891] WN 165. See also the dictum of Lord Blanesburgh in *Bell* v *Lever Bros* [1932] AC 161 at p. 195.

[73] *Re Thompson* [1930] 1 Ch 203.

[74] Excepting negligent breaches of his or her common law duties.

[75] For instance in *In Plus Group Ltd* v *Pyke* [2002] 2 BCLC 201, the Court of Appeal held that there was no completely rigid rule that a director could not be involved in the business of another company which was in competition with a company of which he was a director, and they stressed that every situation was 'fact-specific'.

4 Nominee directors

Another area which is a good candidate for infringing the no-conflict rule is the practice of appointing 'nominee' directors. A nominee director is a director who has been appointed specifically to represent and protect the interests of some outside party,[76] perhaps a venture capital company which has agreed to lend or subscribe capital only on condition that it can 'keep an eye' on the company by having its nominee on the board.[77] The practice of appointing nominees is well recognised in the case law as are the dangers they face from a position which involves a potential conflict of interest.

It is clear that nominees must be careful not to get themselves into difficulties with conflicts of interest. Lord Denning gave this warning:

> It seems to me that no one who has duties of a fiduciary nature to discharge can be allowed to enter into an engagement by which he binds himself to disregard those duties or to act inconsistently with them ... take a nominee director ... There is nothing wrong in it ... so long as the director is left free to exercise his best judgment in the interests of the company which he serves. But if he is put upon terms that he is bound to act in the affairs of the company in accordance with the directions of his patron, it is beyond doubt unlawful.[78]

The matter was explored in *Kuwait Bank* v *National Mutual Life*.[79] By virtue of a 40% shareholding the bank had nominated two directors to the board of a company which was a money broker involved in deposit-taking activities. The company had gone into insolvent liquidation and the depositors lost money. The question arose as to whether the bank, the nominator, could be held liable for the negligence of its nominees. In the process of trying to establish this, it was argued that the bank was vicariously liable because the nominees were appointed by the bank, were employed by it and carried out their duties as directors in the course of their employment by it. It was held that the bank was not vicariously liable because the nominee directors were bound (because of their fiduciary duty to the company) to ignore the wishes of their employer, the bank. An argument that the nominees were agents of the bank similarly failed; they were agents of the company.

The case shows the court applying quite a robust presumption that the nominee directors were obeying the precepts of company law and to that extent it gives strong judicial support to the general practice of appointing nominees. If it becomes clear that they are not complying with their duties, then they are in difficulties. This could arise by gradually drifting into a situation which is legally untenable or by deliberate fraud. In *SCWS* v *Meyer*[80] the articles of association of company A permitted company B to nominate three out of its five directors. This happened. Later,

---

[76] Sometimes called the 'patron' or the 'nominator'.

[77] The term 'nominee' director needs to be distinguished from a 'shadow director'. A shadow director is a statutory concept, which was first introduced in the Companies Act 1980, so that the various statutory provisions regulating directors' activities could be made to have a wider impact. The concept is explored with reference to its operation in the field of wrongful trading at p. 33 above.

[78] *Boulting* v *ACTT* [1963] 2 QB 606 at p. 626.

[79] [1990] 3 All ER 404, PC.

[80] [1959] AC 324.

the directors stood accused of failing to defend the interests of company A against the depredations of company B. Lord Denning put the problem in this way:

> So long as the interests of all concerned were in harmony, there was no difficulty. The nominee directors could do their duty by both companies without embarrassment. But as soon as the interests of the two companies were in conflict, the nominee directors were placed in an impossible position . . .[81]

In *Selangor United Rubber Co. Ltd v Cradock (No. 3)*[82] the two nominee directors, L and J, were involved in causing the company to provide funds to Cradock to enable him to purchase shares of the company contrary to what is now s. 151 of the Companies Act 1985.[83] Ungoed-Thomas J held the directors liable for the misapplication of the company's funds:

> It seems to me, however, that both L and J were nominated as directors . . . to do exactly what they were told by Cradock, and that is in fact what they did. They exercised no discretion or volition of their own and they behaved in utter disregard of their duties as directors . . . They put themselves in [Cradock's] hands . . . as their controller.[84]

The *Selangor* case is an example of nominee directors who committed a clear breach of their basic fiduciary duty. *SCWS* v *Meyer* also involved the situation where the breach of duty was evidentially established, although the circumstances were less deliberate than *Selangor*. These cases are not examples of the no-conflict rule operating. They are proven breaches of fiduciary duty.

However, there is then the question as to whether the nominee director phenomenon is one which inherently infringes the no-conflict rule as applied in *Regal (Hastings) Ltd* v *Gulliver* and *Keech* v *Sandford*.[85] In other words, the position of the nominee is highly likely to lead to a situation where he covertly prefers the interests of his nominator to those of the company. It would usually be impossible to prove. Just the kind of situation to attract the no-conflict rule. The courts, however, seem disinclined to take this approach.[86] On the contrary, the decision in *Kuwait Bank* v *National Mutual Life* seems to be operating a presumption which is almost the opposite of the no-conflict rule, namely that the nominator could not be vicariously liable, because the nominees owed a duty to ignore the bank's instructions by virtue of their paramount duty to the company.

It would perhaps be unwise to rule out the application of the no-conflict rule in all cases. There may well be situations where the circumstances show that the nominee is in an impossible position of conflict, and so even without any actual or proved breach of duty, he will be in breach of the no-conflict rule. But this would be rare. The practice of appointing nominees is so well established in commercial practice that the approach of the courts seems to be to make a finding against the

---

[81] *Ibid.* at p. 366.
[82] [1968] 1 WLR 1555.
[83] Some aspects of the legislation have changed; see generally Chapter 16 below.
[84] [1968] 1 WLR 1555 at p. 1613.
[85] Above.
[86] See *Boulting* v *ACTT* [1963] 2 QB 606 at p. 618, *per* Lord Denning 'There is nothing wrong in it . . .' (see p. 173 above).

nominees if, but only if, it can be shown that they are actually in breach of fiduciary duty.

5 Contracts with the company

The law has not always sought to regulate directors' conflicts of interest by requiring the director to hand over his profit to the company. A less severe technique would be to set up some procedure which would go some way towards providing a safeguard against a director breaching his duty. This approach has been adopted for many years where the conflict situation is that the director has a personal interest in some contract that he is making with the company, perhaps because he is selling an item of his own property to the company, or because he is negotiating a contract with the company under which the company will supply him with goods. In recent years, the American expression 'self-dealing' is sometimes used to describe this kind of situation.

At first, the case law required disclosure to the general meeting and approval by it. In default of this, the contract was (and still is) voidable at the option of the company.[87] Then it became common for the articles of association to require disclosure to the board – an easier process than disclosure to the general meeting. The legislature became concerned to ensure that the articles did not dispense with the disclosure requirement altogether and enacted what is now s. 317 of the Companies Act 1985. The effect of s. 317 is to make disclosure to the board a *minimum* duty and to prevent the articles from dispensing with it, but it does not authorise disclosure to the board instead of the general meeting and unless the articles give permission for disclosure to the board, then the basic case law duty of disclosure to the general meeting will govern the situation.[88] In practice, most companies adopt the Table A provisions. These were amended in 1985 and obviate some of the problems which had occurred under the previous Table A. The current provisions are arts 85 and 86, which provide that a director can be interested in a contract with a company, provided that he has disclosed that interest to the board. He may not vote at any directors' meeting on any such contract unless it falls within certain narrow exceptions.[89] The disapplication of the common law requirement to disclose to the general meeting is contained in art. 85, which makes it clear that he 'shall not, by reason of his office, be accountable to the company for any benefit which he derives' from the transaction and the transaction is not 'liable to be avoided on the ground of any such ... transaction'. It is arguable that s. 310 conflicts with this, because it makes void any provisions in the company's articles[90] for exempting any officer of the company from liability for default or breach of duty. It is an ongoing problem and does not seem capable of satisfactory resolution. It is probable that the courts will strive to give effect to the Table A provisions on one basis or another.[91]

---

[87] *Aberdeen Railway Co.* v *Blaikie* (1854) 1 Macq 461, HL; *North-West Transportation Co.* v *Beatty* (1887) 12 AC 589.
[88] Companies Act 1985, s. 317 (9). Disclosure to the board will also be required.
[89] Table A, art. 94. Article 95 will disapply him from the quorum if he is not entitled to vote.
[90] '... [O]r otherwise'.
[91] See e.g. *Movitex Ltd* v *Bulfield* (1986) 2 BCC 99,403.

Some aspects of this area are subject to additional and to some extent overlapping regulation by virtue of ss. 320–322A of the Companies Act 1985[92] and it should also be mentioned that a number of transactions which might conceivably otherwise fall within the self-dealing principle, such as loans to directors are subject to stringent statutory regulation.[93]

C Duty in respect of employees

Section 309 of the Companies Act 1985 dates from 1980 and provides that: 'The matters to which the directors of a company are to have regard in the performance of their functions include the interests of the company's employees in general, as well as the interests of its members.' The section goes on to make it clear that the duty is a fiduciary duty and is owed to the company (and the company alone). The provision is of great significance in the development of company law, even if it is not of great significance in legal practice.[94]

9.4 RELIEF FOR DIRECTORS

A Ought to be excused

Section 727 of the Companies Act 1985 will sometimes be of assistance to a director[95] who has been subjected to proceedings for breach of duty, negligence, default etc. Under it, directors may seek relief, on the basis that although they may be liable, they nevertheless have acted honestly and reasonably and 'ought fairly to be excused'. It will often cover the situation where they have committed merely a technical breach of duty, although it is wider than that. Relief under s. 727 is often claimed by directors but in most cases, especially where the breach of duty is substantial, the application for relief is given fairly short shrift. Thus, in *Dorchester Finance Ltd* v *Stebbing*[96] Foster J said: '. . . I have no hesitation in concluding that they should not be relieved under the provisions of this section.'[97]

B Exemption and insurance

The extent to which the articles of a company could effectively relieve a director of liability has for many years been resticted by s. 310 of the Companies Act 1985 which, broadly speaking, made void, provisions in articles or contracts (or otherwise) for exempting him from liability attaching to him by virtue of various breaches of duty in relation to the company.

---

[92] Subject to various exceptions and extensions, s. 320 prohibits any arrangement (falling within certain limits) whereby a director acquires a 'non-cash' asset from the company or sells one to it. Additionally, s. 322A will make voidable certain transactions entered into between the company and its directors (and others) where the board of directors are exceeding their authority.

[93] See p. 179 below.

[94] See p. 60 above.

[95] Or auditor or officer.

[96] [1989] BCLC 498 at p. 506.

[97] See also *Bairstow* v *Queens Moat Houses plc* [2002] BCLC 91, CA.

In view of recent concerns that potential liabilities of directors have increased to the extent that able people are being deterred from holding office as directors, the Company (Audit, Investigations and Community Enterprise) Act 2004 has introduced new ss. 309 A–C into the 1985 Act. These provisions are designed to ameliorate the position of directors of the company. They do not apply to auditors, who thus continue to be regulated in this regard by the regime in s. 310 (suitably amended). It seems that company officers other than directors or auditors (such as the company secretary) fall outside both sets of provisions.

Sections 309A(1)–(2) provide that any provision which purports to exempt a director from liability attaching to him in connection with any negligence, default, breach of duty or breach of trust by him in relation to the company, is void. However, under s. 309A(5), the company may purchase and maintain insurance against such liability, in respect of a director of the company or associated company (as defined).

Furthermore, by s. 309A(3), any provision by which a company provides an indemnity for a director of the company or associated company against such liability is void. To this prohibition on indemnities there are complex exemptions contained in ss. 309A(4) and 309B–C, permitting what are referred to as 'qualifying third party indemnity provisions'. Lastly, it should be mentioned that the position as regards the company's funding of directors' expenditure on defending proceedings has been ameliorated in certain circumstances by the insertion into the 1985 Act of s. 337A.

9.5 DUTY NOT TO COMMIT AN UNFAIR PREJUDICE

Unfair prejudice is a concept which is usually seen as a liability, namely a liability that a member will petition under s. 459 of the 1985 Act 'on the ground that the company's affairs ... have been conducted in a manner which is unfairly prejudicial to the interests of its members generally or of some part of its members ...'. On the other hand, when the unfair prejudice jurisdiction was first created in 1980, there seemed to be more litigation against directors in the first few years under those provisions than there had been in the previous 100 years under the general law. It is true that some of the points raised in that litigation added nothing substantive[98] to the existing liability of directors, because they were merely references to the existing common law or fiduciary duties. On the other hand, the unfair prejudice cases may sometimes contain instances where the directors would have probably escaped any liability under their common law or fiduciary duties, but find that the case goes against them because they infringed some aspect of the wider concept of unfair prejudice. These cannot be examined in detail here, but should be borne in mind when studying the concept of unfair prejudice in Chapter 13. An important note of caution here is that there is an artificiality and an insufficiency in seeing directors' duties solely from the traditional angle of common law and fiduciary

---

[98] They often added liability at a procedural level because the rule in *Foss v Harbottle* is generally not available to prevent the bringing of proceedings based on conduct which is alleged to be unfairly prejudicial, whereas it is available to stifle proceedings based on breach of common law or fiduciary duties.

duties. Because of the unfair prejudice jurisdiction, the liability of directors is wider and more subtle than will be suggested solely by an examination of those traditional duties.

9.6 COMPANY LAW REVIEW AND LAW REFORM

As part of their inquiry into the adequacy of present corporate governance mechanisms, the Review carried out a major analysis of the role and function of directors.[99] In particular, the scope and content of the duties of directors was put under examination. This followed on from the work of the Law Commission, which had recommended that there needed to be a statement of the general duties of directors contained in the Companies Act. After wide consultation, the Review generally accepted the idea[100] and set out a Trial Draft. The subsequent government White Paper contained a draft of a codification of directors' duties, headed 'General Principles by which Directors are Bound'.[101] It is likely that a version of this will eventually reach the statute book and it may well help to bring to the notice of directors what is expected of them by the law, in general terms.

---

[99] Law Com. Report No. 261 (1999).
[100] DTI Consultation Document (March 2000) *Developing the Framework* paras 3.8–3.16.
[101] See *Modernising Company Law* (London: DTI, 2002), draft Companies Bill, cl. 19 and Sch. 2. Available on the DTI website http://www.dti.gov.uk/cld.

10

OTHER LEGAL CONSTRAINTS ON DIRECTORS' POWERS

10.1 CONSTRAINTS ON DIRECTORS' POWERS

This chapter will examine the way in which, aside from directors' common law and fiduciary duties, the law has sought to constrain the power of the directors. Some of the rules are flat prohibitions on certain types of transactions which are thought to be unacceptable. Many of the statutory prohibitions in Part X of the Companies Act 1985 fall into this category. Other rules are gateway provisions which seek to prevent an unfairness coming into the situation by establishing a procedure to be followed.[1] Other types of rules seek to operate, as it were, *in terrorem*, and enable some other party to set in motion something which the directors will find adverse, such as removal under s. 303, or wrongful trading proceedings. In addition to all these, there is another group of rules which can really be seen as setting up structures which will have some monitoring function in regard to the directors.

10.2 STATUTORY CONTROLS AFFECTING DIRECTORS

A Introduction

The Companies Act 1985 contains many provisions which seek directly to regulate the conduct of directors. They mainly relate to transactions and situations which have been seen, over the years, to give rise to abuses. To some extent they overlap with the common law and fiduciary duties in that, if the statutory provisions were not there, it might be possible to attack the transaction on the basis that it was a breach of duty in some respect or other.

B Part X enforcement of fair dealing

Part X of the Companies Act 1985, ss. 311–347, contains a range of provisions which are designed to enforce fair dealing. Some of these have already been looked at in various situations, in particular ss. 317, 320–322A, which seek to reduce the potential damage flowing from various situations involving 'self-dealing'.[2]

Sections 323–329 seek to regulate certain share dealings by directors and their

---

[1] Such as Companies Act 1985, s. 317 and its attendant case law.
[2] See p. 175 above.

families. Since the Companies Act 1967 directors have been prohibited from dealing in options in shares in certain circumstances, it being felt that this was a likely way of their abusing insider knowledge. It was not part of a general attempt to regulate insider dealing, which had to wait until 1980.[3] The option provisions are now contained in ss. 323 and 327 of the Companies Act 1985.

In certain circumstances a director will have a statutory duty to notify the company as to his interest in shares in it (and/or debentures). The provisions are widely drafted and will also require, for instance, notification of certain events, such as if he enters into a contract to sell the shares. 'Interest' is widely defined, and in some circumstances, shares held by the director's spouse and children must be disclosed. The company must keep a register containing the information thus received and notify the Stock Exchange if the shares are listed.[4] Besides making insider dealing more difficult, these disclosure provisions can operate as a barometer of the directors' levels of confidence in the company so that if they have just sold most of their holdings, their proclamations of confidence in the company's future at a subsequent general meeting can be judged accordingly.[5]

The making of a loan by the company to a director is a situation which is open to abuse in a number of ways. The loan may be at an unrealistically low rate of interest and therefore be disguised remuneration. If the loan is not repaid over a long period of time, it can be a form of disguised gift. The Companies Act 1948 contained provisions to regulate loans to directors which eventually came to be seen as inadequate and widely circumvented. The Companies Act 1980 set out to rectify this and the provisions are now contained in ss. 330–347 of the 1985 Act. The provisions are complex and are designed to prevent directors getting benefits from the company by way of loan, property transfers or by various other methods, so in addition to regulating loans there is regulation of 'quasi-loans', 'credit transactions' and 'assignments' and 'arrangements'. The provisions are broadly drafted so that they will catch many obvious avoidance techniques like making the loan to the director's spouse, and others not so obvious. Sometimes the provisions are made subject to certain exceptions such as where the amounts involved are below a stated figure or for certain purposes. Detailed analysis of these is beyond the scope of this book and the whole area has recently been the subject of a painstaking review and consultation by the Law Commission.[6] The matter was taken up by the Company Law Review and it is likely that there will be many amendments to the provisions in due course; and few repeals.[7]

---

[3] See further p. 377 below.
[4] Companies Act 1985, ss. 324–326, 329. There are extensions to spouses and children of directors in s. 328.
[5] Directors dealing in shares of their company are in an exposed position as regards insider dealing liability. The matter is dealt with at p. 381 below.
[6] Law Com. Report No. 261 (1999).
[7] See DTI Consultation Document (March 2000) *Developing the Framework* paras 3.86–3.89.

C Controls over issue of shares

The power to issue shares is obviously one which is open to abuse by directors. Past examples[8] include: issuing shares to themselves, to water down the voting rights of another so as to assist them in a battle for control within the company,[9] or to make them less vulnerable to removal,[10] or issuing shares to the bidder in a takeover to help produce what they saw as a favourable outcome.[11] Prior to 1980 there was no statutory regulation of the power to issue shares. The power was generally assumed to reside in the directors by virtue of art. 80[12] of the 1948 Act's Table A. The Companies Act 1980 tightened up on the provisions by introducing what are now ss. 80 and 89–96 of the Companies Act 1985.

Section 80 limits the power of the directors to issue shares.[13] Generally, they may not do so unless authorised by the company in general meeting or the articles. Such authorisation may be given for a particular exercise of the power or for its exercise generally and conditions may be attached.[14]

Sections 89–96 provide existing equity shareholders of the company with preferential subscription rights[15] in the event of a further issue of shares. The provisions are complex, but, in outline, the position is as follows. A company proposing to allot 'equity securities'[16] must not allot them to anybody unless it has first made an offer of allotment to the existing holders of either 'relevant shares' or 'relevant employee shares'.[17] The offer must be on the same of more favourable terms and in more or less the same proportion to the size of his existing stake in the company.[18] Section 90 makes detailed provision as to the method of making the offer. Private companies may exclude the preferential rights in their memorandum

---

[8] The directors' efforts in these cases were unsuccessful and the share issues were set aside. The unfair prejudice jurisdiction has uncovered similar ingenuity and reacted against it; see *Re Cumana Ltd* [1986] BCLC 430; *Re DR Chemicals Ltd* (1989) 5 BCC 39; *Re Kenyon Swansea Ltd* (1987) 3 BCC 259; *Re a Company 007623/84* (1986) 2 BCC 99,191; *Re a Company 002612/84* (1984) 1 BCC 92, 262; *Re a Company 005134/86* [1989] BCLC 383 and see generally Chapter 13 below.

[9] *Piercy* v *Mills* [1920] 1 Ch 77.

[10] *Punt* v *Symons* [1903] 2 Ch 506.

[11] *Howard Smith* v *Ampol Petroleum* [1974] AC 821.

[12] Similar to art. 70 of the 1985 Table A in the sense that it vested the power to manage the business of the company in the board; there are important differences.

[13] With certain exceptions.

[14] In addition to the various detailed provisions in s. 80, s. 80A provides exemptions for private companies and s. 88 requires a return of allotments to be made to the Registrar of Companies. Further provisions relating to public offerings of public company shares are dealt with in Chapter 20.

[15] These are sometimes referred to as pre-emption rights, which can be confusing since the term 'pre-emption' usually refers to a right of first refusal of something which is already in existence being offered for sale. The term 'pre-emption' does not appear in the body of the legislation itself, only in the heading, which may perhaps be regarded as a draftsman's error, although perhaps nothing turns on it.

[16] Defined in s. 94 so as to exclude subscriber shares, bonus shares, employee shares and certain preference shares but so as to include certain convertible debentures and warrants.

[17] Defined in s. 94 so as to exclude some types of preference shares.

[18] Section 89 (1). The offer must remain open for at least 21 days and in the meantime the company may not allot any of the securities, unless it has earlier received notice of the acceptance or refusal of every offer (ss. 89 (1), 90 (6)). Allotments under an employee share scheme are exempt (s. 89 (5)), as are allotments of equity securities which are to be wholly or partly paid up otherwise than in cash (s. 89 (4)). Special provisions apply, sometimes enabling a modified form of offer to be made, where the company has more than one class of equity share in existence (s. 89 (2), (3)).

or articles.[19] Both public and private companies may sometimes disapply the preferential rights.[20] Contravention of the provisions can result in the company and the officers responsible being liable to compensate any person to whom an offer should have been made for loss or damage suffered as a result.[21]

D Statutory provisions *in terrorem*

1 Introduction

Under this *in terrorem* heading are gathered together a group of statutory provisions which might have a salutary influence on the behaviour of directors. Each one of them is a drastic measure and often each will only actually be put into effect after the undesirable behaviour has occurred. Nevertheless, their existence will sometimes help to convey in advance to directors the feeling that wrongdoing may carry adverse consequences for them. The list below is not exhaustive; although these are the main provisions of this nature.

2 Removal of directors

Under s. 303 of the Companies Act 1985, a company may remove a director before the expiration of his period of office. The power is exercisable by ordinary resolution and cannot be taken away by anything in the articles or in any agreement.[22] The power to remove directors merely by passing an ordinary resolution is an important shareholder right. This is particularly so in view of the fact that it is not necessary to show any wrongdoing. The director is liable to removal 'without cause', although presumably in general meeting it will often be tactically necessary to produce some reasons.

Section 303 will sometimes have an effect on directors' behaviour by deterring wrongdoing which if discovered would lead to their removal. It is also an important adjunct to the operation of an efficient takeover market in which boards of directors who underperform, in the sense of getting a poor return on the resources at their disposal, may find that they become the target of a takeover bid. Once control has passed to the bidder, it will be in a position to remove the target board under s. 303. The threat of this can operate as a spur to incumbent management to increase their performance.[23]

In some situations there will be significant restrictions on the use of s. 303. These can come about in a number of ways. In a large plc one practical reason might be

---

[19] Section 91.

[20] Under s. 95, which provides that where the directors are given a general authorisation under s. 80 (to allot shares) they may be given power by the articles, or by special resolution of the company, to allot equity securities pursuant to that authority as if s. 89 did not apply, or as if it applied with modifications chosen by the directors. Various procedures are set out in s. 95. In the case of public companies which are also listed on the Stock Exchange, the FSA Listing Rules contain further requirements; see FSA Listing Rules, paras 9.16–9.23.

[21] Section 92.

[22] Section 303 (1). Special notice is required; see further p. 153 above.

[23] On the theoretical aspects of the market for corporate control, see further p. 390 below. Section 303 also becomes significant in a proxy battle.

the political necessity to keep the director reasonably well disposed towards the company, especially if he is the only one being removed. He may well be aware of wrongdoing by other directors which they would rather not have mentioned. In such a situation, the likely outcome might be for the company to pay him off with a huge financial settlement; confidentiality comes at a price. The public are regularly baffled when they read in the financial press that a director has been found to have been implicated in the incompetent running of the company and its subsequent poor performance, and then paid off with a settlement running into millions.

Another factor which restricts the use of s. 303 is that in the case of an executive director who has a fixed term employment contract, removal may be a breach of that contract, giving rise to substantial damages. The company's liability is expressly preserved by s. 303 (5).

Use of s. 303 runs another risk, particularly in small partnership style companies. The removal of a director will often give him the right to petition the court under s. 459 to complain of unfairly prejudicial conduct. This may involve the other shareholders or directors in having to find the money to purchase his shares. Alternatively, in rare circumstances, a director excluded from management could seek to have the company wound up under s. 122 (1) (g) of the Insolvency Act 1986. This kind of litigation is often catastrophic for those involved in a small company.[24]

The last problem which will sometimes arise with s. 303 is that in some situations the company's articles will have effectively excluded its use. The effectiveness of such provisions was tested in *Bushell v Faith*.[25] Faith and his two sisters each had 100 £1 shares. The sisters tried to remove him under s. 303 but failed because of a clause in the articles which uplifted his voting power by three votes per share on a resolution to remove a director. He thus polled 300 votes on the resolution against their 200. The argument that the voting uplift was void as being contrary to statute was not accepted by the House of Lords who took the view that the clause was really in the nature of a voting agreement, the legality of such had long been recognised.[26] Voting agreements of this nature can therefore create a high degree of entrenchment, but are probably limited to small and medium-sized companies for it is unlikely that the Stock Exchange or the FSA would permit the listing of a company which had such a clause in its articles.

3 Wrongful trading

Section 214 of the Insolvency Act 1986 contains provisions under which in some circumstances, directors of an insolvent company will become liable to contribute to the assets of the company in the liquidation.[27] Their liability will in no way depend on fraud being proved or a dishonest state of mind. Conduct, which could be loosely described as being 'negligent',[28] is sufficient to trigger this liability. Thus

---

[24] See further Chapter 13.

[25] [1970] AC 1099.

[26] For a similar approach in a different context, see *Russell v Northern Bank Development Corp* [1992] BCC 578, HL, discussed at p. 96 above.

[27] See further at p. 33 above.

[28] In fact, some quite specific standards are laid down in s. 214 (2)–(5); see further p. 34 above.

directors may find that if they carry on trading when the company is in financial difficulties and when insolvency is looming, then money will have to be found from their own pockets. In the first reported case on wrongful trading the directors were required to pay £75,000 to the liquidator because they struggled on trading for longer than they should have.[29] It was a huge sum when compared to the amounts that they had been drawing from the company over the years. It is highly probable that the section has had a significant effect on boards of directors and their advisers.[30]

4 Disqualification

Under the Company Directors Disqualification Act 1986 the court can disqualify persons from acting as directors.[31] Currently about 1,500 such orders are made each year. Although orders for disqualification are made in civil proceedings, rather than criminal proceedings, the process must inevitably be extremely unpleasant for the director at the receiving end. He is being put through a trial of his competence as a professional director, a trial which will trawl through a large slice of his past business conduct.[32] At the end of it, if he is unsuccessful in defending his position, he will be banned from carrying on as a director for at least two years. This may well destroy permanently or temporarily his ability to earn a living. Most of the cases brought seem to relate to small businesses where the management were usually basically honest but found themselves in difficult situations which gradually slipped out of control. All in all, disqualification proceedings form a major part of the depressing vista which the law creates for businessmen who fail to live up to the standards which are now thought to be necessary.

5 Other insolvency provisions

Insolvency proceedings can involve a wide range of remedies and processes which will subject the director to investigation, and possible disgorgement of assets, in addition to the danger of wrongful trading liability and disqualification.[33]

10.3 MONITORING OF DIRECTORS

A Introduction

Part of the picture of the legal regulation of the environment in which directors operate are mechanisms which result in the directors being monitored. Sometimes, the monitoring will then produce a reaction from some organisation which will impact on the directors.

---

[29] *Re Produce Marketing Consortium Ltd (No. 2)* (1989) 5 BCC 569.
[30] See further p. 36 above.
[31] And from holding other positions. On all this, see Chapter 23 below.
[32] Unless the summary procedure is being used; see p. 423 below.
[33] See Chapter 22 below.

B The policy of disclosure of the financial affairs of the company

Disclosure is a fundamental regulatory tool[34] which is as old as UK company law itself. The Joint Stock Companies Act 1844 had contained a requirement for companies to publish their annual balance sheet and in later years the extent of disclosure required was increased and made more complex, although periodically, the legislature has exhibited a change of heart and produced measures which for a time have required less disclosure than before; so the growth in the requirements has not been steady. It continues to fluctuate at the present day as the legislature strives to find a balance between protecting those who deal with companies on the one hand, and the needs of commerce to be free of unnecessary burdens, on the other.

Disclosure is a fundamental technique of that area of company law known as capital markets law, or securities regulation. Disclosure of financial information is merely one aspect of disclosure technique, although an important one nevertheless. Not only does it provide information about the performance of the company but it also helps to prevent fraud. Similarly, disclosure is also of great significance in the area of company law these days known as corporate governance, for by providing public information about the affairs of the company it enhances the ability of the markets to monitor the performance of management.[35] It is probable that Orders which may be made under the Electronic Communications Act 2000 will enhance the ability of shareholders to monitor management by enabling them to access annual reports and other information through electronic means. It is difficult to be precise about whether disclosure of financial information by a company should be considered as part of company law or part of the law of securities regulation; it clearly belongs to both, and provides further illustration of the artificiality of the boundaries between company law and capital markets law.

C Accounts and reports

The Companies Act 1985[36] casts the main responsibility for financial reporting[37] firmly on the board of directors. It is they who have to ensure that accounting records are kept, that these are sufficient to show and explain the company's transactions, and disclose with reasonable accuracy the financial position of the company, and enable the proper preparation of the balance sheet and the profit and loss account.[38] Accordingly, the directors 'shall prepare' a balance sheet and a profit

---

[34] For a wider analysis of the role of disclosure in company law and securities regulation, see generally, Chapter 17.

[35] See p. 53 above.

[36] In addition to the statutory requirements and the accounting standards which are mentioned in this chapter, a listed plc will need to comply with the relevant requirements of the FSA Listing Rules.

[37] Many matters in relation to financial reporting are the responsibility of the Financial Reporting Council (FRC) and its 'subsidiary' bodies. Descriptions of these important bodies and their very important work are available on http://www.frc.org.uk. The Companies (Audit, Investigations and Community Enterprise) Act 2004 increases the powers and resources of the FRC so as to enable it to take over the functions of the Accountancy Foundation in respect of setting of accounting and audit standards, and overseeing the major accountancy bodies.

[38] Companies Act 1985, ss. 221–222.

and loss account[39] for each financial year[40] of the company. The company's annual accounts need to be approved by the board of directors and duly signed by a director on behalf of the board.[41]

These accounts must comply as to form and content with Schedule 4 to the 1985 Act.[42] Schedule 4 contains *inter alia* a statement of accounting principles and rules but departure from these is allowed where this is necessary to show what the legislation calls a 'true and fair view'.[43] Behind the statements of principle in Sch. 4 lie the more detailed Statement of Standard Accounting Practice (SSAPs) and Financial Reporting Standards issued by the Accounting Standards Board (FRSs).[44] In practice these SSAPs (and FRSs) are usually followed by accountants, for although they are not given the force of law by the Companies Act, there is a requirement for it to be stated whether the accounts have been prepared in accordance with applicable accounting standards[45] and any material departures from the standards must be mentioned and reasons given.[46] If the company is a parent company within the meaning of the Act, then as well as preparing individual accounts, the directors must prepare group accounts which comprise a consolidated balance sheet dealing with the state of affairs of the parent company and its subsidiary undertakings and a similar profit and loss account.[47]

International Accounting Standards (IAS)[48] have been developed and issued by the International Accounting Standards Board (IASB) with a view to setting and encouraging the use of global standards.[49] These have now been adopted as law in the EU, and so EU companies which are traded publicly must prepare their consolidated accounts in line with IAS.[50] UK government policy is to permit the use of IAS in other situations also,[51] and legislation is being prepared to bring this about.[52]

---

[39] *Ibid.* ss. 226, 231–232. If the company is a parent company, group accounts will sometimes be required as well as the company's individual accounts: ss. 227–232 (the s. 226 accounts are referred to in s. 226 (1) as the company's 'individual' accounts to distinguish them from group accounts).

[40] Defined in ss. 223–225.

[41] Companies Act 1985, s. 233. If necessary defective accounts can be revised in accordance with s. 245 and the DTI have powers to require revised accounts and may apply to the court if necessary: ss. 245A–245C.

[42] Schedule 4A in the case of group accounts.

[43] Companies Act 1985, s. 226 (5).

[44] In some circumstances Urgent Issues Task Force (UITF) Abstracts will also be relevant. Certain small companies or groups can choose to apply the Financial Reporting Standards for Smaller Entities (FRSSE).

[45] Defined in Companies Act 1985, s. 256.

[46] *Ibid.* Sch. 4, para. 36A.

[47] These accounts must comply with the provisions of Sch. 4A to the 1985 Act as regards form and content. By virtue of s. 228, in some circumstances a parent company which is included in the accounts of a larger group is exempt. Sections 229–230 make further provision in relation to group accounts.

[48] Standards which are issued on 6 April 2004 and thereafter are being referred to as International Financial Reporting Standards (IFRS). Existing standards (i.e. issued prior to that date) will continue to be referred to as IAS.

[49] At a global level their main rivals are the Americans who have developed and continue to hold to US GAAP (US Generally Accepted Accounting Principles).

[50] With effect from 1 January 2005. This is as a result of the EC Regulation of July 2002. For further details of this, see p. 12 above.

[51] I.e. in the individual accounts of publicly traded companies and in the individual and consolidated accounts of most other companies.

[52] With effect from 1 January 2005.

Until recently, there was almost always an additional requirement for the participation of auditors in this financial reporting process. For many companies, particularly the larger ones, this is still the case, because s. 384[53] contains a basic requirement for the company to appoint an auditor or auditors. The main exceptions were first introduced in 1994[54] and exempt certain small companies from the obligation to appoint auditors and the audit process.[55] This was done as part of various reforms designed to remove burdens on small businesses.

In addition to the accounts, the directors are required to prepare a directors' report[56] containing a 'fair review[57] of the development of the business of the company and its subsidiary undertakings during the financial year and of their position at the end of it' and also a statement as to the amount of dividend which they are recommending. Additionally, the directors' report must contain the matters required by Sch. 7. Of special note is the requirement that the directors' report must contain particulars of directors' emoluments.[58] The statutory responsibilities for the preparation of the accounts and directors' report cannot be shifted onto the auditors, even if they are retained as the accountants to the company and so in fact are the people most directly involved in the actual work of preparing the figures out of the mass of internal documentation which the directors have handed over to them. This point has become particularly apparent in relation to wrongful trading cases where it has been held that the directors cannot escape liability by arguing that they were unaware of the financial state of the business because the accounts were not ready in time.[59]

An Operating and Financial Review (OFR) is also soon to be required for quoted companies.[60] This was an idea much commended by the Company Law Review[61] as an improvement to corporate governance and which the government is acting speedily on. Many companies of course already produce this kind of review on a voluntary basis. Although the detailed standards are being developed by the Accounting Standards Board it is likely that it will be a narrative review covering such matters as past performance, future prospects, business, objectives and strategy, and possibly employees, social and community issues, environment.

Companies are also obliged to deliver[62] an annual return to the Registrar in the pre-

---

[53] See generally Companies Act 1985, ss. 384–394A.
[54] Companies Act 1985 (Audit Exemption) Regulations 1994 (SI 1994 No. 1935). The regulations added ss. 249A–249E to the Companies Act 1985. There have been subsequent amendments.
[55] In certain circumstances, the audit report is replaced by a report to be made by a 'reporting accountant': Companies Act 1985, ss. 249C–249D.
[56] Companies Act 1985, s. 234, with approval required in accordance with s. 234A.
[57] The requirements for the contents of the directors report will change when the Modernisation Directive (2003/51/EC) is implemented. This is likely to have happened by the time this book is published. The Directive defines the 'fair review' as 'a balanced and comprehensive analysis of the development and performance of the company's business and of its position, consistent with the size and complexity of the business'.
[58] The Directors' Remuneration Report Regulations 2002 (SI 2002, No. 1986) have recently introduced rules designed to achieve more transparency on directors' remuneration.
[59] *Re Brian D Pierson (Contractors) Ltd* [1999] BCC 26; see also *Re Produce Marketing Consortium Ltd (No. 2)* (1989) 5 BCC 569.
[60] Although not yet passed into law at the time of writing, the legislation is likely to be the Companies Act (Operating and Financial Review and Directors' Report) Regulations 2004.
[61] See Company Law Review Final Report, paras. 6.8–6.16, 8.1–8.144.
[62] Within certain time periods.

scribed form,[63] which must contain information[64] such as the address of the company's registered office, the names and addresses of every director and various other details. Much of this information remains the same each year and the procedure has been made more efficient by the introduction of a 'shuttle' system whereby a document is sent from the Registrar containing the previous year's information and requiring only necessary amendments to the document which is then returned.

D Publicity

The legislation contains a range of processes and requirements designed mainly with a view to getting the accounts and reports thoroughly publicised throughout the company and put on public file. The accounts in respect of each financial year must be laid before the company in general meeting within the periods prescribed.[65] Additionally, the accounts must be delivered to the Registrar of Companies where they will be placed on public file.[66] Provided that the prescribed procedure is followed, private companies may elect to dispense with the laying of accounts.[67] A copy of the annual accounts must be sent to every member, debentureholder and any other person entitled to receive notice of general meetings, within prescribed time limits.[68] Furthermore, any member or debentureholder is entitled to demand a copy of the company's last annual accounts.[69] If a company publishes its accounts, then there are various prescriptions designed to ensure that they are complete and that certain misleading impressions are not created.[70]

E Non-statutory reports

Accounts usually contain more than the balance sheet and profit and loss account required by the legislation. In particular, accounting standards require a cash flow statement.[71] Often also there are reports containing a review of the company's financial needs, resources and treasury management, a report on operations, on community programmes. Listed plcs have for many years used the need to circulate annual accounts to shareholders as a way of promoting the image of the company and so the accounts and related non-statutory reports are presented in a glossy magazine format designed to present the company in its best light.[72]

---

[63] Companies Act 1985, s. 363.

[64] Set out in ss. 364 and 364A.

[65] Companies Act 1985, ss. 241, 244. Special rules apply in respect of certain overseas or other subsidiaries which have been excluded from the group accounts: s. 243.

[66] *Ibid.* s. 242. Sections 246–249 contain provisions enabling companies and groups which qualify as 'small' or 'medium-sized' to file with the Registrar accounts which contain less information than those which they must circulate to the shareholders, sometimes referred to as 'modified accounts' or 'abbreviated accounts'.

[67] Subject to members' rights to require laying: Companies Act 1985, ss. 252–253.

[68] Companies Act 1985, s. 238; there are certain exceptions.

[69] *Ibid.* s. 239; the company must comply within seven days.

[70] *Ibid.* s. 240.

[71] FRS 1.

[72] On the importance of annual reports generally, see S. Bartlett and R. Chandler 'The Private Shareholder, Corporate Governance, and the Role of the Annual Report' [1999] JBL 415.

F The role of the auditors

The auditors are a significant part of the overall mechanism for the protection of shareholders and the corporate governance process generally. They have an important statutory function which establishes them as a kind of independent checking mechanism. This comes about through the operation of s. 235 of the Companies Act 1985, which requires that the auditors must make a report to the company's members on all annual accounts of the company of which copies are to be laid[73] before the company in general meeting during their tenure of office. This auditors' report must state whether in the opinion of the auditors the annual accounts have been properly prepared in accordance with the 1985 Act and whether a true and fair view is given. They must also consider whether the information given in the directors' report is consistent with the accounts, and if not, they must state that in their report.[74] The auditors have a duty to carry out sufficient investigations to enable them to form an opinion as to whether proper accounting records have been kept by the company and proper returns adequate for their audit have been received from branches not visited by them and also whether the company's individual accounts are in agreement with the accounting records and returns.[75] If these or any of the other matters are not satisfactory, the auditors must state that in their report. In a listed company an adverse report by the auditors can lead to a DTI investigation.

Events in the last 15 years have turned a spotlight on the liability of auditors for their audit reports. Although the House of Lords' decision in *Caparo plc v Dickman*[76] provided some amelioration for them by limiting the scope of their liability for negligent misstatement in tort, their contractual liability to the company was more than sufficient to give rise to a plethora of claims against them where the standard of their efforts had arguably fallen below the reasonable care implied in their contracts. The claims were brought by the liquidator or administrator of the failed company and since these were usually partners from the top accountancy firms the result was that most of the firms found themselves pitted against each other in what in financial terms were life or death struggles.[77] There were plenty of corporate scandals around to provide the basis for actions: Barlow Clowes, Maxwell, Polly Peck to name but a few. Some of the claims were huge; the largest was probably the action brought by the liquidators of Bank of Credit and Commerce International (BCCI) against Price Waterhouse and Ernst & Whinney,[78] claiming £5.2bn.[79]

Accountants had traditionally pursued their professional activities as partnerships and those who are partners are jointly liable for the contract debts of the firm.[80]

---

[73] On the laying process, see pp. 153 and 188 above.

[74] Companies Act 1985, s. 235 (3).

[75] *Ibid.* s. 237.

[76] [1990] 2 AC 605. However, if the auditors have 'assumed a duty of care' to the claimants, this may lead to liability: see *Henderson v Merrett Syndicates* [1995] 2 AC 145, HL; *ADT v BDO Binder Hamlyn* [1996] BCC 808; *Electra Private Equity Partners v KPMG Peat Marwick* [2000] BCC 368, CA.

[77] In the Barings Bank collapse, the administrators were the accountancy firm Ernst & Young and the defendants were Coopers & Lybrand (London and Singapore) and Deloitte Touch (Singapore).

[78] Later called Ernst & Young.

[79] *Financial Times*, 5 August 1994. It was eventually drastically scaled down (to around £250m) and settled.

[80] And jointly and severally liable for tort debts; see Partnership Act 1890, ss. 9, 10 and 12.

Professional indemnity insurance provided protection only to a certain level. Beyond that, the partners were personally liable. The accountancy profession developed various ideas on how their problems might be mitigated.[81] They were largely instrumental in setting up the Cadbury Committee on the Financial Aspects of Corporate Governance, the Report of which produced a revolution in the self-regulatory aspects of corporate governance.[82] The problems faced by the accountancy profession were the initial incentive for the development of the Limited Liability Partnership.[83] To some extent, provisions in the Companies (Audit, Investigations and Community Enterprise) Act 2004 will improve their position.[84] It will give auditors rights to require information from a wider group of people than at present, and introduce a new offence for failing to provide information or explain. There will also be a duty cast upon directors to consider whether they have supplied the information necessary for a successful audit, and the accounts will contain a statement certifying that the directors have not withheld information necessary for the auditors to form their opinion.[85]

G Company secretary

The existence of other officers of the company, such as the company secretary,[86] could in some circumstances help to provide a check on the activities of directors. Every company must have a secretary.[87] The legislation has prohibitions on who can be a secretary in certain situations.[88] Since the Companies Act 1980, the rules on who can be the secretary of a public company have been tightened up with the overall aim of ensuring that the secretary of a public company is, broadly, a 'professional'. The statute provides that it is the duty of the directors to take all reasonable steps to secure that the secretary[89] is a person who appears to them to have the requisite knowledge and experience to discharge the functions of secretary. Additionally, they must also satisfy one of the detailed requirements set out in s. 286 of the Companies Act 1985.[90] The terms of appointment of the secretary are usually governed by the articles and in particular art. 99 of Table A provides in effect that the appointment, remuneration and removal of a secretary is in the hands of the directors. The

---

[81] Besides improving their own internal procedures. One proposal was to put a 'cap' on their liability to clients, based on a multiple of their audit fee. This is progressing: see DTI Consultative Document *Director and Auditor Liability* (London: DTI, 2003).

[82] See Chapter 11.

[83] See p. 20 above.

[84] When in force.

[85] See ss. 8–18. The Act also seeks to strengthen auditor independence by requiring companies to publish detailed information in their annual accounts as to the non-audit services which their auditor has provided. The idea being that shareholders will be able to judge from this whether the auditor is subject to conflicts of interest which may affect the objectivity of the audit.

[86] See the definition in s. 744 of the Companies Act 1985: 'officer ... includes a director, manager, or secretary.'

[87] Companies Act 1985, s. 286 (1).

[88] As regards who can be a secretary, it is provided that a sole director may not also be the secretary (and nor may another company be the secretary if the sole director of that is the same sole director of the company, and similarly, nor may it have as sole director of the company, a corporation the sole director of which is secretary to the company: s. 283 (3), (4)).

[89] And each joint secretary.

[90] The appointee must have been secretary (or assistant or deputy) on 22 December 1980; or for at least three of the five years immediately preceding the appointment, held office as secretary of a public

company secretary may sometimes become liable for failures to perform his duties. Often the legislation penalises the 'officers' of the company for, for instance, failing to deliver a document to the Registrar of Companies. As we have seen, the secretary is an officer by virtue of the definition in s. 744. In some circumstances he might become personally liable for debts and other payments.[91] Disqualification of a company secretary is also possible in certain limited circumstances.[92]

It is difficult to be precise about the nature of the duties and role of the company secretary. Much will depend on the contractual terms of his employment and the size of the company involved. Usually the company secretary will be expected to ensure that the company complies with all the 'disclosure' requirements in the legislation so that, for instance, he will be responsible for the operation of the various registers, books and particulars required to be kept at the company's registered office.[93] The summoning and arranging of meetings and other legislative requirements like the annual return will also usually fall to him. He may also find that extensive liaison with the auditors is necessary, particularly if they are being dilatory about preparing the annual audit, delay with which can now attract severe penalties. In smaller companies in particular, the company secretary may often be required to provide a legal service also, dealing with matters like drafting of contracts and employment law. Sometimes he will have an executive or commercial function and may have actual or apparent authority to bind the company in contracts.[94]

H Government and other agencies

The activities of companies are monitored in various ways by a number of government and non-governmental agencies and organisations; these include the Department of Trade and Industry, the London Stock Exchange, the Financial Services Authority, the Insolvency Service, as well as the police, the Serious Fraud Office and the Crown Prosecution Service.[95] General monitoring of the management and affairs of companies is carried out by the DTI which has various statutory powers of investigation.[96] There are two main types of DTI investigation – s. 447 requisitions and s. 432 investigations.[97]

---

company; or be a barrister, advocate or solicitor called or admitted in any part of the UK; or be a member of any of various specified bodies (these include the accountancy bodies, and the Institute of Chartered Secretaries and Administrators, the Institute of Cost and Management Accountants and the Chartered Institute of Public Finance and Accountancy); or be a person who, by virtue of his holding or having held any other position or his being a member of any other body, appears to the directors to be capable of discharging those functions.

[91] See e.g. Companies Act 1985, s. 349 (4).

[92] See e.g. Company Directors Disqualification Act 1986, ss. 4 (1) (b), 22 (6), and Companies Act 1985, s. 744.

[93] See Companies Act 1985, ss. 169, 211, 287–290, 325, 352–362, 382–383, 407.

[94] See e.g. *Panorama Developments Ltd* v *Fidelis Furnishing Fabrics Ltd* [1971] 3 All ER 16.

[95] See generally Chapters 17–23.

[96] These are contained in the Companies Act 1985, ss. 431–453 and make detailed provision for the investigation of companies. The DTI also has powers in relation to insider dealing offences; these are dealt with at p. 383 below.

[97] It should also be mentioned that under s. 442 inspectors may be appointed by the DTI to investigate the ownership of a company's shares. Also under s. 431 inspectors may be appointed at the formal request of the company in certain circumstances, although this power is very rarely used.

Under s. 447 the Secretary of State (in practice the DTI's Companies Investigation Branch)[98] has power to require the production of documents if he thinks that there is good reason to do so. A s. 447 inquiry is unannounced and, for those on the receiving end, sudden. It enables the DTI to get enough information[99] to decide whether to do anything further. In the year ending 31 March 2004 there were 189 such investigations,[100] some as a result of requests from the public, some on the DTI's own initiative, and some as a result of a request from a variety of other sources such as other regulators. Many such investigations lead no further. Some do, however, and may result in criminal investigations and proceedings, or perhaps winding up.[101] Occasionally such an investigation is a preliminary to a s. 432 investigation.

Section 432 provides various grounds for the DTI to appoint inspectors to investigate a company. These are generally carried out by outside inspectors, often a Queen's Counsel and an accountant, and lead to a detailed report which is usually published. The investigations are very rare events, and so for instance, in the year to 31 March 2004, only one such investigation was completed.[102]

10.4 CONCLUSIONS

This chapter has provided a résumé of the legal constraints which constitute the environment in which directors operate. It hardly seems possible to conclude that the law is 'woefully inadequate' or some similar epithet; indeed, as it currently stands, it is not inadequate. The scandals of the 1980s were largely the product of a very different legal regime; a regime formed in the 1960s and 1970s, and earlier. Much of the law changed in the 1980s, and the way in which it was operated by the regulators changed too.

The unfair prejudice remedy dates from 1980 but took some years to develop, by which time it had become clear that it had revolutionised shareholder litigation to the extent that, far from being almost impossible to set up, it had by the 1990s become almost a crippling nuisance.[103] Most of the insolvency law reforms date from 1985 and they also took a while to impact; but eventually it became clear that the environment had changed. Wrongful trading cases became a more frequent sight in the law reports and a jurisprudence developed on the issue of the liability of a parent company for wrongful trading through its subsidiary.[104] Disqualification cases became more common in the late 1980s after the passing of the Company Directors Disqualification Act 1986 and these have steadily grown to the current annual figure of 1,500. The system for filing of accounts had become notorious due to accounts being years out of date but the introduction of substantial civil fines has

---

[98] For detail on the work of the CIB see their website: http://www.dti.gov.uk/cld/comp_inv.htm.

[99] The Companies (Audit, Investigations and Community Enterprise) Act 2004 seeks to strengthen the investigations regime by increasing the DTI's powers in relation to obtaining information and increasing remedies available against people who fail to provide information.

[100] See *Companies in 2003-04* (London: DTI, 2004) p. 19.

[101] Under s. 124A of the Insolvency Act 1986.

[102] See reference in n. 100 above, *ibid.* p. 17.

[103] See further p. 233 below on judicial efforts to contain unfair prejudice litigation.

[104] See further at pp. 34–36 above.

largely succeeded in changing this. The regulatory climate was changing. As regards the regulators themselves, the scene changed out of all recognition from 1986 onwards. The old DTI-operated system of licensing of share dealers under the Prevention of Fraud (Investments) Act 1958 gave way to comparatively ferocious regulation of the wider financial services industry under the Securities and Investments Board,[105] now replaced by the Financial Services Authority.[106] This and other changes[107] produced a marked shift in the culture of the business industry. Businessmen had not grown to like business law, but they had certainly begun to realise that it could not be ignored without undesirable results.

Many of these matters will be taken up later in this book. But this much is clear. It is important not to assess the UK system of corporate governance by reference to the past, looking at past scandals and looking at a legal climate which has since moved on. We will see in the next chapter that for larger companies, there is also now a substantial layer of regulation emanating from the self-regulatory committees. This too has had its impact.

10.5 COMPANY LAW REVIEW AND LAW REFORM

The Final Report of the Review makes various recommendations for changes to Part X of the Companies Act 1985, and to financial reporting.[108]

---

[105] Set up by the Financial Services Act 1986.

[106] Now operating under the statutory authority of the Financial Services and Markets Act 2000.

[107] E.g. the enhanced enforcement of insider dealing law.

[108] See *Modern Company Law for a Competitive Economy Final Report* (London: DTI, 2001) paras. 6.8–6.16, 8.1–8.144. See also the subsequent government White Paper, *Modernising Company Law* (July 2002, Cmnd. 5553) and *Company Law. Flexibility and Accountability: A Consultative Document* (London: DTI, 2004).

11

ROLE OF SELF-REGULATION

11.1 RELIANCE ON SELF-REGULATION

It has been seen[1] how the corporate scandals of the 1980s and the exposed legal position of statutory auditors prompted a reconsideration of the adequacy of corporate governance mechanisms and that the Cadbury Committee was set up in May 1991 by the Financial Reporting Council, the London Stock Exchange and the accountancy profession to examine the financial aspects of corporate governance. The resultant Cadbury Report,[2] issued in 1992, reviewed the structure and responsibilities of boards of directors, the role of auditors and the rights and responsibilities of shareholders. The recommendations as regards directors were summarised in a 'Code of Best Practice'. Although the report was expressed to focus on those aspects of corporate governance specifically related to financial reporting and accountability, the committee intended that their ideas would seek to contribute to the promotion of good corporate governance as a whole.[3]

The chief distinguishing feature of the Cadbury Report was its reliance mainly on self-regulation. It was not a report which produced a long list of recommended changes to the law[4] and which thereby postponed the resultant hoped-for improvements until some remote future date after the legislature had acted on the recommendations. The Cadbury Report took effect swiftly and without reliance on the law.[5] Some time after the report was issued the London Stock Exchange added force to the recommendations of the report by amending the Listing Rules so as to require listed companies to make a statement about their level of compliance with

---

[1] See at p. 190 above.

[2] *Report of the Committee on the Financial Aspects of Corporate Governance* (London: Gee, 1992).

[3] The literature is immense. See e.g. D. Prentice and P. Holland (eds) *Contemporary Issues in Corporate Governance* (Oxford: Clarendon Press, 1993); N. Maw, P. Lane, M. Craig-Cooper *Maw on Corporate Governance* (Aldershot: Dartmouth Publishing, 1994); S. Sheikh and W. Rees (eds) *Corporate Governance and Corporate Control* (London: Cavendish, 1995); G. Stapledon *Institutional Shareholders and Corporate Governance* (Oxford: Clarendon Press, 1996); K. Hopt and E. Wymeersch (eds) *Comparative Corporate Governance* (Berlin: de Gruyter, 1997); J. Kay and A. Silberston 'Corporate Governance' in F. Patfield (ed.) *Perspectives on Company Law: 2* (Deventer: Kluwer, 1997) p. 49. See also the footnote references in Chapter 3 above, pp. 53-58. For a detailed comparative study of European corporate governance codes, see the report on behalf of the European Commission by the firm, Weil Gotshal & Manges LLP; available at http://europa.eu.int/comm/internal_market/en/company/company/news/corp-gov-codes-rpt-part1_en.pdf and also http://europa.eu.int/comm/internal_market/en/company/company/news/corp-gov-codes-rpt-part2_en.pdf.

[4] There were some, but these formed a minor aspect of the Cadbury Report's overall approach (see e.g. para. 4.41 (Companies Act to be amended to require shareholder approval for directors' service contracts exceeding three years)).

[5] Although it was mindful of the legal background.

the Cadbury Code of Best Practice and give reasons for non-compliance. The Cadbury Report also made the point, as is often made by regulators in the context of self-regulation, that if the self-regulatory mechanisms were seen not to be working, then legislation would become inevitable.[6]

The Cadbury Report gave renewed impetus to the debate about the merits or demerits of self-regulation for a similar controversy had already surrounded the self-regulatory Code on Takeovers and Mergers.[7] Much of the early public reception given to the Cadbury Report and the idea of self-regulation in corporate governance was sceptical.[8] Self-regulation has its disadvantages, chiefly in relation to enforceability, and there is an obvious theoretical objection to allowing those who are likely to benefit most from a weakly regulated regime, to be responsible for regulating it. And yet, by 1995, evidence was beginning to emerge of significant levels of compliance with the Cadbury Code, albeit with lower levels among smaller companies.[9] The Company Law Review expressed the view that the evidence[10] suggested a fairly high level of compliance with the Combined Code and that it was increasing.[11] The Review cited a survey by PIRC[12] which shows that 93% of a sample of FTSE All Share Index companies had a board made up of one-third or more non-executive directors.[13] It is arguable that self-regulation is superior in some repects to regulation by statute: its potential for cultural change is likely to be greater because, deriving from public debate and perceived consensus within the sector to be regulated, it commands greater respect within that sector than rules imposed by an external lawgiver. It is also more flexible and can respond more quickly to change. Enforcement mechanisms, while not as final and crushing as legal enforcement, can nevertheless be very varied and create a supportive environment for a self-regulatory code.[14] The use of self-regulatory codes is widespread, and, while it could be a grand exercise in self-deception, it is more likely that the current public enthusiasm for them is based on a shared intuitive perception that they have a contribution to make. As a caveat to this it is worth observing that there may be some matters which are not amenable to self-regulation and where legislation may be needed, particularly where there is no consensus on the matter within the sector being regulated.

---

[6] Cadbury Report, paras 1.10, 3.6.

[7] See e.g. G. Morse 'The City Code on Takeovers and Mergers – Self-regulation or Self-protection?' [1991] JBL 509.

[8] In its Lex column the *Financial Times*, 28 May 1992, swung its weight against the idea with a piece entitled 'Cadbury's Soft Centre'. Doubts were expressed by both academics and practitioners: see e.g. Finch 'Board Performance and Cadbury on Corporate Governance' [1992] JBL 581 at p. 595; N. Maw, P. Lane, M. Craig-Cooper *Maw on Corporate Governance* (Aldershot: Dartmouth Publishing, 1994).

[9] See the 1994 Report of the Cadbury Committee's Monitoring Sub-Committee. For further empirical analysis in this area, see A. Belcher 'Regulation by the Market: The Case of the Cadbury Code and Compliance Statement' [1995] JBL 321; A. Belcher 'Compliance with the Cadbury Code and the Reporting of Corporate Governance' (1996) 17 *Company Lawyer* 11.

[10] By March 2000.

[11] See DTI Consultation Document (March 2000) *Developing the Framework* para. 3.129.

[12] Pensions Investment Research Consultants.

[13] Although there are gaps in compliance in other respects.

[14] The Cadbury Report stressed the role to be played by financial institutions, and a wide range of public bodies; also the role of the media in drawing attention to governance issues of public or shareholder concern: Cadbury Report, para. 3.14.

11.2 TECHNIQUES OF CADBURY

A Different approaches

In order to achieve its aim of an improvement in the quality of corporate governance, the Cadbury Report attacked the problems from different angles, with the overall intention of changing the environment in which companies operate. Three approaches can be identified:

(1) structural and functional alterations designed to spread the balance of power;
(2) increases in assumptions of responsibility;
(3) enhanced quality of disclosure.

These will now be examined.

B Structural and functional alterations

Some of the Cadbury Report's key recommendations were designed to ensure that power is spread around within the governance structure and not concentrated in one person, or in one small group. It was seen as important to get the structure working; in particular, to get the board working as a group and to provide proper checks and balances[15] so that the board does not simply agree to do whatever the chief executive wants and does not have too much power. The Cadbury Committee evolved an enhanced status and function for non-executive directors (NEDs), of whom there had to be at least three.[16] The idea, broadly, is that the NED is someone who is not involved full-time in the running of the company.[17] Accordingly, he is not dependent on it for his livelihood, and he is not going to be in the pocket of the chief executive or the rest of the board. Because he derives only a small part of his overall income from the company (he might be a NED on several boards), he will not risk his reputation and overall earning capacity by getting involved in corporate malpractices. In short; he is independent. As such, he is in a position to carry out the task assigned by the Cadbury Report, which is to bring an 'independent judgement to bear on issues of strategy, performance, resources, including key appointments, and standards of conduct'.[18] Thus the NEDs would form an independent element within the board, playing a normal directorial role in the leadership of the company but also exercising a kind of monitoring and control function. Additionally, the report envisaged the NEDs playing an important role on subcommittees of the board.[19]

Spreading of power was enhanced by the recommendation that there should be a division of responsibilities at the head of the company, that the role of the chairman of the board should, in principle, be separate from that of the chief executive.[20] It had been found that in companies where corporate governance had gone badly

---

[15] *Ibid.* para. 4.2.
[16] *Ibid.*, para. 4.11. There was no definition of 'non-executive director'.
[17] In other words, is not an executive director on a full-time employment contract.
[18] Cadbury Report, para. 4.11.
[19] *Ibid.* paras 4.35 (b) and 4.42.
[20] *Ibid.* para. 4.9.

wrong, it was common to find that the powerful positions of chairman and chief executive had been combined in one person, who was thus in a position to stifle board discussion.

The establishment of sub-committees of the board was another area explored by the Cadbury Committee, which came to the conclusion that boards should appoint 'audit committees'. This would enable a board to delegate to such a committee, a thorough review of audit matters. It would enable NEDs to play a positive role in audit matters and also offer auditors a direct link with the NEDs.[21] Additionally, it was recommended that boards should appoint 'remuneration committees', consisting wholly or mainly of NEDs, to make recommendations as to the level of remuneration of the board. Thus, executive directors should play no part in deciding what their remuneration should be.[22]

The role of the company secretary was given an enhanced status, with responsibilities for ensuring that board procedures are both followed and regularly reviewed and that all directors have access to the company secretary's advice and services.[23]

C Assumptions of responsibility

The Cadbury Committee was concerned to ensure that people within the governance structure knew where their responsibilities began and ended, and also concerned that people assumed those responsibilities and got on and discharged them properly. Various provisions within the report were geared to bringing this about. Thus it was recommended that there should be a statement of directors' responsibilities for the accounts and a counterpart statement by the auditors about their auditing responsibilities.[24] In similar vein, the responsibility of the board to ensure that a proper system of control over the financial management of the company was highlighted, by recommending that the directors should make a statement about it in the report and accounts.[25] Institutional investors were to be encouraged to make greater use of their voting rights (and hence exercise more responsibility for the monitoring of board performance) by requiring them to make a policy statement about their use of their voting power.[26]

D Enhanced quality of disclosure

Much of the Cadbury Report was geared to enhancing the quality of financial information being disclosed by companies. The disclosure of financial information is an important regulatory tool. If the information is accurate, it enables the market to react appropriately and is thought to result in an accurate valuation of the company's securities.[27] Accordingly, the Report's recommendations were directed

---

[21] *Ibid.* para. 4.36.
[22] *Ibid.* para. 4.42.
[23] *Ibid.* paras 4.25–4.27.
[24] *Ibid.* para. 4.28.
[25] *Ibid.* para. 4.32.
[26] *Ibid.* paras 6.9–6.12.
[27] *Ibid.* para. 4.48.

towards ensuring that the system of financial reporting and the audit function were working well.[28] In particular the Report addressed the problem of different accounting treatments being applied to essentially the same facts. It also supported and proposed measures to increase the effectiveness and objectivity of the audit, which it saw as an important external check on the way in which financial statements are prepared and presented, and regarded the annual audit as one of the cornerstones of corporate governance, an essential part of the checks and balances required.[29]

11.3 THE GREENBURY REPORT

The next self-regulatory initiative on corporate governance occurred in January 1995 when, in response to a public debate fuelled by media stories of excessive remuneration of directors, the Confederation of British Industry set up the Study Group on Directors' Remuneration chaired by Sir Richard Greenbury. The resultant 'Greenbury Report' in July that year contained a Code of Best Practice for Directors' Remuneration. The Code reinforced the Cadbury Committee's ideas relating to the establishment of remuneration committees and contained a requirement for the audit committee to submit a full report to shareholders each year, explaining the company's approach to remuneration. It also required much more detail about the remuneration package of each director than was required by the law existing at that time.[30]

11.4 THE HAMPEL REPORT: EVOLUTION OF THE COMBINED CODE 1998

The Cadbury Report had recommended the appointment of a new committee by the end of June 1995 to examine compliance, and to update the Cadbury Code.[31] The Greenbury Committee expressed similar sentiments as to a successor body.[32] In the event, this took the form of the 'Committee on Corporate Governance' chaired by Sir Ronald Hampel. It was established in November 1995 on the initiative of the Chairman of the Financial Reporting Council. It produced a preliminary report in August 1997 and a final report in January 1998. The Hampel Committee then produced a draft document which was a set of principles and a code which embraced Cadbury, Greenbury and their own work. The document was passed to the London Stock Exchange which then published, in March 1998, a consultation document setting out the draft Combined Code[33] and the proposed related changes to the Listing Rules. Consequent upon consultation, the London Stock Exchange made a number of changes to the draft.[34]

---

[28] *Ibid.* paras 4.47–4.59, 5.1–5.37.
[29] *Ibid.* para. 5.1.
[30] Greenbury Report, Section 2, Code Provisions A1–A9, B1–B12. Other parts of the Code contained guidelines and advice on company remuneration policy and directors' service contracts and compensation for dismissal; *ibid.* C1–C12, D1–D6.
[31] Cadbury Report, para. 3.12.
[32] Greenbury Report, para. 3.11.
[33] Also, an annotated version of the Code prepared by the Hampel Committee, showing derivations.
[34] With the Hampel Committee's agreement.

The Combined Code was issued by the London Stock Exchange on 25 June 1998. Its status was that of an appendix to what are now the FSA Listing Rules, and it did not form part of the Rules. Subtitled 'Principles of Good Governance and Code of Best Practice', it brings together the work of the Cadbury, Greenbury and Hampel Committees on corporate governance. The Combined Code is a consolidation of the work of those committees and was not a new departure.[35]

The basic feature of the Combined Code which distinguished it from the Cadbury and Greenbury Codes was the emphasis on the desirability of complying with broad principles and, in addition, complying with more specific provisions contained in a code of best practice. This feature came about as a result of the Hampel Committee's disapproval of what they called 'box ticking'. They recounted how the actual experience of many companies with regard to implementation of the Cadbury and Greenbury Codes was that the codes had been treated as sets of prescriptive rules, and that the focus of interest had narrowed to the simple question of whether the letter of the rule had been complied with, if yes, then the 'box' on a checklist[36] would receive a tick. The Hampel Committee deprecated box ticking on the basis that it took no account of the diversity of circumstances and experience among companies and on the further basis that it could lead to arrangements whereby the letter of the rule is complied with, but not the substance. Their conclusion was that good corporate governance was not just a matter of prescribing structures and rules, but there was also a need for broad principles.[37] Thus, it helps with understanding the name 'Combined Code' if the name is seen as signalling that it is a *package* consisting of principles *and* code (although the other meaning of the name is that it is derived from and is a consolidation of the work of past committees and the existing codes). It is clear that much of the Cadbury 'Code of Best Practice' has been subsumed into the provisions of the Combined Code, but it is worth observing that, less obviously, many of the principles and code provisions in the Combined Code were derived from recommendations or suggestions in the text of the Cadbury Report which did not find their way into the Cadbury Code of Best Practice.[38]

11.5 THE HIGGS REVIEW AND THE COMBINED CODE 2003

In 2002 the UK government commissioned Sir Derek Higgs (as a senior independent figure from the business world) to lead a short independent review of the role and effectiveness of non-executive directors in the UK. On 7 June 2002 a Consultation Paper was published entitled 'A Review of the Role and Effectiveness of Non-Executive Directors'. A final report was published on 20 January 2003.[39]

---

[35] Combined Code, Preamble, para. 7.

[36] See generally Hampel Report, paras 1.11–1.14.

[37] The broad principles needed to be applied flexibly and with common sense to the varying circumstances of individual companies and this was how the Cadbury and Greenbury Committees intended their ideas to be implemented.

[38] Although some of them were code provisions in Cadbury which are elevated to the status of principles in the Combined Code; e.g. Cadbury Code of Best Practice, para. 1.2 becomes part of Combined Code, Principle A.2.

[39] Available at http://www.dti/gov/uk/cld/non_exec_review.

Consequent upon the Higgs Review,[40] on widespread public comment, and on further work by various groups, a new version of the *Combined Code on Corporate Governance* was issued by the Financial Reporting Council[41] on 23 July 2003.

The Higgs Review followed the tradition of recent developments in UK corporate governance under which self-regulation in the application of governance codes forms a major part and most of his recommendations were presented as modifications of the existing Combined Code 1998. On the important matter of the role of the board, the Review saw no case for abandoning the unitary board structure in favour of a continental-style supervisory board and executive board, and saw benefit in the unitary board having executive knowledge within the board, alongside non-executive directors who can bring in wider experience.[42] The role of the Chairman was seen as 'pivotal' in creating board effectiveness and lent support to the idea that the roles of the Chairman and Chief Executive should be separate.[43] A more controversial proposal was that the Code should provide that a chief executive should not thereafter become chairman of the same company.[44] As regards non-executive directors, the Review felt that there was no essential contradiction between the monitoring role and the strategic role; both needed to be present.[45] However, concerned to strengthen independence on the board, the Review recommended that at least half the members of the board[46] should be independent[47] non-executive directors,[48] although it was recognised that widespread compliance might take time to achieve. The procedures relating to recruitment and appointment of non-executives to the board were seen as being in need of formalising[49] and nomination committees should consist of a majority of independent non-executives.[50] New non-executives needed an induction process.[51] The Review welcomed the report by Sir Robert Smith, recommending that the audit committee needed to include at least three members, all independent non-executives. The remuneration committee needed to work closely with the nomination committee so as to ensure that incentives are appropriately structured.[52] Guidance was formulated on the difficult matter of the legal liability of non-executive directors.[53] Support was voiced for the Institutional Shareholders' Committee's Code of Activism.[54] In relation to smaller listed companies[55] it was recognised that it may take more time for compliance and some of the Code's provisions may be less relevant, although the Review

---

[40] And also consequent upon the Smith Report on Audit Committees; available on http://www.frc.org.uk/publications.
[41] The FRC has responsibility for the contents of the Code and for updating it.
[42] Higgs Review, para. 4.2.
[43] *Ibid.* paras 5.1–5.2.
[44] *Ibid.* para. 5.7.
[45] *Ibid.* para. 6.2.
[46] Excluding the chairman.
[47] The Review formulated a detailed definition of independence; *ibid.* para. 9.11.
[48] *Ibid.* para. 9.5.
[49] *Ibid.* para. 10.9.
[50] *Ibid.* para. 10.9ff.
[51] *Ibid.* para. 11.1.
[52] *Ibid.* para. 13.10ff.
[53] *Ibid.* draft guidance statement, Annex A.
[54] *Ibid.* para. 15.24.
[55] I.e., listed companies outside the FTSE 350.

stopped short of differentiating Code provisions for different sizes of companies.[56] It will be apparent from the summary of the Combined Code in the next section, that many of the ideas and concerns espoused in the Higgs Review have found their way into the new Combined Code.[57]

11.6 THE COMBINED CODE 2003[58]

A Listing Rules compliance statements[59]

The primary 'enforcement' mechanism[60] is modelled on that which had been adopted for the earlier Codes, namely the FSA Listing Rules' requirement for a statement of compliance. Under the heading 'Corporate Governance', para. 12.43A requires the following 'additional'[61] items to be included in the annual report and accounts:

(a) a narrative statement of how it has applied the principles set out in Section 1 of the Combined Code, providing explanation which enables its shareholders to evaluate how the principles have been applied;

(b) a statement as to whether or not it has complied throughout the accounting period with the Code provisions set out in Section 1 of the Combined Code. A company that has not complied ... or complied with only some ... must specify the ... provisions ... and give reasons for any non-compliance.

There is also a sub-paragraph (c) under the heading 'Directors' remuneration'.[62] It is important to note that the compliance statements required by sub-paragraphs (a) and (b) above relate only to compliance with what is described as Section 1 of the Combined Code. Broadly speaking, Section 1 contains the principles, supporting principles and code provisions which are applicable to UK listed companies and which relate to the governance of those companies. Section 2 contains principles and code provisions which relate to institutional shareholders and to their role in monitoring and ensuring the proper governance of the companies in which they hold shares. [63]

---

[56] *Ibid.* para. 16.8.

[57] Also emanating from the Higgs Review is the increased use of suggestions for good practice. These are set out in the Combined Code pp. 59–79 and provide a range of useful items such as summaries of duties of committees, checklists and guidance.

[58] Available on the UKLA part of the FSA's website: http://www.fsa.gov.uk.

[59] In due course the FSA as UKLA will perhaps amend the rules so as to take account of the fact that the principles in the new Combined Code 2003 are in fact now designated as 'Main Principles' and 'Supporting Principles'. The Combined Code itself is untroubled by this; see Preamble, para. 4.

[60] On question of 'enforcement' in the context of self-regulation, see further p. 195 above.

[61] In other words, *additional* to para. 12.43.

[62] There then follows a provision under the heading 'Requirements of auditors' which sets out the auditors' duties in relation to review of the company's statement and the auditors' report.

[63] This format can be traced back to the Hampel Committee which had felt that it was inappropriate to include matters in Section 2 within the listing requirement.

B Excerpts and summary of the main provisions

1 General format of the Combined Code

For the reasons just described, the Combined Code is split into two sections: Section 1, 'Companies', and Section 2, 'Institutional Shareholders', which sets out the role of the institutional shareholders in corporate governance. Section 1 deals with four areas: A. Directors; B. Remuneration; C. Accountability and Audit; D. Relations with Shareholders. These will now be examined. At the outset, it is worth observing that one of the main innovations in format compared to the previous Combined Code is the division of 'principles' into 'main principles' and 'supporting principles'.

2 Directors

A.1 The Board
Main Principle: Every company should be headed by an effective board, which is collectively responsible for the success of the company.
Supporting Principles: The board's role is to provide entrepreneurial leadership of the company within a framework of prudent and effective controls which enables risk to be assessed and managed. The board should set the company's strategic aims, ensure that the necessary financial and human resources are in place for the company to meet its objectives and review management performance. The board should set the company's values and standards and ensure that its obligations to its shareholders and others are understood and met.

All directors must take decisions objectively in the interests of the company.

As part of their role as members of a unitary board, non-executive directors should constructively challenge and help develop proposals on strategy. Non-executive directors should scrutinize the performance of management in meeting agreed goals and objectives and monitor the reporting of performance. They should satisfy themselves on the integrity of financial information and that financial controls and systems of risk management are robust and defensible. They are responsible for determining appropriate levels of remuneration of executive directors and have a prime role in appointing, and where necessary removing executive directors, and in succession planning.

Code Provisions
A.1.1 The board should meet sufficiently regularly to discharge its duties effectively. There should be a formal schedule of matters specifically reserved for its decision. The annual report should include a statement of how the board operates, including a high level statement of which types of decisions are to be taken by the board and which are to be delegated to management.
A.1.2 The annual report should identify the chairman, the deputy chairman (where there is one), the chief executive, the senior independent director and the chairmen and members of the nomination, audit and remuneration committees. It should also set out the number of meetings of the board and those committees and individual attendance by directors.
A.1.3 The chairman should hold meetings with the non-executive directors without the executives present. Led by the senior independent director, the non-executive directors should meet without the chairman present at least annually to appraise the chairman's performance (as described in A.6.1) and on such other occasions as are deemed appropriate.

A.1.4 Where directors have concerns which cannot be resolved about the running of the company or a proposed action, they should ensure that their concerns are recorded in the board minutes. On resignation, a non-executive director should provide a written statement to the chairman, for circulation to the board, if they have any such concerns.

A.1.5 The company should arrange appropriate insurance cover in respect of legal action against its directors.

The relationship between the *principles* and the *code provisions* which go with it (both here and elsewhere in the Combined Code) is not entirely clear. Presumably Code Provisions A.1.1–A.1.5 are not meant to be exhaustive in the sense that they are the only things necessary to achieve a successful application of the principles. But if they are not exhaustive, then what are they? Presumably they are a list of the main specific things which are thought to be needed in order to help bring about the broader goals set out in the principle – things which the various committees had noticed as being areas where things had gone wrong in the past. But, obviously, a whole host of other things might be necessary in various circumstances in order to secure good corporate governance. And to emphasise the need to keep an eye on the background, it is only necessary to recall that there are various statute and case law principles which set out the legal duties of directors and govern the way companies are run. Thus, whatever the second supporting principle A.1 rather vaguely says about directors having to 'take decisions objectively in the interest of the company', they will obviously have to take pains to do this in such a way as to discharge their duties of care and skill to the standards set by law.

The linking of the role of chairman and chief executive has long been identified as a potential source of trouble in companies. The Cadbury Committee had felt that if the two roles were combined in one person it represented a considerable concentration of power and recommended that there should be a clearly accepted division of authority, although if the roles were combined, then there needed to be a strong and independent element on the board.[64] A similar attitude has been taken by the subsequent Reports and this is reflected in the provisions in A.2 below. Perhaps one slightly strange feature is the requirement that the chairman should 'ensure that the directors receive accurate, timely and clear information' because the companies legislation clearly casts onto the board of directors the duty to prepare reports and accounts, and so presumably with it the ancillary duty to themselves to make sure that they get proper information.[65]

A.2 Chairman and chief executive
Main Principle: There should be a clear division of responsibilities at the head of the company between the running of the board and the executive responsibility for the running of the company's business. No one individual should have unfettered powers of decision.

Supporting Principle: The chairman is responsible for leadership of the board, ensuring its effectiveness on all aspects of its role and setting its agenda. The chairman is also responsible for ensuring that the directors receive accurate, timely and clear information. The chairman should ensure effective communication with shareholders. The chairman should

---

[64] Cadbury Report, para. 4.9 and see p. 196 above.
[65] Companies Act 1985, ss. 221–222, 226, 231–232, 233.

also facilitate the effective contribution of non-executive directors in particular and ensure constructive relations between executive and non-executive directors.

Code Provisions

A.2.1 The roles of chairman and chief executive should not be exercised by the same individual. The division of responsibilities between the chairman and chief executive should be clearly established, set out in writing and agreed by the board.

A.2.2[66] The chairman should on appointment meet the independence criteria set out in A.3.1 below. A chief executive should not go on to be chairman of the same company. If exceptionally a board decides that a chief executive should become chairman, the board should consult major shareholders in advance and should set out its reasons to shareholders at the time of the appointment and in the next annual report.

Many people would probably agree that when the Cadbury Committee delivered its Report in 1992, the single most significant (and controversial) element of it was the enhanced and pivotal role given to NEDs.[67] In the ten years that followed, much public debate became centered around the question of the extent to which such NEDs should be independent (whatever that meant). Progress on this issue is now reflected in the latest version of the provisions dealing with board balance and independence:

A.3 Board balance and independence

Main Principle: The board should include a balance of executive and non-executive directors (and in particular independent non-executive directors) such that no individual or small group of individuals can dominate the board's decision taking.

Supporting Principles: The board should not be so large as to be unwieldy. The board should be of sufficient size that the balance of skills and experience is appropriate for the requirements of the business and that changes to the board's composition can be managed without undue disruption.

To ensure that power and information are not concentrated in one or two individuals, there should be a strong presence on the board of both executive and non-executive directors.

The value of ensuring that committee membership is refreshed and that undue reliance is not placed on particular individuals should be taken into account in deciding chairmanship and membership of committees.

No one other than the committee chairman and members is entitled to be present at a meeting of the nomination, audit or remuneration committee, but others may attend at the invitation of the committee.

Code Provisions

A.3.1 The board should identify in the annual report each non-executive director it considers to be independent.[68] The board should determine whether the director is independent in character and judgment and whether there are relationships or circumstances which are likely to affect, or could appear to affect, the director's judgment. The board should state its reasons if it determines that a director is independent notwithstanding the exist-

---

[66] The Combined Code also provides: 'Compliance or otherwise with this provision need only be reported for the year in which the appointment is made.'

[67] Cadbury Report, paras 4.1–4.6, 4.10–4.17.

[68] The Combined Code here by footnote provides that: 'A.2.2 states that the chairman should on appointment, meet the independence criteria set out in this provision, but thereafter the test of independence is not appropriate in relation to the chairman'.

ence of relationships or circumstances which may appear relevant to its determination, including if the director:

- has been an employee of the company or group in the last five years;

- has, or has had within the last three years, a material business relationship with the company either directly, or as a partner, shareholder, director or senior employee of a body that has such a relationship with the company;

- has received or receives additional remuneration from the company apart from a director's fee, participates in the company's share option or a performance-related pay scheme, or is a member of the company's pension scheme;

- has close family ties with any of the company's advisers, directors or senior employees;

- holds cross directorships or has significant links with other directors through involvement in other companies or bodies;

- represents a significant shareholder; or

- has served on the board for more than nine years from the date of their first election.

A.3.2 Except for smaller companies,[69] at least half the board, excluding the chairman, should comprise non-executive directors determined by the board to be independent. A smaller company should have at least two independent non-executive directors.

A.3.3 The board should appoint one of the independent non-executive directors to be the senior independent director. The senior independent director should be available to shareholders if they have concerns which contact through the normal channels of chairman, chief executive or finance director has failed to resolve or for which such contact is inappropriate.

The remaining matters dealt with by the Combined Code under the heading 'Directors' relate to appointments to the board, information and professional development, performance evaluation, and re-election. Here again, the pattern is repeated: suggestions and code provisions originally in Cadbury, followed by approval and amendments from Hampel, followed by amendments, new ideas and amplification from the Higgs Review. The principles and code provisions in the Combined Code relating to these matters are as follows:

A.4 Appointments to the Board
Main Principle: There should be a formal, rigorous and transparent procedure for the appointment of new directors to the board.
Supporting Principles: Appointments to the board should be made on merit and against objective criteria. Care should be taken to ensure that appointees have enough time available to devote to the job. This is particularly important in the case of chairmanships.

The board should satisfy itself that plans are in place for orderly succession for appointments to the board and to senior management, so as to maintain an appropriate balance of skills and experience within the company and on the board.

The Combined Code then sets out Code Provisions A4.1–A.4.6 relating to these principles, and covering such matters as the role of the nomination committee, job specifications, details in letters of appointment.

---

[69] The Combined Code by footnote here provides: 'A smaller company is one that is below the FTSE 350 throughout the year immediately prior to the reporting year.'

A.5 Information and professional development
Main Principle: The board should be supplied in a timely manner with information in a form and of a quality appropriate to enable it to discharge its duties. All directors should receive induction on joining the board and should regularly update and refresh their skills and knowledge.

Supporting Principles: The chairman is responsible for ensuring that the directors receive accurate, timely and clear information. Management has an obligation to provide such information but directors should seek clarification or amplification where necessary.

The chairman should ensure that the directors continually update their skills and the knowledge and familiarity with the company required to fulfil their role both on the board and on board committees. The company should provide the necessary resources for developing and updating its directors' knowledge and capabilities.

Under the direction of the chairman, the company secretary's responsibilities include ensuring good information flows within the board and its committees and between senior management and non-executive directors, as well as facilitating induction and assisting with professional development as required.

The company secretary should be responsible for advising the board through the chairman on all governance matters.

The Combined Code then here sets out Code Provisions A.5.1–A.5.3 relating to these Principles, covering such matters as induction, independent advice, and role and appointment of the company secretary.

A.6 Performance evaluation
Main Principle: The board should undertake a formal and rigorous annual evaluation of its own performance and that of its committees and individual directors.

The Combined Code then here sets out a supporting principle and a code provision A.6.1.

A.7 Re-election
Main Principle: All directors should be submitted for re-election at regular intervals, subject to continued satisfactory performance. The board should ensure planned and progressive refreshing of the board.

The Combined Code then here sets out Code Provisions A.7.1–A.7.2 relating to this principle and covering such matters as informational details and periods of appointment.

3 Remuneration

Part B of Section 1 of the Combined Code is taken up with remuneration. The Hampel Committee had earlier made it clear that directors' remuneration should be embraced in the corporate governance process since the handling of remuneration can damage a company's public image and have an adverse effect on morale within the company.[70] The code provisions relating to the principles in this field are long and complex and it is not practicable to set them out in full here. Instead, it is proposed to look briefly at the principles and include references to the code provisions. The principles relating to remuneration are as follows:

---

[70] *Ibid.* para. 2.9.

B.1 The Level and Make-up of Remuneration
Main Principles: Levels of remuneration should be sufficient to attract, retain and motivate directors of the quality required to run the company successfully, but a company should avoid paying more than is necessary for this purpose. A significant proportion of executive directors' remuneration should be structured so as to link rewards to corporate and individual performance.
Supporting Principle: The remuneration committee should judge where to position their company relative to other companies. But they should use such comparisons with caution, in view of the risk of an upward ratchet of remuneration levels with no corresponding improvement in performance. They should also be sensitive to pay and employment conditions elsewhere in the group, especially when determining annual salary increases.

With Principles B.1 go Code Provisions B.1.1–B.1.6, and also Schedule A to the Combined Code, which make detailed prescription with regard to remuneration policy, service contracts and compensation.

B.2 Procedure
Main Principle: Companies should establish a formal and transparent procedure for developing policy on executive remuneration and for fixing the remuneration packages of individual directors. No director should be involved in deciding his or her own remuneration.

Here again the supporting principles and Code Provisions B.2.1–B2.4 make detailed prescription about the role of remuneration committees.

4 Accountability and audit

Here again, the picture is one of ideas in the Cadbury Report being supplemented by further thoughts and refinement in the later reports. Many of the points were already in the Cadbury Code and the current position in the Combined Code is as follows:

C.1 Financial Reporting
Main Principle: The board should present a balanced and understandable assessment of the company's position and prospects.
Supporting Principle: The board's responsibility to present a balanced and understandable assessment extends to interim and other price-sensitive public reports and reports to regulators as well as to information required to be presented by statutory requirements.

This is supplemented by further details in Code Provisions C1.1–C.1.2:

C.2 Internal Control[71]
Main Principle: The board should maintain a sound system of internal control to safeguard shareholders' investment and the company's assets.

---

[71] The Combined Code here, by way of footnote, states that: 'The Turnbull guidance suggests means of applying this part of the Code.' The Turnbull Report had been issued by the Institute of Chartered Accountants of England and Wales (ICAEW, 1999). The Turnbull guidelines require the monitoring and management of important risks. The report encourages NEDs to play an active and professional role on boards of directors. Companies are required to disclose in their accounts that they

This is supplemented by Code Provision C2.1.

C.3 Audit Committee and Auditors
Main Principle: The board should establish formal and transparent arrangements for considering how they should apply the financial reporting and internal control principles and for maintaining an appropriate relationship with the company's auditors.

Code Provisions C.3.1–C.3.7 require the board to establish an audit committee and set out some of its duties.

5 Relations with shareholders

The importance of the shareholder input to corporate governance was recognised by the Cadbury Committee[72] although none of their ideas made it into the Cadbury Code. It has been taken further by subsequent reports, although it is fair to say these have not seen the shareholder input as a panacea and place their main emphasis in corporate governance in getting the board to function properly of its own accord.

D.1 Dialogue with Institutional Shareholders
Main Principle: There should be a dialogue with shareholders based on the mutual understanding of objectives. The board as a whole has responsibility for ensuring that a satisfactory dialogue with shareholders takes place.[73]
Supporting Principles: Whilst recognising that most shareholder contact is with the chief executive and finance director, the chairman (and the senior independent director and other directors as appropriate) should maintain sufficient contact with major shareholders to understand their issues and concerns.

The board should keep in touch with shareholder opinion in whatever ways are most practical and efficient.

The Code Provisions relating to this are D1.1–D1.2.

It seems that there is considerable activity developing in this regard.[74] It is well known that the majority of shares in public listed companies are held by financial institutions.[75] The Company Law Review has described[76] that these institutions exercise their membership rights, not through attendance at the shareholders meeting, but through a process of meeting and dialogue with the management. This process usually takes place in the interval between the company publishing its

---

have an ongoing process for dealing with internal risks that complies with the Turnbull guidelines. It is also necessary to declare what processes the board has undertaken to ensure that the system works. The full text of the Turnbull Guidance is set out in the Combined Code under the heading 'Related Guidance and Good Practice Suggestions' pp. 27–41.

[72] Cadbury Report, paras 6.1–6.16.
[73] The Combined Code by footnote here provides that: 'Nothing in these principles or provisions should be taken to override the general requirements of law to treat shareholders equally in access to information.'
[74] For a picture of the wide range of monitoring activity and involvement by institutions, see the very interesting websites of Pensions Investment Research Consultants (PIRC) and Hermes. These, respectively, are: http://www.pirc.co.uk and http://www.hermes.co.uk.
[75] Between 70% and 80%. See DTI Consultation Document (October 1999) *Company General Meetings and Shareholder Communications* para. 20.
[76] See previous note.

preliminary results and its full accounts. Quite often the institutions are represented by financial analysts. Searching questions are asked and a considerable amount of information[77] is obtained about the company's performance and prospects. There is considerable anecdotal evidence available that this is becoming very common.

D.2 Constructive Use of the AGM
Main Principle: The board should use the AGM to communicate with investors and to encourage their participation.

Going with this are Code Provisions D.2.1–D.2.4, which make prescription with regard to procedures at and prior to meetings. It is important to be aware that Section 2 of the Combined Code, E. Institutional Shareholders, contains principles and code provisions which seek to place certain obligations on institutional share-holders,[78] in particular the responsibility to make considered use of their votes. The reasons for putting these matters into a section separate from the provisions applying to companies have already been explained.[79]

11.7 THE 'PROFESSION' OF DIRECTOR?

It has already been seen how the Companies Act comes close to professionalising the office of company secretary in relation to public companies.[80] The legislature has nevertheless stopped short of doing anything similar as regards directors. The matter has been taken up by the self-regulatory sector and interesting progress is being made.

The Cadbury Report took the view that it was highly desirable that all directors should undertake some form of internal or external training. This was particularly important for board members who had no previous board experience. In addition to this, new board members should be entitled to expect an induction into the company's affairs.[81] The Report made reference to plans then afoot to set up a course covering the full range of directors' responsibilities and suggested that the successor committee keep the matter under review.[82] Subsequent reports have taken a less radical stance. However, in June 1999 the Institute of Directors (IOD) launched a new professional qualification for directors, the certificate of Chartered Director (C.Dir). It involves a three-hour examination and requires directors to subscribe to a code of professional conduct and to undertake ongoing training.[83] This looks like a worthwhile development towards establishing company directors

---

[77] Participants have to be careful not to get involved in insider dealing or market abuse in this situation. The US SEC have adopted (on 21/8/2000) the solution of requiring contemporaneous disclosure of any non-public information which is given by the board; see SEC Regulation FD (Fair Dealing), rule 100: http://www.sec.gov.

[78] In the context of self-regulation and investment institutions, of interest is the Myners Report *Institutional Investment in the United Kingdom: A Review* which requires certain institutional investors to comply with principles of investment decision making or explain the reasons for failure to comply. See http://www.hm-treasury.gov.uk.

[79] See p. 201 above.

[80] See p. 190 above.

[81] Cadbury Report, para. 4.19.

[82] *Ibid.* para. 4.20.

[83] The IOD has offered a Company Direction Programme since 1983 leading to an IOD Diploma in Company Direction.

as professionals even though it will probably only be available to a few hundred candidates a year.[84]

11.8 CONCLUSIONS

For the larger companies[85] the self-regulatory input of the 1990s will undoubtedly have caused major changes. Many, of course, already had good practice in corporate governance and for them the codes would not have required too much upheaval. Others would have had more work to do, in order to be able to claim that they were in line with the requirements. The UK's surge in interest in corporate governance matters during the 1990s coincided with a growth in interest worldwide, and people in many countries have looked with interest at the work of the UK committees on corporate governance.[86]

It is likely that the flowering of activity in this field has largely died down, and the advent of the Combined Code heralds a more settled future in corporate governance. There will always be frauds and corporate malpractice. The law has not eliminated these, and nor will self-regulation. It is nevertheless likely that the self-regulatory input will slowly operate on the minds of those involved in corporate governance and change their values and the ways in which they go about their tasks.

11.9 COMPANY LAW REVIEW AND LAW REFORM

As part of its overall analysis of the functioning of the UK system of corporate governance, the Company Law Review considered the proper role of codes of practice, and in particular, the Combined Code 1988.[87] It identified four areas for examination:

(1) whether the Combined Code 1998 was having a beneficial effect, in the sense of contributing to a climate where companies deliver optimal creation of wealth;
(2) whether compliance is adequate;
(3) whether the substantive provisions of the Code need improvement;
(4) whether other mechanisms would be more effective.[88]

Additional consultation matters which they identified included the question of whether the Combined Code 1998 rules relating to the monitoring role of the

---

[84] There are 3.2 million directors in the UK.
[85] Technically the Combined Code only applies to listed companies, but it is intended, as was the Cadbury Report, to set standards which would have an impact on companies generally.
[86] See generally A. Dignam 'Exporting Corporate Governance: UK Regulatory Systems in a Global Economy' (2000) 21 Co Law 70; for the OECD principles of corporate governance, see the website: http://www.oecd.org/daf/governance/principles.htm; for information on European scene, see the website of the European Corporate Governance Network (ECGN): http://www.ecgn.ulb.ac.be. For a comparative UK/US perspective, see C. Riley 'Controlling Corporate Management: UK and US Initiatives' (1994) 14 *Legal Studies* 244.
[87] DTI Consultation Document (March 2000) *Developing the Framework* paras 3.112–3.153.
[88] *Ibid.* para. 3.125.

NEDs needed to be strengthened and whether any of its provisions needed to be incorporated into law or made mandatory.[89]

In the Final Report the Review adopts many of the ideas originally in the Cadbury Report in relation to the role of institutional investors in corporate governance. Additionally, it considers some of the problems raised by the concept of 'fiduciary investors' (i.e. funds managers and other institutions which control shares on behalf of others).[90] However, when considering the Review's comments, subsequent developments, in particular the effects of the Higgs Review and the role of the FRC, need to be borne in mind.

---

[89] *Ibid.* para. 3.132.

[90] *Modern Company Law for a Competitive Economy Final Report* (London: DTI, 2001) paras. 6.19–6.40. See also the subsequent government White Paper *Modernising Company Law* (July 2002, Cmnd. 5553).

12

SHAREHOLDER LITIGATION:
COMMON LAW

12.1 INTRODUCTION: SHAREHOLDER LITIGATION
GENERALLY

The possibility that shareholders might sue the directors for breach of duty was mentioned in Chapter 8 as one of the many constraints on the activities of directors.[1] The discussion of the mechanisms involved was postponed until this chapter on account of the length and complexity of the subject.

Shareholder litigation can take place either at common law or under statute. Litigation at common law is characterised by doctrinal confusion and (partly as a consequence) very few reported cases. Conversely, litigation under statute is characterised by relatively simple flexible concepts and (partly as a consequence) an unmanageable deluge of cases. Further, it will be seen that the development of litigation at common law has been stultified by a judicial attachment to the 'floodgates' argument, namely that the opportunities for shareholder litigation need to be restricted otherwise the courts would be unable to cope with the volume of litigation. By contrast (again), the development of litigation under statute has been influenced by judicial attempts to shut the opened floodgates and to try to stem the tide of litigation.

One thing needs to be made clear at the outset. As we have seen,[2] directors owe their duties to the company; this is the rule in *Percival* v *Wright*.[3] The result is that the cause of action for breach of duty accrues to the company. The company therefore may bring an action for breach of duty against the directors. Normally, of course, it will not, because the directors will not allow the company to bring proceedings against themselves. But in certain situations, control of the company will pass to others, perhaps to a liquidator in a liquidation, or to a new board elected by a successful takeover bidder. Such circumstances sometimes provide rare examples of litigation by the company itself against the directors. We have already looked closely at the litigation in *Regal (Hastings) Ltd* v *Gulliver*[4] and seen how the company there turned on its former directors once they had sold control to a purchaser and the purchaser had elected a new board. The board of directors control

---

[1] See p. 146 above.
[2] Above at p. 161.
[3] [1902] 2 Ch 421.
[4] [1967] 2 AC 134, [1942] 1 All ER 378; and see p. 167 above.
[5] By virtue of their general powers of management in art. 70 of Table A. In some circumstances, the power to commence litigation rests with the majority of shareholders in general meeting; this difficult matter is discussed further at p. 226.

the use of the company's name in litigation[5] and the new Regal board instigated the company's action against the former directors. But that is not shareholder litigation; it is litigation by the company. As such, it is relatively problem-free.[6] The circumstances in which shareholders may launch litigation discussed below are far more problematic. Because of the size of this topic and the widely differing approaches, litigation at common law will be considered in this chapter, leaving litigation under statute to the next chapter.

12.2 THE DOCTRINE OF *FOSS* V *HARBOTTLE*

The doctrine of *Foss* v *Harbottle*[7] was well stated by Lord Davey in *Burland* v *Earle*[8] (more clearly than in *Foss* itself) where he said:

> It is an elementary principle of the law relating to joint stock companies that the Court will not interfere with the internal management of companies acting within their powers, and in fact has no jurisdiction to do so. Again it is clear law that in order to redress a wrong done to the company, or to recover money or damages alleged to be due to the company, the action should prima facie be brought by the company itself. These cardinal principles are laid down in the well-known cases of *Foss* v *Harbottle* and *Mozley* v *Alston* (1847) 1 Ph 790.[9]

There are really two separate rules here. The second of them is often elevated to the status of being 'the rule' in *Foss* v *Harbottle*; such an approach produces boundless scope for confusion, as will be seen below when we consider the 'exceptions' to *Foss* v *Harbottle*.[10]

The first of the two rules is the very broad statement that the courts will not interfere in the internal management of companies. On the face of it, it has the consequence that a minority shareholder who wishes to complain about the way something has been done will find that he is barred from litigating the matter. There are two ideas behind this policy. One is that there will be an unmanageable deluge of litigation if matters occurring within a company can become the subject of litigation (the 'floodgates' argument). The other probably is that the courts dislike interfering in business decisions reached by a company and regard the shareholders as far better placed to decide what should be done than the judge is.

The second of the two rules is that for wrongs done to the company, the proper claimant is the company itself; sometimes abbreviated to the 'proper claimant' rule. This rule is the embodiment of several technical ideas. First, it incorporates the rule in *Percival* v *Wright*[11] that directors' duties are owed to the company and not to the shareholders. Secondly, it embodies the *Salomon* doctrine, that the company is a separate entity from the shareholders and thus has its own assets, its own rights to sue. And so the right to sue is vested and remains vested in the company, and does

---

[6] Subject to the discussions referred to in the previous note.
[7] (1843) 2 Hare 461.
[8] [1902] AC 83, PC.
[9] *Ibid.* at p. 93.
[10] It is also simpler in some ways, but involves drawing the exceptions differently; e.g. the personal rights exception referred to below ceases to be an exception at all, the rule simply does not apply to it. See further pp. 215 and 217 below.
[11] [1902] 2 Ch 421, see p. 174 above.

not flow through to the shareholders. The full significance of this 'proper claimant' rule is only apparent when it is considered how its operation is affected by the principle of majority rule.

12.3 THE PRINCIPLE OF MAJORITY RULE

It has been seen that the shareholders in general meeting are the residual source of authority in the company.[12] The courts have evolved the principle that, in the event of disagreements between the shareholders, this authority can be exercised by a bare majority vote.[13] It has also been decided that the shareholders are entitled to vote selfishly, in their own interests, and that they do not owe a fiduciary duty to the other shareholders or to the company to vote 'bona fide'.[14] The authority usually cited for this doctrine is *North-West Transportation Ltd* v *Beatty*[15] which, although only a Privy Council case, has usually been applied generally ever since. The doctrine was well expressed by Baggallay J:

> Unless some provision to the contrary is to be found in the charter or other instrument by which the company is incorporated, the resolution of a majority of the shareholders, duly convened, upon any question with which the company is legally competent to deal, is binding upon the minority, and consequently upon the company, and every shareholder has a perfect right to vote upon any such question, although he may have a personal interest in the subject matter opposed to, or different from, the general or particular interests of the company.[16]

An interesting recent case is a rare example of a court denying a shareholder the right to use his votes in his own interests. In *Standard Chartered Bank* v *Walker*[17] the company was in acute financial difficulties and a meeting had been called to approve a restructuring agreement between the company and various creditor banks. It was also proposed to remove Walker from his post as non-executive director. Walker controlled 10% of the votes. One of the banks sought an order either restraining Walker from voting his shares, or ordering him to vote in favour of the restructuring. There was evidence that the company would collapse if the restructuring agreement was not adopted, and then, all the shares would become worthless. Vinelott J held that it was only in extreme cases that an injunction would be granted to stop a shareholder voting his shares, but that this was such a case.[18]

The majority rule doctrine has great significance for the 'proper claimant' part of the *Foss* doctrine, because the ultimate expression of the will of the company as to whether it will sue or not is the majority of shareholders in general meeting. Thus

---

[12] See p. 151 above.

[13] An ordinary resolution; unless the company's constitution or the legislation requires some special majority in the circumstances.

[14] But, if the articles are being altered, or they are voting in a class meeting, the position is different; see pp. 98 and 285 above.

[15] (1887) 12 AC 589.

[16] *Ibid.* at p. 595.

[17] [1992] BCLC 603.

[18] It is possible that the case can be explained on the ground that the court was preventing the destruction of an asset which stood charged to secure a debt. The banks had charges over some of the shares and if the shares became worthless then the security would be destroyed.

when a shareholder seeks to get the company to use its name to litigate some matter concerning it, the courts tend to concentrate on what the majority have decided. Lord Davey, in *Burland* v *Earle*[19] said:

> ... It should be added that no mere formality or irregularity which can be remedied by the majority will entitle the minority to sue, if the act when done regularly would be within the powers of the company and the intention of the majority of shareholders is clear.

Similar sentiments were expressed by Mellish LJ in *McDougall* v *Gardiner*:[20]

> In my opinion, if a thing complained of is a thing which in substance the majority of the company are entitled to do, or if something has been done irregularly which the majority of the company are entitled to do regularly, or if something has been done illegally which the majority of the company are entitled to do legally, there can be no use in having litigation about it, the ultimate end of which is only that a meeting has to be called, and then ultimately the majority gets its wishes.

The discussion of the principle of majority rule will be resumed in various places in the analysis which follows.

12.4 THE 'EXCEPTIONS' TO *FOSS* V *HARBOTTLE*

It is clear that an unrestrained principle of majority rule or a total fetter on litigation by shareholders could often work injustice. For instance, the majority of the shareholders could vote to divide the assets of the company among themselves, leaving the minority with nothing and with no remedy. That would be absurd and so the courts have developed exceptions. Partly due to the influence of academic writers over the years[21] an orthodoxy has grown up over the way this is presented and the exceptions are usually grouped under various headings. These are:

(1) *Ultra vires* and illegality: it has long been held that where the act is *ultra vires* or illegal by statute, the individual cannot be prevented from litigating the matter, merely by an ordinary resolution in general meeting.[22] The standing given to the member by the case law in circumstances of *ultra vires* is preserved by s. 35 (3) of the Companies Act 1985.

(2) Special majorities: this heading refers to the situation where the constitution of the company requires, say, a special resolution, as necessary to do some act. Then, if the company tries to do it by ordinary resolution, the individual minority shareholder can litigate it.[23]

(3) Personal rights: sometimes the articles of association give the shareholders rights which they can enforce against the company. These cannot be taken

---

[19] [1902] AC 83 at p. 93.

[20] (1875) 1 Ch D 13 at p. 18.

[21] See e.g. *Gower's Principles of Modern Company Law* 4th edn (London: Stevens, 1979) at pp. 644–645; the current 7th edn by P. Davies has a different approach. The traditional list of exceptions had its roots in the case law; see e.g. *Edwards* v *Halliwell* [1950] WN 537 at p. 538, *per* Jenkins LJ (although not including the general 'personal rights' category).

[22] See *Hutton* v *West Cork Railway Co. Ltd* (1883) 23 Ch D 654 (*ultra vires*); and *Ooregum Gold Mining Co.* v *Roper* [1892] AC 125 (illegal issue of shares at a discount).

[23] See *Edwards* v *Halliwell* [1950] 2 All ER 1064 at p. 1067.

away by ordinary resolution. The case *Wood* v *Odessa Waterworks Co.* has already been seen to be an example of the supremacy of rights in the articles over an ordinary resolution in general meeting.[24] It is probable that not all the provisions in the articles can be enforced in this way.[25]

(4) Fraud on a minority: this is a general concept, difficult to define, and is discussed further below. Not all breaches of duty by directors will amount to a fraud on a minority.[26] If the majority of the shareholders were to divide the assets of the company amongst themselves, to the exclusion of the minority, as mentioned above, then it is clear on the case law that this would amount to a fraud on a minority. This is what the directors and majority shareholders were doing in *Cook* v *Deeks*[27] and it was held that an ordinary resolution of the shareholders could not deprive the minority of the ability to maintain an action against the directors.[28]

The above four categories of exception have the potential to confuse. This is because they are presented as exceptions to *the* rule in *Foss* v *Harbottle*, whereas, as we have seen, the doctrine really involves two rules. Consider the fourth exception, fraud on a minority; it is actually an exception to both rules in the *Foss* v *Harbottle* doctrine. The first was that the courts would not interfere in the internal management of companies. Clearly, in *Cook* v *Deeks*, they were doing just that, so fraud on a minority is an exception to that first rule. But it is also an exception to the second rule, the proper claimant rule, since there, the wrongs were done to the company (they were breaches of directors' duty owed to the company), and yet the minority shareholders were able to litigate. This is not problematic.

However, the third head of exception, personal rights, is capable of causing some confusion, for whilst the enforcement of a personal right by a shareholder can readily be seen to be an exception to the first rule, that the courts will not interfere in the internal management, it does not seem to be any sort of exception to the second rule, the 'proper claimant' rule. The denial of a personal right is a wrong done to the shareholder in his capacity as such; it is not a wrong done to the company, and the company is not the proper claimant. The proper claimant rule does not 'bite' on the situation at all. This is more than just a semantic subtlety[29] because, as will be seen below, whether a shareholder action is founded on a personal right of the shareholder, or on a right of the company, will produce crucial differences to the procedural and substantive law governing that action.

What about the illegality part of the first exception? Is illegality an improper action by the company which gives the shareholder a personal right to require the company to abstain from the illegality, or is it a wrong perpetrated on the company by its directors and giving the company a cause of action against them? The case law does not give a definitive answer to this. In *Smith* v *Croft (No. 2)*[30] Knox J took

---

[24] See p. 90 above.

[25] See the discussion of the insider/outsider doctrine at p. 91 above.

[26] It is sometimes called 'fraud on *the* minority'; nothing turns on this.

[27] [1916] AC 554.

[28] The ability of a shareholder to maintain an action for fraud on a minority is subject to further limitations; these are discussed at pp. 221–226 below.

[29] Or lack of subtlety, perhaps.

[30] [1987] 3 All ER 909 at p. 945; and see further p. 221 below.

the view that it depended on whether the illegality had taken place or not; a shareholder had a personal right to restrain the commission of a threatened illegality, but thereafter, the company had a right to recover damages against those who had caused it to commit an illegal act.

All this goes to show that a simple and orthodox statement of the *Foss* v *Harbottle* doctrine and its list of exceptions conceals some deep waters.[31] On the other hand, once the problems are understood, the orthodox type of presentation can be seen to convey a reasonable overview of the effect of a jumble of case law, spanning 150 years.

12.5 MEANING OF 'FRAUD ON A MINORITY'

The concept of fraud on a minority needs further examination. It was stated earlier that it is difficult to define. This is partly due to the coyness of the judiciary in what is obviously a difficult field. The approach of Megarry J in *Estmanco (Kilner House) Ltd* v *GLC*[32] was pragmatic, but epitomises the judicial unwillingness to develop the doctrine at a theoretical level:

> As I have indicated, I do not consider that this is a suitable occasion on which to probe the intricacies of the rule in *Foss* v *Harbottle* and its exceptions, or to attempt to discover and expound the principles to be found in the exceptions. All that I need say is that in my judgment the exception usually known as 'Fraud on a minority' is wide enough to cover the present case, and that if it is not, it should now be made wide enough.

Paradoxically, Megarry J came up with an expression elsewhere in his judgment which might be taken as a basic working definition.[33]

In a broad and somewhat crude sense, fraud on the minority is conduct which the judges think is so bad that the majority should not be allowed to get away with it. More acceptable and juristic language can perhaps be found in Megarry J's expression in *Estmanco* that it was conduct 'stultifying the purpose for which the company was formed'.[34] The important point though, is to realise that if a type of act has been judicially categorised as a fraud on the minority then the majority rule principle will cease to govern the situation. It will make no difference, therefore, if the act complained of has been 'ratified', that is, approved of, or forgiven, by the majority in general meeting. The ratification will be invalid, because the breach of duty was in law 'non-ratifiable'. What matters is not whether the breach of duty has been ratified, but whether the breach is regarded as ratifiable.

The case law has developed slowly over the years and has produced a gradual

---

[31] One aspect of the deep water which has recently been causing controversy is the difficult question which arises when a minority shareholder argues that because a director has broken a fiduciary duty and caused damage to the company, he personally has a right to recover damages for the consequent diminution in the value of his shareholding. This will not be allowed where his loss is merely reflective of the company's loss which is recoverable by derivative action. Only if the shareholder's loss is separate and distinct from the loss suffered by the company will he be permitted to make a personal claim. See: *Johnson* v *Gore Wood & Co (No. 1)* [2001] BCLC 313, HL; *Walker* v *Stones* [2001] BCC 757, CA; *Giles* v *Rhind* [2001] 2 BCLC 582; *Day* v *Cook* [2002] BCLC 1, CA.

[32] [1982] 1 All ER 437 at pp. 447–448.

[33] This is mentioned in the next paragraph.

[34] [1982] 1 All ER 437 at p. 448.

categorisation of types of breach of directors' duty. Some are fraud on the minority and non-ratifiable, others do not amount to fraud on the minority and are ratifiable. *Cook* v *Deeks*[35] can be seen as the paradigm example of a non-ratifiable breach of duty, the taking of corporate assets. Conversely, *Pavlides* v *Jensen*,[36] establishes that negligence[37] is not fraud on the minority and is therefore a ratifiable breach of duty. Other decisions establish that various other types of breach of duty are ratifiable, in particular, the issue of shares for a collateral purpose has often been looked upon benignly by the courts.[38] It should not be forgotten that each case will often depend on its own facts and it would be misguided to assume that the issue of shares for a collateral purpose could never amount to a fraud on a minority. The presence of bad faith or other factors could swing the matter.[39] A recent illustration of this is the Court of Appeal decision in *Barrett* v *Duckett*,[40] where some fairly typical claims for fraud on the minority were rejected by the court because they were brought for personal motives rather than bona fide for the benefit of the company.

Two other points need to be made here. The first is that even if it has been the case in the past that the fact that the breach is non-ratifiable will then entitle the shareholder to litigate the matter, there is now a further doctrine and procedure which has been layered on top of the fraud on a minority exception as a result of the decisions in *Smith* v *Croft (No. 2)*[41] and *Prudential Assurance Co. Ltd* v *Newman Industries and others (No. 2)*.[42] This is dealt with below[43] and the above account of fraud on the minority needs to be read in the light of the effect of those decisions. The other matter is that it is necessary to bear in mind that the operation of the 'shareholder consent'[44] doctrine might affect the position. The 'ratification' discussed above is a ratification by ordinary resolution. In other words, the issue really is whether the doctrine of majority rule, which normally governs corporate decision-making, is also being allowed to govern the bringing of litigation. It is highly likely that if the shareholders have 'consented' to what has been done, or will be done, then there can be no litigation. It might be thought that not much turns on this, because the shareholder consent doctrine requires consent by 100% of the shareholders, and if that has happened there will be no minority shareholders who are wanting to litigate; so, no problem arises. However, the matter may not be quite that simple. Unlike some other systems,[45] English law does not seem to have a 'contemporaneous ownership' rule when it comes to shareholder litigation. What this means is that a shareholder can buy shares in a company after a non-ratifiable breach of duty has occurred, and then seek to litigate it. He will not be barred by a

---

[35] [1916] AC 554, PC.
[36] [1956] Ch 656.
[37] I.e. breach of the director's common law duty of care and skill.
[38] See e.g. *Hogg* v *Cramphorn* [1967] Ch 254; *Bamford* v *Bamford* [1970] Ch 212.
[39] *Daniels* v *Daniels* [1978] Ch 406 was argued on the basis that the conduct of the directors had been negligent, but it can perhaps be seen as a case where the fact that the directors made a profit out of their negligence was held to make the negligence non-ratifiable and hence a fraud on the minority.
[40] [1993] BCC 778.
[41] [1987] 3 All ER 909.
[42] [1982] Ch 204.
[43] At pp. 219–226.
[44] On 'shareholder consent' see pp. 158–159 above.
[45] Such as some American states.

rule that his ownership of the shares had to be contemporaneous with the breach of duty; in other words, he can 'buy in' to a cause of action. However, if 100% of the shareholders have consented to the breach of duty, there will be no cause of action remaining in the company, and no cause of action for an outsider to buy into.

Lastly, by way of simple illustration of how the *Foss* v *Harbottle* doctrine is alive and well, and capable of restricting the ability of a shareholder to bring litigation, it is only necessary to consider the fate of the litigants in *Re Downs Wine Bar Ltd*[46] and *Stein* v *Blake*,[47] where both actions were unceremoniously struck out because they involved complaints about matters that did not fall within the exceptions to *Foss* v *Harbottle*.

12.6 THE STRIKING OUT OF DERIVATIVE ACTIONS

A Introduction

As suggested earlier, as a result of comparatively recent decisions, the fraud on the minority concept has another layer of doctrine imposed on it. The consequence of this is to restrict further the circumstances in which a shareholder can bring litigation. The whole area is closely bound up with procedural considerations and these will be dealt with as and when appropriate. First, it is necessary to look more closely at the types of litigation which a minority shareholder might bring.

B Types of action and costs

It has been seen, with reference to the *Regal* case,[48] that if an action is brought in the name of the company, then that is not shareholder litigation,[49] it is an action in the name of the company, a corporate action, brought by the company at the behest of the board.[50] The vast majority of actions brought every day in the name of the company are brought against other companies for commercial reasons and in no way concern internal disputes with shareholders or directors. *Regal* was a rare example of litigation in the name of the company concerning internal matters.

Shareholder litigation brought under the exceptions to *Foss* v *Harbottle* falls into two categories: the personal action and the derivative action.[51] These actions are not merely procedurally different; the underlying theory of the substantive law is different. The action is called a personal action when the shareholder is claiming that some personal right of his has been infringed which gives him a right to sue. The most obvious example of this is the litigation in *Wood* v *Odessa Waterworks Company*,[52] where the shareholder was claiming that he had a personal right to have

---

[46] [1990] BCLC 839.
[47] [1998] BCC 316.
[48] At p. 212 above.
[49] Although it might have started as shareholder litigation and been adopted later by the company; see *Prudential Assurance Co. Ltd* v *Newman Industries Ltd and others (No. 2)* [1982] Ch 204 where by the time the shareholder's action had reached the Court of Appeal, the company had adopted it.
[50] Or conceivably, the general meeting; see further p. 227 below.
[51] Both the personal and the derivative action are often brought in the representative form.
[52] (1889) 42 Ch D 636 and see p. 90 above.

a particular clause of the articles enforced against the company. In such cases, the company is a substantive defendant, and damages may be awarded against it, or an injunction may be granted against it. It may also have to pay the shareholder's costs. The action will be a personal action only where the shareholder can be seen to have some cause of action vested in him personally. It has been seen that this can happen as regards parts of the constitution as a result of s. 14 of the Companies Act 1985.[53] But he cannot bring a personal action where there is no cause of action vested in him. Given the rule that directors owe their duties to the company and not to the shareholders,[54] then it is clear that the shareholder will not be able to bring a personal action for breach of duty by directors. Since in practice, most matters which a shareholder would want to litigate in fact arise from a breach of duty by one or more of the directors, the availability of a personal action is often not going to be an effective solution.

To deal with this problem, the courts have developed what is called the 'derivative' action.[55] The derivative action enables the shareholder to enforce the right which is vested in the company to sue its directors for breach of duty. It gets its name from the idea that the shareholder's right to sue is *derived from* the company's right. In a sense, the shareholder is suing as agent of the company, on behalf of the company. Any damages recovered will go to the company. This last point, of course, raises the question of why the shareholder would want to bother bringing such an action if he obtains no personal benefit from it and is at risk of paying the costs if he loses. Often he will not bother, and that is one of the reasons why there has been so little shareholder litigation at common law since the development of the *Foss* v *Harbottle* doctrine. A shareholder will, indirectly get a pro-rata benefit from any damages which swell the assets of the company, and, it has to be realised, that people will sometimes litigate things in order to make a point of principle which has become important to them.[56]

To mitigate the costs problem with derivative actions, the courts have developed a process known as 'Wallersteiner orders'. First conceived by Lord Denning MR in *Wallersteiner* v *Moir (No. 2)*,[57] it is basically a system under which the minority shareholder who is bringing the action can obtain from the company, an indemnity for costs he may become liable for. In the case in question, Moir had been bringing litigation as a minority shareholder, against one of the directors. Moir had run out of money. In Lord Denning's immortal style, the problem was as follows:

> The only way he has been able to have his complaint investigated is by action in these courts. And here he has come to the end of his tether. He has fought this case for over 10 years on his own ... has expended all his financial resources on it and all his time and labour ... In this situation he appeals to this court for help in respect of the future costs

---

[53] See p. 90 above and the discussion in the context of the exceptions to the *Foss* v *Harbottle* doctrine at p. 215.

[54] See p. 161 above.

[55] It has been called many names (most of them misleading) including: a 'minority shareholders' action', a '*Foss* v *Harbottle* action', a 'fraud on the minority action'. The adoption by the Law Commission of the term 'derivative action' can be taken to have settled the matter.

[56] See e.g. *Wallersteiner* v *Moir (No. 2)* [1975] QB 373, where Moir seems to have been struggling for many years for issues of principle.

[57] [1975] QB 373.

of this litigation. If no help is forthcoming ... Mr Moir will have to give up the struggle exhausted in mind, body and estate.[58]

That was in 1975. Eventually, Wallersteiner orders came to be seen as having the potential for being oppressive. They were usually made without notice to the other side, shortly after the the beginning of proceedings, and on affidavit evidence. The result would be that the company would thereafter find itself paying for an action, which it almost invariably did not want brought, and which would usually put the whole management under intense pressure. It would often then later be discovered that the shareholder's complaints were groundless, with the result that the whole matter had been an expensive waste of time. These kinds of factors were present in *Smith v Croft (No. 1)*[59] and Walton J took the opportunity to redirect the judicial approach. On the facts he took the view that an independent board of directors would not want the action to go ahead and he struck out the Wallersteiner order. Part of the claim was that the directors had taken excessive remuneration and on this, the learned judge felt that they were 'entitled to stand astonished at their own moderation, as Lord Clive once said'.[60]

C Striking out derivative actions

As mentioned earlier, there is another layer of doctrine superimposed on the ortho-dox list of the exceptions to *Foss v Harbottle*. The seeds of it were sown by the Court of Appeal in *Prudential Assurance Co. Ltd v Newman Industries Ltd and others (No. 2)*[61] but the ideas in that case were taken up and developed by Knox J in *Smith v Croft (No. 2)*.[62]

The *Prudential* case is chiefly[63] remembered for its insistence that there is no fifth category of exception to *Foss v Harbottle* and that it was necessary for the claimant to establish a *prima facie* case that the company was entitled to the relief claimed and that the action fell within 'the proper boundaries[64] to the rule in *Foss v Harbottle*'.[65] At first instance, Vinelott J had based his approach on a general 'interests of justice' exception, as it was not clear whether the conduct complained of fell within any of the normally recognised exceptions to the *Foss v Harbottle* doc-trine. On this basis, the first instance trial lasted 72 days. The matter went to the Court of Appeal, who were less than happy with the approach which had been taken by Vinelott J. It had become apparent by then that some of the allegations made by the minority shareholder were only partly substantiated. It had also become clear that the rule in *Foss v Harbottle* had ceased to be of much relevance

---

[58] *Ibid.* at p. 380.
[59] [1986] 2 All ER 551.
[60] *Ibid.* at p. 561. The facts appear in more detail below, in the discussion of the subsequent litigation in *Smith v Croft (No. 2)* [1987] 3 All ER 909.
[61] [1982] Ch 204.
[62] [1987] 3 All ER 909.
[63] There are many points of importance in it. In particular, the Court of Appeal took the view that the claimant needed to show that the defendants were in control of the company. This point and others are taken up in the discussion of *Smith v Croft (No. 2)* below.
[64] Meaning, the orthodox list of exceptions; see p. 215 above.
[65] [1982] 1 Ch 204 at pp. 221–222.

because the company[66] had decided to adopt the judgment in its favour made by Vinelott J; this technically made the Court of Appeal's comments *obiter dicta*, but they have generally been regarded as binding authority ever since.[67]

In *Smith* v *Croft (No. 2)* Knox J's careful reading of the *Prudential* case became apparent and he developed and applied other aspects of the Court of Appeal's comments. It has already been seen how in *Smith* v *Croft (No. 1)* Walton J had struck out the Wallersteiner order. No doubt heartened by this success, the directors decided to try to get the derivative action struck out as well. The facts were complicated, but can be simplified. A minority shareholder was bringing a derivative action which had two different claims in it. The first was, that in breach of fiduciary duty, the directors of the company had used their power to pay themselves wholly excessive remuneration, that the excess was an *ultra vires* gift, and a fraud on the minority. The second was a claim to recover compensation on behalf of the company arising out of payments made allegedly in breach of s. 151 of the Companies Act 1985[68] and therefore illegal and *ultra vires*. The directors had commissioned the accountancy firm Peat Marwick to investigate the allegations and produce a report. The report had concluded that the remuneration was not excessive but that there were some technical breaches of s. 151.

The Court of Appeal in *Prudential* had made it clear that a judge faced with a derivative action should ask himself the question 'ought I to be trying a derivative action?' and had suggested that the matter be dealt with as a preliminary issue.[69] Knox J abstracted the essence of the decision in *Prudential* which he felt required a judge, faced with the prospect of trying a derivative action, to address his mind to two questions. One is to ask whether the claimants have established a *prima facie* case that the company is entitled to the relief claimed.[70] The other is to ask 'whether . . . the action falls within the proper boundaries of the exception to the rule in *Foss* v *Harbottle*'.[71]

The idea in the first of these questions is to hold a sort of mini-trial to see if the evidence of wrongdoing is likely to be sufficient to enable the minority to win the case. Here, the judge would look at the pleadings and the affidavits and try to make up his mind. In this context, it should be remembered that this approach originated in the Court of Appeal in *Prudential*, where to a considerable extent the bold claims made by the minority shareholder were not substantiated once the matter was looked into. In essence, the court is being asked to try to form a view as to whether the action is going to be a good one, or not. The idea in the second of the questions

---

[66] Newman Industries Ltd.

[67] Megarry J tried to apply the Court of Appeal's reasoning in *Estmanco* and Knox J clearly felt bound by *Prudential* in *Smith* v *Croft (No. 2)*.

[68] See further p. 294 below.

[69] Megarry J in *Estmanco (Kilner House) Ltd* v *GLC* [1982] 1 All ER 437 had been the first judge to struggle with implementing the Court of Appeal's sentiments: 'It is clear from the decision of the Court of Appeal in [*Prudential*] that it is right that a *Foss* v *Harbottle* point should where possible be decided as a preliminary issue and not left for determination at the trial. On such an application the court has to do the best it can on the evidence and other material which the parties have chosen to put before it, even though further evidence and other material may well be put forward later, and perhaps lead to other conclusions': *ibid.* at p. 447.

[70] [1987] 3 All ER 909 at pp. 922, 937.

[71] *Ibid.* at p. 914.

is that at the outset the judge (and the parties) must get the theory of the derivative action right. And the theory is basically the exceptions in *Foss* v *Harbottle*. In other words, the claim must be formulated to and actually fit within the straightjacket of the orthodox statement of the exceptions to the rule in *Foss* v *Harbottle*. Thus far, Knox J's analysis was not in any sense radical, at least not in the light of *Prudential*. On the facts he disposed of that part of the claim based on excessive remuneration by holding that it did not satisfy the first question, namely that there was no *prima facie* case. It was obvious, given the expertise of the directors involved, that the remuneration was modest. As Walton J had said in the earlier proceedings, they were '... entitled to stand astonished at their own moderation'.[72] The claim based on breach of s. 151 could not be felled so easily, particularly since the Peat Marwick report had established that there were breaches of the section. It could not be said that there was no *prima facie* case. Knox J turned to apply the second question to it, inquiring whether it fell within the exceptions to *Foss* v *Harbottle*. He had a tricky question to deal with at the outset, namely whether an action complaining about conduct made illegal by statute[73] was personal or derivative. The learned judge disposed of this by holding that it was personal if it related to future acts but derivative if, as here, it related to pursuing claims for money or property lost as a result of past illegality.[74] Thus, this was held to be a derivative action amounting to a fraud on the minority.[75]

Thus far, again, there is nothing radical in the analysis and it seemed to be a normal working out of the *Prudential* ideas. However, at this point, the expected conclusion would be that the action could go ahead, because, having established a *prima facie* case, and having established that the claim was for fraud on the minority and therefore lay within 'the proper boundaries of the exceptions to the rule in *Foss* v *Harbottle*', the minority shareholder would have an indefeasible right to go ahead and litigate. But this was not the conclusion Knox J reached.

Knox J decided that one could look at the views of the 'independent shareholders', the 'views of the majority inside a minority', what he referred to as, the 'secondary counting of heads'. An example might help: if 60% of the shareholders

---

[72] See p. 221 above. The company was involved in the film industry and had world famous directors.

[73] And thus *ultra vires*; see p. 942 at (a).

[74] At p. 945 at (h–j).

[75] Although nothing of substance turns on this, it is worth observing, for the avoidance of confusion in reading the case, that Knox J was using a narrow definition of the scope of the rule in *Foss* v *Harbottle* so that, on his analysis, the rule only applied, so as to prevent litigation, where the action properly accrued to the company. There are several statements in the judgment that show that this was his underlying concept; see [1987] 3 All ER 909 at p. 914.

In effect, if reference is made to the way that the doctrine is explained at p. 213 above, it is as if there is only one rule, the proper claimant rule. Knox J's approach in this is not unusual, and it is certainly true that the main thrust of the rule lies in the aspect of it which establishes that for wrongs done to the company, the proper claimant is the company itself. The difference can be illustrated by considering what would have happened if Knox J had held that the action for breach of statute was personal. He would have concluded that the rule in *Foss* v *Harbottle* did not apply to it and the action could therefore go ahead as a personal action. By contrast, an application of the 'two rule' approach to the doctrine on p. 213 would have reached the conclusion that the rule did apply (not the proper claimant part of the rule, but the general statement that the courts would not interfere in internal matters) but that the action fell within the personal rights exception.

were the alleged wrongdoers, one would inquire what the majority of the remaining 40% wanted. If more than half of these (i.e. more than 21% of the total shareholding) wanted the action to go ahead, then it would. It involves regarding the 40% minority as a sort of untainted organ of the company which represents the true company and which thus retains the power and the ability to take decisions on behalf of the company.

Knox J stated:

> [I]n all cases of minority shareholders' actions to recover money for the company in respect of acts which constitute a fraud on the minority, will the court pay regard to the views of the majority of shareholders who are independent of the defendants to the action on the question of whether the action should proceed? ... In my judgment the concern of the Court of Appeal [in *Prudential*] in making [the statement that when looking at the question of whether the defendants are in control the judge trying the preliminary issue may grant a sufficient adjournment to enable a meeting of the shareholders to be convened by the board] ... was to secure for the benefit of the judge ... what was described as the commercial assessment whether the prosecution of the action was likely to do more harm than good. The whole tenor of the Court of Appeal's judgment was directed at securing that a realistic assessment of the practical desirability of the action going forward should be made and should be made by the organ that has the power and ability to take decisions on behalf of the company ... In my judgment, the word 'control' was deliberately placed in inverted commas by the Court of Appeal in *Prudential* ... because it was recognised that voting control by the defendants was not necessarily the sole subject of investigation. Ultimately the question which has to be answered in order to determine whether the rule in *Foss* v *Harbottle* applies to prevent a minority shareholder seeking relief as plaintiff for the benefit of the company is, 'Is the plaintiff being improperly prevented from bringing these proceedings on behalf of the company?' If it is an expression of the corporate will of the company by an appropriate independent organ that is preventing the plaintiff from prosecuting the action he is not improperly but properly prevented and so the answer to the question is 'No'.[76]

On the facts, it was clear here how the votes would be cast, and so there was no need to call a meeting of the independent shareholders. They did not want the derivative action and Knox J struck it out.

Knox J's ideas were firmly rooted in the tenor of the judgment in *Prudential*. Elsewhere, across the Atlantic, the same conclusions had already been reached in dealing with similar problems.[77] In *Zapata Corp* v *Maldonado*[78] the minority shareholder was bringing a properly founded derivative action but the board of directors had formed an independent sub-committee of the board to make proper inquiries into the allegations which formed the substance of the derivative suit. The company brought a pre-trial motion to dismiss the derivative suit and succeeded. The

---

[76] [1987] 3 All ER 909 at 942 (first sentence) and 955–956 *passim*.

[77] Care needs to be taken when making direct comparisons with shareholder litigation in the USA because most states have not developed a rigid form of the rule in *Foss* v *Harbottle*. However, the US legal system has nevertheless had to address the problem of opening the floodgates, and has had resort to various restrictive rules, some of which have similar theoretical suppositions to the English common law; thus, a ratification will sometimes shut down a derivative action. Other rules are technical bars designed to discourage derivative suits, such as the requirement for a minority derivative litigant to post a bond (i.e. give security).

[78] 430 A 2d 779 (1981).

Delaware Supreme Court held that the shareholder did not have an indefeasible right to bring the action and had regard to the conclusions reached by the sub-committee of the board. The action was struck out.

The *Zapata* case goes a little further than *Smith* v *Croft (No. 2)* because it identified the sub-committee of the board as being the appropriate independent organ of the company which could properly reach a conclusion on behalf of the company as to the desirability of derivative litigation. But the expression 'appropriate independent organ' used in *Smith* v *Croft*[79] and *Prudential*[80] would be sufficient in an appropriate case to extend the idea in England also, to a board sub-committee rather than the independent shareholders.[81] We may therefore be at the stage where it would be an effective tactic for a board faced with what it saw as inappropriate derivative litigation to form a sub-committee to look into the matter. If the sub-committee commissioned a firm of accountants to look into it, and their report exonerated the defendants, the sub-committee could resolve to terminate the derivative action. It may well be that the sub-committee would then be held to be an appropriate independent organ within the *Smith* v *Croft* doctrine. This extension of the doctrine is probably necessary if it is to work in the long run, because in a large company the practicalities of identifying the independent group among thousands of shareholders would probably prove insurmountable.

Is *Smith* v *Croft (No. 2)* a development which is dangerous for minority shareholders? The point has been made that there were already many disincentives to bringing a derivative action.[82] The decision makes it clear that a minority shareholder no longer has an indefeasible right to bring a derivative action for acts which would normally be categorised as fraud on the minority. The would-be litigant now has to be able to pursuade more than half the independent shareholders that the action should be brought. There is perhaps no good reason why an adapted version of the doctrine of majority rule should suddenly spring up at this juncture and be used to stifle litigation. Perhaps it would make more sense if the doctrine was confined to the question of whether the company would pay for the litigation rather than whether it can be brought at all. If the doctrine is extended to give the dismissal decision to a sub-committee of the board, the ability to litigate will have been removed from the shareholders altogether in some situations. All in all, the *Smith* v *Croft* development seems difficult to justify and it remains to be seen how it will fare in future cases.

Subsequent to these developments, the court procedure was amended to ensure that the questions of whether there is a *prima facie* case (the mini-trial) and whether the action falls within the exceptions to the rule in *Foss* v *Harbottle* were dealt with at a very early stage of the proceedings. Under RSC Ord. 15, r. 12A, it was made clear that a derivative action was to stop once the defendant has given notice of intention to defend. If the claimant wanted it to continue he needed to seek the leave of the court, the idea being that *Foss* v *Harbottle* matters would be dealt with at that application for leave.[83] The claimant was permitted to include in his

---

[79] [1987] 3 All ER 909 at p. 915.
[80] [1982] Ch 204 at p. 222.
[81] The phrase used.
[82] See p. 220 above.
[83] RSC Ord. 15, r. 12A (2).

application a request 'for an indemnity out of the assets of the company in respect of costs incurred or to be incurred.'[84] Thus the question of whether a Wallersteiner order[85] should be made would normally be dealt with then also. With the coming into force of the Civil Procedure Rules[86] on 26 April 1999, implementing the Woolf reforms contained in the *Access to Justice, Final Report*, derivative claims are governed by r. 19.9 of those rules. This provides (in para. 3) that: 'After the claim form has been issued the claimant must apply to the court for permission to continue the claim and may not take any other step in the proceedings – except . . . where the court gives permission.' This will largely have the same effect as the old RSC Ord. 15, r. 12A which it replaced, since the overall impact of RSC Ord. 15, r. 12A was to introduce a form of 'case management' and the new rule does the same within the CPR case management system.

12.7 THE *BRECKLAND* PROBLEM

It is clear that the case law on *Foss* v *Harbottle* is very much rooted in the idea that the majority in general meeting control the decision of whether litigation in the name of the company should be brought. It has been seen that only if the circumstances fall within one of the exceptions to the rule, can the minority shareholder litigate. And yet, in a relatively recent case, the majority shareholder found that the court took the view that the decision on whether to litigate or not rested with the board. *Breckland Group Ltd* v *London & Suffolk Properties Ltd*[87] concerned a company which had adopted art. 80 of the 1948 Act's Table A, which vested the management of the business of the company in the board of directors.[88] Breckland Ltd controlled 49% of the shares in London & Suffolk Properties Ltd and the other 51% were held by Crompton Ltd. Crompton Ltd commenced an action in the name of London & Suffolk Properties Ltd against Avery (among others) who was the managing director of London & Suffolk Properties Ltd. Avery also controlled Breckland Ltd. Although there were other matters which influenced the result,[89] Harman J clearly took the view that art. 80 'confides the management of the company to the directors and in such a case it is not for the general meeting to interfere'.[90] Accordingly, the court ordered that the action should proceed no further until the directors' meeting had decided whether to ratify it or not.

It is likely that *Breckland* will one day need to be reconsidered. There is strong support for the view that whatever the effect of art. 80[91] on normal day-to-day busi-

---

[84] *Ibid.* r. 12A (13).
[85] For a recent unsuccessful attempt to obtain a Wallersteiner order see *Halle* v *Trax BW Ltd* [2000] BCC 1,020.
[86] SI 1998 No. 3132.
[87] (1988) 4 BCC 542.
[88] Article 70 of the 1985 Table A has a similar overall effect although there are differences about the extent to which the shareholders can give directions to the board.
[89] In the circumstances, since a shareholder agreement made it necessary for both Breckland Ltd and Crompton Ltd to agree to any litigation by London & Suffolk Properties Ltd, it was pretty clear that the litigation was not going any further at all.
[90] (1988) 4 BCC 542 at pp. 546–547.
[91] Or the modern art. 70.

ness, as regards the conduct of litigation, the general meeting has the right to commence proceedings in the company's name and that this right is collateral to and subsists alongside the board's right. This has judicial support. For instance, in *Alexander Ward Ltd* v *Samyang Navigation Co Ltd*[92] Lord Hailsham gave his approval (*obiter*) to the passage in Gower's *Modern Company Law*[93] where it was stated:

> [A]lthough the general meeting cannot restrain the directors from conducting actions in the name of the company, it still seems to be the law (as laid down in *Marshall's Valve Gear Co* v *Manning Wardle & Co* [1909] 1 Ch 267) that the general meeting can commence proceedings on behalf of the company if the directors fail to do so.

In *Breckland* the *Marshall's Valve* case was criticised and various authorities against it were cited. On the other hand, a slavish attachment to art. 80[94] will produce some curious results. It is well established that the minority of shareholders may bring a derivative action on behalf of the company (although not in its name) against directors and others who have wronged it, if they can show a fraud on the minority and meet the other requirements discussed above. *Breckland* does not purport to overrule this and indeed to do so would have been ineffective in view of the longstanding authority and practice behind it. But it seems odd that 30% of shareholders could bring an action in this way, but 60% could not, being less than the required 75% for a special resolution in accordance with what is now art. 70 and not being able to show that they were a *minority* who were entitled to bring a derivative action. It may be argued that the remedy for the majority in this situation is to remove the directors under s. 303 of the Companies Act 1985 but there are sometimes restrictions on the use of that section and it would not always be a commercially desirable solution.

It is clear that *Breckland*, which vests control of litigation exclusively in the board as a result of what is now art. 70, is difficult to reconcile with *Foss* v *Harbottle*, which is rooted in the idea that the majority control the litigation. At least part of the problem arises from the fact that the interpretation of the article upon which *Breckland* relies only dates from 1906,[95] whereas many of the *Foss* v *Harbottle* authorities are much earlier. Prior to 1906 the directors of a company were usually regarded simply as agents of the shareholders rather than as a separately functioning organ of the company. Overall, it is perhaps likely that in future cases the words of art. 70 'the business of the company shall be managed by the directors' will be held to relate primarily to the commercial business of the company and not exclude the concurrent jurisdiction of the majority in general meeting over the use of the corporate name in litigation.

---

[92] [1975] 2 All ER 424, HL.
[93] 3rd edn, pp. 136–137.
[94] Or the current art. 70.
[95] See *Automatic Self-Cleansing Filter Sindicate Co Ltd* v *Cuninghame* [1906] 2 Ch 34.

12.8 COMPANY LAW REVIEW AND LAW REFORM

A The work of the Law Commission

The whole area of shareholder litigation, both common law and statute,[96] has recently been given a most thorough going-over by the Law Commission for England and Wales in consultation with the Scottish Law Commission. The painstaking process started with a 284-page consultation paper[97] in 1996 which contained an analysis of the problems and some possible solutions. This was followed by extensive nationwide consultation which led to the report *Shareholder Remedies*.[98]

The central plank of the Law Commission's proposed reforms is that there is to be a new statutory derivative action to replace the common law derivative action and that the legislation will set out in modern and accessible form the circumstances in which the courts will permit the derivative action to be brought. The derivative action will only be available 'if the cause of action arises as a result of an actual or threatened act or omission involving (a) negligence, default, breach of duty or breach of trust by a director of the company, or (b) a director putting himself in a position where his personal interests conflict with his duties to the company. The cause of action may be against the director or another person (or both)'.[99]

Rather like the situation under CPR, r. 19.9, at an early stage of the proceedings, the claimant will need to seek permission to continue it. This will be at a case management conference. The following issues are to be relevant to the grant of leave:

(8) There should be no threshold test on the merits.[100]

(9) In considering the issue of leave the court should take account of all the relevant circumstances without limit.

(10) These should include the following:
  (i) the good faith of the applicant (which should not be defined);
  (ii) the interests of the company (having regard to the views of directors on commercial matters);
  (iii) the fact that the wrong has been or may be approved by the company in general meeting (but effective ratification should continue to be a complete bar);
  (iv) the fact that the company in general meeting has resolved not to pursue the cause of action;
  (v) the views of an independent organ that for commercial reasons the action should or should not be pursued.
  (vi) the availability of alternative remedies;

---

[96] The proposed reforms to the statutory area are dealt with at p. 000 below.
[97] Law Com. Consultation Paper No. 142 (1996).
[98] Law Com. Report No. 246 (Cm. 3769, 1997). Subsequently, the DTI produced a Consultation Document *Shareholder Remedies* (November 1998).
[99] Law Com. Report No. 246, para. 6.49.
[100] In other words, there should be no need to establish a *prima facie* case, no 'mini-trial'.

(11) The court should not grant leave to continue the proceedings if it is satisfied that the action is not in the interests of the company.[101]

It is clear that the main thrust of this new approach is to free up the area and reduce what the law has presented as rules of law to the status of 'matters to be taken account of'. The existing legal rules purport to provide a logical structure which will present a would-be litigant with a clear answer to his position. Thus, if the wrong is ratifiable he cannot litigate,[102] if the independent organ has decided that it does not want the litigation then he cannot litigate,[103] if the action is brought in bad faith then he cannot litigate.[104] This rigidity is to be replaced by a more open-textured environment in which there are merely a list of matters which have to be taken into account. The approach recognises that issues in shareholder litigation cases are rarely as clear cut as the case law rules which have been developed would suggest.

Nevertheless, there are perhaps going to be some problems. The statutory derivative action will float above the common law principles, which will be largely redundant since the common law derivative action will no longer be available. But in practice it will be difficult for the courts to remain detached from developing principles or from applying the principles which have been developed, for they represent a compromise between the pragmatic commercial principle of majority rule on the one hand and the need to prevent injustice on the other. The situations which the courts are faced with are not likely to change or be any different from those which have formed the substance of shareholder litigation for the century-and-a-half since *Foss* v *Harbottle* was decided. The maxim that justice requires like cases to be treated alike will inexorably lead the courts to pay close regard to the ways in which applications for leave have been dealt with in the past. Given that the common law was rarely as fixed as the doctrine of *stare decisis* would sometimes lead us to believe, will things really look much different 100 years from now, or will the situation be significantly different from what would have developed if the matter had been left in the hands of the common law?

B Company Law Review and law reform

In the DTI Consultation Document of March 2000, *Developing the Framework*, the Company Law Review has continued the work on shareholder remedies. The Review 'broadly supports'[105] the proposals of the Law Commission, but it set in motion work and consultation on several areas, for instance the effect of ratification, whether breach of the duty of care and skill should ground a derivative action, and also the question of whether the qua member doctrine surrounding s. 14 of the Companies Act 1985 should be retained.[106]

---

[101] Law Com. Report No. 246, n. 94 above, para. 8.11.

[102] *McDougall* v *Gardiner* (1875) 1 Ch D 13; *Burland* v *Earle* [1902] AC 83; *Pavlides* v *Jensen* [1956] Ch 656; *Hogg* v *Cramphorn* [1967] Ch 254; *Bamford* v *Bamford* [1970] Ch 212.

[103] *Prudential Assurance Co.* v *Newman Industries and others (No. 2)* [1982] 1 All ER 354; *Smith* v *Croft (No. 2)* [1987] 3 All ER 909.

[104] *Barrett* v *Duckett* [1993] BCC 778.

[105] DTI Consultation Document (March 2000) *Developing the Framework* para. 4.115.

[106] The Law Commission's view was that this issue is not important in practice and should be left as it is.

The Final Report of the Review[107] recommends that obligations imposed by the company's constitution should be enforceable by members (unless otherwise stated). It also comes down in favour of the proposals for a statutory derivative action.

The government White Paper, *Modernising Company Law*[108] made reference to the 'difficult and complex area' of codification of civil remedies for breach of directors' duties but it was clear that the government were not yet committed to this and intended to see 'if a workable scheme can be devised'. The subsequent DTI publication, *Company Law. Flexibility and Accessibility: A Consultative Document* of May 2004 seems to have come down in favour of putting derivative actions on a statutory footing.

---

[107] *Modern Company Law for a Competitive Economy Final Report* (London: DTI, 2001), paras. 6.19–6.40.
[108] July 2002, Cmnd. 5553 (London: DTI, 2002) para. 3.18.

13

SHAREHOLDER LITIGATION: STATUTE

13.1 WINDING UP

By analogy with their ancient equitable jurisdiction to dissolve partnerships where the partners had lost their close bonds of trust and good faith, the courts have developed a jurisdiction to wind up companies in similar circumstances. It is based on s. 122 (1) (g) of the Insolvency Act 1986, which provides that the court may wind up a company if it is 'just and equitable that the company should be wound up'. The winding up is available in various circumstances where the company is of the type where it could be described as an incorporated partnership[1] and the necessary bonds of trust and co-operation have broken down.[2] The usual situation where it is invoked in practice these days is where there is a company, which we might call Paradigm Ltd, which has, say, three members with equal shareholdings who are also directors. There is an understanding between them that they will all participate in management and share equally in the profits of the business. They choose not to pay dividends and instead take any profits as directors' fees. The members quarrel and two of them combine their votes to dismiss the third from his directorship under s. 303 of the Companies Act 1985. He thus no longer has any managerial role and, because there are no dividends, receives no return on his capital investment in the company. To make matters worse, his capital investment is locked in because, being a small private company, the shares are not publicly quoted on any market, and in the circumstances, even a private buyer is not going to want to pay much for the shares for more or less the same reasons that the director wants to get shot of them: they give no income, no control and no management participation.[3] In such circumstances,[4] the courts will often grant a winding-up order.[5]

---

[1] 'Quasi-partnership' is the expression often used.
[2] The leading authoritative summary of the circumstances in which the jurisdiction will be exercised is the speech of Lord Wilberforce in *Ebrahimi* v *Westbourne Galleries Ltd* [1973] AC 360 at p. 379.
[3] If the articles of association give the directors the power to refuse to register a transfer, there will be additional difficulties; see generally p. 272 below.
[4] Other examples include 'deadlock', see *Re Yenidje Tobacco Ltd* [1916] 2 Ch 426; and 'justifiable lack of confidence in the management of the affairs of the company', see *Loch* v *John Blackwood Ltd* [1924] AC 783, PC.
[5] There is another unrelated set of circumstances where the courts have traditionally wound up under s. 122 (1) (g) of the 1986 Act or its forerunners. The courts will wind up where the 'substratum' has failed. That is, where the objects clause in the memorandum of association stipulates a particular purpose of incorporation and that purpose has failed or been achieved so that, either way, the company no longer has any reason for existence, and its substratum has gone; see generally *Re German Date Coffee Company* (1882) 20 Ch D 169, *Re Perfectair Ltd* (1989) 5 BCC 837. Invocation of this doctrine is extremely rare and, in view of the usual broadly drafted objects clauses and flexibility of alteration, it is not currently of great importance.

In many ways it is an unsatisfactory remedy, particularly if the company has made its profits mainly out of its 'know-how' and business contacts, for on a winding up there may be very little in the way of assets left over for distribution to the shareholders.[6] Because of this, there is a major restriction on the 'just and equitable' jurisdiction. Section 125 (2) of the Insolvency Act 1986 provides in effect that the court may not make a winding-up order on the just and equitable ground if the court is of the opinion both that some other remedy is available and the petitioners are acting unreasonably in seeking to have the company wound up rather than pursue the other remedy. In practice, a fair offer to purchase the shares of the petitioner, made by the other side, the respondents to the petition, will often disentitle him from pursuing the winding up under s. 122 (1) (g).[7] Also, the possibility of an unfair prejudice petition will sometimes produce this result, but not always.[8]

13.2 UNFAIR PREJUDICE

A The alternative remedy failure

In response to influential calls for reform, Parliament enacted s. 210 of the Companies Act 1948, as an 'alternative remedy' to the jurisdiction to wind up on the just and equitable ground. The intention was to vest in the courts a discretion to make an order which was appropriate to the circumstances. The section required that the petitioner could show that there had been conduct which was oppressive.[9] In the event, there were very few successful reported petitions.[10] One which showed what imaginative use might be made of the new jurisdiction was *Re Harmer Ltd*.[11] It was a small family company involved in a stamp-dealing business. The father was very old and his sons, themselves in their sixties, were finding their father very difficult to get on with. The father had founded a branch of the business in the US without consulting the sons and there were other matters of contention. The sons sought some way of controlling their father and petitioned the court. Harman J made a sensitive order, under which the old man would be president for life of the company, but without any powers.

The judges developed a rule which effectively killed off the jurisdiction in the circumstances in which it was most needed. In the sort of situation discussed above,[12] in the example with Paradigm Ltd, it was held that the director who had been dismissed under what is now s. 303 had been oppressed in his capacity as a director,

---

[6] Although if there will be none at all, then winding up on this ground will not be available, because the petitioner must show a *prima facie* case that there will be a surplus of assets over liabilities: *Re Rica Gold Washing Co Ltd* (1879) LR 11 Ch D 36.

[7] See *Re a Company* 002567/82 (1983) 1 BCC 98,931.

[8] See further pp. 237–243 below. On the interaction between the just and equitable jurisdiction and the unfair prejudice remedy, see p. 248 below.

[9] It was also necessary to show that the facts would otherwise justify the making of a winding-up petition on the just and equitable ground.

[10] Three: *SCWS v Meyer* [1959] AC 324; *Re Harmer Ltd* [1959] 1 WLR 62 (see below); and *Re Stewarts* [1985] BCLC 4 (although this was a preliminary application).

[11] [1959] 1 WLR 62.

[12] At p. 231.

and not in his capacity as a member, as the statute impliedly required.[13] His membership (i.e. shareholder) rights were said to be unaffected by his dismissal as director and loss of directors' fees. Thus the s. 210 jurisdiction was a failure. The courts seemed reluctant to take the steps necessary to put the situation right and preferred to wind up the companies instead.

B Unfair prejudice

1 Section 459 replaces s. 210

In 1980, Parliament tried again.[14] It repealed s. 210 of the 1948 Act and replaced it with a new remedy based on a new concept: unfair prejudice. The provisions are now contained in ss. 459–461 of the Companies Act 1985 and were slightly amended in 1989. By virtue of s. 459 (1):

> A member of a company may apply to the court by petition for an order . . . on the ground that the company's affairs are being or have been conducted in a manner which is unfairly prejudicial to the interests of its members generally or of some part of its members (including at least himself) or that any actual or proposed act or omission of the company (including an act or omission on its behalf) is or would be so prejudicial.

The remainder of s. 459 and ss. 460–461 contain further provisions relating to the basic idea in s. 459 (1) and, in particular, provide that the court, if satisfied that the petition is well founded, may make 'such order as it thinks fit for giving relief in respect of the matters complained of'.[15]

Parliament's second attempt was successful. So successful in fact that the floodgates of litigation, firmly shut for so long by *Foss* v *Harbottle*, were well and truly thrown open. The judges were flexible and innovative in their use of the new jurisdiction. By the late 1980s there were dozens of reported cases. These represented only the tip of the iceberg, for many cases were settled before getting into court, the petition having served its usefulness as a mechanism for bringing the other side to the bargaining table. Gradually, it was realised that the availability of the new remedy was capable of being oppressive towards respondents and some of the judges sought to develop ways of restricting the number of cases.[16] The reform proposals in the Report of the Law Commission on *Shareholder Remedies* reflect the concern that the availability of litigation to an aggrieved shareholder can bring problems as well as advantages.[17]

2 Scope of s. 459

There are no hard and fast rules for deciding whether conduct can amount to unfair prejudice, although certain general principles have emerged. There are two main areas

---

[13] See *Re Lundie Bros Ltd* [1965] 1 WLR 1051.
[14] This time on the recommendation of the Jenkins Committee.
[15] Companies Act 1985, s. 461 (1).
[16] See below.
[17] See p. 248 below.

of development. The first is that the judges have made various general statements about how the jurisdiction should be exercised. The second is that quite a lot of case law has developed around the problem of where to draw the line between the shareholders' private matters (which cannot form the substance of an unfair prejudice petition) and matters which can properly be seen as conduct of the company's affairs and which unfairly prejudice some of the members.

The early cases contained various attempts by judges to elaborate in a general way on the idea of 'unfairness' and 'prejudice' in the context of the running of commercial companies. It was decided very early on that the test of unfairness was objective in the sense that the respondents need not have acted as they did in the conscious knowledge that it was unfair to the petitioner, or be in bad faith and that the test was 'whether a reasonable bystander observing the consequences of the conduct would regard it as having unfairly prejudiced the petitioner's interests'.[18] The overall approach came to be reviewed by the Court of Appeal in *Re Saul Harrison plc*.[19] The petition had been struck out by the judge, and the petitioner appealed. The gist of the petitioner's main complaint was that the company had some valuable assets but poor business prospects and that by carrying on its business the directors were dissipating those assets, and any reasonable board would have closed the company down and distributed the assets to the shareholders. In a landmark judgment, Hoffmann LJ reviewed the development of the case law on unfair prejudice, holding that a petitioner would only be entitled to a remedy if she could establish that the powers of management had been used for an unlawful purpose or the articles otherwise infringed. The exception to this would be where she had been able to show that the circumstances were such that because of the personal relationship between her and those who controlled the company, there was a 'legitimate expectation' that the board and the general meeting would not exercise whatever powers they were given by the articles of association. But she would have to show that the relationship was not purely a commercial one, and that there was 'something more' so that the letter of the articles did not fully reflect the understandings upon which the shareholders were associated. In the circumstances she failed to show that there was 'something more' and moreover failed to show any bad faith on the part of the directors in the exercise of their powers.

Re Saul Harrison also contained what looked like an attempt to restrict the circumstances in which a remedy under s. 459 would be granted, to those circumstances in which it had already been granted. Hoffmann LJ recalled the objective reasonable bystander test[20] and, while accepting that the test was objective, he stressed that the standard of fairness must necessarily be laid down by the court and that it was more useful to examine the factors which the law actually took into account in setting the standard, rather than appealing to the views of an imaginary

[18] *Per* Slade J in the unreported case of *Re Bovey Hotel Ventures Ltd*; approved and cited by Nourse J (as he then was) in *Re RA Noble and Sons (Clothing) Ltd* [1983] BCLC 273. Nourse J (as he then was) took the view in *Re RA Noble and Sons (Clothing) Ltd* [1983] BCLC 273 that a petitioner who had behaved badly himself would not get a remedy, but in a later case, *Re London School of Electronics Ltd* (1985) 1 BCC 99,394, he seemed to retract this in favour of the approach that although he need not come to the court with clean hands, his own conduct could affect the remedy which he received.
[19] [1994] BCC 475.
[20] See *Re Bovey Hotel Ventures Ltd*, n. 18 above.

'company watcher'. Whether Hoffmann LJ intended his approach to be restrictive or not, very soon after, a judge of the Chancery Division put down a marker that this was not the last word on the matter and that it was not open to the Court of Appeal to limit the general words of the statute:

> [I]n my judgment, it is not the effect of *Re Saul Harrison* that a remedy under section 459 can be given only if the directors have acted in breach of duty or if the company has breached the terms of its articles or some other relevant agreement. These matters constitute in most cases the basis for deciding what conduct is unfair. But the words of the section are wide and general and, save where the circumstances are governed by the judgments in *Re Saul Harrison*, the categories of unfair prejudice are not closed.[21]

Re Saul Harrison was an example of the courts being concerned as to the possible oppressive effects of the opening of the floodgates of litigation and it was not the first time that Hoffmann LJ had attempted to stem the tide.[22] As will be seen below, *Re Saul Harrison* has now largely been superseded by the House of Lords' decision in *O'Neill* v *Phillips*, but since *O'Neill* v *Phillips* also deals with various other ideas and developments which have not yet been explained here, it is necessary to consider these in their historical context before turning to an analysis of *O'Neill* v *Phillips*.

The second area of development has been in respect of the 'qua member' idea encountered in the example of Paradigm Ltd discussed above,[23] and the related matter of whether the acts complained of amount to conduct of the company's affairs as opposed to the member's private affairs. Given the devastation wrought on the old s. 210 of the 1948 Act by the judicial doctrine that the dismissal of a director in a quasi-partnership company was not oppression 'qua member' as the statute was said to require, it became very important to see what the judges would do with that problem under the new unfair prejudice provisions in the 1980 Act. The wording was similar and so there was nothing on the face of the statute to require a different approach. The judges of the Chancery Division of the 1980s made a point of circumventing the problem by admitting the principle that the prejudice had to be qua member but taking a wide view of what membership rights entailed in a quasi-partnership company. The matter was put well by Hoffmann J (as he then was) in *Re a Company (No. 00477 of 1986)*:[24]

> In principle I accept [the] proposition [that the section must be limited to conduct which is unfairly prejudicial to the interest of the members as members. It cannot extend to conduct which is prejudicial to other interests of persons who happen to be members] ... but its application must take into account that the interests of a member are not necessarily limited to his strict legal rights under the constitution of the company. The use of the word 'unfairly' in section 459, like the use of the words 'just and equitable' in [s. 122 (1) (g)],

---

[21] *Re BSB Holdings (No. 2)* [1996] 1 BCLC 155, *per* Arden J at p. 243.

[22] See p. 239 below.

[23] At p. 231.

[24] (1986) 2 BCC 99,171 at p. 99,174. The same judge took a similar approach in *Re a Company 008699 of 1985* (1986) 2 BCC 99,024. As did Nourse J (as he then was) in *Re RA Noble and Sons (Clothing) Ltd* [1983] BCLC 273 and Vinelott J in *Re a Company 002567 of 1982* [1983] 2 All ER 854, and in *Re Blue Arrow plc* [1987] BCLC 585. An earlier narrow decision of Lord Grantchester QC in *Re a Company* [1983] Ch 178 was not followed.

enables the court to have regard to wider equitable considerations ... Thus in the case of a managing director of a large public company who is also the owner of a small holding in the company's shares, it is easy to see the distinction between his interests as a managing director employed under a service contract and his interests as a member. In the case of a small private company in which two or three members have invested their capital by subscribing for shares on the footing that dividends are unlikely but that each will earn his living by working for the company as a director, the distinction may be more elusive. The member's interests as a member who has ventured his capital in the company's business may include a legitimate expectation that he will continue to be employed as a director and his dismissal from that office and exclusion from the management of the company may therefore be unfairly prejudicial to his interests as a member.

Thus a new chapter in company law was born; a remedy was available in the kind of situations where previously, only a winding up on the just and equitable ground would have been granted. But the genie was out of the bottle, and within a few years the judges were trying to develop ways of restricting the jurisdiction.

The related matter of whether the acts complained of amount to conduct of the company's affairs as opposed to the member's private affairs has received attention in several cases. The difficulty stems from the fact that in small private companies, the shareholders may be interacting with each other in various ways: as members, obviously, but perhaps also as father and son, or as sisters, and perhaps also as joint owners of a piece of land leased to the company, or as participants in a huge family business involving several companies. In these kinds of situations, when faced with an unfair prejudice petition, the court finds that it has to sort out which matters constitute conduct of the company's affairs, and which therefore fall to be taken into account in judging the petition, and which matters constitute conduct of private matters between the members themselves and which are therefore irrelevant to the petition.

Re Unisoft Ltd (No. 2),[25] was a case which also shows judicial concern with the way in which s. 459 can become oppressive to the respondents, and perhaps also to the petitioners. The case was estimated to last three months:

> Petitions under section 459 have become notorious to the judges of this court – and I think also to the Bar – for their length, their unpredictability of management, and the enormous and appalling costs which are incurred upon them particularly by reason of the volume of documents liable to be produced. By way of example, on this petition there are before me upwards of thirty lever-arch files of documents. In those circumstances it befits the court, in my view, to be extremely careful to ensure that oppression is not caused to parties, respondents to such petitions, indeed, petitioners to such petitions, by allowing the parties to trawl through facts which have given rise to grievances but which are not relevant conduct within even the very wide words of the section.[26]

This was a case where there were the normal allegations of exclusion of a director and removal from office. However, there were also various complaints about dealings between the shareholders themselves, relating to sales of shares, and shareholder agreements. These matters were struck out as they were about their private

---

[25] [1994] BCC 766.
[26] *Ibid.* at p. 767, *per* Harman J.

position as shareholders and not about unfair conduct of the company's business.[27] It is clear that this is an area which will lead the courts into making some subtle distinctions in future cases.

3 Share purchase orders

We have seen that the courts are prepared, in appropriate cases, to give a remedy to the shareholder director who is dismissed from a quasi-partnership company. This kind of situation is by far the most common which comes before the courts. The remedy usually sought and granted in such cases is an order that the respondents purchase the shares of the petitioner, although such an order is by no means confined to these situations, and it will be seen later that unfair prejudice proceedings are used to remedy a wide range of problems.[28]

The share purchase order almost invariably requires a majority to buy out a minority. An order the other way around is likely to be an extremely rare event. Hoffmann J[29] expressed the view in *Re a Company 006834/88*[30] that it would be:

> ... very unusual for the court to order a majority shareholder actively concerned in the management of the company to sell his shares to a minority shareholder when he is willing and able to buy out the minority shareholder at a fair price.

But, sooner or later, rare events occur and there has been at least one case where the situation was so unusual that a majority shareholder was ordered to sell out to a minority petitioner.[31]

The question of how the shares are to be valued has given rise to a number of issues, as well as the fairly complex matter of how the valuation is to be arrived at.[32] These cannot be considered in detail here,[33] but one point which has cropped up in many important recent cases needs to be explained. In *Re Bird Precision Bellows Ltd*[34] the judge at first instance had valued the shares on a pro-rata basis, without any discount for the fact that they were a minority holding. The Court of Appeal held that this was fair in the circumstances and ever since then, valuation without discount has generally been regarded as the *prima facie* norm in unfair prejudice cases.[35] The idea is of great benefit to the minority shareholder. If the share value is discounted to reflect the fact that the petitioner's shares are a minority holding, then it will produce a much lower value than a pro-rata valuation. A pro-rata valuation would fix a value for the whole company, and then give 40% of that figure to someone who had a 40% holding of the shares in the company. A discounted valuation would be done

---

[27] Similar points arose in *Re JE Cade Ltd* [1991] BCC 360. The argument was raised in *R & H Electrical Ltd* v *Haden Bill Ltd* [1995] BCC 958, but failed.
[28] See p. 243 below.
[29] As he then was.
[30] (1989) 5 BCC 218 at p. 220.
[31] *Re a Company 00789 of 1987* (1989) 5 BCC 792, [1991] BCC 44. See also the proceedings in *Re Copeland Ltd* [1997] BCC 294, CA.
[32] And the date of valuation; for the principles as to this see *Profinance Trust SA* v *Gladstone* [2002] 1 BCLC 141, CA.
[33] See e.g. *Re OC Transport Services Ltd* [1984] BCLC 251; *Re Cumana Ltd* [1986] BCLC 430.
[34] [1984] Ch 419, [1986] Ch 658, CA.
[35] But there are rare exceptions; see for instance *Elliott* v *Planet Organic Ltd* [2000] BCC 610.

on the assumption that the 40% holding was really worth a lot less than 40% of the total value of the company. The reasons why this might be are obvious: the minority holding carries no control, can vote no director onto the board, can remove no director, and is dependent on the majority for any dividends.

The main developments in this field have centred around trying to find an answer to one specific question: where a petitioner is seeking an order that the respondents purchase his shares, what effect does it have on that petition if the respondents make an offer to purchase the petitioner's shares? There can be no definitive answer to cover every situation, but a number of dominant ideas have developed steadily over nearly 20 years. We have already seen that in the closely related situation of a winding up on the just and equitable ground the existence of s. 125 (2) of the Insolvency Act 1986 can mean that, in some circumstances, an offer to purchase can terminate the petition.[36] In the early 1980s, it was soon established that the same might be true for an unfair prejudice petition, on the basis that whatever harm the petitioner had suffered at the hands of the respondents, a proper offer from them to purchase his shares made the situation no longer unfair and so it would often be appropriate to accede to the respondent's motion to strike out the petition. But the doctrine acquired a sharp edge in the hands of Hoffmann J, for at that time he and a number of the other judges of the Chancery Division seemed concerned to find a fair way of restricting the number of petitions. The learned judge expounded and applied his striking-out doctrine in cases where the articles of association of the companies contained mechanisms designed to govern the valuation of shares in certain circumstances.[37] Strictly speaking, those circumstances had not always arisen and so the approach involved an element of extension of the provisions of the articles.[38] The provisions usually provided for valuation by an accountant acting as an expert, the practical consequence of which was that the valuer would not have to give reasons for his valuation and nor would it be possible to ensure that he did not apply a discount to the valuation because the shares were a minority holding. Hoffmann J set out the background and rationale for his approach:

> This is an ordinary case of breakdown of confidence between the parties. In such circumstances, fairness requires that the minority shareholder should not have to maintain his investment in a company managed by the majority with whom he has fallen out. But the unfairness disappears if the minority shareholder is offered a fair price for his shares. In such a case, section 459 was not intended to enable the court to preside over a protracted and expensive contest of virtue between the shareholders and award the company to the winner.[39]

> In general ... if a petitioner is complaining of conduct which would be unfairly prejudicial only if accompanied by a refusal on the part of the majority to buy his shares at a fair price, and the articles provide a mechanism for determining such a price, he should not be

---

[36] *Re a Company 002567/82* (1983) 1 BCC 98,931; see further p. 232 above.

[37] These were usually share transfer or expropriation provisions in common form; see *Re a Company 004377 of 1986* (1986) 2 BCC 99,520 (also called *Re XYZ Ltd* in some reports), *Re a Company 007623 of 1984* (1986) 2 BCC 99,191 and *Re a Company 006834 of 1988* (1989) 5 BCC 218.

[38] See e.g. *Re a Company 006834 of 1988* (1989) 5 BCC 218, where it really could not be said that the articles actually covered the situation that had arisen.

[39] *Re a Company 006834 of 1988* (1989) 5 BCC 218 at p. 221.

entitled to petition ... until he has invoked or offered to invoke that mechanism and the majority have refused to buy at the price so determined.[40]

This approach quickly ran into trouble. Hoffmann J struck out the petition in *Re Abbey Leisure Ltd*[41] but the petitioner appealed. The respondents had offered to purchase his shares at a price fixed by an accountant and the petitioner was worried that the accountant would discount the price because the petitioner had a 40% minority holding. The Court of Appeal reinstated the petition, holding that, in the circumstances, it was not fair to expect the petitioner to run the risk that the accountant would apply a discount.[42] For a time, this put a stopper on the striking-out process. The effect of *Re Abbey Leisure Ltd* was described by Harman J in a later case:

> ... The decision ... was one which in my judgment plainly changed the whole approach of the court to petitions under sections 459 and 461 ... What [the passage in the case] says is that a petitioner is entitled to refuse to accept a risk – any risk – in an accountant's valuation of his interest if such a risk can be seen to be one that would depreciate in any way the valuation.[43]

However, the striking-out process did not die. It is apparent from recent litigation that if the offer really is a fair one in all the circumstances, then the court may well take the view that there is nothing to be gained from litigation. The offer in *Re a Company 00836 of 1995*[44] was a clever one in the sense that it took account of most of the objections that were being raised to offers in previous cases. Although it is also clear that the judge was not imbued with a sense that the litigation here was essential:

> This is the latest instalment in a long running[45] feud between father and son. The feud has been conducted through the medium of the Companies Court ... It has cost, I am told, so far at least £1m, and possibly nearer £2m, for both sides. In one corner is [the father] ... He is 85 ... In the other corner is his younger son ... who fell out with his father in the late 1980s ...[46]

Both had petitioned against the other and both applied to strike out the other's petition. The son, the majority shareholder, made an offer to purchase his father's shares. The offer had been drafted to avoid most of the points that might be taken against it and so it was a pro-rata offer – the price for the minority holding to be the proportion of the net asset value of the company that those shares bore to the whole of the issued share capital, both sides could have their own accountants make written representations to the expert valuer, and the valuer had to give reasons for the figure to be produced. The judge took the view that:

---

[40] *Re a Company 007623 of 1984* (1986) 2 BCC 99,191 at p. 99,199.
[41] [1990] BCC 60.
[42] The case largely concerned a petition for winding up (although there was also a petition for unfair prejudice) but the principles were felt to be the same as in unfair prejudice cases.
[43] *Re a Company 00330 of 1991, ex parte Holden* [1991] BCC 241 at p. 245.
[44] [1996] BCC 432.
[45] There had been earlier litigation, reported as *Re Macro Ltd* [1994] BCC 781.
[46] [1996] BCC 432 at p. 433, *per* Judge Weeks QC.

[T]here is no substance in the objection [that the petitioner is entitled to his day or week or month in court, and that it is inappropriate to have these matters effectively decided by an accountant rather than the court] . . . and an independent accountant can perfectly well, with the assistance of a solicitor, if he thinks it desirable, make the valuation which he is required to do under the terms of that offer, and that way of proceeding is as good as the method of proceeding before the court with cross-examination, valuers on both sides, and a protracted hearing . . .[47]

Although the court's jurisdiction to strike out is one that must be exercised sparingly,[48] it is clear that a fair offer followed by striking-out proceedings will remain an important and sometimes successful tactic in future unfair prejudice cases.

Many of the doctrines and ideas discussed above arose again in the landmark case of *O'Neill* v *Phillips*.[49] Phillips (the respondent) owned the share capital of the company which consisted of 100 £1 shares. The company operated a business in the construction industry. O'Neill (the petitioner) was originally employed as a manual worker, but later he was promoted and then eventually was given 25 shares and made a director. Phillips told O'Neill that he hoped that O'Neill would eventually take over the day-to-day running of the business and would then have 50% of the profits. Phillips then retired and O'Neill ran the company as de facto managing director. The profits were shared 50/50 thereafter and bonus shares were issued pro rata to existing holdings. O'Neill guaranteed the company's bank account. There were discussions about the allotment of more shares, to take O'Neill to a 50% holding when certain asset targets were reached. But this never happened due to a recession and Phillips resumed control of the company. Meanwhile, O'Neill ran the operations abroad. There was an acrimonious meeting, when Phillips told O'Neill that he would no longer receive 50% profits and would only get salary and any dividends on his 25% holding. O'Neill then terminated the guarantee and set up a competing business abroad. O'Neill petitioned, alleging unfair prejudice by reason of Phillips' terminating the equal profit sharing, and repudiation of an alleged agreement to allot more shares.

At first instance the petition was dismissed on the basis that no concluded agreement for profit sharing had been reached, and refusal to allot more shares was not prejudice to O'Neill in his capacity as a member. The Court of Appeal (reported as *Re Pectel Ltd*) allowed the petition, on the basis that although there was no concluded agreement for more shares, O'Neill had a legitimate expectation that he would get them when the targets were reached and a legitimate expectation of 50% of profits. In the House of Lords, the petition was dismissed. Lord Hoffmann's

---

[47] *Ibid.* at p. 441. The judge also made the point that *Re Abbey Leisure* was a case of a winding-up petition and that this diminished its authority. It is respectfully suggested that this is not necessarily a strong criticism because since the early 1980s the courts have assimilated their approach to striking out summonses whether under s. 125 (2) of the Insolvency Act 1986 on the ground that the offer is a reasonable alternative which makes pursuing the petition unreasonable, or under s. 459 of the Companies Act 1985 on the ground that the unfairness has ceased. Furthermore, it is clear from the passage quoted above from the judgment of Harman J in *Re a Company 00330 of 1991, ex parte Holden* that he felt bound by *Re Abbey Leisure Ltd* in the proceedings that were before him even though they were in respect of alleged unfair prejudice.

[48] See *Re Copeland Ltd* [1997] BCC 294, CA.

[49] [1999] BCC 600.

speech[50] reviewed many of the ideas which had been developing and can be taken as clearly settling the approach to be adopted in future cases. It is also a state-of-the-art account of the rationale of this area of law and so is worth quoting at length:[51]

> In section 459 Parliament has chosen fairness as the criterion by which the court must decide whether it has jurisdiction to grant relief ... [content of fairness] will depend upon the context in which it is being used ... and background.
>
> In the case of section 459, the background has the following two features. First, a company is an association of persons for an economic purpose, usually entered into with legal advice and some degree of formality. The terms of the association are contained in the articles of association and sometimes in collateral agreements between the share-holders. Thus the manner in which the affairs of the company may be conducted is closely regulated by rules to which the shareholders have agreed. Secondly, company law has developed seamlessly from the law of partnership, which was treated by equity, like the Roman *societas*, as a contract of good faith. One of the traditional roles of equity, as a separate jurisdiction, was to restrain the exercise of strict legal rights in certain relationships in which it considered that this would be contrary to good faith. These principles have, with appropriate modification, been carried over into company law.
>
> The first of these two features leads to the conclusion that a member of a company will not ordinarily be entitled to complain of unfairness unless there has been some breach of the terms on which he agreed that the affairs of the company should be conducted. But the second leads to the conclusion that there will be cases in which equitable considerations make it unfair for those conducting the affairs of the company to rely upon their strict legal powers. Thus unfairness may consist in a breach of the rules or in using the rules in a manner which equity would regard as contrary to good faith.
>
> This approach to the concept of unfairness in section 459 runs parallel to that which your Lordships' House in *Re Westbourne Galleries Ltd* [1973] AC 360, adopted in giving content to the concept of 'just and equitable' as a ground for winding up ...
>
> ... So I agree with Jonathan Parker J when he said in *Re Astec (BSR) plc* [1999] BCC 59 at p. 86H: 'in order to give rise to an equitable constraint based on "legitimate expectation" what is required is a personal relationship or personal dealings of some kind between the party seeking to exercise the legal right and the party seeking to restrain such exercise, such as will affect the conscience of the former ...'
>
> In *Re Saul Harrison* ... I used the term 'legitimate expectation', borrowed from public law ... It was probably a mistake to use this term, as it usually is when one introduces a new label to describe a concept which is already sufficiently defined in other terms ... The concept of legitimate expectation should not be allowed to lead a life of its own, capable of giving rise to equitable constraints in circumstances to which the traditional principles have no application. This is what seems to have happened in this case.
>
> The Court of Appeal found that by 1991 the company had the characteristics identified by Lord Wilberforce in *Re Westbourne Galleries* ... as commonly giving rise to constraints upon the exercise of powers under the articles. They were (1) an association formed or continued on the basis of a personal relationship involving mutual confidence, (2) an understanding that all, or some, of the shareholders shall participate in the conduct of the business and (3) restrictions on the transfer of shares, so that a member cannot take out his stake and go elsewhere. I agree. It follows that it would have been unfair of Mr Phillips

---

[50] With which the other Lords of Appeal concurred.
[51] [1999] BCC 600, pp. 603–613 *passim*.

to use his voting powers under the articles to remove Mr O'Neill from participation in the conduct of the business without giving him an opportunity to sell his interest in the company at a fair price. Although it does not matter, I should say that I do not think that this was the position when Mr O'Neill first acquired his shares ... He received them as a gift and an incentive and I do not think that in making that gift Mr Phillips could be taken to have surrendered his right to dismiss Mr O'Neill from the management without making him an offer for the shares. But over the following years the relationship changed ... [worked in business, guaranteed overdraft] ...

The difficulty for Mr O'Neill is that Mr Phillips did not remove him from participation in the management of the business ... he remained a director and continued to earn his salary as manager of the business in Germany ... [as regards whether Mr O'Neill] had a legitimate expectation of being allotted more shares when the targets were met ... Mr Phillips never agreed to give them ... there is no basis consistent with established principles of equity, for a court to hold that Mr Phillips was behaving unfairly in withdrawing from the negotiation ... Where, as here, parties enter into negotiations with a view to a transfer of shares on professional advice and subject to a condition that they are not bound until a formal document has been executed, I do not think it is possible to say that an obligation has arisen in fairness or equity at an earlier stage.

The same reasoning applies to the sharing of profits ... Mr Phillips had made no promise to share the profits equally in [the circumstances when he had come back to running the business] ... and it was therefore not inequitable or unfair for him to refuse to carry on doing so.

The judge, it will be recalled, gave as one of his reasons for dismissing the petition the fact that any prejudice suffered by Mr O'Neill was in his capacity as an employee rather than as a shareholder ... [A]ssuming there had been [unfair prejudice] I would not exclude the possibility that prejudice suffered from the breach of that obligation could be suffered in the capacity of shareholder ... As cases ... [have shown] ... the requirement that prejudice must be suffered as a member should not be too narrowly or technically construed. But the point does not arise because no promise was made.

Lord Hoffmann went on to consider the consequences of the fact that the respondent had made an offer to purchase the petitioner's shares at a fair price. Although his Lordship's comments were strictly *obiter* (since it had been held that there was no unfair prejudice), he nevertheless felt that the matter should be considered, because of the practical importance of the effect of an offer by a respondent to purchase the shares of the petitioner.[52] On the facts of *O'Neill* v *Phillips* it was said that the petitioner was justified in rejecting the offer because it did not provide for his costs which had been accumulating in the almost three years since the presentation of the petition. Nevertheless, Lord Hoffmann's general observations are important guidelines:[53]

If the respondent to a petition has plainly made a reasonable offer, then the exclusion as such will not be unfairly prejudicial and he will be entitled to have the petition struck out. It is therefore very important that participants in such companies should be able to know what counts as a reasonable offer.

In the first place, the offer must be to purchase the shares at a fair value. This will ordinarily be a value representing an equivalent proportion of the total issued share capital, that is, without a discount for its being a minority holding ... This is not to say that there

---

[52] See the discussion at p. 238 above.
[53] [1999] BCC 600 at pp. 613–615.

may not be cases in which it will be fair to take a discounted value ...

Secondly, the value, if not agreed, should be determined by a competent expert ...

Thirdly, the offer should be to have the value determined by an expert as an expert. I do not think that the offer should provide for the full machinery of an arbitration or the half-way house of an expert who gives reasons. The objective should be economy and expedition, even if this carries the possibility of a rough edge for one side or the other (and both parties in this respect take the same risk) compared with a more elaborate procedure ...

Fourthly, the offer should, as in this case, provide for equality of arms between the parties. Both should have the same right of access to information about the company which bears upon the value of the shares and both should have the right to make submissions to the expert, though the form (written or oral) which these submissions may take should be left to the discretion of the expert himself.

Fifthly, there is the question of costs ... [p]ayment of costs need not always be offered ... the majority shareholder should be given a reasonable opportunity to make an offer ... before he becomes obliged to pay costs ...

It is fitting that Lord Hoffmann, who played such a major judicial role in the development of the unfair prejudice remedy from the early 1980s onward, should ultimately have been in a position to expound and clarify these important concepts. *O'Neill* v *Phillips* did much to provide guidance to future litigants.[54]

4 Examples of situations remedied

The discussion thus far has largely[55] centred on cases where a share purchase order has been sought, and where the core of the matters complained of relate to exclusion of a shareholder director from management in a quasi-partnership company. But unfair prejudice proceedings have been used to remedy a wide variety of abuses and the judges have taken seriously the jurisdiction of the court to make, in the words of the statute, 'such order as it thinks fit'.[56] However, in spite of this wide discretion, petitioners are expected to state the nature of the relief they seek, and not simply pour out a list of grievances and then leave it up to the court to do something appropriate.[57]

Cases in the early years of the jurisdiction showed it being used to maintain the status quo, pending, say, the holding of a meeting.[58] It has been used successfully to complain of failures to run a company properly such as ignoring the need to hold meetings or produce accounts.[59] A wide variety of abusive share issues or share watering situations have triggered successful petitions.[60] In some circumstances it is possible that failure to declare dividends could be unfairly prejudicial conduct.[61]

---

[54] The principles in *O'Neill* are being applied in many cases; see for instance *Re G H Marshall Ltd* [2001] BCC 152; *Re Phoenix Office Supplies Ltd* [2003] 1 BCLC 76, CA.

[55] Though not exclusively.

[56] Companies Act 1985, s. 461 (1).

[57] See Companies (Unfair Prejudice Applications) Proceedings Rules 1986 (SI 1986 No. 2000).

[58] *Whyte, Petitioner* (1984) 1 BCC 99,044; *Re a Company 002612 of 1984* (1984) 1 BCC 99,262.

[59] *Re a Company 00789 of 1987* (1989) 5 BCC 792, and [1991] BCC 44, CA.

[60] Examples are: *Re a Company 007623 of 1984* (1986) 2 BCC 99,191; *Re a Company 005134 of 1986* (1989) BCLC 383.

[61] *Re Sam Weller Ltd* (1989) 5 BCC 810. But the argument failed on the facts in *Re Saul Harrison Ltd* [1994] BCC 475.

It has even been held possible for a court to make a buy-out order against a third party.[62] In the early days after 1980, lawyers eagerly discussed whether negligence could ever form the substance of a successful petition.[63] Derivative litigation by a minority had not generally been permitted since it was a ratifiable breach.[64] Would it be 'prejudice' but not 'unfair'? Arguably, it was a commercial risk that you accepted by risking your capital when buying into a company. If a person chooses to invest in a company run by fools that was a bad investment decision, and for the law to interfere with that was to cut across the principle of sanctity of bargain in the making of contracts and relieve a party of the consequences of a bad bargain freely made. These considerations have not won the day and the courts have recently made it clear that they are prepared to regard negligence or mismanagement as a matter which could form the subject of a successful petition if it is sufficiently serious.[65]

A useful illustration of the power of the unfair prejudice jurisdiction occurred in the *Windward Islands* saga,[66] which is a rare example of the unfair prejudice jurisdiction being used to overturn directly the effect of a statutory provision. The Companies Act 1948, s. 132[67] contained an important minority shareholders' power whereby members holding 10% or more of the voting shares could require the directors of the company to requisition a meeting. The obvious purpose of it was to enable a minority to get a forum within the company to discuss and resolve matters of dispute. The section provided that: 'The directors of a company . . . shall . . . on the requisition of members . . . forthwith proceed duly to convene . . . [a meeting].' On 13 April 1982 the minority deposited a requisition with the company with the aim of having a meeting to remove two of the directors and 16 days later the directors sent out a notice convening the meeting. It was going to be held several months later, at lunchtime, on Sunday 22 August. Nourse J carried out an impeccable clinical analysis of the statutory provisions and correctly held that this was lawful. The distinction between *convening* a meeting and *holding* one, was there in the statutory provisions.[68] It was an old trick and, as the judge pointed out, had

---

[62] This occurred in *Re Little Olympian Each-Ways Ltd (No. 3)* [1995] 1 BCLC 636, where the petitioner complained that the company's business had been transferred at an undervalue to another company under the same control as the transferor, and it was held that the court had jurisdiction under s. 461 of the Companies Act 1985 to make the buy-out order against that other company. Relief against a third party was similarly granted in *Re Fahey Ltd* [1996] BCC 320. Some aspects of the proceedings in this case had the substance of a derivative action and yet, curiously, it was held that legal aid was available to the petitioner. It was clear that legal aid would not have been available for a derivative action. It remains to be seen whether this is an isolated example, or whether it represents a softening of the rule against aiding corporate claimants in these kinds of cases.

[63] There was also a technical problem connected with the wording of s. 459 which was remedied by amendment in the Companies Act 1989. The words 'or members generally' were added to obviate the argument that certain wrongs, like negligence, damaged the whole company, and not merely the petitioner and so were not within the section; see A.J. Boyle 'The Judicial Interpretation of Part XVII of the Companies Act 1985' in B. Pettet (ed.) *Company Law in Change* (London: Stevens, 1987) pp. 23–27.

[64] *Pavlides v Jensen* [1956] Ch 656; and see further p. 000 above.

[65] *Re Elgindata (No. 1) Ltd* [1991] BCLC 959; *Re Macro Ltd* [1994] BCC 781.

[66] *Re Windward Islands Ltd* (1988) 4 BCC 158.

[67] Now s. 368 of the Companies Act 1985.

[68] See Companies Act 1948, s. 132 (3), which incorporated the distinction between 'convened' and 'held': 'If the directors do not within twenty-one days from the date of the deposit of the requisition

been criticised 20 years earlier by the Jenkins Committee[69] but the recommendations had not been implemented. It was, as he said, 'An oddity, in regard to a section whose evident purpose was to protect minorities . . .'[70] However, once the
statutory provisions were put under the scrutiny of the unfair prejudice jurisdiction,
the result was astonishingly different. In *McGuinness, Petitioners*[71] some of the shareholders deposited their requisition with the company on 4 November 1987 and
'forthwith' on 23 November, their Glasgow based company convened the meeting,
to be held, in London, the following June. The Court of Session affirmed the analysis of Nourse J in *Windward Islands* but held that the shareholders were entitled to
expect that the meeting would be held within a reasonable period and that in the
circumstances this was unfairly prejudicial to their interests. Thus, when applied
head-on against a statutory anomaly, s. 459 can simply reverse the result.[72]

5 Relationship with derivative actions

An obvious problem for analysis is to consider the relationship which the unfair
prejudice action has with the common law[73] derivative action. Does the would-be
litigant sometimes have the choice of bringing either a derivative action or, alternatively, unfair prejudice proceedings? If so, which is the most advantageous procedure? Or will it depend on the circumstances?

The case law now[74] makes it clear that a complaint by a minority shareholder,
which is in substance derivative, in the sense that he is seeking to litigate a breach
by a director of a duty owed to the company, can be the substance of unfair prejudice proceedings. For instance, in *Re Fahey Ltd*[75] the unfairly prejudicial conduct
involved the diversion of company funds, and it was held that the petitioner was
entitled to seek an order against members and directors involved in the unlawful
diversion, for payment to the company itself.[76] Now that the principle has been
established, it is clear that in many ways a derivative claim can be brought more
easily under s. 459 of the Companies Act 1985 than at common law. The exceptions to *Foss* v *Harbottle* are a relatively narrow gateway, negligence is ratifiable,[77]

---

proceed duly to convene a meeting, the requisitionists . . . may themselves convene a meeting, but any
meeting so convened shall not be held after the expiration of three months from the said date.'
[69] Cmnd. 1749, 1962, para. 458.
[70] *Ibid.* para. 161.
[71] (1988) 4 BCC 161.
[72] This problem has now been resolved by s. 368 (8) of the Companies Act 1985, which provides: 'The
directors are deemed not to have duly convened a meeting if they convene a meeting for a date more
than 28 days after the date of the notice convening the meeting': inserted by the Companies Act 1989,
Sch. 19, para. 9.
[73] Or statutory, perhaps, in the future; see p. 228 above.
[74] The early technical worry that the wording of s. 459 of the Companies Act 1989 precluded a complaint about a breach of duty owed to the company was eradicated by an amendment in the
Companies Act 1989. It had been held that a breach of duty which affected all members equally was
not within the section; see *Re Carrington Viyella plc* (1983) 1 BCC 98,951 at p. 98,959, *per* Vinelott
J.
[75] [1996] BCC 320. See also *Re Sherbourne Park Residents Co. Ltd* (1986) 2 BCC 99,528 (where the
point was *obiter*), and *Re a Company 005287 of 1985* (1985) 1 BCC 99,586.
[76] Also against a third party company.
[77] See p. 218 above.

improper share issues are sometimes ratifiable,[78] and yet, under s. 459, there are no such restrictions, and in some situations for instance, negligence can form the substance of a successful complaint under s. 459,[79] as can a range of matters connected with the issues of shares.[80] An additional advantage with using s. 459 to mount a derivative claim is that a wide mix of claims is possible. Litigation at common law can run into judicial resistance if, for instance, personal claims are mixed with derivative claims.[81] Under s. 459 there would normally be no problem if, for example, the petitioner mixed a claim that he was a shareholder director in a quasi-partnership company who had been excluded from management, with a claim that the respondents should replace assets which they had removed from the company. Another advantage which might be enjoyed by unfair prejudice proceedings may be put in the form of a question. Would the derivative litigation mounted in *Smith* v *Croft (No. 2)*[82] have been struck out, if the claimant had brought the proceedings under s. 459? Perhaps they would. It has already been seen[83] that if fairness requires that the proceedings should no longer be continued, then the courts have not hesitated to strike out. And it is arguable that if an action is in substance derivative, and if the theory of *Smith* v *Croft (No. 2)* is right, why should the court not do the same, merely because the proceedings are brought under s. 459? But it would not, surely, have been so easy to strike out. Section 459 gives *locus standi* to the petitioner to bring his complaint to court. Why should the rather curious concept of seeking the opinion of the majority inside a minority be accorded any influence on the situation? The theory of *Smith* v *Croft (No. 2)* is that that is where the untainted decision-making organ of the company at that moment resides. But is there any reason to suppose that the will of the company has any relevance to the bringing of proceedings under the statutory jurisdiction of s. 459? After all, other matters, negligence for example,[84] lie within the grip of the majority at common law, so that ratification prevents a derivative action. But it has been held that this does not cross into s. 459.[85] So why should we assume that *Smith* v *Croft (No. 2)* will cross over?

Are there any situations remaining in which a claimant would ever choose to bring a common law derivative action? There may be a few. First, Wallersteiner orders. It has been seen[86] that in an appropriate case the court will, in effect, order a company to pay for the derivative litigation by granting an indemnity to the minority claimant. The action is being brought to benefit the company and so, the argument runs, the company can be made to pay for it. It is questionable whether the court would do the same in proceedings raising the same substantive matters under s. 459. The theoretical difficulty lies in the point that at common law, the claimant's

---

[78] See p. 218 above.
[79] See p. 244 above.
[80] See p. 244 above.
[81] The joinder of a derivative claim with two personal claims was held to be misconceived in *Prudential Assurance Company Ltd* v *Newman Industries Ltd and others (No. 2)* [1982] Ch 204. Personal claims arising under the articles would normally not fall to be regarded as outside the scope of s. 459.
[82] See p. 222 above.
[83] See further p. 239 above.
[84] And certain abuses of power.
[85] See p. 244 above.
[86] See p. 221 above.

right to sue is derived from the company's right to sue its directors for breach of their duties owed to it. The action is derivative. But that is hardly true under s. 459, the action is statutory. It is not 'derived' from anything. It is given, directly, to a member, to enable him to complain that the company's affairs are being conducted in a manner which is unfairly prejudicial to the interests of the members generally or of some part of its members. It is not therefore so easy to argue that the company should pay for the proceedings, even though the end result might benefit the company, as it would for instance, in the case of an order that the respondents replace assets of the company which they have diverted to themselves. Apart from the theoretical problem that the action is not derivative, there is the wider point that it is clear that as a matter of general policy, the courts have resisted allowing the members to drag companies into paying for s. 459 litigation.[87]

Secondly, it may be that for a shareholder in a large company, litigation at common law is often going to be his only chance of getting a result. Although it is not a hard and fast rule, it is possible that the flexible equitable considerations which normally give rise to the court's decision to grant a remedy are seen as inappropriate in large company where its shares are publicly traded and where the market participants have a right to expect that their purchase decisions are made on the basis of the information which is available to them. This idea was developed by Vinelott J in *Re Blue Arrow plc*.[88] The petitioner had set up various businesses which she ran through a small private company of which she was a director and was the president. She held 45% of the shares. Some years later, the company was converted to a public company and floated on the USM.[89] As a result of the expansion in the number of shareholders, the petitioner's own holding was reduced to only 2% of the overall value of the shares in issue. However, she continued to hold her presidency by virtue of an existing provision in the company's articles of association. For various reasons, the directors had decided that they wanted to remove her and they proposed an alteration of the articles to bring that about. She petitioned under s. 459 to prevent the company from putting to the annual general meeting the proposal to alter the articles, arguing that she had a legitimate expectation that she would participate in the management and affairs of the company. It was held that since outside investors were entitled to assume that the whole of the constitution of the company was contained in the articles, there was therefore no room for any 'legitimate expectations' founded on some agreement made between her and the other directors and kept up their sleeves and not disclosed to the public buying on the USM. It is therefore possible that such reasoning will often put paid to a claim by a petitioner who is a shareholder in a company where there exists a public market for the shares. In some circumstances, a cause of action under the common law exceptions to *Foss* v *Harbottle* will give the shareholder a better chance of success, although that was clearly not the case in *Blue Arrow*.

[87] See e.g. *Re Kenyon Swansea Ltd* [1987] BCLC 514; *Re a Company 004502 of 1988, ex parte Johnson* [1991] BCC 234. For an analysis of these issues in the light of *Clark* v *Cutland* [2003] EWCA Civ 810, [2004] 1 WLR 783, [2003] 4 ALL ER, see A. Reisberg 'Indemnity Costs Orders under S. 459 Petition?' (2004) 25 Co Law 118.

[88] [1987] BCLC 585. The principle has since been confirmed in *Re Astec (BSR) plc* [1999] BCC 59.

[89] The Unlisted Securities Market. It no longer exists and the current broad equivalent is the Alternative Investment Market (AIM).

Thirdly, a claimant might sometimes see an advantage in bringing a common law derivative action because she or he can be fairly sure of limiting the remedy which is granted, whereas under s. 461, she or he could conceivably find themselves getting a result which the court thought was appropriate but which the petitioner would not have wanted. It is fairly unlikely that a court would do this, but it is a theoretical possibility.

6 Relationship with just and equitable winding up

In the early years of the judicial development of the unfair prejudice jurisdiction, it was common for an unfair prejudice petition to include, as an alternative, a claim for winding up on the just and equitable ground.[90] This often also had an *in terrorem* element, since a winding-up order would kill off the company and perhaps the inclusion of it would help to coerce the respondents into making the offer to buy out the petitioner. The practice has been less common since the 1990 *Practice Direction*,[91] which required that a claim for winding up must not be made as a matter of course, and should only be included if winding up is the remedy which is preferred or if it is thought that it might be the only relief available.[92] If no winding-up claim is made but the court concludes that the share purchase order sought in respect of unfair prejudice is an inappropriate remedy, it seems that the court has no power under s. 461 to make a winding-up order instead. In such circumstances a court recently told the petitioner to present a winding-up petition.[93]

The effect of s. 125 (2) of the Insolvency Act 1986 has already been noted[94] but it is worth alluding to again in this context because, the availability of an unfair prejudice remedy might, in some circumstances be held to disentitle the petitioner to wind up.[95] It would be a different remedy and in some circumstances the court might take the view that the petitioner was being unreasonable in not pursuing that remedy.

7 Law Commission reform proposals

The Law Commission, in its reform proposals,[96] was concerned to deal both with the excessive length and cost of unfair prejudice petitions and also to try to reduce the amount of litigation.[97] The Law Commission proposed that the problems of

---

[90] As to which, see the cases referred to on p. 234, n. 18 above.

[91] [1990] 1 WLR 490.

[92] Though facts which fall short of achieving an unfair prejudice remedy will also often fail to achieve a just and equitable winding up because the basic ideas behind these two remedies are similar; see for instance *Re Guidezone Ltd* [2000] 2 BCLC 321.

[93] *Re Full Cup Ltd* [1995] BCC 682.

[94] See p. 232 above.

[95] See *Re a Company 002567 of 1982* [1983] 2 All ER 854; *Re a Company 003843 of 1986* [1987] BCLC 562; *Coulon Sanderson and Ward Ltd* v *Ward* (1986) 2 BCC 99,207, CA; *Re a Company 001363 of 1988* (1989) 5 BCC 18; *Re Abbey Leisure Ltd* [1990] BCC 60, CA.

[96] Law Com. Report No. 246 (Cm. 3769, 1997); and see further p. 228 above.

[97] There were also various technical recommendations relating to other matters, including the operation of the winding-up remedy. As regards this, the Law Commission recommended *inter alia* that winding up should be added to the list of remedies available to a petitioner in unfair prejudice proceed-

excessive length and cost should be dealt with primarily by active case management to be dealt with in the context of the new Woolf rules of court. These would involve techniques such as greater use of the power to direct that preliminary issues be heard, giving the court power to dismiss parts of a case which had no realistic prospect of success, adjournment to facilitate alternative dispute resolution, and increased flexibility on costs orders.

There were also several proposals which would have the effect both of reducing the amount of litigation being brought in the first place and also shorten it up if it was brought. The Law Commission recommended that in certain circumstances[98] there should be a legislative presumption that unfair prejudice will be presumed where the shareholder has been excluded from participation in the management of a private company. This would no doubt act as a major deterrent to litigation in many cases, since it will put considerable pressure on the respondent to settle, as he otherwise faces an uphill task. However, if litigation nevertheless occurs and the presumption is not rebutted, then a second presumption arises, namely that if the court feels that a share purchase order is the appropriate remedy, then that order should be on a pro-rata basis.[99] The other Law Commission suggestion which, if implemented, might arguably operate to prevent litigation arising, is that appropriate provisions should be included in Table A to encourage parties to sort out areas of potential dispute. In particular here, they recommend that Table A contains what they call an 'exit article' the broad effect of which is that the shareholder will have a right to be bought out if he is removed as director.[100]

8 Company Law Review and law reform

The Company Law Review considered the recommendations of the Law Commission in the light of the responses to the DTI's subsequent consultation. The Review strongly supported the proposal for stronger case management (although this is already in operation under the Civil Procedure Rules 1998). However, it was felt that the exit article would not be used in practice owing to its inflexibility; it was impossible to prescribe in advance what would be a fair exit regime.[101] Other matters were also considered (including the desirability of the decision in *O'Neill* v *Phillips*), although the view was expressed that winding up should not be included as remedy under s. 459.[102] In the Final Report the Review came down in favour of not reversing *O'Neill*.[103]

---

ings, that leave should be required before a petitioner under s. 459 could apply for winding up, and, most significantly, leave should be required before a petitioner could apply for winding up in conjunction with an unfair prejudice petition.

[98] The conditions are, broadly, that: the company is a private company limited by shares; that the petitioner has been removed as director or has been prevented from carrying out all or substantially all of his functions as a director; that all, or substantially all the members were directors; that immediately before the exclusion the petitioner held shares giving him 10% of the voting rights; see further Law Com. Report No. 246 (Cm. 3769, 1997) para. 8.4.

[99] *Ibid.* paras 8.5–8.6.

[100] *Ibid.* para. 8.9.

[101] DTI Consultation Document (March 2000) *Developing the Framework* para. 4.103.

[102] *Ibid.* paras 4.104–4.111.

[103] *Modern Company Law for a Competitive Economy Final Report* (London: DTI, 2001), paras 7.41–7.45.

PART IV

CORPORATE FINANCE LAW

14

TECHNIQUES OF CORPORATE FINANCE

14.1 SOME BASIC CONCEPTS OF CORPORATE FINANCE

A Assets and capital

In order to perform a trading or manufacturing activity a company will need assets. What exactly is needed will depend on the type, size and complexity of the business operations to be conducted, but one could imagine that it might need to take a lease of premises, perhaps a factory, install machinery, acquire office furniture, computers and communications equipment, storage facilities and hire staff. Decisions will have to be made about the acquisition of each of these items and once the company is up and running, decisions will continue to have to be made about the purchase of further assets, even if this is simply confined to replacing existing assets which have become worn out or have been used up. Each of these decisions is an investment decision, and the financial success or failure of the company will depend, in large measure, on these decisions being well made. They are of course, decisions about how the company's money is to be invested.

Which brings us to the next[1] question: 'Where does the money come from?' The broad answer is that companies sell claims against them in return for money, for capital. That capital can then be used to finance the company's investment decisions. The claims that they sell will fall into one or other of two categories; equity or debt. The term 'equity' can mean different things in different contexts, but here it means the risk bearing shares, usually[2] what are called ordinary shares. A purchaser of an ordinary share will usually be purchasing a package of rights which can be described as 'residual' in the sense that he or she and the other ordinary shareholders, in proportion to their shareholdings, will lay claim to what remains of the assets[3] of the company after those with fixed money sum claims (i.e. the creditors) have been paid. The term 'debt' denotes a claim against the company

---

[1] 'Next' for the purposes of this account. In a practical sense, answering it and taking effective action on it is a prerequisite to the company's being able to put into effect any investment decisions.

[2] The position is complicated by hybrid types of shares such as participating preference shares, particularly where the participation is as to capital; see e.g. *Bannatyne* v *Direct Spanish Telegraph Co.* (1886) 34 Ch D 287. In some situations, preference capital can turn into equity in the sense of becoming residual owners as a result of a rationalisation of loss of capital; see *Re Floating Dock* [1895] 1 Ch 691. These cases are discussed at p. 285 and 283 below respectively.

[3] Obviously under the *Salomon* doctrine, they are not, qua shareholders, entitled to the assets of the company; but behind this legal doctrine lies the financial reality that in a liquidation, the ordinary shareholders are the residual owners of the assets of the company.

for the payment at a future date of a fixed money sum, usually with interest accruing pending repayment of the principal sum. Thus a company will raise the money it needs to finance its investment decisions by issuing equity securities, or by borrowing, either by obtaining loans from banks or by issuing debt securities.[4] In order to operate efficiently the company will need to raise the capital as cheaply as possible, by issuing its shares for the highest prices possible and issuing debt securities at the lowest interest rates possible.[5]

B The aims of the company

In modern corporate finance doctrine, the aims of the company will normally be to maximise shareholder wealth or as it is often called, shareholder value.[6] Maximising shareholder wealth/value is not the same as maximising profits, although in the long term the latter will have much bearing on the former. Profits are an accountancy-based concept which depend upon measuring net gains according to accountancy practice over a defined period of time, usually a year. Shareholder wealth is concerned with the flow of dividends to the shareholder over a long period of time. The current share price on the market will reflect the expected future dividend flow and so the current share price is taken as the measure of shareholder wealth. Thus the basic financial goal for the board of directors will be to get and keep the share price as high as possible.[7]

C Cash flows and capital raising

Much of the work of the finance director with overall responsibility for the financial well-being of the company is taken up with the management of cash flows and hence a considerable portion of corporate finance theory is concerned with cash flow. One of the basic problems which confronts a company is that there is a time gap between its outgoing cash flow when it purchases assets and the incoming cash flow when it sells a product or service which it has created out of those assets. Developing techniques to bridge these gaps is a fundamental part of corporate finance theory.

In order to create shareholder value, a firm needs to generate more cash flow than it uses, by buying assets that generate more cash than they use, and selling financial instruments in order to raise cash.[8] Seen in terms of cash flow, shareholder value will have been created where the cash flows out of the firm to the shareholders (and loan creditors) are higher than the cash flows which they put into it.[9]

---

[4] On the different types of equity and debt securities, see pp. 262–275 below.

[5] See generally S. Ross *et al. Corporate Finance* 5th edn (Boston, MA: Irwin Mcgraw-Hill, 1997) pp. 1–5.

[6] This of course assumes that the company has not decided to operate in a way which elevates some other aim above the pursuit of maximum shareholder wealth. As has been seen (p. 61 above) some aspects of stakeholder philosophy might appear to require this, although as has also been argued, if stakeholder policies result in efficiency gains, then there may be no conflict with the principle of maximising shareholder wealth. Aside from stakeholder doctrine, some companies sometimes make the decision to operate on a broader basis than profit motive, such as co-operative societies.

[7] See generally G. Arnold *Corporate Financial Management* (London: Financial Times Management, 1998) pp. 4–14.

[8] See Ross *et al.*, n. 5 above, at p. 5.

[9] *Ibid.*

The techniques of managing cash flows[10] are very much the province of specialist books on corporate finance.[11] These books also deal in detail with the techniques of capital raising; and here there is an overlap with the study of company law. Since a considerable part of company law is concerned with the law relating to how companies finance themselves, it is useful to examine briefly the techniques which companies employ to raise the finance needed to fund their activities.

14.2 FINANCING THE COMPANY

A Initial finance

In the first instance, for most companies, the initial source of finance comes from cash provided by the entrepreneur promoters themselves, or by a bank. Typically, the promoters will utilise their savings, or use money from a recent redundancy, or remortgage their houses, or persuade relatives to let them have money.[12] Wherever it comes from, the promoters will use the money to subscribe for equity shares in the company.[13] They could endeavour to persuade others to take shares, but of course, this may mean diluting their control and they may be reluctant to do this. Quite often a person can be found, perhaps through business contacts such as the firm's accountant, who will be prepared to take a small equity stake in the company and give advice to the promoters. In modern jargon such persons are referred to as 'business angels'[14] but the type is not new.[15]

Many companies will also rely on bank finance to provide initial capital. This will not always be forthcoming, owing to the very high risk of failure of the business at this stage and the bank will usually require a floating charge over the company's assets[16] and security over the promoter's own assets and/or personal guarantees from him and any others whom he can persuade to support him. In an attempt to overcome this problem the government operates a small firms loans guarantee scheme.[17] In some circumstances, other sources of financial help might be available such as hire purchase, credit sale and leasing agreements.

If the company's initial capital requirements are well beyond what can be raised through any of the above sources, then it will need to turn to the venture capital

---

[10] And many other aspects of corporate finance techniques.

[11] See Arnold, n. 7 above, at pp. 49–133; Ross *et al.*, n. 5 above, at pp. 5–41.

[12] The members will not always wish to bring their capital to the company in the form of money. It is possible to make contributions in kind (although subject to the rules on share discounts discussed at p. 276 below) and a particularly common form of this is where the promoter is already operating some form of small business either as a sole trader (or in partnership with others) and desires to incorporate that business. He will sell and transfer the business he owns to the company and in return receives an allotment of fully paid-up shares in the company.

[13] Instead of taking equity shares, a promoter may wish to form a company with only one £1 issued share but finance its business activities by making a loan from himself to the company. If the loan is secured by a floating charge it will give him priority over the trade creditors in a subsequent liquidation. The *Salomon* case (p. 23 above) is a striking example of the effectiveness of this.

[14] See further 'Venture capital financing' below.

[15] The person who provided the debenture to Salomon's new company (Mr Broderip) could perhaps be described as a 'business angel'; see p. 24 above.

[16] Obviously in priority to any taken by the promoter.

[17] See the Business Support section in the DTI's website: http://www.dti.gov.uk.

industry for initial financing, or, in rare cases of initial financing, make an offer of shares to the public and seek a stock exchange quotation.[18]

B Venture capital financing

Venture capital[19] is most commonly seen as a middle stage of finance suitable for companies which are growing in size but which are not yet ready to make a public offering of shares and seek a stock market quotation.[20] However, as has been suggested above, it is sometimes available for companies which have not yet started trading. Entrepreneurs seeking venture capital will usually be concerned to ensure that they do not part with control of the company on a permanent basis. For this reason, redeemable securities are often used, or other arrangements which enable the entrepreneurs to free themselves from the venture capitalist within, say, a five-year period.

The venture capital industry has seen enormous growth since the early 1980s, and since 1984 has invested more than £50bn in around 22,000 companies. In 2003, around 1,500 UK companies received a total of £6.4bn in venture capital financing.[21] Venture capital comes from two main sources: 'business angels' and venture capital firms. The former are individuals who have expertise in entrepreneurial activity and spare money to invest. Business angels usually invest between £40,000 and £500,000 in a company.[22] Venture capital firms obtain their capital from various sources, principally from institutions such as pension funds, but also from banks and individuals. They usually target firms which are seeking an investment of over £100,000. In 2002, the overall average deal size was around £2.7m.[23] Recent years have seen an internationalisation of venture capital, especially in continental Europe as UK and US venture capital companies seek to find new investment opportunities; for instance, 3i Group plc[24] has recently been reported as having eight offices and more than 60 executives in Europe.[25]

The venture capital industry broadly categorises the investment stages of a company's life into: seed corn (to finance the development of a business idea, prior to trading), start-up (further developments prior to trading), early stage (finance for the commencement of trading), expansion (finance for a successful company, to enable further growth),[26] management buy-outs (MBOs, where the managers buy

---

[18] As happened with the financing of the Channel Tunnel, for which the initial equity finance (of £976m) needed to be raised by an international placing and offers for sale in the UK and France. Without such public offerings, the project would not even have seemed viable at the outset; see further T. Stocks *Corporate Finance: Law and Practice* (London: Longman, 1992) pp. 55–72. Additionally, there was £5,000m of debt finance from banks.

[19] Or 'private equity' as it is often called.

[20] Or a placing; see p. 261 below.

[21] Statistics from BVCA Report on Investor Activity 2003; see the British Venture Capital Association (BVCA) website: http://www.bvca.co.uk.

[22] See Business Angel Finance 2003–2004, on the BVCA website; see previous note.

[23] See previous note.

[24] The UK's oldest and largest venture capital organisation.

[25] 'European Private Equity' *Financial Times*, 10 October 1997.

[26] Although it perhaps should be emphasised that much of the finance which is available to companies for growth comes from retained profits; equity and debt finance (and various other sources) provide the remainder.

the business), management buy-ins (MBIs, where a group of managers from out-side the company buy the business).[27] Owing to the high risks involved with new companies, most venture capital firms will confine their inputs to expansion, MBOs and MBIs, leaving the business angels to provide seed corn, start-up, and early stage finance. The venture capital provider will usually make his money out of the capital gain arising on the equity shares or other investments which he took in return for the capital which he provided. Various methods of realising the gain are employed: selling the shares to another company in the sector which needs the business,[28] share repurchase by the company or its management, refinancing,[29] or, in the very successful cases, a flotation of the company on the Stock Exchange or some other market which will provide liquidity.

C Public offerings of securities

1 Effects on management

When a company needs very large amounts of capital to enable it to expand to the size which the directors think would be economically beneficial, it will usually need to make an offering of shares to the public and arrange to have the shares publicly quoted on a stock exchange. Usually in this situation, the company will have a long and successful trading record and will have grown to its present size as a result of inputs of venture capital. This is not always the case and sometimes, although rarely, a company will not have started trading prior to making a public offering, as happened with Eurotunnel which needed to raise large sums of money before it could see its way ahead sufficiently to commence the vast project.[30] In recent years a number of 'dot.com' Internet companies have produced versions of this phenomenon, having very little trading base but seeking large amounts of public capital.

Seen from the point of view of managers seeking to expand their company there are three main advantages of a public offering:

(1) Assuming that the company is financially attractive, they will be in a position to raise almost unlimited amounts of capital over a long period of time, in the initial offering and in later offerings.
(2) The shares will be made more attractive to buyers (with the effect that the cost of the capital to the company will be lower) because they are liquid investments by virtue of the fact that there will be a ready market which will enable share-holders to 'exit' whenever they wish.
(3) With publicly quoted shares the company will be in a position to grow by making share for share takeover bids for other companies.

For the management, these advantages come at a price. The Stock Exchange quotation will bring pressures on them through increased monitoring by the financial

---

[27] Venture capital also has a role to play in 'rescue situations' when the company has got into difficulties.
[28] Trade sale.
[29] I.e. selling the shares to another venture capital company.
[30] See the Eurotunnel example, n. 18 above.

press, through continuing obligations to maintain the quotation,[31] and through increased self-regulatory burdens such as the Combined Code. They will also become subject to market disciplines, because with a public offering will come dispersed ownership of the shares making the company potentially subject to a hostile takeover bid. The risk of this will increase if the company is seen to be underperforming other companies in that sector of industry. Very often, a public offering will mean that the entrepreneurs who founded the company will find that their controlling shareholding in the company is massively diluted after flotation. They may not like the loss of influence and control which this brings, nor perhaps fully appreciate the consequences of it in advance.[32] Very occasionally, a company which has gone public in this way will be taken private again by its former entrepreneur, who, for whatever reasons, has become disenchanted with the new situation.

2 The London Stock Exchange – initial public offerings and flotation

The London Stock Exchange (LSE) plays an important role in the facilitation of UK corporate finance mainly by providing the mechanisms of the market for the trading of shares which have been issued to the public. In addition to complying with the Stock Exchange's rules for admission to trading,[33] a company seeking access to the market will also have to comply with the Listing Rules issued by the Financial Services Authority as the UK Listing Authority.[34] Before the securities can be admitted to that market, they will need to be sufficiently widely held by the public that their marketability when listed can be assumed. Thus a company coming to the market for the first time will normally make an initial public offering (IPO) by one of the methods approved by the Stock Exchange.[35] Closely co-ordinated, there will then be a second stage[36] of the overall process, often called 'flotation',[37] in which the securities of the company are admitted to the market and trading in them begins.[38] Prior to flotation its shares will have been relatively closely held by management and other private individuals, venture capital companies and possibly by a few other financial institutions. After making an IPO and subsequent flotation on the LSE, its share ownership will be widely spread among very many financial institutions and private individuals worldwide. Its shares will be traded on a daily basis and thereafter its reputation and fortunes will largely depend on its current share price in the market.

The LSE currently operates two markets for the trading of shares which have been issued to the public. The Main Market,[39] and also a smaller market for

---

[31] See further p. 369 below.
[32] See e.g. *Re Blue Arrow plc* discussed at p. 247 above.
[33] *The Admission and Disclosure Standards*; see p. 365 below.
[34] UKLA.
[35] And UKLA; see further below.
[36] These two stages are sometimes loosely referred to as the primary market and the secondary market.
[37] The word 'flotation' is not really a term of art and both stages together, seen as a unified whole are quite often referred to as 'flotation'.
[38] The London Stock Exchange is not the only secondary market in the UK but in terms of trading volume and capitalisation it is by far the most significant.
[39] This used to be called the 'Listed Market' but since the transfer of the LSE's functions under the Listing Directives to the Financial Services Authority (FSA) as the UK Listing Authority (UKLA) that name has been dropped; see further p. 362.

younger 'fledgling' companies, called the Alternative Investment Market (AIM). The regulatory criteria for AIM are less onerous than for the Main Market and so securities marketed on AIM are generally a riskier investment.[40] There are around 1,900 companies listed on the Main Market, and 790 quoted on AIM.[41] Although the LSE is not quite the world's biggest market for domestic securities[42] it has the largest volume of non-domestic trading. Trading on the Main Market has for many years been based on a system of competing market makers, under which the market makers throughout the trading day[43] offer buying and selling prices in the shares for which they are registered as market makers and for which they are committed to quoting buy and sell prices, making their living from the margin (i.e. difference) between the buying and selling price. Market makers deal with financial institutions direct, whereas members of the public need to go through a broker/dealer.[44] In recent years the trading systems have been subjected to a rolling programme of modernisation. Buying and selling prices are displayed on an automated price information system, called SEAQ.[45] This ensures that information about available prices and volume of trading is readily available throughout the market. Actual trading is done by telephone, although the process is becoming computerised. Settlement[46] of trades is mainly done through a paperless system called CREST,[47] which enables shareholders to hold their shares in a CREST account in a manner similar in some ways to a bank account, rather than by holding paper share certificates.

For the very largest companies[48] in which there is a very high volume of daily trading, a new fully computerised trading system called SETS[49] has been implemented. SETS permits an alternative to market making trading by allowing brokers to place on-screen offers to buy and sell only those blocks of shares which they wish to trade at that moment. This 'order-driven' system aims to give investors a better deal since it cuts out the market makers and their profit. It is also intended that it will make the London Stock Exchange more competitive as an international exchange.

As an institution, the London Stock Exchange has recently been going through upheavals as great as at any time in its history.[50] The main impetus for this has been

---

[40] However, the term 'market' is fluid, and it should also be mentioned that there is also a new facility called techMARK which is available for innovative technology companies which have been admitted to the Main Market; in effect it is a market grouping, or market within a market. On similar lines there is also techMARK Mediscience, and landMARK (regional groupings). For international securities there is the International Order Book and the International Bulletin Board.

[41] See LSE website: http://www.londonstockexchange.com. Site visited in September 2004.

[42] The New York Stock Exchange and the Tokyo Stock Exchange are bigger.

[43] I.e. during the mandatory quote period, which runs from 08.00hrs to 16.30hrs.

[44] I.e. stockbroker.

[45] Stock Exchange Automated Quotation. Trading on AIM is carried out on an automated trading system called SEATS PLUS (Stock Exchange Alternative Trading Service), a computer system which is specially adapted to securities where there is much less trading taking place; and often only one market maker for each stock.

[46] I.e. transfer of shares from seller to buyer and corresponding payment.

[47] Replacing the older and only partially computerised system called TALISMAN.

[48] Currently the FTSE 100 and a few others.

[49] Stock Exchange Electronic Trading System. Also called the 'order book'. There is also a new hybrid system called SETS mm.

[50] Save perhaps the great changes which occurred in the 1986 'Big Bang', which permitted firms which were not members of the Stock Exchange to take ownership stakes in member firms, thus opening the

the internationalisation of capital markets[51] and the consequent competition from securities exchanges in other countries. Developments have occurred all of which can be attributed, at least in part, to the relentless pressure on the Stock Exchange to modernise and become more commercially orientated in order to compete successfully with other international exchanges. First, the London Stock Exchange has demutualised. Its former status was as a 'mutual',[52] owned by the member firms; its new status as a public limited company is intended to enable it to raise the capital needed in future times to maintain or improve its position in the world league.

The second development has been the transfer of the regulatory and monitoring functions required by the EC Directives on Listing to the Financial Services Authority (FSA) acting as the UK Listing Authority (UKLA). These matters are discussed in some detail in Chapter 20 and the reasons for the transfer are explored there. However, it is important to observe here that although a company wishing to list in the UK will need to comply with the FSA Listing Rules in order to be admitted to the Official List by UKLA, it will also have to comply with the London Stock Exchange's Admission and Disclosure Standards.[53]

Thirdly, as trading on Europe's securities markets becomes ever more internationalised and the markets themselves become less easy to identify with particular territorial bases, then the London Stock Exchange has been facing increased competition from other markets and trading platforms such as Euronext.[54] The growth in alternative trading systems (ATSs) operated by investment firms has also provided a source of competition.[55]

3 Methods of flotation

There are currently five[56] main methods by which a company which is coming to the Main Market for the first time can make an IPO: an offer for sale, offer for subscription, a placing, an intermediaries offer,[57] or by book-building.

Historically, the offer for sale has often been used for large flotations partly

---

way for foreign (mainly US) firms to establish a presence in the City of London, and increased competition by abolishing minimum commissions.

[51] One feature of this is that companies have sometimes found it worth their while to seek an additional listing in another country; for further discussion of the implications of this phenomenon see p. 58 above.

[52] I.e. an unincorporated association usually regarded as being owned by the members from time to time.

[53] These are designed to run in parallel with the Listing Rules to avoid unnecessary duplication.

[54] Euronext was formed by a merger of the stock exchanges of Amsterdam, Brussels, Paris and Lisbon. It also took over the London International Financial Futures and Options Exchange (LIFFE); see http://www.euronext.com. Other markets providing elements of competition are Virt-x (formed by a merger between Tradepoint and SWX); see http://www.virt-x.com and OFEX (Off-Exchange Trading Facility) see http://www.ofex.com. The LSE has recently opened a new European market called EUROSETS, and a new derivatives market called EDX London.

[55] The traditional stock exchanges in the US have faced similar competition from the development of their over-the-counter markets such as the National Association of Securities Dealers Automated Quotation (NASDAQ), which specialises in high growth technology stocks.

[56] If the company already has sufficient securities in issue, it will sometimes be able to obtain entry to the Main Market without the need for an IPO. This is known as an 'introduction'. Sometimes other methods will be permitted. If the company already has shares listed then other methods will be open to it; see p. 262 below.

[57] The point in the previous note might often be applicable here also.

because the Listing Rules limited the size of placings to raising £15m.[58] This limit has been lifted and so placings are currently being used for much larger flotations than was formerly the case. The legal mechanism of an offer for sale involves the company allotting the shares to an investment bank which will then offer[59] the shares to the public. From the company's point of view the issue is effectively underwritten because if the bank cannot sell the shares it will be left with them, unless it has made its own arrangements for other banks to underwrite the issue. If the issue is very large then a syndicate of banks will jointly offer the shares for sale. As well as getting the public to purchase the shares the process of flotation involves ensuring that the shares become listed on the Stock Exchange. This aspect of it will also be handled by the investment bank in their capacity as sponsors.[60] It is they who will prepare the company for listing by UKLA and admission to the Main Market by the LSE.[61] In addition, a flotation will require an accountant who will be required to carry out a thorough investigation into the company's affairs and to produce financial information or a report.[62] Solicitors will be needed to advise the parties and to draft much of the necessary documentation. It will also be necessary to appoint a firm of registrars to handle the huge volume of applications.

An 'offer for subscription' is a variant of the offer for sale, where the shares are not allotted to the investment bank but instead the bank makes the offer on behalf of the company which then allots the shares to the applicants. It is sometimes combined with an offer for sale. Underwriting will also normally be arranged.

A 'placing' involves the company allotting shares[63] to the investment bank which will then 'place' the shares with its institutional investor clients. It does not involve an offer to the general public and avoids the expense of advertising and other matters associated with an offer for sale or offer for subscription. Coupled with the placing will be an arrangement for the shares to be admitted to the Main Market.

An 'intermediaries offer' is similar to a placing but the shares are offered to other intermediaries (i.e. investment banks) for them to allocate to their own clients.

In recent years a technique called 'book-building', originally developed in the US, has come to be used in European IPOs, particularly by US investment banks operating in Europe. In the UK, versions of it were used by the Treasury in many of the major privatisations to enable them to compile a picture of the strength of institutional demand over a range of prices. It involves an investment bank seeking information from institutional investors about how many shares they are willing to take at particular prices. When all the information is compiled it enables the bank to determine the appropriate offer price.

---

[58] Or £30m if the intermediaries offer mechanism was used, which would result in the shares being more widely disseminated than under a normal placing.

[59] In technical legal terms the offer is actually made when members of the public respond to the advertisement and offering to buy the shares; see *Re Metropolitan Fire Insurance Co.* [1900] 2 Ch 671.

[60] The FSA Listing Rules require the appointment of a sponsor if an application for listing is being made; FSA Listing Rules, Chap. 2, para. 2.3. In some circumstances such as where there is a public sector issuer involved the appointment of a listing agent will be required instead; *ibid.* para. 2.5.

[61] The obligation to publish a prospectus and similar matters are dealt with below in Chapter 19.

[62] FSA Listing Rules, Chap. 12, paras 12.1–12.7.

[63] Or agreeing to allot.

This brief account has dealt with a flotation on the Main Market. An AIM flotation will be subject to the AIM Rules rather than the FSA Listing Rules and the LSE Admission and Disclosure Standards, and these are generally more relaxed, although they do require the company to have a nominated adviser as a prerequisite to AIM membership. This role is similar to that of sponsor in a Main Market flotation and will normally be filled by an investment bank. An IPO on AIM is normally carried out by a placing.

4 Subsequent capital raising – rights issues

At some stage after flotation, a company will often find that it needs further capital. It will often seek to obtain this by way of a 'rights issue'.[64] A rights issue is an offer of shares to the existing shareholders of the company in proportion to the size of their existing holdings. Rights issues have been very much part of the culture of the City and additionally ss. 89–96 of the Companies Act 1985 require an offer of equity shares to be made to existing shareholders[65] although provisions can be disapplied. The offer is usually made attractive to the shareholders by making it at a discount of 10–15% to the quoted price of the existing shares; occasionally a deep discount technique of around 50% is employed.[66] The terms of the offer will ensure that the rights can only be taken up within a short period of time. Quite often, the rights issue is of the type known as an open offer, under which the rights cannot be subsequently traded; this is sometimes thought to have the effect of increasing the pressure on the existing shareholders to take up the offer.

5 Raising capital through debt

As has been seen,[67] companies also raise capital through debt.[68] Debt finance comes from two main sources, bank lending and the capital markets, although only the very large companies will use the capital markets to finance their borrowings. Bank lending usually takes the form of short-term overdraft facilities, or medium-term loans where the borrowed sum and interest is repaid in instalments throughout the term,[69] or by the supply of revolving credit facilities. The bank will often seek security.[70] In the case of a very large loan a syndicate of banks will each contribute a portion of it.

---

[64] In addition, a company which already has shares listed will have other methods of bringing the securities to listing; see FSA Listing Rules, Chap. 4, para. 4.1.

[65] See further p. 283 below. Further rules are made in the Listing Rules, Chap. 4, paras 4.16–4.21; Chap. 9, paras 9.16–9.23.

[66] The shareholders are initially given 'letters of right' which they can sell if they do not wish to take up the offer themselves.

[67] At p. 255 above.

[68] Detailed analysis of this is beyond the scope of this book. For an excellent account of the role of debt in corporate finance and the legal aspects see E. Ferran *Company Law and Corporate Finance* (Oxford: OUP, 1999) pp. 457–564. See further E. Ferran 'Creditors' interests and "core" company law' (1999) 20 Co Law 314.

[69] Sometimes called 'term loans'.

[70] For the effect of this in liquidation, see p. 413 below.

Companies wishing to raise debt finance from the capital markets will usually do so by issuing bonds or other securities. Bonds (or debentures)[71] are documents which acknowledge a debt (owed by the company to the lender). They are usually long-term finance in the sense that the principal sum is often expressed to be repayable up to a decade in the future. Shorter-term arrangements are often referred to as loan notes or commercial paper. In addition there are many other forms of debt financing, in particular the Eurobond market which falls outside the control of the UK regulatory authorities.[72]

A company which chooses to have debt as part of its capital structure in addition to equity shares will find that it may make the market share price more volatile and the ratio of debt to equity which a company chooses is a fundamental decision that may affect its financial well-being or survival. The debt/equity ratio is known as gearing; a company which has a lot of debt compared to equity is described as highly geared. High gearing can make the share price volatile by creating a business in which the equity shareholders have provided only a small part of the overall working capital. Since they are the residual owners of the company, when the company is doing well they will be entitled to all the profits of the largely debt-financed business after the interest on the debt has been paid; thus the profits are shared among a relatively small group of people. Conversely, if the company's fortunes change, it will quickly find that the profits are eaten up in servicing the debts with the result that there will be little or nothing remaining for the equity shares.

14.3 THE LAW RELATING TO SHARES

A Definitions of share capital

The memorandum of association of a company contains a capital clause which *inter alia* must 'state the amount of share capital with which the company proposes to be registered and the division of the share capital into shares of a fixed amount'.[73] Thus, it will state, for example, 'The company's share capital is £50,000 divided into 50,000 shares of £1 each'. Several points about this emerge.

The reference in the capital clause to 'the amount of share capital with which the company proposes to be registered' is a reference to what is usually termed its 'authorised' capital (sometimes though less commonly, it is called 'nominal' capital). This 'authorised' capital bears virtually no relationship to the actual money that is being put into the company when it is first formed and it simply means the amount of share capital which the company is allowed to issue without needing to alter the capital clause in the memorandum to sanction the issue of more. Thus, in the example above, which comes from Table B, the authorised capital is £50,000 but the example in Table B then continues on the basis that the two subscribers to the memorandum are only actually taking *one* share each. It should finally be noted that this 'authorised' capital refers to the total amount which the company is

---

[71] If the bond is secured it will usually these days be referred to as a 'debenture'.
[72] Although it is subject to forms of self-regulation.
[73] Companies Act 1985, s. 2 (5) (a). There are certain exceptions, *ibid*.

authorised to issue without needing to change its memorandum; it does not mean that the directors of the company are necessarily authorised to go ahead and issue shares up to that amount.[74]

The capital clause in the memorandum speaks of 'the division of the share capital into shares *of a fixed amount*'. The need for a share to have a 'fixed amount' is often described as its having a 'nominal' value. When the company is first formed the nominal value of its issued shares will usually bear a reasonably close relationship to the real or market value. After a very short time, this is no longer the case. For instance, a company formed at the beginning of the week with 100 £1 shares may have lost in trading the £100 thus raised, by the end of the week. The shares will still have a nominal value of £1 but probably no market value.

Reform committees have recommended that companies should be permitted to issue shares having no nominal value[75] but no action has ever been taken on this; probably because people are used to operating under the present system and there has been little advantage seen in any change.[76] It has been held that it is not necessary for the 'fixed amount' to be in UK currency. It is possible even to have different classes of shares each denominated in a different currency. In *Re Scandanavian Bank Group plc*[77] the company was intending to have a share capital of £30m, US$30m, SFr30m, and DM30m. Each of these four classes of shares were to be divided into 300 million shares of, respectively, 10 pence each, 10 US cents each, 10 Swiss centimes each and 10 German pfennigs each. Harman J held that this was permissible and was within s. 2 (5) (a) of the Companies Act 1985.

It is common practice to issue shares on the basis that the allottee need not pay, for the time being, the whole nominal value of the shares. If a share of a nominal value of £1 is issued on terms that only 75 pence needs to be paid up, then that 75 pence is referred to as the 'paid up' share capital and the £1 share is said to be 'partly paid'. The remaining 25 pence will be made payable at a future date, possibly only on the occurrence of a certain contingency such as liquidation. With a public company, s. 101 of the 1985 Act provides that its share must be 'paid up at least as to one-quarter of its nominal value and the whole of any premium'.

Certain provisions in the Companies Act 1985 mention or relate to called up share capital[78] and for the sake of clarity s. 737 gives a definition of called up share capital. In essence, the Act provides that the called up share capital means the total of capital already paid up, together with any share capital which must be paid on a specified future date by virtue of provisions contained in the articles, the terms of allotment or other arrangements relating to payment.

The term 'issued share capital' refers to the total nominal value of the shares which have been allotted to shareholders. A company's unissued share capital is the difference between its issued share capital and the amount of capital it is permitted to issue[79] by the capital clause in the memorandum.

---

[74] See further at p. 266 below.
[75] See the Gedge Committee, in 1954, Cmd. 9112 and the Jenkins Committee, in 1962, Cmnd. 1749.
[76] The matter is again under consideration by the law reform agencies; see at p. 292 below.
[77] (1987) 3 BCC 93.
[78] E.g. Companies Act 1985, ss. 43 (3) and 264 (1).
[79] I.e. its authorised capital.

For a public company there is a minimum issued share capital requirement, the 'authorised minimum' which is currently £50,000 which as with all public company share capital, must be paid up to at least a quarter of the nominal value and the whole of any premium on it.[80]

B Increase and alterations of capital

Section 121 (1) of the Companies Act 1985 provides for the alteration of share capital and accordingly of the capital clause in the memorandum, provided that power is contained in the articles and other procedures are carried out.[81] In the 1985 Table A the power is provided by art. 32, which makes it clear that it can be exercised by ordinary resolution. Section 121 (2) sets out the possibilities, and provides that the company may:

(a) increase its share capital by new shares of such amount as it thinks expedient; [This means that it can increase the authorised capital.]

(b) consolidate and divide all or any of its share capital into shares of larger amount than its existing shares; [This means that for instance 5 shares of 20 pence may be consolidated into shares of £1 nominal value.]

(c) convert all or any of its paid up shares into stock, and re-convert that stock into paid up shares of any denomination; [Share stock differs from shares in that the shares out of which the stock is created are treated as merged into one fund which can then be transferred as a complete unit. Thus 100 £1 shares converted into £100 worth of stock could then be transferred in units of as little as 1 pence, whereas as shares, the minimum transferable unit here would be £1. The articles of association have often provided, however, that the minimum amount of stock that can be transferred is, for instance, £1. If so, this negates the advantage of having stock rather than shares. Formerly, stock also had certain administrative advantages but this is no longer the case.]

(d) subdivide its shares, or any of them, into shares of smaller amount than is fixed by the memorandum ... [but subject to subsection (3) which provides] ... in any sub-division under subsection (2) (d) the proportion between the amount paid and the amount, if any, unpaid on each reduced share must be the same as it was in the case of the shares from which the reduced share is derived. [This enables the company to reduce the nominal value of shares when the actual stock market value has risen to more than a few pounds since for reasons of practice it is felt that shares become less marketable when they acquire a value of more than a few pounds.][82]

(e) cancel shares which, at the date of the passing of the resolution to cancel them, have not been taken or agreed to be taken by any person, and diminish the amount of the company's share capital by the amount of the shares so cancelled. [This it is stressed, is not a reduction of capital within s. 135[83] but is

---

[80] Companies Act 1985, ss. 117–118, 101 (1).
[81] *Ibid.* ss. 122–123.
[82] See G. Holmes and A. Sugden *Interpreting Company Reports and Accounts* 3rd edn (Cambridge: Woodhead-Faulkner, 1987) at p. 15.
[83] See p. 282 below.

merely the converse of para. (a) above, namely a reduction in authorised capital.]

C Authority to issue share capital

Section 80 of the Companies Act 1985 limits the power of the directors to issue shares.[84] Generally, they may not do so unless authorised by the company in general meeting or the articles. Such authorisation may be given for a particular exercise of the power or for its exercise generally and conditions may be attached. In addition to the various detailed provisions in s. 80, s. 80A provides exemptions for private companies from authorisation and s. 88 requires a return of allotments to be made to the Registrar. Public offerings of public company shares are subject to further provisions.[85]

D Preferential subscription rights

The legislation provides existing equity shareholders of the company with preferential subscription rights in the event of an issue of further shares.[86] The highly complex provisions are contained in ss. 89–96 of the 1985 Act. Briefly, the position is as follows: a company proposing to allot 'equity securities'[87] must not allot them to anybody unless it has first made an offer of allotment to the existing holders of either 'relevant shares' or 'relevant employee shares'.[88] The offer must be on the same or more favourable terms and in more or less the same proportion to the size of his existing stake in the company.[89] The offer must remain open for at least 21 days and in the meantime the company may not allot any of the securities, unless it has earlier received notice of the acceptance or refusal of every offer.[90] Allotments under an employee share scheme are exempt[91] as are allotments of equity securities which are to be wholly or partly paid up otherwise than in cash.[92] Special provisions apply,[93] sometimes enabling a modified form of offer to be made, where the company has more than one class of equity share in existence.[94]

In some circumstances the preferential rights given by s. 89 can be disapplied. Private companies may exclude them in their memorandum or articles.[95] Public and private companies may sometimes disapply the preferential rights under s. 95 which provides that where the directors are given a general authorisation under

---

[84] With certain exceptions.
[85] See Chapter 19 below.
[86] See at p. 262 above for a discussion of this in relation to rights issues.
[87] Defined in s. 94 so as to exclude subscriber shares, bonus shares, employee shares and certain preference shares but so as to include certain convertible debentures and warrants.
[88] Defined in s. 94 so as to exclude some types of preference shares.
[89] Companies Act 1985, s. 89 (1).
[90] *Ibid.* ss. 89 (1) and 90 (6).
[91] *Ibid.* s. 89 (5).
[92] *Ibid.* s. 89 (4).
[93] *Ibid.* s. 89 (2), (3).
[94] *Ibid.* s. 90 makes detailed provisions as to the method of making the s. 89 offer and s. 92 governs the consequences of contravening the various provisions.
[95] *Ibid.* s. 91.

s. 80 (to allot shares) they may be given power by the articles, or by special resolution of the company, to allot equity securities pursuant to that authority as if s. 89 did not apply, or as if it applied with the modifications chosen by the directors. Various procedures are set out in s. 95. In the case of public companies which are also quoted on the Stock Exchange, the FSA Listing Rules contain further requirements.[96]

E Nature of shares and membership

The most helpful judicial definition of a share is to be found in *Borland's Trustee* v *Steel Bros & Co Ltd*[97] where Farwell J said:

> A share is the interest of the shareholder in the company measured by a sum of money, for the purpose of liability in the first place, and of interest in the second, but also consisting of a series of mutual covenants entered into by all the shareholders in accordance with [section 14 of the Companies Act 1985].

The reference to liabilities in the definition is, in the case of a company limited by shares, mainly a reference to the member's liability to pay any amount on his shares which is not yet paid up. There may also be liability for the company's debts in some circumstances, such as under s. 24. In addition to the points made in the definition it should be noticed that a share is also a piece of property which can be bought and sold, mortgaged, charged and left by will. It is classified as 'personal' property rather than 'real' property.[98] Ownership of shares gives ownership of the company (in proportion to the share) but not of course of any assets in the company.[99] It is this concept of being an owner of the company, a proprietor, which distinguishes a share from a debenture or bond, for debentures give rights against the company and not in it; a debentureholder or bondholder is a creditor.

When the company is first formed the subscribers to the memorandum are deemed to have agreed to become members, and are accordingly entered in the register of members.[100] In every other case, membership is acquired in accordance with s. 22(2), which requires, first, an agreement to become a member and, secondly, entry of name on the share register. The share register is required to be kept by the company and made available for inspection.[101] It should be noted that in two situations it is possible as a matter of technicality, for a person to be a shareholder and not a member: (1) where renounceable letters of allotment are used during the course of an offer for sale, the holder of the allotment letter will be a shareholder and yet not a member, since he is not yet entered on the share register; (2) where share warrants are issued, the warrant holder is a shareholder but since his name will not be on the share register he is not a member (although sometimes the articles will deem him to be a member).[102]

[96] FSA Listing Rules, Chap. 4, paras 4.16–4.21, Chap. 9, paras 9.16–9.23.
[97] [1901] 1 Ch 279 at p. 288.
[98] Companies Act 1985, s. 182 (1) (a).
[99] See p. 24 above.
[100] Companies Act 1985, s. 22 (1).
[101] *Ibid.* ss. 352–362.
[102] See further p. 270 below.

At present, the law usually requires that a shareholder is given a share certificate in respect of his shares within two months of allotment or lodgement with the company of an instrument of transfer.[103] The share certificate is *prima facie* evidence of the member's title to the shares[104] and the certificate is intended to facilitate commercial dealings with the shares by the member, so that, for instance, he can transfer them, or create an equitable mortgage of the shares merely by deposit of the certificate.[105] There is a considerable body of case law (most of it fairly old) concerned with the situation where the share certificate is stolen by a thief and then used to help represent (falsely) to a purchaser that he is the owner of the shares. In this, and other similar circumstances, the company can become liable for damages by virtue of the representation contained in s. 186.[106] Problems in this area are rare these days, presumably because company secretaries, aware of the dangers, are more careful when registering transfers. In the case of a Stock Exchange transfer under CREST the requirement for a share certificate is dispensed with by statutory instrument.

F Classes and types of shares

1 Ordinary shares

Prima facie all shares rank equally.[107] Thus if nothing is stated in the terms of issue, articles or memorandum, then the shares will have equal rights to dividend, return of capital in a winding up, and voting. Such shares are usually referred to as 'ordinary' shares, although sometimes these days the American expression 'common' share is used. However, companies often issue other classes of shares. In the absence of some express restriction a company will have the right to issue shares which carry rights which are preferential to the ordinary shares already issued.[108]

2 Preference shares

Most preference shares carry preferential rights to a fixed preference dividend while the company is a going concern and prior return of capital on a winding up. They are thus a comparatively safe form of investment and when issued by the larger plcs they are often similar in quality to debenture stock or government bonds in that the capital is expected to be mainly secure and the rate of preference dividend is fixed and will bear a close relationship to the interest rates prevailing at the time of issue. Often preference shares are issued as redeemable preference shares, redeemable either at the option of the company or sometimes the shareholder, or as is more usual 'convertible' preference shares, giving the holder the right to convert them

---

[103] Companies Act 1985, s. 185.
[104] *Ibid.* s. 186.
[105] See p. 272 below.
[106] See e.g. *Re Bahia and San Francisco Railway Co.* (1868) LR 3 QB 584; *Balkis Consolidated Ltd v Tomkinson* [1893] AC 396.
[107] *Birch v Cropper* (1889) 14 AC 525, HL.
[108] *Andrews v Gas Meter Co.* [1897] 1 Ch 361.

into ordinary shares in certain circumstances. Preference shares are usually expressed to have no voting rights, or to have voting rights which are restricted to certain circumstances such as a right to vote on whether the company goes into liquidation or not.

Not all preference shares follow the usual pattern of giving a preference as to fixed dividend and return of capital on a winding up. Hybrid versions are encountered, which perhaps give a right to a fixed preference dividend and then an entitlement to share profits rateably with the ordinary shareholders, with similar[109] provisions on a winding up. Such shares are usually known as 'participating' preference shares. Such 'participating' rights will need to be spelled out very clearly in the articles or terms of issue, for if the terms provide for a fixed dividend and prior return of capital on a winding up, it will not be open for the shareholder to argue that he is also entitled to share in profits, rateably with the ordinary shareholders, nor will it be possible for him to contend that, if the terms give him a right to a prior return of capital on a winding up, he can also share in surplus assets.[110] Nor will it help him, when seeking to imply participating rights as to capital, to point to his express rights to participating dividend rights.[111]

3 Deferred shares

Deferred shares are shares which have rights which are deferred to the ordinary shares; thus, they will only get any dividend after a specified minimum has been paid to the ordinary shareholders, and as regards return of capital on a winding up they similarly rank behind the ordinary shares (which in turn will be ranking behind any preference shares). Deferred shares are sometimes known as 'founders' shares' because it used to be the practice that promoters would agree to take founders' shares to demonstrate their confidence in the company's ability to pay dividends. Founders' shares fell into disrepute because they would often give the promoters a large share of the profit if the business was successful and they were usually structured with enhanced voting rights so as to permit retention of control. Deferred shares are now a rare phenomenon.

4 Non-voting and multiple voting shares

Sometimes non-voting ordinary shares are issued, usually to enable the present controlling group to retain their control and at the same time raise more capital without resorting to issuing preference shares. Such non-voting shares are sometimes given the label 'A' shares to distinguish them from the normal ordinary shares.

Another device used by a controlling group to acquire or maintain control is to issue shares which have an enhanced voting strength. These can produce the situation where a management group lock themselves in to the company so that

---

[109] I.e. prior return of capital and then rateable share in surplus assets.
[110] *Will v United Lankat Plantations* [1914] AC 11.
[111] *Scottish Insurance Corporation v Wilson and Clyde Coal Co.* [1949] AC 462; *Re Isle of Thanet Electricity Co.* [1950] Ch 161.

although an outsider owns more than 51% of the market value of the company's shares he or she nevertheless has no control over the company. A good example of this was the long-running saga of the attempt by Trust House Forte to take over the Savoy Hotel. The takeover battle began in the 1950s and ended in the late 1980s when Trust House Forte finally abandoned its attempt.[112]

5 Share warrants

The term 'warrant' is used in two senses in modern parlance. In its non-technical sense it is used to describe a form of call option which gives the holder a right to call for a share at a fixed price at a future date if he or she so chooses. Such 'warrants' are often offered to the target company's shareholders by a takeover bidder as part of his offer package, which often consists of shares in the bidder itself, cash and warrants.

The second and more technical meaning of 'share warrant' refers to bearer shares. It is provided[113] that a company may, if authorised by its articles, issue with respect to any fully paid shares a warrant stating that the bearer of the warrant is entitled to the shares specified in it. The share warrant is then probably a negotiable instrument so that title to the shares may be transferred by mere delivery of the warrant.[114] The company is further empowered (if authorised by its articles) to provide, by coupons or otherwise, for the payment of the future dividends on the share included in the warrant. Voting is usually allowed only if the warrant has been deposited with the company. The holder of the warrant is not technically a member of the company[115] and on the issue of the share warrant the company must strike out of its register of members the name of the member then entered in it as if he or she had ceased to be a member. In place of the member's name must be entered the fact that the warrant has been issued, a statement of the shares included in the warrant and date of issue of the warrant.[116]

6 Depositary receipts

Depositary receipts, usually issued by a bank, are negotiable receipts certifying that a stated number of securities of an issuer have been deposited on behalf of the holder in a financial institution. Increasing numbers of depositary receipts are being listed on the London Stock Exchange.

Depositary receipts are often used to enable a company in a country which has an undeveloped economy to make its shares attractive to overseas investors by, in effect, attaching a different currency and regulatory package to the shares. Thus with American Depositary Receipts (ADRs), for example, the ADRs will be issued by a US Depositary Bank,[117] and the shares will be deposited in a branch of the

---

[112] The story is outlined in *Re Savoy Hotel Ltd* [1981] 3 WLR 441.
[113] Companies Act 1985, s. 188.
[114] *Webb, Hale and Co. v Alexandria Water Co.* (1905) 93 LT 339.
[115] Unless the articles deem him to be a member of the company, although this is subject to the Companies Act 1985, s. 355 (5).
[116] Companies Act 1985, s. 355 (1).
[117] Usually Citibank, JP Morgan or the Bank of New York.

bank in the issuer's home country. Dividends are collected from the company by the branch and remitted to the bank in the US and will be paid to the holder of the receipt in US dollars. The US regulatory system will apply to the ADRs.

G Transfer of and transactions in shares

1 Transfers on sale

Once a contract for the sale of shares[118] has come into existence,[119] then provided that it is specifically enforceable (and it will be, in the absence of some vitiating factor), the equitable interest in those shares will pass to the purchaser; on the principle that 'equity regards that done which ought to be done'.[120] Thus the vendor remains legal (though not equitable) owner and in effect is holding the shares on trust for the purchaser, subject to receipt of purchase money. The purchaser will not become the full legal owner until his name is entered on the share register of the company. To get that to happen, the following procedures need to be complied with.

Section 182 (1) (b) of the Companies Act 1985 provides that the shares[121] of a member are 'transferable in the manner provided by the company's articles but subject to the Stock Transfer Act 1963'. In the 1985 Table A, arts 23–28 deal with transfer of shares, but art. 23 is particularly relevant in this context since it provides that the instrument of transfer may be in 'any usual form' or in any other form approved by the directors. In practice the form adopted will usually be that set out in the Stock Transfer Act 1963 which provides that the form need be executed by the transferor only, and need not be attested but it must specify the particulars of the consideration, describe the shares and give the numbers or amounts of shares, details of the transfer and name and address of the transferee. The Stock Transfer Act does not apply to partly paid shares but will normally be followed, with the additional requirement (to comply with art. 23) of the signature of the transferee. Whatever form is used, it must be one which it is possible to regard as a 'proper instrument of transfer' within s. 183 (1) for it is unlawful for a company to register a transfer unless such a 'proper instrument' has been delivered to it.[122]

The normal procedure is for the transferor to hand over the transfer instrument and share certificate to the transferee who then sends them to the company for registration. Assuming that the registration is not liable to be refused,[123] the transferee's name will be entered on the share register and he will then be sent a certificate in respect of the shares. If the transferor is selling only part of the holding to

---

[118] Different procedures apply to the transfer of shares on the death of a shareholder; see Table A, arts 31–32 and Companies Act 1985, s. 183 (3).

[119] There are special procedures for the transfer of shares which are the result of a sale on the Stock Exchange; see p. 259 above.

[120] *Wood Preservation Ltd* v *Prior* [1969] 1 WLR 1977. On the difficult question of voting rights in this situation see *Michaels* v *Harley House (Marylebone) Ltd* [1999] 1 All ER 356, CA.

[121] Or other interest.

[122] Although there are exceptions for transfers of government stock and other similar securities which are dealt with on a computerised basis under the provisions of the Stock Transfer Act 1982 and other exceptions where the shares are transmitted by 'operation of law' (e.g. bankruptcy of member) or by a personal representative (death of member); see Companies Act 1985, s. 183 (1)–(3).

[123] See p. 272 below.

which his certificate relates, a procedure known as 'certification of transfer' is followed (to avoid fraud) whereby the transferor sends the share certificate and instrument of transfer to the company to be endorsed by the company secretary to the effect that there has been produced to the company a certificate in respect of the transfer.[124] This certification procedure is needed because the vendor would be unwilling to hand over a certificate for 1,000 shares to the transferee if, for instance, he has only sold and been paid for 200.

2 Security interests in shares

Shares are an important item of wealth and over the years the law has developed ways in which the wealth locked up in a share can be used as collateral for borrowing. There are three types of security interest commonly granted over shares: mortgages, charges and liens.

Mortgages of shares are usually 'equitable' mortgages, meaning that the mortgagor remains on the share register as 'legal' owner but holds his shares subject to the equitable interest of the mortgagee. Legal mortgages are uncommon because if the mortgagee's name is entered on the share register he will be personally liable for any calls on the shares.[125] An equitable mortgage of shares is usually created by deposit of the share certificate. Alternatively, an equitable charge on shares will come into existence provided that the parties have agreed that those shares should stand as security for the satisfaction of a debt.[126] A lien is a form of equitable charge which is security for the payment of money. It is quite common for the articles of association of companies to provide that the company shall have a lien on the shares of a member in respect of any debts owed by him to the company.[127] Since 1980, and now contained in the Companies Act 1985, public companies can only have liens over their own shares in certain circumstances.[128]

3 Restrictions on transfer

Public or private companies may contain provisions in their constitutions restricting the transferability of shares, although a public company which is seeking a Stock Exchange quotation or a dealing arrangement on AIM will find that this is unacceptable. Many private companies have restrictions on transfer, usually with a view to keeping control within the family or other small group of individuals. Such restrictions are commonly of two types, usually both being present: directors' discretion to refuse transfer, and pre-emption clauses. A power for the directors to refuse to register a transfer is commonly contained in the articles of association of private companies. The clause will read something like: 'The directors may, in their absolute discretion and without assigning any reason therefore, decline to register the transfer of any share, whether or not it is a fully paid share.' The 1985 Table A

---

[124] Companies Act 1985, s. 184.
[125] *Re Land Credit Company of Ireland* (1873) 8 Ch App 831.
[126] *Swiss Bank Corp* v *Lloyds Bank* [1982] AC 584.
[127] Article 8 of Table A gives a lien over partly paid shares in respect of moneys due on that share.
[128] Companies Act 1985, s. 150.

contains what looks deceptively like a similar clause but which in reality has a very restricted ambit since it mainly only applies to shares which are not fully paid.[129] Over the years, the courts have established the principle that the shareholder has a basic right of transfer of his shares and so unless there is an effective and proper exercise of the directors' power of refusal, the transfer right will remain intact.[130] It is also clear that the effect of s. 183 (5) and (6) is that almost invariably the directors must exercise their power of refusal within two months if such refusal is to be valid.[131] Like all directors' powers, the power of refusal must be exercised '... bona fide in what they consider – not what a court may consider – is in the interests of the company and not for any collateral purpose'.[132] Generally, if the clause gives an unfettered discretion, the directors are not required to give reasons for their decision but it appears that if they do give reasons then the court may review them.[133] If the clause gives a right of refusal on certain grounds, it seems that as long as they state the grounds of refusal they similarly need not give reasons.[134]

Pre-emption clauses are often contained in the articles of private companies, long and elaborate they are designed to give the directors or members the right to buy the shares of any member who wishes to sell his shares.[135] Poor drafting of the clauses, perhaps combined with a lack of efficiency in carrying out the prescribed procedures can lead to complex litigation and difficult priority problems if third party rights intervene.[136]

4 Disclosure of interests in shares

The Companies Act 1985 contains three sets of provisions relating to the disclosure of interests in shares. These are: provisions requiring disclosure of 3% interests;[137] provisions enabling the company to investigate the ownership of its shares;[138] and provisions requiring directors to disclose shareholdings in their company.[139] These disclosure provisions are ostensibly designed to ensure that information is available to the market so that buyers and sellers of a company's shares are in a position to know who controls it and who is building a stake in it. In fact, also, the provisions are very useful to incumbent management who are sometimes able to obtain early warning of a potential takeover bidder before he manages to build a sizeable stake in the company from which to launch his bid. The directors' disclosure provisions are useful in that, among other things, they can operate as a barometer of the directors' levels of confidence in the company so that if they have just sold most of their

---

[129] Table A, art. 24.
[130] *Re Copal Varnish* [1917] 2 Ch 349.
[131] *Re Swaledale Cleaners* [1968] 3 All ER 619; *Re Zinotty Properties Ltd* [1984] BCLC 375.
[132] *Re Smith & Fawcett* [1942] Ch 304 at p. 306, *per* Lord Greene MR.
[133] *Re Bell Bros* (1891) 65 LT 245.
[134] *Re Coalport China* [1895] 2 Ch 404.
[135] See e.g. *Borland's Trustee* v *Steel Bros & Co Ltd* [1901] 1 Ch 279.
[136] *Tett* v *Phoenix Ltd* (1986) 2 BCC 99,140.
[137] Companies Act 1985, ss. 198–211.
[138] *Ibid.* ss. 212–220.
[139] *Ibid.* ss. 324–326, 328–329.

holdings, their assertations of confidence in the company's future can be judged in that light.

The provisions requiring disclosure of 3% interests[140] apply in respect of all public companies (whether listed or not) and require notification to the company of the acquisition or disposal of an 'interest of 3 per cent or more' in the 'relevant share capital' and also notification of any subsequent changes that take the holding through a whole percentage point. The notification must be made within two business days. The provisions also extend to becoming aware of the acquisition or disposal and 'relevant share capital' and 'interest' are widely defined. The company must keep a register of interests in shares, containing the details of any notification it receives and keep the register open for public inspection.[141] There are also anti-avoidance provisions, popularly known as the 'concert party' provisions. Basically these are designed to prevent avoidance of the 3% threshold by, for instance, four people holding 1% and agreeing to act together for certain purposes. The concert party provisions are widely drafted and will catch agreements in certain circumstances, even though they do not necessarily amount to binding contracts.[142]

The second set of provisions[143] permit a company to investigate who are the 'real' owners of the company's shares, for often shares are held by nominees on trust for the real holders and disclosure under s. 198 does not reveal anything very useful (or alternatively the company may suspect that the concert party provisions are being ignored). By issuing a s. 212 notice the company can require the registered holder to state for whom he holds on trust. A series of s. 212 notices can be used if a chain of trustees has been used to try to avoid the investigation. Breach of the provisions attract criminal penalties. A favourite avoidance device is to take the chain out of the jurisdiction so that the company comes up against a nominee who simply ignores the s. 212 notice. In practice, this is very effectively dealt with by the company applying to the UK court for an order under s. 216 applying restrictions to the shares in question. The restrictions, set out in s. 454, include suspending voting rights and distribution rights, and voiding transfers. Furthermore, the courts require a very speedy response to the s. 212 notice; in one case, *Lonrho plc v Edelman*[144] two clear days was the maximum allowed for a recipient of the notice abroad, and it was said that even less time is available for a UK recipient.

Lastly, there are provisions[145] which require a director to notify the company as to his interest in shares in it (and/or debentures). The provisions are widely drafted and will also require, for instance, notification of certain events, such as if he enters into a contract to sell the shares. 'Interest' is widely defined and in some circumstances, shares held by the director's spouse and children must be disclosed. The company must keep a register containing the information thus received.

---

[140] *Ibid.* ss. 198–211.
[141] In addition, a listed public company must notify without delay the Company Announcements Office of the Stock Exchange which will then publicise it; see FSA Listing Rules, Chap. 9, paras 9.11–9.15.
[142] Breach of these provisions is a criminal offence.
[143] Companies Act 1985, ss. 212–220.
[144] (1989) 5 BCC 68.
[145] Companies Act 1985, ss. 324–326, 328–329.

14.4 THE LEGAL NATURE OF DEBENTURES (AND BONDS)

The important role of loan capital in corporate finance has already been discussed.[146] It is necessary to consider briefly some of the legal aspects of debt finance.[147] It has already been observed that a debentureholder is not a member of the company and he has rights against the company, as a creditor, rather than rights in it. A debenture is, essentially, a document which acknowledges a debt, but the notion usually also connotes some degree of permanence, or absence of short-term quality.

Debenture is defined in s. 744 of the Companies Act 1985 as including 'debenture stock, bonds and any other securities of a company, whether constituting a charge on the assets of the company or not'. Thus, it is important to realise that although the commercial world draws a rough distinction between a debenture and a bond based mainly on the idea that the former is secured, the Companies Act will regard a bond as a 'debenture' for the purposes of the Act's provisions.

A debenture will sometimes specify a repayment date, or it may be reserved to the company to choose when to pay it off, with no fixed date, or it may be made irredeemable. Usually a debenture will be repayable if the company defaults on its payment of interest.[148] A common feature of modern corporate finance are debentures which contain provisions enabling them to be converted into shares in certain circumstances; these are usually referred to as 'convertible debentures'. A debenture (as opposed to a bond) will usually be secured by fixed and floating charges. If the charge is to be valid it will need to be registered in accordance with s. 395.[149]

14.5 COMPANY LAW REVIEW AND LAW REFORM

The Final Report of the Review recommends that directors should be obliged to give reasons when exercising any discretion to refuse to register transfers of shares.[150] Additionally, there were various other technical recommendations connected with shares.[151] It is clear from the document *Company Law. Flexibility and Accessibility: A Consultative Document* (London: DTI, 2004) that a number of reforms are likely in this area.

---

[146] See pp. 269–272, 279–280 above.

[147] Detailed analysis of this is beyond the scope of this book; see n. 70 above for suggested further reading on this subject.

[148] In certain rare cirumstances permitted by the Enterprise Act 2002 this may entitle the debentureholder to appoint a receiver, who will in certain circumstances be an administrative receiver within the Insolvency Act 1986; see p. 406 below.

[149] Detailed consideration of these matters is beyond the scope of this book.

[150] *Modern Company Law for a Competitive Economy Final Report* (London: DTI, 2001) paras. 7.44–7.45.

[151] *Ibid.* paras. 7.27–7.32.

15

RAISING AND MAINTENANCE OF CAPITAL

15.1 INTRODUCTION

This chapter is concerned with principles mainly developed and settled by the courts by the end of the 19th century. As a result of the need to comply with the EC Second Harmonisation Directive,[1] some of the principles can now be found in the companies legislation in a codified form.[2] The broad principle which infuses this field is that of creditor protection, and in this context this idea leads to some very fundamental rules which are designed to regulate the way in which the company's capital is dealt with. Whether these rules actually serve any useful purpose, or could be replaced by something better, is currently the subject of inquiry.[3]

15.2 THE RAISING OF CAPITAL – DISCOUNTS AND PREMIUMS

A Introduction

It has been seen[4] how in English company law, when shares are issued they have to be given a nominal (or 'par') value, such as £1. This has enabled the development of two rules, designed to regulate the situation where the company receives, first, less than the nominal value for the share (which is then said to be issued at a 'discount') and, secondly (and conversely), more than the nominal value of the share (which is then said to be issued at a 'premium').

B Discounts

A discount occurs where a share of, say, £1 nominal value is issued in return for, say, 80 pence. The discount is 20 pence. It was firmly settled at the end of the 19th century in *Ooregum Gold Mining Co v Roper*[5] that the issue of shares at a discount is illegal. The rationale for the rule is that without it, the company could easily give a

---

[1] 77/91/EEC. The Directive was implemented by the Companies Act 1980.
[2] It will be seen that the input of the European Commission here has sometimes been to open up differences between the regime applicable to public companies and that applicable to private companies, since the requirements of the Second Directive apply only to 'public limited liability companies'.
[3] See further p. 292 below.
[4] See p. 263 above.
[5] [1892] AC 125, HL.

false impression that at some stage in its past, a certain sum of money had been raised for its venture, when, if the shares had been issued at a discount, a much smaller sum had in fact been raised. This might mislead people who were at a later date considering whether to give credit to the company, or to invest in shares in it. As part of the UK's obligations under the EC Second Directive[6] the rule was effectively codified and is now to be found in s. 100 (2) of the Companies Act 1985. If shares are allotted in contravention of the prohibition, the allottee is liable to pay an amount equal to the discount.[7]

If shares are allotted for cash then obviously a share discount is relatively easy to spot and the scope for avoidance of the legislation is limited. However, once it is seen that shares could be allotted in return for a non-cash consideration, then it can be imagined that it would not be difficult to avoid the rule. As a result of the implementation of the EC Second Directive, public companies are subjected to various statutory prohibitions and procedures, designed to ensure that the share capital is properly paid for and also to avoid hidden discounts. The regime applicable to private companies is less onerous.

The basic position as regards payment for shares is that[8] shares allotted by a company, and any premium on them, may be paid up in money or money's worth (including goodwill and know-how).[9] However, a public company may not accept, in payment for shares, an undertaking given by any person that he or another should do work or perform services for the company or any other person.[10] Nor should a public company allot shares (otherwise than in cash) if the consideration for the allotment is or includes an undertaking which is to be, or may be, performed more than five years from the date of the allotment.[11]

With particular relevance to the prevention of discounts are rules contained in ss. 103 and 108 of the 1985 Act which prevent a public company from allotting shares in return for a non-cash consideration unless the consideration has been independently valued.[12] These provisions are not applicable to private companies and so these continue to be governed by the common law as set out in *Re Wragg Ltd.*[13] The facts illustrate quite well the operation of the discount principle in circumstances where a non-cash consideration is given for the allotment and also provide us with another example of the manoeuvre which is extremely common in company law, whereby an existing business is incorporated by being sold to a newly formed shell company in return for shares and

---

[6] EC Second Directive, art. 8.

[7] Plus interest (Companies Act 1985, s. 100 (2)).

[8] Subject to what appears hereafter.

[9] Companies Act 1985, s. 99 (1); EC Second Directive, art. 7.

[10] Companies Act 1985, s. 99 (2); EC Second Directive, art. 7.

[11] Companies Act 1985, s. 102; EC Second Directive, art. 9 (2). There are also provisions which restrict subscribers to the memorandum from transferring non-cash assets to a public company in return for shares unless the assets have been independently valued (ss. 104–105, 109) and prohibitions from giving anything other than cash for shares taken pursuant to an undertaking in the memorandum (s. 106).

[12] See Companies Act 1985, ss. 103 and 108, which prescribe various conditions. Mergers by share exchange are excluded from the ambit of these provisions; see *ibid.* s. 103 (5) and Second Directive, art. 10.

[13] [1897] 1 Ch 796.

other consideration.[14] Wragg and Martin carried on a coach business in partnership. After some years they decided to turn it into a limited company, which they did by forming a company and then selling the assets of the partnership to it at a price fixed at £46,300. In return, they received cash, debentures, and shares. Soon afterwards, the company went into insolvent liquidation and the liquidator argued that when one looked at the actual values of the assets which had been sold to the company, it was clear that the shares had been issued at a discount and therefore, Wragg and Martin were still liable to the company for the discount. The Court of Appeal refused to accept this and held that directors were under a duty to make a bona fide valuation of the asset but in the absence of any evidence showing bad faith, the court will not substitute a valuation of its own.

C Premiums

Shares are issued at a premium if, say, a share of £1 nominal value is issued in return for £1.30. The 30 pence is the premium. Prior to 1948, the premium was not treated as share capital. This meant that the premium was free of the legal restrictions which normally apply to share capital. As will be seen,[15] one of the main restrictions is that the company cannot use share capital to pay a dividend to the shareholders. In 1937 in *Drown v Gaumont Picture Corp Ltd*[16] it was confirmed that a company could use a premium to pay a dividend to shareholders. However, the Companies Act 1948 contained a provision[17] which required the premium to be credited to a share premium account on the balance sheet which means, in effect, that it was largely to be treated, for legal purposes, as if it were share capital. The statutory requirement for the share premium account is now contained in s. 130 of the Companies Act 1985. It provides that if a company issues shares at a premium, whether for cash or otherwise, a sum equal to the aggregate amount or value of the premiums must be transferred to an account called 'the share premium account'.[18] The share premium account must be treated as capital,[19] so that, for instance, the rules on reduction of capital[20] apply just as if the share premium were capital. The basic rationale of this is that if a company issues shares at a premium, then the actual capital which has been raised is the full consideration received, including the premium, and the balance sheet has to reflect this. The rule is the direct result of the concept of the nominal (or par) value of shares.

Shortly after the 1948 Act was passed, the effect of the new legislation became clear in *Henry Head & Co Ltd v Ropner Holdings Ltd*.[21] Here the defendant company

---

[14] The example of how Salomon did this has already been considered at p. 23 above.
[15] See further p. 290 below.
[16] [1937] Ch 402.
[17] Section 56.
[18] *Ibid.* s. 130 (1).
[19] *Ibid.* s. 130 (3). This is subject to exceptions in respect of using the share premium account to issue bonus shares to the members and writing off the company's preliminary expenses (or expenses or commissions etc allowed on any issue of shares or debentures) or it may be used in providing for the premium payable on redemption of the company's debentures (s. 130 (2)).
[20] See further p. 282 below.
[21] [1952] 1 Ch 124.

had entered a sum onto its balance sheet in what was called a share premium account. For reasons which will gradually become apparent, the claimant thought that this produced very undesirable consequences and sought an injunction restraining the defendant from doing this. In effect, the claimant was challenging what was then a new statutory requirement, and hoping that it was not really as compulsory as it seemed. The background to the case indicates that the various participants had not realised what the effect of the new section on their transaction would be.[22] The circumstances concerned an amalgamation of two shipping companies which were being carried on separately, but under the same management. The amalgamation was to be carried out by forming a shell company (the defendant Ropner Holdings Ltd) and then getting the shareholders in the two shipping companies to sell their shares to it, in exchange for shares in it. By the time the amalgamation was carried out, various steps had been taken to ensure that the shares in each of the shipping companies were worth the same, and so it was fair, and made financial sense, for the amalgamation to be carried out by 'a pound-for-pound capitalisation – that is to say, a pound of the new company's shares for a pounds worth, nominal, of the constituent company's shares'.[23] Thus the shareholders in the shipping companies were getting a £1 share in Ropner Holdings Ltd in return for the handing over of each of their £1 shares in the shipping company. In all, in this way, Ropner Holdings Ltd issued shares having a nominal value of £1,759,606. However, the actual value of the assets in the shipping companies was about £5m more than that. So, in a sense, Ropner Holdings Ltd was getting a premium of about £5m when it issued its shares to the shareholders of the shipping companies. And that £5m was entered in a share premium account on the balance sheet. What the claimant objected to was this: the entry of the £5m in a share premium account as the statute seemed to require, had the effect that the £5m was treated as capital. This greatly restricted the way in which the company's assets could be used. As Harman J said:

> [I]t fixes an unfortunate kind of rigidity on the structure of the company, having regard to the fact that an account kept under that name, namely, the Share Premium Account, can only have anything paid out of it by means of a transaction analogous to a reduction of capital. It is in effect, as if the company had originally been capitalised at approximately £7,000,000 instead of £1,750,000.[24]

It is not clear exactly what particular aspect of the rigidity was worrying the claimant company in this case. It is probable that it was upset at the prospect of £5m becoming 'undistributable' in the sense that after the amalgamation it could no longer be used to pay a dividend to shareholders because it was share capital, whereas prior to the amalgamation, it would have been a 'distributable' reserve,

---

[22] The judge referred to the 'sense of shock' in some quarters ([1952] 1 Ch 124 at p. 127). It is not uncommon for practitioners to find that the technicalities of company law legislation largely ruin the effect of a well-intentioned reconstruction carried out for bona fide commercial reasons. The operation of s. 151 of the Companies Act 1985 is well known for causing these problems; see further p. 294 below.

[23] [1952] 1 Ch 124 at p. 126, *per* Harman J.

[24] *Ibid.* at p. 127. The judge was rounding the figures somewhat. On reduction of capital see further at p. 282 below.

which could have been used to pay dividends because it was merely accumulated profits and not share capital. The claimant failed to get an injunction. Its argument that the statute only applied to a cash premium and not, as here, a premium thrown up by the asset values on the balance sheet, failed. The statute clearly said 'whether for cash or otherwise' and so Harman J held that the sum of £5m had been correctly shown in the share premium account.

The share premium account problem also arose in the similar context of a takeover by share exchange. Thus, for instance, when the bidder issued shares (in itself) to the shareholders of the target company, in return for its shares in the target, there was a potential for a share premium to arise. City practitioners tried to minimise the effects of this by ensuring that there was nothing to upset the assumptions made by the parties involved that the value of the shares received by the bidder was equal to the nominal value of the shares issued by it, and hence, no premium. Then in 1980, Walton J in *Shearer* v *Bercain Ltd*[25] made it clear that a proper valuation needed to be made of what the bidder was getting. This was then likely to throw up a share premium and the legislation would then require the establishment of a share premium account which would often have the effect that pre-acquisition distributable reserves would become undistributable after the takeover. The Conservative government of the time responded very quickly to City pressure and the Companies Act 1981 contained provisions designed to provide some relief from the requirement to establish a share premium account in a takeover situation. These 'merger accounting' provisions are now contained in ss. 131–134 of the Companies Act 1985.[26]

15.3 THE MAINTENANCE OF CAPITAL

A The meaning of the doctrine

In a series of leading cases towards the end of the 19th century, the courts[27] established the doctrine of maintenance of capital[28] under which the share capital of a company[29] must be maintained as a fund of last resort for the creditors of the

---

[25] [1980] 3 All ER 295. For a detailed account of this saga see the article by R. Pennington 'The Companies Act 1981 (2)' (1982) 3 Co Law 66.

[26] The main provision as regards takeovers and mergers is s. 131 which will apply where the company which issues the shares (i.e. the bidder) had secured at least a 90% equity holding in another company (the target) in pursuance of an arrangement providing for the allotment of equity shares in the issuing company on terms that the consideration for the shares allotted is to be provided either by the issue or transfer to the issuing company of equity shares in the other company (the target) or by the cancellation of any such shares not held by the issuing company (bidder); see s. 131 (1). It is then provided that a premium arising on the issuing company's shares is exempt from the s. 130 requirement to establish a share premium account (s. 131 (2)). There is also provision for relief from share premium accounts in situations involving group reconstructions where a company in the group issues shares to another in the group in return for non-cash assets (s. 132).

[27] As a result of the implementation of the EC Second Directive, much of the case law has (since 1980) been codified in the Companies Act 1985; see EC Second Directive, arts 15–22.

[28] The doctrine relates only to 'capital' in the strict sense of *share* capital. The term 'capital' is often used in common parlance to refer to all the funds which are available to the company to operate its business, whether arising from the issue of shares (equity capital) or from debt (loan capital).

[29] Including any quasi-capital funds such as share premium account.

company to look to. Put in this form the maintenance doctrine makes little sense because companies often go into insolvent liquidation and the creditors frequently then get little or nothing back. The idea of the capital being maintained as a fund of last resort is at best a rather general concept and there are a number of important qualifications to it. First, the capital needs to be maintained only so far as the ordinary risks of business allow. If a company is capitalised with 1,000 £1 shares and loses this capital through bad luck or negligent trading, that is not a breach of the maintenance of capital rule and the rule provides no remedy in that situation.[30] Secondly, there is no requirement that the debt which a company takes on should bear any relationship to its share capital in the sense of there being a fixed ratio. Thus it is possible to form an English company with 100 £1 shares and a loan from the bank of £1m.[31] Thirdly, and this may have altered, there is no basic requirement in English law that a company be adequately capitalised. In other words if it is formed with a share capital of 1,000 £1 shares, then there is no fundamental legal doctrine which lays down limits as to the size of the business that it undertakes. However, it is possible that case law on wrongful trading may have indirectly introduced a form of capitalisation requirement; this is discussed above.[32] In effect then, the maintenance of capital doctrine is heavily qualified, and really amounts to a group of rules which restrict the circumstances in which capital can be given to, or back to, the shareholders.

There are three areas which can properly be viewed as maintenance of capital problems. The first, reduction of capital, is perhaps the most obvious example of the maintenance concept, for certain types of reductions involve handing money back to the shareholders and reducing the share capital on the company's balance sheet. Also easy to see as a maintenance problem is the purchase by a company of its own shares, since it is a very similar mechanism to some reductions, in that the company gives the shareholder money and then scrubs out the corresponding shares on the balance sheet. The third area, dividends, is less obviously a maintenance problem, although it has long been seen in this light. Dividends are a payment of money to the shareholder, by the company, and it is clear that unless the company has made profits at least equal to the amount of the dividend, then the distribution to the shareholder will diminish the assets available to the creditors.[33] Hence the courts developed the rule that dividends can only be paid out of profits.

There is a fourth area which is sometimes seen as an example of the maintenance of capital principle.[34] It is the problem of a company giving financial assistance to enable someone to purchase[35] some of its existing shares from another

---

[30] There may be other remedies, such as an unfair prejudice petition.

[31] Other jurisdictions have different rules and it is not uncommon to find a prescribed debt/equity ratio in corporations legislation.

[32] At p. 36. A public company will need to have an issued share capital of at least the authorised minimum (£50,000) but this is a fixed amount and not a concept of capital adequacy; see p. 15 above.

[33] Although it is also clear that no diminution in the share capital as stated on the balance sheet is being contemplated.

[34] See e.g. the DTI Consultation Document (February 1999) *The Strategic Framework* para. 5.4.20: '[ss. 151–158] ... normally regarded as part of the capital maintenance regime'.

[35] The use of the word purchase is not wholly accurate, although that is the usual situation; see p. 296 below.

person.[36] It is usually simply referred to as 'financial assistance'. Such an activity less obviously involves a breach of the maintenance principle, for no diminution of the undistributable elements on the balance sheet occurs, nor is there necessarily any payment made to the shareholders. It might perhaps tentatively be argued to represent an example of a broader maintenance principle which forbids any payment or arrangement made other than for the legitimate purposes of the company's business or objects. There are two problems with this. One is that it is highly doubtful whether the case law on maintenance really justifies this view, and the second is that if it was really possible to see the financial assistance problem as covered by the maintenance principle then it would not have been necessary to introduce special legislation in 1929 to deal with it.[37] Financial assistance is more properly seen as a discrete problem which is largely unrelated to the maintenance principle, and for this and other reasons, financial assistance forms a chapter on its own in this book.[38]

B Reduction of capital

1 Statutory procedure

Reductions of capital essentially involve a diminution in the share capital[39] on the balance sheet. Under the doctrine of maintenance of capital this entails a threat to the interests of creditors, therefore the courts and the legislature have adopted a policy which allows reductions to take place only under strict safeguards designed to protect the interests of those who might otherwise be adversely affected by it.[40] Since reductions traditionally have involved an application to the court they are time-consuming and expensive.[41]

Sections 135–141 of the Companies Act 1985 contain the statutory regime governing reductions of capital. The main provision is s. 135 which provides that: 'Subject to confirmation by the court,[42] a company . . . may, if so authorised by its articles, by special resolution reduce its share capital in any way.'[43] Article 34 of Table A will give the necessary authorisation if Table A has been adopted. Creditors are protected by ss. 136–137 which require the notification of creditors and give them, in some circumstances, the right to object to the reduction at the court proceedings for confirmation and also make their consent necessary.[44]

---

[36] To be carefully distinguished from the situation where a company purchases its own shares!
[37] See s. 45 of the Companies Act 1929. The present much modified provisions are contained in the Companies Act 1985, ss. 151–158; see Chapter 16.
[38] For a similar view, see W. Knight 'Capital Maintenance' in F. Patfield (ed.) *Perspectives on Company Law: 1* (London: Kluwer, 1995) p. 49.
[39] 'Share capital' in its broadest sense, including quasi-capital funds such as the share premium account.
[40] As will be seen below (at p. 284) it is not only the creditors who need protection because where there are different classes of shares there will be complicated issues between them.
[41] In limited circumstances, if the reduction is returning capital to the shareholders and the company is a private company, then the procedure can be simplified if the transaction is carried out via a purchase by the company of its own shares; see further p. 289 below.
[42] Reductions are now normally dealt with by a Registrar; see Practice Direction [1999] BCC 741.
[43] Without prejudice to the generality of s. 135 (1), subs. (2) goes on to give examples of the types of reduction most commonly desired.
[44] As an alternative to getting their consent, the court may order the company to secure the debt (s. 136 (5)).

2 Examples of reduction

Reductions often fall into two main categories: those where the company has more capital than it needs or wants and so involve paying back capital to the shareholders; and those where no capital is being returned to the shareholders but, instead, the reduction involves a write-off against share capital.

An example of the former type of reduction occurred in *Re Chatterley-Whitfield Collieries Ltd*[45] where the company was engaged in coal mining and after the coal mines were nationalised in 1948 the company decided to carry on mining in Ireland though it obviously needed less capital than before. Hence it returned capital to the shareholders. It was returning the preference share capital in this case which was expensive in the sense that, with a reduction in profits flowing from the reduced scale of operations, little or nothing would be left for the ordinary shareholders after the preference shares had been serviced. The preference shares had been entitled to a dividend in priority to the ordinary shareholders. In other cases, preference capital is being returned because the preference shares have rights to a fixed preference dividend of say 14%, issued at a time when interest rates were around that figure. Later, when rates have dropped to 7%, that capital is expensive and the company may want to pay off the preference shares in a reduction and either issue some more at a lower dividend or obtain finance in some other way.

A good example of the second type of reduction, the 'write-off' against share capital, occurred in *Re Floating Dock Ltd*.[46] Over many years some promoters were, through the companies which they formed from time to time, engaged in constructing and operating a floating dock on St Thomas in the West Indies.[47] It was an 'iron and wooden structure' and cost £100,000 to build. From time to time storms came and the dock sank and was duly raised again. The progress of the companies mirrored those of the dock and they were periodically wound up. Eventually, in 1878, the company which was the subject matter of the petition, was formed. It had a capital of £20,800 as ordinary shares and £70,994 as first preference shares and £71,823 as second preference shares. But the storms came again – and then it was eventually found that modern steamers were too big for the dock. The upshot was that by 1894 the assets of the company were only worth £50,000, but the company had a total issued share capital of £163,618. This would have produced the difficulty (among others) that it was difficult to raise any further capital by the issue of shares since any shares issued would immediately be worth less than their nominal value[48] and an issue at less than nominal value was not feasible as it would involve an illegal discount. Hence, a reduction by cancellation of capital was necessary to bring the share capital into line with the available assets.[49]

---

[45] [1949] AC 512, HL, [1948] 3 All ER 593, CA.

[46] [1895] 1 Ch 691.

[47] As Chitty J ([1895] 1 Ch 691 at p. 695) put it: 'The circumstances connected with this floating dock [were] somewhat remarkable', although the fact that for 30 years the dock behaved more like a submarine than a pontoon must have been a source of continuing dismay to the incorporators.

[48] An option here might have been the creation of a new class of preference shares ranking in priority to any of those already issued.

[49] Other aspects of this seminal case are dealt with at p. 285 below.

3 Exercise of the judicial power to confirm reductions

The classic statement of the judicial approach to reaching a decision as to whether to confirm a reduction or not was made by Evershed LJ in *Re Chatterley-Whitfield Collieries Ltd*[50] when he said that: '[T]he court must be satisfied not only of the formal validity of the steps taken by the ... company, but also that the reduction proposed is one that is fair and equitable to the shareholders or classes of shareholders affected.' At first sight, this looks straightforward enough. However, where there is more than one class of shares in existence in the company, the application of these basic principles has given rise to disputes and a large number of hard-fought cases. The test 'fair and equitable' to the classes of shareholders is applied and interpreted to mean that the reduction will usually satisfy the test, provided that the shareholders are being treated in accordance with their rights on a winding up as set out in the company's constitution or terms of issue of the shares. This seems a strange proposition. Why should the rights of the shareholders who are being unwillingly paid off in a reduction be judicially equated with what their rights would have been, had the company been in liquidation? The answer lies in the realisation that to some extent, a reduction is a mini winding up, a winding up *pro tanto*, because, in the reduction, the shareholder is being pushed out of the company, to the extent that his shareholder rights are being reduced. Thus it makes some sense, and produces a type of fairness, to draw the analogy with a winding up. The 'rights' which the courts are primarily having regard to in this context are therefore their rights to a return of capital. It will be seen that the cases turn on such matters as: whether the shares have a prior[51] right to repayment on a winding up, and whether the shares have a right to participation in surplus assets on a winding up.[52]

It is often said that in a reduction of capital, the rule is that the preference shareholders are first to be paid off. Indeed, authorities can be found where that is clearly what is happening.[53] It is argued that preference shareholders cannot complain as they know when they take their shares that this is part of the bargain.[54]

But there is a two-part problem with this approach if it becomes a substitute for thinking through the principles and appropriateness of what is happening in each

---

[50] When the case was in the Court of Appeal, see [1948] 2 All ER 593 at p. 604. See also at p. 283 above.

[51] 'Prior' meaning that they rank in priority to other classes of shares such as ordinary shares.

[52] Where there is only one class of shares, the 'fair and equitable' test will normally require equal treatment of the shareholders, although in unusual circumstances a different result might be reached; see *British and American Trustee Corporation* v *Couper* [1894] AC 399.

[53] *Re Chatterley-Whitfield Collieries Ltd* (above) and *House of Fraser plc* v *ACGE Investments Ltd* (1987) 3 BCC 201.

[54] *Per* Lord Greene MR in *Re Chatterley-Whitfield Collieries* [1949] AC 512 at p. 596. The repayment in such a reduction is at par, i.e. they get the nominal value, since this is all they would have been entitled to in a winding up. If interest rates have fallen since the shares were issued it is likely that they will stand at a premium to the nominal value. It is usual these days for the terms of issue to mitigate the possibility of a repayment reduction by including a clause which ties the repayment on a reduction to the market price. The preference shares in *House of Fraser plc* v *ACGE Investments Ltd* (1987) 3 BCC 201 contained a detailed version of such a clause (at p. 204) which is sometimes referred to as a 'Spens formula'. Another way of protecting the preference shareholders is to include a provision in the articles to the effect that a reduction of capital is deemed to be a variation of class rights. This will trigger the procedure in s. 125; see *Re Northern Engineering Co. Ltd* [1994] BCC 618 and p. 285 below.

case. The first aspect of the problem is that preference shares do not always carry the same kinds of rights. Most do have a prior right to a return of capital on a winding up. But some shares, which would still broadly be referred to as preference shares,[55] have a prior right to a dividend while the company is a going concern, but rank equally (*pari passu*) with ordinary shares on a winding up.[56] In such circumstances it is patently wrong to rely on the rule of thumb that the preference shareholders 'go first'; they do not. On a winding up, they rank equally with the ordinary shares and must be treated in the same way. In order to satisfy the test of 'fair and equitable to the ... classes of shareholders', the reduction would need to bear equally on all the shareholders, preference and ordinary.[57]

The second aspect of the problem, is that if the reduction involves, for example, a cancellation of capital rather than a repayment of capital, then the application of the 'fair and equitable' test will produce a result which is the converse of the idea that 'preference shareholders go first'.[58] Thus, in *Re Floating Dock Ltd*[59] although the (first) preference shareholders had a priority to a return of capital on a winding up, they did not go first in the reduction. They were the last to be cancelled.[60] This is because in a cancellation reduction the whole theory of what is happening is different from the repayment reduction. The cancellation reduction is about bearing losses of capital. In *Floating Dock*, the first preference shares were the class which under the articles had the highest priority to a return of capital in a winding up, and so they were the last to be reduced in the cancellation reduction.

4 Variation of class rights

What happens if the reduction is not in conformity with the 'fair and equitable' test? The basic result is that the proposed reduction is a variation of class rights. It can still be confirmed by the court, provided that the procedures in s. 125 for variation of class rights are complied with. As with the comparable area of company law, schemes of arrangement, it is possible to find that conflicts of interest problems can make it difficult to hold meetings which can satisfy the court that they were an adequate safeguard of class rights.[61] This occurred in *Re Holders Investment Trust Ltd*.[62] The redeemable preference shares carried a right to a 5% fixed preference

---

[55] There is no definition; see p. 268 above.

[56] See e.g. the reduction in *Bannatyne v Direct Spanish Telegraph Ltd* (1886) 34 Ch D 287 where, in the words of Cotton LJ, the preference shares 'were constituted without any preference as regards capital, though they had a preference as regards dividend'. But, it is important to be aware, in reading this case, that it is not a repayment reduction but is instead a cancellation reduction. It is therefore also an example of the second aspect of the problem referred to in the text above.

[57] Sometimes referred to as an 'all round reduction'.

[58] Unless the first aspect of the problem is also operative, as it was in *Bannatyne v Direct Spanish Telegraph Ltd* (n. 56 above).

[59] The facts are given at p. 283 above.

[60] They were partially cancelled; by £1 per share of a nominal value of £3.10. The ordinary shareholders and the second preference shareholders were wiped out entirely by the cancellation. In effect, as a result of the elimination of the other classes, the first preference shares were recognised to be the residual owners of the company; in a sense they had become 'equity' shares.

[61] See the discussion of *Re United Provident Assurance Ltd* at p. 107 above.

[62] [1971] 1 WLR 583. This case is also important for showing that members of a class have a duty, in class meetings, to vote bona fide for the benefit of the class.

dividend while the company was a going concern and a prior right to a return of capital on a winding up. The reduction proposed to cancel the preference shares and in return substitute loan stock which carried 6% but which had a later redemption date. It was common ground that the reduction involved a variation of class rights and after the company had passed the special resolution to reduce the capital as proposed, a class meeting of the preference shares was convened and held, at which an extraordinary resolution of the class was passed, consenting to the reduction. At the hearing of the petition for confirmation Megarry J refused to sanction the reduction. It had become clear that 90% of the preference shares were vested in some trustees who also held 52% of the ordinary shares. The ordinary shares stood to gain from the reduction. The trustees admitted that they had voted in the class meeting on the basis of what was for the benefit of the trust as a whole, not bona fide that they were acting in the interests of the general body of members of that class. Megarry J held that there was therefore 'no effectual sanction for the modification of class rights'[63] and that it was therefore incumbent on those proposing the reduction to prove that it was fair;[64] on the evidence, he held that it was unfair.

C Company purchase of own shares

1 The rationale of prohibition

In 1887 the House of Lords took the decision to prohibit companies from buying their own shares. The case which gave rise to this opportunity was *Trevor v Whitworth*.[65] The insolvent company was in liquidation and was faced with a claim from the executor of a deceased shareholder for the balance of the purchase price of shares which the shareholder had sold to the company.[66] The articles of association provided that: '[A]ny share may be purchased by the company from any person willing to sell it, and at such price, not exceeding the marketable value thereof, as the board think reasonable.'[67] The decision largely proceeded on the technical basis that the purchases were *ultra vires* the company as being neither 'in respect of or as incidental to any of the objects specified in the memorandum'.[68] But it is clear that their Lordships felt that the practice was thoroughly undesirable and unlawful for reasons other than being beyond the powers of the company as defined in the memorandum – indeed, Lord Macnaghten went so far as to say that even 'if the power to purchase its own shares were found in the memorandum of association . . . it would necessarily be void'.[69]

---

[63] [1971] 1 WLR 583 at p. 589.

[64] A difficult burden to discharge once it is agreed that the proposal is a variation of class rights.

[65] (1887) 12 AC 409.

[66] There was an issue as to whether the shares were being purchased by a director on his own account but it was held that the purchase was in fact made by him on behalf of the company: (1887) 12 AC 409 at p. 413.

[67] Article 179. By art. 181 it was provided that: 'Shares so purchased may at the discretion of the board be sold or disposed of by them or be absolutely extinguished, as they deem most advantageous to the company.'

[68] (1887) 12 AC 409 at p. 416, *per* Lord Herschell.

[69] *Ibid.* at p. 436.

The main thrust of the rationale against allowing share purchase was expressed in the form that a proponent of the practice was on 'the horns of a dilemma'[70] (and a dilemma which was made 'perfect'),[71] namely that if the shares purchased by the company were going to be resold, then this was 'trafficking' in shares and if they were not, then it was a reduction of capital which was unlawful because it fell outside the statutory provisions regulating reductions.[72] The need for careful regulation of reductions in accordance with the maintenance of capital principle was stressed:

> The creditors of the company which is being wound up . . . find coming into competition with them persons, who, in respect only of their having been, and having ceased to be shareholders in the company, claim that the company shall pay to them a part of that capital . . . The capital may, no doubt, be diminished by expenditure upon and reasonably incidental to all the objects specified. A part of it may be lost in carrying on the business operations authorised. Of this all persons trusting the company are aware and take the risk. But I think they have a right to rely, and were intended by the legislature to have a right to rely, on the capital remaining undiminished by any expenditure outside these limits, or by the return of any part of it to the shareholders.[73]

Although the courts developed a few marginal exceptions,[74] *Trevor* v *Whitworth* remained the main source of authority until the legislature intervened in the early 1980s.

2 A residual prohibition

The Companies Act 1980 was enacted and contained provisions codifying the basic common law rule on company purchase of own shares.[75] While this legislation was passing through Parliament, moves were afoot to consider the possibility of extending the exceptions to the legislation, to the extent permitted by the EC Second Directive.[76] The DTI issued a Consultative Document[77] and in due course the Companies Act 1981 brought in the wider exceptions.

All the relevant legislation is now contained in ss. 143–149 and 159–181 of the Companies Act 1985. The basic prohibition is contained in s. 143 (1) which provides: 'Subject to the following provisions, a company limited by shares or limited by guarantee and having a share capital shall not acquire its own shares, whether by purchase, subscription or otherwise.' The sanctions are contained in s. 143 (2)

---

[70] *Ibid.* at p. 425, *per* Lord Watson citing James LJ in *Hope* v *International Society* (1876) 4 Ch D 335.
[71] (1887) 12 AC 409 at p. 419, *per* Lord Herschell citing Brett JA in *Hope* v *International Society* above.
[72] Then contained in the Companies Act 1867, ss. 9–13 (now ss. 135–138 of the Companies Act 1985). 'When Parliament sanctions the doing of a thing under certain conditions and with certain restrictions, it must be taken that the thing is prohibited unless the prescribed conditions and restrictions are observed': (1887) 12 AC 409 at pp. 437–438, *per* Lord Macnaghten.
[73] *Ibid.* at pp. 414–415, *per* Lord Herschell. On the facts it seemed fairly clear that a systematic breach of the maintenance principle was being perpetrated despite the argument that the purchases were being carried out to facilitate the retention of family control.
[74] See *Kirby* v *Wilkins* [1929] 2 Ch 444; *Re Castiglione's Will Trusts* [1958] Ch 549.
[75] Companies Act 1980, ss. 35–37.
[76] Mainly arts 19–22, 24 and also art. 39 (redeemable shares).
[77] *The Purchase by a Company of its Own Shares: A Consultative Document* (Cmnd. 7944, 1980) paras 15–16. The document was written by Professor Gower.

which provides for a fine for the company and fines or imprisonment for the officers in default. The purported acquisition is void. It has been held in *Acatos & Hutcheson plc* v *Watson*[78] that s. 143 was not contravened when a company acquired another company which held shares in it.

The exceptions are set out in a list in s. 143 (3) and by subs. (3) (a) the prohibition is expressed not to apply to 'the redemption or purchase of shares in accordance with [ss. 159–181]'.[79] Section 162 (1) then provides: 'Subject to the following provisions of this Chapter, a company limited by shares or limited by guarantee and having a share capital may, if authorised to do so by its articles,[80] purchase its own shares (including any redeemable shares)'. Shares purchased are normally treated as cancelled[81] although, as a result of recent reform, it is now possible in some situations[82] for companies to hold the shares 'in treasury'. The DTI felt that the facility of using treasury shares might come to be seen as a less cumbersome and less expensive process than a conventional buyback and fresh issue.[83] It is also possible that it might enable companies to take advantage of capital growth in their own shares by selling small numbers of treasury shares opportunistically.[84]

The procedure required for a company to purchase its own shares, depends on whether the share purchase is an 'off-market'[85] purchase or a 'market'[86] purchase. The main examples in practice of market purchases are those made of shares listed on the London Stock Exchange or quoted on the Alternative Investment Market (AIM). With off-market purchases the company may only make the purchase if the contract is approved in advance.[87] Obviously this would not be possible in the case of a market purchase and so the legislation here requires merely prior authorisation in general meeting.[88] The provisions make various other specifications applying to share purchases, so that the shares must be fully paid up,[89] there may be no pur-

---

[78] [1995] 1 BCLC 218.
[79] Companies Act 1985, s. 143 (3) (b)–(d) is mainly a gathering together list of exceptions which already exist or are already dotted about in other parts of the Act. Section 143 (3) also makes it clear that a company may acquire any of its own fully paid shares 'otherwise than for valuable consideration' such as by way of gift. In ss. 144–149 there are complex provisions dealing with companies having beneficial interests in their own shares and designed to prevent circumvention of the prohibition in s. 143.
[80] The necessary authority is normally supplied by art. 35 of Table A.
[81] CA 1985, ss. 162(2) and 160(4).
[82] There are various conditions, such as: the shares need to be those which are traded on a regulated market, and not more than 10% of the aggregate nominal value of the issued share capital or of any class of share capital may be held in treasury. See generally the Companies (Acquisition of Own Shares) (Treasury Shares) Regulations 2003 (SI 2003, No. 1116); there have been subsequent amendments.
[83] DTI Consultative Document (May 1998) *Share Buybacks*, which raised the question of whether companies should be allowed to hold their repurchased shares 'in treasury' for resale at some later date.
[84] Possibly a dangerous procedure; see Chapter 20 below on Insider Dealing and Market Abuse.
[85] The 1985 Act provides a complex definition of 'off-market' in s. 163 (1) and (2).
[86] Defined in Companies Act 1985, s. 163 (3) as '... a purchase made on a recognised investment exchange, other than a purchase which is an off-market purchase by virtue of [s. 163 (1) (b)]'.
[87] The terms of the proposed contract must be authorised by special resolution before the contract is entered into (s. 164). Not surprisingly, the owner of the shares is effectively barred from voting on the resolution (s. 164 (5)) and there are various other conditions and extensions (ss. 164, 165).
[88] Companies Act 1985, s. 166 (1). Various conditions are laid down in s. 166.
[89] *Ibid.* ss. 162 (2) and 159 (3).

chase if as a result of the purchase there would no longer be any member of the company holding shares other than redeemable shares[90] and there is a requirement for disclosure by delivery of particulars to the Registrar of Companies.[91]

3 Payment for the shares

It is in the provisions concerning the payment for the shares that Parliament meets some of the challenges posed by the rationale of *Trevor* v *Whitworth*. One of the main objections was that it would operate as an unlawful reduction of capital:

> The shareholders receive back the moneys subscribed, and there passes into their pockets what before existed in the form of cash in the coffers of the company, or of buildings, machinery, or stock available to meet the demands of the creditors.[92]

This problem is avoided by requiring that the shares may only be purchased out of the proceeds of a fresh issue of shares made for the purpose or out of distributable profits of the company. The drafting by which this is achieved is convoluted to say the least. The approach adopted is to import these rules (by s. 162 (2)) from the provisions governing the redemption of redeemable shares (s. 160) where the underlying principles concerning maintenance of capital are identical. On the other hand, also applicable here, but standing alone and not imported, are the provisions of s. 170 which require the establishment of a capital redemption reserve to the extent that the payment for the purchase[93] of the shares is out of distributable profits. The capital redemption reserve effectively makes those profits undistributable and so preserves the capital.

With private companies, it is possible to reduce capital in some circumstances. Where various conditions set out in ss. 171–177 are satisfied the Act permits the use of capital to the extent of what is called 'the permissible capital payment'.[94] The *Trevor* v *Whitworth* objection is met to a large extent by the existence of numerous safeguards such as the need for directors' declarations as to solvency and enhanced protection for creditors.

The other main objection emanating from *Trevor* v *Whitworth* was that a purchase of own shares would enable the company to traffic in its own shares, i.e. buy and sell for profit. This is effectively prevented by provisions that the shares purchased are treated as cancelled.[95] There is an additional safeguard in the background here. If the company were to buy its own shares in an effort to force up or support the market price the directors and the company itself could face liability under the Financial Services and Markets Act 2000.[96]

---

[90] *Ibid.* s. 162 (3).
[91] Respectively *ibid.* ss. 162 (2) and 159 (3), 162 (3) and 169. Other matters are dealt with in s. 167 (assignment) and s. 178 (effect of failure to purchase).
[92] *Trevor* v *Whitworth* (1887) 12 AC 409 at p. 416, *per* Lord Herschell.
[93] Or redeemable shares redeemed under Companies Act 1985, ss. 159–160.
[94] *Ibid.* s. 171 (3).
[95] See *ibid.* ss. 162 (2) and 160 (4).
[96] See Chapter 20.

4 Commercial uses of share buy-backs

In recent years, the statutory facility permitting companies to purchase their own shares has become popular. It has even acquired a popular name: share 'buy-backs'. Listed plcs have been setting up share buy-backs in a variety of circumstances. In 1995–96 £1.4bn worth of share buy-backs were conducted in the UK market.[97] Share buy-backs have become an essential component of the finance director's armoury in his battle to manage the company's capital flexibly and efficiently.

Many different commercial reasons can lie behind the decision of a company to set up a buy-back. One of the reasons for the current frequency of buy-backs is that during the early 1990s favourable economic conditions left many plcs with very substantial earnings. Companies which have cash which is surplus to their current needs will sometimes find that this dilutes their average earnings per share. This is because they get a higher return on their trading and acquisition activities than they can by investing the money. If this is the situation, a share buy-back will enhance the future earnings per share of the remaining shares. This will tend to make the shares more attractive and thus bolster the market price.[98] Earnings per share might also be enhanced by a buy-back in other situations such as where the cancelled share capital was to be replaced by a cheaper source of funding. Another example of commercial use has been occurring where the situation is that the traded price of the shares of the company is thought by the directors to be undervaluing its assets. Assuming that the directors' view of the situation is correct, a buy-back will provide a method of increasing the value of the remaining shares and so wipe out or reduce the discount in the traded price.[99]

D Dividends and distributions

Unless the company is making profits out of which dividends can be paid, the payment of dividends will gradually reduce the stock of assets which are available to creditors. It will not diminish the amount of share capital entered on the balance sheet as such, and in this important sense, the problem differs from those so far examined, which have been concerned with reduction of capital and share purchases that essentially involve striking out capital from the balance sheet and thereby decreasing the undistributable reserves of the company. As such, the payment of dividends represents a less overt threat to the maintenance of capital doctrine. Nevertheless, the rule was established in *Re Exchange Banking Co., Flitcroft's Case*[100] that dividends could only be paid out of profits.

Thereafter, the way that the rules were developed and applied over many years produced a situation where the legal rules were considerably less stringent than those which would normally have been applied by prudent businessmen or

---

[97] *Financial Times*, 25 March 1996. The USA has seen similar developments. According to Lehman Brothers, share buy-backs in 1996 amounted to $14bn (*Financial Times* 22 March 1997). For an account of developments in Australia, see J. Cotton (1995) 16 Co Law 287.

[98] A reason suggested by S. Edge 'Do We Have an Imputation System or Not?' (1996) 375 *Tax Journal* 2.

[99] A reason advanced by H. Nowlan and I. Abrahams 'Share Buy-Backs' (1994) 278 *Tax Journal* 10.

[100] (1882) 21 Ch D 519.

accountants. An example of this can be seen in *Ammonia Soda Co.* v *Chamberlain*,[101] where it was made clear that trading losses occurring in previous accounting periods could be ignored in such a way that the trading periods in the accounts became separate from each other. This threw the losses onto capital, in the sense, at least, that the assets of the company would be diminished by the amount of the dividend. Suppose, for instance, that in its first year of trading, the company made a trading loss of £1,000, and in its second year a £1,200 profit. A distribution of the second year's profit as dividend would mean that, taking a two-year perspective, the company's assets available to creditors was still £1,000 less than when it started.

In 1980, in fulfilment of the UK's obligations under the EC Second Directive, the case law rules were replaced by statutory provisions which are more in line with normal business and accountancy practice. These provisions are now contained in ss. 263–281 of the Companies Act 1985. The basic prohibition is contained in s. 263 (1), which provides that a company may not make a 'distribution' except out of profits available for the purpose. 'Distribution' is defined as meaning every description of distribution of a company's assets to its members, whether in cash or otherwise.[102] Crucially, the profits available for distribution are defined in s. 263 (3) as follows:

> ... [A] company's profits available for distribution are its accumulated, realised profits, so far as not previously utilised by distribution or capitalisation, less its accumulated, realised losses, so far as not previously written off in a reduction or reorganisation of capital duly made.

The wording contains some subtle effects. For instance, the use of the word 'accumulated' reverses the *Ammonia Soda Case* because it shows that the profit and loss account is to be treated as a continuum, in that it may not be split up into artificial and isolated trading periods. Similarly, the presence of the word 'realised' ends another earlier dispute between the cases on whether unrealised profits[103] could be used to pay dividends. It is now clear that unrealised profits cannot be so used, although an unrealised profit can be used to pay up bonus shares, since these are not a 'distribution' within s. 263 (2).[104] Whether or not distribution may lawfully be made is to be determined by reference to the company's accounts.[105]

Public companies are subjected to further conditions before a distribution can be made. It is necessary that at the time of the distribution the amount of the public company's net assets is not less than the aggregate of its called up share capital and undistributable reserves and that the distribution does not then reduce the

---

[101] [1918] 1 Ch 266.

[102] Companies Act 1985, s. 263 (2). However, distribution does not include an issue of bonus shares, redemption or purchase of the company's own shares out of capital (including the proceeds of any fresh issue of shares) or out of unrealised profits. Nor does it include certain reductions of share capital or distributions of assets to members of the company on its winding up; *ibid.*

[103] In other words, those arising merely from a revaluation of assets in the books of the company rather than an actual sale. For the earlier case law dispute, see *Dimbula Valley (Ceylon) Tea Co.* v *Laurie* [1961] Ch 353; *Westburn Sugar Refineries Ltd* v *IRC* 1960 SLT 297, 1960 TR 105.

[104] Companies Act 1985, s. 263 (2) (a). 'Realised' loss may in some circumstances within s. 269 include development costs.

[105] *Ibid.* ss. 270–276.

net assets below that aggregate.[106] The 'undistributable reserves' referred to means, broadly, the share premium account, capital redemption reserve, the amount by which the accumulated unrealised profits exceed its accumulated unrealised losses (unless the profits or losses have, respectively, already been capitalised, or written off).[107] What this provision is actually doing is requiring that a public company keep its share capital intact, before it can pay a dividend, even in respect of unrealised capital losses. Thus if the fixed assets of the company have fallen in value, this will reduce its net assets in the balance sheet and so the company will be unable to pay a dividend unless this shortfall is made good. A private company is not troubled by such a downwards revaluation because it is not a 'realised loss' within s. 263 (3).

Distributions made in breach of the legislation are dealt with by s. 277 which provides that the member is liable to repay it if at the time of the distribution, the member knows, or has reasonable grounds for believing that it is made in breach of the provisions. Section 277 (2) preserves any case law obligation to repay. Over the years, the judicial method of requiring a recipient to repay a sum or asset received in breach of the doctrine of maintenance of capital has been to hold that it is *ultra vires*.[108] The link with *ultra vires* has enabled the court to move speedily to the conclusion that the money could be recovered by the imposition of a constructive trust. It is unlikely that the courts will be so keen to utilise the *ultra vires* doctrine in this way in future cases in view of the fact that since the 1989 reforms, *ultra vires* acts can be ratified by special resolution.[109] Directors who authorise payments in breach of the provisions may find themselves liable for breach of fiduciary duty and liable to restore any loss to the company.[110]

15.4 COMPANY LAW REVIEW AND LAW REFORM

One of the 'key issues' selected by the Company Law Review[111] in *The Strategic Framework*[112] was 'capital maintenance'. Subsequently, in *Company Formation and Capital Maintenance*,[113] the recommendations were set out and consultation began. The Steering Group noted that many major creditors attached little importance to the company's nominal capital and looked to other indicators of creditworthiness.

Very many reforms were proposed, the main ones being: first, to abolish par (i.e. nominal value) for private companies[114] so that a share would then merely repre-

---

[106] *Ibid.* s. 264 (1). By s. 264 (2) the term 'net assets' means here the aggregate of the company's assets less the aggregate of its liabilities. Further relevant provisions are contained in s. 264 (4) and Sch. 4, para. 89.

[107] And also any other reserve which the company is prohibited from distributing by any other enactment or by its memorandum or articles; see generally s. 264 (3).

[108] See *Re Precision Dippings Ltd* (1985) 1 BCC 99,539; *Aveling Barford Ltd* v *Perion Ltd* (1989) 5 BCC 677 (discussed at p. 119 above). The idea was also very much present in *Trevor* v *Whitworth* (p. 289 above).

[109] Companies Act 1985, s. 35 (3).

[110] *Bairstow* v *Queens Moat Houses plc* [2002] BCC 1000, CA.

[111] See generally Chapter 4 above.

[112] DTI Consultation Document (February 1999).

[113] DTI Consultation Document (October 1999).

[114] The public company position is constrained by the Second Directive.

sent a proportion of the company's value.[115] This would mean that the concept of the share premium account would become redundant and would be replaced by a requirement that on the issue of new shares the undistributable reserves on the balance sheet would be increased by the net proceeds of the shares.[116] Secondly, it was proposed to relax the rules regulating reductions of capital and to do away with the burdensome requirement of an application to the court for confirmation of the reduction.[117] For public companies in order to comply with the Second Directive, creditors would be given a right to apply to the court to cancel the reduction. In a subsequent DTI Consultation Document *Capital Maintenance: Other Issues*,[118] in the light of various criticisms raised by consultees, the Steering Group expressed the view that the merits of the proposals concerning par value and the related concepts of share premium and share discounts remained uncertain.

Eventually, the Final Report of the Company Law Review came down in favour of retaining the capital maintenance regime, but recommended further relaxations for private companies. The concept of par (i.e. nominal) value is to be retained; this is to be welcomed, since it was always highly questionable whether creating a separate regime for private companies and public companies on such fundamental matters as par value and undistributable reserves is a reform, which looking at company law as a whole, is necessarily to be seen as an improvement, particularly in view of the fact that the Second Directive has sought to harmonise the position. However, they recommended the abolition of the requirement for companies to have an 'authorised share capital' so that in effect the company no longer need have a ceiling on the amount of capital it can issue. Also, capital reduction requirements are to be streamlined so as to reduce the number of situations in which reduction needs confirmation by the court.[119]

It is clear from the document *Company Law. Flexibility and Accessibility: A Consultative Document* (London: DTI, 2004) that a number of reforms are likely in this area.

---

[115] DTI Consultation Document (October 1999) *Company Formation and Capital Maintenance* para. 3.8.

[116] *Ibid.* para. 3.18.

[117] *Ibid.* paras 3.27 *et seq.*

[118] June 2000. The document seeks consultation on further matters, especially on clarifying the concepts of 'distribution' and 'realised losses'.

[119] *Modern Company Law for a Competitive Economy Final Report* (London: DTI, June 2001) paras.4.4–4.5, 10.1–10.7.

16

FINANCIAL ASSISTANCE FOR THE ACQUISITION OF SHARES

16.1 BACKGROUND TO THE PRESENT LAW

This chapter is concerned with an area of statute law and the case law which has sprung from it, which has a long history of failure. Failure, in the sense of not preventing the abuses it was designed to prevent, and failure in the sense of smashing up transactions which have been carried out for bona fide commercial reasons. Dating from 1929,[1] it continues to engage practitioners on a daily basis and provides a fruitful source of income for the Chancery Bar who are frequently asked to provide opinions on an area almost unrivalled for its ability to cause trouble.[2]

Broadly speaking, s. 151 of the Companies Act 1985 penalises the provision of financial assistance by a company for the acquisition of its own shares by another. Sections 151–158 originated in 1981,[3] when the government embarked on a radical restructuring of the existing provisions then contained in s. 54 of the 1948 Act. The mischief which the provisions were originally designed to prohibit was clearly described by the Greene Committee[4] in 1926:

> A practice has made its appearance in recent years which we consider to be highly improper. A syndicate agrees to purchase from the existing shareholders sufficient shares to control a company, the purchase money is provided by a temporary loan from a bank for a day or two, the syndicate's nominees are appointed directors in place of the old board and immediately proceed to lend to the syndicate out of the company's funds (often without security) the money required to pay off the bank ... Thus in effect the company provides money for the purchase of its own shares.

That the statutory provisions were not very successful in the prevention of this type of abuse became well known[5] and was illustrated by the glaring examples of it in

---

[1] Companies Act 1929, s. 45.

[2] It nevertheless found its way into the Second EC Company Law Directive (79/91/EEC) from where it continues to dismay our European partners; art. 23 provides: 'A [public] company may not advance funds, nor make loans, nor provide security, with a view to the acquisition of shares by a third party.'

[3] First enacted as ss. 42–44 of the Companies Act 1982 and then consolidated in 1985.

[4] Cmd. 2657, 1926, para. 30.

[5] Section 54 was described by Neville Faulks QC in the Board of Trade Investigation into the Affairs of H. Jasper and Company Ltd as 'honoured more in the breach than in the observance' (London: HMSO, 1961) para. 161 (B).

Selangor United Rubber Estates Ltd v *Cradock (No. 3)*[6] and *Wallersteiner* v *Moir*.[7] The penalty of £100 fine in s. 54 of the 1948 Act was hardly a realistic deterrent. It was not until 1980 that breach of the provisions could carry up to two years' imprisonment.[8]

On the other hand, for all its feebleness, s. 54 was seen by others as a thorough nuisance, capable of penalising and preventing many desirable commercial transactions. Lord Seebohm said (in the debates on the 1981 reforms): 'I joined Barclays Bank in 1929 the year in which section [45] of the Companies Act [1929] came into force. Ever since that time it has been a plague for those operating in the banking field.'[9] For by contrast to the insignificant criminal penalties, the civil consequences[10] of breach of the section were (although sometimes uncertain) far-reaching and draconian. A security or other financial assistance given in breach of the section was void;[11] the sale of the shares itself was liable to be set aside unless it could be severed from the illegal parts of the transaction; directors who participated in breaches were liable to recoup the company for any loss suffered; and worst of all, from the point of view of the business community in general, *Selangor United Rubber Estates Ltd* v *Cradock (No. 3)* established a wide constructive trust liability for banks and others who unintentionally became participants in complex schemes which were in breach of the section.

Two situations in particular had been seen to give difficulty. The first was the kind of situation where the small private company was owned by, say, a 65-year-old managing director[12] who wanted to retire and had found a buyer for his shares. The buyer needed a loan from a bank in order to help him fund the purchase. The bank was prepared to lend but wanted security. The purchaser's house was already second-mortgaged to pay school fees and had no security to give. Could the company help out by giving a floating charge over its undertaking? If the bank lent on this basis it would find that its security, the floating charge was illegal and void, since the company had given financial assistance for the purchase of its shares.

The second situation was where company A buys an asset from company B at a fair price. The asset is one that company A genuinely wants for bona fide commercial reasons. Because the purchase money passes to company B, the transaction also has the incidental effect of putting company B in funds to buy shares in company A. When discussing this situation in the Court of Appeal case of *Belmont Finance Corporation Ltd* v *Williams Furniture Ltd (No. 2)*,[13] Buckley LJ expressed the view that where the sole purpose was to put B in funds to acquire the shares, this clearly contravened the legislation, but, somewhat alarmingly, he suggested that it might

---

[6] [1968] 1 WLR 1555.
[7] [1974] 1 WLR 991.
[8] Companies Act 1980, s. 80, Sch. 2. Now in Companies Act 1985, s. 730, Sch. 24.
[9] *Hansard*, HL, vol. 418, col. 973.
[10] The current position is examined in detail below.
[11] Probably; see further p. 305 below.
[12] Some versions of this example could contravene the directors' loan provisions (Companies Act 1985, ss. 330 *et seq.*).
[13] [1980] 1 All ER 393 at p. 401 d–h.

also have contravened it where putting B in funds was merely one of a number of purposes.

In 1962, the Jenkins Committee[14] recommended reform on the basis that: 'From the evidence we have received, we are satisfied that s. 54, as it is now framed, has proved to be an occasional embarrassment[15] to the honest without being a serious inconvenience to the unscrupulous.' Thus, by 1981, the time was long due for major reform of the section, the previous year having seen two cases which further demonstrated both the vagueness of the section and its undesirably wide ambit.[16]

16.2 THE MODERN SCOPE OF THE PROHIBITIONS

The general prohibition is contained in s. 151 of the Companies Act 1985. Section 151 (1) provides:

> ... [W]here a person is acquiring or is proposing to acquire shares in a company, it is not lawful for the company or any of its subsidiaries to give financial assistance directly or indirectly for the purpose of that acquisition before or at the same time as the acquisition takes place ...

It is clear that this relates only to what might be termed '*pre*-acquisition assistance'. However, s. 151 (2) extends the prohibition to a situation which might be termed '*post*-acquisition' assistance. Thus, s. 151 (2) provides:

> ... [W]here a person has acquired shares in a company and any liability[17] has been incurred (by that or any other person), for the purpose of that acquisition, it is not lawful for the company or any of its subsidiaries to give financial assistance directly or indirectly for the purpose of reducing or discharging the liability so incurred ...

It is generally thought that s. 151 (1) and (2) give separate treatment to *pre*- and *post*-acquisition assistance in order to prevent problems arising in the kind of situation where a parent company (H Co.) gives a debenture (to D Bank) which requires all its assets and those of its subsidiaries to be charged by way of floating charges, and H Co. later acquires a new subsidiary (S Co.) by purchase of the shares (from V Co.). A floating charge given on the assets of the new subsidiary would possibly have been in breach of the old s. 54 provisions[18] since it was arguably given (in a loose sense) '... in connection with a purchase ... of ... shares ...'. Now, however, (i.e. since 1981) there is clearly no breach of s. 151, for s. 151

---

[14] Cmnd. 1749, 1962, paras 176, 170–187.

[15] This was in 1962. After *Selangor* (1968) this became something of an understatement.

[16] One of these was the *Belmont Finance* case (discussed in the text above), the other was *Armour Hick Northern Ltd* v *Whitehouse* [1980] 1 WLR 1520.

[17] By s. 152 (3), this is expressed to include 'changing his financial position by making an agreement or arrangement (whether enforceable or unenforceable, and whether made on his own account or with any other person) or by any other means ...'.

[18] Section 54 of the Companies Act 1948 provided: 'Subject as provided in this section, it shall not be lawful for a company to give, whether directly or indirectly, and whether by means of a loan, guarantee, the provision of security or otherwise, any financial assistance for the purpose of or in connection with a purchase or subscription made or to be made by any person of or for any shares in the company, or, where the company is a subsidiary company in its holding company.' The legislation contained exceptions.

(1) is clearly inapplicable and under s. 151 (2) the issue is whether assistance is given for the purpose of reducing or discharging a liability incurred (with V Co.) for the purpose of the acquisition and the charge in favour of D Bank is clearly not being given to discharge a liability incurred for the purpose of the acquisition.[19]

Another significant difference between s. 151 and the old s. 54 is that, for the prohibition under s. 151 to apply, the financial assistance needs to be given '*for the purpose of*[20] that acquisition' which is considerably narrower[21] in ambit than the words 'in connection with' in the old s. 54. In view of the emphasis laid on the concept of 'purpose' in the legislative exceptions which are discussed below, it is worth emphasising this threshold test of purpose.

It is clear from s. 151 that the giving of assistance by a subsidiary can be within the prohibition. This aspect was examined by Millett J in *Arab Bank plc v Mercantile Holdings Ltd,*[22] a case which nicely illustrates the complexity of companies legislation. Mercantile Holdings Ltd[23] had given a charge over some of its property in favour of Arab Bank plc in order to secure a loan facility which the bank had given another company to enable that other company to acquire the shares of the parent company of Mercantile Holdings Ltd. The bank wished to realise its security by selling the property and to prevent this happening, Mercantile Holdings Ltd sought to argue that the security had been given in breach of s. 151 and was therefore void. Without more, the parties were agreed that the giving of the charge was a breach of s. 151. However, Mercantile Holdings Ltd had been incorporated in Gibraltar and had received legal advice at the time it created the charge that because it was a foreign subsidiary the transaction was not caught by the section and it then entered into the transaction honestly and in good faith in reliance on that advice. It now suited it to maintain that the transaction was in fact unlawful.

The first question which Millett J addressed was whether the mere giving of financial assistance by the subsidiary *ipso facto* also constituted the giving of such assistance by the parent company. The answer to this was:

[P]lainly 'no'. The statutory prohibition is, and always has been, directed to the assisting company, not to its parent company. If the giving of financial assistance by a subsidiary for the acquisition of shares in its holding company necessarily also constituted the giving of financial assistance by the holding company, s. 73 of the 1947 Act would not have been necessary.[24] Moreover, ss. 153–158 of the 1985 Act are clearly predicated on the assumption that it is the conduct of the subsidiary alone which needs statutory authorisation.[25]

---

[19] See Standing Committee A, 30 June 1981, col. 298 and also *Hansard*, HC, vol. 10, cols 206–207.

[20] Emphasis added.

[21] This also helps to produce the result in the example given above.

[22] [1993] BCC 816.

[23] The name is confusing. Although called 'Holdings', in fact Mercantile Holdings Ltd was the subsidiary here.

[24] The point being that s. 45 of the Companies Act 1929 first introduced the prohibition on a company from giving financial assistance in connection with the purchase of its own shares and it was s. 73 of the Companies Act 1947 which extended it to the giving of financial assistance in connection with the purchase of shares in the company's holding company. It did this by enacting that s. 45 of the 1929 Act should apply to shares in a company's holding company as it applied to shares in the company itself.

[25] [1993] BCC 816 at p. 819.

On the other hand, if a parent company were to procure the unlawful acts of the subsidiary, then this would be an offence (assuming those acts were actually unlawful). Also, there clearly may be situations where a parent company's conduct might make it liable for the indirect provision of financial assistance even if the act of the subsidiary itself was not unlawful. The example given[26] by Millett J was that of an English company which hives down an asset to a foreign subsidiary in order for it to be made available to finance an contemplated acquisition of shares of the English company.

The second question which arose, was whether s. 151 made it unlawful for a foreign subsidiary of an English parent company to give financial assistance for the purpose of the acquisition of shares of its parent company. Millett J observed that if read literally, s. 151 did make the assistance unlawful and, in the circumstances, Mercantile Holdings Ltd was certainly a 'subsidiary'[27] within the meaning of the Companies Act 1985, for s. 736 sets out the circumstances in which one company may be deemed to be a subsidiary of another. In it, the word 'company' includes any 'body corporate'.[28] The term 'body corporate' is defined by s. 740 to include a company incorporated elsewhere than in Great Britain. This position differed from that which pertained under the previous version of the legislation[29] and was attributed to a change in drafting style rather than any parliamentary intention to change the law.[30] It explains Millett J's opening remarks in the case which, in the current maelstrom of reform of company law, may perhaps be seen as a timely warning about disturbing settled law in complex areas:

> The case illustrates the dangers which are inherent in any attempt to recast statutory language in more modern and direct form for no better reason than to make it shorter, simpler and more easily intelligible.[31]

The judge reached the conclusion that: ' "any of its subsidiaries" in s. 151 must be construed as limited to those subsidiaries which are subsidiary companies, that is to say English companies'.[32] Such a departure from the literal meaning of a statute needs strong justification, and so, perhaps with this in mind, Millett J listed no fewer than 10 reasons for his decision.[33] For the purposes of the general law, the most significant of these were probably the private international law considerations, namely:

> 2. There is a presumption that in the absence of a contrary intention expressed or implied, UK legislation does not apply to foreign persons or corporations outside the UK whose acts are performed outside the UK. Some limitation of the general words of s. 151 is

---

[26] *Ibid.* at pp. 819–820. The example is predicated on the basis (as was later held) that s. 151 did not make unlawful the conduct of the foreign subsidiary itself.

[27] Although it was not a 'company' within the Companies Act 1985, because s. 735 (1) (a) defines a company as 'a company formed and registered under this Act'. Having an established place of business in Great Britain, it was in fact an 'oversea company' (s. 744).

[28] Companies Act 1985, s. 736 (3).

[29] I.e. 'old' s. 54.

[30] [1993] BCC 816 at p. 819.

[31] *Ibid.* at p. 816.

[32] *Ibid.* at p. 821.

[33] *Ibid.* at pp. 821–822.

necessary in order to avoid imputing to Parliament an intention to create an exhorbitant jurisdiction which is contrary to generally accepted principles of international law
. . .

5. The capacity of a corporation, the regulation of its conduct, the maintenance of its capital and the protection of its creditors and shareholders are all matters for the law of the place of its incorporation, not the law of the place of incorporation of its parent company.[34]

The obvious criticism to be levelled at this decision is that in some circumstances it may make it possible to evade the statutory provisions by arranging things so that when financial assistance is needed, and is not going to be within any of the legitimate statutory exceptions, then it is given by a foreign subsidiary. However, as suggested earlier, this may in any event make the parent company liable for providing indirect assistance[35] although the prosecution will often find it difficult to show that the parent was sufficiently involved with the structuring of the subsidiary and the use of its assets. Overall, it is clear that Millett J reached the right conclusions in law as to the scope of the statute, and to the extent that it exists, the danger of evasion is the result of unstated legislative policy or defective legislating.

16.3 MEANING OF FINANCIAL ASSISTANCE

The scope of the prohibition on giving 'financial assistance' in s. 151 is circumscribed by s. 152 which deals in considerable detail with what is meant by 'financial assistance'. The previous legislation[36] also used the expression 'financial assistance' but without much elaboration as to its meaning, beyond the addition of the phrase 'whether by means of a loan, guarantee, the provision of security or otherwise'. In *Charterhouse Investment Trust Ltd* v *Tempest Diesels Ltd*[37] Hoffmann J (as he then was) took the view that:

> One must examine the commercial realities of the transaction and decide whether it can properly be described as the giving of financial assistance by the company, bearing in mind that the section is a penal one and should not be stretched to cover transactions which are not fairly within it.

This was a decision on the old legislation but it has since been held that a similar approach must be taken when construing section 152.[38]

16.4 PRINCIPAL/LARGER PURPOSE EXCEPTIONS

A salient and problematic feature of the current legislation is the inclusion of a general purpose based exception to the prohibitions, partly as a result of the

---

[34] *Ibid.*
[35] Although not for procuring, since the foreign subsidiary is not in breach of s. 151 and is therefore doing nothing unlawful.
[36] I.e. 'old' s. 54 of the Companies Act 1948.
[37] [1986] BCLC 1 at p. 10.
[38] See *Barclays Bank plc* v *British & Commonwealth Holdings plc* [1996] BCLC 38, CA; *Chaston v SWP Group plc* [2003] 1 BCLC 675, CA; *MT Realisations Ltd (In Liquidation) v Digital Equipment Co Ltd* [2003] 2 BCLC 117, CA.

recommendations earlier made by the Jenkins Committee and partly in response to the observations of the Court of Appeal in the *Belmont Finance* case.[39]

The relevant provisions are s. 153 (1) and (2) which, like the corresponding provisions in s. 151 to which they provide exception, give separate treatment to *pre-* and *post-*acquisition assistance. Thus s. 153 (1) provides:

> Section 151 (1) does not prohibit a company from giving financial assistance for the purpose of an acquisition of shares in it or its holding company if:
> (a) the company's principal purpose in giving that assistance is not to give it for the purpose of any such acquisition, or the giving of the assistance for that purpose is but an incidental part of some larger purpose of the company, and
> (b) the assistance is given in good faith in the interests of the company.

In similar terms, s. 153 (2) is designed to provide exception in circumstances of post-acquisition assistance:

> Section 151 (2) does not prohibit a company from giving financial assistance if:
> (a) the company's principal purpose in giving the assistance is not to reduce or discharge any liability incurred by a person for the purpose of the acquisition of shares in the company or its holding company, or the reduction or discharge of any such liability is but an incidental part of some larger purpose of the company, and
> (b) the assistance is given in good faith in the interests of the company.

Since 1988, the effect of s. 153 has been completely overshadowed by the House of Lords' decision in the complicated case *Brady* v *Brady*.[40] Two brothers, Jack and Bob, ran the company T. Brady & Sons Ltd ('Brady') and relations between the brothers had broken down. A complex scheme was proposed and agreed upon which would enable them to separate, each with different parts of the business, but also keeping the company alive and trading. The brothers reached a contractual agreement to reconstruct the company along certain lines but Bob, feeling that he was not getting a fair deal, refused to go ahead with the arrangements. Jack brought an action for specific performance. Bob argued that specific performance should not be awarded because the scheme was illegal under s. 151 (2).

The illegality problem arose because at one stage of the elaborate scheme prepared by the professional advisers to the parties, a company called Motoreal Ltd purchased the shares of Brady and in doing so incurred a liability. At a later stage in the scheme, Motoreal Ltd caused Brady to transfer half its assets to another company (Actavista Ltd) to discharge the liability that Motoreal Ltd had incurred in the purchase of the shares. All the parties accepted that this transaction was in breach of s. 151 (2), and the main issue[41] which confronted the House of Lords was whether it was saved by s. 153 (2). The judgment of the House of Lords was delivered by Lord Oliver. It was held that the scheme, as proposed, contravened s. 151 (2) and that it was not saved by s. 153 (2). Whereas the majority of the Court of

---

[39] See at p. 295 above.
[40] [1988] BCLC 579.
[41] It was also argued *inter alia* that the scheme was *ultra vires*. This contention had succeeded in the Court of Appeal but ultimately failed in the House of Lords.

Appeal[42] had felt that the difficulty with the scheme lay in para. (b) of s. 153 (2), the House of Lords felt that the difficulty with the scheme lay with para. (a).[43] The House of Lords' analysis is set out at length in a difficult passage in the speech of Lord Oliver.[44] He held that s. 153 (2) (a) contemplates two alternative situations:

> ... The first envisages a principal and, by implication, a subsidiary purpose. The inquiry here is whether the assistance was given principally in order to relieve the purchaser of shares in the company of his indebtedness resulting from the acquisition or whether it was principally for some other purpose – for instance the acquisition from the purchase of some asset which the company requires for its business. That is the situation envisaged by Buckley LJ in the course his judgment in the *Belmont Finance* case as giving rise to doubts. That is not this case, for the purpose of the assistance here was simply and solely to reduce the indebtedness incurred by Motoreal ...

Lord Oliver went on to say that the second alternative situation in s. 153 (2) (a) was where:

> ... [I]t is not suggested that the financial assistance was intended to achieve any other object than the reduction or discharge of the indebtedness but where that result (that is, the reduction or discharge) is merely incidental to some larger purpose of the company. These last three words are important. What has to be sought is some larger overall purpose in which the resultant reduction or discharge is merely incidental ... [P]urpose is, in some contexts, a word of wide content but in construing it in the context of the fasciculus of sections regulating the provision of finance by the company in connection with the purchase of its own shares there has always to be borne in mind the mischief against which s. 151 is aimed. In particular, if the section is not, effectively, to be deprived of any useful application, it is important to distinguish between a purpose and the reason why a purpose is formed. The ultimate reason for forming the purpose of financing an acquisition may, and in most cases probably will be more important to those making the decision than the immediate transaction itself. But 'larger' is not the same thing as 'more important' nor is 'reason' the same as 'purpose'. If one postulates the case of a bidder for control of a public company financing his bid from the company's own funds – the obvious mischief at which the section is aimed – the immediate purpose which it is sought to achieve is that of completing the purchase and vesting control of the company in the bidder. The reasons why that course is considered desirable may be many and varied ... It may ... be thought ... that the business of the company would be more profitable under his management than it was heretofore. There may be excellent reasons but they cannot, in my judgment, constitute a 'larger purpose' of which the provision of assistance is merely an incident. The purpose and the only purpose of the financial assistance is and remains that of enabling the shares to be acquired[45] and the financial or commercial advantages flowing from the acquisition, whilst they may form the reasons for forming the purpose of providing the assistance, are a by-product of it rather than an independent purpose of which the assistance can properly be considered to be an incident.

---

[42] [1988] BCLC 20 at pp. 26–27, 41.
[43] Of s. 153 (2) (b) it was said: 'The words "in good faith in the interests of the company" form, I think, a single composite expression and postulate a requirement that those responsible for procuring the company to provide the assistance act in the genuine belief that it is being done in the company's interest': [1988] BCLC 579 at p. 597.
[44] Lords Keith, Havers, Templeman and Griffiths concurring.
[45] Here, Lord Oliver is referring to s. 153 (1) by way of example, rather than s. 153 (2).

This reasoning was then applied to the facts of the *Brady* case itself with the result that the only 'purpose' of the scheme was said to be the acquisition of the shares and the wider benefits such as freedom from management deadlock were merely the 'reasons' for doing it. In an almost bizarre ending to the case, it was held that the exception for private companies contained in ss. 155–158 could still be utilised, because the contractual obligation to reconstruct was still subsisting and was sufficiently broadly drawn to permit different ways of performing the contract. So, ultimately, the parties were required to use that method and accordingly, subject to compliance with those sections,[46] the scheme was not illegal under s. 151.

The House of Lords thus adopted a very narrow construction of s. 153 (2), which would have had the effect in *Brady* (absent the s. 155 point) of allowing s. 151 (2) to wreck what was a completely normal commercial transaction. Lord Oliver's policy in adopting the narrow approach was so as not to provide a 'blank cheque for avoiding the effective application of s. 151 in every case'.[47] It is arguable that this approach does not give enough consideration to the fact that the principal/larger purpose concept is only the first stage in a carefully drafted two-stage gateway. Paragraph (b) in s. 153 (1) and (2) requires that 'the assistance is given in good faith in the interests of the company' and this might often close the gate on undesirable or improper transactions.

Soon afterwards, *Plaut* v *Steiner*[48] provided a further demonstration of the vulnerability of commercial reconstructions of businesses and that post-*Brady*, the exemption provisions in s. 153 (1) and (2) are often going to be next to useless. The case was concerned with a complex agreement designed to separate family businesses which had become 'commercially integrated'. The splitting was necessary because of friction between the personalities involved and increasing deadlock. The agreement was designed to enable the families to exchange certain shareholdings in the companies. It arose out of a 'reversible offer' from the Steiners containing two packages described as options and contained provisions designed to make either option equally attractive. Before the agreement was fully executed, various external circumstances changed, and the Steiners felt that the deal had gone badly and wished to turn the clock back. The Plauts sought specific performance. The hearing of the action was postponed to await the decision of the House of Lords in *Brady*. When the action came on, it was held that certain elements of the agreement amounted to financial assistance within s. 152. The main issue was whether the financial assistance was given 'for the purpose' of the acquisition within s. 151 and if so, whether the prohibition was removed or excepted by s. 153 (1). No doubt with the need to avoid *Brady* in mind, it was argued that the purpose of the companies was to effect a division of the commercially integrated business between them and while the reason or motive for that purpose may have been to enable the families to exchange their shareholdings, such reason or motive was irrelevant. Morritt J rejected this as 'ingenious' but wrong; the financial assistance was not necessitated

---

[46] And subject to the right of the respondents to raise certain points which they had agreed not to raise earlier in the litigation.

[47] [1988] 2 All ER 617 at p. 633.

[48] [1989] 5 BCC 352.

by the division of the integrated business between the companies. In the circumstances the financial assistance was:

> [D]irected entirely to the need to make each option equally attractive. There was no need to make the options equally attractive to the companies, only to the shareholders in those companies ... [I]t is plain that the financial assistance was to be given for the purpose of the acquisition by the Steiners of the Plauts' shares ... and by the Plauts of the Steiners' shares ...[49]

Morritt J then used the logic of this to break up the contention based on s. 153 that the principal or larger purpose of the companies was to effect a division of the commercially integrated business between them so that the purpose of the financial assistance either was not the principal purpose or was an incidental part of that larger purpose:

> As I have already said in relation to s. 151 (1), the financial assistance had nothing to do with the division of the business between the companies; therefore the principal purpose in giving that assistance cannot have been and was not to effect that division. Likewise the giving of the assistance cannot have been and was not an incidental part of the larger purpose of effecting the division. The division of the business between the companies could have been effected without the financial assistance.[50]

The learned judge went on to hold that s. 153 (1) (b) was not satisfied here either, mainly because the giving of the assistance would have rendered insolvent one of the companies providing it. Nor was it possible lawfully to perform the agreement in some other way, for alternative performance had to be within the framework of what had been agreed, and in the circumstances, it was not. Nor were any of the ways suggested within the framework lawful; in particular (and unlike in *Brady*) owing to the financial position of the companies involved, s. 155 could not be used.[51] Thus the claim for specific performance was dismissed; the defence of illegality had succeeded.

16.5 PRIVATE COMPANY EXCEPTION

One of the main defects of the s. 54 of the Companies Act 1948 had been the obstacles which it created in the situation of a management buy-out. Often the management would need a loan to enable them to purchase the shares. It was usually necessary for the loan to be secured and the company itself would be prevented from charging its own assets as security by s. 54 which would render the charge void.[52] In this context, the 1981 legislation (now contained in ss. 155–158 of the Companies Act 1985) made the major innovation of permitting private companies to give financial assistance provided that the procedures prescribed are followed. This made institutional finance more readily available and was one of the factors behind the increase in management buy-outs in the early 1980s.[53]

---

[49] *Ibid.* at p. 369.
[50] *Ibid.*
[51] *Ibid.* at pp. 371–376 *passim.*
[52] As described at p. 295 above.
[53] See M. Wright, J. Coyne and A. Mills *Spicer and Pegler's Management Buy-outs* (1987) pp. 3–4 and D. Sterling 'Financial Assistance by a Company for the Purchase of its Shares' (1987) 8 Co Law 99.

The 1985 Act requires[54] a special resolution of the company and the directors have to make a statutory declaration containing such matters as particulars of the assistance to be given and a statement as to the solvency of the company accompanied by an auditor's report. An elaborate timetable is laid down for all this. The procedures are complicated and it is easy to get things wrong. The case law shows that the courts are adopting a facilitative approach and so are sometimes prepared to condone small technical breaches of the procedures.[55]

16.6 OTHER EXCEPTIONS

In addition to the above exceptions, the remainder of s. 153 contains a list of specific transactions which are expressed not to be prohibited by s. 151. Section 153 (3) (a) refers to a 'distribution[56] of a company's assets by way of dividend lawfully made or a distribution made in the course of the company's winding up'. The Jenkins Committee[57] had felt that the payment of a dividend was unobjectionable in principle (although probably in breach of old s. 54 of the 1948 Act) even in the situation where 'A borrows the money to buy control of company B and then causes company B to pay a dividend, which company B can properly do, and uses the dividend to repay the loan'. The reasons given were that: 'the payment of a dividend properly declared is no more than the discharge of a liability and we cannot see why the discharge by a company of a lawful liability should be regarded as giving financial assistance to the creditor. Such a payment cannot prejudice the rights of creditors, while minority shareholders will directly benefit from it.' It is arguable that the Jenkins Committee were unwise to view this situation as unobjectionable. The potential difficulties were pointed out by Lord Mackay of Clashfern in debate in the House of Lords where he said: 'Permitting otherwise lawful dividends would for example, allow a predator to borrow sufficient funds to acquire control of a cash-rich company, in the knowledge that he could then declare a lawful, substantial dividend from the assets of the company and repay funds borrowed from this dividend.'[58] This warning went unheeded, for the government felt[59] that Pt III of the Companies Act 1980[60] (which was new at that time), with its provisions that dividends could only be paid out of profits, was sufficient to protect the minority shareholder and creditor. The government's view was that prior to 1980, the real danger was that the company could declare an unusually large dividend which was clearly an objectionable practice but which by 1981 had already been foreclosed by the provisions in the 1980 Act, hence no further protection was needed from s. 151. However, the government did acknowledge that in exempting lawful dividends from s. 151 they were 'widening the scope for a company's liquid funds to be extracted from it'. But this is precisely one of the main dangers which is even worse

---

[54] Companies Act 1985, ss. 155–158.
[55] See eg *Re S H & Co. (Realisations) Ltd* [1993] BCC 60; *Re N L Electrical Ltd* [1994] 1 BCLC 22.
[56] Defined in Companies Act 1985, s. 263 (2) (s. 152 (1) (c)).
[57] Cmnd. 1749, 1962, at para. 175.
[58] *Hansard*, HL, vol. 419, col. 1298.
[59] In committee; see Standing Committee A, 30 June 1981, col. 300.
[60] Now Pt VII of the Companies Act 1985; see p. 290 above.

where there is a distribution made in a winding up, which s. 153 (3) (a) also permits. Section 151 was passed for the wider purpose of preventing objectionable schemes whereby a company's shares are purchased using its own assets and s. 151 may often fail to prevent that, to the extent that a scheme utilises either limb of s. 153 (3) (a).[61]

The remainder of s. 153 (3)[62] exempts from s. 151 the allotment of bonus shares,[63] and then various transactions which are already regulated by statute elsewhere.[64] Section 153 (4) contains further exceptions, namely the lending of money where this is part of the ordinary business of the company and the lending is in the ordinary course of the business; the provision by the company in accordance with an employees' share scheme of money for the acquisition of fully paid shares in the company or its holding company; the making of loans to persons (other than directors) employed in good faith by the company, with a view to enabling those persons to acquire fully paid shares in the company to be held by them by way of beneficial ownership.[65]

16.7 CIVIL CONSEQUENCES OF BREACH

The civil effects of breaches of s. 54 of the Companies Act 1948 were not defined in the statute itself and it fell to the courts to work these out. The provisions in s. 151 of the 1985 Act use substantially the same words[66] as s. 54, namely '. . . it is not lawful . . .' and it is reasonable to assume therefore that the pre-existing case law applies to s. 151 also. A number of questions arise: What is the validity of a security (or other assistance) given in breach of the section? The result reached by Fisher J in *Heald* v *O'Connor*[67] was that a security given in breach of the section was void. In these circumstances the voidness benefits the company and serves to protect the company from having its assets misused (since the security is unenforceable). Where, however, the company makes a loan in breach of the section, voidness is not such an attractive result since *prima facie* the company cannot recover its loan[68] under the void contract and would have been in a better position if the transaction

---

[61] The *Brady* case also illustrates the curious results produced by this exception since it was pointed out there that the scheme, unlawful under s. 151, and not saved by s. 153 (2), could nevertheless be carried out lawfully by using the dividend exception: [1988] BCLC 579 at p. 582.

[62] Companies Act 1985, s. 153 (3) (b)–(g).

[63] It is possible that this too is unwise and may be open to abuse, particularly in view of the fact that safeguards in the Companies Act 1985, ss. 263 *et seq.* do not apply to distributions made by way of bonus shares; see s. 263 (2) (a).

[64] Namely, transactions under ss. 37, 159–181, 425 of the Companies Act 1985 and ss. 1–7, 110 of the Insolvency Act 1986.

[65] But for public companies, s. 153 (4) of the Companies Act 1985 authorises the giving of financial assistance only if the company has net assets which are not thereby reduced, or if they are reduced, then only out of distributable profits; see s. 154.

[66] Section 54 had '. . . it shall not be lawful . . .'.

[67] [1971] 1 WLR 497.

[68] It is clear from *Selangor* (above) that in some circumstances the company may recover by way of constructive trust and the illegality created by the section will not prevent this. It is also possible that since the illegality was created for the protection of one of the parties to the transaction (i.e. the company), then the innocent party may recover; see *Wallersteiner* v *Moir* [1974] 1 WLR 991 at p. 1014, *per* Lord Denning MR; *Hughes* v *Liverpool Victoria Friendly Society* [1916] 2 KB 482.

had been voidable at the option of the company, or even valid. However, the position is not without doubt and an earlier case[69] regarded security given in breach of the section as valid and enforceable.

Another question which arises is if the scheme or transaction as a whole involves a breach of s. 151 because it contains illegal financial assistance, what is the effect of this on the actual contract to purchase the shares? The main English authority on this is the Court of Appeal decision in *Lawlor* v *Gray*,[70] where it was said that a vendor of shares owed a statutory duty to the company and a contractual duty to the purchaser to perform the agreement without any breach of the section,[71] but on the facts of this particular case it was possible for the sale of the shares to have been carried out lawfully. In other cases, this might not be the position. A subsequent Privy Council case has taken this further. In *Carney* v *Herbert*[72] the transaction for the purchase of the shares involved sales agreements, a guarantee and mortgages in a composite transaction. It was held that the mortgages were illegal since they amounted to provision by a subsidiary company of financial assistance in connection with the purchase of shares in the holding company[73] but that the remainder of the transaction could be enforced if the mortgages were severable from it. Here the mortgages were severable as they were ancillary to the basic sale contract (in that they did not go to the heart of the transaction) and the elimination of the mortgage would leave unchanged the subject matter of the contract and the primary obligations of the vendors and the purchaser. There was also no public policy objection to the enforcement of the contract from which the mortgage had been divorced.

The liability of directors and others who deliberately breach the section is well settled: the directors themselves are liable for breach of fiduciary duty if they misapply assets of the company in this way;[74] and so also are nominee (or shadow) directors in some circumstances.[75] As an alternative, there may be liability for the tort of conspiracy whereby the company can recover the loss which is reasonably forseeable as flowing from the unlawful transaction.

The most spectacular civil effect of breach of the section is undoubtedly the wide constructive trust liability applied in *Selangor United Rubber Estates Ltd* v *Cradock (No. 3)*,[76] where the District Bank Ltd became involved in a circular cheque transaction in breach of s. 54 of the Companies Act 1948. The bank's officers had acted in good faith but due to their inexperience had failed to realise the significance of what was happening. The bank was held liable because it had knowledge of the circumstances which made the transaction a breach of trust and a dishonest intention

---

[69] See *Victor Battery Co. Ltd* v *Currys Ltd* [1946] Ch 242.

[70] An unreported Court of Appeal decision but noted in (1980) 130 New LJ 31. Also in *Brady*, the House of Lords adopted a comparable approach.

[71] A similar approach (in a slightly different context) was adopted by the Privy Council in *Motor and General Insurance Co. Ltd* v *Gobin* [1987] 3 BCC 61.

[72] [1985] AC 301.

[73] Contrary to s. 67 of the Companies Act 1961 (New South Wales).

[74] *Wallersteiner* v *Moir* [1974] 1 WLR 991; *Belmont Finance Corporation Ltd* v *Williams Furniture Ltd (No. 2)* [1980] 1 All ER 393; *Re in a Flap Envelope Ltd* [2004] 1 BCLC 64.

[75] See *Selangor United Rubber Estates Ltd* v *Cradock (No. 3)* [1968] 1 WLR 1555.

[76] [1968] 1 WLR 1555.

on its part was unnecessary. There then followed a series of cases in which the courts either followed this approach,[77] or swung towards ameliorating the position of third parties by requiring something amounting to dishonesty before a constructive trust could be imposed.[78] The very full discussion in the Privy Council case of *Royal Brunei Airlines Sdn Bhd v Tan*[79] has settled[80] the matter. An insolvent company called Borneo Leisure Travel owed money to an airline. The company had been a general travel agent for the airline for the sale of passenger and cargo transportation. It was required to account to the airline for all amounts received from sales of tickets and it was common ground that the effect of the agreement of appointment was to constitute the company a trustee of the ticket money for the airline. In practice the money received by the company was not paid into a separate account but into its ordinary current account. The company was poorly run with heavy overhead expenses and the money was lost in the ordinary course of business. The airline sued Tan who was the company's principal director and shareholder. The claim against Tan was that he was liable as constructive trustee for assisting with knowledge in a dishonest and fraudulent design on the part of the trustees.

Their Lordships began by changing the 'shorthand' terminology often used in this field as a result of the existing judicial distinction between 'knowing receipt' and 'knowing assistance'.[81] 'Knowing receipt' was referred to as being 'concerned with the liability of a person as a recipient of trust property or its traceable proceeds'. 'Knowing assistance' is concerned with the 'liability of an accessory to a trustee's breach of trust'.[82] In the context of ss. 151–158, the chief interest in the lengthy judgments in this case lies in what was said about the role and nature of dishonesty in 'accessory liability'. First, it was made clear that 'dishonesty' is a necessary ingredient of accessory liability[83] and that:

[I]n the context of the accessory liability principle acting dishonestly . . . means simply not acting as an honest person would in the circumstances . . . Honesty . . . [has] . . . a strong

---

[77] *Karak Rubber Co. Ltd v Burden (No. 2)* [1972] 1 WLR 602; *Baden v Société Generale* [1992] 4 All ER 161.

[78] See e.g. *Belmont Finance Ltd v Williams Furniture Ltd* [1979] Ch 250 at pp. 267 and 274; *Re Montagu's Settlement Trusts* [1987] Ch 264 at p. 285; *Agip v Jackson* [1990] Ch 265 at p. 293; *Eagle Trust plc v SBC Ltd* [1992] 4 All ER 488 at p. 499; *Polly Peck International plc v Nadir (No. 2)* [1992] 4 All ER 769 at p. 777.

[79] [1995] 3 All ER 97.

[80] Probably. In theory, since it is only a Privy Council case, of persuasive rather than binding authority, the dispute could restart at some future date. This seems unlikely, however, particularly in the light of the endorsement of the subjective approach by the House of Lords in *Twinsectra Ltd v Yardley* [2002] 2 All ER 377, where it was held that there could be liability as accessory only where it was established that the conduct had been dishonest by the ordinary standards of reasonable and honest people *and* that the defendant himself had realised that by those standards his conduct was dishonest. However, other views continue, and Lord Millett delivered a strong dissenting speech.

[81] The liability of third parties was set out by Lord Selborne in *Barnes v Addy* (1874) 9 Ch App 244 at p. 251: '[S]trangers are not to be made constructive trustees . . . unless [they] receive and become chargeable with some part of the trust property, or unless they assist with knowledge in a dishonest and fraudulent design on the part of the trustees.'

[82] [1995] 3 All ER 97 at p. 99.

[83] *Ibid.* at p. 105.

subjective element[84] in that it is a description of a type of conduct assessed in the light of what a person actually knew at the time, as distinct from what a reasonable person would have known or appreciated ... Unless there is a very good and compelling reason, an honest person does not participate in a transaction if he knows it involves a misapplication of trust assets ... Nor does an honest person in such a case deliberately close his eyes and ears, or deliberately not ask questions, lest he learn something he would rather not know, and then proceed regardless.[85]

Ultimately, Tan was held liable. The company had committed a breach of trust by using the money in its business instead of simply deducting its commission and holding the money intact until it paid the airline, and Tan's conduct, by causing or permitting his company to apply the money in a way he knew was not authorised by the trust of which the company was trustee, was dishonest. It was also held 'for good measure' that the company also acted dishonestly in that Tan was the company and his state of mind was to be imputed to the company. Overall, the decision should have provided some relief for banks and others whose commercial functions put them at risk from this type of liability. However, any sense of relief should perhaps be tempered with the reflection that the notion of dishonesty set out in the judgment is of a very robust quality. It does not give a general exemption from making inquiries, for in some circumstances an honest person would have made them.

16.8 COMPANY LAW REVIEW AND LAW REFORM

In November 1992 the Department of Trade and Industry set up a working party of business people, members of the accountancy and legal professions and DTI officials to examine the law regulating financial assistance for the acquisition of shares. This led in October 1993 to the publication of a consultation document[86] setting out three main approaches[87] to the reform of the law affecting public companies: (1) to amend the existing ss. 151–154; (2) to reproduce art. 23 of the EC Second Directive;[88] or (3) to restructure ss. 151–154. As they observed in the Consultation Document, the third of these possibilities appeared to offer the greatest scope for improvement of the existing legislation. In a subsequent paper in September 1994 the DTI set out proposals for future reform of the area, opting for a substantial restructuring of the legislation to take account of the various criticisms which have

---

[84] It was also said to be an objective standard in the sense that 'if a person knowingly appropriates another's property, he will not escape a finding of dishonesty simply because he sees nothing wrong in such behaviour'.

[85] [1995] 3 All ER 97 at pp. 105–107 *passim*.

[86] DTI Consultative Document (October 1993) *Proposals for Reform of Sections 151–158 of the Companies Act 1985*.

[87] *Ibid*. para. 4.

[88] 77/91/EEC. Obviously any possible future reforms will be circumscribed by the need to implement the Directive, which at present is done by s. 151. Article 23 (which by art. 1 (1) only applies to public companies) provides: '(1) A company may not advance funds, nor make loans, nor provide security, with a view to the acquisition of its shares by a third party.' There are then exceptions, subject to conditions, in art. 23 (2) in respect of transactions concluded by financial institutions in the course of business and in respect of employee shares. Article 23 (3) contains another exception in respect of certain shares issued by investment companies.

been levelled at it over the years, in particular those consequent on the *Brady* case. It was proposed that *Brady* might be disposed of by rewording the general 'purpose' based exceptions in s. 153 (1) and (2) along the lines that the assistance is not prohibited if the 'predominant reason' for the giving of the assistance is not to enable that person to acquire its shares, even though the immediate effect of that transaction may be to assist that person to do so.

In a letter of November 1996, the DTI indicated that it had abandoned the attempt to construct an overall scheme embracing both public and private companies. The law relating to public companies would be amended along the lines of the 'predominant reason' test, and private companies would be permitted to give financial assistance, provided that the assistance was not 'materially prejudicial' to the company or the members of the company approved the transaction in advance. Subsequently, there has been another internal review of the area within the DTI.

The Company Law Review then took the matter in hand. The area was considered in the Consultation Document of February 1999, *The Strategic Framework*, and in more detail in the later Consultation Document of October 1999, *Company Formation and Capital Maintenance*. The kind of issues which were raised for consultation were whether the ban on financial assistance should be removed entirely, for private companies, and whether the 'principal purpose' exception can be satisfactorily redrafted. In addition, many small technical changes were considered.[89] Subsequently, in the Consultation Document *Completing the Structure*,[90] it seemed that the view had been reached that ss. 151–158 should be amended so as to apply only to public companies and therefore the s. 155 whitewash procedure for private companies would no longer be needed. The *Company Law Review Final Report* largely endorsed this.[91]

It seems clear from the document *Company Law. Flexibility and Accessibility* (London: DTI, 2004) that the government's current view is that reform will produce the result that private companies are exempt from the provisions.

---

[89] DTI Consultation Document (October 1999) *Company Formation and Capital Maintenance* paras 3.41 *et seq.*
[90] Paragraph 7.12 *et seq.*
[91] Paragraphs 4.4 and 10.6.

PART V

SECURITIES REGULATION

17

POLICY AND THEORY IN SECURITIES REGULATION/CAPITAL MARKETS LAW

17.1 THE RELATIONSHIP BETWEEN TRADITIONAL COMPANY LAW AND SECURITIES REGULATION

One of the main aims of this book is to move the study of securities regulation (or 'capital markets law')[1] closer to traditional company law. Securities regulation is concerned with the way in which the marketing of shares and other financial products is regulated, either by the state or by the financial services industry itself.

Thus it will involve rules regulating the offer of shares[2] to the public; it will involve rules covering the way in which the secondary market for trading in those shares is run, by supervision of the market participants and by rules about how the market itself must be conducted, such as rules against insider dealing. Takeovers essentially involve the buying and selling of shares, but since corporate control is usually at stake, there will be extra rules to ensure fairness and other matters; so takeover regulation forms part of securities regulation. Many of these are matters which would feature in one way or another in a book on mainstream company law: public offerings of shares, insider dealing, takeovers, are all the stuff of traditional company law.

However, by including a whole section on securities regulation, this book focuses on why these parts of company law are sufficiently different from the mainstream that they can profitably be examined as a separate group. The point really is that if public offerings, takeovers and insider dealing are examined not (as is usual in company law textbooks) as, respectively, part of the techniques of capital raising, restructuring and directors' duties but rather, as part of securities regulation, then a quite fundamental culture difference becomes apparent. It becomes clear that the emphasis in mainstream company law is on providing the business community with the legal structures that it needs to create and run efficient businesses.[3] It is mainly private law and is concerned with the contractual relationships which the various participants in companies enter into. Securities regulation, on the other hand, owes much to public law. Although the commercial relationships (i.e. the buying and selling of securities) are contractual in nature, the central fact of securities regulation is the pervasive presence of the state, in the form of the regulator who seeks to achieve the requisite degree of investor protection. The *laissez-faire* culture of

---

[1] Capital markets law is the European term for securities regulation.
[2] And other securities.
[3] See the earlier analysis at pp. 3–8 above.

company law is replaced by an environment in which the state claims (and will enforce) the right to regulate in minute detail exactly how each bargain is to be struck – the regulation including authorisation requirements for industry participants, fitness requirements, prudential rules for the structure of firms, conduct of business rules requiring, for example, suitable advice to be given.

To be sure, all these arguments can be partially reversed. Does mainstream company law not have areas of state regulation in the form of competition law, or DTI investigations? Why confine the idea of efficient business structures to company law; is not the goal of securities regulation also efficiency in the sense of providing efficient primary and secondary markets which facilitate capital raising and economic growth? But these counter observations merely indicate that the distinction is one of degree or emphasis rather than of unbridgeable principle.

This leads on to the next point. The boundaries between what falls within traditional company law and what forms part of securities regulation are fluid, and in recent years it is common knowledge that there have been examples of migration from company law to securities regulation. To take one example:[4] insider dealing has its theoretical origins in the idea that insiders are breaching a fiduciary duty of confidentiality owed to the company whose securities are being traded, and in the US and the UK the law has reflected that. However, within the EU, that principle has taken a back seat since the adoption of the Directive on insider dealing.[5] The Directive is based on the securities regulation policy of ensuring a fair market and not on the company law fiduciary concept. Hence, since the implementation in the UK of the Directive in 1993, UK law on insider dealing, largely follows EU capital markets law and its theoretical basis is the securities regulation concept of market egalitarianism.[6] The existence of this migration process makes it increasingly difficult to justify the study of mainstream company law without also securities regulation.

Lastly, because of the close and interdependent relationship between company law and securities regulation, it is often the case that quite technical points feed from one area into the other. Without some understanding of both, these angles are often simply not seen. For instance, in the last decade or so, the self-regulatory nature of the City Code on Takeovers and Mergers has in practice been largely illusory for the very technical reason that the investment banks and other professionals engaged in takeovers have been firms who required authorisation under the Financial Services Act 1986.[7] As authorised persons they have then been bound by conduct of business rules emanating from their self-regulating organisations (SROs)[8] and these rules require, broadly, observance of the Code.[9]

---

[4] For another example, see p. 361 below.
[5] See p. 378 below.
[6] For a more detailed account of this, see p. 379 below.
[7] Now repealed and replaced by the Financial Services and Markets Act 2000.
[8] See at p. 319 below.
[9] The FSMA 2000 gives a wide range of support to the Code; see Chapter 21 below.

17.2 THE BIRTH OF SECURITIES REGULATION

Modern securities regulation in a systematic and sophisticated form began in the US in 1933 with the passing of the Securities Act,[10] which set up an elaborate federal system of regulation of public offerings of securities, in other words, of the primary market.

In the following year the Securities Exchange Act put in place regulation of the secondary market, the brokers, dealers, exchanges and other matters. Also with this Act, Congress established the Securities and Exchange Commission,[11] the SEC, which became and has remained globally a name which evokes an image of rigorous and comprehensive securities enforcement.

The events which had led to these Acts had been cataclysmic. The Wall Street crash of 1929 had produced an economic depression and shattered public confidence in the banking system and capital markets.[12] The supply of capital to industry had consequently dried up. The Roosevelt government of 1933 brought in a series of 'New Deal' reforms aimed at restoring confidence in capitalism. The Securities Act and the Exchange Act were fundamental to this, along with important legislation on the structure of banking.[13]

As suggested above, the 1933 and 1934 Acts can reasonably be regarded as the birth of 'modern' securities regulation in the sense that they laid down in a comprehensive way policies and formats which are largely followed and copied throughout the world. But elements of partial (and not very effective) systems of securities regulation were in existence prior to that. In the US, securities frauds and stock market crashes of the first decade of the 20th century invoked a response at state government level in the form of state legislation which required disclosure and, often also, compliance with standards of fairness.[14] The first of these[15] statutes was enacted in Kansas in 1911 and state legislation remains a feature of US securities regulation at the present day.[16]

In the UK, securities regulation can be traced to the early provisions for the licensing of brokers who acted as agents and who were required to take an oath to be of good behaviour.[17] And so already there were two basic techniques of securi-

---

[10] This and other federal securities legislation can be found in the 'Securities Lawyer's Deskbook' at http://www.law.uc.edu./CCL/intro.html.

[11] The 1933 Act was administered by the Federal Trade Commission until the creation of the SEC.

[12] These events have served as a paradigm for the securities regulation concept of 'systemic risk' which is the risk that the collapse of one bank or financial institution within a system will trigger a series of collapses in others who are not structured with sufficient capital to be able to absorb the damage caused by the initial failure.

[13] The so called 'Glass–Steagall' Act, after the Members of the Congress who were involved in drafting it. It required the separation of deposit-taking banking business from investment banking (i.e. business related to dealing in securities). Some provisions of the Act have recently been repealed.

[14] Usually referred to as a 'merit' test.

[15] State public utility regulation pre-dated even this.

[16] State legislation on public offerings of securities is known as 'blue sky law' after the story that the legislation was aimed at promoters who 'would sell building lots in the blue sky in fee simple'; see L. Loss *Fundamentals of Securities Regulation* (Boston, MA: Little, Brown, 1988) p. 8. Similarly, going through the processes of making sure that a public offering complies with state law is known as 'blue skying' an issue.

[17] A Statute of Edward I in 1285. See generally B. Rider, C. Abrams and M. Ashe *Guide to Financial Services Regulation* 3rd edn (Bicester: CCH, 1997) pp. 3–4; G. Gilligan 'The City of London and the

ties regulation operating: registration of market participants and, albeit very basic, an early version of conduct of business rules. Further licensing provisions were enacted in 1697. And then there was that ultimate blunt tool of securities regulation: the Bubble Act 1720. The story of this has been told many times[18] but it is worth emphasising that the securities regulation technique being used was, in effect, *suppression* of the securities activity rather than regulation of it because the 1720 Act tended towards prohibiting the creation of the companies themselves and prohibiting the issuance of transferable stock. The importance of the Joint Stock Companies Act 1844 has been noted with regard to its setting up of the system of incorporation by registration, but it also had significance for securities regulation, for it introduced a requirement for registration of a prospectus when shares were issued to the public.[19]

Despite this and many subsequent developments, such as the introduction of legislation against insider dealing in 1980,[20] it is fair to say that the UK had no comprehensive system of securities regulation until the Financial Services Act 1986 set up the Securities and Investments Board (SIB). By then, the Barlow Clowes affair had revealed both the inadequacy of the system of DTI regulation of share dealers required by the Prevention of Fraud (Investments) Act 1958 and the inadequacy of the response by the various City regulators which involved a feast of buck-passing between them.[21] As will be seen below, even the SIB system was not considered sufficiently comprehensive, and events have now moved on with the passing of the Financial Services and Markets Act 2000.

17.3 THE SEC

A major feature of systems of securities regulation is the high profile presence of the state, in the form of the regulatory authority. Historically, nowhere has this been more clear than in the US with the federal government making itself felt through the agency of Securities and Exchange Commission. The SEC has its headquarters in Washington, DC and is comprised of five commissioners, appointed by the President in consultation with the Senate.[22] They have five-year terms, with one expiring each year. There is a support staff of around 3,000 made up of lawyers, accountants, economists, computer experts and administrators.

The Securities Act 1933 and the Securities Exchange Act 1934 together provide the core of the legislation which the SEC is responsible for administering. In addition there are five other statutes which, together with the 1933 and 1934 Acts, make up what are often referred to as 'the SEC statutes'. They are the Public Utility Holdings Company Act 1935, which regulates utility companies; the Trust

---

Development of English Financial Services Law' in B. Rider (ed.) *The Corporate Dimension* (Bristol: Jordans, 1998) at p. 3.

[18] See for instance Loss, n. 16 above, at p. 2.

[19] Joint Stock Companies Act 1844, s. 4.

[20] See p. 377 below.

[21] See generally L. Lever *The Barlow Clowes Affair* (London: Macmillan, 1992). Ultimately it led to the DTI agreeing to pay compensation to the investors for the government's role in handling the matter.

[22] Not more than three may be members of the same political party.

Indenture Act 1939, which supplements the 1933 Act where a distribution consists of debt securities; the Investment Company Act 1940, which regulates collective investment schemes; and the Investment Advisers Act 1940, which requires the registration of investment advisers and the Securities Investor Protection Act 1970, which insures customers against broker insolvency. While these statutes provide a solid background of legislation, in practice much of the day-to-day regulation by the SEC is carried out under its rule-making powers which legislative provisions delegate to it. The dramatic corporate scandals which have rocked corporate America in recent years, such as Enron, have prompted a reaction as drastic as that epitomised by the 1933 and 1934 Acts, namely the passing of the Sarbanes-Oxley Act of 2002. It makes widespread changes to US corporate governance, such as requiring all listed companies to have fully independent audit committees. Notably, it fixes the Chief Executive Officer (CEO) and the Chief Finance Officer (CFO) with liability for the financial statements of the company.[23]

The above-mentioned power to make rules and regulations has enabled the SEC to put flesh on the bones of the statutory provisions, to meet new developments, or to clarify matters. Such delegated legislation is usually the result of a three-stage procedure involving a concept release seeking public views on how to approach the problem, then a rule proposal, also for public consultation before, finally, rule adoption. A visit to the SEC website shows that this process is very much ongoing.[24]

Much can be learned from the SEC's enforcement processes,[25] and indeed as will be seen below, the UK regulator has recently adopted some of the SEC's techniques.[26] The SEC itself has no powers to begin criminal proceedings. However, if the facts found by the SEC are sufficiently serious that it is felt that the public interest would be served by criminal proceedings being brought, then the matter will be brought to the attention of the US Department of Justice which will work with the SEC in setting up the criminal processes. In spite of this, the SEC is an extremely effective enforcement agency.[27] Enforcement is carried out through an array of civil processes, which, coupled with the SEC's formidable reputation (which usually causes targets to settle actions by the SEC against them) provide effective sanctions.[28] Broadly, there are two types of process used: Civil Injunctive Actions and SEC Administrative Proceedings.

Civil Injunctive Actions are a frequently used mechanism and a variety of remedies are available to the SEC under these proceedings if it appears that any person is

---

[23] For an interesting analysis of the effects of this on US corporate governance see L. Ribstein 'Raising the Rent on US Law: Implications of the Sarbanes-Oxley Act 2002' (2003) 3 JCLS 132.

[24] http://www.sec.gov.

[25] For an excellent analysis of this and other aspects of enforcement from a comparative perspective, see J. Fishman 'A Comparison of Enforcement of Securities Law Violations in the UK and US' (1993) 14 Co Law 163.

[26] E.g. the adoption of civil (as opposed to criminal) processes for combatting insider dealing and other forms of market abuse; see p. 384 below.

[27] E.g. in 2003 the SEC obtained disgorgements of profits from securities laws violators of US $900m, and civil money penalties of US $1.1bn; see *SEC Annual Report* 2003.

[28] Prior to an enforcement process, the SEC will mount an investigation and it has wide-ranging powers to require the production of documents and the giving of information. Quite often, the SEC will feel that all that is necessary is a private cautionary letter which will advise the recipient of violations of the securities laws or the likelihood of violation in the circumstances.

engaged or is about to engage in violation of the Securities Acts or rules made under them.[29] The civil burden of proof makes it an easier remedy to obtain than any criminal penalty would be, and the courts are empowered to give a range of ancillary relief such as rescission, restitution and civil monetary penalties.[30] Several hundred civil actions are brought annually and most are settled.[31] The settlement process is greatly helped by the device of the consent decree[32] under which the person accused agrees not to repeat his conduct, agrees to pay a money penalty but does not need to admit wrongdoing. Most enforcement actions are settled in this way.

SEC Administrative Proceedings are available in many situations and are often used.[33] They are available where a person is registered with the SEC under the 1934 Act or has registered securities with it[34] and that person appears to have violated one of the provisions of the Act or rules or regulations made under it.[35] The proceeding is in effect a trial conducted by an SEC official. On a finding that the person has broken a rule the official can impose sanctions which may include censure or restriction of his activities, revocation of registration, civil money penalties, disgorgement of profits, or a 'cease and desist order'.[36] Often the matter is settled. The SEC occasionally then uses the rulings which are made in Administrative Proceedings to create a kind of 'judicial' precedent as regards the interpretation of its rules and regulations.[37]

This brief look at the SEC has given a glimpse of some of the techniques used by the world's leading regulator; many of the ideas have found their way into other regulatory systems and sure enough, when we look at the UK's Financial Services Authority, its powers and methods of operation, much of it will seem familiar.

17.4 THE FINANCIAL SERVICES AUTHORITY

A The self-regulation era – the SIB

Some of the events which led up to the Financial Services Act 1986 and the establishment of the Securities and Investments Board (SIB) have already been alluded to;[38] the technical aspects have not. Towards the end of the 1970s the DTI asked Professor Jim Gower to look into ways of improving investor protection in the UK.[39] This ultimately led to the publication of his *Review of Investor Protection – A*

---

[29] Securities Exchange Act 1934, s. 21, as amended.
[30] *Ibid.* Also available under s. 21 are bars against persons acting as officers or directors.
[31] In 2003 the figure was 271; see *SEC Annual Report* 2003.
[32] See Fishman, n. 25 above, at p. 166.
[33] In 2003 the figure was 365; see *SEC Annual Report* 2003.
[34] See Securities Exchange Act 1934, s. 12.
[35] Securities Exchange Act 1934, s. 15 (c) (4).
[36] *Ibid.* ss. 21B, 21C.
[37] See e.g. the importance of the SEC decision in the *Cady, Roberts* case, discussed at p. 376 below.
[38] E.g. the Barlow Clowes scandal, p. 316 above. Other events include: one of the periodic Lloyd's debacles had helped to undermine confidence in the City during the late 1970s; see further J. Gower ' "Big Bang" and City Regulation' (1988) 51 MLR 1. The setting up of the SIB coincided (in 1986) with major changes in Stock Exchange practice which became known as the 'Big Bang'.
[39] See the detailed and racy account of this by B. Rider in B. Rider, C. Abrams and M. Ashe *Guide to Financial Services Regulation* 3rd edn (Bicester: CCH, 1997) pp. 13–22.

Discussion Document[40] and, subsequently, a *Review of Investor Protection – Part 1*[41] and *Part 2*.[42] The government set out its views in the White Paper *Financial Services in the United Kingdom: A New Framework for Investor Protection*,[43] emphasising that improvements in the system should come about primarily through self-regulatory mechanisms. Although it wanted to appear to be firm with the City, the government had no stomach for the setting up of a tough SEC-style public regulator[44] and the City itself wanted regulation to be left largely in its own hands. The resulting compromise was the Financial Services Act 1986 and various subsequent Orders. In effect, the UK's first general system of investor protection was to be characterised as a feature of the private sector rather than state regulation; investor protection was to remain company law, rather than become securities regulation. In fact, as soon emerged, the self-regulatory aspect of it was probably a good deal less in evidence than the City lobby had expected, as Gower observed in his lecture at the London School of Economics in 1987 when he expressed the view that the government's description of the system in their White Paper as 'self-regulation within a statutory framework' was more accurately expressed as 'statutory regulation monitored by self-regulatory organisations recognised by, and under the surveillance of, a self-standing Commission'.[45]

In essence it worked as follows: the Act set up the Securities and Investments Board (SIB)[46] with the role of overseeing the carrying on of investment business in the UK. In order to carry on such business it was usually necessary to get 'authorised', and the main way of doing this was by joining a self-regulating organisation (SRO). There were originally nine of these but by the time the regime reached its final phase, as a result of mergers, there remained only three: the Securities and Futures Authority (SFA), the Investment Managers Regulatory Organisation (IMRO) and the Personal Investment Authority (PIA). The SROs were organisations designed to regulate certain sectors of the financial services industry while at the same time ensuring that the business interests of the participants in those industries were properly taken account of in the process of deciding what regulatory burdens to impose. In the early years some firms obtained their authorisation direct from the SIB but as time went by this became increasingly rare and the role of the SIB became more focused on regulating the SROs themselves since they were, what it termed, the 'front line regulators'.

In the years immediately following the passing of the Act the SIB concentrated on producing a model rulebook containing detailed prescription as to how various

---

[40] London: DTI, 1982.

[41] Cmnd. 9125, 1984.

[42] London: DTI, 1985. Part 2 was published after the government's White Paper referred to in the next note; it reflected differences of opinion between Gower and the DTI.

[43] Cmnd. 9432, 1985.

[44] The SEC's unpopularity in the City of London probably owed much to the fierce stance it took on its jurisdictional reach, which often threatened to ensnare UK business activities in the requirements of the US Securities Acts; see e.g. *Manley v Schoenbaum* 395 US 906 (1968). Recent years have seen a moderation of the position.

[45] Gower, n. 38 above, at p. 11.

[46] In fact in a technical sense the Act did not set this up because it merely gave power to the DTI to transfer powers to a designated agency; when the powers were transferred, the agency was the SIB; see Financial Services Act 1986, s. 114 (1)–(2).

types of investment business should be operated. The SROs, feeling bound by what the SIB had thought was needed, tended to transmute these rules largely unaltered into their own rulebooks. This was widely felt to have produced over-heavy regulation and led to the reforms contained in the Companies Act 1989. These reforms, dubbed the 'New Settlement',[47] brought in some softer regulatory techniques, such as the laying down of broad principles.[48]

By the mid-1990s it began to be apparent that the writing was on the wall for this system. It does not really seem to be the case that the regulation was ineffective or weak. On the contrary, SRO disciplinary proceedings were clearly capable of imposing high levels of fines on their own members and it will be seen that their widespread practice of both expelling a member (thus shutting down his business) and giving him a hefty money penalty has been discontinued in the new legislation.[49] Nor were the SROs really seen as failing organisations; in many ways they were confident and hard-hitting.[50] A combination of reasons lay behind the decision for change: there were overlaps in the self-regulatory system, so that multi-function financial services institutions had to join more than one SRO; there were doubts about the need for the 'two-tier' system with the SIB supervising the SROs and it began to seem to make more sense to roll the SROs into one regulator; furthermore, the pensions mis-selling scandal had exacerbated tensions between the SIB and the SROs; there were also strong arguments for widening the scope of the powers of the regulatory authority so that it would cover areas of finance and business which were currently covered by a variety of other regulators, such as Lloyd's, the building societies and the Bank of England. Ultimately, although the pressure for change was building before the Labour government came to power in 1997 there may have simply been a political aspect: that the self-regulatory system should be replaced with a system which more overtly derived its authority from the state.

The transition from the 1986 Act's regime to the new system under the Financial Services and Markets Act 2000 was a work[51] of thoughtful legal and administrative creativity. The SIB changed its name to the Financial Services Authority (FSA), which was the name it wanted to have under the system to be brought in, although in legal terms it broadly remained the same old SIB.[52] Then the SROs were rolled into the FSA by co-locating their staff and arranging for the staff of the SROs to become employed by the FSA which then leased them back to the SROs to enable the SROs to continue to perform their functions. In substance the organisation began to function as one entity, almost as the future FSA would function when the Financial Services and Markets Bill became law, while legally the old system remained, with the SROs as the front-line regulators carrying out their usual

---

[47] Note the cultural links being made with Roosevelt's 'New Deal' and the big brother regulator, the SEC.

[48] For an excellent account of this see A. Whittaker 'Legal Technique in City Regulation' (1990) 43 *Current Legal Problems* 35.

[49] See p. 356, n. 105 below.

[50] They were staffed by professionals with expertise in law and finance.

[51] Under the then FSA chairmanship of Sir Howard Davies.

[52] Although most of the banking regulatory functions of the Bank of England were transferred to it by the Bank of England Act 1998.

authorisation and disciplinary functions, and the SIB (now called FSA) monitoring their functions, and preparing the policy documents for the new regime. The system risked challenge, perhaps on the basis that in substance the FSA and the SROs were one organisation and that accordingly the FSA was exceeding its powers and illegally purporting to regulate members of SROs. In the event, there seems not to have been great difficulty.

So marked the end of an era. In the 14 years between 1986 and 2000 regulatory policy in the UK had undergone a marked shift. In 1986, all that seemed politically acceptable and therefore possible[53] was a beefed-up version of the self-regulatory approach to investor protection which owed more to company law, with its emphasis on private law and minimal state interference, than to anything else. By 2000 the UK had acquired a statutory commitment to an SEC-style regulator,[54] the state in human form, with responsibilities ranging across almost the entire spectrum of financial activity; and widespread powers of enforcement. US-style[55] securities regulation had reached the UK.

B Statutory securities regulation: accountability issues

The Financial Services and Markets Act 2000 provides that the Financial Services Authority is to have the functions conferred on it by the Act.[56] The detail of its statutory functions and enforcement powers fall to be discussed below.[57] At this point it is useful to consider the extent to which the FSA is made accountable, as the problem of controlling the regulator is a fundamental policy consideration in the field of securities regulation. During the long passage through Parliament of the Financial Services and Markets Act 2000 it became clear that there were grave fears about the sufficiency of the mechanisms of accountability of the state's new creature which seemed set to dominate the financial world.

Schedule 1 sets out the constitution of the FSA and it is important to see what checks and balances it provides, both internally in terms of procedures and structures and externally in terms of monitoring by outsiders. As regards the internal controls, it is provided that the constitution of the FSA must continue to provide for it to have a chairman and a governing body (i.e. a board) and that the board must have a majority of members who are non-executives (i.e. outsiders who are not involved in the day-to-day functioning of the FSA).[58] This last provision is perhaps of considerable theoretical significance, for it requires the FSA board to act in such a way as to be able to carry the support of the informed public. Also to be part of the constitution is a 'non-executive committee', which has the role of monitor-

---

[53] It seems that the Conservative government of the time was not willing to upset City interests by a wholesale departure from a tradition of self-regulation.

[54] See generally the Financial Services and Markets Act 2000 and p. 338 *et seq.* below.

[55] Although in some respects the remit of the FSA is even broader than that of the SEC.

[56] Section 1. Its current form is the merged form described above and consists of an organisation of around 3,000 staff (about the same size as the SEC) with a similarly wide range of skills, located mainly on one site in Canary Wharf. For details of the organisation and other matters the reader is referred to the website: http://www.fsa.gov.uk.

[57] See pp. 327 and 338 respectively below.

[58] Financial Services and Markets Act 2000, Sch. 1, paras 2 and 3.

ing the FSA as to its efficient use of resources, its financial controls and as to the remuneration of the chairman and executive members of the governing body.[59] Additionally, the FSA is required to have regard to such generally accepted principles of corporate governance as it is reasonable to regard as applicable to it.[60]

There are various mechanisms for external monitoring. In an attempt to replace some aspect of the industry input which was an important feature of the previous system, the 2000 Act requires outsider panels. By s. 8, the FSA must consult practitioners and consumers on the extent to which its general policies and practices are consistent with its general duties under s. 2. The Act requires the existence of Practitioner and Consumer Panels to represent the interests of those groups.[61] A notion of wider democracy is evident from the provision[62] that there has to be a public meeting at least once a year, to consider the annual report and to enable members of the public to ask questions. In a light-hearted moment the then Chairman of the FSA suggested that perhaps this would provide a long-term use for the Millennium Dome.[63] There is also an independent Complaints Commissioner who hears and investigates complaints[64] made against the FSA. Under this 'complaints scheme' the Complaints Commissioner produces a report to the FSA and the complainant. It will often be published and a further report may be published on how the FSA responded.[65]

An important external monitoring input comes from the role of the Treasury, which is of course of constitutional significance, since it represents input from a democratically elected government. The Treasury has significant powers over the FSA. It has power to appoint and remove the chairman and members of the board.[66] An annual report to the Treasury is required[67] which Treasury ministers will lay before Parliament where it will probably come under the scrutiny of the Treasury Select Committee of the House of Commons. If past practice is anything to go by, the Treasury Select Committee will periodically summon the chairman for public questioning. The Treasury can commission a 'value for money' audit of the FSA's operations[68] under which a person independent of the FSA conducts a review of the economy, efficiency and effectiveness with which the FSA has used its resources in discharging its functions. A major inquiry can be ordered by the Treasury where there has been an occurrence of what might be described as a regulatory 'meltdown'; i.e. where something has gone very fundamentally wrong in such

---

[59] *Ibid.* Sch. 1, paras 3 (1) (b), 4.

[60] *Ibid.* s. 7.

[61] Sections 9–10. These functions are carried out by the Financial Services Practitioner Panel, and by the Financial Services Consumer Panel; see respectively, http://www.fs-pp.org.uk and http://www.fs-cp.org.uk.

[62] Financial Services and Markets Act 2000, Sch. 1, para. 11.

[63] H. Davies 'Financial Regulation and the Law', speech of 3 March 1999, p. 4.

[64] There may be an investigation by the FSA itself in the first instance; a complaint will normally only proceed to be investigated by the Commissioner if the complainant is then dissatisfied with the FSA's determination or handling of his complaint. See generally *FSA Handbook of Rules and Guidance*, Complaints against the FSA, available on http://www.fsa.gov.uk.

[65] Financial Services and Markets Act 2000, Sch. 1, paras 7 and 8.

[66] *Ibid.*, Sch. 1, para. 2 (3).

[67] *Ibid.*, Sch. 1, para. 10.

[68] *Ibid.*, s. 12.

a way that it could precipitate systemic failure, and the regulatory system has seriously failed in relation to it. Inquiries may also arise where there has been fraud or failure in relation to a collective investment scheme, failure or misbehaviour of persons which posed a grave risk to the financial system,[69] or failures in relation to listed securities or issuers, and these events might not have occurred or the risk or damage might have been reduced, but for a serious failure in the regulatory system.[70] Thus, overall there are significant opportunities for the representatives of the electorate to exercise influence over the FSA. To what extent these will be effectively exercised or sufficient remains to be seen.

In addition, there are other constraints on the FSA. It has been clear for some time that the FSA and its predecessor, the SIB,[71] are subject to judicial review.[72] However, since judicial review is a remedy of last resort, in that statutory remedies have to be used up first, then, in view of the existence of mechanisms such as the complaints procedure discussed above, it is likely that resort to judicial review will be rare.[73] More likely to make appearances in this field is the European Convention on Human Rights, which was incorporated into UK law by the Human Rights Act 1998 in October 2000. The likely impact of this is discussed in the next chapter, in the context of FSA enforcement powers, where of course, there is potential for the oppressive use of powers.[74]

It is clear that the FSA is subject to considerable constraints[75] and that care has been taken to build some powerful checks and balances into the structure.[76] The sufficiency of these will no doubt be tested in the years which lie ahead.

17.5 LEGAL THEORY IN SECURITIES REGULATION

A Aims of securities regulation

In considering what are the aims of securities regulation we find ourselves confronted with a series of rather basic underlying questions. Why do we have securities regulation at all? Why do we have markets?[77] Some rudimentary answers are necessary before a discussion of the aims of securities regulation can be attempted.

Markets exist because of the general increase in social welfare which results from specialisation facilitated by the exchange process. Our ancient ancestors, prior to the existence of markets of any kind, had, each one, to be self-sufficient; then the

---

[69] For example, the collapse of Barings Bank.

[70] Financial Services and Markets Act 2000, ss. 14–18.

[71] And indeed the SROs; IMRO was held to be subject to judicial review in *Governor and Company of the Bank of Scotland, Petitioners* [1989] BCLC 700.

[72] See e.g. *R v Securities and Investments Board, ex parte IFAA* [1995] 2 BCLC 76.

[73] Other rare possibilities include actions for misfeasance in public office; see generally *Three Rivers District Council v Bank of England (No. 3)* [2003] 2 AC 1, HL.

[74] At p. 355.

[75] In addition to the ones discussed above, there are various other examples scattered throughout the 2000 Act, such as the restrictions on the disclosure by the FSA of confidential information; see ss. 348–353. To be balanced against this is the immunity granted to the FSA and its employees in some circumstances by Sch. 1, para. 19.

[76] For a thoughtful analysis of striking the balance, see E. Lomnicka 'Making the Financial Services Authority Accountable' [2000] JBL 65.

[77] For discussion of the related question of why we have companies, see p. 3 *et seq* above.

practice grew up of swapping goods and resources; exchange was born, and a hunter who has killed two rabbits could swop one of them for some vegetables to make himself a more nourishing stew than would otherwise be the case; presumably also the recipient of the rabbit felt enriched by his market exchange. In the modern world, all this is taken for granted and we all are daily surrounded by goods and services which are the products of specialisation and then exchange on countless markets.

Markets channel scarce resources into various sectors of the economy. If the man who produces the vegetables finds that no one wants them, he may well decide to channel his scarce resource (of labour) into pursuing the rabbits; absent demand for a product and the supplier will find that his choice of specialisation may need to be reassessed. Modern day capital markets perform this function of channelling scarce resources (i.e. capital) into the various sectors of the economy. This is particularly obvious as regards markets for new issues of shares (the primary markets). An efficient looking company in a rising sector of the economy will be able to raise new capital easily, whereas one operating in a dying sector will not. The subsequent trading of those shares on the market supports the primary market by making the initial share investment highly liquid and therefore more attractive.[78]

This process of allocation of scarce resources on the markets is a fundamental feature of capitalist systems. Without it, it becomes necessary to make some sort of administrative allocation of labour and raw materials to manufacturing organisations. However, in order for the capitalist system to function reasonably well, it is necessary for the allocation to be accurate. If the allocative process is distorted by, for instance, the dissemination of false information, then the allocative function of the market will become inefficient. Thus 'allocative efficiency' is an important goal of capital markets.

It is now possible to consider the goals of securities regulation. The SEC's position in the US is that the primary purpose of securities laws is the protection of investors, and that investors can best be protected by making certain that they all trade on the basis of equal[79] information; this is often referred to as 'market egalitarianism'. This leads to the two main principles which govern the SEC's position:

(1) There is a need for mandatory disclosure of information; in other words, information that is deemed useful in evaluating securities must be disclosed publicly by issuers of shares so that it will be equally available to all investors.[80]

(2) There is a need for regulation of insider dealing so that information not equally

---

[78] And obviously if the securities are getting a rough time on the secondary market this diminishes the ability of the company to raise more capital (attract more scarce resources) by a fresh issue of securities.

[79] Roughly equal.

[80] In pinning its colours to the mast of adequate disclosure or as it has been called 'truth in securities' law, the SEC turned away from the 'merit' approach to securities regulation operated by some state blue sky law systems under which there would be an evaluation of the fairness of the offer, and instead put its faith in the disclosure mechanisms themselves as being sufficient to create an adequate level of investor protection. Thus the primacy of freedom of contract is preserved, so that the investor is free to make a bad bargain, but the disclosure should ensure that the bargaining game is played 'on a level playing field'.

available to all investors through this egalitarian disclosure mechanism cannot be used unfairly to earn excessive profits.[81]

The SEC's approach to securities regulation came to be challenged by the development of a theory known as the Efficient Capital Markets Hypothesis (ECMH). The broad thrust of the theory is this:[82] that capital markets are efficient, which means that security prices fully reflect all available information and adjust to new information almost instantaneously; and that prices move randomly, so that traders will not be able to spot patterns so as to enable them to beat the market.[83] Arguments were made along the lines that, since investors cannot be cheated in an efficient market, the SEC should encourage the use of all sources of information rather than trying to ensure that information passes through its narrow disclosure mechanisms before reaching the public.[84] In due course counter-arguments supportive of the SEC's position were developed[85] and the SEC's policy remains unchanged.[86]

For a clear and comprehensive statement of the objectives of securities regulation, reference may be made to the statement contained in the influential IOSCO[87] document *Objectives and Principles of Securities Regulation*.[88] The document argues that there are three objectives upon which securities regulation is based and that although there are differences in market structures they form a basis for an effective system of securities regulation.[89] It recognises that the objectives are closely related and in some respects overlap.[90] The core objectives focus on the need to secure the protection of investors, and the integrity of markets in the sense that they embrace fairness, efficiency and transparency, and also on the need to reduce systemic risk.

It is clear that none of this is particularly new and they can all, one way or another, be traced to the New Deal legislation and its subsequent interpretation by the SEC. On the other hand it is useful to find a statement of these fundamental ideas at the highest level of international co-operation.

---

[81] See generally C. Saari 'The Efficient Capital Markets Hypothesis, Economic Theory and the Regulation of the Securities Industry' 29 Stan LR 1031 (1977) at pp. 1032–1033.

[82] See generally the excellent account in G. Arnold *Corporate Financial Management* (London: Financial Times Management, 1998) pp. 595–633.

[83] *Ibid.* at p. 596.

[84] See e.g. C. Saari 'The Efficient Capital Markets Hypothesis, Economic Theory and the Regulation of the Securities Industry' 29 Stan LR 1031 (1977).

[85] See e.g. J. Coffee 'Market Failure and the Economic Case for a Mandatory Disclosure System' 70 Vir LR 717 (1984); see also V. Brudney and W. Bratton *Corporate Finance* 4th edn (Westbury, NY: Foundation Press, 1993) pp. 128–147.

[86] Although, challenges continue to appear; see e.g. R. Romano 'Empowering Investors: A Market Approach to Securities Regulation' in K.J. Hopt, H. Kanda, M.J. Roe, E. Wymeersch, S. Prigge (eds) *Comparative Corporate Governance – The State of the Art and Emerging Research* (Oxford: OUP, 1998) p. 143, advocating a system under which securities issuers could choose a federal or state regime to govern their securities, thus creating competition between regimes and so ensuring a greater alignment of securities laws with investor interests.

[87] International Organisation of Securities Commissions; the nature and function of IOSCO is discussed below at p. 329.

[88] May 1998. Available on the IOSCO website: http://www.iosco.org.

[89] IOSCO *Objectives and Principles of Securities Regulation*, p. 1.

[90] *Ibid.* p. 6.

B Techniques of securities regulation

Most of the main techniques of securities regulation have been described above. Disclosure is obviously the mainstay of the US system and it will be seen[91] that this is true of the UK also. Disclosure can operate in a number of ways[92] but in securities regulation its main *modus operandi* is informative, being designed to make sufficient information available to the investor to empower him when making his investment decisions.

Regulation and registration of market participants is another mainstay regulatory technique which has ancient origins.[93] It can be found almost everywhere from the US Exchange Act's requirement for the registration of brokers or dealers[94] to the basic requirement for authorisation of persons carrying on regulated activities contained in the Financial Services and Markets Act 2000. This kind of registration will usually encompass a screening process as to whether the person is fit and proper and the application of general principles thereafter.

Conduct of business rules are rules which regulate both in general and in detail how business is to be conducted by the market participants. They may involve general principles of conduct such as honesty and fair dealing and detailed principles of conduct such as the duty to give appropriate advice to a client who is considering buying a product.

Prudential regulation and supervision are techniques used to ensure that the structure and financial standing of financial services firms is suitable to the activities they are carrying on. It will often require the firm to have sufficient capital to withstand the knocks that are likely to come to it in the business in which it is engaged. Prudential regulation is one of the major ways of reducing systemic risk.

Rescue systems are a technique used to deal with systemic risk. They occur mainly in banking regulation[95] and involve national or international structures which are able to support a bank which has got into difficulties before that bank collapses and possibly causes a wave of failures throughout the system.

Investor compensation schemes are an important method of investor protection used to meet the situation when all the other regulatory techniques have failed and the firm which owes its clients money has become insolvent. Compensation schemes are a kind of insurance mechanism under which either the state or other firms in the industry are required to contribute towards paying compensation to the investors who have lost out.

Rules against insider dealing and other forms of market abuse are important

---

[91] In the next chapter.

[92] These are: (1) the 'enforcement effect', where disclosure is being used as an aid to the enforcement of a law which contains a substantive prohibition of conduct and the disclosure requirement helps to draw attention to the violation; (2) the 'public disapproval' effect, where disclosure merely draws attention to what is happening and then public reaction makes some kind of adverse input on the perpetrator; (3) the 'informative effect' where disclosure informs people and enables them to act so as to protect their own interests; see the note entitled 'Disclosure as a Legislative Device' 76 Harv LR 1273 (1963).

[93] See p. 315 above.

[94] Securities Exchange Act 1934, s. 15 (1) (a).

[95] Which is largely outside the scope of this book.

methods of ensuring that markets are fair and efficient in the sense that they are able to perform their function of allocation of scarce resources.

Separation of function is used in different situations to create safeguards or prevent abuses which would otherwise be likely to arise. The paradigm example of this was the US Glass–Steagall Act, which required the separation of deposit taking from investment banking.[96]

Suppression of the activity is a securities regulation technique of last resort. Mention has already been made of the UK's Bubble Act in this regard[97] although this is an extreme example. A softer option, containing prohibitions on an activity for certain periods of time, might be seen in the Stock Exchange's Model Code for Transactions in Securities by Directors etc, which puts a ban on share dealings by directors for a period, in certain circumstances.[98]

The next four chapters contain accounts of the UK regulatory structure, insider dealing, public offerings of shares and takeover regulation. Throughout these the reader will find many examples of all of these techniques operating.[99]

C The statutory objectives and the FSA's duties

It is interesting to consider the regulatory objectives which are set out in the Financial Services and Markets Act 2000. These represent a modern and sophisticated statement of the objectives of securities regulation. Of particular interest is the way in which they capture the dilemmas which face the regulatory authority; for instance, its need to balance investor protection against the need not to stifle the financial services industry with unnecessary burdens.

The regulatory objectives are:

(1) Market confidence:[100] this is described as 'maintaining confidence in the financial system'.[101]
(2) Public awareness:[102] described as 'promoting public understanding of the financial system' it is expressed to include '(a) promoting awareness of the benefits and risks associated with different kinds of investment or other financial dealing; and (b) the provision of appropriate information and advice.'[103] Here the FSA is being cast in the role of educator.[104]
(3) The protection of consumers:[105] the protection of consumers objective is

---

[96] See n. 13 above.

[97] See p. 316 above.

[98] See generally, FSA Listing Rules, Chap. 16, Appendix.

[99] Attention will also be given to the enforcement mechanisms which back up the various types of regulation.

[100] Financial Services and Markets Act 2000, s. 2 (2) (a).

[101] *Ibid.* s. 3 (1). By s. 3 (2) the financial system means: 'the financial system operating in the United Kingdom and includes—(a) financial markets and exchanges; (b) regulated activities; and (c) other activities connected with financial markets and exchanges.'

[102] *Ibid.* s. 2 (2) (b).

[103] *Ibid.* s. 4.

[104] This is not uncommon among securities regulators.

[105] Financial Services and Markets Act 2000, s. 2 (2) (c). It is clear from s. 5 (3) that the word 'consumers' is not being used to convey anything significantly different from what the use of the word 'investors' would have done.

described as 'securing the appropriate degree of protection for consumers'. It is provided that:

> [I]n considering what degree of protection may be appropriate, the Authority must have regard to:
>
> (a) the differing degrees of risk involved in different kinds of investment or other transaction;
> (b) the differing degrees of experience and expertise that different consumers may have in relation to different kinds of regulated activity;
> (c) the needs that consumers may have for advice and accurate information; and
> (d) the general principle that consumers should take responsibility for their decisions.[106]

Paragraph (d) above is particularly interesting because it is possible to see the contractual doctrine of sanctity of bargain[107] having an effect on regulatory policy. The statutory provision as drafted makes the point that the public are expected to become aware of the risks so that they can take responsibility for the bargain which they are making. Securities regulation systems are perhaps often prone to creating the impression that the investor should be immersed in a cocoon of rules designed to protect him from invariably unscrupulous suppliers of financial products. There is, however, a balance to be struck and it is clear that the underlying principle of sanctity of bargain has not changed under the new legislation.

(4) The reduction of financial crime:[108] this objective is described as 'reducing the extent to which it is possible for a business carried on by a regulated person[109] to be used for a purpose connected with financial crime'.[110] Here the legislature is giving a high profile to one of the major factors threatening any system of financial services and requiring the FSA to focus on it. This seems appropriate, in view of the damage evident from past financial collapses.[111]

The Financial Services and Markets Act 2000 also lays down the FSA's general functions. Not surprisingly, in discharging its general functions it has to try to meet the regulatory objectives.[112] The general functions are delineated as:

> (a) its function of making rules (considered as a whole);
> (b) its function of preparing and issuing codes under this Act (considered as a whole);
> (c) its functions in relation to the giving of general guidance (considered as a whole); and

---

[106] *Ibid.* s. 5 (2).

[107] Under which parties to a contract remain free to make a bad bargain and there is no general doctrine of fairness or reasonableness operating to give one or other of them a way out.

[108] Financial Services and Markets Act 2000, s. 2 (2) (d).

[109] Or someone who should be regulated.

[110] See Financial Services and Markets Act 2000, s. 6, which contains various provisions.

[111] E.g. Barlow Clowes, Barings, BCCI, and the constant threat of drug-related crime and money laundering.

[112] Thus it is provided that 'the Authority must, so far as is reasonably possible, act in a way (a) which is compatible with the regulatory objectives; and (b) which the Authority considers the most appropriate for the purpose of meeting those objectives': Financial Services and Markets Act 2000, s. 2.

(d) its function of determining the general policy and principles by reference to which it performs particular functions.[113]

The 2000 Act seeks to build into the FSA's *modus operandi* a wide range of policies. It is provided that:

In discharging its general functions the Authority must have regard to:

(a) the need to use its resources in the most efficient and economic way;
(b) the responsibilities of those who manage the affairs of authorised persons;
(c) the principle that a burden or restriction which is imposed on a person, or on the carrying on of an activity, should be proportionate to the benefits, considered in general terms, which are expected to result from the imposition of that burden or restriction;
(d) the desirability of facilitating innovation in connection with regulated activities;
(e) the international character of financial services and markets and the desirability of maintaining the competitive position of the United Kingdom;
(f) the need to minimise the adverse effects on competition that may arise from anything done in the discharge of those functions;
(g) the desirability of facilitating competition between those who are subject to any form of regulation by the Authority.[114]

The provision that the FSA must 'have regard' to these matters shows that the balance and mix of these policies is in the hands of the regulator. This is clearly an important list of considerations; in particular the principle of proportionality in relation to benefits and burdens of regulation (in para. (c)) is part of several measures designed to ensure that the regulatory environment is not unnecessarily heavy.[115]

D IOSCO and global convergence

Recent years have seen the increasing internationalisation[116] of securities markets, not just in the sense of markets for dealings in shares, but generally as regards the marketing of investment products. These kinds of developments pose challenges for securities regulators, in terms of detection of fraud or improper practices, and as a result of the existence of weak national regimes of securities regulation which can provide a haven for unscrupulous activity.[117] Securities commissions have sought various ways of meeting these challenges.[118]

---

[113] *Ibid.* s. 2 (4).
[114] *Ibid.* s. 2 (3).
[115] See also e.g. s. 155 (2) (a) of the 2000 Act, which requires a cost benefit analysis of proposed new rules.
[116] As an example of this trend mention could be made of the World Trade Organisation (WTO) Pact on Financial Services 1997, under which there was agreement to relax or eliminate restrictions on foreign banks and other financial institutions; see General Agreement on Trade in Services (GATS), Fifth Protocol: http://www.wto.org/english/tratop_e/servfi_e/fiback_e.htm.
[117] Some types of criminal activity which sometimes have a bearing on securities and corporate frauds will fall to be dealt with by ICPO-Interpol or by Europol.
[118] For a full account, see H. Baum 'Globalizing Capital Markets and Possible Regulatory Responses' in J. Basedow and T. Kono (eds) *Legal Aspects of Globalization: Conflict of Laws, Internet Capital Markets and Insolvency in a Global Economy* (The Hague: Kluwer, 2000) p. 77.

Probably of paramount importance here is the existence of the International Organisation of Securities Commissions (IOSCO), currently based in Madrid. The common goals of the securities commissions which are members of IOSCO provide for co-operation in the promotion of high standards of regulation of markets in order to secure fairness, efficiency and international surveillance. With a view to promotion of domestic markets, there is to be focus on the need for commissions to exchange information on their regulatory experiences. Another important aim is for the commissions to provide mutual assistance in the promotion of standards and in enforcement.[119]

IOSCO is not a securities regulator; it has no power over the nationals of any state. On the other hand, its role in providing a forum for discussion of problems, and formulating principles[120] for the guidance of the world's regulators is an important one. In the long run, it seems possible that through its influence, the world's securities regulation regimes will increasingly take on similarities.[121]

In 1985 the SEC and the UK's SIB signed what was probably the first major memorandum of understanding (MOU) between securities regulators.[122] MOUs are declarations of intent by which, in a non-legal way, regulators agree to co-operate with each other.[123] They involve an exchange of information about the regulators and the systems in operation in their respective countries and agreements for the exchange of information in certain circumstances. There are several hundred MOUs[124] in existence and they perform an important role in combatting the difficulties presented by internationalisation.[125]

E Financial market integration in the EU

1 The internal market in financial services

Within the EU, securities regulation has become inseparably bound up with the creation of the European Single Market.[126] The basic mechanisms for many areas

---

[119] See the IOSCO website http://www.iosco.org.

[120] Reference has already been made to its publication, *Objectives and Principles of Securities Regulation*, May 1998; it is amended periodically.

[121] For an interesting exploration of the idea of a World Financial Authority, see J. Eatwell and L. Taylor 'New Issues in International Financial Regulation' in E. Ferran and C. Goodhart (eds) *Regulating Financial Services and Markets in the 21st Century* (Oxford: Hart Publishing, 2001) p. 35.

[122] For a description of the FSA's relations with the international regulatory community see: http://www.fsa.gov.uk/international.

[123] S. Bergstrasser 'Cooperation between Supervisors' in G. Ferrarini (ed.) *European Securities Markets: The Investment Services Directive and Beyond* (London: Kluwer, 1998) p. 373.

[124] *Ibid.* p. 376, suggesting 200.

[125] IOSCO has recently been developing a Multilateral MOU for Securities Regulators; see http://www.iosco.org.

[126] See generally P. Clarotti 'The Completion of the Internal Financial Market: Current Position and Outlook' in M. Andenas and S. Kenyon-Slade (eds) *EC Financial Market Regulation and Company Law* (London: Sweet & Maxwell, 1993) p. 1; L. Garzaniti and D. Pope 'Single Market-Making: EC Regulation of Securities Markets' (1993) 14 Co Law 43; E. Lomnicka 'The Single European Passport in Financial Services' in B. Rider and M. Andenas (eds) *Developments in European Company Law* (Deventer: Kluwer, 1996) p. 181.

of creation of the internal market were the Treaty of Rome provisions coupled with the case law of the European Court of Justice (ECJ). In the field of financial services this would have been theoretically possible by use of the relevant Treaty provisions.[127] Article 43[128] gives a right of establishment.[129] Article 49[130] gives a freedom to provide services on a cross-border basis.[131] The case law of the ECJ has established that arts 43 and 49 are directly applicable[132] and so, for instance, in the financial services field could be used to bring about recognition of the rights of establishment of a financial services firm in another Member State and the right to offer cross-border financial services.[133] However, in the field of financial services law, it was felt that what was needed was something more detailed than the Treaty provisions.[134] The approach which was finally adopted was set out in the European Commission's White Paper *Completing the Internal Market*[135] involving the use of Directives which required minimal co-ordination of rules.[136] The key concept

---

[127] See Lomnicka, n. 126 above, at p. 182 and references cited there.

[128] Its pre-Amsterdam Treaty numbering was art. 52.

[129] '... restrictions on the freedom of establishment of nationals of a Member State in the territory of another Member State shall be abolished by progressive stages ... Such progressive abolition shall also apply to restrictions on the setting up of agencies, branches or subsidiaries by nationals of any Member State established in the territory of any Member State.'

[130] Article 59, pre-Amsterdam.

[131] '... [R]estrictions on freedom to provide services within the Community shall be progressively abolished ... in respect of nationals of Member States who are established in a State of the Community other than that of the person for whom the services are intended.'

[132] See on arts 43 and 49 respectively, Case 2/74 *Reyners* v *Belgian State* [1974] ECR 631; Case 33/74 *Van Binsbergen* v *Bedrijfsvereniging Metaalnijverheid* [1974] 1 ECR 1229.

[133] For use in the financial services field, see Case C-101/94 *EC Commission* v *Italy (Re Restrictions on Foreign Securities Dealers)* [1996] 3 CMLR 754.

[134] See Lomnicka, n. 126 above, at p. 182.

[135] COM (85) 310.

[136] The main Capital Markets Directives, both prior and subsequent to the Commission's 1985 White Paper, are listed below. Many have been amended and the current amended versions can be found on the European Union's website http://www.europa.eu.int. Most of these Directives are discussed in this and in the following four chapters of this book.

Directive 79/279/EEC co-ordinating the conditions for the admission of securities to official stock exchange listing (the 'Admissions Directive'); Directive 1980/390/EEC co-ordinating the requirements for the drawing up, scrutiny and distribution of the listing particulars to be published for the admission of securities to official stock exchange listing (the 'Listing Particulars Directive'); Directive 82/121/EEC on information to be published on a regular basis by companies the shares of which have been admitted to official stock exchange listing (the 'Interim Reports Directive'); Directive 85/345/EEC (the 'Second Banking Co-ordination Directive'); Directive 85/611/EEC on EC Undertakings for Collective Investment in Transferable Securities (the 'UCITS Directive'); Directive 87/345/EEC on the mutual recognition of listing particulars (the 'Mutual Recognition Directive'); Directive 88/627/EEC on the information to be published when a major holding in a listed company is acquired or disposed of (the 'Major Shareholdings Directive'); Directive 89/298/EEC co-ordinating the requirements for the drawing-up, scrutiny and distribution of the prospectus to be published when transferable securities are offered to the public (the 'Prospectus Directive'); Directive 89/592/EEC co-ordinating regulations on Insider Dealing (the 'Insider Dealing Directive'); Directive 91/308/EEC (the 'Money Laundering Directive'); Directive 93/6/EEC (the 'Capital Adequacy Directive'); Directive 93/22/EEC on investment services in the securities field (the 'Investment Services Directive'); Directive 97/9/EC on investor compensation schemes; Directive 2000/12/EC relating to the taking up and pursuit of the business of credit institutions. In recent years, following the impetus created by the Financial Services Action Plan, the pace of EC legislation has increased, and it defies listing in totality here. And as will be seen in appropriate parts of this book, many of the above have been replaced, although in many cases it will be some years before the

employed was the European 'passport', which would give EC-wide recognition to the authorisation by each Member State of its own firms. To illustrate this it is useful to consider the 1993 Investment Services Directive,[137] which contains the fundamental techniques, many of which survive into the 2004 Directive which is replacing it.

2 1993 The Investment Services Directive (ISD)

The Investment Services Directive is expressed to apply to all 'investment firms'.[138] An investment firm is defined so as to mean 'any legal person the regular occupation or business of which is the provision of investment services for third parties on a professional basis'.[139] 'Investment service' is defined as meaning 'any of the services listed in Section A of the Annex relating to any of the instruments listed in section B of the Annex that are provided for a third party'. Section A of the Annex then lists various services which broadly speaking can be said to cover the activities carried out by brokers, dealers, investment managers and underwriters. Section B of the Annex lists the instruments such as 'transferable securities'. Interestingly, there is also a Section C list of non-core services which can only be carried out under the passport if an activity in Section A has been authorised.[140] The giving of investment advice or matters such as advising companies about takeovers are Section C activities.[141] Behind this lies the background that in some EU Member States, these activities are not subjected to authorisation or regulation requirements and it would therefore not have been appropriate to subject them to the authorisation requirements of the Investment Services Directive.[142]

The basic principle of 'Home State' authorisation is contained in art. 3, which requires that: 'Each Member State shall make access to the business of investment firms subject to authorisation for investment firms of which it is the Home Member

---

replacement legislation comes into force. For instance, the first three above have been consolidated into Directive 2001/34/EC, there is a new Prospectus Directive 2003/71/EC, a Directive on Takeover Bids 2004/25/EC, a Directive on Insider Dealing and Market Manipulation (Market Abuse) 2003/6/EC, and a replacement for the Investment Services Directive called the Directive on Markets in Financial Instruments 2004/39/EC (MiFID).

[137] Directive 93/22/EEC on investment services in the securities field. See generally G. Ferrarini (ed.) *European Securities Markets: The Investment Services Directive and Beyond* (London: Kluwer, 1998). The Investment Services Directive was implemented in the UK by the Investment Services Regulations 1995 (SI 1995 No. 3275). Also of general relevance to investment firms, but not examined here, is the Capital Adequacy Directive (93/6/EEC), which seeks to impose capital requirements on investment firms with a view to ensuring that they have adequate capital to meet business risks. The Directive has been subsequently amended and there is an ongoing wide-ranging review of capital adequacy rules within the EC.

[138] Article 2 (1).

[139] Article 1 (2). This would obviously exclude UK partnerships and so there are special rules for these and other business organisations which are not legal persons. There are also various exclusions from the definition of investment firm, e.g. members of professions (such as solicitors and accountants) conducting investment services incidentally to the practice of their profession; see generally art. 2 (2).

[140] Article 3 (1).

[141] Section C, paras 6 and 4.

[142] See G. Ferrarini 'Towards a European Law of Investment Services and Institutions' (1994) 31 *Common Market Law Review* 1283 at p. 1289.

State.'[143] Article 14 gives effect to the passport[144] by providing that: 'Member States shall ensure that investment services ... may be provided within their territories ... either by the establishment of a branch or under the freedom to provide services ...' These passport rights are subject to notification provisions[145] under which a firm wishing to use its passport abroad must notify its own competent authorities who will then require information from it which will be communicated by them to the Host State's competent authorities.

One of the most problematic aspects of the Investment Services Directive is the division of functions between the Home and Host States with regard to the rules which investment firms have to observe. The basic idea is that a passporting firm must observe two sets of rules, 'prudential rules' and 'rules of conduct', the former relating mainly to organisation and structure of the firm and the latter pertaining to the way in which it carries out its business transactions. But it must observe the prudential rules which emanate from its Home State, and the rules of conduct which emanate from the Host State.[146] The prudential rules are set out in art. 10, which stipulates that: 'Each Home Member State shall draw up prudential rules which investment firms shall observe at all times.'[147] They involve, for instance, having sound administrative and accounting procedures, making adequate arrangements for the safeguarding of the funds belonging to investors, arranging for records of transactions to be kept, and being structured so as to avoid conflicts of interest.

Rules of conduct are covered by art. 11, which requires Member States[148] to 'draw up rules of conduct which investment firms shall observe at all times'. The rules must implement the principles set out, such as ensuring that an investment firm acts 'honestly and fairly in conducting its business activities in the best interests of its clients and the integrity of the market' and 'acts with due skill, care and diligence ... ' and 'makes adequate disclosure of relevant material information in its dealings with its clients'. Also, and significantly, it is required to comply with 'all regulatory requirements applicable to the conduct of its business activities so as to promote the best interests of its clients and the integrity of the market'.[149] It is

---

[143] It is further provided (art. 3) that: '... such authorisation shall be granted by the Home Member State's competent authorities ... The authorisation shall specify the investment services referred to in Section A of the Annex which the undertaking is authorised to provide. The authorisation may also cover one or more of the non-core services referred to in Section C of the Annex.'

[144] See also art. 15, which gives a right to passporting firms to have access to or become members of securities exchanges of Member States.

[145] In arts. 17 and 18.

[146] Articles 10 and 11.

[147] Although, whatever the content of these rules, there are some fundamental requirements imposed by art. 8 (1), (2) and (3); capital adequacy and fitness. Article 8 (3) makes it clear that the prudential supervision of an investment firm is the responsibility of the Home Member State, although this is expressed to be 'without prejudice to those provisions of this Directive which give responsibility to the authorities of the Host Member State.'

[148] The Host Member State is given responsibility for implementation and supervision of compliance; see art. 11 (2).

[149] There is also art. 13, which enables Host Member States to make rules about advertising (these are not specifically mentioned in art. 11), although the power to do this is limited by the concept of the general good; for discussion of this see in the text.

possible that the power of Member States to draw up rules of conduct is limited by a requirement that the rules must be such that they can only be justified by reference to the ECJ concept of the 'general good'.[150] This limitation does not appear from the wording of art. 11, but other parts of the Investment Services Directive arguably proceed on the basis that art. 11 is so limited.[151]

3 The Financial Services Action Plan (FSAP)

As the end of the 1990s approached, it became apparent that the success of the Investment Services Directive and the other Capital Markets Directives has been limited. The Commission Communication *Financial Services: Implementing the Framework for Financial Markets – Action Plan*[152] assessed the situation as:

> A single market for financial services has been under construction since 1973. Important strides have been made towards providing a secure prudential environment in which financial institutions can trade in other Member States. Yet, the Union's financial markets remain segmented and business and consumers continue to be deprived of direct access to cross-border financial institutions . . .[153]

The document went on to say that the introduction of the euro provides an opportunity for further action and then set out detailed proposals for future action. These ideas were endorsed at the Lisbon European Council in March 2000, and thereafter the progress towards carrying out this Financial Services Action Plan (FSAP) gathered pace. By June 2004, 39 measures had been produced, many of them major pieces of EC legislation in the form of directive or regulation, others are Commission communications. Many of the most important ones are dealt with in appropriate places in this book. The EC Commission has provided summaries of progress on the europa website. These are useful, in view of the magnitude of the legislation.[154] All this has presented an awesome challenge to the securities commissions of the Member States. Our own FSA (in conjuction with the Treasury) has recently produced its latest analysis of the task it faces and how it proposes to carry it out.[155]

Alongside this revolution in the substantive law and rules of EU securities regulation, events have occurred which have in themselves changed forever the shape of securities regulation in Europe. In 2001 the Lamfalussy Report on the Regulation of European Securities Markets was published.[156] The Report's perspective on the malaise in the progress towards an integrated EU securities market was that the legislative system was not working. Its processes were too slow to enable it to mould the regulatory structure appropriate to markets where the pace of change was accelerating, and the use of Directives meant that there were considerable divergences

---

[150] Which perhaps broadly 'translates' as 'public interest'.
[151] See further Lomnicka, n. 126 above, at pp. 198–199.
[152] COM (1999) 232, 11 May 1999.
[153] *Ibid.* p. 3.
[154] http://europa.eu.int/comm/internal_market/en/finances/actionplan/index.htm.
[155] The EU Financial Services Action Plan: Delivering the FSAP in the UK (FSA, May 2004).
[156] Final Report of the Committee of Wise Men on the Regulation of European Securities Markets (The Lamfalussy Report), Brussels 15/2/2001.

between Member States on how they were implemented. They recommended a four-level legislative structure, making use of the comitology procedures which had been developed many years earlier for use in other areas of the internal market. The four levels have been restated and re-explained by various institutional sources ever since, and it may well be that the concept of four 'levels', whilst having a user-friendly feel to it, does not really get to grips with the detail of what is happening in legal legislative terms, but nevertheless, using that format, the approach is broadly as follows:

Level 1: This consists of a Directive (or EC Regulation) setting out broad principles. So, for instance, in the field of market conduct, we have recently had the enactment of the Directive on Insider Dealing and Market Manipulation (Market Abuse),[157] sometimes known as the 'MAD'. The principles are kept at a high level of generality so that Member States can easily agree to them. The detail will come later.

Level 2: Here come the details, which are needed to properly implement the broad principles of level 1. At level 2, the Commission makes legislation, known as 'implementing measures', in conjunction with the ESC.[158] In fact, the Commission in doing this will have had the benefit of detailed thought, research and advice from another committee, the Committee of European Securities Regulators (CESR) which under the four level classification mainly stars at level 3, although its non-constitutional advisory role in the background of level 2 is crucial. So, for instance, in relation to the MAD, the Commission made a series of formal technical requests (mandates)[159] to the CESR for advice on what was needed to fill in the detail of some of the broad principles in the MAD. After various working documents and consultations, the comitology process then led to three implementing measures on really detailed and complex matters: one on the question of defining (and disclosing) inside information and defining market abuse,[160] another on presentation of investment recommendations and disclosure of conflicts of interest,[161] and a third on exemptions for buy-back programmes and stabilisation of financial instruments.[162]

Level 3: At this level we find the Committee of European Securities Regulators (CESR), an independent committee made up of the heads of the Securities Commissions[163] of Europe's Member States, and based in Paris. It replaces the earlier less formal grouping known as FESCO[164] and takes over its functions and

---

[157] 2003/6/EC, OJ 2003, L 96/16. On this generally see Chapter 20 below.
[158] European Securities Committee. This is a committee consisting of high-level government representatives from each Member State. The ESC fulfils a constitutional function in the enactment of the 'implementing measures' rather than making any input of expertise. Although needed for constitutional and legal aspects of the comitology process, its role in the four level picture is very much in the background.
[159] EC Commission Mandate of 27 March 2002, and EC Commission Mandate of 31 January 2003 (Ref: MARKT/G2 D(2003), leading to CESR's Advice on Level 2 Implementing Measures for the proposed Market Abuse Directive (Ref: CESR/02.089d).
[160] Commission Directive 2003/124/EC, OJ 2003, L 339/70.
[161] Commission Directive 2003/125/EC, OJ 2003, L 339/73.
[162] Commission Regulation (EC) No 2273/2003, OJ 2003, L 336/33.
[163] More technically, 'the heads of the national public authorities competent in the field of securities'.
[164] Forum of European Securities Commissions.

agreements. As we have seen, it operates as an advisory group to the Commission in the preparation of implementing measures, and in advising the Commission generally on the development of the EU's regulation of securities. It also has the function of ensuring a consistent day to day implementation of the legislation, and will work towards enhanced co-operation between the States. It will produce guidance and codes. Perhaps in this body we can see the beginning of the development of true Pan-European Securities Regulation; it is indeed an interesting development.[165] Already, its ability to speak effectively for the whole of Europe is bringing a new dimension to global securities regulation for it has already led to an agreement on enhanced collaboration between the SEC and the EU.[166]

Level 4: This seems to be an exhortation to the Commission to strengthen its enforcement powers. It is clear that this will involve liaison between all the bodies involved in this process.

4 The new ISD 2 is called MiFID

The 1999 Financial Services Action Plan, among all the other ideas, criticised the Investment Services Directive as being:

> [I]n urgent need of upgrading if it is to serve as the cornerstone of an integrated securities market ... host country authorities are unwavering in applying their conduct of business rules. However, there may ultimately be a need to reconsider the extent to which host country application of conduct of business rules – which is the basic premise of the ISD – is in keeping with the needs of an integrated securities market.[167]

In the ensuing years, there followed many drafts and consultations on what was then described as the proposal for the 'ISD 2'. At a comparatively late stage of gestation the proposal underwent a name change, and the Directive which was ultimately adopted on 21 April 2004[168] was called the Directive on Markets in Financial Instruments, popularly known as 'MiFID'. The Lamfalussy process has been getting into gear to produce the Level 2 implementing legislation, and Member States have until 30 April 2006 to bring the Directive into force; also on that date the repeal of the old Investment Services Directive[169] will take effect.

The MiFID carries forward many of the basic ideas in the ISD, such as home state authorisation and prudential supervision. It seeks to avoid the problem of host state imposition of conduct of business rules on incoming firms, by including a large measure of harmonisation of the principles contained in COB rules. In this way it seeks to ensure that the passport does actually enable firms to do business in other Member States without interference by the regulatory authorities of those host states, and in particular by the host authorities imposing their own COB rules.

---

[165] They have an informative website: http://www.cesr-eu.org.

[166] Press Release, CESR 11-04, 4 June 2004.

[167] *Ibid.* at p. 5. In this regard, the document focuses on the possibility of developing the concept of letting 'sophisticated investors' choose the conduct of business regime which will apply to their contract.

[168] Directive 2004/39/EC, OJ 2004, L 145/1.

[169] Directive 93/22/EC.

Under MiFID the powers of the host state are relatively limited, usually extending only to monitoring compliance with COB rules.[170]

The MiFID deals with many other matters, such as broadening the range of investment services which need authorisation (so as to include, for instance, the giving of investment advice), clarifying and expanding the types of financial instrument that can be traded on regulated markets and by firms, clarifying standards for regulated markets and markets run by investment firms.[171] All of this will need a great deal of work at level 2, and in the securities commissions of Member States when they implement it in their own legislation and regulatory rules.

---

[170] E.g. arts 32(7) and 61–62.
[171] Known as MTFs (Multiple Trading Facilities).

18

THE REGULATORY MACHINERY OF THE FINANCIAL SERVICES AND MARKETS ACT 2000

18.1 INTRODUCTION AND ASSUMPTIONS

The previous chapter, in the context of the policy and theory of securities regulation, has described the role and duties of the Financial Services Authority as set out in the Financial Services and Markets Act 2000, and also considered its accountability.

This chapter gives an account of the main features of the complex system of regulation established by the Financial Services and Markets Act. It will be seen that many aspects of the regime established by the Financial Services and Markets Act 2000 relate to what are often termed 'intermediated securities'. These are products which are formed out of securities originally issued by companies to large financial institutions, or purchased by them, but which in the hands of such intermediaries have been fashioned into a product which is suitable for domestic consumers.[1] An example would be a collective investment scheme, such as a unit trust, operated by an investment bank intermediary. Such an intermediated product is attractive to domestic consumers because it (1) spreads risk and (2) is available in small amounts. These intermediated products are economically very important because they ensure that domestic capital[2] forms part of the overall picture of corporate finance. As will be seen, the effect that they have on the regulatory structure is that the regulator feels obliged to establish a high degree of consumer protection, which would probably have been unnecessary had the transaction merely taken place between the intermediary and the company or secondary market where the shares were being traded.

18.2 SCOPE OF THE ACT

A The general prohibition

The most fundamental provision of the Act is s. 19, which provides:

---

[1] In an economic sense, holders of intermediated products are still shareholders, although in technical terms, within traditional company law, this is not the case and shareholder rights will fall to be exercised by the intermediary.

[2] I.e. that part of a householder's income which she or he has decided should, for whatever reasons, be set aside as savings.

(1) No person may carry on a regulated activity in the United Kingdom, or purport to do so, unless he is:

    (a) an authorised person; or

    (b) an exempt person.

(2) The prohibition is referred to in this Act as the general prohibition.

A person who contravenes this is guilty of a criminal offence[3] and enforceability of agreements may be affected.[4]

Thus, people wanting to carry on a regulated activity have to get authorised, or be exempt.

B Regulated activities

1 Relationship between the Act and the Order

The legislature has adopted a two-stage approach to defining 'regulated activities'. There is a very general provision in the Act and then detailed but fundamental provisions in a statutory instrument, the Financial Services and Markets Act (Regulated Activities) Order.[5] The rationale behind this approach is that the Order can easily be adjusted as necessary to cope with market developments. It is a recognition of the fact that commercial practice is fast changing and the law needs to be as well. To amend an Act takes valuable parliamentary time, but it is comparatively simple to amend a statutory instrument.

The general provision in the Act (s. 22) provides that:

(1) An activity is a regulated activity for the purposes of this Act if it is an activity of a specified kind which is carried on by way of business and:

    (a) relates to an investment of a specified kind; or

    (b) in the case of an activity of a kind which is also specified for the purposes of this paragraph, is carried on in relation to property of any kind.

(2) Schedule 2 makes provision supplementing this section.

(3) Nothing in Schedule 2 limits the powers conferred by subsection (1).

(4) 'Investment' includes any asset, right or interest.

(5) 'Specified' means specified in an order made by the Treasury.

This general provision actually reveals very little about which activities are regulated activities, since it is not clear which *activities* and/or *investments* are *specified*. Referring to Sch. 2 is hardly more helpful since it is a list of examples of matters

---

[3] Subject to a penalty of up to two years' imprisonment (s. 23 (1)). It appears that no *mens rea* is required unless perhaps something can be implied from the words 'carry on'. See also s. 24 (1), which contains criminal penalties for making false claims to be authorised or exempt. It is necessary to distinguish s. 20, the effect of which is dealt with in the context of the 'permissions' regime at p. 344 below.

[4] See generally ss. 26–28, under which agreements made by or through unauthorised persons become unenforceable against the other party.

[5] Financial Services and Markets Act 2000 (Regulated Activities) Order 2001 (SI 2001, No. 544). It is frequently amended.

which might be specified by the Treasury.[6] The answer to the question as to what the expression 'regulated activity' covers is to be found in the Order.

The Regulated Activities Order (RAO) is not an easy document to construe and the account which follows is not an exhaustive analysis but instead provides an introduction to some of its more important aspects. The first point is that the Order seems to ignore comprehensively Sch. 2 to the Act, in the sense that it imposes many detailed conditions and exceptions and ignores the layout of the Schedule. Secondly, Part II of the Order lists specified activities and Part III lists specified investments.

2 The 'Business' test

However, there is a fundamental condition which usually needs to be fulfilled before the activity counts as a regulated activity for the purposes of s. 22 of the Act. This is what is called the 'Business' test (or business requirement). In other words, a person will only be regarded as engaging in an activity within s. 22 if it is carried on by way of business. There is no general definition of 'carried on by way of business'[7] and so it is necessary to rely on past case law on similar ideas elsewhere in law, or under the previous regime. Various questions spring to mind. Do the words 'carry on' add much? Do they import a requirement that there must be a degree of repetition and continuity in the activity[8] and that an isolated occasion would not be sufficient? On the other hand, a one-off transaction might be very large and of great commercial significance. It is not proposed to discuss this at length here, but the judgment in *Morgan Grenfell* v *Welwyn Hatfield DC*[9] can give useful guidance in this regard. It was held there that for the purposes of the words 'by way of business' in s. 63 of the Financial Services Act 1986, the test is whether:

> [I]n ordinary parlance [it] would be described as a business transaction, as opposed to something personal or casual ... As regards the test of the frequency with which the relevant type of transaction is entered into, this can be no more than a guide. Regularly entering into a certain type of transaction for the purpose of profit is a good indication that the party doing so is doing so by way of business. But it is equally possible that the very first time it enters into such a contract it is doing so by way of business because it is doing so as part of its overall business activities.[10]

---

[6] Thus: 'The matters with respect to which provision may be made under s. 22 (1) in respect of activities include, in particular, those described in general terms in this ... Schedule.' It seems that this provision currently has no discernible legal effect.

[7] Although in some circumstances exemptions and definitions are applied by the Financial Services and Markets Act 2000 (Carrying on Regulated Activities by Way of Business) Order 2001 (SI 2001 No. 1177). See, in particular, art. 3, which provides that in relation to a range of activities relating to investments: 'A person is not to be regarded as carrying on by way of business an activity to which this article applies, unless he carries on the business of engaging in one or more such activities.'

[8] Some support for this interpretation can be gained from the judgment in *Lloyd* v *Poperly and another* [2000] BCC 338 (case decided on similar words in the FSA 1986).

[9] [1995] 1 All ER 1.

[10] *Ibid.* at pp. 13–14, *per* Hobhouse J.

C Examples of prescribed 'activities' and 'investments'

The wide scope of the regulatory power wielded by the Financial Services Authority is apparent from a perusal of the Regulated Activities Order. In some circumstances[11] the following[12] will be specified activities: accepting deposits; effecting contracts of insurance; establishing a collective investment scheme; dealing in investments; managing investments; issuing electronic money; safeguarding and administering investments; managing investments; advising on investments; various activities at Lloyd's; regulated mortgage contracts; agreeing to carry on certain activities. These are only examples, and it is thus clear that the new regime covers a very wide range of financial services.

The following are some examples of what in some circumstances will be prescribed investments: deposits; electronic money; contracts of insurance; shares etc; instruments creating or acknowledging indebtedness; government and public securities; instruments giving entitlement to investments; certificates representing certain securities; units in a collective investment scheme; options; futures; contracts for differences etc; Lloyd's syndicate capacity and syndicate membership; regulated mortgage contracts; rights to or interests in investments. As above, this list is not exhaustive.

D Territorial scope of the general prohibition

The territorial scope of the general prohibition is stated simply in s. 19 (1), which contains a prohibition on carrying on a 'regulated activity in the United Kingdom'. This relatively simple statement is then supplemented and altered in effect, by provisions which regulate 'inward' and 'outward' scope. Inward scope is dealt with in art. 72 of the Regulated Activities Order and creates exemptions for people overseas in some circumstances. Outward scope is dealt with in s. 418 of the Act, which, broadly is dealing with the question of how far jurisdiction can be claimed over people who are located in the UK, but do business abroad. The purpose of s. 418 is to enable the UK to claim jurisdiction to regulate financial services which are being offered from the UK because if they are unregulated it could damage international confidence in the UK as a place to invest and do business. It is not unusual for countries to be concerned about their image as a fair market and the idea is broadly in line with the tenor of the ECJ's approach in *Alpine Investments*,[13] where it was held that concern for the reputation of Dutch securities markets was a valid reason for the imposition of controls on Dutch securities traders who were based in Holland but selling their securities out of the country. The provisions also give effect to the rights and obligations of passporting firms[14] under the Capital Markets Directives.

---

[11] The actual wording of the Regulated Activities Order needs to be looked at carefully as there are many conditions, definitions and exceptions in it.

[12] This list is not exhaustive.

[13] Case C–384/93 *Alpine Investments BV* v *Minister van Financien* [1995] ECR 1–1141.

[14] See p. 330 above.

E The financial promotion regime

It has been seen that the key to avoiding contravention of the general prohibition in s. 19 is by becoming authorised, or by being exempt. These matters are dealt with later. It is necessary here to consider the effect of the financial promotion regime which is set out in s. 21 of the FSMA 2000 and in the Financial Services and Markets Act 2000 (Financial Promotion) Order.[15] It should be noted that the drafting of the Financial Promotion Order is complex and in some places considerably alters the effects of the primary legislation.

Obviously, most promotional activity is carried out by *authorised* persons operating within the financial services sector by way of business. And they will be authorised by the FSA in order to carry on those businesses. Their promotional activities will be regulated by the special conduct of business rules issued by the FSA.[16] Also, authorised persons will have to comply with the FSA's Principles for Businesses which apply to authorised persons generally.[17] Thus, in particular, Principle 7 requires that 'a firm must pay due regard to the information needs of its customers, and communicate information to them in a way which is clear, fair and not misleading'.[18] So, for authorised persons engaging in financial promotion, the system makes detailed provision.

The FSMA 2000 provides definitions of financial promotion and the Financial Promotion Order provides various exemptions. None of this is very remarkable (though the legislation is complex). However, the legislation also seeks to do one further thing; it seeks to extend the regime to promotions by unauthorised persons by requiring them to get the content of the financial promotion approved by an authorised person.

All these matters are clearly reflected in s. 21 of the Act, which provides:

(1) A person ('A') must not, in the course of business, communicate[19] an invitation or inducement to engage in investment[20] activity.
(2) But subsection (1) does not apply if:
 (a) A is an authorised person; or
 (b) the content of the communication is approved[21] for the purposes of this section by an authorised person.

A deceptively simple definition of 'engaging in investment activity' is given in s. 21 (8), but in fact, because of the link made there to the concept of 'controlled activity', the legislature is using the definition to fine-tune the scope of the regime. This is because, behind s. 21 (8), lies some complex subordinate legislation by statutory instrument. Section 21 (8) provides:

---

[15] SI 2001, No. 1335.
[16] These are in the FSA Handbook of Rules and Guidance, Conduct of Business COB, Chap. 3.
[17] See p. 348 below.
[18] Also relevant is Principle 6 (customers' interests).
[19] By s. 21 (13), ' "Communicate" includes causing a communication to be made'.
[20] By s. 21 (14), ' "Investment" includes any asset, right or interest'.
[21] In deciding whether to give approval, authorised persons will be required to have regard to the rules mentioned above, e.g. the FSA COB Rules and FSA Principles for Businesses.

'Engaging in investment activity' means—
  (a) entering or offering to enter into an agreement the making or performance of which by either party constitutes a controlled activity; or
  (b) exercising any rights conferred by an investment to acquire, dispose of, underwrite or convert an investment.

The concept of 'controlled activity' and hence, largely, the scope of the financial promotion regime, depends on Treasury 'specification'.[22] The relevant provisions are contained in the Financial Services and Markets Act (Financial Promotion) Order.[23] Schedule 1 to the Order defines 'controlled activity'. It lists the controlled activities and specifies the investments to which they relate. Other parts of the Financial Promotion Order contain many exotically worded exemptions, such as where shares are offered around to rich or sophisticated persons.[24]

The territorial scope of the financial promotion regime is dealt with by s. 21 (3), which provides that: 'in the case of a communication originating outside the United Kingdom, subsection (1) applies only if the communication is capable of having an effect in the United Kingdom.' This is a very broad territorial claim. However, as with much of the legislation in the Financial Services and Markets Act 2000, the effect of the provision in the primary legislation is substantially altered by the subordinate legislation, and there are many provisions in the Financial Promotion Order which narrow the effect of this.[25]

18.3 AUTHORISATION AND EXEMPTION

A Methods of authorisation

It has been seen that, by virtue of s. 19, in order to avoid the 'general prohibition', a person engaging or purporting to engage in a regulated activity in the UK must be authorised or an exempt person in relation to that activity.

Authorisation is covered by s. 31:

(1) The following persons are authorised for the purposes of this Act:
  (a) a person who has a Part IV permission to carry on one or more regulated activities;
  (b) an EEA firm qualifying for authorisation under Schedule 3;
  (c) a Treaty firm qualifying for authorisation under Schedule 4;
  (d) a person who is otherwise authorised by a provision of, or made under this Act.

Some explanation of this is required. Authorisation by the FSA is what is being referred to in s. 31 (1) (a) and is the primary route from within the UK. This is examined in detail below under the heading 'Part IV Permissions'.

EEA firms qualifying for authorisation under Sch. 3 are what are generally referred to as 'passporting firms'. As has been seen, under the Capital Markets Directives, such as the Investment Services Directive,[26] it is possible for a person to

---

[22] Section 21 (9), (15).
[23] See n. 15 above.
[24] Thus providing an exemption for business angels; see arts. 48–50.
[25] See e.g. art. 12.
[26] See further p. 330ff. above.

obtain a passport to enable them to provide investment services in another Member State without needing to get authorised there. Broadly, the idea is that a firm can get authorised in its Home State, and this gives it a passport. It can then do business throughout the EEA, thus giving substance to the EU concept of a single market in financial services.[27]

Treaty firms are persons established in other Member States of the EU who, by virtue of being authorised or permitted to carry on certain other activities in their Home State, have rights to carry on regulated business in the UK which go beyond the rights referred to by the Capital Markets Directives.

Section 31 (1) (d), on persons 'otherwise authorised ...', in fact refers to operators or trustees of collective investment schemes which are undertakings for collective investment in transferable securities (within the meaning of the UCITS Directive).[28]

B Part IV permissions

Getting a Part IV permission is in fact the primary way of getting authorised and as a description of being authorised, the wording of s. 31 (1) (a) is thus somewhat backhanded.[29] Nevertheless, the effect is clear. A person intending to carry on a regulated activity in the UK must apply to the FSA for a permission.[30] If he or she gets it, he or she is 'authorised'.

The permissions regime is set out, unsurprisingly, in Part IV of the Act.[31] The essence of it, and the effect of it, is that being an authorised person does not mean being in a position to carry out each and every type of regulated activity. A person will be in a position to carry out the regulated activities for which permission has been given, and it is the intention of the legislature that that person will not get permission for activities which he or she is not suited for. This is achieved by imposing on the FSA a requirement that it must specify the permitted regulatory activity or activities.[32]

It is provided that the FSA may give permission: 'only in such terms as are, in its opinion, appropriate for the purpose of ensuring that the qualifying conditions set out in Schedule 6 will be satisfied, and continue to be satisfied, in relation to all of the regulated activities for which permission is being given.'[33] These 'threshold con-

---

[27] Although it may need to comply with e.g. conduct of business rules of the Host State; see ss. 193–202.

[28] See further p. 350 below.

[29] The sections fit together in this way: s. 19 introduces the term 'authorised person' by prohibiting the carrying on of a regulated activity (etc) unless he is an 'authorised person ... [or ...]'. The term 'authorised person' is defined in s. 31 (2) as 'a person who is authorised for the purposes of this Act'. And then s. 31 (1) gives the list of those persons who are 'authorised for the purposes of this Act', the first in the list of these, being 'a person who has a Part IV permission ...'.

[30] The word person seems to have a broader meaning here than the law would normally give it. Section 40 (1) provides that: 'An application for permission to carry on one or more regulated activities may be made to the Authority by: (a) an individual; (b) a body corporate; (c) a partnership; (d) an unincorporated association.' Neither of the last two categories (in England) would usually be regarded as legal persons.

[31] Sections 40–55.

[32] Section 42 (2).

[33] Section 41 (2).

ditions' impose requirements such as adequate resources and suitability. Thus, it is provided that the 'resources of the person concerned ... must be adequate in relation to the regulated activities that he seeks to carry on, or carries on' and 'the person ... must satisfy the Authority that he is a fit and proper person having regard to all the circumstances'.[34] The FSA has set out its policies on how it intends to approach this and other threshold conditions.[35]

Obviously, over the years, the business direction of a firm carrying on regulated activities might well change. The Act makes provision for this by enabling the FSA to vary the permission by, for instance, adding a regulated activity to those for which it gives permission, or removing an activity.[36] It is important to consider what would happen if a firm exceeds its Part IV permissions. Does this mean that it ceases to be an authorised person, and thus contravenes the general prohibition in s. 19? The question is answered by s. 20 which provides that:

(1) If an authorised person carries on a regulated activity in the United Kingdom, or purports to do so, otherwise than in accordance with permission:
   (a) given to him by the Authority under Part IV, or
   (b) resulting from any other provision of this Act,
   he is to be taken to have contravened a requirement imposed on him by the Authority under this Act.

What this means, in effect, is that if an authorised person carries on a regulated activity otherwise than in accordance with permission, then it will fall to be treated as a breach of the FSA's rules and thus be regarded as rendering the person liable to FSA disciplinary proceedings.[37]

C The Register

Section 347 requires the FSA to maintain a public record containing certain details about all authorised firms, including a description of the regulated activities they are permitted to undertake. It is on the internet[38] and constitutes an important plank in the FSA's consumer protection objective.

18.4 EXEMPT PERSONS AND EXEMPTION OF APPOINTED REPRESENTATIVES

It will be recalled that the general prohibition in s. 19 makes it clear that in order to avoid committing a criminal offence, a person who carries on, or purports to carry on, a regulated activity in the UK must be an authorised person or, an exempt person in relation to that activity. It is now necessary to examine the concept of 'exempt person'.

---

[34] Schedule 6, paras 4 (1), 5.
[35] FSA Handbook of Rules and Guidance, Threshold Conditions, COND.
[36] Sections 44–50. Under these sections the FSA may also cancel permissions in certain circumstances.
[37] See further p. 355 below; and s. 20 (2), (3).
[38] See the FSA website: http://www.fsa.gov.uk.

Section 38 gives power to the Treasury to make an exemption order and under this power it has made the Financial Services and Markets Act (Exemption) Order.[39] The Order makes various official bodies exempt, such as the Bank of England, and the central banks of other EU Member States.

Of more complexity is the provision in s. 39 which provides:

(1) If a person—
    (a) is a party to a contract with an authorised person (his 'principal') which:
        (i) permits or requires him to carry on business of a prescribed[40] description, and
        (ii) complies with such requirements as may be prescribed,[41] and
    (b) is someone for whose activities in carrying on the whole or part of that business his principal has accepted responsibility in writing,

he is an exempt person in relation to any regulated activity comprised in the carrying on of that business for which his principal has accepted responsibility.[42]

A person who is exempt under the section is called an appointed representative.[43] A largely similar exemption of appointed representatives was in operation under the 1986 Act regime. It is designed to deal with the fact that self-employed sales representatives often work under the auspices of an 'umbrella' organisation which takes responsibility for what they do. The idea of the system is that the principal needs to be authorised and needs to accept responsibility for the acts of his appointed representative. If so, then the appointed representative does not need to get authorised himself. However, it is clear from *Re Noble Warren Investments Ltd*[44] that the system must be seen to work in fact. In that case the principals lost their authorisation under the 1986 Act because *inter alia* they had failed to train or supervise the appointed representatives.

18.5 CONDUCT OF BUSINESS

A Textures of regulation

The regime under the 1986 Act produced a crop of huge rulebooks which financial services firms were expected to follow. These emanated from the SIB as well as from the SROs, which people usually had to join if they were to gain authorisation. Aspects of this regime have already been discussed.[45] As it developed, from 1986 to 1999, the system tried out various different techniques of regulation giving rise to what has been described as 'textures' of regulation.[46] At one stage, in 1989, a three-tiered structure was introduced as part of the so called 'New Settlement'. The New

---

[39] SI 2001, No. 1201.

[40] Certain businesses are prescribed by the FSMA 2000 (Appointed Representatives) Regulations 2001 (SI 2001, No. 1217) as amended; see art. 2.

[41] See art. 3 of the regulations referred to in the previous footnote.

[42] There are further provisions which deal with the responsibility of the principal, and other matters; see s. 39 (3)–(6).

[43] Section 39 (2).

[44] Noted by E. Lomnicka [1989] JBL 421.

[45] See p. 318 above.

[46] The term was used by A. Whittaker in 'Legal Technique in City Regulation' (1990) 43 *Current Legal Problems* 35.

Settlement was designed to restore industry confidence in a regulator who had come to be perceived as unnecessarily heavy handed and rule orientated. It produced three tiers of rules. At the top were ten general principles of conduct of business; these were applicable to all authorised persons. They were general in nature and became known as the 'Ten Commandments'. The middle tier consisted of core rules which applied to all authorised persons. The bottom tier consisted of the detailed rulebooks produced by the SROs and the rules in these applied to those who had been authorised by the SROs,[47] the idea being that each SRO would develop rules that were 'industry specific' which would be sensitive to the actual business situations confronting the members of that particular SRO.

Under the new system brought in by the Financial Services and Markets Act 2000, some aspects of this 'textured' approach remain. Gone, of course, are the SROs. The FSA now regulates those areas formerly covered by the SROs. However, we can still see different textures. There are high level principles which are applicable throughout the financial services industry, similar in generality to the 'Ten Commandments'; although there are eleven of them now. And there are detailed rules, not of general application, but applying to particular sectors of the industry, tailor-made to cover widely different situations.

A kind of texturing can be seen in the different types of rule-making power which the Act gives to the FSA. Section 138 gives the FSA a wide enabling power to make *rules*. As subordinate legislation these rules will have the force of law, and they will be capable of imposing binding obligations upon authorised persons.[48] But also there is power, in s. 127, for the FSA to issue *guidance* on its rules and other regulatory matters. Guidance will not be legally binding but will be a way of putting flesh on principles or rules to bring out their bearing on a particular problem or situation. The FSA has now issued Guidance on many matters and it is clear that this is a major feature in the new regime.[49]

B The FSA Handbook of Rules and Guidance

The FSA Handbook of Rules and Guidance lies at the heart of the regulatory structure established by the Financial Services and Markets Act 2000. Much of it is familiar material in the sense that it is the progeny of the SIB/FSA and SRO rulebooks of the previous regime. Change has been made where circumstances have made it necessary, but much of the old wisdom and ways of doing things are reflected in its current format. Over the years, it can be expected that there will be further redrafting and rationalisation. Its early format owed much to the need to

---

[47] For those who had direct authorisation from the SIB, the SIB rulebook applied instead.
[48] In contrast to the position under the previous regime, there is no separate power to state 'principles' and it is intended that the general rule-making power in s. 138 will enable the FSA to lay down requirements anywhere along the spectrum from broad principle to detailed requirement. (There are also more specific rule-making powers in Pt X.) There is also a power (in s. 148) for the FSA to give *waivers*; i.e. to disapply its rules on a case by case basis and power in s. 143 for the FSA to endorse a code issued by another body, if the FSA itself would have had power to make rules on the matters in question.
[49] See generally the FSA Handbook of Rules and Guidance.

get the new regime up and running within the tight time frame which was available but its current state reveals that much work is being done on it to rationalise and clarify.

C The FSA Principles for Businesses[50]

The aim[51] of the FSA Principles for Businesses is to formulate succinct high-level precepts stating the fundamental obligations of regulated businesses.[52] Firms would then have a basic standard to guide their behaviour. The Principles will apply to all authorised persons. It is intended that the existence of these principles will mean that the regulatory system need never be completely silent on an issue, even if rapid changes in the business environment have meant that gaps have appeared in the more detailed Conduct of Business rules. Furthermore, often the detailed COB rules will flesh out the more basic ideas in the Principles, but the COB rules will not exhaust the effect of the general Principle which will still be there to plug any gaps. It is clear that some of the Principles overlap, but the FSA have expressed the view that this is inevitable when drafting at this level of generality.[53]

It is fundamental that breach of FSA rules such as detailed conduct of business rules will give rise to the possibility of FSA disciplinary action against the authorised person concerned.[54] However, interestingly, the FSA has made it clear that it is possible to imagine a situation where breach of a Principle would, of itself, be the cause for initiating disciplinary action.[55] Such cases are likely to be rare, but the possibility adds a significant dimension to the regulatory armoury and will probably do much to raise the profile of the Principles in day-to-day conduct.

The Principles give quite a comprehensive picture of the spectrum of situations which frequently need to be addressed by the regulator and it is worth setting them out in full.[56] At the time of writing, the current version[57] is as follows:

1. Integrity
A firm must conduct its business with integrity.

2. Skill, care and diligence
A firm must conduct its business with due skill, care and diligence.

---

[50] These replace the 'Ten Commandments' under the previous regime: there are eleven of them.
[51] The FSA's policy behind the Principles is set out in various places in *Consultation Paper 13* (September 1998) and in *Response on Consultation Paper 13* (October 1999).
[52] *Consultation Paper 13* (September 1998) p. 5.
[53] *Response to Consultation Paper 13* (October 1999) p. 8.
[54] See further p. 356 below.
[55] *Response to Consultation Paper 13* (October 1999) p. 7. It is not envisaged by the FSA that breach of the Principles alone would give rise to civil liability under s. 150 in the way that breach of the rules may do. The Principles have been devised as a statement of regulatory expectations, not as a set of legal rights at large. Nor would such breach give an entitlement to payments under the Compensation Scheme, since the general principles are not designed to create rights or liabilities in civil law; see generally *Consultation Paper 13* (September 1998) p. 11.
[56] For a detailed commentary on their meaning the reader is referred to *Response to Consultation Paper 13* (October 1999), available on the FSA website http://www.fsa.gov.uk.
[57] August 2004, FSA Handbook of Rules and Guidance, Principles for Businesses, PRIN.

3. Management and control

A firm must take reasonable care to organise and control its affairs responsibly and effectively, with adequate risk management systems.

4. Financial prudence

A firm must maintain adequate financial resources.

5. Market conduct

A firm must observe proper standards of market conduct.

6. Customers' interests

A firm must pay due regard to the interests of its customers and treat them fairly.

7. Communications with clients

A firm must pay due regard to the information needs of its clients, and communicate information to them in a way which is clear, fair and not misleading.

8. Conflicts of interest

A firm must manage conflicts of interest fairly, both between itself and its customers and between a customer and another client.

9. Customers: relationships of trust

A firm must take reasonable care to ensure the suitability of its advice and discretionary decisions for any customer who is entitled to rely on its judgment.

10. Clients' assets

A firm must arrange adequate protection for clients' assets when it is responsible for them.

11. Relations with regulators

A firm must deal with its regulators in an open and cooperative way, and must disclose to the FSA appropriately anything relating to the firm of which the FSA would reasonably expect notice.

D Ancillary regimes

The Financial Services and Markets Act 2000 contains a number of provisions relating to conduct of business and designed to extend regulatory reach beyond merely authorised persons. These relate to approval of special categories of employee, controllers of authorised persons, and employment of prohibited persons.

We have already seen that the regulatory framework focuses primarily on those businesses which will require authorisation by the FSA. However, where the authorised person is a firm (as opposed to a sole trader), it has been decided that the FSA should also have regulatory powers which it can use against certain of the employees of those firms, namely the significant ones like the senior managers and also salespersons who have direct contact with the customers. The Act accordingly contains provisions[58] which make the appointment of the special categories[59] of employee subject to FSA approval before they take up their employment, with the aim of ensuring that they are fit and proper to occupy the post in question. Thereafter, they become subject to the FSA Principles for Businesses.

---

[58] Sections 59–63.
[59] Which categories of job need to be subject to the approval regime will be kept under review by the FSA.

A similar regime[60] exists in relation to persons who have control over authorised persons. Controllers of firms such as major shareholders and 'shadow' directors can have significant influence over how the firms operate, for often it is they who will choose the board and the senior managers. The provisions require that any person who acquires influence or additional influence over a regulated firm has to notify and be cleared by the FSA who will need to be satisfied that the applicant is fit and proper to exercise the relevant degree of influence, so that the interests of consumers would not be threatened.

Lastly, the FSA is given power[61] to make a 'prohibition order' against any person where it considers that that person is not fit and proper to perform a function or type of function in relation to certain regulated activities. Authorised persons then come under a duty to take care that they do not employ prohibited persons. This provision is similar to the above two regimes in that it is designed to operate against people who are not authorised, but who have managed to become involved in regulated activities by, for instance, being employees or owners of a business.

18.6 COLLECTIVE INVESTMENT SCHEMES

A Background

Before the present regulatory structure relating to collective investment schemes (CISs) is examined, it is useful to gain some idea of the purpose and nature of such schemes, and the regulatory background. Obviously investments carry risk and a pooling of investments might help to reduce that risk. Thus, a fund of 60 different shares is likely to remain largely intact even if a few of the companies selected under-perform or collapse altogether. However, sharing in a fund of shares has other advantages than just spreading the portfolio, since it can be arranged that the fund can be invested by expert managers and they will be able to achieve economies of scale. Historically, the UK has seen three main[62] types of pooling of investment capital.

The oldest type is the investment (trust) company. These companies date from the middle of the 19th century. In business form they are merely companies registered under the Companies Act 1985.[63] They are not based on trusts law and the use of the word 'trust' in the name is inappropriate. The basic aim of investment (trust) companies is to make profits by trading in the shares of other companies. Investors in the companies buy and sell their shares in the ordinary way, through the stock market. This raises a problem, since the price investors get for their shares will not necessarily depend on the actual asset value of the investments which the investment (trust) company holds. Market factors will have an influence on the price and this has tended to make them unpopular as investment vehicles. The recurrent problem seems to be that the shares of the company trade at a discount

---

[60] Sections 178–192.
[61] Sections 56–58.
[62] These are the main ones, but there are many other schemes and ideas in operation.
[63] And its predecessors.

of 10–20% to the net asset value. This is perhaps because there is an excess of supply in the market which depresses the price. The lack of demand may be partly due to their being unpopular with investment fund managers. In recent years one way of mitigating this has been for the company to buy back its shares on the open market. This increases the underlying value of the remaining shares[64] and helps to mop up excess supply and so increases the market price.

During the 1930s an alternative investment vehicle, the unit trust became popular, and its popularity has remained ever since. The investors here pool their capital. The resultant fund is held and invested by trustees, acting on the advice of managers, who are expert in the fields in which they are investing. There is no corporate structure involved and the assets are held by the trustees for the benefit of investors who get certificates stating that they hold units in the fund. They are popular with investors because they are bought and sold by the trust itself; no 'complicated' stock exchange mechanisms are involved. The price paid reflects the value of the assets held by the fund. There is usually a 6% spread between the bid to offer price[65] which is a kind of premium the investor pays for joining the fund, to cover administrative costs etc and to discourage people from trading in and out very frequently, and including 5% for the manager's initial charge. Additionally, the managers take 1% a year for their fees and administration. Many different types of unit trust have grown up, some offering high income at the expense of capital growth, some offering capital growth at the expense of high income, some specialising in the shares of smaller companies, some in European shares, some in Japan, some in the USA. Recently, unit trusts have been permitted to move to a single pricing system, having a single unit price based on a mid-market valuation.

The third main type of mechanism for the pooling of capital[66] is the open-ended investment company (OEIC).[67] These are a form of collective investment vehicle which has only recently become allowed in the UK. Indeed, these companies are more popular in continental countries where the UK unit trust, based on antiquated rules of trust law, is regarded as a strange creature. Difficulties in marketing the unit trust in Europe mean that there is a need to offer OEICs to compete successfully there. The name comes from the feature that OEICs can issue shares to investors and buy them back again.

They are open-ended, as opposed to closed-ended companies, which cannot buy back their shares. For many years the formation of open-ended companies was illegal in the UK. It became possible after 1981 when the Companies Act of that year permitted companies to purchase their own shares. However, the complex rules on maintenance of capital made such companies inappropriate vehicles for the formation of investment companies and, once it was decided that the UK needed

---

[64] Since the market price of 100 shares is less than the actual proportion of the net asset value that 100 shares represents and the excess accrues to the remaining shares, in proportion.

[65] 'Bid' means the price the trust will pay the investor for his units, 'offer' means the price at which units are offered to the public.

[66] Unit trusts, OEICs and Investment Trust Companies are the main three. However, various other arrangements, such as limited partnerships or informal pools operated by stockbrokers, are sometimes used to create collective investment schemes in land, metals and minerals.

[67] For a detailed account, see E. Lomnicka 'Open-Ended Investment Companies – A New Bottle for Old Wine' in B. Rider (ed.) *The Corporate Dimension* (Bristol: Jordans, 1998) p. 47.

OEICs, a special sort of company, tailor-made for the purpose, was created by legislation. OEICs have a single pricing structure and the FSA is considering making this compulsory for unit trusts since it is confusing to have two price structures operating side by side. But in reality many OEICs charge an initial charge of 5% on entry which is what the dual-pricing structure was about anyway. Some have argued that concern over dual pricing is exaggerated, that the two-price system is readily understood by the public and is similar to the system operating when foreign exchange is bought at a bank or travel agent. The pricing of an OEIC, like the pricing of a unit trust, is based on the net asset value per share and so unlike investment trusts, OEICs will not trade at a discount or premium to net asset value per share. In recent years many investment trust companies have converted to OEICs; the conversion removes the discount and the possibility of marketing in Europe is attractive. Similarly, many unit trusts have converted.

From the regulatory point of view, collective investment schemes pose high risks. They involve very large sums of money which come under the control of the operators and the opportunity for fraud on a grand scale is significant. The Financial Services Act 1986 introduced a regulatory regime for the regulation of collective investment schemes. The existing scheme was regarded as working well and so with a few minor changes it was re-enacted in Part XVII of the Financial Services and Markets Act 2000. To some extent, the background to these new provisions is the UCITS Directive[68] which was concerned to harmonise the laws of the Member States with regard to UCITS, to ensure equivalent protection for unit-holders, so that the conditions of competition are not distorted, and overall to help bring about a European Capital Market. The Directive requires that UCITS cannot carry on activities unless they have been authorised by the competent authorities of the Member State in which they are situated[69] and lays down many other structural and regulatory details, such as disclosure requirements.

It is interesting to notice that the old investment trust companies did not fall within either the Directive or the UK legislation.[70] They were not collective investment schemes. This is still the case; the FSMA 2000 provided that the Treasury could make regulations specifying that certain arrangements do not amount to collective investment schemes, and the regulations they made exclude investment trust companies.[71] Investment trust companies, while not falling within the regulatory regime applicable to collective investment schemes, nevertheless attract a considerable amount of regulation under the FSA Listing Rules,[72] and if, as is common, they appoint a separate investment management company to manage the funds,

---

[68] Directive 85/611/EEC on EC Undertakings for Collective Investment in Transferable Securities. For an account of the provisions of the Directive see: F. Wooldridge 'The EEC Directive on Collective Investment Undertakings' [1987] JBL 329. The UCITS Directive has been amended by the 'Product Directive' (2001/108/EC) and the 'Management Directive' (2001/107/EC) which, respectively, extended the range of products which can qualify for the passport and produced tougher regulatory rules for management companies.

[69] UCITS Directive, art. 4.

[70] *Ibid.* art. 2 (1) and Financial Services Act 1986, s. 75 (7).

[71] FSMA 2000, s. 235 (5), and FSMA 2000 (Collective Investment Schemes) Order 2001 (SI 2001, No. 1062), art. 3 and Sch., para. 21.

[72] Chapter 19.

that company will need normal FSA authorisation (i.e. Part IV permission), otherwise it will breach the general prohibition in s. 19 of FSMA 2000. Additionally, if FSA-authorised intermediaries are involved in selling the securities of investment trust companies, they will need to comply with any relevant COB rules.[73]

B The basic regulatory position under the FSMA 2000

The basic regulatory position is that the FSMA 2000 defines a collective investment scheme, and then, broadly, requires persons involved in running such things to be FSA authorised under Part IV. The definition of 'collective investment scheme' is as follows:

> 235.—(1) In this Part 'collective investment scheme' means any arrangements with respect to property of any description, including money, the purpose or effect of which is to enable persons taking part in the arrangements (whether by becoming owners of the property or any part of it or otherwise) to participate in or receive profits or income arising from the acquisition, holding, management or disposal of the property or sums paid out of such profits or income.
> (2) The arrangements must be such that the persons who are to participate ('participants') do not have day-to-day control over the management of the property, whether or not they have the right to be consulted or give directions.
> (3) The arrangements must also have either or both of the following characteristics:
> > (a) the contributions of the participants and the profits or income out of which payments are to be made to them are pooled;
> > (b) the property is managed as a whole by or on behalf of the operator of the scheme.[74]

This is the basic definition in FSMA 2000, but there is however, a range of exemptions contained in the FSMA 2000 (Collective Investment Schemes) Order[75] covering for instance 'schemes not operated by way of business'[76] and the situation where 'the predominant purpose of the arrangements is to enable the participants to share in the use or enjoyment of property, or to make its use or enjoyment available gratuitously to others'.[77]

Having thus defined what is meant by the term 'collective investment scheme' the legislation requires, in effect, the persons running it to get authorised, otherwise they will break the general prohibition in s. 19. This is largely achieved by art. 51 of the Regulated Activities Order,[78] which provides that the following are specified kinds of activity: '. . . establishing, operating or winding up a collective investment scheme . . . '[79] The result is that such persons will of course have to comply with the FSA Handbook of Rules and Guidance, and in particular the Principles for Businesses, COB rules, and CIS rules.

---

[73] The FSA has recently been developing enhanced COB rules to deal with recent problems relating to 'split-capital' investment trusts.

[74] Financial Services and Markets Act 2000, s. 235 (4) further provides: 'If arrangements provide for such pooling as is mentioned in subsection 3 (a) in relation to separate parts of the property, the arrangements are not to be regarded as constituting a single collective investment scheme unless the participants are entitled to exchange rights in one part for rights in another.'

[75] SI 2001, No. 1062.

[76] Article 4.

[77] Article 14.

[78] See n. above.

[79] This is an excerpt, there are further provisions in art. 51.

C The marketing of collective investment schemes: restricted

Section 238 of the 2000 Act imposes a special restriction on the marketing of collective investment schemes. Section 238 (1) prohibits authorised[80] persons from promoting collective investment schemes. However, various exemptions have been made in relation to, for instance, marketing between investment professionals.[81]

However, there is a more general exemption from the restriction. This is contained in s. 238 (4), which provides that: 'Subsection (1) does not apply in relation to— (a) an authorised unit trust scheme; (b) a scheme constituted by an authorised open-ended investment company; . . .'[82] The upshot of this is to prevent generally the marketing of collective investment schemes in the UK unless they are unit trusts or OEICs where the schemes themselves have been given an *authorisation order* by the FSA.[83] It will be seen in the following two paragraphs that getting that order will involve compliance with detailed rules.

D Authorised unit trust schemes

The FSMA 2000 contains various provisions which set out fundamental rules about authorisation[84] of the scheme and its organisation. One of the main protection mechanisms against fraud is the provision for separate roles for the scheme manager and the holder of the assets, the trustee. Either the manager or the trustee has to apply for authorisation of the scheme.[85] They must be corporate bodies[86] and they must be different persons.[87] Participants must be entitled to have their units redeemed in accordance with the scheme at a price related to the net value of the property to which the units relate, or if arrangements are made for sale on an investment exchange at a similar price.[88]

In addition to these provisions in the Act, many other aspects are regulated by the complex provisions in the FSA Handbook of Rules and Guidance, Collective Investment Schemes, CIS. These cover organisational structure, pricing and dealing, investment powers and duties of the managers and trustees.

E Open-ended investment companies

The basic legal existence and nature of open-ended investment companies (OEICs)[89] is set up by the Open Ended Investment Companies Regulations

---

[80] Unauthorised persons who do this would anyway be in breach of ss. 19 and/or 21.
[81] FSMA 2000 (Promotion of Collective Investment Schemes) (Exemptions) Order 2001 (SI 2001, No. 1060).
[82] Note that s. 238 (4) (c) refers to a third category which is permitted, namely certain overseas schemes, confusingly referred to as 'a recognised scheme'. See at p. 355 below.
[83] See further s. 237(3).
[84] If they fall within the scope of the UCITS Directive, the product will get the passport. There are in existence some non-UCITS authorised unit trusts, but these are only a small part of the market. In other words, they are authorised by the FSA for the purposes of UK law, but are investing in products which the Directive does not extend to, so they do not get the passport.
[85] *Ibid.* s. 242. Both must themselves be authorised persons, see s. 243 (7).
[86] *Ibid.* s. 242 (5).
[87] *Ibid.* s. 242 (2).
[88] *Ibid.* s. 243 (10), (11).
[89] Often these days referred to as ICVCs (Investment Companies with Variable Capital).

2001.[90] An OEIC is formed by the act of the FSA making an 'authorisation order'.[91] Again, as with the unit trusts, there is provision for a split between the holding of the property and the management of it. Thus, the property must be looked after by a depositary.[92] There is to be authorisation by the FSA.[93] In addition, the Regulations set up a new company law code, a 'corporate code' setting out a set of company law rules specially for OEICs.[94] These are broadly similar to normal company law, but specially tailored for OEICs.

There is also a whole range of matters provided for by the FSA Handbook, CIS. The rules cover in detail such matters as prospectus, pricing and dealing and generally have the effect of making OEICs similar to unit trusts. Of particular note is the fact they make provision for the existence of an Authorised Corporate Director, who basically acts as manager.[95]

F Overseas collective investment schemes

Sections 264–283 of the Financial Services and Markets Act 2000 make provision for the recognition of overseas collective investment schemes which are then regarded as 'recognised[96] schemes' and may be marketed to the public in the UK. Section 264 gives automatic recognition to UCITS schemes constituted in another EEA state. Under s. 270, certain schemes in designated countries can be recognised and under s. 272 the FSA can recognise foreign schemes on an individual basis.

18.7 ENFORCEMENT

A 'Policing the perimeter'

Persons who carry on[97] a regulated activity in the UK without being authorised[98] fall outside the perimeter fence of the FSA's now vast domain, within which it wields disciplinary powers over its authorised disciples who are bound by the 'Eleven Commandments' and other FSA rules. They face criminal penalties.[99] Over the years the FSA (and the former SIB) has adopted a flexible hard/soft approach to what it has called 'policing the perimeter', i.e. dealing those who are discovered to have contravened the authorisation requirement. Annually it has been investigating several hundred cases, most of whom were people who were unaware

---

[90] SI 2001, No. 1228.
[91] *Ibid.* reg. 3.
[92] *Ibid.* reg. 5.
[93] *Ibid.* reg. 9.
[94] *Ibid.* regs. 28–64.
[95] If they fall within the scope of the UCITS Directive, then, as with Authorised Unit Trusts, they will get passporting rights.
[96] A name which seems unnecessarily confusing.
[97] Or purport to carry on.
[98] Or exempt persons in relation to that activity.
[99] See the analysis of the effect of s. 19 at p. 338 above and the financial promotion regime at p. 342. Note that the effect of exceeding a Pt IV permission by an authorised person falls within 'the perimeter' and is to be dealt with as an FSA disciplinary matter; see s. 20 and p. 345 above.

that they were in breach of the statutory requirements and who would usually merely receive a warning letter from the FSA, requiring compliance with the authorisation procedures or cessation of the activity. However, recalcitrance or calculated infringement has elicited a tougher response.

B Disciplinary measures

Trouble for authorised persons suspected of committing infringements of the FSA's rules usually starts by the exercise of the FSA's wide powers to call for information. If they have queries about specific matters, the FSA can require by notice in writing, an authorised person to provide specified information or documents.[100] If they have general concerns about a firm but there are no circumstances suggesting any specific breach they may start an investigation into the matter if there is 'good reason'.[101] The investigators then have wide powers to require the person to attend for questioning or otherwise provide information or documents.[102]

The provisions in ss. 205–211 of the Financial Services and Markets Act 2000 are the core of the FSA's enforcement machinery. It is these provisions which replace the contractual powers of the SROs to levy money penalties for breach of their rules.[103] The centrepiece is s. 206, which authorises the FSA to impose a penalty of such amount as it considers appropriate, if it considers that an authorised person has contravened a requirement imposed on him by or under the Act. Additionally, the FSA may cancel a person's Pt IV permission,[104] which has the effect of removing their authorisation; effectively shutting down their business, at least in so far as it involves regulated activities. Obviously it is likely that this sanction will be reserved only for the more severe cases.[105] There is also the possibility of public censure.[106] Court orders are available to restrain a likely contravention of the Act or the FSA's rules, or to restrain the continuance or repetition of a contravention.[107]

---

[100] Financial Services and Markets Act 2000, s. 165 (1).

[101] Under *ibid*. s. 167.

[102] *Ibid*. s. 171. There are restrictions on the extent to which and manner in which the answers given can be used against the person in subsequent criminal proceedings; broadly, only where the accused during the criminal proceedings has made reference to the answers which he gave in the earlier proceedings (s. 174). The need for this narrow gateway came about after the decision of the European Court of Human Rights in *Saunders* v *United Kingdom* [1997] BCC 872, where statements made to DTI inspectors operating under powers in the Companies Act 1985 were used to help secure a conviction in subsequent criminal proceedings. It was held that this deprived the defendant of a fair hearing, contrary to art. 6 of the European Convention on Human Rights.

[103] The SROs found that they had extremely effective powers to exact money penalties. In order to get authorised under the 1986 Act, it was necessary for a person to join an SRO (unless he was directly authorised by the SIB/FSA, which became very rare). By joining the SRO, a person became contractually bound to comply with its rules and also contractually bound to pay up if its disciplinary procedures required a money penalty from him. Towards the end of the 1986 Act's regime, penalties in excess of £250,000 were being exacted by the SROs.

[104] Under the power in ss. 33 and 54 of the Financial Services and Markets Act 2000.

[105] Section 206 (2) makes it clear that the FSA is not empowered both to withdraw authorisation *and* make the person pay a money penalty. This is designed to reverse the practice of the SROs whereby they would order a person to be expelled from the SRO (thus withdrawing their authorisation under the 1986 Act) and also impose a money penalty as a parting shot.

[106] Financial Services and Markets Act 2000, s. 205.

[107] *Ibid*. s 380. By s. 381 these powers also apply to cases of market abuse, on which, see Chapter 20 below.

During the long and stormy passage through Parliament of the Financial Services and Markets Act 2000, the disciplinary structure which the FSA was proposing to adopt came under attack on human rights grounds, mainly on the basis that the hearing process in disciplinary proceedings was vitiated by being too closely linked with the rest of the FSA and therefore in breach of art. 6 of the European Convention on Human Rights. With this in mind the FSA has carefully developed internal mechanisms which are designed to minimise the risk of human rights breaches. Disciplinary matters which are likely to be contentious[108] are dealt with by a Regulatory Decisions Committee (RDC),[109] which is a body outside the FSA's management structure, where, apart from the Chairman, none of the members is an FSA employee. The RDC will have a matter referred to it by the FSA staff member investigating it and the RDC will then decide whether or not to take the matter further by taking disciplinary action against the authorised person. The trump card in terms of fending off Human Rights cases lies in the fact that if that person is not content to accept the penalty imposed on them, they have the right to refer the matter[110] to the Financial Services and Markets Tribunal, which is a tribunal independent of the FSA.[111] They will hear the matter *de novo*. It is likely that this will usually be sufficient to avoid successful human rights challenges.[112]

C Restitution, private actions for damages and insolvency

The FSA may apply to the court for a restitution order if a person has contravened the Act or rules,[113] or been knowingly concerned in the contravention, and profits have been made or loss sustained as a result, or an adverse affect. The court has power to order the person to pay to the FSA, such sum as appears just, having regard to the profits or loss.[114]

With regard to private actions for damages, the Act provides that a contravention by an authorised person of a rule, is actionable at the suit of a private person who suffers loss as a result of the contravention.[115] This is a very important provision. The legislation is in effect giving an action in tort for breach of statutory duty. It is limited to actions by private persons. This is done with a view to preventing large firms from suing each other for technical breaches of the rules. However, exceptions can be made for certain rules if the FSA wishes, thus opening the way for it to use

---

[108] Such as restricting regulated activities, making prohibition orders, imposing financial penalties. Matters not likely to be contentious (e.g. requiring a firm to send in more reports or a business plan) are dealt with by Executive Procedures, meaning by members of FSA staff of appropriate seniority.

[109] On all this, see generally FSA Handbook of Rules and Guidance, Enforcement (ENF), and also Decision making (DEC).

[110] See *ibid*. s. 208 (4).

[111] See generally *ibid*. ss. 132–137, and Sch. 13.

[112] In the first reported case, the Court of Appeal made it clear that the courts would allow judicial review only in the most exceptional circumstances. Thus, normally the aggrieved person's right to go to the FSMA Tribunal and then (on a point of law) to the Court of Appeal, would be a sufficient remedy. See: *R (Davies and others)* v *Financial Services Authority* [2003] 4 ALL ER 1196.

[113] Financial Services and Markets Act 2000, s. 382.

[114] For market abuse (as to which see Chapter 20 below) there are similar restitution possibilities, but here, the FSA can require it, without the intervention of the court; see *ibid*. ss. 383–384.

[115] *Ibid*. s. 150.

the threat of civil actions by powerful firms as an additional way of securing compliance with certain rules; an interesting regulatory technique.[116]

The FSA is given a number of rights, enabling it to participate in insolvency proceedings[117] so that if, for instance, there is a voluntary arrangement being entered into by a firm and its creditors, the FSA might feel it necessary to become involved in certain circumstances. Of particular importance, is the provision that the FSA can present a petition for winding up of a body or partnership which has been an authorised person, or appointed representative, or carrying on a regulated activity in contravention of the general prohibition.[118] Similarly, it can petition for a bankruptcy order in respect of an individual.[119]

18.8 INVESTOR COMPENSATION

Compensation schemes are an important part of the mechanisms used to achieve one of the basic goals of securities regulation: investor protection. They operate as a kind of enforced insurance mechanism whereby investors are to some extent insured against the insolvency or bankruptcy of financial services suppliers. If the scheme is funded by a levy on the financial services industry, then compensation schemes can also have the effect of operating as an encouragement on the industry as a whole to monitor the other players.

This is an area which is particularly circumscribed by part of the EU legislation designed to bring about the internal market in financial services. The Investor Compensation Schemes Directive[120] requires that Member States shall ensure that a scheme or schemes are operative and that no investment firm can carry on investment business unless it belongs to such a scheme.[121] The cover must not be less than 20,000 euros. Member States can provide that the investor will get only 90% of his claim.[122] This is with a view to diminishing the tendency of an investor to cease to act carefully in his choice of investment firm. The Directive keys in to the Investment Services Directive[123] so that an investor who deals with a passporting firm knows that there are at least minimum provisions for compensation in force in the Member State which that firm comes from. The matters in respect of which claims can be made are limited, so that they will usually only involve getting money or investments back[124] and the ability to make claims only arises where the competent authority has decided that the firm is not going to be able to meet its financial commitments or a court has made an order which has the effect of suspending investors' ability to make claims against it.[125]

---

[116] For definitions and conditions see the FSMA 2000 (Rights of Action) Regulations 2001 (SI 2001, No. 2256).
[117] *Ibid.* ss. 355–379.
[118] *Ibid.* s. 367.
[119] *Ibid.* s. 372.
[120] Directive 97/9/EEC.
[121] *Ibid.* art. 2.
[122] *Ibid.* art. 4.
[123] See p. 332 above.
[124] Directive 97/9/EEC, art. 2 (2).
[125] E.g. a winding-up order.

The UK's implementation of the Investor Compensation Schemes Directive is contained in the Financial Services and Markets Act 2000.[126] This sets up a single scheme of compensation to replace the five schemes previously in existence and in particular to replace the Investor Compensation Scheme established under s. 54 of the Financial Services Act 1986. The new scheme, called the Financial Services and Markets Compensation Scheme is a separate organisation from the FSA, but accountable to it. It is a limited company, and will carry out the functions cast upon the 'scheme manager' by the Act. The FSA sets the maximum levels of compensation to be offered and makes rules on the circumstances in which it is to be paid, although it is clear[127] that it is a scheme for compensating persons where the investment firm is unable or likely to be unable to satisfy claims made against it. The scheme will be funded by levies on the industry but the cost of paying compensation will fall on firms in the same area[128] of financial services business; so that defaults will affect their contribution levels rather than those of unrelated firms.[129]

18.9 FINANCIAL OMBUDSMAN SERVICE

Prior to the regime under the Financial Services and Markets Act 2000, there were eight ombudsman schemes in existence which enabled consumers to pursue a complaint about a financial services provider. The FSA put forward proposals[130] for the new scheme, which is a single financial services ombudsman scheme. Membership of that scheme is compulsory for firms that are authorised by the FSA. The legislature has preferred the ombudsman approach rather than arbitration because one of the main differences between the two processes is that an ombudsman can bind the firm whilst leaving complainants free to pursue their claim before the courts if they wished, whereas an arbitration can only take place where both parties agree in advance to be bound by the arbitrator's decision. The ombudsman has power to direct a firm to take remedial steps to pay compensation for financial loss and for distress and inconvenience.[131]

18.10 REGULATION OF INVESTMENT EXCHANGES AND CLEARING HOUSES

The Financial Services and Markets Act 2000 largely continues[132] the 1986 Act's regime in relation to recognised investment exchanges (RIEs) and recognised clearing houses (RCHs). Broadly speaking, the system is that the FSA issues a recognition order in respect of, say, the London Stock Exchange[133] which then becomes exempt from the general prohibition[134] as respects any regulated activity which is carried on as part of the Stock Exchange's business as an investment exchange or

---

[126] Sections 212–224.
[127] From s. 213 (1) of the Financial Services and Markets Act 2000.
[128] This helps to enhance the monitoring effect described above.
[129] On all this see FSA Handbook of Rules and Guidance, Compensation, COAF.
[130] In Consultation Paper 4 *Consumer Complaints*.
[131] See generally ss. 225–234 and the website http://www.financial-ombudsman.org.uk.
[132] See ss. 285–301.
[133] Section 285 (1) (a).
[134] Section 19.

which is carried on for the purposes of, or in connection with, the provision of any clearing services by it.[135] In order to be recognised, an exchange will need to meet certain conditions as thereafter be subject to the FSA's supervision.[136] However, such market infrastructure providers have a choice between being recognised as an RIE or just authorised as firms.[137] The Over-the-Counter (OTC) markets such as the alternative trading systems (ATSs) of broking firms have largely opted for authorisation rather than RIE status, and in that context the FSA has developed a light-touch regulatory regime in certain respects.[138] A major difference between the recognised body regime (RIE) and the authorised regime is that recognised bodies are themselves regulators who establish rules governing the conduct of their members or participants and are required to have an in-house regulatory resource to monitor and enforce compliance with those rules,[139] subject to oversight by the FSA. Thus, in a very real sense they are an important manifestation of the survival of self-regulation in some areas of the regulatory scene.[140] On the other hand, being an RIE will give greater flexibility in the regulatory regime (the FSA cannot make rules for recognised bodies) and some tax advantages.

18.11 FINAL MATTERS

The account in this chapter has provided an overview of the main[141] concepts and mechanisms being employed by the Financial Services and Markets Act 2000 in the regulation of financial services activity in the UK. It is now possible to turn to consider three other core areas of securities regulation: the regulation of public offerings of shares; the regulation of insider dealing and market abuse; and the regulation of takeovers.

---

[135] Section 285 (2).

[136] Sections 286, 293, 296.

[137] See: *The FSA's Approach to Regulation of the Market Infrastructure* (Financial Services Authority, January 2000), available on http://www.fsa.gov.uk, pp. 7–8.

[138] See FSA Handbook of Rules and Guidance, Market Conduct, MAR 3 Inter-professional conduct; MAR 5 Alternative Trading Systems.

[139] Thus they have their own disciplinary procedings.

[140] Another, obviously, is the Takeover Panel; see Chapter 21 below.

[141] Certain matters have not been covered, such as the regulation of Lloyd's (ss. 314–324) and of professionals who engage in financial services activities as ancillary to their main profession (ss. 325–333). However, some further aspects of the Financial Services and Markets Act 2000 are considered below. For a full account of the effect of the 2000 Act and the rules, see A. Whittaker (ed.) *Butterworths Financial Services Law and Practice* (London: Butterworths, looseleaf).

19

THE REGULATION OF PUBLIC OFFERINGS OF SHARES

19.1 MIGRATION INTO CAPITAL MARKETS LAW

The regulation of public offerings of shares has an ancient pedigree as a subject falling within mainstream company law. It is dealt with in this Part of the book on Securities Regulation because it is another of those areas of mainstream company law which arguably have migrated[1] into capital markets law. This migration had become fairly apparent, at least by 1986, when some of the provisions governing public offerings of shares were included in the Act which set up the UK's first comprehensive system of securities regulation, the Financial Services Act 1986. More recently there has been a graphic confirmation of it when the functions of the London Stock Exchange as the competent authority under the Listing Directives[2] were transferred to the Financial Services Authority, mainly because it was felt that there was a conflict of interest between the money-making functions of the Stock Exchange as a private body and its public functions as competent authority.[3] Thus, the final vestiges of the company law aspects of the public regulation of public offerings of shares had literally[4] decamped into securities regulation. The commercial functioning of the Stock Exchange and its role in facilitating corporate finance are clearly still part of mainstream company law and in this book have been dealt with accordingly.[5]

19.2 BEFORE THE EC DIRECTIVES

Prior to EC legislation dating from 1979, listing of shares on the Stock Exchange[6] was mainly governed by the detailed requirements of the Stock Exchange Regulations on Admission of Securities to Listing. However, by virtue of a provision in the then prevailing Companies Act,[7] an offer of shares to the public was prohibited unless accompanied by a 'prospectus' which complied with the require-

---

[1] The concept of migration is well known among European scholars.
[2] See below.
[3] See further below.
[4] In view of the consequent staff transfers between the London Stock Exchange and the Financial Services Authority.
[5] In Chapter 14.
[6] The current name, the London Stock Exchange, is relatively recent; its predecessor having been the International Stock Exchange of the United Kingdom and Northern Ireland.
[7] Companies Act 1948, s. 38 (3).

ments set out in Sch. 4 to that Act. The original requirement for a prospectus can be traced back to the Joint Stock Companies Act 1844.[8]

Thus before any EC intervention, the regulation of public offerings of shares was governed largely by the twin devices of control by the Stock Exchange over listing and, whether or not the shares were to be listed,[9] legislative requirements on disclosure in a prospectus of details relating to the securities being offered. In addition, the common law background to this area provided important contractual doctrines and tortious remedies.[10] Broadly speaking, this twin approach, of regulating the trading of shares and the offering of shares to the public, continues at the present day although the legal mechanisms governing both listing and prospectus requirements have been subjected to EC Directives which have brought changes.

19.3 THE LISTING DIRECTIVES AND THE PROSPECTUS DIRECTIVE

As has already been observed, the EC Directives in the securities regulation field were adopted with a view to establishing a European capital market. In the field of public offerings of shares, a series of Directives were issued governing trading of securities and public offerings of securities.

The Listing Directives aimed to regulate the Stock Exchange listing of securities. Historically, there were three of them, although they are now consolidated into one. The first to appear was the Directive co-ordinating the conditions for the admission of securities to official stock exchange listing,[11] in 1979, usually known as the 'Admissions Directive'. It set out minimum conditions for what it called 'official listing' on a stock exchange in a Member State and which requires the process of listing to be overseen by a 'competent authority' designated by each Member State. This was followed, in 1980, by the Directive co-ordinating the requirements for the drawing up, scrutiny and distribution of the listing particulars to be published for the admission of securities to official stock exchange listing;[12] usually known as the 'Listing Particulars Directive'.[13] Lastly, the Directive known as the 'Interim Reports Directive'[14] supplemented the reporting requirements in the Admissions Directive by requiring half-yearly reports on their activities in the first six months of each financial year. This area is now governed by a consolidating Directive.[15]

---

[8] Section 4. Although not in this form.

[9] Technically, listing is not a prerequisite for a public offering of shares, as long as the prospectus rules are complied with, although if it is to have much chance of success, a public offering will need to have made arrangements for listing (or these days a quotation on AIM) and for the issue to be underwritten; see further p. 258 above.

[10] See p. 372 below. Cases are rare, but practitioners need to be mindful of the common law here.

[11] 79/279/EEC, OJ 1979 L66/21.

[12] 80/390/EEC, OJ 1980 L100/1.

[13] The principles of mutual recognition and Home State control (see p. above) were added by an amending Directive in 1987; see the Directive on the Mutual Recognition of Listing Particulars (87/345/EEC).

[14] Directive on information to be published on a regular basis by companies the shares of which have been admitted to official stock exchange listing; 82/121/EEC, OJ 1978, L222/11.

[15] Directive on the Admission of Securities to Official Stock Exchange Listing and on information to be published on those Securities; 2001/34/EC, OJ 2001, L 184/1. This Directive is sometimes referred to as the Consolidated Admissions and Reporting Directive (CARD).

The Prospectus Directive[16] requires the publication of an information document called a prospectus when securities are offered to the public for the first time.[17] At the time of writing, this Directive is still in force and the following account of current UK law reflects that. However, on 1 July 2005 this Directive will be repealed and replaced by a *new* Prospectus Directive. This is dealt with below at paragraph 19.7 under the heading 'The *New* Prospectus Directive and the FSA's Review of the Listing Regime'.

19.4 UK IMPLEMENTATION

A The 'competent authority'

The implementation of these Directives in the UK has had a very complex history which need not be investigated here. Nevertheless, the current position appears to be reasonably clear and the drafting of the legislation is a great improvement on the old. The requirements for official listing are dealt with in Pt VI of the Financial Services and Markets Act 2000. The Act provides that the Financial Services Authority is to be the 'competent authority'[18] to carry out the functions conferred on it by this Part of the Act. Previously, the London Stock Exchange was the competent authority and the transfer of this function to the Financial Services Authority (FSA) was actually made under the pre-existing legislative regime.[19] The reasons for this were that the demutualisation of the Stock Exchange might have led to conflicts of interest between its role as a regulator and its new status as a profit seeker. Also, there was dissent from its competitor exchanges at that time, about the London Stock Exchange's wide powers of regulation which could sometimes extend over shares marketed on their exchanges.

The London Stock Exchange continues to function as a commercial enterprise providing quotation and dealing facilities,[20] but it has lost its functions under the Directives. Rather than perpetuate the term 'competent authority', the FSA has adopted what it calls, the UK Listing Authority or 'UKLA'. Thus the position is that the FSA is acting as the UKLA. Under the 2000 Act the UKLA has the role of maintaining the 'Official List' and in accordance with the Directives (and the Listing Rules) will decide upon which securities can be admitted to the Official List and thus traded on the Stock Exchange's Listed Market (the Main Market).[21] Compliance with the Stock Exchange's own admission rules will also be necessary.[22] Listed

---

[16] Council Directive co-ordinating the requirements for the drawing-up, scrutiny and distribution of the prospectus to be published when transferable securities are offered to the public; 89/298/EEC, OJ 1989 L124/8. This Directive was amended in 1990 so as to add the principle of mutual recognition by the Directive usually known as the 'Integration Directive'; 90/211/EEC. In the case of unlisted securities mutual recognition will only be accorded after compliance with the regime in s. 87 of the Financial Services and Markets Act 2000.

[17] Unless they are already officially listed; see further p. 364 below.

[18] Section 72.

[19] See the Official Listing of Securities (Change of Competent Authority) Regulations 2000 (SI 2000 No. 968).

[20] See p. 258 above.

[21] Financial Services and Markets Act 2000, ss. 74–75. On the markets see p. 259 above.

[22] See Listing Rules (hereafter 'LR' in these footnotes), rule 3.14A, 'Admission to Listing and Admission to Trading will together constitute admission to official listing on a Stock Exchange'.

companies have to comply with the Listing Rules, which are detailed requirements for listing which help to implement the Directives as well as embodying the Stock Exchange's procedures which have grown up over many years.[23] Failure to comply with the Listing Rules has traditionally attracted censure or very rarely, delisting. UKLA has the power to fine for breaches of the Listing Rules.[24]

B Prospectuses and listing particulars

As has been seen, apart from setting up a regulatory structure for listing, the Directives regulate the documentation to be issued when shares are issued to the public. In some circumstances a document called a 'prospectus' is required, in other, rarer circumstances, a document called 'listing particulars' is required. The starting point for an understanding of this area is the Prospectus Directive.

The Prospectus Directive is expressed to apply to transferable securities 'which are offered to the public for the first time in a Member State provided that these securities are not already listed on a stock exchange [there]'.[25] Where it applies, then publication of a prospectus is required by the person making the offer.[26] Thus, the Directive does not apply where (a) the securities are not being offered to the public *for the first time* or (b) where they are *already listed* on an exchange. There is one further complication. The prescribed content of the prospectus will vary, depending on whether the shares are in the process of being admitted to the Stock Exchange. If they are, then the prospectus must follow the rules originally laid down by the Listing Particulars Directive[27] (although it is still called a 'prospectus'). If they are not soon going to be admitted to the Stock Exchange,[28] then the prospectus must follow the rules laid down in the Prospectus Directive.[29] The UK legislation which reflects these distinctions is described in the next paragraph.

The Financial Services and Markets Act 2000 provides that 'new' securities cannot be admitted to the Official List unless a prospectus has been approved and published.[30] The Public Offers of Securities Regulations 1995[31] provide that the Regulations apply 'to any investment which is not admitted to official listing, nor

---

[23] The Listing Rules (and the Guidance) are available on the FSA website: http://www.fsa.gov.uk.

[24] See s. 91 of the Financial Services and Markets Act 2000.

[25] Prospectus Directive (89/298/EEC, OJ 1989 L124/8) art. 1.

[26] *Ibid.* art. 4.

[27] Now consolidated, as described above.

[28] In fact most Prospectus Directive securities will be marketed on AIM, but this is not the Official Listed Market and so the securities are not technically being 'admitted to the Stock Exchange'.

[29] All this is achieved by art. 7 of the Prospectus Directive, which provides that: 'Where a public offer relates to [transferable securities] which at the time of the offer are the subject of an application for admission to official listing ... the contents of the prospectus and the procedures for scrutinising and distributing it shall ... be determined in accordance with [the Listing Particulars Directive]' and by art. 11, which provides that: 'Where a public offer relates to transferable securities other than those referred to in arts 7 and 8, the prospectus must contain the information ... [set out in art. 11 of the Prospectus Directive].'

[30] Section 84 (1). 'New securities' are defined as 'securities which are to be offered to the public ... for the first time before admission to the official list': s. 84 (2). 'Prospectus' is defined as meaning 'a prospectus in such form and containing such information as may be specified in the listing rules', i.e. following the Listing Particulars Directive. 'Offered to the public' is defined extensively in Sch. 11.

[31] SI 1995 No. 1537.

the subject of an application for listing'[32] and that 'when securities are offered to the public in the UK for the first time the offeror shall publish a prospectus'.[33] Sometimes, as has been seen, a prospectus is not required, but the document called 'listing particulars' will be required if securities are being admitted to the Official List. This might occur say when there is a placing[34] of securities with a very small group of institutional investors, coupled with an introduction (i.e. listing onto) the Stock Exchange. Here, no prospectus is required because no securities are being 'offered to the public' within the Prospectus Directive.[35]

19.5 LISTED SECURITIES

A Introduction

The Financial Services and Markets Act 2000 provides[36] that the UKLA shall not admit any 'securities' to the Official List unless the application has been made in accordance with the Listing Rules and complies with them.[37] As well as admitting securities to the list, the UKLA has power to discontinue or suspend the listing in some circumstances[38] which it will exercise when it is necessary to protect investors and ensure the smooth operation of the market.[39]

What follows is a brief outline of the main structure of the rules governing a new listing of an issue of equity shares by a UK company, although the length of the Listing Rules is such that very many details are necessarily omitted. It should also be made clear that not every applicant will necessarily be a normal public company; for instance, an issuer of government bonds will usually be a nation state. It is also important to realise that since the transfer of the London Stock Exchange's functions as competent authority to UKLA, there is now a two-stage process for admission to the Official List, and compliance with the London Stock Exchange's Admission and Disclosure Standards and consequent admission to trading is also necessary.[40]

---

[32] Public Offers of Securities Regulations 1995, reg. 3 (1) (a).

[33] *Ibid.* reg. 4 (1). The content shall be in accordance with Sch. 1 (which in fact implements the Prospectus Directive); see reg. 8.

[34] See p. 260 above.

[35] The complex drafting and structure of the legislation is partly due to the fact that it is heavily based around the concept of 'listing particulars' rather than the word 'prospectus' because the Prospectus Directive was a much later piece of EC legislation. Section 86 of the 2000 Act provides in effect that quite often in the Act, 'listing particulars' provisions also apply to 'prospectus'. LR paras. 5.1(d),(e) make similar provision in relation to the Listing Rules. See also the UKLA Guidance Manual 2.1.2, 'For the avoidance of doubt, in this guidance manual any reference to listing particulars is defined, unless the context otherwise require, to include a reference to a prospectus.'

[36] In ss. 74–76.

[37] 'Security' is defined widely in s. 74 (5) of the 2000 Act.

[38] Financial Services and Market Act 2000, ss. 77–78 and LR paras 1.15–1.23.

[39] LR paras 1.19–1.21.

[40] See also p. 363 above, and LR para. 3.14A. A copy of the application for admission to trade must be included with the application for listing; paras 7.5 (1), 7.11 (f) and 7.12 (e).

B Background conditions

The company applying for a listing must comply with a number of basic conditions if its application is to have any hope of being successful. The UKLA will ensure the the company complies with the Listing Rules but it may make admission subject to any special condition if this is considered appropriate.[41] In any event, it is made clear that mere compliance with the Listing Rules will not necessarily ensure admission to the Official List, and the UKLA may refuse an application for listing if it considers that the applicant's situation is such that admission of the securities would be detrimental to the interests of investors.[42] It is interesting to speculate as to the way UKLA will exercise its discretion here. It is likely that refusal on those grounds will be rare and will not develop into the kind of procedures employed in some US states which have a merit test[43] in their 'blue sky' laws, in which they make an assessment of aspects of the commercial desirability of the security rather than merely check compliance with disclosure standards.

It is provided that the company must be duly incorporated under the law of the place where it is incorporated and obviously it must be a public company.[44] It is also made clear that the securities must comply with the law of the place where the applicant is incorporated, and be duly authorised according to the requirements of the company's memorandum and articles.[45] Also any necessary authorisations (such as those required under the Companies Act 1985, s. 80) must have been given and there must be compliance with the preferential subscription rights provisions.[46]

The applicant must also have published or filed accounts covering a period of three years preceding the listing application although in some circumstances the UKLA will accept a shorter period if that is desirable in the interests of the company or investors and provided that the investors will have the necessary information available to arrive at an informed judgment on the company and the securities for which listing is sought.[47] Further requirements relate to transferability of shares, share certificates, nature and duration of business activities, directors (expertise and experience), and many other matters.

The Listing Rules, in Chapter 2, make it clear that, in certain circumstances, the company will need to appoint a sponsor who will normally be corporate brokers or an investment bank but may also be certain other professional advisers. The sponsor then has various duties, such as, satisfying itself 'to the best of its knowledge and belief, having made due and careful enquiry of the issuer and its advisers, that the issuer has satisfied all applicable conditions for listing and other relevant requirements of the listing rules'.[48]

The minimum market value of the securities for which initial listing is sought is £700,000 (less for debt securities) although securities of a lower value can be admit-

---

[41] LR paras 1.1, 3.1.
[42] LR para. 1.4 (a); and in certain other circumstances; see LR para. 1.4 (b), (c).
[43] See p. 315 above.
[44] LR para. 3.2. A private company may not issue shares to the public; Companies Act 1985, s. 81.
[45] LR para. 3.14.
[46] *Ibid.* See p. 266 above.
[47] LR paras 3.3 (a), 3.4.
[48] LR para. 2.9 (a).

ted provided that the UKLA is satisfied that adequate marketability is expected. Further issues of shares of a class already listed are not subject to these limits.[49]

C Methods of issue

The main methods of issue have been discussed from the corporate finance perspective in Chapter 14.[50] Here it is sufficient to recall that applicants without equity shares already listed may bring securities to listing by any of the following methods: offer for sale to the public by a third party; direct offer to the public for subscription; a placing; an intermediaries offer where the shares are offered to intermediaries for them to allocate to their own clients; an introduction; or in some circumstances other methods will be permitted.[51]

D Application procedures

When an issuer applies for admission to the list of its securities which are to be offered to the public in the UK for the first time before admission a document called a 'prospectus' must be submitted to and approved by the London Stock Exchange. The technical legal background to this has been described above and as has been seen, sometimes the document will be called 'listing particulars'. A large part of the Listing Rules is thus taken up with providing rules governing the submission, approval, publication and contents of the prospectus/listing particulars. In the following account, the term 'prospectus' will be used.

There is a requirement for publication of the prospectus in accordance with the detailed requirements in Chapter 8 of the Listing Rules which vary according to the circumstances, size and method of offer but which will, for instance, usually require publication by making the prospectus available at the Document Viewing Facility[52] and advertisement in at least one national daily newspaper.[53] However, the prospectus may not be published until it has been formally approved by the UKLA.[54] It is also necessary for it to be delivered to the Registrar of Companies for registration before it is actually published.[55] At least ten clear business days prior to the intended publication date of the prospectus, the prospectus and various other necessary documents, such as circulars, application forms to subscribe, must be submitted (in draft) for approval.[56]

The application for admission of the securities for listing must then be submitted at least 48 hours (two *business* days) before the hearing of the application for listing by the UKLA, accompanied by various documents including a copy of each newspaper containing the published prospectus.[57] Other documents must be submitted

---

[49] LR paras 3.16–3.17.
[50] At p. 260 above.
[51] LR para. 4.2.
[52] In accordance with LR para. 8.4.
[53] In accordance with LR para. 8.7.
[54] LR paras. 5.12, 8.1.
[55] Financial Services and Markets Act 2000, s. 83.
[56] LR paras 5.9–5.13.
[57] LR para. 7.5.

on the day itself, or later.[58] Assuming that the application for admission to the Official List is granted, the date for the commencement of dealings which is requested by the applicant will usually also be approved at the hearing of the application. Admission of securities only becomes effective when the decision of the UKLA to admit the securities to listing has been announced in accordance with para. 7.1 (usually by being disseminated by the electronic system used by the UKLA for communication with the public).

E Contents of the prospectus

Much of the Listing Rules is taken up with extremely detailed requirements as to the precise form and contents of the prospectus, but before briefly considering these it is necessary to allude to a more general disclosure requirement contained in s. 80 of the Financial Services and Markets Act 2000 which provides:

(1) Listing Particulars [i.e. prospectus][59] submitted to the competent authority must contain all such information as investors and their professional advisers would reasonably require, and reasonably expect to find there, for the purpose of making an informed assessment of (a) the assets and liabilities, financial position, profits and losses, and prospects of the issuer of the securities; and (b) the rights attaching to those securities.

(2) That information is required in addition to any information required by:
(a) listing rules, or
(b) the competent authority, as a condition of the admission of the securities to the official list.

(3) Subsection (1) applies only to information:
(a) within the knowledge of any person responsible for the listing particulars; or
(b) which it would be reasonable for him to obtain by making enquiries.

(4) In determining what information subsection (1) requires to be included in listing particulars by virtue of this section, regard shall be had (in particular) to:
(a) the nature of the securities and their issuer;
(b) the nature of the persons likely to consider acquiring them;
(c) the fact that certain matters may reasonably be expected to be within the knowledge of professional advisers of a kind which persons likely to acquire the securities may reasonably be expected to consult; and
(d) any information available to investors or their professional advisers as a result of requirements imposed on the issuer of the securities by a recognised investment exchange, listing rules or under any other enactment.

Section 80 thus puts significant pressure on issuers and their advisers to give very careful consideration to the contents of their prospectus.

The requirements for the contents of the prospectus for the admission of shares are set out mainly in Chapter 6 of the Listing Rules. Details (the description of which covers some 38 printed pages of the Listing Rules) are required under the following headings:

---

[58] LR paras 7.7, 7.8.
[59] See s. 86.

A – The persons responsible for the prospectus, the auditors and other advisers.

B – The shares for which application is being made.

C – The issuer and its capital.

D – The group's activities.

E – The issuer's assets and liabilities, financial position and profits and losses.

F – The management.

G – The recent development and prospects of the group.

These matters are supplemented by Chapter 12, which makes prescription as to accountants' reports and financial information.

It should finally be noted here that if at any time after the preparation of the prospectus for submission to the UKLA and before dealings begin there is any significant change or new matter affecting the prospectus, then a supplementary prospectus will need to be submitted, approved and published.[60]

F Continuing obligations

Once the formalities connected with the listing have been complied with, matters do not end there, for the Listing Rules, in Chapter 9, set out what are referred to as 'Continuing Obligations', that is to say 'Obligations which a listed company is required to observe once any of its securities have been admitted to listing'.[61] Broadly speaking, Chapter 9 requires notification of information about changes affecting the company. Other Continuing Obligations are set out in other chapters, namely: transactions (Chapter 10); transactions with related parties (Chapter 11); financial information (Chapter 12); documents not requiring prior approval (Chapter 13); circulars (Chapter 14); purchase of own securities and provisions relating to shares held in treasury (Chapter 15); and directors (Chapter 16).

G Other provisions

Chapter 17 contains provisions dealing with overseas companies and contains various adaptations of the prospectus, exemptions, mutual recognition and provisions dealing with foreign companies which have a secondary listing on the London Stock Exchange. Chapters 18–27 deal with special situations: property companies, mineral companies, scientific research based companies, investment entities, public sector issuers, specialist securities (including Eurobonds), securitised derivatives, innovative high growth companies, venture capital trusts, and strategic investment companies.

---

[60] LR paras 5.14–5.16; and see Financial Services and Markets Act 2000, s. 81.
[61] See also s. 96.

19.6 UNLISTED SECURITIES

A The Alternative Investment Market (AIM)

The Alternative Investment Market (AIM) exists as the lightly regulated alternative to the Main Market, for younger companies.[62] Entry to AIM is governed by the conditions set out in the London Stock Exchange's AIM Rules. These are similar to the provisions in the Listing Rules although much less detailed and onerous. An AIM company which makes a public offering of shares will usually need to comply with the prospectus requirements of the Public Offers of Securities Regulations 1995 unless the offer falls within the exemptions.

B Prospectuses

As has been described,[63] the offer to the public of shares which are not listed on the London Stock Exchange pursuant to Pt VI of the Financial Services and Markets Act 2000 is governed by the Public Offers of Securities Regulations 1995.[64] The basic position, in outline, is as follows:

Regulation 4 (1) provides:

> When securities are offered to the public in the United Kingdom for the first time the offeror shall publish a prospectus by making it available to the public, free of charge, at an address in the United Kingdom, from the time he first offers the securities until the end of the period during which the offer remains open.

The Regulations contain various definitions. The main point about the word 'securities' in this context is that it means (primarily) any investment which is not admitted to official listing nor the subject of an application for listing.[65] The expression 'to the public' is dealt with in reg. 6:

> A person offers securities to the public in the United Kingdom if, to the extent that the offer is made to persons in the United Kingdom, it is made to the public; and, for this purpose, an offer which is made to any section of the public, whether selected as members or debenture holders of a body corporate, or as clients of the person making the offer, or in any other manner, is to be regarded as made to the public.

There are then various exemptions so that some offers are deemed not to be offers to the public, for example where the securities are offered to no more than 50 persons, or are offered to 'a restricted circle of persons whom the offeror reasonably believes to be sufficiently knowledgeable to understand the risks involved in accepting the offer'.[66] A security which falls outside the regime will sometimes then fall within the rules relating to financial promotion.[67]

The prospectus must contain all such information as investors would reasonably require, and reasonably expect to find there, for the purpose of making an informed

---

[62] See further p. 259 above.
[63] See at p. 364 above.
[64] SI 1995 No. 1537.
[65] See Public Offers of Securities Regulations 1995, regs 2 (1) and 3.
[66] See generally *ibid.* reg. 7.
[67] On the financial promotion regime, see p. 342 above.

assessment of the financial position and prospects of the issuer and the rights attaching to the securities.[68] This is in addition to the detailed list of information required by reg. 8 of and Schedule 1 to the Regulations. The information must be presented in a form that is easy to analyse and comprehend.[69]

19.7 THE *NEW* PROSPECTUS DIRECTIVE AND THE FSA'S REVIEW OF THE LISTING REGIME

With effect from 1 July 2005 the existing Prospectus Directive is repealed and replaced by the *New* Prospectus Directive.[70] This, and the advent of other EC legislation in this field (the Transparency Directive[71] and the Market Abuse Directive),[72] has prompted the FSA to carry out a thorough review of the Listing Regime. At the time of writing they are currently drafting rules which will implement a new regime to come into effect in the summer of 2005. Further changes will be made over the following year (implementing the Transparency Directive and the MAD).

The *New* Prospectus Directive is intended to improve the framework for raising capital on an EU wide basis. There are currently many different practices within the EU regarding the content and layout of prospectuses, and the existing mutual recognition system has not succeeded in providing a single passport for issuers. The new Directive introduces a system of notification, whereby the competent authority of the issuer's Member State will merely have to notify their counterparts in other Member States in order for the prospectus to be accepted in those host states; thus the host states will no longer have the right to request additional information to be included in the prospectus. There is also a new language regime under which, if the prospectus is drafted in a language customary in international finance (normally English) then the host state will have to accept that, and can require further in their own language only a summary of the prospectus. The financial disclosure content of the prospectus will be on the basis of a single set of accounting standards as a result of the recent requirement that consolidated accounts be prepared in accordance with International Accounting Standards (IAS). Various formats of prospectus will be permitted, in particular one designed for fast-track new issues for frequent issuers whereby the prospectus is in two parts. One part will be a registration statement containing details about the issuer, the other will be a securities note containing details of the securities being issued and admitted to trading. As with the other recent Capital Markets Directives

---

[68] Public Offers of Securities Regulations 1995, reg. 9 (1).

[69] *Ibid.* reg. 8 (3).

[70] Directive on the Prospectus to be Published when Securities are Offered to the Public or Admitted to Trading, 2003/71/EC, OJ 2003, L 345/64.

[71] Directive on Transparency Requirements with Regard to Information on Issuers whose Securities are Admitted to Trading on a Regulated Market. The EC Council has reached political agreement on the draft directive which is likely to be formally adopted in the autumn of 2004. It will amend and upgrade provisions of the Consolidated Admissions Directive 2001/34/EC with regard to the information which companies are required to supply to investors. It will also improve the dissemination of the information by, for instance, requiring companies to make it available on their websites.

[72] See Chapter 20 below.

developed under the Financial Services Action Plan, many of the details will be worked out under the comitology procedures recommended by the Lamfalussy Report; they can also be kept under review so as to cope with developments in market conditions.

In the context of the need to implement these Directives, the FSA has inaugurated a general review of the listing regime[73] which will be implemented by changes to the rules in accordance with the timetable mentioned above. The review also aims to modernise the listing regime and proposes a range of reforms such as the introduction of a set of high level Listing Principles.

19.8 REMEDIES FOR INVESTORS

Part VI of the Financial Services and Markets Act 2000 contains provisions giving legal remedies to investors in a number of circumstances.[74] The main provisions relevant to prospectuses/listing particulars[75] are contained in s. 90.[76] Persons responsible[77] for the prospectus are liable to pay compensation to any person who has acquired any of the securities and suffered loss in respect of them as a result of any untrue or misleading statement in the prospectus (or omission from them of matters required to be included). However, there is no liability if the person responsible satisfies the court that at the time when the prospectus was submitted to the UKLA he reasonably believed (having made whatever inquiries he should reasonably have made) that the statement was true and not misleading or that the matter whose omission caused the loss was properly omitted. It is also necessary for him to show that he continued in that belief until the time when the securities were acquired.[78] There are various other situations where a defence is available, such as:[79] where the statement is made by or on the authority of an expert and various conditions (similar to the above) are satisfied;[80] or where the defendant has published or tried to publish a correction;[81] or where the statement is made by a public official;[82] or that he reasonably believed that a change or new matter was not

---

[73] See Consultation Paper 203, *Review of the Listing Regime*, FSA October 2003.

[74] There are analogous provisions in regs 13–16 of the Public Offers of Securities Regulations 1995 covering unlisted securities. These are similar to those in Pt VI of the 2000 Act and will not be given separate treatment here.

[75] The terms are used interchangeably in the 2000 Act; see s. 86.

[76] And Sch. 10 to the 2000 Act.

[77] Regulations have been made to cover this; see s. 79 (3) and the Financial Services and Markets Act 2000 (Official Listing of Securities) Regulations 2001 (SI 2001 No. 2956). Thus, for instance, directors are responsible for listing particulars.

[78] *Or* that they were acquired before it was reasonably practicable to bring a correction to the attention of persons likely to acquire the securities in question, *or* that before the securities were acquired he had taken all such steps as it was reasonable for him to have taken to secure that a correction was brought to the attention of those persons, *or* that he continued in that belief until after the commencement of dealings in the securities following their admission to the Official List and that the securities were acquired after such a lapse of time that he ought in the circumstances to be reasonably excused (Financial Services and Markets Act 2000, s. 90 (2) and Sch. 10).

[79] See, generally, Financial Services and Markets Act 2000, Sch. 10.

[80] *Ibid.* Sch. 10, para. 2.

[81] *Ibid.* Sch. 10, para. 3.

[82] *Ibid.* Sch. 10, para. 5.

sufficient to require the issue of a supplementary prospectus.[83] Obviously, also, there is no liability if the person suffering the loss knew of the falsity or omission.[84]

There are also rules and doctrines developed by the case law (occasionally modified by statute) which may be of relevance in a situation where a person suffers loss as a result of relying on prospectuses or other documents published in connection with share issues such as what are referred to as 'mini prospectuses' which are often used in connection with share offers.[85] In brief, the types of such common law remedies which may become available are: rescission of the contract for misrepresentation,[86] damages for misrepresentation (whether fraudulently made or not),[87] damages for common law deceit, or for negligent misstatement. There has been a steady trickle of case law over a long period of time on the question of when the prospectus becomes 'spent' in the sense that it is no longer reasonable to regard it as a representation. It has been held that a person cannot rely on the prospectus if he subsequently buys shares in the secondary market,[88] or similarly where the prospectus was addressed to the claimant for a particular purpose, such as a rights issue, then he could not rely on it for another purpose, namely the purchase of shares on the market.[89] On the other hand, if the circumstances are such that the prospectus can be treated as a continuing representation then it can sometimes be relied on.[90]

---

[83] *Ibid.* Sch. 10, para. 7.

[84] *Ibid.* Sch. 10, para. 6.

[85] See LR paras 8.12–8.13, 8.24.

[86] Or damages in lieu of rescission under s. 2 (2) of the Misrepresentation Act 1967.

[87] Under s. 2 (1) of the Misrepresentation Act 1967.

[88] *Peek* v *Gurney* (1873) LR 6 HL 377.

[89] *Al Nakib Ltd* v *Longcroft* [1990] BCC 517.

[90] See *Andrews* v *Mockford* [1896] 1 QB 372 where false information had been published in a newspaper to revive interest in the prospectus; similarly in *Possfund* v *Diamond* [1996] 2 BCLC 665 it was held that the defendants intended to inform and encourage after-market purchasers. On measure of damages, see *Smith New Court* v *Scrimgeour Vickers (Asset Management) Ltd* [1997] AC 254, HL.

20

THE REGULATION OF INSIDER DEALING AND MARKET ABUSE

20.1 REGULATION OF MARKET CONDUCT

Until fairly recently, the regulation of market conduct has emphasised the way in which particular markets attempt to regulate the problem of insider dealing. Other methods of regulation, such as the prohibition of misleading statements designed to affect investment decisions and create a false market, while historically sometimes predating insider dealing regulation have nevertheless maintained a lower profile in securities regulation. For this reason, this chapter will approach the topic of the regulation of market conduct by first looking at the development of regulation of insider dealing. However, it will then be necessary to have regard to the wider picture, both at European level and in the UK. For at European level we now have a *new* Directive on Insider Dealing and Market Manipulation (Market Abuse),[1] and in the UK the FSA has recently begun to develop a regulatory technique of civil penalties for *market abuse*, a term which under the legislation and accompanying code, spans a wide range of regulation of market conduct, including manifestations of insider dealing.

20.2 INSIDER DEALING AND MARKET EGALITARIANISM

It will be seen that case law and legislative systems of insider dealing regulation have produced some very subtle concepts of what amounts to insider dealing. However, for the sake of this introductory discussion, the facts of *SEC v Texas Gulf Sulphur Co*[2] can give a basic idea. The directors of a company learned that huge deposits of copper and zinc had been discovered under land owned by the company. Some of them purchased more shares[3] and later, when the discovery had become common knowledge and the market price had risen, they sold their shares at a profit. The SEC brought a civil action for violation of r. 10b-5[4] by 'insider dealing'.

The regulatory stance against insider dealing toughened from the 1960s. In the

---

[1] Directive 2003/6/EC, OJ 2003, L 96/16.
[2] 401 F 2d 833, 394 US 976, 89 S Ct 1454, 22 L Ed 2d 756 (1969).
[3] There were other significant facts concerning their denial of a rumour about the discovery of the zinc, but these have been omitted for present purposes.
[4] On this, see p. 375 below.

US in 1961 there was the landmark case of *Cady, Roberts & Co.*[5], which for the first time held that insider dealing could violate the general anti-fraud provision of r. 10b-5.[6]

In 1980 the UK passed legislation which was a complicated and detailed attempt at comprehensive regulation of insider dealing.[7] In 1989 the European Community adopted a Directive 'Co-ordinating regulations on insider dealing'[8] designed to bring about a high level of co-ordination of regulation and to combat the problem that many Member States had no legislation at all against insider dealing.[9]

As a backdrop to this decisive regulatory activity, a debate has simmered[10] as to whether there should be regulation against insider dealing. The arguments which have been ranged against regulation proceed along the lines that it is compensation for entrepreneurial activity, and that no one is harmed by it.[11] The pro-regulatory block has mounted various responses, which have often been mirrored in the jurisprudence of the case and statute law. Arguments for regulation are that insider dealing is wrong because it involves a breach of fiduciary duty by the director or insider, or that it involves a misappropriation of confidential information, or that it is contrary to basic notions of market fairness.[12] This last view is dominant in Europe, since market fairness is the rationale adopted by the relevant Directive. In practical terms, the battle has been won and IOSCO and regulatory authorities generally take the view that regulation against insider dealing is an essential part of any system of securities regulation.

20.3 DEVELOPMENT OF REGULATION AGAINST INSIDER DEALING

A The cradle: SEC r. 10b–5

Systematic regulation against insider dealing is the result of SEC administrative and judicial interpretation in the USA. It came about as a result of interpretation of a general anti-fraud provision. Rule 10b-5 was promulgated by the SEC in 1942

---

[5] 40 SEC 907 (1961). See further p. 376 below.

[6] In effect this meant that, thereafter, the SEC could take action against insider dealing. Until *Cady, Roberts* the main US regulatory plank against insider dealing was s. 16 (b) of the Securities Exchange Act 1934, which sought to prevent directors and other corporate insiders and certain shareholders from making profits from e.g., purchase and resale of shares within a six-month period. It was certainly designed with insider dealing in mind: 'For the purpose of preventing the unfair use of information which may have been obtained by [a director . . .] by reason of his relationship with the issuer.' However, it has never been or become a general proscription of insider dealing.

[7] Companies Act 1980, ss. 68–73. Provisions prohibiting directors from dealing in options were first contained in the Companies Act 1967, it then being felt that this was the most likely area where directors could abuse insider knowledge. They are now contained in the Companies Act 1985, ss. 323, 327.

[8] 89/592/EEC.

[9] On implementation see: J. Black 'Audacious But Not Successful? A Comparative Analysis of the Implementation of Insider Dealing Regulation in EU Member States' [1998] CFILR 1.

[10] It is still current: see H. McVea 'What's Wrong with Insider Dealing?' (1995) 15 *Legal Studies* 390; D. Campbell 'Note: What *Is* Wrong with Insider Dealing?' (1996) 16 *Legal Studies* 185.

[11] See generally H. Manne *Insider Trading and the Stock Market* (New York: Free Press, 1966).

[12] Sometimes called 'market egalitarianism'.

under s. 10 (b) of the Securities Exchange Act 1934. It was not intended to apply to insider dealing[13] and its wording was not apposite to do so:

> It shall be unlawful for any person, directly or indirectly, by the use of any mails or instrumentality of interstate commerce, or of the mails, or any facility of any national securities exchange,[14]
>
> (a) to employ any device, scheme, or artifice to defraud,
> (b) to make any untrue statement of a material fact or omit to state a material fact necessary in order to make the statements made, in the light of the circumstances under which they were made, not misleading, or
> (c) to engage in any act, practice or course of business which operates or would operate as a fraud or deceit upon any person,
>
> in connection with the purchase or sale of any security.

Since basic insider dealing simply involves buying or selling shares on a market (albeit with some special insider knowledge), none of this looks very promising as a basis for proscribing it. However, in *Cady, Roberts & Co*[15] the SEC held that insider dealing does violate para. (c) of r. 10b-5.[16] On the face of it, it does not look as though para. (c) could be breached by insider dealing activity, because the act which operates as a fraud or deceit is 'keeping quiet' (i.e. not revealing that inside knowledge) and does not seem to be covered by the wording in para. (c). However, it was held that persons who are seeking to deal in shares and have inside knowledge are under a fiduciary duty to disclose to the counterparty that they have the knowledge,[17] or to abstain from dealing. The existence of this positive duty is the judicial device which then enables insider dealing to fall under para. (c).[18] This approach, founded on the insider's fiduciary duty, became known as the 'classical' theory of liability.

The limitations of r. 10b–5 soon became apparent. The legal system was forced to confront the question of whether someone to whom insider knowledge was passed and who then made use of it to deal and make a profit or avoid a loss, could be liable. Persons in that kind of position have colloquially been referred to as 'tippees'.[19] The difficulties which the classical theory faced in extending liability to tippees became apparent in *Chiarella* v *US*.[20] Chiarella was a printer who was involved in printing documents for takeover bids and although the names of the parties were omitted, he managed to work out who was involved. He purchased

---

[13] It had been introduced to deal specifically with the problem of directors who had been dishonestly telling their shareholders that the company was doing badly (when it was not) and then buying their shares at a reduced price.

[14] By the inclusion of these technical words, Congress was signalling that it was claiming federal application for its new law.

[15] 40 SEC 907 (1961). This was an SEC administrative action.

[16] Confirmed in later cases; see e.g. *Chiarella* v *US* 445 US 222 (1980).

[17] Since it would affect his investment judgment. The duty arises from (1) the existence of a relationship affording access to inside information intended to be available only for a corporate purpose, and (2) the unfairness of allowing a corporate insider to take advantage of that information by trading without disclosure. See *Chiarella* v *US* 445 US 222 (1980) at p. 227.

[18] It was later held that r. 10b-5 could not be breached by negligent conduct. '*Scienter*' was required (i.e. dishonesty); see *Ernst and Ernst* v *Hochfelder* 425 US 185 (1976).

[19] Someone in receipt of a 'tip'.

[20] 445 US 222 (1980).

shares in the targets and when the bids were announced and the market price went up, he took his profit. He was indicted for violating r. 10b–5 and convicted but the conviction was reversed by the US Supreme Court. It was held, in accordance with the *Cady, Roberts* approach, that his use of the information was not a fraud under r. 10b–5 unless he was subject to an affirmative duty to disclose it before trading. Here, there was no such duty: he was not a corporate insider and received no confidential information from the target company, and the information upon which he relied related only to the plans of the acquiring company. *Chiarella* produced an uncomfortable result and later cases have been at pains to point out that a tippee will be under a fiduciary duty to the shareholders of a corporation not to trade on material non-public information if (1) the insider has breached his fiduciary duty to the shareholders by disclosing the information to the tippee and (2) the tippee knows or should know that there has been a breach.[21]

Chiarella was revisited in *US* v *O'Hagan*.[22] O'Hagan was a partner in a law firm which was representing the bidder in a takeover bid. Although he was not involved in the bid himself, O'Hagan learned who the parties were by overhearing it being discussed at lunch, and bought stock and options out of which he in due course made a profit. Here again, the limitations of the classical theory became apparent. As a 'lawyer'[23] to the bidder, he owed no fiduciary duty to the target or its shareholders in the market to disclose the information or refrain from dealing. The Supreme Court felt the need for something more than the classical theory and adopted a doctrine, additional to the classical theory, which had been set out in Burger J's dissenting judgment in *Chiarella* and which is generally referred to as the 'misappropriation theory'. Burger J put it in this way:

> ... A person who has misappropriated nonpublic information has an absolute duty to disclose that information or to refrain from trading ... The evidence shows beyond all doubt that Chiarella, working literally in the shadows of the warning signs in the printshop, misappropriated ... valuable nonpublic information entrusted to him in the utmost confidence. He then exploited his ill-gotten informational advantage by purchasing securities in the market. In my view, such conduct plainly ... violates Rule 10(b)–5.[24]

B UK legislation

1 The 1980 legislation

The UK's early attempt to construct a regime against insider dealing was permeated with a theory of liability based broadly on the US classical theory. Thus, the statute laid stress on the need for the 'individual knowingly connected with a company' (i.e. the insider) to have information which 'it would be reasonable to expect a person and in the position by virtue of which he is so connected not to disclose except for the proper performance of the functions attaching to that

---

[21] See e.g. *Dirks* v *SEC* 463 US 646 (1983) at p. 660.
[22] 117 S Ct 2199 (1997). See further K. McCoy 'Supreme Court Affirms Second Theory of Liability for Insider Trading' (1997) 18 Co Law 335.
[23] I.e. member of the law firm which was acting for the bidder.
[24] 445 US 222 (1980) at p. 245.

position ...'.[25] Here lies the theoretical emphasis on his position, and the confidentiality and limitations on use arising from that position; in other words, the fiduciary duty of the insider to the company.

With tippee liability, the 1980 Act adopted the kind of structure seen in the US law above, of making the tippee liable where the insider has breached his fiduciary duty to the company by giving it to the tippee in the first place, and, where the tippee knows or should know that there has been a breach of fiduciary duty and so is affected by the same trusts as the insider. This is reflected in the provisions of the 1980 Act which deal with tippee liability. The tippee was liable if he dealt in circumstances where he had:

> [I]nformation which he knowingly obtained ... from another individual who is connected with a particular company ... and who the former individual knows or has reasonable cause to believe held the information by virtue of being so connected; and ... the former individual knows or has reasonable cause to believe that, because of the latter's connection and position, it would be reasonable to expect him not to disclose the information except for the proper performance of the functions attaching to that position.[26]

Thus, the theoretical building blocks of the 1980 UK law were closely linked to the case law concepts being developed in the US.[27] In the 1985 consolidation, the insider dealing provisions of the Companies Act 1980 were re-enacted in the Company Securities (Insider Dealing) Act 1985. This Act was then repealed and replaced by the Criminal Justice Act 1993, which contains the current UK law. What had happened in the meantime was the adoption of the 1989 Directive[28] on insider dealing and this produced some subtle changes.

2 The Directive and the shift to 'market egalitarianism'

By the time the EC Directive 'Coordinating regulations on insider dealing'[29] was adopted,[30] the European Commission's programme of creating the EC-wide capital market was well advanced and it seemed possible to take some bold steps with insider dealing policy. As ever, the Preamble to the Directive reflects the policy background and it traces the link between the basic need to create the structure of the internal market and a small plank in that structure, insider dealing regulation:

> Whereas ... the Treaty states that the Council shall adopt the measures for the approximation of the provisions laid down by law, regulation or administrative action in Member States which have as their object the establishment and functioning of the internal market;

---

[25] Companies Act 1980, s. 68 (1) *passim*.

[26] *Ibid.* s. 68 (3) *passim*.

[27] For this view, see B. Rider, C. Abrams and M. Ashe *Guide to Financial Services Regulation* 3rd edn (Bicester: CCH, 1998) at p. 222.

[28] Subsequently this has been replaced by a *new* Directive on Insider Dealing and Market Manipulation (Market Abuse), which will usher in further changes in the law by the summer of 2005. This is dealt with in more detail at para. 20.6 below. This new Directive will not change the UK's criminal provisions on insider dealing contained in the CJA 1993, which will thus continue to reflect the influence of the 1989 Directive; see further n. 71 below.

[29] 89/592/EEC.

[30] I.e. 1989.

Whereas the secondary market in transferable securities plays an important role in the financing of economic agents;

Whereas, for that market to be able to play its role effectively, every measure should be taken to ensure that market operates smoothly;

Whereas the smooth operation of the market depends to a large extent on the confidence it inspires in investors;

Whereas the factors on which such confidence depends include the assurance afforded to investors that they are placed on an equal footing and that they will be protected against the improper use of inside information;

Whereas, by benefiting certain investors as compared with others, insider dealing is likely to undermine that confidence and may therefore prejudice the smooth operation of the market;

Whereas the necessary measures should therefore be taken to combat insider dealing . . .

Gone is the Anglo/US company law basis for insider dealing regulation, with its emphasis on breach of duty by fiduciaries. In its place stands capital markets law. Company law has here migrated into capital markets law; company law has become capital markets law.[31] This is discernible in the current UK legislation.

3 UK enactment of the Directive – the current law

The detail of the current UK provisions reflects the policy shift. Liability is no longer based on having received information as a result of a breach of fiduciary duty by a corporate insider. Instead, liability is based on knowing that you have inside information, and it does not matter much how you acquired it; it does not have to come through an official who is acting in breach of duty.[32]

The offences and defences to them are set out in ss. 52 and 53 of the Criminal Justice Act 1993. There are basically three ways of committing the offence of insider dealing: (1) dealing in securities; (2) encouraging another person to deal; and (3) disclosing information. These are now examined in more detail:

(a) Dealing in securities
The main elements are set out in s. 52 (1) which provides:

An individual who has information as an insider is guilty of insider dealing if, in the circumstances mentioned in subsection (3),[33] he deals in securities that are price-affected securities in relation to the information.

The legislation contains various definitions of the terminology being used. 'Securities' is defined widely[34] so that it includes not only certain shares and debt

---

[31] For this idea generally see P. Davies 'The European Community's Directive on Insider Dealing: From Company Law to Securities Markets Regulation' (1991) 11 OJLS 92.

[32] See Rider, Abrams and Ashe, n. 27 above, at pp. 222–223.

[33] Criminal Justice Act 1993, s. 52 (3) provides that: 'The circumstances . . . are that the acquisition or disposal in question occurs on a regulated market, or that the person dealing relies on a professional intermediary or is himself acting as a professional intermediary.'

[34] In Criminal Justice Act 1993, s. 54 and Sch. 2. The actual definition is complicated by the detailed

securities, but also, for instance, certain options and futures. 'Dealing' is also given a wide definition.[35]

Sections 57 sets out the concept of 'insiders':

(1) ... a person has information as an insider if and only if:
    (a) it is, and he knows that it is, inside information, and
    (b) he has it, and knows that he has it, from an inside source.
(2) For the purposes of subsection (1), a person has information from an inside source if and only if:
    (a) he has it through:
        (i) being a director, employee or shareholder of an issuer of securities; or
        (ii) having access to the information by virtue of his employment, office or profession; or
    (b) the direct or indirect source of his information is a person within paragraph (a).

This needs to be read in the light of s. 56, which provides further definitions.[36]

It can be seen from ss. 52 and 57 that the essence of the offence under the Criminal Justice Act 1993 is, broadly, knowing that you have information as an insider and then dealing. This represents a subtle shift from the theoretical basis of liability under the previous legislation, which was predicated on the basis of a breach of fiduciary duty along the lines of the US classical theory. However, in fact, the insider dealer will usually be in breach of a fiduciary duty of confidentiality.

The same shift of emphasis is apparent as regards the basis of tippee liability within ss. 52 and 57. A tippee will be caught by the offence in s. 52 in circumstances where it can be said that he '... has information as an insider ...' within that section and within the definition of those words in s. 57. It is clear that s. 57 (2) needs to be satisfied in order for s. 57 (1) to be satisfied. The part of s. 57 (2) which relates to tippees is s. 57 (2) (b)[37] 'the direct or indirect source of his

---

extra conditions imposed by arts 4–8 of the Insider Dealing (Securities and Regulated Markets) Order 1994 (SI 1994 No. 187). This Order is also of relevance for the definition of 'regulated market' in s. 52 (3) above. Section 62 deals with the fairly complex territorial scope of the provisions.

[35] In Criminal Justice Act 1993, s. 55.

[36] Section 56 of the Criminal Justice Act 1993 states:
'(1) For the purposes of this section and section 57, "inside information" means information which—
(a) relates to particular securities or to a particular issuer of securities or particular issuers of securities and not to securities generally or to issuers of securities generally; (b) is specific or precise; (c) has not been made public; and (d) if it were made public would be likely to have a significant effect on the price of any securities.
(2) For the purposes of [ss. 52–64], securities are "price-affected securities" in relation to inside information, and inside information is "price-sensitive information" in relation to securities, if and only if the information would, if made public, be likely to have a significant effect on the price of the securities.
(3) For the purposes of this section "price" includes value.'
There are then further definitions of 'made public', 'professional intermediary' and various other terms; see generally ss. 58–60.

[37] It could be argued that a tippee might fall within s. 57 (2) (a) in some circumstances. Consider the example of *O'Hagan* (p. 377 above) who, although not himself involved with the takeover bid, heard the information over lunch. Could he be said to fall within s. 57 (2) (a) (ii) as having the information 'by virtue of his employment, office or profession'? He was, after all, in the building and at the lunch table by virtue of some or all of those things. Perhaps the better view is that para. (a) is only meant to apply to the situation where the information comes to the person in the course of him exercising

---

information is a person within paragraph (a)'. Therefore, although the person giving the tippee the information will often in fact be in breach of a fiduciary duty of confidentiality, the statute does not require this as a precondition of liability.

The offence is however subject to the defences set out in s. 53 (1) which provides that:

> An individual is not guilty of insider dealing by virtue of dealing in securities if he shows:
> (a) that he did not at the time expect the dealing to result in a profit attributable to the fact that the information in question was price-sensitive information in relation to the securities,[38] or
> (b) that at the time he believed on reasonable grounds that the information had been disclosed widely enough to ensure that none of those taking part in the dealing would be prejudiced by not having the information, or
> (c) that he would have done what he did even if he had not had the information.[39]

As regards these defences, para. (a) seems to be importing a kind of intent requirement into the offence, although the burden of proof is the reverse of the normal situation where the prosecution has to prove the mental intention as part of the elements of the offence. Paragraph (b) is an important provision since it is often not going to be clear to someone who deals on the basis of information whether or not the information has been made public.[40] Paragraph (c) is designed to prevent injustice in what will probably be quite rare cases where there are overlapping causes of the events. Thus, for instance, if a person is planning to sell shares on Wednesday to pay for his daughter's wedding taking place on Saturday, even if the prosecution can make out the elements of the offence in s. 52 (1), it is clear that they are not an operative cause of the actions being taken.

All in all, even taking into account the availability of these defences, these provisions are quite tough. They have a tendency to reverse the burden of proof so that the prosecution has to prove only some matters related to the concept of 'insiders'. The prosecution does not have to prove intention to make a profit, nor does it have to prove a breach of fiduciary duty of confidentiality. On the other hand, as will be seen below, it is notoriously difficult to detect insider dealing and then manage to bring a successful prosecution and so perhaps there is no real element of overkill in the statutory provisions.[41]

---

functions in relation to the employment, office or profession; the words 'has it through' in para. (a) might help this construction. Thus, O'Hagan would perhaps more properly fall under para. (b).

[38] By s. 53 (6) 'profit' here includes avoidance of loss.

[39] Also by s. 53 (4) there are various exemptions for market makers and by s. 63 (1) for individuals acting on behalf of public sector bodies in pursuit of monetary policies.

[40] If it has, it is no longer 'inside information' within s. 56 (1) (c).

[41] Listed companies are required to comply with the Stock Exchange's Model Code for Securities Transactions contained in the Appendix to Chapter 16 of the Listing Rules. The Code provides that there are circumstances when it would be undesirable for a director and certain employees to buy or sell their company's securities, even though this would not of itself amount to a breach of the insider dealing legislation.

(b) Encouraging another person to deal

The main elements of the second way of committing the offence of insider dealing are set out in s. 52 (2) (a), which provides:

> An individual who has information as an insider is also guilty of insider dealing if:
> (a) he encourages another person to deal in securities that are (whether or not that other knows) price-affected securities in relation to the information, knowing or having reasonable cause to believe that the dealing would take place in the circumstances mentioned in subsection (3) . . .

The defences to this are set out in s. 53 (2) and are broadly similar to those which pertain to the offence under s. 52 (1). There are then various definitions; these have been mentioned in more detail under (a) above.

(c) Disclosing information

The main elements of the third way of committing the offence of insider dealing are set out in s. 52 (2) (b), which provides:

> An individual who has information as an insider is also guilty of insider dealing if: . . .
> (b) he discloses the information, otherwise than in the proper performance of the functions of his employment, office or profession, to another person.

The defences to this are set out in s. 53 (3) and are similar to the ones already discussed except that they omit the third defence contained in s. 53 (1) (c) and (2) (c), which would clearly be inappropriate in the circumstances covered by s. 52 (2) (b).

20.4 ENFORCEMENT

In the US, insider dealing will in most instances be dealt with by the SEC bringing a civil action for disgorgement of profit, a monetary penalty,[42] and an injunction against future violations. The action will then usually be settled. Over the years this has provided a cheap and expeditious means of dealing with insider dealing.[43] In the more serious cases, the SEC civil action will be put on hold pending the outcome of a criminal indictment brought by the District Attorney in the District Court. For detection of the insider dealing violation, the SEC relies on its own computer monitoring of the market and denouncements by private individuals. Many a UK visitor to the SEC website[44] will be bemused to find it using the old 'Wild West' technique of offering 'bounty' to people who supply it with information of insider dealing violations.

---

[42] Normally about the same amount as the profit. The power to impose a civil monetary penalty was first granted in the Insider Trading Sanctions Act 1984 and is now contained in the Insider Trading and Securities Fraud Enforcement Act 1988 which amended and codified the 1984 Act. As a result of the 1988 Act there is also the possibility of a private right of action under s. 20A of the Securities Exchange Act 1934, although damages are limited to profits gained or loss avoided and are subject to reduction for amounts paid in actions brought by the SEC. There is also a possibility of action at common law, based on fiduciary duties; see *Diamond* v *Oreamuno* 24 NY 2d 494 (1969) NY Ct App.

[43] See further J. Fishman 'A Comparison of Enforcement of Securities Law Violations in the UK and US' (1993) 14 Co Law 163.

[44] http://www.sec.gov.

In the UK, criminal proceedings in respect of alleged insider dealing may only be brought by or with the consent of the Secretary of State (i.e. the DTI) or the Director of Public Prosecutions or the FSA.[45] Many cases of suspected insider dealing are referred to the DTI from the Stock Exchange which has its own insider dealing monitoring department. The Stock Exchange has one of the most advanced computer market monitoring systems in the world called IMAS.[46] In 1998 this highlighted over 10,000 significant price movements and the Stock Exchange carried out 1,150 subsequent inquiries, resulting in 28 referrals to the DTI. However, the number of prosecutions has remained fixed at only one or two a year. In the past these have rarely resulted in prison sentences[47] and many of those convicted have been minor offenders. In view of this, it is perhaps not surprising that the FSA has pioneered the inclusion in the Financial Services and Markets Act 2000 of civil monetary penalties for market abuse.[48]

The Criminal Justice Act 1993 makes no provision for any civil remedy and it is certainly arguable that directors who deal in their company's securities using insider knowledge commit a breach of fiduciary duty so that the company could recover their profit.[49] Similar liability might even apply to people who are not directors but who can be shown to have received confidential information and made a profit out of it.[50] So far there has been no reported litigation in the UK along these lines, but it is possible that some encouragement might have been given by the litigation in *Chase Manhattan Equities Ltd* v *Goodman*,[51] a first instance case decided under the previous legislation, which established that, despite the wording of s. 8 (3) of Company Securities (Insider Dealing) Act 1985, in some circumstances a transaction by an insider dealer could be set aside for illegality. The sale was by a director of the company (via nominees) to Chase Manhattan Equities in circumstances where the director was using unpublished price-sensitive information to avoid a loss. The transaction was not fully carried out on the Stock Exchange and just before the transaction would have been delivered into the TALISMAN system,[52] Chase sought to rescind the sale agreement. It was held *inter alia* that the agreement was tainted by the illegal insider dealing and was therefore unenforceable. This was so, in spite of s. 8 (3) of the Company Securities (Insider Dealing) Act 1985, which provided that 'No transaction is void or voidable by reason only that it was entered into ...' in contravention of the insider dealing prohibitions. The judge took the view that s. 8 (3) was enacted for the purpose of preventing the disruption and unwinding of completed Stock Exchange transactions and did not cover the present case because the transaction had not been put through the Stock Exchange completion machinery and only the parties to the original dealing were involved. Section 8 (3) is now replaced by s. 63 (2) of the 1993 Act, which provides that 'No

---

[45] Criminal Justice Act 1993, s. 61; Financial Services and Markets Act 2000, s. 402 (1) (a).
[46] Integrated Monitoring And Surveillance System.
[47] The maximum prison sentence was increased from two years to seven years by the Criminal Justice Act 1987.
[48] See p. 384 below.
[49] See at p. 168 above.
[50] See e.g. *Seager* v *Copydex* [1967] 2 All ER 415.
[51] [1991] BCC 308.
[52] The Stock Exchange's settlement system at that time, now mainly replaced by CREST.

contract shall be void or unenforceable by reason only of section 52.' It is possible that the new word 'unenforceable' has overturned this case, although this is far from clear.

Given the internationalisation of the world's securities markets during the 1980s, insider dealing has become an international problem and this is being reflected in increasing co-operation between countries.

20.5 UK REGULATION AGAINST MARKET ABUSE

A The criminal law background

Apart from some early common law offences, the first major legislation occurred in the Prevention of Fraud (Investments) Act 1939, largely re-enacted in 1958. This, broadly, made it a criminal offence to induce an investment transaction, by making a false statement either dishonestly or recklessly, or by dishonestly concealing a material fact.[53] These 'misleading statements' provisions are now contained in s. 397 of the Financial Services and Markets Act 2000 (FSMA 2000), where there are various amplifications and defences. A common example of the kind of offence which these provisions are aimed at is what the Americans refer to as 'pump and dump' such as where a person puts out false information about a company in which he holds shares, in order to boost the share price; when the share price rises he sells out.

In 1986 the regulatory armoury was augmented by legislation[54] against 'market manipulation', which is also now contained in s. 397.[55] In essence, the provisions are aimed at engaging in an act or course of conduct which creates a false or misleading impression as to the market in an investment or price or value of it. The example often given of this is what the Americans refer to as a 'boiler house' operation, in which fraudsters buy and sell shares to each other, thus misleading investors into thinking that there is a lively market in the shares. The FSA currently has power to prosecute for all these offences, as well as offences under the Money Laundering Regulations. Criminal provisions relating to insider dealing have been dealt with above.

B Civil penalties for market abuse

Experience has shown that it has been difficult to bring successful prosecutions under the criminal legislation and perhaps having cast a few longing glances at the SEC's very effective civil enforcement remedies in respect of insider dealing, the FSA ensured that the FSMA 2000 gave it additional tools in the fight against insider dealing and other forms of market abuse. The new tools are civil penalties,[56]

---

[53] Section 13(1).
[54] Financial Services Act 1986, s. 47(2).
[55] There are detailed provisions and various defences.
[56] Often referred to as 'administrative' enforcement in some jurisdictions.

and it is probable that infringements will be readily settled by firms on the receiving end of the FSA's investigations.

The Act provides that the FSA will have power to impose a financial penalty for market abuse,[57] both where he has engaged in market abuse, or by taking or refraining from any action has required or encouraged another person to engage in behaviour which [if he had done it] would amount to market abuse. An appeal lies to the Financial Services and Markets Tribunal if the person does not accept the findings and the penalty. The power applies generally and may therefore be used against not only authorised persons, but also non-authorised persons (in other words, against anyone who happens to be trading on the market). Instead of a penalty, the FSA may issue a statement of censure. The FSA's policy as to how it intends to use these new provisions, and elaborate and detailed guidance, is set out in its Code of Market Conduct.[58]

Market abuse is defined in s. 118:[59]

(1) For the purposes of this Act, market abuse is behaviour . . .:[60]

    (a) which occurs in relation to qualifying investments traded on a market to which this section applies;

    (b) which satisfies any one or more of the conditions set out in subsection (2); and

    (c) which is likely to be regarded by a regular user of that market who is aware of the behaviour as a failure on the part of the person or persons concerned to observe the standard of behaviour reasonably expected of a person in his or their position in relation to that market.[61]

(2) The conditions[62] are that:

    (a) the behaviour is based on information which is not generally available to those using the market but which, if available to a regular user of the market, would or would be likely to be regarded by him as relevant when deciding the terms on which transactions in investments of the kind in question should be effected;

    (b) the behaviour is likely to give a regular user of the market a false or misleading impression as to the supply of, or demand for, or as to the price or value of, investments of the kind in question;

    (c) a regular user of the market would, or would be likely to, regard the behaviour as

---

[57] Financial Services and Markets Act 2000, ss. 118 (1)–(10), 123–131. In some circumstances [injunctions and restitution orders], the court may order a penalty (s. 129).

[58] Available on the FSA website, in the FSA Handbook of Rules and Guidance, MAR 1. Detailed examination of these complex provisions is outside the scope of this book.

[59] See generally *ibid.* ss. 118 (1)–(10) and 119–131.

[60] '(whether by one person alone or by two or more persons jointly or in concert)'.

[61] Here, under this 'regular user test', the standard is being set by the hypothetical regular users of the market. Thus, in 'determining whether behaviour amounts to market abuse, it is necessary to consider objectively whether a hypothetical reasonable person, familiar with the market in question, would regard the behaviour as acceptable in the light of all the relevant circumstances' (see MAR 1, section 1.2.2); there follows (*ibid.*) futher detailed elaboration of the ideas involved.

[62] It is tempting, at first sight, to see these three conditions as paraphrases of the existing three criminal offences of insider dealing, misleading statements, and market manipulation. However, on closer inspection, especially when the detailed elaborations in the Code are taken into account, it is clear that this approach is not helpful, and the conditions are perhaps best regarded as *sui generis*. The Code, in enormous detail, treats them as giving rise to a situation where market abuse is defined as one of three types of behaviour: (i) misuse of information, (ii) misleading statements and impressions, (iii) market distortion.

behaviour which would, or would be likely to, distort the market in investments of the kind in question.

By way of defences, it is provided that the FSA may not impose a penalty if there are 'reasonable grounds for it to be satisfied that (a) he believed, on reasonable grounds that his behaviour did not [amount to market abuse], or (b) that he took all reasonable precautions and exercised all due diligence to avoid behaving in a way which [amounted to market abuse].' It is also clear that the Code will itself in many circumstances provide defences and safe harbours.[63]

By August 2004 there had been three market abuse cases completed under the new regime which had resulted in the imposition of civil money penalties. The first two were separate examples of the misuse of unpublished confidential information involving individuals who had traded in shares for personal profit. Both were separately fined £15,000.[64] The third case was at the other end of the size spectrum, involving the giant petroleum company Shell,[65] which had made false or misleading announcements in relation to its hydrocarbon reserves and reserves replacement ratios between 1998 and 2003. For this market abuse behaviour consisting of misleading statements and impressions,[66] the FSA levied the unprecedented fine of £17 million.[67]

20.6 THE *NEW* EC MARKET ABUSE DIRECTIVE

As part of the Financial Services Action Plan, the EC Commission has developed a new Directive in the field of insider dealing and market abuse, with a view to a more detailed harmonisation Europe-wide, of regulation in this area. The Directive on Insider Dealing and Market Manipulation (Market Abuse)[68] is a framework 'principles' directive operating at Level 1 under the Lamfalussy processes. Below that, at level 2, the comitology procedure of the CESR assisted by the ESC[69] has developed detailed legislation in certain areas covered by the Directive.[70]

The timetable for UK implementation of the changes which this will bring about is designed to produce legislative amendments by early in 2005 and at the time of writing the FSA is still consulting on draft proposals. While much of the UK regime on insider dealing and market abuse is in line with the new Directive, changes will be needed in a number of areas to upgrade our provisions. In other areas the FSA are planning to leave our more wide-ranging provisions in force, so that in some respects the UK regime will go beyond that required by the Directive. In particu-

---

[63] On the effect of the Code, see s. 122. Also relevant in the context of defences is s.118(8).

[64] FSA Market Watch; issue 10, July 2004.

[65] Shell Transport and Trading Company, Royal Dutch Petroleum Company, and the Royal Dutch/Shell Group of Companies.

[66] There were also breaches of the Listing Rules.

[67] See FSA Press Release of 24 August 2004. The FSA also perhaps felt constrained to point out that: 'Financial penalties are not treated as income by the FSA. They are applied for the benefit of authorised persons . . . as appropriate, and so given back to the industry in subsequent years.'

[68] For reference see n. 1 above.

[69] For an explanation of these acronyms and the processes which they give rise to see p. 335 above.

[70] Commission Directive 2003/124/EC, Commission Directive 2003/125/EC and Commission Regulation (EC)2273/2003, available at http://europa.eu.int/comm/internal_market/en/finances/mobil.

lar, certain defences which are at present available under our 'regular user test' are not available under the Directive and our legislation will change to reflect that. The territorial scope will change with the result that the regime may have a wider effect in some circumstances than at present reflected by UK law; also there will be a wider definition of investment instruments covered than at present. Since the Directive is only concerned with establishing a civil (administrative) regime for insider dealing and market abuse, the UK's current criminal provisions in this regard will not change.[71]

At the time of writing the plan is to implement the Directive by changes to UK legislation, in particular by producing a new s. 118 of the FSMA 2000. The current[72] draft of it is as follows:[73]

118 Market abuse
(1) For the purposes of this Act, market abuse is behaviour (whether by one person alone or by two or more persons jointly or in concert) which:
   (a) occurs in relation to qualifying investments traded or admitted to trading on prescribed market or in respect of which a request for admission to trading has been made, and
   (b) falls within any one or more of the types of behaviour set out in subsections (2) to (8).
(2) The first type of behaviour is where an insider deals, or attempts to deal, in a qualifying investment or related investment on the basis of inside information relating to the qualifying investment.
(3) The second is where an insider discloses inside information to another person otherwise than in the proper course of the exercise of his employment, profession or duties.
(4) The third is where the behaviour (not falling within subsection (2) or (3)):
   (a) is based on information which is not generally available to those using the market but which, if available to a regular user of the market, would be, or would be likely to be, regarded by him as relevant when deciding the terms on which transactions in qualifying investments or related investments should be effected, and
   (b) is likely to be regarded by a regular user of the market as a failure on the part of the person concerned to observe the standard of behaviour reasonably expected of a person in his position in relation to the market.
(5) The fourth is where the behaviour consists of effecting, or participating in effecting, transactions or orders to trade (otherwise than for legitimate reasons in conformity with accepted market practices on the relevant market) which:
   (a) give, or are likely to give a false or misleading impression as to the supply of, or demand for, or as to the price or value of, one or more qualifying investments or related investments, or
   (b) secure the price of one or more such investments at an abnormal or artificial level.
(6) The fifth is where the behaviour consists of effecting, or participating in effecting, transactions or orders to trade which employ fictitious devices or any other form of deception or contrivance.
(7) The sixth is where the behaviour consists of disseminating, or causing the dissemination of, information by any means which gives, or is likely to give, a false or mislead-

---

[71] See generally the joint FSA/Treasury consultation document of June 2004: UK Implementation of the EU Market Abuse Directive (Directive 2003/6/EC) available at http://www.fsa.gov.uk.
[72] Excerpts from annex A of the consultation document mentioned in the previous note.
[73] Certain parts and words are omitted.

ing impression as to a qualifying investment or related investment by a person who knew or could reasonably be expected to have known that the information was false or misleading.

(8) The seventh is where the behaviour (not falling within subsection (5), (6) or (7)):

    (a) gives, or is likely to give, a regular user of the market a false or misleading impression as to the supply of, demand for or price or value of, qualifying or related investments, or

    (b) would be, or would be likely to be, regarded by a regular user of the market as a failure on the part of the person concerned to observe the standard of behaviour reasonably expected of a person in his position in relation to the market.

The draft proposed legislation then goes on to set out provisions in relation to a range of related matters, such as territorial scope, safe harbours, definitions of insider and inside information.[74]

---

[74] See draft ss. 118A, 118B and 118C.

21

THE REGULATION OF TAKEOVERS

21.1 TAKEOVER BATTLES

The hostile takeover bid[1] is an extraordinary phenomenon which has a long history in the UK, and in the US,[2] and is gradually being extended to other countries.[3] In the UK it will usually take the form of a predator company making an offer to the shareholders of the target company to buy its shares at a price which is a premium to the market price.[4] The offer will remain open for period of time, during which the target shareholders will consider whether to accept the offer. Played out in the full glare of the financial press, the management of the target company is subjected to whirlwind pressure over a period of weeks. The word 'battle' has been coined and it is not an exaggeration. The management teams of the target and the bidder will spend most of that time locked in frantic conference with their investment bank and legal advisers. Both sides become tempted to 'bend the rules', for the stakes are high; the target management team who lose will be at the mercy of a successful bidder and will usually lose their jobs; with them will go reputation and large measures of self-esteem. The newspapers will carry pictures of the losers with exhaustion and the shock of defeat etched in their faces, juxtaposed to ecstatic winners drunk on adrenalin. In takeover battles the winners really do win; and the losers lose heavily.

---

[1] Currently only about 14% of UK bids would be classified as hostile; see statistics on p. 21 of The Takeover Panel 2003–04 Report, showing that during that year there were 134 takeover or merger proposals that reached the stage where formal documents were sent to shareholders and that 19 offers remained unrecommended at the end of the offer period. There are many types of agreed takeover and a full account is beyond the scope of this book. See L. Rabinowitz (ed.) *Weinberg and Blank on Takeovers and Mergers* 5th edn (London: Sweet & Maxwell, 1989, looseleaf).

[2] US takeovers have different rules for the players but some of the outcomes are similar.

[3] See generally T. Ogowewo 'The Underlying Themes of Tender Offer Regulation in the United Kingdom and the United States of America' [1996] JBL 463; G. Barboutis 'Takeover Defence Tactics Part I: The General Legal Framework on Takeovers' (1999) 20 Co Law 14; and Part II: (1999) 20 Co Law 40.

[4] There is another form of hostile takeover where the predator does not attempt to gain more than a small percentage of shares in the target, but as an insurgent within the company wages a campaign designed to 'win the hearts and minds' of the target shareholders so that they then vote in a new management team who are nominees of the predator. Called a 'proxy battle' because it involves getting the target shareholders to complete their proxy forms in favour of the insurgents this form is more common in the US although it is by no means unknown in the UK. Although it is relatively cheap, it has the obvious disadvantage that without voting control the influence obtained could be transitory if the company is either subjected to a full bid or the voters change their minds again.

21.2 DISCIPLINING MANAGEMENT – THE MARKET FOR CORPORATE CONTROL

The appearance and rapid growth of the phenomenon of the hostile takeover in the US and UK in the 1960s quickly led to the beginning of systematic regulation in both of the systems. In the US, in 1968, it was public regulation, primarily federal legislation, in the form of the Williams Act 1969.[5] In the UK, in 1968, it was self-regulation in the form of the City Code on Takeovers and Mergers promulgated and administered by the Takeover Panel. The hostile takeover phenomenon and the appearance of regulation were the catalysts for a long-lasting academic and political debate. Economists engaged themselves in precise monitoring of the effects of takeovers on share prices; the effects of the bid, the effects of defences and subsequent developments.[6] The desirability of takeovers was put under scrutiny. To some extent, it can be said that they have survived the scrutiny process in that regulatory authorities have not decided to ban them totally. Given the amount of positive evidence which has emerged about their economic effects and their role, this is not surprising.[7]

Three main functions or economic benefits of takeovers can be identified. First, the possibility of hostile takeovers is often seen as a way of disciplining corporate managers to use the assets of the company in an efficient (and therefore socially optimal) way.[8] The second function of takeovers, which is broader, in the sense that it is not mainly related to hostile takeovers but will relate to the whole range of agreed takeovers and mergers, is that the bidder will often make gains from the resulting business combination.[9] Thirdly, there exists considerable empirical evidence about the positive effect of takeovers on shareholders' wealth, particularly the target shareholders.[10]

21.3 GOALS OF TAKEOVER REGULATION

A The struggle for a Europe-wide regulatory policy

It is obviously necessary to consider why we regulate takeovers and what the goals of that regulation are. Apart from US law, UK experience and ideas on the fundamentals of takeover regulation have the oldest pedigree in the world, and many of our ideas are to be found in the new European (partial) consensus[11] on regulatory

---

[5] Amending ss. 13 and 14 of the Securities Exchange Act 1934. US public regulation of takeovers has been further enhanced by state takeover statutes and a substantial case law on directors' duties.

[6] See e.g. p. 54, n. 53 above.

[7] See generally: H. Manne 'Mergers and the Market for Corporate Control' (1965) 73 *Journal of Political Economy* 110; M. Jensen and R. Ruback 'The Market for Corporate Control' (1983) 11 *Journal of Financial Economics* 5.

[8] See M. Mandelbaum 'Economic Aspects of Takeover Regulation with Particular Reference to New Zealand' in J. Farrar (ed.) *Takeovers, Institutional Investors and the Modernization of Corporate Laws* (Auckland: OUP, 1993) pp. 203, 206.

[9] *Ibid.* at p. 207.

[10] See the summary in F. Easterbrook and D. Fishel *The Economic Structure of Corporate Law* (Cambridge, MA: Harvard University Press, 1991) p. 171.

[11] A broad consensus, with some divergences, as will be seen.

techniques and goals in this field. The story of Europe's Takeover Directive[12] is an amazing 15-year saga which eventually seemed to catch the imagination of Member State governments all over the Union; it was as if the mere idea of exciting takeover battles had spilled over into the discussion about the regulation of them, so that, the regulatory scene itself became a battleground.

The first draft proposal[13] on what was then referred to as the 13th Directive on Takeovers had been put forward in 1989. It was amended in 1990 but there was no agreement between the Member States on the first proposal and negotiations were suspended in 1991. In was then realised that detailed harmonisation was not going to be the way forward here, and an amended proposal, a streamlined 'framework' Directive, was presented by the Commission in 1996.[14] However, this too met opposition. An amended proposal was put forward in 1997 which made better progress and on 21 June 1999 the EU's Council of Internal Market Ministers reached political agreement on this amended proposal, subject only to settling a dispute with Spain concerning Gibraltar! Although the proposal was subsequently redrafted and renumbered to some extent, it remained unchanged in substance and the Common Position on this proposed Directive was eventually reached on 19 June 2000. Subsequently, the European Parliament proposed amendments which the Council did not approve of and eventually an agreement was reached within the Conciliation Committee on 6 June 2001. On 4 July the European Parliament rejected the compromise text in unusual circumstances; a historic tied vote of 373 each side. Undaunted, the Commission decided to construct a new proposal for a Directive, aimed at meeting the concerns of the European Parliament but without departing unnecessarily from the basic principles approved unanimously in the Council's common position of 19 June 2000. The Commission established the High Level Group of Experts in Company Law under the chairmanship of the Dutch lawyer, Professor Jaap Winter, asking them to find a way of resolving the matters which had been causing concern to the European Parliament.

The 'Winter Report'[15] was published on 10 January 2002. The Report argued that there were two distinct stages of a bid: The first stage commences when the bid is announced and the second is the stage commencing after the successful completion of the bid. The Report focused[16] on the desirability of implementing two main principles in both stages of the bid: (i) that in the event of a takeover bid, the ultimate decision must be with the shareholders; (ii) that there should be proportionality between risk-bearing and control, so that only risk-bearing capital should carry control rights, in proportion to the risk carried.

With respect to the first stage of a bid, the Directive would require the board of the offeree to be 'neutral'[17] after the bid has been announced (a revolutionary proposal in some European countries). As regards the second stage, a bidder who

---

[12] Directive on Takeover Bids, 2004/25/EC, OJ 2004, L 142/12.
[13] COM (88) 823 final – SYN 186; 16 February 1989.
[14] COM (95) 655 final; 95/0341 (COD) 7 February 1996.
[15] Report of the High Level Group of Company Law Experts on Issues Related to Takeover Bids: http://europa.eu.int/comm/internal_market/en/company/company/official/index.htm.
[16] It also dealt with other matters which had become contentious.
[17] Sometimes referred to as 'board passivity' in European circles.

acquires 75% should be allowed to 'breakthrough' mechanisms and structures in the constitution of the company which would otherwise frustrate the bid by denying control (another revolutionary proposal). Neither of these ideas can have been popular among industrialists in some of the Nordic countries, particularly Germany and the Netherlands, where elaborate devices are often in place to protect incumbent management from a hostile bidder. On a wide spectrum of human ingenuity, these range from the simple concept of shares with voting uplift, to the esoteric legally robotic devices of the Netherlands whereby a kind of guardian foundation offshore will automatically react to defend a target against the bid, by for instance, issuing a steady trickle of shares to supporters of the management.

On 2 October 2002 the Commission published its renewed proposal for a Directive[18] stating that it had taken 'broad account' of the recommendations in the Winter Report but making it clear that they were not taking up all the recommendations. The Commission's October proposal had a rough ride thereafter and underwent many amendments. By 28 April 2003 the proposal had acquired the title 'the Revised Presidency Compromise Proposal'.[19] Throughout the summer of 2003 the fortunes of the proposal waxed and waned in various committees and meetings, sustained by what became known as the 'Portuguese option' whereby versions of the controversial breakthrough rights where made optional for Member States, in effect creating a two-track regulatory policy for Europe. In November 2003 agreement was finally reached and the Directive formally and finally adopted on 21 April 2004, coming into force at the end of that month. Article 21 of the Directive makes it clear that Member States have until 20 May 2006 to bring the Directive into force in their own lands.

B The ideas in the new Directive

An examination of the stated objectives of the Directive can be a useful summary of the aims which a regime of takeover regulation might usefully seek to achieve. The 1st and 3rd Recitals to the Preamble to the Directive contain the policy of EC-wide co-ordination of regulation. The 2nd Recital refers to the need to 'protect the interests of holders of securities of companies ... when those companies are the subject of takeover bids or of changes of control and at least some of their securities are admitted to trading on a regulated market', making explicit the main thrust of the takeover policy, which is to protect target shareholders. There is also perhaps a hint of protecting the reputation of the capital markets.[20] Recital 9 contains the policy for the mandatory offer: 'Whereas Member States should take the necessary steps in order to protect holders of securities having minority holdings after the purchase of the control of their company ...' Recital 5 contains the idea that Member States must have a supervisory authority. Recitals 13, 14, 16 contain extra provisions with regard to proper information in offer documents, time limits for the bid, and prohibition of frustrating action.[21]

---

[18] Proposal for a Directive on Takeover Bids (COM) (2002) 534 final.
[19] Interinstitutional File 2002/0240 (COD).
[20] The 12th Recital, aiming to 'reduce the scope for insider dealing ...' contains a more overt protection of capital markets provision.
[21] Overall, it has to be said that the Preamble is curiously thin on economic rationale, unlike most of the

Thus the outlines[22] of the basic model of a regulatory system emerge: takeovers in the EU are to be subject to regulation by a supervisory authority, subject to timetables, transparency requirements and sharing of the control premium. This last point needs some explanation.[23] The control premium arises because in an unregulated system, a purchaser seeking to acquire control of a target will normally need to acquire around only 30% of the shares and for the last few blocks of shares which take his holding of say 25% up to 30% will be prepared to pay a price which is above the prevailing market price. This premium price is being paid because the purchaser knows that those shares are very valuable to him, because they will give him control over the company. From the regulatory standpoint the problem with this is that most of the shareholders do not get a chance to get a share of the premium that is being paid when control passes and thus some system of ensuring that they do share is needed. The UK system and that to some extent adopted in the Directive is to have a requirement that the purchaser who has acquired control must extend his offer to all the shareholders of the company. An underlying policy may also be that a company should not be able to take over a target merely by acquiring around 30% of its shares and it should be a company with sufficient means to buy the whole of the target issued share capital.

What does the new Directive say about the much debated 'breakthrough rights'? As heralded above, there is an option. Article 12 is headed 'Optional Arrangements' and provides that Member States 'may reserve the right not to require companies ... which have their registered offices within their territories to apply Article 9(2) and (3) and/or Article 11'. And in those articles we find enshrined the essence of an open market for corporate control: prohibition on frustrating action by the board in circumstances of a bid (art. 9), and restrictions on arrangements designed to deny control to a successful bidder (art. 11). On this crucial policy issue the Directive thus creates a two-track regulatory environment in Europe.[24]

21.4 THE UK SYSTEM

A The Takeover Panel and self-regulation

It is well known that, the City Code on Takeovers and Mergers has no statutory or other legal authority.[25] It is promulgated, supervised in execution and administered by the Takeover Panel,[26] which comprises a select body of representatives mainly from those financial institutions primarily engaged in the business of takeovers and certain other relevant bodies. The practically binding but non-legal effect of the Code has enabled the Takeover Panel to operate with great flexibility. It is available

---

other Capital Markets Directives. There is no mention of other recognised goals of takeover regulation, such as encouraging efficient allocation of resources, encouraging competition for corporate control and monitoring management, although these must surely underlie the Directive, even if they are unstated; of course, the statement of such objectives might have been politically difficult.

[22] The Directive also deals with many other matters.

[23] The prohibition on frustrating action is examined below in connection with defences.

[24] For further commentary on this and other aspects of the Directive, see p. 400 below.

[25] The likely effects of the Directive on this position are discussed below.

[26] See generally the website of the Takeover Panel: http://www.thetakeoverpanel.org.uk.

to the parties for consultation on the applicability and meaning of the Code and, in making speedy decisions, gives effect to the spirit rather than the letter of the rules.

However, it is almost equally well known that, while the City Code has been self-regulatory in the sense that those engaged in the takeover industry are by and large the people who make an input into the content and operation of the Code, it has nevertheless not been voluntary. There have been considerable practical pressures which have made compliance with the Code essential.

Historically (until the transfer of its 'competent authority' functions to the FSA as UKLA in 2000), the Stock Exchange lent its support to the Takeover Panel, and the Takeover Code, even to the extent of suspending the listing of a company.[27]

The courts have generally expressed approval of the City Code and its administration and even though judicial review of Takeover Panel decisions is possible, it is done in such a way that it will not undermine the Takeover Panel's authority in the particular case, merely being declaratory of the position for the future. With the aim of not interfering with the outcome of the bid, the relationship of the courts with the Panel has been expressed to be 'historic rather than contemporaneous'.[28] The result of this attitude, and the fact that the rules of the Code are non-legal, is that takeover battles in the UK are largely immune from tactical litigation designed to thwart the bid, and can thus be left open for the outcome to be freely determined by market forces and the economics of the situation. The experience of the US with its public systems of legal regulation of takeovers has been that the outcome of takeovers is often in the hands of the lawyers rather than the shareholders.[29]

In 1986 a new form of support for the self-regulatory regime emerged. Under the partially self-regulatory system established by the Financial Services Act 1986, support was given to the Takeover Panel and the City Code. For instance, in the Securities and Futures Authority's conduct of business rules, there was a rule[30] in a section headed 'Market Integrity, Support of the Takeover Panel's Functions'. Breach of that rule could lead to an SFA disciplinary hearing, with possible expulsion from the SFA and consequent withdrawal of authorisation to conduct investment business. The FSA 1986 has now been replaced by the FSMA 2000 which has ushered in a new version of this kind of support for the Panel, and containing a redefining of the relationship which the statutory regulator, the FSA, has with the Panel.

The new relationship is set out in the FSA Handbook of Rules and Guidance.[31] Using its powers under FSMA 2000, s. 143, the FSA has 'endorsed' the Takeover

---

[27] See the account of the St Piran saga by G. Morse 'Attempting to Enforce a Mandatory Bid' [1980] JBL 358.

[28] *R v Panel on Takeovers and Mergers, ex parte Datafin* (1987) 3 BCC 10.

[29] See e.g. Langevoort's analysis of board duties in a takeover situation and his account of associated litigation, in 'The Law's Influence on Managers' Behaviour in Control Transactions: An American Perspective' in K. Hopt and E. Wymeersch (eds) *European Takeovers – Law and Practice* (London: Butterworths, 1992) at p. 255.

[30] Rule 48 provided: '(1) A firm must not act or continue to act for a specified person . . . in connection with a takeover . . . unless it has the consent of the Takeover Panel. (2) Subject to the provisions of the Takeover Code, a firm must (a) provide . . . such information as the Takeover Panel requests . . . and (b) otherwise render all such assistance as the firm is reasonably able to provide to enable the Takeover Panel to perform its functions.'

[31] Market Conduct, MAR 4: Endorsement of the Takeover Code.

Code.[32] The main effect of this is that at the request of the Panel, the FSA may take enforcement action against a firm[33] which contravenes the Code. It is further provided,[34] in effect, that a firm must not act for a person in a takeover if it has reason for believing that the person is not going to comply with the Code. Although the new regime under FSMA 2000 permits and facilitates the Takeover Panel to retain its regulatory functions, it is arguable that, to some extent at any rate, the Panel is to henceforth be seen as operating under the umbrella of the statutory regulator, the FSA. For the FSA rules provide that their endorsement has effect in relation to the Code because the FSA has notified the Panel 'that it is satisfied with the Takeover Panel's consultation procedures, and not withdrawn that notification, in accordance with section 143(6) of the Act'.[35] Furthermore, the FSA have carefully stated that in some circumstances they even envisage taking action without the request of the Panel, although there would no doubt be careful consultation before they did so.[36]

B The operation of the City Code

The City Code on Takeovers and Mergers applies to offers for all public companies (listed or unlisted) resident in the UK.[37] It also applies to offers for certain resident private companies which have in some way been involved in public markets, but only where certain requirements are also satisfied.[38] It is made clear that 'offer' in this context includes partial offers, offers by a parent for shares in its subsidiary and certain other transactions where control of a company is to be obtained or consolidated.

The City Code comprises 10 general principles and 38 detailed rules with notes, together with an introduction, definitions and appendices. The overall aim is to ensure that all shareholders are treated fairly and equally in relation to takeovers. Part of the mechanism for doing this lies in the orderly framework and timetable which the Code lays down, designed to prevent shareholders from being panicked into accepting an offer without time to consult with their financial advisers. Great emphasis is laid on equality and high standards of information, both in offer documents and in advertisements and announcements.

---

[32] MAR 4.2. Also the SARs are endorsed. For an explanation of these see p. 397 below.

[33] Firms as described in MAR 4.2.1 and also against approved persons.

[34] MAR 4.3.

[35] MAR 4.2.2.

[36] See the FSA Handbook of Rules and Guidance: Enforcement, ENF 14.10.4: 'The FSA is only able to take enforcement action under section 143 of the Act in respect of a breach of the Takeover Code ... at the request of the Takeover Panel. However, if the behaviour in question, leaving aside any breach of the Takeover Code ..., could also constitute a breach of the rules [i.e. FSA Handbook], or in relation to an approved person, a Statement of Principle, the FSA may use its enforcement powers whether a request has been received from the Takeover Panel or not. It that situation, however, the FSA will consult the Takeover Panel and give due weight to its views.'

[37] And in some cases outside the UK, 'residence' to be determined by the Takeover Panel; see City Code, Introduction, para. 4.

[38] See generally City Code, Introduction, para. 4 (a). Offers for private companies falling outside the definitions there are not wholly unregulated and in some circumstances an offer document may fall within the financial promotion regime; see p. 342 above.

One of the striking features of the City Code is the acceptance condition, which is contained in rule 10. Rule 10 regulates what the Code refers to as the 'voluntary offer', that is to say, the normal case,[39] such as where a company wishes to make a full takeover bid for the target company and has gone ahead and done so. Rule 10 imposes an acceptance condition. It provides that it must be a condition of an offer[40] which 'if accepted in full, would result in the offeror holding shares carrying over 50% of the voting rights of the offeree company[41] that the offer will not become or be declared unconditional as to acceptances, unless the offeror has acquired or agreed to acquire[42] ... shares carrying over 50% of the voting rights ...'. What this means, in effect, is that the offeror not only has a get-out if the bid has failed to win him *de jure* control[43] of the company, but also that there is a require-ment that he give up and admit defeat. This is only clear in the light of some fur-ther explanation. The basic mechanism of the voluntary bid is that the offeror will make an offer to the shareholders of the target. Under the terms of the City Code, the offer must remain open for at least 21 days.[44] During that period the target shareholders will send in their indications to the offeror's receiving agents as to whether they wish to accept or not. The offeror makes the contract binding once he announces that the offer is 'unconditional as to acceptances', meaning that his acceptance of the tenders is no longer subject to any condition.[45] By this rule 10 mechanism, the City Code seeks to ensure both that the offeror is not stuck with a bid which has failed, in the sense that it has left him with 45%, and also that he is not permitted to try to run the company from that position.

Perhaps the other most important feature of the City Code, and certainly the one for which it is most famous internationally, is the mandatory bid requirement. The policy which lies behind this has already been explained.[46] A mandatory offer will be required in two situations:[47] (1) where any person acquires[48] shares which[49] carry 30% or more of the voting rights of a company; (2) where any person[50] hold-ing not less than 30% but not more than 50% of the voting rights acquires[51] additional shares which increase his percentage of the voting rights.[52] The details of the mandatory offer are set out in rule 9. In essence, an offer must be made to the

[39] The term voluntary offer is used to distinguish the 'mandatory offer' which is discussed below. Although an actual mandatory offer is a rare event, this fact should not be allowed to obscure the importance of the existence of the provisions which require the mandatory offer in certain circum-stances.
[40] For voting equity share capital. The Takeover Panel may waive the rule in certain circumstances.
[41] I.e. it is not a bid for a small block of shares.
[42] Either pursuant to the offer or otherwise.
[43] I.e. more than 50% of the votes.
[44] Rule 31.1.
[45] I.e. as to his getting 50.1% of the votes. Although if the 90% acceptance condition is satisfied, the offeror is not required to make a declaration.
[46] See p. 393 above.
[47] City Code, rule 9.1.
[48] Whether by a series of transactions over a period of time or not.
[49] Taken together with shares held or acquired by persons acting in concert with him; for a discussion of 'acting in concert', see rule 9.1, note.
[50] Together with persons acting in concert with him.
[51] Such acquisition may be by the person or any person acting in concert with him.
[52] This is for the July 2000 version of the Code, and subsequent versions. Earlier versions permitted a 'creeping' increase in the holding.

shareholders,[53] and it must be in cash[54] at not less than the highest price paid by the offeror[55] for shares of that class during the offer period and within 12 months prior to its commencement.[56]

C Other provisions applying to takeovers

Also promulgated by the Takeover Panel are the Substantial Acquisitions Rules, which apply (with exemptions) to shares of UK (etc) resident companies listed on the Stock Exchange or dealt in on the Unlisted Securities Market. They are designed to restrict the speed with which a person may increase his holding of shares and rights over shares to a total of between 15% and 30% of the voting rights of a company.[57] The aim being to reduce the effectiveness of the 'dawn raid' and to ensure a more fair market. Additionally, rule 4 of the Substantial Acquisitions Rules contains detailed provisions relating to tender offers, designed to protect the shareholders.

In addition to the above, companies subject to the UKLA Listing Rules will need to comply with its detailed provisions regarding takeovers.[58] Under the Competition Act 1998 a merger is liable to be referred to the Competition Commission if certain conditions are satisfied, and it will then be for the Commission to decide whether the merger operates against the public interest. Certain large mergers above the prescribed financial thresholds and having a 'Community Dimension' are required to be notified to the European Commission which will have exclusive jurisdiction and which may then eventually prohibit such mergers.[59] Rule 12 of the City Code recognises the significance to certain takeovers of these reference and notification requirements since it provides that it must be a term of an offer that it will lapse if there is a reference to the Competition Commission or if the European Commission initiates proceedings (or takes certain other actions).

Various legislative provisions may have significance for certain takeovers, not necessarily applying only to takeovers which fall under the scope of the City Code. Most of these have been considered in detail elsewhere and are merely listed here. Sections 131–134 of the Companies Act 1985 provide exemption from share premium account in certain takeover situations.[60] Sections 151–158 of the Companies Act 1985 prohibit financial assistance for the acquisition of shares, which may sometimes have relevance in the takeover context. Sections 198–220 of the 1985 Act relate to disclosure of interests in shares.[61] Sections 312–316 of the Companies

---

[53] Various classes: equity shares voting or non-voting, and voting non-equity shares; see City Code, rule 9.1.
[54] Or accompanied by a cash alternative; see rule 9.5.
[55] Or any person acting in concert with it.
[56] There are various other conditions, including a rule about the circumstances in which the offer must become unconditional as to acceptances; see City Code, rule 9.3.
[57] Substantial Acquisitions Rules, Introduction, para. 2.
[58] In particular, Chap. 10.
[59] Regulation (EEC) 4064/89.
[60] See further p. 280 above.
[61] See p. 273 above.

Act 1985 will apply to payments made to directors in some takeover situations.[62] Insider dealing legislation will often be relevant. If the offeror company is allotting shares as part of the takeover, this will of itself activate various legal considerations; e.g. s. 103 (5) of the Companies Act 1985. Finally, reference should be made here, to the complex provisions in ss. 428–430F of the Companies Act 1985, under which in some circumstances an offeror who acquires 90% of shares may compulsorily buy out or be required to buy out the remaining 10%.

Although litigation is rare in the context of UK takeovers, the courts have occasionally become involved in making pronouncements about various aspects of takeover regulation and so a small body of law has grown up. Some aspects of this have already been mentioned; e.g. judicial review of the decisions of the Takeover Panel. However, many aspects of company law could sometimes have been relevant in takeover situations. In particular, the courts have had to consider the duties owed by directors of the target company in the context of, for instance, conflicting or competing bids.[63]

D Defences

Takeover defences in the UK are heavily circumscribed by what seems to be a prevailing attitude among City institutions and business that hostile bids are beneficial and even if not actually encouraged, they should not be stifled. Some of the economic arguments on this topic have already been alluded to.[64] The salient fact is that the bid will be at a price which is higher than the current market price for the shares and the feeling is that the shareholders should not be deprived of an opportunity of taking up the offer.

Prior to the bid being made, boards of directors no doubt consider various possibilities for putting themselves into the best possible position (1) to discourage a predator from mounting a bid and (2) to win the takeover battle if it starts. Whatever they choose to do will obviously have to comply with their basic fiduciary duty to act in good faith in the interests of the company.[65] This has usually been thought to rule out devices like 'poison pills' which have been a recurrent feature of US takeover battles. A poison pill is an arrangement which becomes financially damaging once a company is taken over. The predator who has taken over the company will thereby have swallowed the pill. As an anti-takeover device it is obviously necessary for the predator to be aware of the pill's existence prior to making a bid so that he decides not to go ahead. A typical poison pill would be a warrant issued to target shareholders which gives them rights to subscribe for further shares in the target at half the prevailing market price if any predator company gets a controlling stake in the target. Over the years, one of the most frequently used defences

---

[62] See p. 179 above.

[63] See *Heron International Ltd* v *Lord Grade* [1983] BCLC 244; *Re a Company 008699/85* (1986) 2 BCC 99,024; *Dawson plc* v *Coats Patons* (1988) 4 BCC 305 and generally *Gething* v *Kilner* [1972] 1 All ER 1166.

[64] See p. 390 above.

[65] For a fascinating (and rare) example of UK litigation on the legality of poison pills, see *Criterion Properties plc* v *Stratford UK Properties LLC* [2002] 2 BCLC 151, [2003] BCC 50, CA, [2004] BCC 570, HL.

has been for the target to seek a merger reference which has the effect of stopping the bid for 12 months. Although this is primarily a post-bid defence, the preparation for it, possibly involving restructuring[66] so as to make it difficult for a particular likely predator to avoid a merger reference, is a pre-bid defence mechanism.

It is the orthodox view that the most effective method of preventing a bid is a well-run company with a high share price. The economics of this make it relatively difficult for the bidder to come up with a higher offer price, or to want to. The corollary of this is the painful fact that if the share price is low and the company appears not to be well run, then there may well not be a great deal which can be done.

After the bid has been made, the position of the target board is governed by General Principle 7 and rule 21 of the City Code, which prevent activities that can generally be described as frustrating action. Additionally, in general it can be said that the timetable under the City Code leaves very little time to mount much by way of defence unless preparations have been made beforehand. Often the most that a target board can do at this stage is to issue reports and interim accounts showing how things are going to improve in the near future. But the tone and quality of such documents is controlled by the City Code.[67] And usually the fact will remain that, faced with an offer at a significant premium to the current share price, the target board faces an unbridgeable credibility gap; the predator has effectively said to target shareholders that the target management is no good and that the company's share price is depressed as a result, and has backed its statement with its offer.

21.5 UK IMPLEMENTATION OF THE DIRECTIVE

Member States are supposed to implement the Directive by 20 May 2006. Many aspects of the Directive are not particularly challenging to the UK, for to a large extent the concepts in it, such as timetables, transparency, supervision, mandatory bid, absence of frustrating action and control passing to a successful bidder, are all matters which our system, one way or another, has embodied in it already. On the other hand, it is possible that the detail of many of these matters will change, and implementation will need some careful thought in the UK. The Takeover Panel has expressed the view that primary legislation will be needed for implementation and has started discussions with the DTI on various matters of concern. It appears that opting in to art. 9 (board passivity) is seen in the UK as largely unproblematic since it is similar in effect to General Principle 7 and rule 21.1 of our existing Code, while opting in to art. 11 (breakthrough) may lead to wide-ranging effects which will need consideration.[68] The other matter which will probably continue to give concern in the UK is the status of our self-regulatory system: (i) will a self-regulatory system be sufficient to implement the Directive?; and (ii) will the implementation of the Directive in some way change the status of the rules and principles of the Takeover Code so as to give rise to US-style litigation in the UK? Both these matters have been on the minds of our various negotiators in Brussels ever since 1989 and

---

[66] I.e. if a particular predator is identified, target could take on a subsidiary business which would put the predator in danger of a reference, were it to mount a bid.

[67] Rule 19.

[68] See the Takeover Panel Report 2003–04, pp. 14–15.

various solutions have been built into the proposals over the years to accommodate us,[69] and versions of these are now in the Directive.[70] How these will work out in the light of any legislation here remains to be seen.

21.6 THE FUTURE IN EUROPE UNDER THE DIRECTIVE

It is interesting to consider what the future under the Directive on Takeovers might hold for Europe. As has been seen, it is largely modelled on the UK's market for corporate control which, unusually for Europe, is open and competitive. Companies, even very large ones, are open to the discipline of takeover bid. Already in recent years we have seen the opening up of the German takeover market. The hostile takeover of the German company Mannesmann by the UK's Vodafone, apart from being an epic battle, was a watershed for the German corporate world. Until then, the Germans referred to their industrial set-up as 'Deutschland AG'[71] indicating that it was organised in such a way as to be impervious to hostile takeovers. The main features of this were: (1) the fact that the German banks hold large stakes in major companies and are traditionally not willing to sell to hostile bidders; (2) the secrecy of the share registers; and (3) that shares are often in the form of warrants held by the banks who will vote the shares in favour of the status quo unless instructed otherwise. The Mannesmann takeover revealed that the German banks were prepared to sell out to the higher offer mounted by Vodafone.

It is arguable that the art. 12 option, creating as it does a two-track regulatory environment for takeovers has made the Directive pointless. This can be overstated as there are many other less controversial features of the Directive which will help to bring about a level playing field for takeovers in Europe. In the course of time it may even be seen that the art. 12 option has the effect of drawing attention to the international capital markets that the management of companies in certain countries are not willing to submit themselves to the market discipline inherent in the open takeover regime. Economic theory would then have it that because their corporate governance mechanisms are softer on them, they will find it harder (i.e. more expensive) to raise capital, and thus be 'punished in the market'. In the long run, the Directive will probably be seen as having made it harder for countries to resist an open market for corporate control.

Lastly, it is clear that there are many features of the Directive which will need clarification and definition. But it is a Lamfalussy Directive[72] and the necessary ideas can be brought forward by the Commission under the comitology procedures, developed by the Member States through the CESR and the ESC. The Takeover Directive has a long history of painstaking negotiation behind it, and in a Union which has many different corporate cultures and economic structures, it may well now be a decade before it can be seen to bear true fruit.

---

[69] And the Swedes, who also have a self-regulatory system.

[70] For example: Recital 7 'Self-regulatory bodies should be able to exercise supervision' and art. 4.1; Recital 8 '... Member States should be left to determine whether rights are to be made available which may be asserted ... in proceedings between parties to a bid' and art. 4.6.

[71] Deutschland Aktien Gesellschaft (i.e. Deutschland Corporation).

[72] Article 18.

PART VI

INSOLVENCY
AND LIQUIDATION

22

INSOLVENCY AND LIQUIDATION PROCEDURES

22.1 THE DEVELOPMENT OF CORPORATE INSOLVENCY LAW

The decision taken by Parliament in 1844 in enacting the Joint Stock Companies Act to permit the creation of companies by registration with the Registrar of Companies also led to the systematic development of a regime for the winding up of companies. The same year saw the passing of an Act for 'Winding up the Affairs of Joint Stock Companies unable to meet their Pecuniary Engagements' and in the years leading up to the passing of the Companies Act 1862 there were various enactments relating to the development of corporate insolvency law.[1] The Companies Act 1862 provided that a company could be wound up voluntarily where the members had resolved that it could not by reason of its liabilities continue its business and that it was advisable to wind up, and made provision for the appointment of a liquidator by the members.[2] The Act also provided that a company might be wound up by the court in certain circumstances, such as where the company was unable to pay its debts, and made provision for the appointment of an official liquidator to administer the proceedings. The Companies (Winding-up) Act 1890 provided *inter alia* that in the case of a winding up by the court, the Official Receiver automatically became the provisional liquidator and that he was responsible for investigating the affairs of the company and acting as liquidator with responsibility for getting in the assets and distributing the proceeds.[3] The Companies Act 1929 introduced a distinction between two types of voluntary liquidation so that if the company was expected to be unable to pay its debts in full, then there would be a creditors' voluntary winding up (rather than a members' voluntary winding up) in which the creditors would be in control of matters such as the appointment of the liquidator.[4] One of the other major innovations in the 1929 Act were the provisions against fraudulent trading. Subsequently, the Companies Acts 1947 and 1948 and the Insolvency Act 1976 introduced further reforms.

In 1977 a committee was appointed by the Secretary of State for Trade under the

---

[1] See generally *Insolvency Law and Practice. Report of the Review Committee* (London: HMSO, Cmnd. 8558, 1982) paras 74–99.
[2] Such a voluntary winding up might later be made subject to the supervision of the court if the court so ordered.
[3] Cmnd. 8558, 1982, para. 79.
[4] *Ibid.* paras 76, 89.

chairmanship of Mr Kenneth Cork[5] to carry out a fundamental and exhaustive reappraisal of all aspects of the insolvency laws of England and Wales. The Report was presented to Parliament in 1982 and recommended wide-ranging reforms.[6] As a consequence, the DTI set out its policy in the White Paper, *A Revised Framework for Insolvency Law*.[7] Its fundamental objectives were stated to be to encourage, and to assist and ensure the proper regulation of trade, industry and commerce and to promote a climate conducive to growth and the national production of wealth.[8]

In pursuing those objectives, the principal role of the insolvency legislation was said to be to establish effective and straightforward procedures for dealing with and settling the affairs of corporate (and personal) insolvents in the interests of their creditors; to provide a statutory framework to encourage companies to pay careful attention to their financial circumstances so as to recognise difficulties at an early stage and before the interests of creditors were seriously prejudiced; to deter and penalise irresponsible behaviour and malpractice on the part of those who manage a company's affairs; to ensure that those who act in cases of insolvency are competent to do so and conduct themselves in a proper manner; to facilitate the reorganisation of companies in difficulties to minimise unnecessary loss to creditors and to the economy when insolvency occurs.[9]

It was stressed that the main task in furthering the DTI's objectives was to ensure that action is taken at an early stage in insolvencies under the control of the court to protect the assets of the insolvent, in the interests of creditors, and to investigate the affairs of insolvents where it appears that the cause of the liquidation or bankruptcy has been malpractice rather than misfortune, so that undesirable commercial or individual conduct is sufficiently deterred.[10] In 1985, legislation now in the form of the Insolvency Act 1986[11] produced the most thoroughgoing reforms in insolvency law for over 100 years.[12]

---

[5] Later Sir Kenneth Cork.

[6] See n. 1 above.

[7] Cmnd. 9175, 1984.

[8] *Ibid.* para. 2.

[9] *Ibid.* It is beyond the scope of the short account in this chapter to consider the theoretical debates which have taken place as to the proper role of insolvency law. For an excellent summary and critique of the leading theories see: R. Goode *Corporate Insolvency Law* 2nd edn (London: Sweet & Maxwell, 1997) pp. 35–52. See further J. Bhandari and L. Weiss (eds) *Corporate Bankruptcy* (Cambridge: CUP, 1996).

[10] Cmnd. 9175, 1984.

[11] And its accompanying Insolvency Rules 1986 (SI 1986 No. 1925), which have since been amended to make them compatible with the Civil Procedure Rules 1998; generally, the effect of the amendments is that the Civil Procedure Rules do not apply to insolvency proceedings, although they will apply to the extent that they are not inconsistent with them. There have also been many other subsequent amendments to the 1986 rules.

[12] Subsequently amendments to various areas have been made by the Insolvency Act 2000, and by the Enterprise Act 2002. The EC Regulation on Insolvency Proceedings EC 1346/2000 came into force in May 2002 and is designed to regulate cross-border insolvency proceedings.

22.2 PRE-INSOLVENCY REMEDIES

A Corporate rescue

One of the main aims of the reforms of 1985 was to make it easier for companies in financial difficulties to rescue themselves or be rescued, so as to prevent if possible, the onset of insolvency. To this end, two new procedures were introduced, both of which have been in frequent use. The company voluntary arrangement (CVA) mechanism was introduced to make it easier for companies to enter into arrangements with their creditors without, for instance, having to go through the more formal mechanisms contained in s. 425 of the Companies Act 1985.[13] The CVA is discussed below.[14] The other major innovation was the administration order which was designed to vest the powers of management of the company in an 'administrator' (usually an insolvency expert from one of the leading firms of accountants or insolvency specialists). It is then hoped that the administrator will have the necessary expertise and detachment which will enable him to make the tough decisions necessary to restructure and revive the company, or at least save some part of it. The administration regime has recently been completely overhauled by the Enterprise Act 2002.[15]

B Administration

The purpose of administration is apparent from the statutory duty which is cast[16] upon the administrator who

> ... must perform his functions with the objective of:
>
> (a) rescuing the company as a going concern, or
> (b) achieving a better result for the company's creditors as a whole than would be likely if the company were wound up...,[17] or
> (c) realising the property in order to make a distribution to one or more secure or preferential creditors.

The legislation then makes further prescription about the duties of the administrator.[18]

A person may be appointed as administrator by order of the court,[19] by the holder of a floating charge,[20] or by the company or its directors.[21] The circumstances and conditions vary according to which of those circumstances of appointment is being adopted. The onset of administration has many legal effects

---

[13] See further, p. 106 above.
[14] At p. 406.
[15] This account is written on the assumption that the Enterprise Act 2002 is actually in force.
[16] By s. 8 of and para. 3(1) of Sch. B1 to the Insolvency Act 1986, as substituted by the Enterprise Act 2002, s. 248.
[17] '... (Without first being in administration).
[18] *Ibid.* paras. 3–4, 67–69 of sch. B1. An administrator must be a qualified insolvency practitioner, and there are other restrictions; see paras. 6–9.
[19] Paragraph 10.
[20] Paragraph 14.
[21] Paragraph 22.

designed to give the administrator a chance to carry out his objectives, so for instance, there is a moratorium on insolvency proceedings and other legal process.[22] The administrator has a broad range of powers, for it is provided that he may 'do anything necessary or expedient for the management of the affairs, business, and property of the company', although without prejudice to the generality of this, some are specified, such as removing and appointing directors.[23] The process of administration is set out in the legislation and, broadly, involves the administrator making a proposal about what he intends to do, and obtaining the approval of the creditors.[24]

C Administrative receivers

Prior to the Enterprise Act 2002 a situation similar to administration could often come about as a result of the appointment of a receiver. If a company created a floating charge to secure a debenture, the terms of the debenture would almost always give the debentureholder power to appoint a receiver. Such a receiver would usually have been a receiver and manager so that he could not only take possession of the company's assets with a view to speedily realising them for the benefit of the debentureholders but also manage the business of the company and keep it going while the assets are being realised. A receiver under a floating charge would usually have been deemed to be an 'administrative receiver' within the terms of the Insolvency Act 1986,[25] with the result that, in addition to any powers set out in the debenture or trust deed, he would have had wide powers of management of the company. However, it had been found that this in practice meant that any administration procedure (discussed in the previous section) needed the concurrence of the institutional lenders, the banks, for their loans, almost invariably secured by floating charges, and would have entitled them to block the appointment of an administrator by appointing an administrative receiver.[26] The Enterprise Act 2002 deals with this by removing the right of a floating charge holder to appoint an administrative receiver,[27] so that only in rare and exceptional cases will appointment of an administrative receiver be possible. [28]

D Company voluntary arrangement or other reconstruction

Sections 1–7 of the Insolvency Act 1986[29] contain provisions designed to produce a method by which the company can reach a legally binding agreement with its creditors without the need to use the fairly cumbersome and elaborate mechanism

---

[22] Paragraphs 40–45.
[23] Paragraphs 59–66.
[24] Paragraphs 46–58.
[25] See s. 29 (2).
[26] Under the former ss. 9–10 of the Insolvency Act 1986.
[27] Enterprise Act 2002, s. 250, inserting new ss. 72A–H into the Insolvency Act 1986.
[28] Instead, as mentioned in the previous section, the floating charge holder may in some circumstances appoint or secure the appointment of an administrator; see Insolvency Act 1986, s. 8 and Sch. B1, paras. 14–21, 35–39.
[29] As augmented by Pt I of the Insolvency Rules 1986 (SI 1986 No. 1925) as amended.

of s. 425 of the Companies Act 1985.[30] In practice the CVA is used only in situations involving smaller companies, because it binds only those creditors who 'in accordance with the rules had notice of' the meeting (s. 5 (2) (b)). In a large company with many creditors, one may be overlooked, and he or she will then be in a position to upset the arrangement by, for instance, putting the company into liquidation. In such situations it will sometimes be preferable to proceed by a scheme of arrangement under s. 425 because that will bind all creditors whether they had notice or not, provided that the scheme has been duly advertised in accordance with the directions of the court.

Broadly, the CVA mechanism is that the directors[31] make a 'proposal' to the company and its creditors for a 'voluntary arrangement'.[32] The term 'voluntary arrangement' means a composition in satisfaction of its debts or a scheme of arrangement of its affairs.[33] A 'proposal' is defined as one which provides for some person, who is called the nominee, to act in relation to the voluntary arrangement either as trustee or otherwise for the purpose of supervising its implementation.[34] The procedure is that a report is submitted to the court by the nominee.[35] Assuming that the nominee thinks that the proposal should go ahead, the report will state that meetings of the company and of creditors should be summoned to consider the proposal. The approval of the meeting binds everybody who was entitled to vote at it.[36]

Protection for minorities is covered by provisions that the court may direct that the meetings shall be summoned,[37] and that the result of the meetings is reported to the court.[38] Also, aggrieved parties can apply to the court in certain circumstances on the ground that the voluntary arrangement approved at the meetings unfairly prejudices the interests of a creditor, member or contributory and/or that there has been some material irregularity at or in relation to either of the meetings.[39]

The CVA procedure had been seen to have defects mainly because there was no provision for a moratorium on enforcement by creditors pending the adoption of the CVA so that unless the company was already in liquidation or administration, the proposal could have been upset by one or more of the creditors.[40] Proposals for change were duly made[41] and the Insolvency Act 2000 provides a mechanism for a moratorium.[42]

---

[30] For this and other methods of reconstruction see the discussion at p. 106 above.

[31] When the company is in liquidation or subject to an administration order, then the directors are not empowered to make a proposal, and the liquidator or administrator may make the proposal instead of the directors and the procedures differ slightly; Insolvency Act 1986, s. 1 (1). These situations are not dealt with here.

[32] *Ibid.* s. 1 (1).

[33] *Ibid.*

[34] *Ibid.* s. 1 (2); the nominee must be a person who is qualified to act as an insolvency practitioner in relation to the company.

[35] *Ibid.* s. 2.

[36] *Ibid.* ss. 3–5.

[37] *Ibid.* s. 3 (1).

[38] *Ibid.* s. 4 (6).

[39] *Ibid.* s. 6.

[40] As to the position of secured or preferential creditors, see s. 4 (3), (4).

[41] See Insolvency Service, Revised Proposals for a New Company Voluntary Arrangement Procedure, April 1995, and DTI Company Voluntary Arrangements Press Notice P/95/839, November 1995.

[42] Section 1 inserts a new s. 1A and Sch. A1 into the Insolvency Act 1986.

22.3 TYPES OF WINDING UP AND GROUNDS

A Voluntary winding up

Section 84 of the Insolvency Act 1986 sets out the circumstances in which a company[43] may be wound up voluntarily:

> A company may be wound up voluntarily:
> (a) when the period (if any) fixed for the duration of the company by the articles expires, or the event (if any) occurs, on the occurrence of which the articles provide that the company is to be dissolved, and the company in general meeting has passed a resolution requiring it to be wound up voluntarily;
> (b) if the company resolves by special resolution that it be wound up voluntarily;
> (c) if the company resolves by extraordinary resolution to the effect that it cannot by reason of its liabilities continue its business, and that it is advisable to wind up.

There are requirements for disclosure and publicity. A copy of the resolution must be sent to the Registrar of Companies and there must be an advertisement in the *Gazette*.[44]

A voluntary winding up commenced under s. 84 will be one of two types. It may be a members' voluntary winding up, or a creditors' voluntary winding up, the basic difference being that in the former type the members are in control of it, whereas the creditors are in the latter type; hence the names. In order for it to be a members' voluntary winding up, it will be necessary for the directors to make a declaration of solvency, for otherwise the winding up will automatically be a creditors' voluntary winding up.[45] The declaration of solvency is a declaration to the effect that the directors have made a full inquiry into the company's affairs and that they have formed the opinion that the company will be able to pay its debts in full (together with interest) within such period (not exceeding 12 months) from the commencement of the winding up as may be specified in the declaration.[46] The legislation further prescribes a timetable, disclosure requirements and tough penalties (imprisonment) for making a false declaration without reasonable grounds. Furthermore, if it turns out that the company cannot pay its debts, there is a rebuttable presumption that the directors did not have reasonable grounds for their opinion.[47]

B Winding up by the court

Section 122(1) of the Insolvency Act 1986 sets out the circumstances in which companies may be wound up by the court:

> A company may be wound up by the court if:

---

[43] As regards the meaning of 'company' in s. 84 and which companies may be wound up voluntarily, see p. 410 below.
[44] Insolvency Act 1986, s. 84 (3) and 85.
[45] *Ibid.* s. 90.
[46] *Ibid.* s. 89.
[47] *Ibid.* s. 89 (2)–(6).

(a) the company has by special resolution resolved that the company be wound up by the court,

(b) being a public company which was registered as such on its original incorporation, the company has not been issued with a certificate under section 117 of the Companies Act (public company share capital requirements) and more than a year has expired since it was so registered,

(c) it is an old public company within the meaning of the Consequential Provisions Act,

(d) the company does not commence its business within a year from its incorporation or suspends its business for a whole year,

(e) except in the case of a private company limited by shares or by guarantee, the number of members is reduced below 2,

(f) the company is unable to pay its debts,

   (fa) at the time at which a moratorium for the company . . . comes to an end, no voluntary arrangement . . . has effect . . .

(g) the court is of the opinion that it is just and equitable that the company should be wound up.

Most of the above categories are self-explanatory but, with the exception of paras (f), (fa) and (g), are fairly rare. Winding up litigation under para (g) is an important remedy for the minority shareholder in a small company.[48] Paragraph (f) is the unsecured creditor's basic remedy of last resort and is frequently used. Inability to pay debts is defined extensively in s. 123. A company will be deemed unable to pay its debts where a written demand (in the prescribed form) has been served on the company by a creditor owed more than £750 and the money is not paid within three weeks;[49] also where it is proved that the company is unable to pay its debts as they fall due or where it is proved that the value of the company's assets is less than the amount of its liabilities.[50]

C Procedure and scope

An application for winding up by the court must be by petition presented by the company, or directors, creditors (including contingent or prospective creditors), or by 'contributories'.[51] The term 'contributory' has the broad technical meaning of 'every person liable to contribute to the assets of a company in the event of its being wound up'[52] and these persons are[53] 'every present and past member', although the legislation goes on to make it clear that not all those who are technically called contributories will in fact actually have to contribute anything, so that, for instance, in the case of a company limited by shares, no contribution is required from any member which would exceed the amount (if any) unpaid on his shares (or former shares).[54]

---

[48] See further p.231 above.

[49] Insolvency Act 1986, s. 123 (1).

[50] *Ibid*. s. 123 (1), (2). If the carrying out of a court order for payment fails to produce sufficient money, then the company will be deemed unable to pay its debts; s. 123 (1) (b).

[51] *Ibid*. s. 124.

[52] *Ibid*. s. 79 (1).

[53] By *ibid*. s. 74.

[54] *Ibid*. s. 74 (2) (d). The right of contributories to petition for winding up is restricted in various ways; ss. 124 (2), (3). Various others are also entitled to petition; ss. 124 (1), (4), (5), 124A. Other statutes, such as the Financial Services and Markets Act 2000, also sometimes give a right to petition; see Financial Services and Markets Act 2000, s. 367.

Both the voluntary winding up provisions[55] and winding up by the court[56] apply to 'a company'. This is defined in s. 735 of the Companies Act 1985[57] as follows: ' "company" means a company formed and registered under this Act, or an existing company.' 'Existing company' is then defined so as to include companies formed under earlier Companies Acts (except some which are there listed). However, the provisions for winding up by the court also apply (with certain exceptions and modifications) to overseas companies and certain other 'unregistered' companies.[58]

22.4 EFFECTS OF WINDING UP, PURPOSE AND PROCEDURE

A Immediate effects of winding up

In a voluntary winding up the company must, from the commencement of the winding up,[59] cease to carry on its business, except so far as may be required for the beneficial winding up.[60] Furthermore, any transfer of shares, unless made with the sanction of the liquidator, and any alteration in the status of the company's members, made after the commencement of the winding up, is void.

In the case of a winding up by the court, the effects are more extensive, for it is provided that any disposition of the company's property and any transfer of shares or alteration in the status of the company's members, made after the commencement of the winding up, is void, unless the court otherwise orders.[61] With a winding up by the court, the commencement of the winding up is deemed to be at the time of the presentation of the petition for winding up (although in some circumstances it will be the time of passing the resolution for the voluntary winding up if such an earlier resolution had been passed).[62] Except with leave of the court, no action or proceeding may be proceeded with or commenced against the company or its property.[63] Various enforcement proceedings put in force after the commencement of the winding up are also void.[64] Carrying on of business by the liquidator is possible, 'so far as may be necessary for its beneficial winding up' but the sanction of the court (or sometimes liquidation committee)[65] is necessary.[66]

---

[55] Insolvency Act 1986, s. 84.
[56] *Ibid.* s. 122.
[57] Imported into the Insolvency Act 1986 by s. 73 thereof.
[58] Insolvency Act 1986, ss. 221, 225 and generally 220–229. The expression 'unregistered company' includes 'any association and any company' but it excludes statutory railway companies.
[59] Which by Insolvency Act 1986, s. 86, is the date of the passing of the resolution for winding up.
[60] *Ibid.* s. 87.
[61] *Ibid.* s. 127. There are exemptions in respect of administration.
[62] *Ibid.* s. 129.
[63] *Ibid.* s. 130 (2).
[64] *Ibid.* s. 128.
[65] As to which see further below.
[66] Insolvency Act 1986, ss. 167 (1) (a), 168, and Sch. 4, Pt II.

B Aims and purpose of liquidation

Although there may be many different reasons for commencing a winding up, once it has started, the overall policy and purpose is the same: to ensure that the creditors (if any) are treated equally (*pari passu*) and, subject to that, the property of the company is to be distributed to the members in accordance with their various rights.[67] However, the principle of equal treatment of creditors is subject to a number of inroads.[68] Sometimes (but rarely) the liquidation process is being used as a technical step in certain types of reconstruction.[69]

C Procedure[70]

1 Appointment of liquidator

In a members' voluntary winding up, the liquidator is appointed by the general meeting 'for the purpose of winding up the company's affairs and distributing its assets', and on his appointment the powers of the directors cease (unless the liquidator or general meeting otherwise decide).[71]

In a creditors' voluntary winding up the liquidator is normally appointed by the creditors' meeting which takes place within 14 days of the resolution to wind up.[72] During the interim the directors have very reduced and limited powers over the company's assets and they must prepare a 'statement of affairs' of the company to lay before the creditors' meeting.[73] The meeting may also appoint a 'liquidation committee' to assist the liquidator.[74] Once the liquidator is appointed, all the powers of the directors cease (unless the liquidation committee or creditors otherwise decide).[75]

Where the winding up is by the court, the official receiver automatically becomes liquidator[76] and continues as such unless he decides to summon meetings of the creditors and contributories to choose a 'private sector' liquidator.[77] Sometimes, if it is necessary to preserve the assets of the company prior to the hearing of the winding-up petition, the court will appoint a liquidator provisionally.[78]

Any liquidator must be properly qualified. The Insolvency Act 1986 regulates anyone who 'acts as an insolvency practitioner', which phrase includes acting as a

---

[67] *Ibid.* s. 107.
[68] These are discussed at p. 412 below.
[69] Insolvency Act 1986, s. 110. This is discussed at p. 110 above.
[70] Insolvency law procedure is complex, and in addition to many sections of the Insolvency Act 1986, there are detailed rules set out in the Insolvency Rules 1986 and various subsequent amendments; for the position as regards the effect of the Civil Procedure Rules 1998, see n. 11 above. What follows here is a brief outline of the remaining main steps in the liquidation process.
[71] Insolvency Act 1986, s. 91.
[72] *Ibid.* ss. 98–100.
[73] *Ibid.* ss. 99, 114.
[74] *Ibid.* s. 101.
[75] *Ibid.* s. 103.
[76] Unless the court appoints a former administrator under s. 140 of the Insolvency Act 1986.
[77] Insolvency Act 1986, s. 136. Alternatively, he can apply to the Secretary of State for the appointment of a liquidator under s. 137.
[78] *Ibid.* s. 135.

liquidator.[79] The person must be an 'individual' (i.e. not a corporate body).[80] He must be authorised to act as an insolvency practitioner, either by membership of a specified professional body (such as the institutes of accountants) and compliance with its rules, or by a direct authorisation granted by the Secretary of State or other 'competent authority'.[81]

2 Collection and distribution of assets

Normally the assets of the company remain its property[82] and the liquidator's function is to 'get in' the assets by taking them under his control, then to realise the assets and then distribute them to those entitled.[83] Liquidators have very wide powers, some exercisable subject (in various circumstances) to permission given by the members, the liquidation committee, creditors or the court, while other powers are exercisable without such restrictions.[84] Powers may also be delegated to the liquidator by virtue of s. 160. Additionally, there are various other powers scattered throughout the Insolvency Act, such as the power to apply to the court for directions in relation to any particular matter arising in the winding up,[85] the power to apply to have the winding up stayed, and the power to disclaim onerous property.[86]

Creditors are entitled to submit their claims to be paid, to the liquidator, technically referred to as 'proving for his debt'.[87] The procedures for proof of debts[88] differ slightly as to which type of liquidation is being conducted. In some cases the liquidator will need to estimate the value of a claim which does not bear a fixed or certain value.[89] If the liquidator feels that the claim is unfounded, he may reject the proof, a process which then sometimes leads to litigation.[90] This is especially so if the law is unclear as to whether the claim can be admitted to proof or not.[91]

Before dealing with the rules as regards priority of payments, it is worth observing that where the liquidation is not an insolvent liquidation, then little turns on the order in which the debts are repaid since everybody is going to get paid and any sur-

---

[79] *Ibid.* ss. 388–398. It also includes, in relation to companies, acting as provisional liquidator, administrator or administrative receiver.

[80] The person must also satisfy s. 390 (3) of the Insolvency Act 1986 and the Insolvency Practitioners Regulations 1990 (SI 1990 No. 439) (as amended) which require a security for the proper performance of his functions, up to a maximum of £5m. There are also certain disabilities listed in s. 390 (4) (e.g. disqualification order, mental patient).

[81] Insolvency Act 1986, ss. 390–393.

[82] Except where an order under s. 145 of the 1986 Act is made.

[83] Insolvency Act 1986, ss. 107, 143–144, 148, and Insolvency Rules 1986 (SI 1986 No. 1925), r. 4.195.

[84] Insolvency Act 1986, ss. 165–168 and Sch. 4.

[85] *Ibid.* ss. 168 (3), 112 (1).

[86] *Ibid.* ss. 178–182. Investigatory powers are discussed below at p. 415.

[87] Insolvency Rules 1986, r. 4.73 (3).

[88] Set out in Insolvency Rules 1986, rr. 4.73–4.94.

[89] Insolvency Rules 1986, r. 4.86.

[90] *Ibid.* rr. 4.82–4.83.

[91] See e.g., the discussion of the litigation in *Re Introductions Ltd* at p. 116 above.

plus will be paid to the shareholders. Where the assets are insufficient to pay everybody in full, then the question of priority becomes important.

It is also important to realise that various legal principles exist which will either swell or reduce the assets available to the creditors in the liquidation. Those which tend to swell the assets are discussed below.[92] As regards diminishing or reducing the assets, there are two main principles of common law which will have this effect. The first is the concept of security under which assets which are charged may be appropriated by the creditor to the satisfaction of his debts, in priority to the unsecured creditors.[93] The second is the doctrine of set-off, under which a creditor who owes, say, £1,000 to the company, but who himself is owed, say, £300 by the company, may deduct the money owed by the company to him, leaving him with a debt of only £700. As regards the £300 here owed to him by the company, the effect of the set-off is that he is, in a sense, paid in full. It should also be mentioned that various other legal grounds exist for claiming that certain assets should not be regarded as assets in the liquidation and thus not available for the creditors. Goods supplied subject to a retention of title clause are sometimes in this category,[94] and trust doctrines may sometimes produce this result.[95]

Subject to the operation of the principles discussed above, the order of priority for the payment of claims will be as follows:

(1) Expenses of the winding up.
(2) Preferential debts.
(3) Section 176 creditors.
(4) General creditors.
(5) Deferred debts.
(6) Shareholders.

These categories need further explanation:

'Expenses of the winding up' basically refers to the liquidator's expenses and remuneration. There are different types of these and they are subject to detailed priority rules set out in the Insolvency Rules 1986[96] and may be varied by the court in some circumstances.[97]

'Preferential debts' are those debts which Parliament has decided should have priority. These relate mainly to certain employee wages set out in ss. 175, 386 of and Sch. 6 to the 1986 Act. Prior to the Enterprise Act 2002 certain 'crown debts' were also deemed preferential, but with a view to improving the lot of the general unsecured creditors, the preference was discontinued.[98]

'Section 176 creditors' are creditors who have distrained on goods of the

---

[92] At p. 416
[93] In certain circumstances the order of priority produced by the normal operation of the legal principles of security and property is set aside. Section 175 (2) of the Insolvency Act 1986 operates to produce a statutory restriction of the normal priority given to the floating chargee as against 'preferential' creditors. For the meaning of 'preferential creditors' see below.
[94] See *Aluminium Industrie Vaassen BV* v *Romalpa* [1976] 2 All ER 552 and subsequent vast case law.
[95] See *Re Kayford* [1975] 1 WLR 279.
[96] Insolvency Rules 1986, r. 4.218. *Re Leyland Daf Ltd* [2004] BCC, HL, established that liquidation expenses are not payable out of assets subject to a floating charge.
[97] Insolvency Act 1986, s. 156.
[98] Enterprise Act 2002, s. 251. This account assumes that this legislation is in force.

company in the period of three months ending with the date of the winding-up order. The goods (or proceeds) are subject to a charge for meeting the preferential claims to the extent that these are otherwise unsatisfied. To the extent that the distraining creditor makes payments under such charge, he is subrogated to the rights of the preference creditors and thus becomes in effect entitled to the same priority as they had as against other creditors.[99]

'General creditors' refers to the ordinary trade or other creditors who have no special priority of deferral.

'Deferred debts' are those which are postponed to the other classes of creditor by virtue of some statutory provision. Certain payments of interest on proved debts are thus postponed.[100] Debts due to any member in his capacity as such (for example, dividends declared but not paid) are deferred.[101]

'Shareholders' means that any surplus remaining should be distributed among the shareholders in accordance with their rights as set out in the memorandum, articles, or terms of issue of the shares.

The process of actually paying the creditors is sometimes a protracted one and often a 'dividend' (i.e. distribution) is paid as soon as it is clear that it can be distributed, with the possibility of a further final dividend in the future. In the past it has often been the case that unsecured creditors end up with little or nothing since the lion's share of the assets are taken by floating charge holders. With a view to amelioration of the position of unsecured creditors, the Enterprise Act 2002 has introduced a concept under which a 'prescribed part of the company's net property' is to be made available for the satisfaction of unsecured debts.[102] It will be interesting to see how this idea develops in practice.

3 Dissolution of the company

As soon as the company's affairs are fully wound up, the liquidator[103] must prepare an account thereof and present this to meetings of members (in the case of a members' voluntary winding up) or of members and of creditors (in every other case).[104] It is up to these final meetings to decide whether or not the liquidator should 'have his release', that is to say, that he is 'discharged from all liability both in respect of acts or omissions of his in winding up and otherwise in relation to his conduct as liquidator'.[105] After the meetings, the liquidator must submit a report to the Registrar of Companies.[106]

Within three months of the day on which the report is registered by the Registrar, the company is deemed dissolved.[107] The company thus ceases to exist, it no longer

---

[99] See *ibid*. s. 176.

[100] *Ibid*. s. 189 (2).

[101] *Ibid*. s. 74 (2) (f).

[102] Enterprise Act 2002, s. 252 inserting a new s. 176A into the Insolvency Act 1986.

[103] Not being the Official Receiver.

[104] Insolvency Act 1986, ss. 94, 106, 146.

[105] *Ibid*. ss. 173 (4), 174 (6). Such release is, however, subject to the courts' powers in relation to any misfeasance by him under s. 212.

[106] *Ibid*. ss. 94 (3), 106 (3), 172 (8).

[107] *Ibid*. ss. 201, 205.

has legal personality. However, the court has power on application made within two years of dissolution to declare the dissolution void.[108] The two-year limit does not apply if the application is being made for the purpose of bringing proceedings against the company for damages in respect of personal injuries or fatal accidents. It is also possible for the liquidator to apply for 'early dissolution' in cases where the company is hopelessly insolvent and the assets will not even cover the expenses of winding up.[109]

Quite often in practice, particularly with small private companies and where the company is solvent, the whole of the liquidation process is by-passed; it is simply never started. Instead, the directors cause it to stop trading, pay off the creditors, and then pay any surplus to the shareholders. The practice has then often been to invite the Registrar of Companies to exercise his powers under s. 652 of the Companies Act 1985 to strike the name of the now defunct company off the register; the Registrar will usually assent to this. However, the dissolution does not discontinue the liability of the directors and members, and it may also be subjected to formal winding-up proceedings later, if necessary. A member or creditor may apply (within 20 years of the publication of the notice in the *Gazette* relating to striking off) to have the company's name restored.[110] The general s. 652 powers still exist, but since the amendments made by the Deregulation and Contracting Out Act 1994, new ss. 652A–F have been inserted into the Companies Act 1985. These set out a procedure under which the directors of a private company which has not been active for three months, other than paying its debts, may apply to the Registrar to have the company's name removed from the register. Liabilities of directors and members similarly continue and the company's name may be restored to the register.[111]

D Misconduct, malpractice and adjustment of pre-liquidation (or pre-administration) transactions

1 Investigation

There are a variety of investigatory powers. A winding up by the court inevitably involves some degree of investigation by the Official Receiver, for by s. 132 of the Insolvency Act 1986, it is the duty of the Official Receiver to investigate the causes of failure of the company (if it has failed) and generally, the promotion, formation, business, dealings and affairs of the company, and then to report to the court if he thinks fit. He has power to apply to the court for public examinations of officers and others.[112] This is in practice rare, although the powers of the court to order a private examination are widely used. These powers[113] are not restricted to the Official Receiver but can also be requested by any liquidator, administrator, administrative

---

[108] *Ibid.* s. 651.
[109] *Ibid.* ss. 202–203.
[110] *Ibid.* s. 653.
[111] *Ibid.*
[112] *Ibid.* s. 133.
[113] Contained in *ibid.* s. 236.

receiver or provisional liquidator[114] and apply to voluntary liquidations as well as winding up by the court. They are used in attempts to obtain explanations from former directors as to their conduct. Obviously, matters discovered in the course of a winding up might also trigger full-scale investigations by the DTI, the Serious Fraud Office, or the DPP. Indeed, s. 218 requires liquidators who have discovered criminal malpractice to submit a report to the Secretary of State.

2 Remedies

Once misconduct has been discovered, the Insolvency Act 1986 makes available a wide range of remedies and penalties to deal with it: fraudulent trading;[115] wrongful trading;[116] misfeasance proceedings;[117] fraud in anticipation of winding up;[118] falsification of company's books;[119] omissions from statement of affairs;[120] false representations to creditors.[121] There are also restrictions[122] designed to prevent the name of the wound-up company from being used again within a five-year period. The provisions relating to disqualification of directors often become relevant in the context of liquidation.[123]

The Insolvency Act 1986 contains a number of provisions designed to adjust or set aside transactions effected prior to a liquidation or administration. Briefly, these are as follows: certain transactions at an undervalue may be set aside under ss. 238 and 340–341. Also certain preferences may be set aside (ss. 239, 240–241). Extortionate credit transactions may be set aside or restructured under s. 244. Under s. 245 certain floating charges can be declared invalid to the extent that the company did not get consideration for them.[124]

---

[114] *Ibid.* ss. 236, 234.
[115] *Ibid.* s. 213; and see p. 33 above.
[116] *Ibid.* s. 214 and see pp. 33–37 above.
[117] *Ibid.* s. 212.
[118] *Ibid.* s. 208.
[119] *Ibid.* s. 209.
[120] *Ibid.* s. 210.
[121] *Ibid.* s. 211.
[122] In *ibid.* ss. 216–217.
[123] See further Chapter 23 below.
[124] For further explanation of these matters, see I. Fletcher *Corporate Insolvency Law* 2nd edn (London: Sweet & Maxwell, 1996) pp. 640–651.

23

DISQUALIFICATION OF DIRECTORS

23.1 BACKGROUND

The provisions for disqualification of directors introduced by the Insolvency Act 1985 were not a wholly new phenomenon in that the Companies Act 1948 had included provisions[1] which permitted the disqualification of directors who were guilty of fraud, breach of duty or liquidation offences. Subsequently, the jurisdiction was steadily extended by legislation over the years until the Insolvency Act 1985[2] produced its current form, now contained in the Company Directors Disqualification Act 1986.[3] As a result of this legislation and changes of policy within the DTI, the number of disqualifications has increased drastically in recent years. In 1983–84, a total of 89 were made,[4] in 1987–88, 197 orders were made, in 1994–95, 493 orders were made but by 1999–2000 the annual total had risen to 1,509.[5] In the year 2003–2004 disqualifications totalled 1,527.[6]

23.2 THE DISQUALIFICATION ORDER

The Company Directors Disqualification Act 1986 (CDDA 1986) consolidated various prior enactments under which the court[7] could disqualify persons from acting as directors (and holding other positions).

Section 1(1) of the CDDA 1986 provides that a disqualification order is an order that:

---

[1] Section 188.
[2] The expansion of the jurisdiction in the Insolvency Act 1985 was largely the result of recommendations contained in the Cork Report (Cmnd. 8558, 1982) and the White Paper, *A Revised Framework for Insolvency Law* (Cmnd. 9175, 1984).
[3] There are accompanying rules governing the procedure: Insolvent Companies (Disqualification of Unfit Directors) Proceedings Rules 1987 (SI 1987 No. 2023). These have been subsequently amended to make them compatible with the Civil Procedure Rules 1998, although broadly the position is that the Civil Procedure Rules do not apply to the Disqualification Rules, except to the extent that they are not inconsistent with them.
[4] Mainly under the Companies Act 1948, s. 188.
[5] See *Companies in 1998–99* (London: DTI, 1999) p. 36 and earlier editions. For analysis of the decision-making mechanisms relating to the bringing of disqualification proceedings, see S. Wheeler 'Directors' Disqualification: Insolvency Practitioners and the Decision-making Process' (1995) 15 *Legal Studies* 283.
[6] See *Companies in 2003–04* (London: DTI, 2004) p. 44. Interestingly, about two thirds of these were under the new procedure of disqualification by undertaking; see p. 423 below.
[7] It also contains two outright prohibitions on persons acting as directors: undischarged bankrupts, s. 11 (see e.g. *R v Brockley* [1994] BCC 131) and (hardly of general application) s. 12.

For a period specified in the order:

(a) he shall not be a director of a company, act as receiver of a company's property or in any way, whether directly or indirectly, be concerned or take part in the promotion, formation or management of a company unless (in each case) he has the leave of the court, and

(b) he shall not act as an insolvency practitioner.[8]

The order need not be a total disqualification and he can be allowed to act in relation to certain companies subject to conditions, while being disqualified from acting for any others.[9] Furthermore, even once disqualified, the legislation effectively enables him to later apply for leave to act in relation to certain companies.[10]

Although disqualification proceedings are a civil proceeding,[11] it is clear that they may also involve matters in respect of which criminal proceedings are sometimes brought and acting in breach of a disqualification order is a criminal offence as well as giving rise to personal liability for the debts of the company.[12] The disqualification is widely construed and in *R v Campbell*[13] it was held that a management consultant who advised on the financial management and restructuring of a company was in breach of the order, in particular, the words in the statute that he should not 'be concerned in' the 'management of a company'. It is clear from *Re Sevenoaks Ltd*[14] that the director cannot be disqualified on the basis of charges which were not formally made against him, but which happened to be made out once the evidence had been given in court.[15]

The jurisdiction is available against 'persons'; the first case against a corporate director was *Official Receiver v Brady*[16] where Jacob J said:

As a matter of practice there may be a useful purpose in being able to disqualify companies as well as the individuals behind them. It means that one of the tools used by people who are unfit to be company directors can themselves be attacked. There may be a host of ... advantages. You may not be able to find the individuals behind the controlling director.[17]

One of the most frequently disputed issues in disqualification proceedings is the question of whether a person can, in the circumstances, be regarded as a shadow director, or as a de facto director, so as to make him liable.[18] In *Re Kaytech International plc*[19] the Court of Appeal discussed various judicial observations on the

---

[8] For practice procedures see *Practice Direction: Directors Disqualification Proceedings* [1999] BCC 717.

[9] See *Re Lo-Line Ltd* (1988) 4 BCC 415.

[10] CDDA 1986, s. 17. See e.g. *Secretary of State for Trade and Industry v Rosenfield* [1999] Ch 413, where it was held that if the applicant was not acting as director, the companies would suffer, with severe consequences for the employees, and so subject to conditions, leave was granted. In *Secretary of State for Trade and Industry v Griffiths* [1998] BCC 836 the Court of Appeal set out detailed guidance on the manner in which s. 17 applications should be dealt with.

[11] *Re Churchill Hotel Ltd* (1988) 4 BCC 112.

[12] CDDA 1986, ss. 1 (4), 13, 15.

[13] [1984] BCLC 83 (a case under s. 188 of Companies Act 1948).

[14] [1990] BCC 765, CA.

[15] Similarly, the disqualification period should be fixed by reference only to the matters properly alleged.

[16] [1999] BCC 258.

[17] *Ibid.* at p. 259.

[18] See e.g. *Re Richborough Furniture Ltd* [1996] BCC 155 and *Secretary of State for Trade and Industry v Tjolle* [1998] BCC 282, where on the facts the respondents were held not to be de facto directors. Different conclusions were reached in *Secretary of State for Trade and Industry v Jones* [1999] BCC 336 and *Re Kaytech International plc* [1999] BCC 390, CA.

[19] [1999] BCC 390, CA.

matter but declined to lay down a firm test for determining de facto directorship other than to pass the fairly general observation that 'the crucial issue is whether the individual in question has assumed the status and functions of a company director so as to make himself responsible under the 1986 Act as if he were a de jure director'.[20]

Lastly here, it could be observed that the cases under the CDDA 1986 provided scant comfort for non-executive directors that they might be under a lower standard of duty than ordinary full-time directors. In *Re Continental Assurance Co of London plc*[21] one of the directors held a senior position at the bank which had financed the company and was effectively a non-executive director with the company appointed to the board to protect the bank's interest. The judge accepted that the facts showed that he did not know what was going on, but that he should have known.[22]

23.3 GROUNDS – UNFITNESS AND INSOLVENCY

A The s. 6 ground

There are numerous grounds for disqualification.[23] The ground where most of the case law has been occurring is s. 6 which provides that it is the duty of the court to disqualify where it is satisfied that he:

> [I]s or has been a director[24] of a company which has at any time become insolvent (whether while he was a director or subsequently) and . . . that his conduct as a director of that company (either taken alone or taken together with his conduct as a director of any other company or companies) makes him unfit to be concerned in the management of a company.

Under this ground[25] the minimum period of disqualification is two years, the maximum is 15 years. The term 'becomes insolvent' is defined very broadly, so it will embrace both voluntary and involuntary liquidation. It covers 'going into liquidation at a time when its assets are insufficient for the payment of its debts and other liabilities and the expenses of the winding up'[26] and also where an administration order is made or an administrative receiver is appointed. The case law has given a wide meaning to the term 'director' so that acting as a director is sufficient, even if there has never been any formal appointment.[27]

The proceedings can only be invoked by the DTI in accordance with s. 7 which empowers them in some circumstances to direct the Official Receiver to bring proceedings. There are also time limits governing the commencement of proceedings, for it is provided[28] that an application for the making under s. 6 of a

---

[20] *Ibid.* at p. 402, *per* Robert Walker LJ.
[21] [1996] BCC 888.
[22] A similar attitude towards non-executives was expressed in *Re Wimbledon Village Restaurant Ltd* [1994] BCC 753 although on the facts, the circumstances were not sufficient to establish unfitness.
[23] The others are dealt with below.
[24] Director in ss. 6–9 of the CDDA 1986 includes shadow director; see ss. 22 (4) and 22 (5).
[25] Other grounds sometimes attract different maximums and there are no minimum periods; see p. 425 *et seq.* below.
[26] CDDA 1986, s. 6 (2).
[27] *Re Lo-Line Ltd* (1988) 4 BCC 415.
[28] CDDA 1986, s. 7 (2).

disqualification order 'shall not be made after the end of the period of 2 years beginning with the day on which the company . . . became insolvent'.[29]

B Unfitness

1 Statutory provisions

Guidance on whether a director is unfit or not is given in s. 9 and Sch. 1 of the CDDA 1986. Schedule 1, Pt I applies to the concept of unfitness generally and lists the matters which the court must have particular regard to, such as: misfeasance, breach of duty, misapplication of property or conduct giving rise to a liability to account, the extent of his responsibility for any transactions set aside under the avoidance provisions in the Insolvency Act, and for any failures to keep accounting records, make annual returns etc.

Part II applies additionally, where the company has become insolvent and covers such matters as: the extent of the director's responsibility for the causes of the company becoming insolvent, for failure to supply goods and services paid for, for transactions and preferences set aside under the Insolvency Act, for failure to call creditors meetings and for failures in connection with his duties in a liquidation (such as preparing a statement of affairs).

2 Commercial morality

In addition to these statutory indicators, the courts have developed a concept of 'commercial morality' in which they try to balance the need to protect the public from those who abuse the privilege of limited liability with the need to be careful not to make it so strict that it stultifies enterprise and with the need to be fair to the directors themselves. Hoffmann J (as he then was) set out the balance in *Re Ipcon Fashions Ltd*[30] where he said:

> The public is entitled to be protected not only against the activities of those guilty of the more obvious breaches of commercial morality, but also against someone who has shown in his conduct . . . a failure to appreciate or observe the duties attendant on the privilege of conducting business with the protection of limited liability.

Thus, limited liability is seen as a privilege which must not be abused. On the other hand, this policy of protecting the public from abusers of limited liability does not stand on its own and it has been made clear that it has to be balanced against the need not to 'stultify all enterprise'.[31] It was also stressed that there was a need to be fair to the directors themselves:

> Looking at it from the point of view of the director on the receiving end of such an application, I think that justice requires that he should have some grounds for feeling that he

---

[29] On the interpretation of this, see *Re Tasbian Ltd* [1990] BCC 318, where it was held that the time limit in s. 7 (2) ran from the happening of the first of the events mentioned in s. 6 (2).
[30] (1989) 5 BCC 733 at p. 776.
[31] See e.g. Harman J in *Re Douglas Construction Ltd* (1988) 4 BCC 553 at p. 557 (a case on the similar jurisdiction in the predecessor to the CDDA 1986, namely, s. 300 of the Companies Act 1985).

has not simply been picked on. There must, I think be something about the case, some conduct which if not dishonest is at any rate in breach of standards of commercial morality, or some really gross incompetence which persuades the court that it would be a danger to the public if he were allowed to continue to be involved in the management of companies.[32]

It is useful to look at the facts of some of the cases falling either side of the line; first, cases where there was held to be a contravention of the principle of commercial morality.

In *Re Ipcon Fashions Ltd*[33] the director knew the company was insolvent and he siphoned off its business to another company with a view to resurrecting it. During all this, the old company was used to incur liability. A five-year period of disqualification was imposed. In *Re McNulty's Interchange Ltd*[34] the main problem was that the director had no new ideas which might have improved the business of the company and he simply went on incurring debts; disqualification for 18 months.[35]

Secondly, there are cases where the conduct was held to be within the boundaries of commercial morality. In *Re Douglas Construction*[36] the director had put a lot of his own money into the company in order to keep it going. In view of this it was held that it was difficult to say he was abusing the concept of limited liability. In *Re Dawson Print Ltd* there was a very young entrepreneur who was only about 20 years old when he started his first companies. He had had some bad luck and some problems with employees. No disqualification was imposed. Hoffmann J made the memorable statement: '. . . [H]aving seen him in the witness box I thought that he was a great deal more intelligent than many directors of successful companies that I have come across.'[37] An interesting issue which arose in this case concerned the relevance of the use by the director of moneys which represented Crown debts. In other words, what weight does the court attach to the fact that the directors have used PAYE and NI money collected from employees to finance the company in its dying days, instead of handing it over to the Inland Revenue or other appropriate authority? Some judges had taken the view that the director was a 'quasi-trustee' of these moneys and that use of these to finance the business was more culpable than failure to pay commercial debts.[38] In the *Dawson* case, the assets realised £3,855 and debts were £111,179 of which about £40,000 represented unpaid PAYE, NI, VAT and rates. Hoffmann J was not prepared to regard the use of these Crown moneys as being especially culpable:

> The fact is that . . . the Exchequer and the Commissioners of Customs and Excise have chosen to appoint traders to be tax collectors on their behalf with the attendant risk. That risk is to some extent compensated by the preference which they have on insolvency. There

---

[32] *Per* Hoffmann J in *Re Dawson Print Ltd* (1987) 3 BCC 322 at p. 324 (Companies Act 1985, s. 300); followed by Browne-Wilkinson J in *Re McNulty's Interchange Ltd* (1988) 4 BCC 533 at p. 536 (Companies 1985, s. 300).

[33] (1989) 5 BCC 733.

[34] (1988) 4 BCC 533.

[35] A case on Companies Act 1985, s. 300.

[36] (1988) 4 BCC 553.

[37] (1987) 3 BCC 322 at p. 324.

[38] See e.g. *Re Lo-Line Ltd* (1988) 4 BCC 415 (Companies 1985, s. 300) and earlier cases.

is as yet no obligation upon traders to keep such moneys in a separate account as there might be if they were really trust moneys, they are simply a debt owed by the company. I cannot accept that failure to pay these debts is regarded in the commercial world generally as such a breach of commercial morality that it requires in itself a conclusion that the directors concerned are unfit to be involved in the management of a company.[39]

This passage was subsequently approved by the Court of Appeal in *Re Sevenoaks Ltd*[40] and they made it clear that non-payment of Crown debts was not to be treated automatically as evidence of unfitness and it was necessary to look closely at each case to see what was the significance of non-payment.[41]

These then are merely examples of cases falling on either side of the line. It is clear that each case will fall to be decided very much on its own facts and that the judges are having to perform some quite subjective assessments of the conduct of individuals.

3 Reference to other companies

The courts have been required to form a view about whether the respondent is able to refer to his subsequent or contemporaneous conduct of other companies by way of mitigation. In *Re Matthews (DJ) (joinery design)*[42] companies had been wound up insolvent in 1981 and 1984 but the respondent argued that the current position was what mattered, that he had learned from his mistakes, and was now running a third company successfully. It was held that although this later company could be some mitigation, it could not entirely wipe out the past. Peter Gibson J put it thus:

> It was submitted that . . . just as there is joy in heaven over a sinner that repenteth, so this court ought to be glad that a director who has been grossly in dereliction of his duties, now wishes to follow the path of righteousness. But I must take account of the misconduct that has occurred in the past, and give effect to the public interest that required such misconduct to be recognised.[43]

In a later case[44] the same judge took the view that the wording of s. 6 (1) (b): 'did not enable the court to look at the respondent's conduct in relation to any company whatsoever. The attention of the court is focused on the conduct of the respondent as a director of one or more companies as specified in that subsection.'[45] Subsequently, in *Re Country Farms Inns Ltd*[46] it has been observed that there is a 'lead company' concept built into s. 6 (1) (b) which is the necessary consequence of the words 'either taken alone or taken together with it', to the effect

---

[39] (1987) 3 BCC 322 at p. 325.
[40] [1990] BCC 765 at p. 777.
[41] On the other hand, it is often a failure to pay Crown debts which causes the s. 6 proceedings to be brought and was the ground upon which the Court of Appeal upheld the disqualification order in *Sevenoaks* itself; see *Re Verby Print for Advertising Ltd* [1998] BCC 656, *per* Neuberger J.
[42] (1988) 4 BCC 513 (Companies Act 1985, s. 300).
[43] *Ibid.* at p. 518.
[44] *Re Bath Glass* (1988) 4 BCC 130.
[45] *Ibid.* at p. 132.
[46] [1997] BCC 801 at p. 808, *per* Morritt LJ.

that conduct relating to the collateral company alone could not justify a finding of unfitness sufficient to lead to a disqualification order under that section. In that case, the issue arose of whether the conduct in relation to the 'collateral' company (or companies) in s. 6 (1) (b) should be the same as or similar to that relied on in relation to the 'lead' company. The Court of Appeal held that there was no requirement for this.[47]

4 Appropriate periods of disqualification

In *Re Sevenoaks Ltd*[48] the Court of Appeal laid down guidelines as to the appropriate periods of disqualification:

> I would for my part endorse the division of the potential 15-year disqualification period into three brackets ...
> (1) The top bracket of disqualification for periods over ten years should be reserved for particularly serious cases. These may include cases where a director who has already had one period of disqualification imposed on him falls to be disqualified yet again.
> (2) The minimum bracket of two to five years' disqualification should be applied where, though disqualification is mandatory, the case is, relatively, not very serious.
> (3) The middle bracket of disqualification for from six to ten years should apply for serious cases which do not merit the top bracket.

In the later case of *Secretary of State for Trade and Industry v Griffiths*[49] the Court of Appeal gave further general guidance on the process of deciding upon the appropriate period of disqualification. In particular it took the view that it is something which ought to be dealt with comparatively briefly and without elaborate reasoning. The Court of Appeal also made it clear that in view of the very large number of cases which have now appeared in the law reports, it would not usually be appropriate for the judge to be taken through the facts of previous cases in order to guide him as to the course he should take in the case before him.[50]

5 The Development of *Carecraft* procedure and its displacement by disqualification undertakings under the Insolvency Act 2000

In *Re Carecraft Construction Ltd*[51] the court was asked to follow a summary procedure in view of the circumstances that there was no dispute about the material facts and no dispute about the period of disqualification. The procedure comprised a schedule of agreed facts. The directors accepted that the court would be likely to find that their conduct made them unfit to be concerned in the management of a company. On that basis, the Official Receiver agreed that it was not necessary for other comparatively unimportant disputes about the facts to be settled and accepted that he would not seek more than the minimum period of disqualification. The court held that it had jurisdiction to proceed in this way.

---

[47] *Ibid*; departing from statements to the contrary in earlier cases.
[48] [1990] BCC 765 at pp. 771–772, *per* Dillon LJ.
[49] [1998] BCC 836.
[50] *Ibid.* at pp. 845–846.
[51] [1993] BCC 336.

Subsequently, many cases have been decided in this way under what has become known as the *Carecraft* procedure.[52] The details of the rationale behind it were recently summarised by Jonathan Parker J in *Official Receiver* v *Cooper*:[53]

> [T]he public interest in relation to proceedings under [section 6] lies in the protection of the public against persons acting as directors or shadow directors of companies who are unfit to do so. That in turn involves ensuring, so far as possible, that disqualification orders of appropriate length are made in all cases which merit such orders and that they are made as speedily and economically as is reasonably practicable ... The *Carecraft* procedure represents, in my judgment, an important means of advancing that public interest. In the first place, it avoids the need for a contested hearing, with the attendant delays and inevitably substantial costs. Not only does this benefit the taxpayer, who ultimately bears the burden of the Secretary of State's costs (in so far as they are not recovered from the respondent) and of the costs of a legally aided respondent, it also avoids the situation where a non-legally aided respondent against whom an order for costs is made is in effect buried under an avalanche of costs, causing his financial ruin in addition to any disqualification order made against him ... In the second place, the *Carecraft* procedure discourages respondents from requiring the Secretary of State to prove at a contested hearing allegations which the respondent knows to be true. In the third place, the *Carecraft* procedure encourages respondents to recognise their wrong doing and to face the consequences of it.[54]

The judge in *Carecraft* proceedings is not bound to make a disqualification order, and is not bound by the length of period of disqualification which the parties have agreed is appropriate. On the other hand, the case comes before him on agreed facts and those are the only facts on which he can base his judgment.[55]

The Insolvency Act 2000 established a regime[56] under which the Secretary of State can accept a 'disqualification undertaking' from a director. The aim of this new administrative procedure was to avoid the need to use the *Carecraft* procedure which although a summary procedure nevertheless involves to some extent, the expense of a court process. The basic rules on disqualification undertakings are set out in s. 1A of the CDDA.[57] Statistically it is looking as though disqualification undertakings are replacing *Carecraft* in most situations in which in the past *Carecraft* would have been used. For instance, in 2003–2004 disqualifications under s. 6 by court order numbered 213, whereas disqualifications under s. 6 by means of disqualification undertakings numbered 1,154.[58] Whereas in the last year prior to the coming into use of disqualification undertakings, there were 1,548 disqualifications under s. 6 by court order.[59]

---

[52] A director who is unwilling to become involved in *Carecraft* procedure is not able to prevent the bringing of full disqualification proceedings by offering undertakings to the court not to act as a director; see *Re Blackspur Group plc* [1998] BCC 11, CA.

[53] [1999] 1 BCC 115. It was held here that the respondent could make the admissions and concessions for the purpose of *Carecraft* proceedings only, and without prejudice to other proceedings.

[54] [1999] 1 BCC 115 at p. 117.

[55] *Secretary of State for Trade and Industry* v *Rogers* [1997] BCC 155, CA.

[56] Insolvency Act 2000, ss. 6–8 amending the CDDA 1986.

[57] And sections 7 and 8.

[58] *Companies in 2003–04* (DTI: London, 2004) p. 44.

[59] *Ibid.*

23.4 OTHER GROUNDS

A Disqualification after investigation

Section 8(1) provides in effect that if it appears to the Secretary of State from a report made by inspectors under various enactments (or from information or documents obtained under certain enactments) that it is expedient in the public interest that a disqualification order should be made against any person who is (or has been) a director,[60] he may apply to the court for an order. The court may make the order where it is satisfied that his conduct in relation to the company makes him unfit to be concerned in the management of a company.[61] Under these provisions therefore, and unlike the s. 6 cases where there is an insolvency, the test of unfitness is to be applied using only Pt 1 of Sch. 1, and the case law.[62] Under this ground the maximum period of disqualification is 15 years.

B Disqualification on conviction of an indictable offence

The court[63] has power to make a disqualification order against a person convicted of an indictable offence[64] in connection with the 'promotion, formation, management, liquidation or striking off of a company, or with the receivership or management of a company's property'.[65] An example of this occurred in *R v Georgiou*.[66] The defendant was convicted of carrying on insurance business without the necessary authorisation under the Insurance Companies Act 1982. He was also disqualified from being a director for five years.[67] His argument that the court had no jurisdiction to disqualify him because he had not used the company as a vehicle for the commission of the offence and so the misconduct was not 'in connection with management' was rejected by the Court of Appeal; carrying on insurance business through a limited company was sufficiently a function of management.

C Disqualification for persistent breaches of the companies legislation

Here, the ground for disqualification is where it 'appears to the court that [the person] has been persistently in default in relation to the provisions of the companies legislation requiring any return, account or other document' to be sent to the Registrar of Companies.[68] If the respondent has been found guilty[69] of three or more such defaults within the five years ending with the date of the Secretary of

---

[60] Or shadow director of any company. See also CDDA 1986, s. 22 (4) and (5).
[61] *Ibid.* s. 8 (2).
[62] *Ibid.* s. 9 (1) (a).
[63] Defined so as to include certain criminal courts; *ibid.* s. 2 (2).
[64] Whether on indictment or summarily.
[65] CDDA 1986, s. 2 (1).
[66] (1988) 4 BCC 322.
[67] Under CDDA 1986, s. 2.
[68] *Ibid.* s. 3 (1).
[69] Technically, CDDA 1986, s. 3 (3) applies here.

State's application for disqualification, it is treated as conclusive proof of persistent default.[70] The maximum period of disqualification is five years.

D Disqualification for fraud in a winding up

It is provided that the court[71] may make a disqualification order against a person if, in the course of a winding up it appears that he:

(a) has been guilty of an offence for which he is liable (whether he has been convicted or not) under section 458 of the Companies Act (fraudulent trading), or

(b) has otherwise been guilty, while an officer or liquidator of the company receiver of the company's property or administrative receiver of the company, of any fraud in relation to the company or of any breach of his duty as such officer, liquidator, receiver or administrative receiver.[72]

Here, the maximum period of disqualification is 15 years.

E Disqualification on summary conviction

This provision permits disqualification in certain circumstances where a person is convicted of certain offences. Broadly, it relates to convictions for failures to comply with companies legislation relating to returns, accounts and similar matters to be sent to the Registrar of Companies.[73] If there have been three of these within the five years ending with the date of the current proceedings[74] then the court may disqualify him for a period of up to five years.[75]

F Disqualification for fraudulent or wrongful trading

Section 10 of the CDDA 1986 fits with the fraudulent and wrongful trading provisions[76] by giving the court power to disqualify in addition to any other order that is being made under those provisions.[77] As many of the facts that give rise to a disqualification order under s. 6 (i.e. unfitness and insolvency) may also trigger liability for fraudulent or (more usually) wrongful trading, this additional power of the court makes sense.

23.5 HUMAN RIGHTS CHALLENGES

It is very possible that proceedings under the CDDA 1986 are going to become fertile ground for challenges on the basis that in some way or other, they have

---

[70] *Ibid.* s. 3 (2).

[71] Defined in CDDA 1986, s. 4 (2).

[72] *Ibid.* s. 4 (1).

[73] See CDDA 1986, s. 5 (1).

[74] Including those proceedings.

[75] See CDDA 1986, s. 5 (2)–(5). There are marked similarities between this and the s. 3 provisions but the main point is that s. 5 applies only where criminal proceedings are ongoing.

[76] See p. 33 above.

[77] See e.g. *Re Brian D Pierson (Contractors) Ltd* [1999] BCC 26.

infringed the European Convention on Human Rights which was incorporated into UK law by the Human Rights Act 1998 and came into force on 2 October 2000.[78] Even prior to this date it has made its appearance in the cases.[79] In *Hinchliffe* v *Secretary of State for Trade and Industry*[80] the director wished to argue that various aspects of the disqualification proceedings infringed art. 6 of the Convention and sought, as the judge put it: 'whatever ... adjournment of the disqualification proceedings is necessary to ensure that they will not be heard before the passage into law of the Bill presently before Parliament for incorporation of the European Convention on Human Rights into English law, so as to give the English court the power and duty to apply the provisions of that Convention.'[81] The director's argument failed, mainly on the ground that it was held that the court could not embark on the speculative course of whether a Bill before Parliament would be passed into law in its then form.

In *EDC* v *United Kingdom*[82] the former director applied to the European Commission of Human Rights against the UK government alleging that there had been unreasonable delays in the disqualification proceedings which constituted a violation of art. 6 of the Convention. The relevant part of art. 6 provided that 'in the determination of his civil rights and obligations ... everyone is entitled to a ... hearing within a reasonable time'. The proceedings had begun in 1991 and ended in 1996 and in all the circumstances of the case had failed to meet the reasonable time requirement in art. 6 (1).[83]

23.6 EPILOGUE

This last chapter in this book has covered the disqualification of directors. The penalty of disqualification in effect makes a public statement that disqualified directors should, for a time at least, no longer be part of the corporate world; that they are not fit to be doing what they have done in the past; that in respect of their efforts at work, the nation is better off without them.

As a final thought, it is worth raising the question whether the government has got the balance right. And not only the balance as regards the operation of the area of law concerned with disqualification, but also as regards all the regulatory aspects of mainstream company law, and as regards the regulation which is imposed on the capital markets, by the EU and UK regulatory authorities.

Disqualifications are now averaging a figure of about 1,500 per year. The process involves the public imposition of very high levels of disapproval by the judicial system, the heavy arm of the machinery of the state. It is cast upon people who were

---

[78] Disqualification cases involving human rights arguments will probably come to be regarded as the exact opposite of *Carecraft* procedure.

[79] Arguments based on art. 6 have also arisen in judicial review proceedings connected with disqualification; see *R* v *Secretary of State for Trade and Industry, ex parte McCormick* [1998] BCC 379.

[80] [1999] BCC 226.

[81] *Ibid.* at p. 227, *per* Rattee J.

[82] Application No. 24433/94 [1998] BCC 370.

[83] Subsequent cases are less encouraging for directors; see e.g. *DC, HS and AD* v *United Kingdom* [2000] BCC 710; *WGS and MSLS* v *United Kingdom* [2000] BCC 719; *Re Westminster Property Management Ltd* [2001] BCC 121, CA.

in the main running small businesses, trying their best to earn a living, and usually providing employment for others in the process. The vast majority will have got into difficulties, not through planned fraud, but by struggling on, trying to pretend to their employees and to their families that they were on top of the problems; hoping that things would turn out for the best. Many will have also suffered personal insolvency as a result of the collapse of their business, or come very close to insolvency. The Company Law Review has expressed the view that the evidence suggests that small firms are the main job creators.[84]

Almost without exception, the agencies of government responsible for setting levels of regulation, and enforcing them, are operated by salaried employees, whose work environments will be very different, and will involve relatively high levels of certainty, of reward, and advancement; certainties which are no part of the life of an entrepreneur. There is a danger that over the years the government agencies will misjudge the balance. If so, in due course, it may be found that fewer able people will choose to make their living through entrepreneurial activity. Arguably, this is happening in other areas of life in the UK, where high levels of regulation and relatively poor rewards are making essential jobs increasingly unattractive; and then it is found that there are shortages.

Although company law has many areas where the rules are permissive, left largely in the hands of business people, the ultimate fact is that if the state acting on behalf of the general populace wants to intervene and make new rules, it will. Company law is, in essence, public regulation of the organisational structures through which production takes place, and of the capital markets through which money is raised to finance the production process. The agencies of the state know that they bear the responsibility for ensuring a stable yet vital commercial environment by means of an unbiased approach to both *laissez-faire* and regulation. If they get the balance wrong, the economy will suffer. It is not an easy balance to strike and there is no panacea.

---

[84] In the sense of new jobs. Thus the example is given of statistics available to the DTI which show that between 1989 and 1991 over 90% of additional jobs created were in firms with fewer than ten employees even though they accounted for only 18% of total employment in 1989; see DTI Consultation Document (February 1999) *The Strategic Framework*, para. 2.19.

INDEX

Accounts and audit, 12, 39, 55,
  185–91, 192–3, 198, 207–8
Agency, 5, 45, 69–71, 73–4, 118,
  131–41
Alternative Investment Market (AIM),
  15, 259, 262, 370
Articles and memorandum of
  association, 40–2, 110–15,
  146–51
  alteration of, 98–101
  capital, 263–7
  company secretary, 190–1
  constitution, 39–42, 87–103, 106,
    109–29
  contracts with the company, 175
  directors, 146–51
  enforcement, 89–91
  entrenchment of rights, 87–103
  incorporation, 39–42
  minority shareholders, 215–16
  shareholder agreements, 95–6
  shares, control over issues of, 181
  voting, 157

Berle and Means companies, 17, 50–3
Branches, 13, 19
Bubble Act, 9, 326
Business organisations, 20

Cadbury Report, 54–5, 80, 190,
  194–9, 209–11
Capital, 16, 253–4, 276–80
  articles and memorandum of
    association, 88, 263–7, 282
  authority to issue, 266
  buybacks, commercial use of, 290
  cash flows, 254–5
  Company Law Review and reform,
    292–3
  debt, role of, 262–3
  discounts, 276–8

dividends and distributions, 290–2
increase and alteration, 265–6
maintenance, 6, 12, 280–93
minimum, 16, 42
premiums, 278–80, 293
preferential subscription rights,
  266–7
purchase of own shares, 286–90
raising, 6, 12, 254–5, 262–3,
  276–80
reduction of capital, 282–6, 293
variation of class rights, 101–6,
  285–6
Capital markets, 3, 6–7, 313–400 *see
  also* theories in securities
  regulation/capital markets law
Charitable donations, 59–60
Chartered companies, 19
Class rights, variation of, 101–6,
  285–6
Collective investment schemes, 350–5
Combined Code, 195, 198–211
Committee of European Services
  Regulators (CESR), 335–6
Community Interest Company (CIC),
  19, 84
Company Law Review and reform, 4,
  46, 74–84, 130, 193, 428
  academics, role of, 81
  agencies of reform, 77–81
  capital, 292–3
  City and institutional input, 80
  Companies (Audit, Investigations
    and Community Enterprise) Bill,
    84, 190
  constitution of the company, 111
  contractual relations, 142
  corporate governance, 210–11
  Department of Trade and Industry
    (DTI), 77–81, 84
  directors, 172, 178

429